Jobs for the Poor

Jobs for the Poor

Can Labor Demand Policies Help?

TIMOTHY J. BARTIK

Russell Sage Foundation
New York, New York

W. E. Upjohn Institute for Employment Research
Kalamazoo, Michigan

The Russell Sage Foundation

The Russell Sage Foundation, one of the oldest of America's general purpose foundations, was established in 1907 by Mrs. Margaret Olivia Sage for "the improvement of social and living conditions in the United States." The Foundation seeks to fulfill this mandate by fostering the development and dissemination of knowledge about the country's political, social, and economic problems. While the Foundation endeavors to assure the accuracy and objectivity of each book it publishes, the conclusions and interpretations in Russell Sage Foundation publications are those of the authors and not of the Foundation, its Trustees, or its staff. Publication by Russell Sage, therefore, does not imply Foundation endorsement.

Library of Congress Cataloging-in-Publication Data

Bartik, Timothy J.
Jobs for the poor : can labor demand policies help? / Timothy J. Bartik.
p. cm.
Includes bibliographical references and index.
ISBN 0-87154-097-5 (hc) ISBN 0-87154-098-3 (pbk)
1. Labor demand—United States. 2. Poor—Employment—United States. 3. Economic assistance, Domestic—United States. I. Title.

HD5706 .B385 2001
331.1′0973—dc21 2001019118

The paper used in this publication meets the minimum requirements of American National Standard for Information Sciences—Permanence of Paper for Printed Library Materials. ANSI Z39.48-1992.

Text design by Suzanne Nichols

RUSSELL SAGE FOUNDATION
112 East 64th Street, New York, New York 10021
10 9 8 7 6 5 4 3 2 1

Contents

Acknowledgments

I appreciate the financial support for this research provided by the Russell Sage Foundation, the Rockefeller Foundation, and the W.E. Upjohn Institute for Employment Research. I thank Eric Wanner, President of the Russell Sage Foundation, for his leadership role in supporting this project from its start through its lengthy development. I thank Randy Eberts, Executive Director of the Upjohn Institute, for his continued enthusiasm for my work on longterm research projects such as this book.

The findings, interpretations, and policy recommendations in this book are my own, and may not reflect the views of any of the sponsors of this research.

I also want to thank the many staff persons at the Upjohn Institute who helped this complex research project develop into a book. I thank: Ken Kline and Wei-Jang Huang for their research assistance; Leslie Lance and Brian Latshaw for keeping the computers running; Linda Richer and Babette Schmitt for library support, including tracking down obscure documents around the U.S.; and Claire Black and Nancy Mack for secretarial support.

The book benefitted greatly from comments on the first draft of the book manuscript from David Weiman of the Russell Sage Foundation and four anonymous reviewers. I also received helpful comments on portions of this manuscript from Kevin Hollenbeck.

Midway through this project, I received a grant from the Joint Center for Poverty Research to look at the displacement effects of welfare reform, and that research project shaped the development of this book. I appreciate comments on the JCPR research from Becky Blank, David Card, and Larry Katz.

Editing this complex manuscript was a difficult task. For their editorial work, I thank Suzanne Nichols, Emily Chang, and Cindy Buck. I also appreciate David Nadziejka's help with the proof-reading. I thank David Haproff for his help in promoting this book.

Finally, in all things I depend on the support of my wife, Deb Wickman, and my two sons, Alex Bartik and Jonathan Bartik.

About the Author

Timothy J. Bartik is senior economist at the W.E. Upjohn Institute for Employment Research.

1

THE CASE FOR LABOR DEMAND POLICIES

How can public policy in the United States be most effective in helping low-income Americans increase their employment and earnings? Current U.S. antipoverty policies emphasize "labor supply policies." Labor supply policies are characterized by direct interactions with the poor to increase the quantity or quality of their labor supply or the wages they receive. Labor supply policies include welfare reform policies that make welfare benefits more difficult to receive as well as job training and education programs.

Current U.S. antipoverty policies place little emphasis on "labor demand policies." Labor demand policies are characterized by direct interactions with employers to provide more of the poor with jobs or to increase the quality of their jobs. Labor demand policies include public-service employment, wage subsidies to private employers, and economic development programs.

This book's main argument is that U.S. antipoverty policy would be more effective if it made greater use of labor demand policies. Using empirical evidence, this book argues that labor supply policies alone have significant limitations, and that labor demand policies can be effective. I also discuss how labor demand policies can be best designed to enhance their effectiveness in increasing earnings and to minimize their negative side effects.

The empirical evidence suggests that labor supply policies are limited because they have only modest effects in helping low-income Americans increase their employment. Even when welfare reform or job training programs help participants obtain jobs, those jobs are no longer available to other low-income Americans who are nonparticipants, thus "displacing" others from jobs. Some education policies may significantly increase participants' earnings but are very expensive. Job training and other labor supply policies also are more effective when overall labor demand is strong and the policies have strong ties to employers.

Labor demand policies are needed because even when overall U.S.

unemployment is low, jobs are in short supply for many groups, such as those with less education, racial minorities, and residents of high-unemployment cities. Increases in aggregate demand in the U.S. economy do significantly help the poor. However, the effects of those increases are not strong enough to come close to "solving" poverty. More targeted labor demand policies are also needed. Such targeted programs would directly induce either public employers or private employers to hire more low-income Americans. Empirical evidence suggests that public-service employment programs or wage subsidy programs for private employers can be effective in increasing the employment and earnings of low-income Americans.

An important point is that labor demand programs can have long-term effects on employment and earnings. How can a program that provides temporary subsidies for employing a low-income individual have long-term effects? The work experience provided during the subsidy period increases the job skills of the participant, particularly the "soft skills" of being able to reliably show up for work and deal effectively with coworkers and supervisors. Work experience also helps a worker build self-confidence, which also increases future employability. Finally, work experience gives a worker a better reputation with employers, who have only very imperfect information about which prospective workers will be most productive.

Targeted demand programs should be designed with features that reduce their displacement and inflation effects, increase the program's attractiveness to employers, and increase the program's long-run political support. To reduce displacement and inflation effects, targeted demand programs should emphasize creating new jobs, target individuals who currently are out of the labor force, and provide only temporary employment opportunities. If programs are also designed to make sure that participants can be productive on the job, private employers will be less likely to "stigmatize" the participants in the targeted demand program as unproductive.

Labor demand policies have usually faced strong political opposition in the United States. To reduce such opposition, targeted demand policies should emphasize subsidies to nonprofit employers and small business employers. This strategy would not invoke the American fear of augmenting the power of big government and big business, a fear that has often motivated opposition to public-service employment or wage subsidies to employers. In addition, labor demand policies should be managed locally by organizations that encompass one local labor market, such as a metropolitan area, to make sure that the design of the targeted labor demand programs matches the labor market conditions and institutions of that local market.

Based on the findings of this book, I would advocate a labor demand program for the United States with two components. First, the United States should increase aggregate labor demand by providing wage subsidies to employers who increase their overall employment. This wage subsidy program should be expanded during recessions and restricted during boom periods to high-unemployment local labor markets. Second, a large-scale labor demand program should be developed that targets those who are outside of the labor force or otherwise unlikely to be employed in regular jobs. When necessary, the targeted demand subsidies should be supplemented by supply-side programs to provide counseling or training to some individuals in the target group. Under the targeted demand program, short-term wage subsidies should be provided to selected public and private employers, particularly small businesses and nonprofits, for newly created jobs that go to selected persons in the target groups. Local agencies familiar with the local labor market should manage the targeted demand program, selecting members of the target group and employers who will be a good match, in that the match will create the largest short-run and long-run effects on employment and earnings. Over time a combined program of aggregate labor demand subsidies and a targeted labor demand program, with complementary supply-side programs, could significantly improve the permanent employment and earnings position of low-income Americans.

What Are Labor Supply and Demand Policies? How Are They Used Today in the United States Compared to Other Countries and the United States in the Past?

The distinction between labor supply and demand policies is fundamental. Each type of policy intervenes on a different side of the labor market. An increase in employment for low-income Americans requires changes on both sides of the labor market: on the supply side, additional persons must be able and willing to work; on the demand side, employers must be willing to hire additional labor.

As discussed in more detail in chapter 2, however, there are many different ways in which each type of policy can be implemented that make a major difference to their effectiveness. Labor demand and supply policies may differ in the instruments used to affect demand and supply, the particular types of labor suppliers and demanders targeted by the policy, the agency that administers the policy, and the degree of administrative discretion of that agency. Among the instruments used by labor demand and supply policies are "carrots" such as wage subsidies to workers or employers. But labor demand and supply policies may also influence the behavior of employers and workers through "sticks"—penalties for not behaving in a certain way, such as cutting off welfare benefits to welfare recipients who do not search for or accept jobs, or imposing legal penalties on firms that engage in racially discriminatory practices in hiring. Supply and demand policies can also influence behavior through information provision, such as providing employers with better information on the productivity of some workers, or providing workers with leads to better jobs.

Labor supply and demand programs may also differ in the workers or firms they target. They may focus on individuals below a certain income level, from a particular racial group, or at a particular stage of the life cycle. For example, U.S. educational and training programs to help the disadvantaged have traditionally devoted most of their resources to education programs for young persons, particularly K-12 programs, though extra attention is also focused on preschoolers and college students. These school and preschool programs are sometimes called "first-chance" programs, in contrast to job training and other postschool educational programs, which are called "second-chance" programs. Programs may also target a particular type of employer, such as public versus private employers, and, within those categories, employers below or above a certain size.

Labor supply and demand programs may also differ in the level of government and type of agency that is responsible for funding and administration. Some programs are administered at the federal level, such as the Earned Income Tax Credit (EITC), which subsidizes earnings for low-income families, and others are run at the state and local levels, such as economic development programs and welfare reform programs.

Finally, programs may be designed with more or less administrative discretion. The program's efforts to influence supply and demand behavior may tend toward automatically subsidizing or penalizing anyone who takes certain actions, on the one hand, or toward allowing the agency administering the program to award subsidies or impose penalties in a discretionary manner, on the other. For example, subsidies to firms for hiring the disadvantaged may be awarded either to any firm that does such hiring or only to firms that apply for such subsidies and are awarded one of a limited number of such subsidies at the discretion of the agency.

All of these different characteristics of supply and demand programs clearly can make a difference in program effectiveness. Although each program is unique and should be judged separately, this book concludes that programs tend to be more effective if they focus on "carrots" such as subsidies and information provision, are targeted at particular groups of interest, are locally administered to take account of the peculiarities of the local labor market, and allow for administrative discretion in handing out program benefits and sanctions.

Overall, the United States devotes far more resources to labor supply than to labor demand policies to reduce poverty, as shown in more detail in chapter 2. This great emphasis on labor supply approaches in the United States is particularly marked if we include first-chance programs that aid low-income Americans from preschool through college.

The U.S. underemphasis on labor demand programs is unusual among Western industrial countries. As shown in chapter 2, the United States devotes a far lower percentage of its economy to labor demand programs than do most other Western industrial countries. The United States also tends to devote fewer resources to labor supply policies to help the disadvantaged, but the differences in labor supply programs between the United States and other Western industrial countries are not as great.

This underemphasis on labor demand programs is also unusual compared to past U.S. policy. Historically the United States has occasionally undertaken labor demand policies that were quite large, such as the Works Progress Administration (WPA) program of the 1930s and early 1940s and the public-service jobs programs under the Comprehensive Employment and Training Act (CETA) in the mid-1970s. The U.S. historical experience with WPA and CETA is discussed in chapters 2 and 7.

Why does the United States devote unusually low levels of resources to labor demand policies? Labor demand policies tend to lack an enthusiastic political base, while arousing fears of big government or big business power. Labor demand policies to create public-service jobs arouse opposition from conservatives opposed to an expansion of big government, as well as from some public-sector labor unions concerned about their members losing jobs because of the new subsidized workers. Labor demand policies that subsidize private employers to create jobs arouse opposition from some liberals as "corporate welfare" and from some businesses and conservatives as an unwarranted interference in the private market. As suggested throughout the book, labor demand policies that focus on encouraging job creation at small nonprofits and small businesses may find more political support.

What Does Our Understanding of the Low-Wage Labor Market Suggest About the Likely Effects of Supply and Demand Policies?

As reviewed in chapter 3, economists and other social scientists already have considerable knowledge about the functioning of low-wage labor markets. Much of this knowledge is quite relevant to understanding the effectiveness of different labor supply and demand policies, including: evidence on the need for and effectiveness of jobs in the low-wage labor market; the responsiveness of labor supply in the low-wage labor market to increased demand; the responsiveness of labor demand for low-wage workers to increased labor supply; the likely displacement and wage effects of labor supply and demand policies; and the geographic scope of low-wage labor markets.

Even though the U.S. economy is currently strong, there are still many low-income Americans who need a job. Compared to past employment rates for some groups, or compared to the need for income, the United States probably needs at least three million to nine million additional jobs for low-income Americans, according to estimates presented in chapter 3. Furthermore, contrary to popular myth, having a full-time full-year worker in each American family would have sizable effects on reducing U.S. poverty rates, cutting the number of persons in poverty by more than 70 percent. Earnings supplements such as the EITC are extensive enough in the United States today that even relatively low-wage jobs can help reduce poverty.

As shown in chapter 3, many of the U.S. poor could work more under the right labor demand conditions. Many Americans in poverty already work, although not always full-time and full-year. Improved demand conditions, which would increase wage rates and lower unemployment rates, have been shown by empirical studies to cause a significant labor supply response, increasing the labor force participation and employment rates of low-income Americans.

Furthermore, as mentioned earlier, the work experience brought about by increased employment can significantly increase the long-run employment and earnings of the poor, according to the research reviewed in chapter 3. Improved job skills, self-image, and reputation with employers all increase a worker's long-run employability and wages. As a result, full-time full-year work increases the long-run earnings of different educational groups in the United States by the same percentage.

As shown in chapter 3, even in today's strong economy, the labor demand for low-income Americans is for many groups and in many areas short of labor supply. For example, though the overall U.S. unemployment rate was 4.5 percent in 1998, unemployment was still 8.9 percent among blacks, and 7.3 percent in the New York metropolitan area. Labor demand for low-income Americans does respond to increased labor supply, but the most plausible estimates suggest that this response is modest and probably considerably less than the increase in labor supply.

One reason that labor demand for low-income Americans may not fully respond to increased labor supply is the poor information that employers have about the productivity of job seekers. Because of poor information, new hires in the low-wage labor market frequently do not work out well and employers become more reluctant to hire in response to increased labor supply. Furthermore, because employers have great difficulty finding productive workers, they often adopt practices that may put many low-income Americans at a disadvantage, such as hiring through referrals from current employees or refusing to hire welfare recipients. In the absence of reliable information on job seekers' productivity, some employers may rationalize their own racial prejudices against minority job seekers. Empirical studies show that racial discrimination in hiring is still common.

The modest responsiveness in low-wage labor markets of both labor supply and demand means that both labor supply and demand policies can increase employment but may also cause displacement. According to estimates presented in appendices 1 and 2, employment increases in response to increased labor supply, but by perhaps one-third to two-thirds of the employment obtained by those persons added to labor supply. This implies that other persons lose their jobs, because of the increased labor supply, or are "displaced" from employment owing to the policy. Similarly, employment increases in response to increased labor demand, but also by perhaps one-third to two-thirds of the employment of those directly employed in subsidized jobs. Other persons lose their jobs because of the increased labor demand or are "displaced."

The appropriate design of labor supply and demand policies depends on the economic conditions, labor market institutions, and mix of businesses in the labor market for low-wage labor. What is the geographic scope of the low-wage labor market? As shown in chapter 3, the available evidence suggests that the relevant labor market is best defined as the area within which most commuting flows are contained, such as a metropolitan area. Within such an area there is sufficient commuting that changes in labor market conditions for similar individuals tend to be transmitted fairly rapidly across the metropolitan area. In larger metropolitan areas labor market conditions for somewhat smaller areas may also be relevant, owing to problems in efficiently transmitting information about job openings and job seekers throughout a large metropolitan area.

Metropolitan areas and other similar labor market areas are relevant to labor supply and demand policies because each labor market area has a particular character of its local labor market institutions, such as local job training agencies, local schools and community colleges, local economic development agencies, and local business groups. The character of these local institutions, and their interrelationships, may influence the types of labor supply and labor demand policies that are most effective in a particular local labor market.

In addition, each metropolitan area has its own mix of industries and sizes of businesses. This business mix affects business hiring, training, and job retention policies. These business policies must be taken into account in designing appropriate labor supply and demand policies.

What Is the Evidence on the Effects of Labor Supply Policies?

Labor supply policies to increase the employment, earnings, and income of low-income Americans include welfare reform, earnings supplements to workers, education policies, and job training. As shown in chapter 4, such labor supply policies can do much good but have significant limitations. It is difficult for labor supply policies to increase significantly *both* the employment and the income of the poor without huge costs. In addition, the significant displacement effects of many labor supply policies can adversely affect employment prospects for low-income Americans who do not participate in labor supply programs.

Welfare reform can significantly increase employment for welfare recipients by making it more difficult to receive adequate welfare benefits, thereby forcing many welfare recipients into the labor force. However, such welfare reform does significantly reduce family income for a sizable proportion of those pushed into the labor force. Under a philosophy of "sink or swim," some sink. Welfare reform also causes significant displacement effects: perhaps half of the new jobs for welfare recipients represent reduced employment for other low-income persons.

"Carrot" approaches seek to increase the labor supply of low-income Americans by providing them with earnings supplements; for example, the Earned Income Tax Credit provides refundable tax credits for extra earnings for low-income families. Such earnings supplements can significantly increase income for many low-income Americans but generally appear to have only modest effects on employment, as reviewed in chapter 4. Supplements have a modest effect on employment in part because the apparent stigma attached to receiving most income-tied earnings supplements may reduce somewhat a family's incentive to alter its work behavior because of the supplement. In addition, those earnings supplements may cause displacement: to the extent to which the earnings supplements encourage some of those receiving supplements to get jobs they otherwise would not obtain, these jobs are unavailable to others.

Education policies can significantly increase both the employment and the income of disadvantaged persons who successfully complete education programs. Any displacement effects of the extra employment of the newly educated tend to be felt by more highly educated persons, and in fact, education may open up some job opportunities for individuals left behind in the low-education job market. However, education programs can be very expensive, particularly considering how many extra jobs are needed (three million to nine million) and the enormous costs of making additional education available to millions of people. Furthermore, any enormous expansion of education levels would require some significant reforms if it is to be accomplished without some diminishment of educational quality.

The enormous costs of significantly expanding the regular first-chance education system increases the interest in perhaps improving job skills more cheaply through more focused job training programs. On the whole, the performance of the average job training program has been disappointing to many social scientists and policymakers. As reviewed in chapter 4, the programs on average increase earnings of training participants by only perhaps $1,000 per year, although this average probably conceals that these earnings benefits are concentrated among the relatively few trainees who gain much more in an annual earnings boost. Furthermore, most training programs in practice have not significantly improved wage rates, so the new trainees are competing for jobs with others who also have modest incomes. Training programs probably have significant displacement effects, so a significant portion of the added jobs for trainees represent reduced employment for others who also have quite moderate to low incomes.

Some training programs have been considerably more effective. Such successful programs tend, like the Center for Employment Training (CET) program, to be located in local labor markets with relatively strong employment growth. In addition, successful programs like CET typically have strong ties to individual local employers; the programs involve these employers in training design and aggressively market program graduates to them. Therefore, labor supply programs such as job training are most successful when labor demand is strong and when the programs make some effort to affect the behavior of employers—that is, when the program adopts some of the characteristics of a labor demand policy.

What Is the Evidence on the Effects of Increased Labor Demand?

As reviewed in chapter 5, a considerable amount of empirical research has estimated the effects of increased labor demand on the employment and earnings of low-income persons. This research suggests that increases in labor demand can make a significant difference to the employment and earnings of low-income Americans, particularly if the increase in labor demand is somehow targeted at low-income Americans who are originally out of the labor force. (Later chapters consider the issues of designing labor demand programs that can actually do this.) Empirical research also suggests that targeted labor demand increases can result in long-term increases in employment and earnings for low-income Americans. Increases in high "wage premium" jobs—those jobs that pay well relative to the skills required—have greater benefits.

Despite the myth that a "rising tide no longer lifts all boats," the empirical work reviewed in chapter 5 shows that increases in overall labor demand still have progressive effects on the income distribution. Stronger overall labor demand and lower average unemployment increase the employment rates and labor force participation rates of those who originally were not employed and allow for occupational upgrading for many persons in lower-paid occupations. As a consequence, lower overall unemployment increases real earnings and income for all education and income groups, but by a higher percentage for those with less education or lower income.

However, the progressive effects of stronger overall labor demand are clearly insufficient to be the only solution to the poverty problem. For example, numerous empirical studies suggest that a 1 percent lower overall U.S. unemployment rate would bring somewhere between one million and three million persons out of poverty. But with more than thirty million Americans in poverty, and a U.S. unemployment rate close to 4 percent, even reducing unemployment to zero would not solve all of the poverty problem, and clearly reducing overall unemployment a huge amount below the current level is infeasible.

As reviewed in chapter 5, the empirical evidence suggests that increases in labor demand targeted at lower-income groups can significantly increase employment and earnings. Studies using a variety of empirical approaches suggest that a targeted increase in labor demand, whether brought about by public policy or by the regular workings of the economy, will in the short run increase employment and earnings of the targeted group by about two-thirds of the initial shock to employment and earnings of that group, implying a "displacement" effect of about one-third. Displacement rates may be somewhat larger in the long run. However, simulations using estimated parameters suggest that long-run displacement rates can be reduced by targeting the increased demand on persons who originally were out of the labor force and by encouraging those targeted for increased labor demand to remain available for other jobs.

The empirical evidence also suggests that increases in labor demand cause long-run increases in employment and earnings. Empirical studies of individuals' earnings suggest that increased work experience for individuals causes increases in wages and employment rates many years later. In addition, empirical work on local labor markets suggests that an increase in labor demand at one point in time causes a local labor market to still have increased employment rates many years later.

The long-run effects of greater labor demand are somewhat higher for increased labor demand that is concentrated in high "wage premium" jobs. Empirical evidence suggests that such jobs tend to be characterized by greater job retention, which promotes greater long-run employment and earnings effects.

Will Increases in Labor Demand Inevitably Increase Inflation?

One argument against policies to increase labor demand for the poor is that such policies could increase inflation. Perhaps labor demand policies, if expanded until unemployment is dramatically reduced, could push unemployment low enough to initiate an upward spiral of accelerating inflation rates. This possibility is based on the theory that there is a level of unemployment below which inflation tends endlessly to accelerate the so-called non-accelerating inflation rate of unemployment (NAIRU).

As chapter 6 explains, potential problems with a NAIRU should not scare policymakers away from labor demand policies, although these problems might affect the design of labor demand policies, for several reasons. First, even in empirical models that estimate that there is a NAIRU, unemployment below the NAIRU only significantly accelerates inflation after a long time. In addition, there is much uncertainty about exactly what unemployment rate is the NAIRU, or indeed whether a NAIRU exists. Given the long-term nature of the potential NAIRU problem and this uncertainty, it may make sense to pursue labor demand policies and simply monitor these policies' possible effects on inflation.

Second, the inflationary effects of increasing labor demand are reduced if the increased labor demand is targeted at those out of the labor force—a sizable group of the adult U.S. poor. To put it another way, the inflationary effects of added labor demand are reduced if the increased labor demand is accompanied by an increase in labor supply. As discussed in chapter 6, empirical work also indicates lower inflationary effects of labor demand increases that are targeted at high-unemployment local labor markets.

Third, the inflationary effects of increasing labor demand are moderated if the newly employed are more readily available for hiring by private employers. For example, if the labor demand policy is to provide public-service jobs for the disadvantaged, these jobs could require periodic job search and be temporary by design, with time limits on how long someone could hold such a job. In addition, setting the wage rate on these special public-service jobs slightly below alternative wages in the private sector would tend to increase work search among the disadvantaged workers who get these jobs.

Finally, if some labor demand policies are implemented in a way that lowers marginal costs for businesses, inflationary pressures may be eased. For example, wage subsidy programs for the disadvantaged tend to lower business marginal costs. As reviewed in chapter 6, there is some empirical evidence that wage subsidies do lower the prices charged by employers.

What Is the Evidence on the Effects of Labor Demand Policies? The Case of Public-Service Employment Programs

Various labor demand programs to increase the employment and earnings of low-income Americans have been proposed or implemented over the years. Chapter 7 considers the most traditional type of labor demand program for the disadvantaged, public-service employment (PSE). Chapter 8 considers labor demand policies that provide wage subsidies to private for-profit employers for employing the disadvantaged. Finally, chapter 9 considers a wide variety of other labor demand programs, ranging from economic development programs to the minimum wage.

As reviewed in chapter 7, public-service employment programs can be effective. The U.S. experience with PSE programs suggests that, if the PSE program is well administered, PSE jobs are productive, delivering valuable services and developing public works. Furthermore, administrative requirements that PSE jobs be new jobs and that existing workers not lose their jobs to PSE hires seem to be reasonably effective in minimizing the displacement of existing public-sector workers by the new subsidized workers.

Well-designed PSE programs can also reduce their effects on the labor market that might cause marketwide displacement and increase the long-run effects on participants' earnings of the PSE jobs, while keeping down the size and cost of the program. PSE programs should target disadvantaged persons who otherwise would be unlikely to get a job, such as persons who were originally out of the labor force and who then were unsuccessful in searching for a regular job. PSE jobs should be limited in the duration of the subsidy period and pay slightly below market wages; the limited duration and low wage will encourage PSE participants to transition to regular jobs. In addition to reducing the displacement effects of PSE, these policies of targeting PSE jobs and limiting their wages and duration also tend to hold down the size and cost of a PSE program.

What Is the Evidence on the Effects of Labor Demand Policies? The Case of Wage Subsidies to Private For-Profit Employers

Another commonly used labor demand policy to increase the earnings of low-income Americans is to give wage subsidies to private employers for hiring persons from various lower-income groups. As reviewed in chapter 8, the empirical evidence suggests that several varieties of wage subsidy programs for employers can be effective in increasing the employment and earnings of low-income Americans. Among the effective wage subsidy programs are general wage subsidies, such as the New Jobs Tax Credit (NJTC) of the mid-1970s, which provided corporate tax credits for employment expansion regardless of who was hired. Another type of effective wage subsidy program is a targeted entitlement wage subsidy, such as the Work Opportunities Tax Credit (WOTC), which provides tax credits to firms that hire individuals from particular disadvantaged target groups, such as welfare recipients. Finally, the type of wage subsidy that has been the most successful in increasing the earnings of the disadvantaged is a discretionary wage subsidy, in which local agencies distribute wage subsidies in a discretionary manner to selected employers for hiring selected disadvantaged individuals.

The type of wage subsidy program that does not work is a voucher program, under which low-income persons are given vouchers entitling their employer to a wage subsidy; the voucher program is then primarily marketed to employers by encouraging individual voucher holders to tell prospective employers of the voucher. This type of program is ineffective because of stigma effects. Some employers contacted by voucher holders appear to use the voucher as a signal that the voucher holder is likely to be less productive. As a result, as discussed in chapter 8, several studies show that voucher wage subsidy programs may actually reduce the hiring prospects of voucher holders.

However, most other forms of wage subsidy programs in practice operate in ways that reduce such stigma effects. General wage subsidy programs do not suffer from stigma effects because employers are not required to hire particular target groups. Because discretionary wage subsidy programs allow local agencies to screen local employers and disadvantaged job seekers, the agencies can screen out the local employers who would be most reluctant to hire disadvantaged job seekers because of stigma effects, and they can provide employers with disadvantaged job seekers for whom there is at least some information suggesting that they can be productive on the job. Finally, in practice entitlement wage subsidy programs seem to be used most heavily by larger low-wage employers who expect to hire many disadvantaged job seekers and are unlikely to use stigma issues arbitrarily to refuse to hire an entire disadvantaged group.

One serious problem in wage subsidy programs for employers is their generally low take-up rates. The reluctance of many employers to use these programs limits the number of additional jobs that they can help create. The low take-up rate appears to be based in part on employer ignorance of the programs, and in part on a reluctance to be too involved with government red tape. As reviewed in chapter 8, some empirical evidence suggests that aggressive marketing of wage subsidy programs to employers can significantly increase these programs' take-up rate.

Wage subsidies, PSE, and job training programs may be seen as complementary programs. Training programs can help disadvantaged persons whose greatest employment need is to improve skills that are best addressed through formal educational programs, whereas subsidized jobs programs can help disadvantaged persons whose greatest employment need is to gain more work experience, job contacts, and credentials. It is easier to target public-service employment programs than wage subsidy programs at more disadvantaged groups. On the other hand, wage subsidies to private employers are more likely to result in "rollover" of the subsidized employers to permanent private-sector jobs.

What Is the Evidence on the Effects of Labor Demand Policies? Other Labor Demand Policies

In addition to PSE and wage subsidies to employers, the United States also has a number of other labor demand policies that, if not primarily aimed at reducing poverty, can be used to increase significantly the employment and earnings of low-income Americans. Chapter 9 reviews the following labor demand policies: state and local economic development policies; labor market intermediary programs; antidiscrimination policies; and minimum-wage or living-wage regulations.

As reviewed in chapter 9, the empirical evidence suggests that state and local economic development policies can increase local employment growth and thereby increase the earnings of low-income local residents. However, for most typical economic development policies, these earnings effects on low-income groups are likely to be modest. Linking state and local economic development efforts with customized training programs that train disadvantaged persons, and with labor market intermediary programs (LMIs) that seek to identify productive workers among disadvantaged job seekers, helps increase the proportion of the earnings benefits of local job growth that accrue to the poor.

Labor market intermediary programs, such as the U.S. Employment Service, seek to increase and improve the matching between job seekers and available jobs. Under the recent Workforce Investment Act, the employment service is supposed to be integrated and coordinated with job training programs and welfare-to-work programs. At the same time, a number of neighborhood-based efforts around the United States have also sought to do a better job of linking the disadvantaged with available jobs. As reviewed in chapter 9, the available evidence suggests that LMIs can indeed result in better job matches. However, LMIs in the United States usually are poorly funded. In addition, by seeking to serve two very different clients, job seekers and employers, LMI services are complex and difficult to deliver consistently in a high-quality fashion. Chapter 9 suggests that perhaps political pressure to improve both the funding for and performance of LMI programs will increase if these programs are perceived as tied to economic development programs, which have greater local community support.

Although many white Americans believe otherwise, the empirical evidence shows that there is still significant hiring discrimination against blacks in the United States, as reviewed in chapter 9. Some evaluation studies suggest that antidiscrimination laws and affirmative action regulations do help to reduce employment discrimination. However, under current procedures, these laws and regulations are easier to enforce against discrimination in promotions than against discrimination in hiring. As suggested in chapter 9, perhaps political support for antidiscrimination efforts would be stronger if the existence of hiring discrimination were regularly demonstrated, perhaps by sending out matched employment testers of different races to apply for job openings in a variety of different occupations in different local job markets. Such employment testing could also be used to improve enforcement of antidiscrimination laws against discrimination in hiring. Firms might also be more willing to change discriminatory practices if testing were linked with assistance from LMI programs or others in improving the effectiveness of overall firm policies in hiring, training, and keeping productive workers.

Minimum-wage regulations are usually applied at the federal or state level to require minimum wages for most employees. A more recent trend is living-wage regulations, which are typically local regulations that require employers that receive contracts or economic development subsidies from the local government to pay "living wages" (higher than current federal minimum wages). As reviewed in chapter 9, most empirical studies suggest that minimum-wage and living-wage regulations have at best modest antipoverty effects. The earnings effects of higher wages for the poor are reduced for those many individuals who are not fully employed year-round, have wages above the minimum, or work for employers that are not covered by the minimum- or living-wage regulation. In addition, minimum wages may cause some employers to reduce employment of less-skilled workers, and living-wage regulations may cause some employers to change their location decisions in response to a city's living-wage requirement for firms receiving economic development subsidies. However, higher minimum wages and living wages have great political popularity. Campaigns for higher minimum or living wages may be a useful organizing tool for getting many groups involved in thinking about the problems of poverty and low earnings. Such campaigns could lead to broader and more diversified efforts to reduce local poverty rates.

What Labor Demand Program Should Be Pursued to Increase the Employment and Earnings of Low-Income Americans?

Based on the findings of this book, what labor demand program makes the most sense to increase the employment and earnings of low-income Americans? As outlined in chapter 10, the most effective program would include two components, the first focusing on ensuring stronger aggregate labor demand in all local labor markets, the second on a large-scale targeted labor demand policy.

Ensuring stronger aggregate labor demand in all local labor markets in part rests on macroeconomic policies that minimize recessions and keep the U.S. economy operating at close to peak levels as much as possible. But stronger aggregate labor demand in all local labor markets would also be encouraged by adopting a revision of the New Jobs Tax Credit of 1976–1977. As outlined in chapter 10, in this modified NJTC all employers (private for-profit, nonprofit, and governmental) in high-unemployment local labor markets would receive refundable tax credits against social security payroll taxes for expanding employment above some base level. (The social security trust fund would be reimbursed for the forgone taxes from general revenues.) When the national unemployment rate is low, such a policy would target expanded labor demand in the local labor markets in which expanded aggregate demand is most likely to be effective in expanding employment, with the lowest inflationary consequences. When the national unemployment rate is high, such a policy would provide subsidies for expanded labor demand in virtually the entire nation. This policy would increase the automatic countercyclical effects of U.S. fiscal policy. This particular expansionary fiscal policy, compared to other types of tax reductions or spending expansions, would tend to increase employment more per dollar of resources, since the tax credits are targeted at employment expansions. Furthermore, it would be possible and desirable to design the refundable tax credits so that the program encourages the expansion of lower-skill jobs. For example, if the tax credit applies only on wages up to some proportion of the social security tax base, the incentive to expand employment would be somewhat greater for lower-wage jobs.

Some rough estimates in chapter 10 suggest that during a recession a revised NJTC could create around two million jobs, about one-quarter of which would go to disadvantaged household heads. This would offset a significant portion—but not most—of the employment losses due to a recession. This revised NJTC might cost around $20 billion per year during recessions.

During a national labor market boom the NJTC subsidies for expansion of aggregate employment in high-unemployment local labor markets are estimated to increase the employment of disadvantaged household heads by around half a million in the long run. As discussed in chapter 3, disadvantaged Americans probably need from three million to nine million more jobs—or, to pick a middle number, about six million jobs. Therefore, although the revised NJTC would have important long-run effects on the employment of the poor, it would deal only with a small portion of their employment problems. During a boom NJTC subsidies would probably cost a little less than $5 billion annually.

As a second component of a labor demand program, I propose a large-scale targeted labor demand policy. This policy resembles a 1980s Minnesota program called MEED but is sufficiently revised that the program is renamed NEED (National Employment and Economic Development).

Under the NEED program, short-term wage subsidies would be provided to selected public and private employers for hiring into newly created jobs selected members of targeted disadvantaged groups. Local agencies familiar with the local labor market would administer the program and decide, within guidelines, which employers would receive wage subsidies and which disadvantaged persons would have their employment subsidized. The disadvantaged workers targeted would be low-income persons who are out of the labor force or otherwise unlikely to be employed in regular jobs. Whether participants are unlikely to receive a regular job would be decided in part by requiring them to undertake a job search before receiving a subsidized job slot. If necessary, an individual in the target group would receive supply-side services, such as counseling or training, before or during their period of subsidized employment.

Job developers would aggressively market the program to local employers. To increase political support, preference for subsidies would go to small businesses and small nonprofit agencies. Subsidized employment would last for up to six months. Preference in giving wage subsidies would go to employers that encourage the "rollover" of subsidized employees into regular jobs. Although firms would pay the market wage to subsidized workers, part of the worker's wages would be "taxed" by the program and paid as a bonus later if the worker meets certain goals for staying employed. This short-term reduction in the subsidized worker's net wage would encourage both long-term job retention and the transition to a regular job.

Empirical estimates suggest that it is feasible to operate a NEED program that, over a ten-year period, would create the five and a half million jobs needed by disadvantaged Americans (the assumed six million minus the half-million provided by the revised NJTC). Doing so would require a NEED program with about three million annual participants. Although such a large-scale program is unusual in the current U.S. policy environment, it is not out of line compared to past U.S. labor demand policies or policies in some Western European countries. The costs of the NEED program are estimated to be a little more than $40 billion per year.

In the end, finding resources for these programs will require a political coalition that is committed to government activism to increase the employment of low-income Americans. This book creates an intellectual case that an increased role for labor demand policies can significantly increase the employment of the poor. But these policies cannot be adopted without an active political coalition involving some combination of business groups, labor groups, community groups, and intellectual groups. Groups on the left must be willing to accept the idea that a key priority for helping the poor is increasing their employment. Groups on the right must be willing to accept the idea that increasing the employment of the poor may require some government activism.

Plan of the Book

Chapter 2 reviews the wide variety of labor demand and supply policies used in the United States and other industrial countries and describes their size and history. Chapter 3 goes on to discuss some features of the workings of the low-wage labor market and their relevance to understanding labor supply and demand policies. Chapter 4 reviews the evidence on the effectiveness of various labor supply policies. Chapter 5 examines the effects on the low-wage labor market of various types of shocks to labor demand, both aggregate and more targeted shocks to labor demand. Chapter 6 considers the effects on inflation of increases in labor demand. Chapters 7, 8, and 9 review the evidence on the effects of various specific labor demand policies, including public-service employment policies, wage subsidies to for-profit employers, and economic development policies. Chapter 10 makes the case for this book's policy recommendations.

2

LABOR SUPPLY AND DEMAND POLICIES: DESCRIPTIONS, CLASSIFICATIONS, CROSS-NATIONAL COMPARISONS, AND HISTORY

THIS CHAPTER describes some of the fundamental features of U.S. labor supply and labor demand policies to increase the employment and earnings of lower-income Americans. This description includes some key distinctions between different types of labor supply and labor demand policies, and comparisons in the scope of labor supply and demand policies between the United States and other countries, and between the United States today and the United States in the past. These descriptions and comparisons provide a context for the discussion of specific labor supply and demand policies in subsequent chapters.

The distinction between labor supply and labor demand policies is fundamental. Labor supply policies directly seek to alter the behavior of low-income Americans, increasing their labor supply or job skills. Labor demand policies directly seek to alter the behavior of employers, increasing their employment, or altering the kind of employee they hire and at what wages. For the employment and earnings of low-income Americans to increase, behavior must change on both sides of the market, among both employers and low-income Americans: employers must hire more low-income Americans, and more low-income Americans must be willing and able to work. These behavior changes on both sides of the market may be effected by policy interventions, or they may occur as reactions to changing market conditions. Whether labor suppliers or demanders are directly targeted by public policy may make a difference to the policy's effectiveness, the best institutional arrangements for implementing the policy, and the political sustainability of the policy.

Labor supply and demand policies can be implemented in many different ways. As discussed in this chapter, one fundamental distinction is between policies that seek to alter the behavior of labor suppliers or demanders through positive incentives to behave in the desired manner or through negative sanctions to behave in the undesired manner. Supply and demand policies also differ in the types of organizations used to implement them, and the specific labor suppliers or demanders whose behavior is targeted by the policy. All of these differences may affect whether a particular labor supply or demand policy is effective.

The United States relies much less on labor demand policies than on labor supply policies. To increase the employment and earnings of low-income Americans, the United States devotes only one-tenth as many resources to labor demand policies as are devoted to labor supply policies. The low U.S. emphasis on labor demand policies contrasts with a much more balanced use of both labor demand and labor supply policies in many Western European countries. The low priority given to labor demand policies in the United States today also contrasts with some U.S. policies in the past, such as the heavy use of public-service employment during the Great Depression. Labor demand policies are probably deemphasized in the United States because they have a weak political base: often vehemently opposed by business interests and conservatives, they have had only lukewarm support from labor and liberals. A recurring issue throughout this book is the challenge of designing labor demand policies that are not only effective but politically sustainable.

The Distinction Between Labor Supply and Labor Demand Policies

Both labor supply and labor demand antipoverty policies seek to increase the employment and earnings of the poor, but they differ in whose behavior is targeted. Labor supply antipoverty policies seek to directly alter the behavior of the poor. Labor demand antipoverty policies seek to directly alter the behavior of employers. Examples of labor supply policies are job training and education. Examples of labor demand policies are public employment, wage subsidies for private employers to hire the poor, and affirmative action programs.

Why is the distinction between labor supply and demand policies so fundamental? The side of the labor market targeted by policymakers may make a big difference in the effectiveness of a policy, substantively, politically, and operationally.

Although the distinction between labor supply and demand policies is fundamental, increases in employment for low-income Americans must at some stage involve both sides of the labor market. For employment to increase, labor demanders must be willing to employ more persons, and labor suppliers must be willing and able to supply more labor. Labor supply and demand policies differ in the side of the labor market they initially target, and in which side then reacts to changes in the market. For a labor supply policy to increase employment, the direct effects of the policy on labor supply must lead to changes in the labor market that then cause labor demanders to be willing to employ more labor. For a labor demand policy to increase employment, the direct effects of the policy on labor demand must lead to changes in the labor market that then cause labor suppliers to be willing and able to be employed. Chapter 3 reviews what we know about the responsiveness of labor supply and demand.

Wage subsidies are one example of the differences in effectiveness of policies targeted at one side of the market rather than the other. Either wage subsidies to low-income Americans or wage subsidies to employers to employ low-income Americans may lead to increased employment.[1] But depending on labor market conditions, wage subsidies to one side of the labor market or the other may be more effective in increasing employment. For example, suppose that employers have imperfect information about the productivity of those they hire. Suppose that disadvantaged workers are assumed, perhaps accurately, to have lower productivity on average. Suppose that normally employers can ascertain whether a job applicant is "disadvantaged" only with considerable error. Then the government introduces a program that pays wage subsidies to employers to hire workers who are given vouchers attesting to their disadvantaged status. It is quite possible that workers with such vouchers will find that their odds of being hired are *reduced:* from the employers' perspective, the expected lower productivity of disadvantaged workers may outweigh the benefits of the wage subsidies. Because of the stigma of being labeled "disadvantaged," the wage subsidy to employers actually reduces employment and earnings among the disadvantaged. There is some empirical evidence to support the belief that stigma effects in hiring the disadvantaged may be important (Burtless 1985). I return to this issue of the stigma effects of wage subsidies in chapter 8, which also considers how such effects can be reduced.

On the other hand, under these imperfect information conditions, wage subsidies to disadvantaged workers may still be quite effective. Subsidies to these workers increases their labor supply. This increased labor supply reduces market wages. Because employers in this case have no greater information about who is disadvantaged, this reduction in market wages should allow some expansion in the quantity of labor that is demanded.

In contrast, suppose that conditions in the labor market are such that wages for low-income Americans are rigid downward. (Market wages could be rigid downward owing to minimum-wage regulations or to social norms that cause lower wages to lead to customer boycotts or dramatic decreases in worker productivity.) Under these conditions, wage subsidies paid to workers have no effects, but wage subsidies paid to employers could have large effects. Wage subsidies paid to workers expand labor supply, but because market wages are rigid downward and thereby do not change, there is no reason for firms to expand their employment. With the expanded labor supply, it is possible that some workers who previously were not employed will become employed. However, each additional worker who becomes employed is matched by a worker who loses his or her job: there is complete displacement. Wage subsidies paid to employers increase labor demand under these conditions, because the labor costs to firms go down because of the subsidy even if the market wage cannot go down. If at the original downward rigid wage there was an excess supply of workers (involuntary unemployment), then it may be possible to accommodate this expanded demand for workers through the existing supply, even if the market wage rate is unchanged.[2]

Labor supply and demand policies are also likely to be fundamentally different in the types of programs needed to affect behavior on these two sides of the market. For example, the types of programs needed to increase the skills of welfare recipients are likely to have little in common with the programs designed to change the hiring decisions of small businesses.

The agencies that carry out labor supply and demand policies are likely over time to develop different personalities. It is certainly normal over time for a government agency to develop a greater understanding of the challenges faced by its clients, even if it is not actually politically "captured" by these clients. Agencies dealing with the labor supply of low-income Americans are likely over time to gain a greater appreciation for the perspective of these citizens on the labor market. Agencies dealing with the labor demand of employers for different disadvantaged groups are likely over time to gain a greater appreciation for the perspective of these employers on the labor market.

The politics of labor supply and labor demand policies are different. Labor supply policies directly aid low-income Americans and interfere little with employers' decisions about whom to hire. The size or scope of labor supply policies may be questioned, but labor supply policies have a solid base of political support from liberals and, with the right research evidence of effectiveness, can gain the support of pragmatic moderates.

In contrast, labor demand policies are directly aimed at the behavior of employers and only indirectly aid low-income Americans. This orientation leads to the suspicion that labor demand policies may benefit only employers, not low-income Americans. This suspicion is likely to be particularly acute among liberal groups when the immediate beneficiaries of the labor demand program are large corporations, as is the case with some wage subsidy programs for employers. In addition, labor demand policies result in either government hiring or government interference with the hiring decisions of employers. This consequence leads to opposition to labor demand policies by free-market conservatives and many businesses. The opposition by these groups may be particularly strong when the labor demand program increases the size of government, but many conservatives

and businesses also oppose government wage subsidies to for-profit businesses as inappropriate government interference. In addition, by encouraging some employers to hire more disadvantaged job seekers, labor demand policies may threaten the jobs of some current workers, including some unionized workers. This threat is particularly obvious for public-service jobs programs. The net result of all these political forces is that labor demand policies may antagonize a wide variety of conservative, business, and union groups, while lacking enthusiastic support from any group.

Different Types of Labor Supply and Demand Policies

The effectiveness of labor supply or demand policies may depend on the policy's specific techniques to alter supplier or demander behavior, the type of organization used to carry it out, the specific groups of suppliers or demanders it targets, the administrative flexibility used in implementing it, and the level of government that finances and authorizes it. Labor supply and demand policies differ widely along all these dimensions. Table 2.1 categorizes supply and demand policies by the instrument or technique used to affect labor demand or labor supply, and table 2.2 categorizes supply and demand policies by their organizational arrangements and clientele.

As emphasized in table 2.1, policy can affect labor supply or labor demand using many techniques. Education and training are the best-known techniques for affecting the labor supply of the poor. The labor supply of the poor is also affected by welfare program rules, incentives to work more, and better information on job opportunities. Among labor demand policies, subsidies for private employers to hire the poor receive the most attention and resources today. In the past, the emphasis was probably on public-service employment for the poor. Demand for the labor of the poor can also be affected by antidiscrimination laws, the minimum wage and other labor market regulations, training programs for the disadvantaged that pay firms to do on-the-job training, economic development assistance that encourages firms to hire the poor, programs that provide employers with better information on qualified job candidates among the poor, and programs that help train employers to deal with a more diverse workforce.

Among these techniques for affecting labor demand or supply, public provision and incentives are the most expensive. The discussion of such policies in subsequent chapters considers ways to keep the costs of public provision and incentives under control. Such expensive public programs become more attractive if they can produce long-term results with a short-term investment—for example, if they lead to better job skills—and these possibilities are also discussed in subsequent chapters. Sanctions and regulations are cheaper for the government in the short term but may have more subtle social costs. For example, government regulation can increase the

TABLE 2.1 *How Labor Supply and Demand Policies Alter the Labor Supply of or Demand for the Poor*

Intervention	Labor Supply Policies	Labor Demand Policies
Direct public provision	?	• Public-service employment • Sheltered workshops • Supported work experience programs
Incentives	• Wage subsidies to workers • Increased earned income disregards in welfare programs • Subsidies for child care and other work-related expenses	• Wage subsidies to employers • On-the-job training subsidies to employers • Economic development programs
Sanctions	• Job search requirements in welfare • Work requirements • Welfare time limits	• Anti-discrimination laws • Affirmative action • Minimum-wage laws, other labor regulation
Training	• Education • Job training	• Diversity training • Job retention services to help employers reduce turnover
Information provision	• Labor exchange services/ job development services—providing information to poor on job openings	• Labor exchange services/ job development services—helping employers find qualified employees among poor

Source: Author's own classification.

minimum wage but cannot force businesses to create jobs at that minimum wage. Welfare recipients can be forced off welfare, but ex-welfare recipients do not necessarily find jobs at decent wages. Education and training have traditionally been held in high regard by Americans, who have great faith in the potential for personal transformation. Education and training also are attractive because they promise that their short-term investment costs will yield long-term increases in earnings. However, actually effecting great personal transformation in an individual can be quite difficult and chancy; the effort often entails great costs and invokes difficult issues of program design. Information provision also promises great improvements in job matching for relatively modest costs. However, information is a somewhat amorphous good that is difficult to produce in a reliably high-quality fashion. Hence, information provision programs always face the issue of how to monitor performance and improve performance over time.

Supply and demand policies can also be categorized by the type of organization that provides the services or subsidies (table 2.2). These organizations are often defined by their particular clientele. Some programs may be narrowly targeted at a very needy clientele, whereas other programs include the needy in services or subsidies provided to a much broader clientele.

The most familiar labor supply and demand antipoverty programs are those that help individuals who are having employment problems after leaving school—"second-chance" programs. Second-chance programs are provided by job training agencies, welfare-to-work agencies, and the employment service. Such agencies provide some services directly to job seekers (labor supply services), such as training and job placement assistance. These agencies also increase the employment of their clients by providing "labor demand" services to employers, including subsidies to private employers, referrals of qualified job seekers to private employers, and public-service employment. Second-chance programs have the advantage of clearly being targeted at a disadvantaged group of potential job seekers. But such targeting also leads to some significant issues, including whether being targeted causes participants to become stigmatized as disadvantaged by employers. In addition, the disadvantaged clients of these programs have not traditionally been in a strong political position to demand improved services, so it remains unclear how to design a system of second-chance programs that provide strong incentives for better performance. I return to these issues in later chapters.

The employment and earnings of the poor are increased not only by second-chance programs but by the general education system: "first-chance" programs. Some education programs are specifically directed at students from disadvantaged backgrounds, but students from low-income families also receive services from the general subsidies provided to public education. Although programs for the poor in the first-chance system may not be stigmatized as special programs for the disadvantaged, sometimes the first-chance system, which is intended to help all students, may not actually help students from disadvantaged backgrounds but rather write them off. In addition, the K-12 educational system historically has been oriented toward preparing individuals for liberal arts colleges rather than preparing students for careers, although some recent school-to-work initiatives have tried to change this orientation. I return to these issues in subsequent chapters.

Economic development agency programs provide subsidies for new and expanding businesses. Such programs usually do not specifically target the employment of the poor, but the employment of the poor is increased by these programs, as we see in chapters 5 and 9. In addition, some modifications in how these programs are operated can make economic develop-

TABLE 2.2 *Organizational Arrangement and Clientele of Supply and Demand Programs That Affect the Employment of the Poor*

Organizational Arrangements and Clientele	Labor Supply Programs	Labor Demand Programs
Second-chance system; employment-related programs	• Job training agencies: programs that provide training and placement • Welfare-to-work agencies: programs that provide training and placement • Employment service: information to job seekers on job openings	• Job training agencies: programs that provide summer public-service jobs to youth, work experience, and wage subsidies to employers for OJT • Welfare-to-work agencies: programs that provide public-service jobs, community service jobs, work experience, and grant diversion to subsidize private employers • Employment service: information to employers on job seekers
First-chance system of education[a]	• Head Start • K-12 public schools • Community colleges • Four-year public colleges and universities	The customized training provided by community colleges to employers is typically funded by economic development agencies, and rarely targeted at the disadvantaged
Economic development programs[b]		Wide variety of subsidies for new and expanding businesses, particularly manufacturing, including: • Customized training (see above) • Discretionary tax subsidies, such as property tax abatements • Subsidized infrastructure
Tax system	Earned Income Tax Credit	Tax credits to employers for hiring disadvantaged groups, such as former Targeted Jobs Tax Credit and current Work Opportunity Tax Credit. Also, some general wage subsidies for hiring were for-

TABLE 2.2 *Continued*

Organizational Arrangements and Clientele	Labor Supply Programs	Labor Demand Programs
		merly used, such as New Jobs Tax Credit of 1977 to 1978.
Labor regulations		• Minimum wage: enforced by federal and state departments of labor • Equal employment opportunity laws: enforced by departments of labor and various civil rights agencies

Source: Author's own classification.

[a] Some education programs are targeted at the poor, but the poor also benefit from general public subsidies for education.

[b] Economic development programs are rarely targeted at disadvantaged persons, but some programs (enterprise zones) are targeted at distressed places.

ment programs more effective in addressing the needs of the poor, as I discuss in chapter 9. The political challenge is to change the traditional focus of economic development agencies on attracting business, any business, rather than on seeking to change the kind of employees businesses hire.

Some supply and demand programs are delivered through the tax system. The appeal of tax subsidies is that they promise to require relatively low government administrative costs and may be more politically feasible than enacting new spending programs. The problem is that tax-based subsidies may be more difficult to control administratively and to fine-tune once the basic rules of the program are set up. Some tax subsidies are highly targeted on the disadvantaged (such as the Earned Income Tax Credit and the Work Opportunity Tax Credit), whereas others are more general subsidies that may also help the poor, such as the New Jobs Tax Credit, which was in place from 1977 to 1978 (see chapter 8 for more details).

Finally, some labor demand programs are administered by government labor departments or other agencies that administer employer regulations. Examples of such programs are the minimum wage and the laws and executive orders banning employment discrimination against minorities.

Policies to affect labor supply or demand also differ across other dimensions. For example, programs differ in whether the assistance provided is an "entitlement" that applies to everyone in a specified category or "discretionary" in that assistance is determined by program managers. For example, the Work Opportunity Tax Credit is an entitlement that goes to every firm that hires a new employee who meets certain criteria for being disadvantaged. In contrast, under the on-the-job training (OJT) program of federal job training programs, subsidies to firms for employing and training some disadvantaged clients go only to firms that have been approved by the local job training agency. Whether assistance is provided as an entitlement or by discretion, and how entitlement is determined and how discretion is used, clearly could make major differences to program effectiveness. This issue is discussed in detail in chapter 8.

Programs also differ in whether they are run privately or by the government, and if by the latter, by what level of government (federal, state, or local). The level of government that runs the program may differ from the level of government that finances it. For example, job training services are largely financed by the federal government but actually run by local workforce investment boards, with considerable supervision by state governments. Services are contracted out by local workforce investment boards to both public and private training providers. In contrast, economic development programs are largely financed and run by state and local governments, with minimal federal government involvement. The degree of local flexibility needed in running labor supply and demand programs depends in part on whether the appropriate policies differ greatly in different local areas, which in turn depends on the nature of the low-wage labor market, a topic considered in chapter 3.

Resources Devoted to Labor Supply and Demand Policies: The United States Past and Present and Compared to Other Countries

Perhaps because of the political problems of labor demand policies, the United States today devotes relatively few resources to labor demand policies to help increase the employment and earnings of disadvantaged groups. That lack of emphasis on labor demand policies is evident in comparisons with both other advanced industrial countries and the past record of the United States itself.

Table 2.3 compares the United States and other advanced industrial countries. The data come from the Organization for Economic Cooperation and Development (OECD), an international organization of the leading industrial nations that tries to promote world trade and economic development. The data show the resources devoted to labor market policies, both labor supply and demand, to deal with unemployment and underemployment in these countries. The "size" of these policies is measured in two

TABLE 2.3 *Comparison of Labor Supply and Demand Policies in the United States and Other Leading Industrial Nations*

Country (Fiscal Year of Data)	Percentage of GDP Devoted to Labor Supply Policies	Percentage of Labor Force Annually Participating in Labor Supply Policies	Percentage of GDP Devoted to Labor Demand Policies	Percentage of Labor Force Annually Participating in Labor Demand Policies
United States (1997 to 1998)	0.11	1.3	0.01	0.2
Canada (1996 to 1997)	0.20	2.1	0.07	0.7
United Kingdom (1997 to 1998)	0.06	0.9	0.15	1.1
Germany (1998)	0.50	2.4	0.55	2.4
France (1997)	0.40	3.3	0.81	6.9
Japan (1997 to 1998)	0.03	na	0.02	na
Sweden (1998)	0.54	5.6	1.07	6.5

Source: Data are derived from author's calculations using Organization for Economic Cooperation and Development (1999, 246–52, table H).

Notes: Labor supply programs include training for unemployed adults (category 2a), measures for unemployed and disadvantaged youth (3a), and vocational rehabilitation (5a). Labor demand programs include training for employed adults (2b), support of apprenticeship and related forms of general youth training (3b), subsidized employment (4, which includes subsidies to regular employment in the private sector, support of unemployed persons starting enterprises, and direct job creation, public or nonprofit), and work for the disabled (5b).

ways. First, the annual amount spent on them is compared with the country's gross domestic product (GDP). This captures how much of the country's resources its political leaders are willing to devote to these policies. Second, the annual number of participants in these policies is compared to the country's labor force. This captures the maximum extent to which the country's labor supply and labor demand might actually be altered by these policies over a one-year period. Of course, policies are more likely to alter labor supply or labor demand significantly if they use greater resources.

As table 2.3 shows, the United States invests considerably less in labor supply policies than do some other countries, such as Sweden, Germany, France, and Canada. However, the United States does devote more resources to labor supply policies than the United Kingdom and Japan.

The disparity between the United States and other leading industrial counties is much greater and more consistent for labor demand policies. By the standards of other countries, U.S. labor demand policies are minuscule. For example, France and Germany each devote more than fifty times as great a percentage of GDP as the United States does to labor demand policies. On the extreme, Sweden devotes more than 1 percent of its GDP to labor demand policies, compared to 0.01 percent in the United States.

One response to table 2.3 is that it provides an argument against labor demand policies. In recent years, European nations and Japan have lagged behind the United States in net job creation; one could thus argue that greater use of labor demand policies may have done more harm than good. However, as Paul Osterman (1999, 119–23) has pointed out, we should be cautious about evaluating labor market policies based on recent aggregate trends. For example, a decade or so ago the perception was that labor market performance was better in Germany, Sweden, and Japan than in the United States. Labor market policies in these countries have not changed drastically in recent years. It is unlikely that recent aggregate labor market trends are due to these countries' long-standing heavier use of labor demand policies. The point of table 2.3 is to show that the choices made by the United States about labor market policies do not exhaust all possibilities. It is possible to use labor demand policies much more.

Table 2.4 presents a more detailed accounting of U.S. labor supply and demand policies to help the disadvantaged.[3] The table also reports past resources devoted to some labor demand policies.

The table shows that the United States devotes far more resources to labor supply than labor demand policies. About 1 percent of GDP is devoted to labor supply policies, almost ten times the resources devoted to labor demand policies. The disparity between labor supply and demand policies is much less if we look only at second-chance programs, for which the resources devoted to labor supply programs exceed those devoted to labor demand programs by a ratio of two to one. But most labor supply and labor demand programs are not administered by second-chance agencies. Tax-based wage subsidies to disadvantaged workers are almost one hundred times as large in budget costs as tax-based wage subsidies to employers for hiring the disadvantaged. Although significant resources are devoted to labor demand initiatives such as economic development programs, minimum-wage regulations, and equal opportunity laws, these are dwarfed by the general education subsidies provided to students from disadvantaged families.

In the past, the United States devoted a much larger share of national resources to demand-side programs. During the New Deal, significant resources were provided to the WPA, which provided a wide variety of public-services jobs and public works jobs to disadvantaged, unemployed persons. At its peak in 1938, the WPA cost more than 2.5 percent of GDP and employed more than 6 percent of the U.S. labor force. In addition, during the Carter administration in the late 1970s, public-service employment for the disadvantaged was also a significant program, costing almost 0.2 percent of GDP and employing more than 0.7 percent of the labor force.

TABLE 2.4 *Resources Devoted to Labor Supply and Labor Demand Programs*

Labor Supply Programs	Percentage Share of GDP	Labor Demand Programs[a]	Percentage Share of GDP
Second-chance programs: training and placement	0.060	Second-chance programs: subsidized employment	0.029
Federal job training programs: skills development, job placement	0.027	Federal job training programs: summer youth jobs, OJT, and work experience	0.013
Welfare-to-work: training and placement	0.027	Welfare-to-work: OJT, work experience, community service jobs, public-service jobs	0.011
Employment service: half allocated to supply side	0.006	Employment service: half allocated to demand side	0.006
First-chance education programs: targeted at disadvantaged	0.215		
Head Start	0.051		
Title 1 spending on disadvantaged students, K-12	0.073		
Pell Grants and state need-based higher education aid	0.091		
First-chance education programs: general subsidies, proportion going to disadvantaged students	0.477	Economic development programs: proportion that benefits the disadvantaged	0.043
Total amount for elementary and secondary education that goes to disadvantaged	0.463		
Total subsidies for higher education that go to disadvantaged students	0.014		
Earned Income Tax Credit	0.353	Work opportunity tax credit and welfare-to-work tax credit	0.004
		Minimum-wage laws: wage increase for low-income workers	0.032
		Equal employment opportunity laws: proportion that benefits disadvantaged	0.010
Total	1.105		0.118

Source: Author's compilation.
Note: More details on the derivation of this table are in chapter 2, note 3.
[a] Past labor demand programs at their peak:

WPA (FY1939)	2.541 percent of GDP
CETA public service employment (FY1979)	0.160 percent of GDP

Thus, large-scale labor demand policies in the United States have so far failed to be politically sustainable. This failure is explained in part by opposition from business and conservatives and by lukewarm support from labor and some liberals. Suspicion of such extensive government intervention in employment, however, appears to run deep in American popular opinion. For example, when Americans were asked in public opinion polls in 1939 to list the greatest accomplishment and the greatest failure of FDR's administration, the WPA headed up both lists (Howard 1943, 105). This widespread public opposition to the WPA contrasts with the quick institutionalization and public support for such New Deal innovations as social security.

Conclusion

As this chapter has emphasized, labor supply and labor demand policies come in many different types. Policies differ in the techniques they use to affect labor supply or demand behavior, the organizations that implement the policies, the specific groups of labor suppliers or demanders they target, and the level of government that finances them. Chapters 4 and 6 through 9 consider in more detail specific types of supply and demand policies and the most effective policy designs. A particularly important issue is whether some specific types and designs of labor demand policies can overcome some of the political problems of these policies. These political problems have limited the size of U.S. labor demand policies compared to other countries and compared to the United States' own history.

Before considering specific types of labor supply and demand policies, we must first consider some basic issues in how labor supply and labor demand policies affect the labor market. As emphasized in this chapter, a fundamental distinction that influences policy effectiveness is that supply and demand policies work on different sides of the labor market. The relative effectiveness of labor supply versus demand policies depends on how the low-wage labor market works, and in particular on how labor supply and labor demand in this labor market respond to market forces. The next chapter analyzes the workings of the low-wage labor market, and their implications for labor supply and demand policies.

3

THE LOW-WAGE LABOR MARKET

An understanding of the effectiveness of labor supply and demand policies to reduce poverty requires an understanding of the low-wage labor market. In this chapter I consider some key features of the low-wage labor market that influence whether and how labor supply and demand policies can increase the employment and earnings of the poor.

This chapter's discussion of the low-wage labor market is divided into five sections:

1. *The overall employment situation:* Are there enough jobs available, and will jobs reduce poverty?
2. *Labor supply:* Can the poor readily supply productive labor in response to increased demand?
3. *Labor demand:* Will employers' demand for the labor of the poor readily respond to more supply?
4. *The interaction of supply and demand:* What employment and earnings outcomes are likely from the interaction of supply and demand when we implement a supply or demand policy?
5. *The geographic scope of the low-wage labor market:* What geographic area most closely approximates a low-wage labor market, and what consequences does this have for policy?

In each of these sections I dispel several myths about the low-wage labor market and replace them with facts. I discuss how these facts influence our views of the effectiveness of labor supply and demand policies in reducing poverty. These discussions are continued in more detail in subsequent chapters, which consider specific supply and demand policies. In analyzing specific policies, those chapters take into account some of the features of the low-wage labor market discussed in this chapter, including:

- More jobs are needed for the poor.
- The labor supply of the poor is likely to be significantly responsive to increased demand.

- Labor demand for the poor is not infinitely or even overwhelmingly responsive to increased supply.
- The spillover effects of labor supply and demand policies may be important.
- The relevant low-wage labor market is best thought of as about the size of a metropolitan area.

The Overall Employment Situation

A crucial issue addressed by this book is whether more employment can do much to solve poverty. Would more jobs for the poor really significantly help reduce poverty? There is a myth that with overall strong employment in the United States, employment is about as high as it needs to be. There is also a myth that the wages of the poor are so low that employment cannot solve poverty. I address each of these myths.

> MYTH: There are plenty of jobs for everyone.
>
> FACT: Even with a strong U.S. labor market, employment would need to increase by several million jobs for there to be an adequate number of jobs for disadvantaged groups compared to past levels, social standards, and economic needs.

As this book was being written, the U.S. economy was in a prolonged boom. One could argue that in a booming U.S. economy, the need for more jobs is nil.

But despite the boom, I contend that employment is short by millions of jobs for disadvantaged groups and the poor compared to where it can or should be. This assertion can be supported by several types of evidence, each of which considers a different way of defining the poor and disadvantaged and a different way of defining how many jobs are needed. One way to see the need for additional jobs is to look at recent trends in the employment rates of lower education groups. Table 3.1 reports employment rates for "prime working-age" (twenty-five to fifty-four) Americans in 1979 and 1998, broken down by gender, marital status, and ethnic group. Even though the overall U.S. labor market was arguably stronger in 1998 than in 1979 (4.5 percent unemployment in 1998 versus 5.8 percent unemployment in 1979), the employment climate has deteriorated for some groups. As can be seen in the table, since 1979 there has been a large decline in the employment rates of men with less than a college education, particularly among high school dropouts and blacks. This large decline is not evident among less-educated women. However, the employment rates among sin-

TABLE 3.1 *Employment Rates for Persons Ages Twenty-Five to Fifty-Four, by Gender, Race, and Marital Status*

	High School Dropouts		High School Graduates		College Graduates	
	1979	1998	1979	1998	1979	1998
Males						
White non-Hispanic	0.846	0.759	0.935	0.905	0.960	0.950
Black non-Hispanic	0.750	0.574	0.867	0.809	0.905	0.918
Hispanic	0.858	0.843	0.912	0.883	0.913	0.917
Other non-Hispanic	0.813	0.735	0.870	0.863	0.893	0.923
Married (spouse present) females						
White non-Hispanic	0.435	0.520	0.551	0.727	0.635	0.791
Black non-Hispanic	0.518	0.577	0.673	0.755	0.833	0.879
Hispanic	0.369	0.435	0.534	0.656	0.626	0.741
Other non-Hispanic	0.429	0.532	0.579	0.669	0.659	0.699
Other females						
White non-Hispanic	0.516	0.480	0.810	0.818	0.893	0.913
Black non-Hispanic	0.423	0.441	0.670	0.731	0.882	0.889
Hispanic	0.414	0.522	0.669	0.738	0.806	0.863
Other non-Hispanic	0.484	0.470	0.791	0.724	0.882	0.826

Source: All employment rates were calculated by the author using data from the Outgoing Rotation Group of the Current Population Survey (CPS-ORG).
Note: The employment rate is the annual average over twelve monthly surveys of those employed last week as a proportion of the total population of each group.

gle women with less than a college education, who presumably have at least as much need as men to support themselves through work, still lag significantly behind those of men.

To get a sense of how many jobs might be needed, I calculated how many additional jobs as of 1998 would be required for men and single women in each of these four ethnic groups, who are high school dropouts or high school graduates without a college degree, to reach the employment rates of white men of the same educational level in 1979.[1] The results of these calculations are reported in table 3.2. The calculation indicates that about five million additional jobs are needed. Of these additional jobs, about 60 percent are needed for single women, and 40 percent for men; 70 percent for high school graduates, and 30 percent for high school dropouts; and a little less than half for white non-Hispanics, a little more than one-third for blacks, and the remainder for other ethnic groups.

Another way to see the need for jobs is to focus on the employment needs of the poor. For example, one can calculate the employment increase required if all non-elderly poor families are to have the equivalent of one full-time, full-year worker—that is, if the sum of work hours in each poor

TABLE 3.2 *Number of New Jobs for Prime-Age Less-Educated Persons Required to Match White Male Employment Rates of 1979*

	Whites	Blacks	Hispanics	Others	Total All Ethnic Groups
High School Dropouts					
Males	0.296	0.265	0.008	0.027	0.596
Unmarried females	0.411	0.318	0.304	0.049	1.082
Total	0.707	0.583	0.312	0.076	1.678
High School Graduates					
Males	0.740	0.538	0.162	0.078	1.518
Unmarried females	0.970	0.687	0.224	0.095	1.975
Total	1.710	1.225	0.386	0.173	3.493
Male total	1.036	0.803	0.170	0.105	2.114
Unmarried female total	1.381	1.005	0.528	0.143	3.057
Total males and unmarried females	2.417	1.808	0.698	0.249	5.171

Source: All data are derived from the author's calculations using the CPS-ORG.
Notes: All job figures are in millions of jobs, as of 1998, needed for persons ages twenty-five to fifty-four to match white male employment rates for that education category and age range in 1979. High school graduate category does not include college graduates. Data are calculated based on employment rates given in table 3.1 and estimated numbers of persons in each ethnic-education-gender category as of 1998. The formula for calculating needed jobs is: needed jobs for ethnic group *r*, education category *e*, gender *g* = number of persons in group (*reg*) × (employment rate for white males in education category *e* in 1979 − employment rate for group [*reg*] in 1998).

family is to exceed 2,000 hours per year. The results of this calculation are reported in table 3.3. As this table shows, for each poor family to have the equivalent of one full-time, full-year worker, 8.6 million additional full-time equivalent jobs must be created. Of these 8.6 million jobs, 4.5 million are needed among whites, and 4.1 million among nonwhites. Families with children need 2.9 million of these jobs.

Another way to assess the job needs of the poor is to calculate how many jobs would be needed to eliminate the "income gap" of the poor, that is, the amount of income needed to bring a poor family's income up to the poverty line. Table 3.4 reports this calculation for families with children, arbitrarily assuming that the poor earn $7 per hour. As the table shows, closing the poverty gap for all families with children would require the equivalent of 2.8 million full-time, full-year jobs. Families with children headed by a single mother would need 1.8 million of these jobs.

In sum, even when the U.S. economy is booming, millions of jobs are still needed by the poor and disadvantaged. The various simulations suggest that between 3 million and 9 million jobs are needed. These jobs are needed in the sense that job increases of this magnitude would be required

TABLE 3.3 *Number of New Jobs Needed for All Non-Elderly Poor Families to Have One Full-Time Worker*

	Full-time Equivalent Jobs Required (Millions)
Total all families with family head less than sixty-five years old	8.6
Families with children	2.9
Single-mother families with children	2.4
White	4.5
Black	2.2
Hispanic	1.5
Families with no adult worker during the current year	5.8

Source: All calculations are derived by the author from the March 1999 CPS.
Notes: For all poor families with a family head less than sixty-five years old, I calculated total annual work hours of all adults in the family. 18.8 percent have combined adult work hours of more than 2,000 hours per year and were excluded from further calculations; 43.2 percent have zero adult work hours, and one full-time job was assumed to be needed for each such family. Another 38.0 percent have work hours between 1 and 1,999 per year. The number of extra annual work hours needed for that family's total to equal 2,000 was calculated. The total number of extra annual work hours needed was divided by 2,000 to get the estimated number of full-time equivalent jobs needed.

to move some groups to the employment rates achieved by white males in the past, to provide one full-time, full-year worker in each poor family, or to bring all poor families with children out of poverty through earnings increases.

MYTH: Because wages for the poor are so low, even full-time, full-year employment will not bring many poor families out of poverty.

TABLE 3.4 *Full-Time Equivalent Jobs Needed to Bring All Families with Children Up to the Poverty Line*

Group	Number of Families Below Poverty Line (Millions)	Mean Income Gap Below Poverty Line	Mean Proportion of FTE Jobs Needed to Bring Family up to Poverty Line[a]	Total FTE Jobs Needed (Millions)[b]
Families with children	5.6	$7,056	0.504	2.8
Single-mother families with children	3.5	$7,215	0.515	1.8

Source: Data are author's calculations based on U.S. Census Bureau (1999, 21, table 4).
[a] A full-time equivalent (FTE) job was assumed to be 2,000 hours per year at $7.00 per hour.
[b] The mean proportion of full-time equivalent jobs multiplied by the number of families.

FACT: Because of the many earnings supplements available to working families, full-time, full-year employment is surprisingly effective in bringing poor families out of poverty.

Would more jobs for the poor actually be effective in reducing poverty? Aren't wages for the poor so low that employment is not really a solution to poverty for most low-income workers?

The empirical evidence suggests otherwise: increasing the employment of the poor would cause large poverty reductions. These poverty reductions occur even though the poor earn low wages. Simulations done by Isabel Sawhill (1999) show what would happen to the poverty rate if all nondisabled and non-elderly heads of poor families worked forty hours a week for fifty-two weeks. Wage rates per hour are predicted for every family head (including those for whom no work hours or wage rates are observed) based on the head's demographic characteristics. Sawhill's simulation shows that full-time, full-year work by all these family heads would reduce the poverty rate by two-thirds, from 12.2 percent to 3.6 percent.

Why is employment so effective in reducing poverty? One reason is that many poor families are relatively small, so that even if the job held by the head of the family pays low wages, full-time, full-year employment will bring the family out of poverty. In addition, in recent years the United States has enormously expanded the Earned Income Tax Credit, which provides refundable tax credits of up to 40 percent of earnings for low-income families (see chapter 4 for more information on the EITC). With the EITC, as well as possibly food stamps, many poor families receive enough income to get out of poverty if at least one adult in the family works full-time year-round.

Getting out of poverty does not imply that a family has achieved middle-class status, or even what most Americans would consider a decent standard of living. For example, the poverty line for a family of four is now \$17,028 per year,[2] which would probably be perceived by most Americans as an extremely paltry annual income for a family of this size. Therefore, raising wages for low-wage workers is still an important issue for public policy. But policy has already taken some *modest* steps forward in helping to make work pay. Work is at least somewhat plausible now as a way for many families to at least reach the very minimal goal of being above the poverty line.

Therefore, significantly more employment of the poor is needed and would be effective in reducing poverty. However, this finding says nothing about which policies would most effectively yield the needed increase in employment. Perhaps there are plenty of jobs that are available, or would readily become available for the poor, and the needed increase in employment is best achieved by labor supply policies, such as policies to increase the skills of the poor or their willingness to accept available jobs. Or labor demand policies might be best. Perhaps a sufficient number of jobs for the poor are not readily available, and the needed increase in employment would best be achieved using policies that directly create additional jobs for the poor through economic development programs, wage subsidies, or public employment. The specifics of the pros and cons of different supply and demand policies in helping the poor is the subject of most of this book. In the rest of this chapter, I consider the implications of what we know about how the low-wage labor market operates for how responsive the employment of the poor is likely to be to labor supply and demand policies.

Labor Supply

For demand policies to have any chance of working, there must be a significant supply of labor from the poor, that is, people who are either not working or not working full-time, and who are able with increased demand to work full-time, full-year. But there are many myths about the availability of the poor to fill jobs that suggest that the poor are unresponsive to improved incentives to work, perhaps because too many barriers impede their ability to work productively, or perhaps because they have inadequate reading and math skills. This section refutes these myths and argues that most (not all) of the poor can work productively full-time in the long run, if demand is adequate.

> MYTH: Economic studies have shown that the labor supply of the poor and other groups is unresponsive to increased wages.
>
> FACT: Studies suggest that when demand for the poor increases, labor supply responds, either owing to the increased wages or the lower unemployment rates brought about by increased demand.

According to long-standing conventional wisdom among economists, the responsiveness of labor supply to wages is zero among men, and modest among women.[3] However, the research on men fails to focus sufficiently on how wages affect labor force participation rates.[4] Effects on labor force participation rates are particularly important for lower-wage men, who are in and out of the labor force more than higher-wage men. Men in the bottom 10 percent of the wage distribution on average spend more than 30 percent of a typical year out of work, while men in the top 40 percent of the wage distribution on average spend less than 5 percent of a typical year out of work.[5] Empirical estimates suggest that labor force participation rates of men are more sensitive to wages than are hours of work conditional on working (Triest 1990). This accords with economic theory: for persons out of the labor force, a wage increase provides an unambiguous incentive to work, while for those already working, a wage increase provides an incentive to work but also provides extra income, which may allow them to forgo overtime or cut back to part-time.

In recent empirical work that specifically focused on labor force participation rates for low-wage men, Chinhui Juhn, Kevin Murphy, and Robert Topel (1991) found modest positive labor supply elasticities with respect to wages for low-wage workers, of perhaps 0.4. That is, a 1 percent wage increase for low-wage males would increase their labor supply, including the effect on the probability of labor force participation, by four-tenths of 1 percent. This is consistent with the general consensus about supply elasticities for women and with research by Robert Moffitt (1983) on the supply elasticities of single mothers.[6]

In addition to responding to increased wages brought about by increased labor demand, the labor supply of the poor can also respond to increased demand by reduced unemployment, which increases employment among the unemployed and also increases labor force participation rates. As discussed later in this chapter, there is considerable evidence that even with a relatively strong U.S. labor market, involuntary unemployment persists for some groups. As shown in Bartik (1991), an increase in employment growth in a metropolitan area leads to considerable short-run reductions in unemployment rates. For every extra 1 percent employment growth in a metropolitan area, unemployment declines in the short run by 0.3 percent or 0.4 percent. This decline in unemployment occurs among all groups but is particularly large among lower-education groups and racial minorities. This lower unemployment directly increases employment among the poor and other groups and thereby represents an effective "labor supply response" to increased labor demand. In addition, the lower unemployment rates increase labor force participation rates, which further increase labor supply and employment. A one-point reduction in the unemployment rate increases labor force participation for most groups by around .5 percent (Bowen and Finegan 1969; Bartik 1999).

In addition to these formal econometric studies of the responsiveness of the labor supply and employment of the poor to changing demand conditions, there is more informal, descriptive evidence that suggests that many poor individuals can work productively under the right demand conditions. For example, the data show that many of the poor do work, at least part-time or part of the year, and hence cannot be considered "unemployable" or "slackers." The latest data show that 57 percent of families who are poor during a given year include at least one individual who worked sometime during the year, although in two-thirds of these "working poor" families (38 percent of all families in poverty), the combined hours of work of all adults in the family amount to less than 2,000 hours per year. Many of these part-time, part-year workers could work more if labor market conditions were right.[7]

Official data include only earnings that poor individuals report to government interviewers. In a recent book, Kathryn Edin and Laura Lein (1997), who relied on more in-depth interviews, reported their finding that unreported work by welfare recipients was far greater than work reported to the welfare department. Welfare provided too little income for a single mother to support her family, so welfare mothers had to obtain unreported income. During a typical month, only 5 percent of women in Edin and Lein's sample reported work to their welfare department. But 41 percent did some sort of unreported or illegal work (mostly unreported legal work). This other work provided 12 percent of these women's income during the months they received welfare (Edin and Lein 1997, 44).[8]

Furthermore, some in the disadvantaged population can work as productively as many workers. In the Youth Incentive Entitlement Pilot Projects Demonstration (YIEPP), conducted from 1978 to 1980, disadvantaged sixteen- to nineteen-year-olds were guaranteed jobs if they remained in school or returned to school. Even though more than 82 percent of all businesses were unwilling to hire these youths with a 100 percent wage subsidy, most businesses who did hire these youths were satisfied with their job performance. More than 80 percent reported that the youths' work habits and attitudes were average or better than average (Ball et al. 1981, 56). In a recent survey of "work experience" programs for welfare recipients, in which welfare recipients are assigned to unpaid public-sector work, supervisors "found that participants performed at comparable levels to entry-level regular employees" (Brock, Butler, and Long 1993, 28).

> MYTH: So many barriers impede the employment of the poor that significantly more employment for the poor is not feasible without addressing all these barriers.
>
> FACT: Although there are significant barriers to the employment of the poor, many, but not all, of the poor are able to overcome those barriers and get a job under the right demand conditions.

Don't the poor have so many barriers to employment, it is sometimes argued, that it is unrealistic to expect additional labor supply and employment from them, even with better labor demand conditions? It is certainly true that the poor experience greater barriers to employment than the nonpoor. A recent study of welfare recipients found that more than one-quarter meet standard mental health screening criteria for depression, twice the percentage of the depressed in the general population (Danziger et al. 1999). Twenty-two percent of welfare recipients gave self-assessments of their mental health that were "very poor"—in the bottom 10 percent of the overall population (Zedlewski 1999, 9).[9] One-third of welfare recipients have academic skills in the bottom 10 percent of the population (Olson and Pavetti 1996).[10] Between 10 and 20 percent of welfare recipients have medical problems that limit work activity, at least twice the average for other women (Danziger et al. 1999; Olson and Pavetti 1996; Zedlewski 1999).

With a sufficient number of severe barriers, some poor persons can be "unemployable." One study found that of welfare recipients who experienced seven or more barriers out of fourteen considered (including barriers related to job skills, work experience, mental and physical health, substance abuse, domestic violence, transportation problems, and problems with discrimination), about 6 percent were employed at least twenty hours per week when contacted seven to ten months later (Danziger et al. 1999).[11] However, so many barriers to employment is uncommon: only 3 percent of welfare recipients experience seven or more barriers to employment.

It is more common for the poor to experience some barriers to employment but for these barriers to still allow employment. As shown in table 3.5, more than one-third of welfare recipients experience either no barriers to employment or perhaps one barrier that does not significantly reduce their odds of getting a job. Perhaps another one-third or more experience two or three barriers to employment. Although two or three barriers significantly reduce the odds of employment, more than half of the mem-

TABLE 3.5 *Barriers to Employment and Work Experienced by Welfare Recipients*

Number of Barriers to Work	Percentage of Welfare Recipients with This Number of Barriers	Percentage Estimated to Work at Least Twenty Hours per Week Seven to Ten Months Later
0	15	81
1	21	71
2 to 3	37	62
4 to 6	24	41
7 or more	3	6

Source: These figures are taken from Danziger et al. (1999, 29, 34, figure 1, and table 5).
Notes: The "percentage estimated to work" are regression-adjusted numbers that hold race, children, age, urban residence, and other demographic characteristics constant. The "percentage estimated to work" is for a welfare recipient who is single, black, living in an urban census tract, twenty-five to thirty-four years old, the mother of one child under two, and a welfare recipient for seven years. Sampling frame draws from single mothers on the welfare rolls of an urban Michigan county in February 1997, and employment status is measured as of an interview in the September 1997 to December 1997 period. The fourteen barriers examined include poor job skills, little work experience, poor mental or physical health, substance abuse, domestic violence, transportation problems, and problems with racial discrimination.

bers of this group were able to get a job. Less than one-third of welfare recipients experience so many barriers that their odds of employment are reduced to less than half.

Many persons with low academic skills can work. Among all women in the bottom decile in academic skills, one-third worked more than fifty weeks during either the year of the survey or the year before the survey (Olson and Pavetti 1996).[12] This survey refers to employment during 1990 and 1991, when the United States was in recession.

These data are consistent with the views of welfare experts. According to the journalist Dana Milbank (1997, 22–23):

> Poverty experts generally split the welfare caseload into thirds. The top third is easy. . . . A middle third has some barriers to employment. . . . The bottom third is where the greater problem is; though only a few are utterly hopeless, the others in this category, though capable of work, have so many obstacles in their path that getting them to meet even the most minimal of employment standards requires far more effort than most industry supervisors or government social workers would consider worth the trouble.

If only one-third or less of welfare recipients have such severe problems, one would expect fewer employability problems with the non-elderly poor who do *not* receive welfare. Less than one-third of the poor population receives cash welfare (U.S. Department of Health and Human Services 1998b). Many of the poor are members of two-parent families (35 percent of the poverty population, according to Blank 1997, 17), whom we would expect to be easier to employ than single-parent families.

> MYTH: The poor have such mediocre reading and math skills that they cannot be expected to supply productive labor in today's economy without much more formal education.
>
> FACT: Although the "hard skills" of the poor, such as reading and math skills, are a significant problem, employers in the low-wage labor market are at least as concerned about "soft skills," such as showing up at work on time and getting along with coworkers and supervisors. Such soft skills are not consistently taught through formal education but may be acquired in part by the additional job experience that can be brought about through stronger labor demand.

Another argument for the inability of the poor to supply productive labor in response to increased labor demand is that they lack the advanced education needed in today's economy. As I will show, this view is an exaggeration. Although some skills that are best transmitted by formal education have become more important in the low-wage labor market, the amount of education needed to acquire such skills is not extremely advanced. The soft skills that are most important for the jobs held by the poor—regular on-time attendance at work, dealing well with supervisors and coworkers—are skills that are probably best acquired through job experience. Job experience is, of course, more readily acquired by the poor if the labor market has strong labor demand.

The importance of soft skills versus hard skills in the low-wage labor market can be seen by looking at the jobs held by the poor. Table 3.6 lists the top ten occupations held by poor men and women. For comparison, table 3.6 also lists the top ten occupations of nonpoor men and women.

As shown in the table, the poor are more concentrated in a few occupations, with a higher percentage of the poor than the nonpoor in the top ten occupations. The jobs in which the poor are concentrated have lower educational requirements and pay lower wages. Even when the poor and nonpoor are in the same occupational classification (for example, cashiers), the poor are concentrated in segments of the occupation that require less education and pay lower wages.

However, even though the jobs held by the poor may not require advanced academic skills, all of these jobs require significant skills. No one who has ever been a waiter or waitress could describe this as an "unskilled" occupation. Many of the occupations held by the poor, such as waitress, cashier, or salesperson, require some skill dealing with money and numbers. Other jobs held by the poor, such as secretary, require skill with the written word. Many of the jobs held by the poor listed in table 3.6 require skills dealing with supervisors, coworkers, and (particularly for jobs held by poor women) customers. All of these jobs require the skill of being able to show up at work consistently on time. Being reliable may require considerable skill for a welfare mother juggling child care and transportation.

More formal studies have confirmed that jobs held by the poor require both some hard (academic) skills and many soft (nonacademic) social skills. For hard skills, surveys of employers show that of all jobs that do not require a college education, 65 percent require the daily use of arithmetic, and 55 percent require the daily reading of paragraphs of written text (Holzer 1996). Acquiring these academic skills may not require college or even high school graduation. But to do a job that involves arithmetic and daily reading, a person may need to really understand and be able to use what he or she learned in elementary and middle schools.

What is distinctive about the low-wage labor market is that hard skills are not as relatively important as soft skills: showing up at work consistently on time, and getting along with supervisors, coworkers, and customers. Hard skills—basic reading and math skills—are important, but they are not the biggest problems facing employers in this market. Most of the evidence for the importance of soft skills comes from surveys of

TABLE 3.6 *Top Ten Occupations of the Poor and Nonpoor*

Occupation	Percentage in Occupation	Median Wage	Percentage High School Dropout
Poor men			
Cooks	5.7	4.62	62
Truck drivers	5.1	5.43	29
Farm workers	4.8	5.36	75
Janitors	4.7	5.08	38
Groundskeepers	4.1	5.00	68
Construction laborers	3.8	5.21	44
Carpenters	3.5	5.19	37
Stock handlers, baggers	3.0	4.90	34
Laborers, except construction	2.3	4.68	36
Cashiers	2.1	5.56	36
Nonpoor men			
Managers, administrators	7.0	22.00	3
Supervisors and proprietors, sales occupations	4.1	15.38	4
Truck drivers	3.9	12.02	21
Janitors	1.9	9.13	34
Carpenters	1.8	11.90	22
Cooks	1.7	6.87	42
Sales representatives, mining, manufacturing, and wholesale	1.5	18.26	3
Laborers, except construction	1.4	9.42	29
Computer systems analysts	1.4	24.96	1
Groundskeepers	1.3	7.69	45
Poor women			
Cashiers	11.1	5.00	37
Nursing aides	6.8	5.73	34
Waitresses	4.7	5.03	27
Cooks	4.4	4.61	43
Janitors	3.5	5.00	43
Maids	3.4	5.05	60
Private household cleaners and servants	2.4	4.82	50
Secretaries	2.4	5.29	13
Sales workers, other commodities	2.2	5.96	36
Early childhood teacher's assistants	1.8	4.95	15
Nonpoor women			
Secretaries	4.6	10.60	4
Cashiers	3.8	6.25	32
Managers, administrators	3.8	15.60	2
Supervisors and proprietors, sales occupations	3.1	10.66	5
Registered nurses	3.0	19.71	0
Nursing aides	2.8	8.17	20

(Table continues on p. 46.)

TABLE 3.6 *Continued*

Occupation	Percentage in Occupation	Median Wage	Percentage High School Dropout
Teachers, elementary schools	2.7	14.95	0
Bookkeepers	2.6	11.06	3
Waitresses	1.8	6.59	25
Receptionists	1.7	8.33	7

Source: Author's calculations from the March 1999 CPS.
Notes: The percentage of each group in its top ten occupations is 39.1 percent for poor men, 25.0 percent for nonpoor men, 42.7 percent for poor women, and 29.9 percent for nonpoor women. All data are based on income and earnings during 1998. Wage rate per hour is defined as earnings of person divided by product of weeks worked during 1998 and usual weekly hours. Hence, this is a rough measure of hourly wages, which may account for some of the median wages that are below the minimum wage. (Subminimum wages may also account for some of this.) All figures use appropriate sampling weights. The wage rate and percentage without a high school degree are calculated separately for each of the four groups for each occupation.

employers, caseworkers, and welfare recipients about the problems with job retention faced by welfare recipients, although some studies have also looked at other disadvantaged workers.

Consider the evidence from fifty interviews conducted with participants in the New Chance program, which provided young welfare mothers with preparation for acquiring a general equivalency diploma (GED) and with job placement help (Quint, Musick, and Ladner 1994). Janet Quint and her colleagues concluded that, "with only a few exceptions, the respondents in this study did not leave their jobs because of inability to perform the required tasks. . . . The difficulties of many young women in the workplace might rather be described as relational—dealing with supervisors, with fellow workers, with apparently arbitrary rules, and with favoritism and discrimination" (1994, 61).

These authors tell the story of one woman who was suspended for a week from her nursing home job because she was late for work. She was late because her boyfriend, a drug dealer, was in jail and could not get her kids off to school for her: "Delores resented her week's suspension and seemed to think that her supervisor should excuse her lateness because she believed she had a good reason for that lateness. . . . She exemplifies this comment by one New Chance staff member: 'They [the program enrollees] think a good excuse for not doing something is as good as doing it'" (Quint et al. 1994, 48).

A similar picture emerges from interviews conducted by Linnea Berg, Lynn Olson, and Aimee Conrad (1991, 14) with fifty-eight participants, and their employers, in Project Match, a Chicago welfare-to-work program:

> We did not find that technical inability to do a job was a primary factor accounting for job loss. In 9 out of 58 cases, employers complained the

> worker did not have the skills to do some part of their job, usually running a cash register. There were only four cases where the inability to perform the work contributed to losing the job within six months. However, even in most of these cases, clearly many factors contributed to the job loss—it was not just a skill deficiency problem. For example, an 18-year-old counter clerk not only had trouble filling orders and running a cash register, her supervisor also felt she chronically made personal phone calls, was absent frequently, could not get along with her co-workers, and was perhaps stealing from the register. The worker, in turn, felt the supervisor was prejudiced and unbearably demanding.

According to Berg and her colleagues, the problems causing job loss include absenteeism and punctuality, questioning orders or "having an attitude" with supervisors, and general difficulties getting along with supervisors and coworkers.

Soft skills are not automatically acquired from other life experiences besides work. Of course, some prior life experience may predispose an individual to better navigate the workplace. For example, many caseworkers who work with welfare recipients have commented that job retention problems are related to problems with self-confidence. One research study on welfare recipients cites a client who "told her case manager that she had quit her job as a word processor because she felt 'out of her league,' overpaid for her skills, and under qualified compared with her coworkers." Another client "felt overwhelmed in her soda shop job when her co-worker stepped outside for a cigarette break and left her alone behind the counter" (Haimson, Hershey, and Rangarajan 1995, 72).

Although prior life experiences affect work performance, there are many differences between the skills needed for daily life in a low-income neighborhood and the skills needed to be productive at work. The usual daily activities of an unemployed welfare recipient consist of child and home care, with no supervisors or coworkers. An unemployed welfare recipient controls her own schedule. Many low-wage jobs involve intense supervision and pressure to deal continually with customers and coworkers.

Conventional classroom teaching may also find it difficult to teach the soft skills of getting along with supervisors, coworkers, and customers. Many cognitive psychologists and education researchers have argued that many people learn best when teaching is accompanied by some hands-on practice (Kazis and Kopp 1997, 36–37). Many individuals have difficulties transferring skills learned in the abstract to a different context such as the workplace. These problems with abstract classroom teaching may be more pronounced among individuals from disadvantaged backgrounds. The implication is that a training program that uses traditional classroom teaching by itself may not improve the productivity of many program participants. Programs may need to consider how training can incorporate either actual or simulated workplace experience.

Soft skills may also in many cases be effectively taught through actual workplace experiences, particularly if employers are able to take a more patient attitude and allow a new hire to move gradually toward good work attitudes during the first months on the job, with informal support from supervisors and coworkers. Employers are more likely to be willing to provide such a supportive work environment if labor demand is high, making it more difficult to find productive replacements.

> MYTH: The long-run productivity and wages of the poor cannot be effectively increased without increasing the acquisition by the poor of more formal education and training.
>
> FACT: In part because of the importance of soft skills and workplace experience, increased labor demand in the short run can increase the employability and wages of the poor in the long run.

Even if increased labor demand could get more poor individuals into jobs, this argument goes, it would only place the poor into dead-end jobs with few possibilities for advancement and wage increases. What would really help is more formal education. The evidence suggests, however, that this argument is invalid. Although education can significantly increase the earnings of the poor, it is also the case that full-time, full-year work experience can increase the long-run employment and earnings of the poor. Therefore, increased short-run labor demand, by increasing the odds of full-time, full-year work experiences, can significantly increase the long-run earnings of the poor just as increased formal education does.

It has long been known in labor economics that more work experience, either with a specific firm or in the labor market in general, is associated with higher wages. The effects of general workplace experience on workers' wages are most pronounced for the first years of experience: wages increase much more as a worker goes from zero to ten years of experience than they do going from twenty to thirty years of experience (Altonji and Williams 1992, 1997; Bratsberg and Terrell 1998; Murphy and Welch 1990). Work experience also has a positive effect on wages for less-educated workers and other disadvantaged groups. Because less-educated groups on average work fewer hours during a year than more-educated groups, wages of less-educated groups increase with time by less than the wages of more-educated groups. However, wages increase with actual work experience about the same for more- and less-educated groups (Gladden and Taber 2000).[13] The effects of actual work experience on wages are probably below average for black males and for females, although work experience raises wages for these groups as well (Bratsberg and Terrell 1998; Gladden and Taber 2000).

It is difficult to demonstrate a cause-and-effect relationship between work experience and wages. Perhaps individuals who, for unobservable reasons, are more productive tend as a result both to earn higher wages and to garner more work experience. But some studies that have tried to control for these unobservables have found evidence that work experience does truly increase wages, and higher wages presumably reflect greater productivity (Altonji and Williams 1992, 1997; Bratsberg and Terrell 1998).

If work experience affects the productivity of workers and supervisors, then demand or supply policies may have "hysteresis" effects on the long-run equilibrium employment rate and wage rate. ("Hysteresis" is a scientific term describing the failure of a system to return to its previous equilibrium after experiencing a temporary external shock.) By temporarily increasing the employment rate, policy may permanently increase equilibrium employment and wages. Such hysteresis effects make the benefit-cost ratio for a policy more favorable because they raise the possibility of having permanent effects on employment and earnings as a result of a short-run policy.

Several different mechanisms may cause greater short-run employment to produce hysteresis effects. First, there is the mechanism that has already been mentioned: work experience in the short run may increase worker productivity. Second, short-run work experiences may improve the self-esteem of a worker, which increases long-run earnings. Third, short-run work experiences may increase the reputation of a worker with employers, thus improving their chance of being hired. Finally, an increase in the overall employment rate may force employers to hire individuals who otherwise might not have been hired. If employers are forced by low unemployment to hire more minorities and welfare recipients, or members of any other disadvantaged group, they may learn to better manage that group and develop different attitudes toward the potential productivity of that group. These attitudes and learning may persist in the future.

In chapters 5, 7, and 8, I explore the empirical evidence on these long-run effects of employment experiences. One issue to be explored is whether some types of employment experiences are more likely to lead to long-run effects on employment and wages. If so, labor supply and demand programs must consider how to encourage these types of employment experiences.

Labor Demand

The evidence and arguments presented so far suggest that the labor supply of the poor can respond to increases in labor demand, and that it is thus possible for labor demand policies to be effective in increasing the employment and earnings of the poor. However, perhaps labor demand policies are unnecessary if labor supply policies are extremely effective in increasing the employment and earnings of the poor. For labor supply antipoverty policies to be extremely effective, labor demand for the poor must be either already readily available or quite responsive to increases in the labor supply of the poor.

The myth is widespread that in today's booming economy, jobs are readily available for all of the poor in this country. In this section, I show that for some groups in some places, high levels of involuntary unemployment nevertheless persist. Jobs are in short supply. The overall number of job slots for which there is employer demand does not automatically respond fully to the number of job seekers supplied to the labor market. Furthermore, there is considerable underemployment: some individuals are in lower-wage jobs than others with similar job skills and personal characteristics. The quality of jobs for which there is employer demand does not automatically respond fully to the capabilities of job seekers. Furthermore, although many economists believe that increases in labor supply cause large increases in labor demand, as labor demand responds to the incentives of the lower wages and higher unemployment, the empirical evidence suggests that the responsiveness of labor demand for the poor to increases in the labor supply of the poor is probably modest. Part of the reason for this modest response is that employers have great difficulty determining which prospective workers will be adequately productive and hence are reluctant to hire new workers who have little previous job experience or have been on welfare. In addition, employers continue to discriminate against blacks and Hispanics in hiring, making it more difficult for new workers from these groups to get jobs.

> MYTH: The unemployment rate is so low today that anyone who wants a job can get one.
>
> FACT: Even at today's low overall unemployment rates, some groups and some local labor markets still have high levels of unemployment. These high unemployment rates appear to reflect a shortage of available jobs and lead to lengthy unemployment and nonemployment spells for some workers.

It is widely believed that with overall U.S. unemployment around 4 percent, jobs must be readily available for all. But to the contrary, even in today's economy, unemployment for some groups is so high that it seems plausible that this unemployment is involuntary and creates significant difficulties in getting jobs. For example, in 1998, when overall unemployment was only 4.5 percent, unemployment among former welfare recipients was 31.4 percent, black unemployment was 8.9 percent, Hispanic unemployment was 7.2 percent, teenage unemployment was 14.6 percent, and unemployment among high school dropouts was 7.1 percent.[14] Of the nation's 329 metropolitan areas, 50 had unemployment of 6 percent or greater, including the New York metropolitan area at 7.3 percent, the Los Angeles metropolitan area at 6.5 percent, and the Miami metropolitan area at 6.5 percent. Of the nation's 50 largest cities, 14 had unemployment rates greater than 6 percent, including Los Angeles at 7.4 percent, New York City at 8 percent, Cleveland at 8.5 percent, and Baltimore at 9.0 percent.

These high unemployment rates appear to reflect a shortage of available jobs. Some researchers have tried to compare the number of job vacancies with the number of job seekers, either in the overall labor market or the less-skilled labor market. For the overall labor market, it appears that the numbers of unemployed exceed the numbers of job vacancies unless unemployment goes below 3 percent (Abraham 1983; Holzer 1989).[15] Some calculations for the Midwest suggest that the supply of low-skilled workers after welfare reform greatly exceeds the expected openings in jobs with low skill requirements due to job growth or turnover; the calculated ratio of job seekers to available jobs is at least two to one (Kleppner and Theodore 1997). Some more elaborate calculations attempt to match workers to available jobs based on their education, skills, race, and car ownership (Holzer and Danziger 1998). These calculations suggest that even when overall unemployment and vacancies are balanced, some disadvantaged workers have trouble finding jobs, because some of the vacancies are for jobs with skill requirements or other requirements that are not well matched to these disadvantaged workers' characteristics. Using data from four cities on employer characteristics and skill requirements, and job seekers' characteristics, Harry Holzer and Sheldon Danziger (1998) calculate that perhaps 9 to 17 percent of all workers have these "mis-match" problems. Mis-match problems are much greater for disadvantaged groups, affecting 30 to 45 percent of high school dropouts and 20 to 40 percent of welfare recipients.

Some economists have argued that unemployment is largely voluntary, implying that high unemployment rates for some groups do not necessarily point to a shortage of jobs; according to this argument, being "unemployed" (nonemployed and telling the Census Bureau they are looking for a job) and "out of the labor force" (other nonemployed who are not looking for a job) are much the same thing. This is contradicted by the exhaustively established finding (see Blanchflower and Oswald 1994) that year-to-year changes in wages in different local labor markets are far better predicted by unemployment rates than by employment rates or labor force participation rates; the suggestion is that the "unemployment" category is meaningful for labor market analysis. In addition, high unemployment rates for some groups do converge to the overall unemployment rate as unemployment is reduced, suggesting that high unemployment rates are *not* immutable characteristics of the group. For example, in research looking at different MSA labor markets (Bartik 2000c), I have found that the high unemployment rates of nonwhite groups decline much faster than white unemployment rates as overall MSA unemployment is reduced; nonwhite and white unemployment rates converge to the same rate at about 2 percent overall unemployment. This suggests that the higher unemployment rates of nonwhite groups at 6 percent unemployment, or even at 4 percent unemployment, do to some extent reflect a lack of labor demand, not simply the characteristics of nonwhite groups.

High unemployment rates and job shortages for some groups do appear to lead to lengthy periods of unemployment and nonemployment for some. (The unemployed make up the subset of the nonemployed who say they are looking for a job.) For example, research by Juhn and her colleagues (1991) shows that in the late 1980s, among prime-age males (one to thirty years after leaving school), more than 40 percent of unemployment was accounted for by men who were unemployed more than half of the year, and more than two-thirds of nonemployment was accounted for by men who were not employed more than half a year. These individuals with lengthy unemployment and nonemployment experiences clearly have significant employment problems. Unemployment and nonemployment are *not* simply about it taking a few weeks or a month to find a job. The proportion of unemployment and nonemployment among prime-age males accounted for by men with lengthy durations of unemployment or nonemployment increased significantly from the late 1960s to the late 1980s. More recent calculations are unavailable. However, earnings inequality among men continued to increase in the 1990s, and the wages and employment rates of less-skilled men continued to deteriorate, suggesting that a significant proportion of unemployed and nonemployed men are probably individuals with significant employment problems.

Even minimum-wage jobs are not easily available to everyone. In the Harlem labor market, according to research by Katherine Newman and Chauncy Lennon (1995), fourteen Harlem residents apply for every fast-food restaurant job opening. Of Harlem residents who applied unsuccessfully for these jobs, about three-quarters were still unemployed a year later, even though most had applied for many other jobs (Newman 1999; Newman and Lennon 1995). Newman and Lennon (1995, 67) conclude that, "in short, it is simply not the case that anyone who wants a low-wage job can get one."

> MYTH: The wage rate of a worker depends solely on that individual's characteristics and the effects of these characteristics on his or her productivity. Therefore, the quality of jobs that are provided by employers responds to the quality of workers supplied to the labor market.
>
> FACT: Wage rates depend on the worker's characteristics, but also—to a modest but significant extent—on the wage strategy followed by the

worker's employer. Some employers may pay higher wages to lower their hiring and worker turnover costs and improve worker productivity. Greater employer use of higher wage strategies may be encouraged by demand as well as supply policies.

As shown by the presence of involuntary unemployment and job shortages, the *number* of jobs demanded by employers does not always expand to match the number of job seekers supplied to the labor market. What about the quality of jobs? Do wages and other components of job quality that employers provide simply respond to the quality of workers supplied to the labor market? Traditional labor economics assumes that wages are identical for similar workers in a particular labor market, with wage rates determined by worker characteristics that influence productivity on the job. But in the real world, similar workers may be employed in "good" or "bad" jobs. Even controlling for all observable worker and job characteristics, similar workers are paid significantly different wages in different industries or firms. Across industries, typical wage differentials for similar workers are around 15 to 20 percent (Katz and Summers 1989). Across firms within an industry, typical wage differentials for similar workers are 10 to 15 percent (Groshen 1991).[16]

These wage differentials across industries and firms are similar for many different types of workers. (Although, of course, the absolute level of wages differs for different workers within an industry or firm; what is similar are the differences among industries and firms.) For example, the wage differential across industries is similar for many different occupations, such as managers, secretaries, and laborers (Katz and Summers 1989). Therefore, it seems likely that industry and firm wage differentials are significant even among low-education workers and are important in understanding why some workers receive low wages and similarly low-skilled workers receive somewhat better wages.

Some economists have argued that such wage differentials are due to unobserved worker or job characteristics. However, the empirical evidence suggests that a significant portion of these wage differentials represent real differences in the quality of the different jobs available to the same worker. Worker quits are lower in industries that pay higher industry wage differentials, suggesting that the jobs are in fact better jobs (Katz and Summers 1989). Workers who switch from one industry to another receive changed wages that resemble those paid other workers, suggesting that the wage differentials are not just due to different unobserved characteristics of workers (Katz and Summers 1989).

What explains these industry and firm wage differentials? These differentials may reflect differences in the degree to which different firms or industries feel that paying higher-than-average wages may lower costs or improve productivity. Higher wages may lower costs by reducing the worker quit rate and making it easier to find new workers. Higher wages may improve productivity by increasing worker morale and giving workers a greater incentive to work hard to avoid being fired. The importance of these considerations may differ across industries and firms. Industries and firms differ in technology, product market competition, profitability, the share of labor in production costs, the ease of monitoring worker productivity, the importance and cost of on-the-job-training, and the costs of recruiting new workers. All of these factors may affect the degree to which particular firms or industries find that raising wages above the market-clearing level is profitable. Empirical studies suggest that industry profitability per worker may be particularly important in determining industry wage differentials, possibly because industry profitability affects workers' views of a "fair" wage, as well as the industry's ability to pay such a wage (Katz and Summers 1989; Dickens and Katz 1987; Akerlof 1982).

These industry and firm wage differentials imply that antipoverty policies must consider the type of employment of the poor that is increased. Labor supply antipoverty policies, such as job placement or job training programs, must consider the industries and firms in which the poor become employed, and the wages and other working conditions that characterize those industries and firms. Labor demand antipoverty policies, such as wage subsidies or economic development policies, must consider the types of industries and firms that respond the most to these policies.

MYTH: In the medium or long run, labor demand for the disadvantaged responds quite elastically to the lower wage rates or higher unemployment rates of the disadvantaged brought about through increased labor supply of the disadvantaged. Therefore, we expect the increase in employer labor demand to absorb easily and fully any increase in the labor supply of the disadvantaged brought about by welfare reform, job training, or other labor supply policies.

FACT: The available empirical evidence, although scant, suggests that labor demand for the disadvantaged is only modestly or moderately responsive to lower wages or higher unemployment rates of the disadvantaged. Therefore, if the labor supply of the disadvantaged increases owing to welfare reform or job training, the employment of the disadvantaged may not fully respond to the increase, even after some time.

Even if the current *levels* of the quantity or quality of the labor of the disadvantaged that is demanded does not always exactly match the *levels* of quantity or quality of the labor of the disadvantaged that is supplied, one could argue that *changes* in labor demand for the disadvantaged are highly responsive to *changes* in the labor supply of the disadvantaged. There are two channels by which changes in the labor supply of the disadvantaged can cause changes in labor demand: by reducing the wage rate of the disadvantaged, or by raising the unemployment rate of the disadvantaged. Therefore, how responsive changes in labor demand for the disadvantaged are to changes in labor supply depends on how responsive labor demand is to changes in the wages and unemployment of the disadvantaged.

The responsiveness of demand for different types of labor is much disputed in the empirical literature in economics.[17] Empirical work using employment of some labor type as a dependent variable finds little effect of wages on employment (Grant 1979). Empirical work using wages of some labor type as a dependent variable finds modest effects of employment of that labor type on wages, suggesting large elasticities of labor demand (Berger 1983; Juhn and Kim 1999; Borjas, Freeman, and Katz 1997). Both of these approaches have problems because wages and employment are endogenous, biasing estimation that uses these variables on the right-hand side of the estimating equation. The most convincing evidence on the responsiveness of demand for less-educated workers to wages comes from the minimum-wage literature. This evidence is convincing because variation in the minimum wage across states or time is a natural "experiment" that exogenously varies the wage faced by employers. The minimum-wage literature finds that minimum-wage increases have modest effects, if any, on the employment of less-educated workers such as teenagers.[18] The minimum-wage literature suggests that the elasticity of demand for less-educated workers is in the modest range from -0.1 to -0.6; that is, a 1 percent reduction in the wage of less-educated workers may increase demand for their labor by between one-tenth and six-tenths of 1 percent.[19] In addition, empirical work suggests that greater unemployment of some labor types has moderate effects on their employment, with 1 percent greater unemployment of a labor type increasing labor demand for that type by around seven-tenths of 1 percent in the short run, and about 1.5 percent in the long run (Bartik 1999).

As explored further in appendices 1 and 2, these elasticities suggest that employment of the disadvantaged responds partially but not fully to an increase in the labor supply of the disadvantaged. For every ten additional disadvantaged persons seeking jobs, employment of the disadvantaged may go up by between three and seven jobs in the short run or the medium run.

Myth: Employers in the low-wage labor market have good information about the capabilities of job seekers. Therefore, employers are readily able to identify productive job seekers among the disadvantaged and to offer them jobs.

Fact: In the low-wage labor market, employer information about which job seekers will be productive employees is extremely sketchy. As a result, employers often adopt hiring practices that reduce the hiring prospects of the poor, such as refusing to hire welfare recipients or relying on current employees to recommend job applicants.

One reason labor demand for the disadvantaged may not be fully responsive to increases in labor supply is that employers in the low-wage labor market face serious information problems in assessing job seekers' capabilities: it is very difficult for employers in the low-wage labor market to find and hire reliable workers. Because hiring the disadvantaged frequently does not work out well, employers may be reluctant to respond to expanded supply by increasing their hiring. In addition, in response to these information problems, employers in the low-wage labor market often adopt hiring practices that make it more difficult for the disadvantaged to get jobs. These hiring practices include refusing to hire current or former welfare recipients and basing hiring primarily on referrals and recommendations of the employer's current workers.

Several studies indicate that employers have weak information about the productivity of job seekers. Interviews with employers of entry-level high school graduates show that these employers do not trust the information on job seekers that can be obtained from schools, teachers, and previous employers (Miller and Rosenbaum 1996). Most employers do not use tests to screen job applicants, owing to concern both that the tests may not predict job performance and that they may violate equal opportunity laws. Instead, many employers rely on their "gut instincts" from interviews in making hiring decisions. But these instincts often prove misleading in predicting job performance. According to one employer, "You know, it is more of a feel that you have [from the interview]. You never really know 'til you get somebody in. I've personally been duped both ways" (Miller and Rosenbaum 1996, 16).

Because of the many problems in obtaining accurate information, many new hires do not perform as well as the employer expected. According to one survey: "Managers of small and medium-sized firms were very often unpleasantly surprised by the performance of new hires. After six months on the job, more than one-quarter of new hires were producing less than 75 percent of what was anticipated when they were hired" (Bishop 1993, 336).

Why is employer information about job seekers' productivity so imperfect? In part, because of the importance of soft skills—how dependable the job seeker is and how well he or she gets along with other people. These skills are not necessarily acquired in school and are difficult for the employer to evaluate except on the job. For example, one employer in Miller and Rosenbaum's study, when asked why he did not use tests to screen job applicants, said, "We're looking for someone with people skills [who is] looking to listen to instructions, the ability to want to learn, this type of thing" (Miller and Rosenbaum 1996, 10). Such skills are not easily tested.

Poor information about job matches contributes to many important features of the low-wage labor market. One effect of poor job match information is that the low-wage labor market suffers from huge turnover, with many quits and fires in the first few months of employment. For example, at one welfare-to-work program, Project Match, researchers found that 46 percent of the program's clients lost their first job by three months, 60 percent by six months, and 73 percent by twelve months.[20]

It is difficult to believe that this extremely high rate of turnover is the most efficient method to develop better job matches, job skills, and productivity. There is some evidence that firms with higher turnover perform more poorly. According to one study, controlling for firm size, age, and industry, firms with higher employee turnover are more likely to die (Lane, Isaac, and Stevens 1997). And though job seekers can learn from their mistakes after losing a job, it would seem better for them to learn how to be more productive while retaining the job.

Poor employer information about job seekers encourages employers to make hiring decisions using imperfect signals of productivity, such as the job seeker's welfare status. Using these signals unfairly discriminates against an entire group of job seekers. Some employers simply refuse to hire welfare recipients. In an experimental study in Gary, Indiana, welfare recipients who were urged to inform employers (accurately) that the employer could receive a tax credit for hiring them were less likely to be hired than a randomly chosen group of welfare recipients who were not given these instructions (13 percent hire rate for those who advertised the tax credit versus 21 percent for the control group) (Burtless 1985). The hiring subsidy was less important to employers than the information that the job seeker was receiving welfare, information that was interpreted negatively by some employers.

Information about job seekers may be improved by hiring based on referrals from current employees. However, this hiring practice disadvantages the poor. Current employees are motivated to recommend job seekers who will be a good match. For jobs that require less than a college degree, more than one-quarter of those hired were referred by current employees (Holzer 1996, 52).[21] Hiring through referrals increases the average productivity level of those hired (Bishop 1993). However, hiring through referrals makes getting a job more difficult for persons with fewer job contacts. The poor on average have fewer job contacts.

Poor information by employers about job seekers has important implications for antipoverty policies. Programs must consider how their training or postplacement follow-up can minimize job turnover, and how to deal with the aftermath of job turnover. Both labor supply and labor demand programs must think about how to provide information to employers that avoids stigmatizing program participants. Programs that can produce information that leads to better job matches will increase the productivity of both employers and the poor and will be in demand from both employers and job seekers. More details on how programs might pursue these goals is provided in subsequent chapters.

> MYTH: Given the civil rights movement and changing social attitudes, racial discrimination by U.S. employers against blacks is no longer a significant problem.
>
> FACT: A wide variety of empirical evidence shows that racial discrimination against blacks is still quite common in hiring.

In an atmosphere of generally poor information about job seekers, employers may also indulge their prejudices and stereotypes and discriminate against blacks and other racial minorities. Empirical evidence strongly suggests that racial discrimination in hiring decisions is still common. For example, interviews with Chicago employers show that many admit they discriminate against blacks in hiring decisions in low-wage labor markets (Kirschenman and Neckerman 1991). Discrimination is rationalized by many employers as a way of screening out the less productive. According to one Chicago manufacturer:

> I would in all honesty probably say there is some [discrimination against blacks] among most employers. I think one of the reasons, in all honesty, is because we've had bad experience in that sector, and believe me, I've tried. And as I say, if I find—whether he's black or white, if he's good and, you know, we'll hire him. We are not shutting out any black specifically. But I will say that our experience factor has been bad. We've had more bad black employees over the years than we've had good. (Kirschenman and Neckerman 1991, 212)

Employers also discriminate based on social class, neighborhood of residence, and gender. According to another Chicago employer: "We have some black women here, but they're not inner city. They're from suburbs and . . . think they're a little bit more willing to give it a shot, you know, I mean they're a little bit more willing [than black men] to give a day's work for a day's pay" (Kirschenman and Neckerman 1991, 217).

Direct evidence of racial discrimination in hiring has been provided by audit studies. In these studies, matched white and minority "testers" were recruited, given similar fake résumés, and sent to the same firm to apply for the same advertised job. In the Washington, D.C., study, the white tester was offered the job in 19 percent of the cases, whereas the job was offered 6 percent of the time to the black tester. In Chicago the white tester was offered the job 10 percent of the time, compared to 5 percent of the time for the black tester (Fix and Struyk 1992). Similar differential treatment of whites and Hispanics was found in Chicago and San Diego. In contrast, an audit study of Denver did not find employer discrimination against black or Hispanic testers. Racial discrimination in hiring may vary in prevalence in different local labor markets. These differences could reflect different cultural attitudes or different demand conditions.

Because of racial discrimination, labor supply policies that add blacks to the labor market may face special difficulties in expanding overall labor demand for black workers. Some type of demand-side intervention to reduce racial discrimination in hiring may be needed. I return to this topic in chapter 9.

The Interaction of Supply and Demand

I have argued that additional jobs are needed for the poor. Because both labor supply and labor demand are moderately responsive to changes in the other side of the labor market, both labor supply and labor demand policies may increase the employment and earnings of the poor. Our almost sole reliance in the United States on labor supply policies assumes that only these policies can be effective in increasing long-run earnings.

The moderate responsiveness of both labor supply and demand of the poor has important consequences for analyzing labor supply and labor demand policies. As I show later, because of the moderate responsiveness of both labor supply and demand, supply and demand policies generally have significant "spillover" effects—that is, effects on the employment or earnings of persons other than those directly targeted by the policies. Spillover effects are ignored in virtually all of the research evaluating supply and demand policies.

MYTH: A labor supply or demand policy affects only the employment or earnings of those directly targeted by the policy, that is, those directly trained or employed by the program. Wage subsidy policies have no effect on market wages.

FACT: Labor supply or demand policies are likely to have significant spillover effects on other persons besides those targeted by the policy. The increased employment of those directly trained or hired by the policy is offset to some extent by reduced employment of the persons "displaced" by the policy. Wage subsidies to either workers or employers are offset somewhat by changes in market wages.

Most evaluations of the effects of labor supply and demand policies on the employment and earnings of the poor assume that there are no spillover effects on nonparticipants in these programs. For example, most evaluations of welfare reform programs estimate the program's effects on employment and earnings by comparing the employment and earnings of welfare reform participants with those of a control group of people (preferably randomly chosen) who did not participate in the program. Such an evaluation ignores the possibility that some of the jobs gained by participants may have come at the expense of jobs lost by nonparticipants, and that the welfare reform may reduce the wages of nonparticipants.

The underlying reason for the spillover effects of labor supply and demand policies is that both labor supply and demand respond to changes in the other side of the labor market with some moderate elasticity, rather than having zero or infinitely elastic responsiveness. For example, a welfare reform program may add workers to the low-wage labor market. This puts downward pressure on the wage rate and increases unemployment. For employment demand to increase enough to absorb a significant share of the increased supply of low-wage labor, the labor supply conditions faced by employers must change significantly: either unemployment must be significantly higher so that it is easier to find and hire low-wage labor, or wages must be lower so that employment of low-wage labor is even cheaper for employers. Higher unemployment and lower wages in turn have some moderate—non-zero but non-infinite—effects on reducing labor force participation rates among persons not involved in the welfare reform. These lower labor force participation rates coupled with the higher unemployment rates reduce employment rates among low-wage workers who were not involved in the welfare reform. Therefore, the welfare reform–induced increase in the labor supply of low-wage labor is accompanied by some overall increase in the employment of low-wage labor, but by less than the increase in employment of the new labor force participants due to welfare reform, with employment falling for low-wage workers who are not welfare recipients. Wages also fall in the low-wage labor market for all workers, including both welfare recipients and nonrecipients. Welfare reform would have quite different effects if either labor demand or supply had infinite or zero responsiveness. For example, if labor demand for low-wage labor had extremely high responsiveness to even slight changes in unemployment or wages, then only very small increases in unemployment or reductions in wages would be needed for employers to be willing to expand employment enough to absorb all the additional labor supply.

The magnitude of spillover effects depends on the magnitude of the responsiveness of labor supply and demand to wages and unemployment rates, and on how wages respond to unemployment rates. Appendices 1 and 2 present both theoretical and empirical models that predict the likely magnitude of the employment and wage effects of different supply and demand policies. Using plausible magnitudes of the sensitivity of demand and supply to wages and unemployment rates, a labor supply or demand policy that adds some quantity to labor supply or demand is likely to have effects on employment of from one-third to two-thirds of the increase in employment of those participating in the labor supply or demand program. This implies that the negative spillover effects reducing the employment of others from a labor supply or demand program offset from one-third to two-thirds of the direct employment effects on program participants. Therefore, the spillover effects on employment are large. The magnitude of spillover effects on wages is much more sensitive to modeling assumptions but is generally modest unless we consider long-run effects or consider a labor supply or demand policy targeted at a group that is a large share of the labor force. However, as explored in later chapters, much depends on the exact design of specific supply and demand policies. In particular, there are ways of targeting wage subsidies so that the costs of these programs may also be kept relatively modest.

The Geographic Scope of the Low-Wage Labor Market

> MYTH 1: Low-wage labor markets are essentially national. Economic forecasts and policies for low-wage workers should be based on national economic trends in demand and supply and on national labor market institutions.
>
> MYTH 2: Low-wage labor markets are essentially neighborhood-oriented because many low-wage workers have limited access to cars and other transportation. Therefore, economic forecasts and policies for low-wage workers should be based on demand and supply trends in workers' neighborhood of residence and on neighborhood-based labor market institutions.
>
> FACT: Low-wage labor markets are essentially local, but larger than the neighborhood level. The geographic scope of the low-wage labor market is best defined as a metropolitan area, or as a rural area that similarly encompasses most commuting flows. Labor market policies should be designed to recognize each metropolitan area's unique labor market conditions and institutions.

The effects of labor market policies on the poor depend on conditions and institutions in the relevant labor market. But what is the relevant labor market, and how do we know it is the relevant one? Discussions of poverty in the national media and social science research often simply discuss trends in the nation as a whole. The natural implication is that differences across local labor markets are unimportant for policy, and that antipoverty policies can be designed as if there were just one national labor market for low-wage labor. Other discussions of poverty focus on the lack of jobs in poor neighborhoods, implying that the labor market for the poor is neighborhood-oriented. What is the labor market for the poor? I argue in this section that the relevant labor market for the poor is a local area such as a metropolitan area. It is the metropolitan area's supply and demand trends and conditions and its economic institutions that must be understood to make better labor market policies for the poor.

Why a Metropolitan Area Approximates the Relevant Labor Market for the Poor

The metropolitan statistical areas (MSAs) used by the Census Bureau are defined so that most commuting from residences in an MSA go to workplaces in that MSA, and most commuting to workplaces in an MSA come from residences in that MSA. Because of commuting, changes in labor market conditions in one part of an MSA affect persons throughout the area. Because labor moves less often across MSA boundaries, the effects of shocks to one MSA on other areas are weaker.

Most workers in the United States work outside the neighborhood where they live. The average travel time to work in U.S. metropolitan areas is twenty-three minutes. Thirteen percent of all metropolitan workers travel forty-five or more minutes to work (U.S. Department of Commerce 1993). In one survey of Chicago employers, the average percentage of employees who lived more than a mile away from the firm was about 70 percent (Reingold 1999). Furthermore, individuals switch jobs a lot. Depending on the year examined, between 20 and 25 percent of all employed males between the ages of twenty and fifty-nine have been at their current job less than eighteen months, and between 25 and 30 percent of all employed females between the ages of twenty and fifty-nine have been at their current job less than eighteen months (Jaeger and Stevens 1999). Even among workers in their forties, more than 10 percent of men and more than 15 percent of women have been at their current job less than eighteen months (Jaeger and Stevens 1999).

Because many individuals can switch jobs, changes in job availability or wages in one part of the metropolitan area spread throughout the area. For example, suburban job growth may help central-city residents, even central-city residents without bus service or cars. Some workers originally working in the central city may take the new suburban jobs, opening up job vacancies in the city. These job vacancies make it easier for central-city residents to find jobs and may increase city wages.

Although labor market conditions throughout a metropolitan area are linked, the earnings of inner-city residents are also affected by nearby job openings, at least for larger MSAs. Some early studies suggested that the earnings of disadvantaged persons were not much affected by proximity to jobs. But the number of nearby jobs may not be a good measure of job availability for the disadvantaged. In more recent research, stronger effects of job access on less-educated workers are found when job access is measured by nearby job growth (Rogers 1997; Raphael 1998). For less-educated workers, nearby job growth may reflect the availability of entry-level jobs (Ihlanfeldt and Sjoquist 1998).

Why does access matter? Recent studies suggest that access may affect information about job openings. Faraway jobs may be physically accessible. But low-wage job seekers are more likely to learn about nearby job openings. A recent study finds that although employers more distant from the black population usually hire fewer blacks, this effect disappears for employers who hire using newspaper ads (Holzer and Ihlanfeldt 1996). Labor submarkets within MSAs may be defined by information availability, not geographic location.

Studies that find job access matters also confirm the importance of overall metropolitan labor demand. For example, Ihlanfeldt (1992) finds that better job access or lower MSA unemployment both increase employment of black teenagers.

The importance of access differs greatly across MSAs. Job access affects black hiring rates more in Atlanta and Detroit, cities with relatively weak public transit systems, than in Boston, a city with a better public transit system (Holzer and Ihlanfeldt 1996). Job access affects black teenage employment rates in MSAs above 800,000 in population, but not in MSAs below 800,000 (Ihlanfeldt 1992). In smaller MSAs, inner-city neighborhoods may be close to job openings. For example, in my home city of Kalamazoo, Michigan, high-poverty neighborhoods are within walking distance of downtown and some industry. Surveys of Kalamazoo employers in high-poverty neighborhoods reveal that less than 5 percent of their employees are neighborhood residents.

Thus, it is best to think of a small or medium-sized metropolitan area as a single labor market. In larger areas there may be geographic submarkets, defined by how information about the labor market is distributed, but labor market conditions throughout the MSA still matter.

There is a great deal less labor mobility across metropolitan areas. Even if jobs become scarce, individuals are reluctant to abandon their home area. One survey, for example, showed that laid-off textile workers were willing to accept 14 percent lower wages to stay in their hometown (Dunn 1979). Moving costs of this magnitude are unlikely to be purely financial. Some part of these moving costs reflects attachments to familiar people and places.

Because of strong ties to home, only 4.4 percent of the population moves into a typical metropolitan area each year.[22] This compares with 9.6 percent of the metropolitan population that moves from elsewhere in the MSA each year, and 20 percent of the population that switches jobs each year.

Cross-MSA mobility rates are lower for low-education persons. For individuals with a high school degree or less, between the ages of twenty-five and sixty-four, only 3.9 percent move into a typical MSA each year. For individuals with a college degree or more, 5.4 percent move into an MSA each year. Perhaps cross-MSA mobility for some high-education professionals (Ph.D. economists?) may be great enough that their labor market is truly national. But this is the exception.

Because of barriers to inter-MSA mobility, increased MSA employment growth does not cause migration to adjust fully. Research shows that in the short run (one year), an increase in a metropolitan area's employment growth of 1 percent increases the area's population by only one-third to one-half of 1 percent (Bartik 1991, 1993a). Thus, a change in MSA labor demand can affect local unemployment and wages. Because many job skills are learned on the job, these short-run changes in labor market experience have long-run effects on individuals' wages and employment. As a result, labor market outcomes in an MSA may persistently diverge from those of the nation. MSAs operate as distinct labor markets.

A few studies have compared national and local influences on labor market outcomes. These studies support the greater effect of the local labor market. For example, MSA employment growth has been found to have significant effects on average family incomes. But once one controls for MSA employment growth, MSA family income is not significantly affected by national growth (Bartik 1994a). Wage rates in a typical American state are far more influenced by the state's unemployment rate than by the overall U.S. rate (Blanchflower and Oswald 1994).

Labor Market Institutions: Private, Public, and Nonprofit

Private, public, and nonprofit institutions may differ across metropolitan areas sufficiently to require different policies. Differences within MSAs may be less important.

Metropolitan areas differ greatly in industry mix and the share of employment in small firms. As mentioned earlier, wages paid for similar workers differ greatly among different industries, and among different firms within the same industry. Wages also tend to be lower for similar workers in smaller firms (Brown, Hamilton, and Medoff 1990). In addition to variations in wages, firms differ in how they advertise job openings, the skills demanded, how they assess applicants' skills, and how much training they provide. A firm's best labor market strategy varies with the industry's technologies, its product market, and the firm's size.

Because of these different business strategies, how low-wage workers can best find jobs or find better jobs varies greatly with the industry and firm size mix of the MSA. Because workers are more mobile across neighborhoods, the industries and firms in the home neighborhood are not as important.

Many public and nonprofit institutions play important roles in local labor markets. Among these institutions are public schools, community colleges, job training agencies, welfare offices, and employment service offices. State and federal funding and policies have important effects on these institutions, but in the end services are delivered by local offices. The geographic scope of such offices is frequently not the metropolitan area but is typically much larger than a neighborhood and much smaller than a state.

These local offices often operate with considerable autonomy. The leaders and staff determine the services that actually get delivered. For example, evaluations of California's welfare-to-work program (GAIN) revealed huge differences in how the program was run in different counties. GAIN in Riverside County had a much stronger employment orientation and greater effects in increasing the earnings and employment of welfare recipients (Ricco, Friedlander, and Freedman 1994). Case study evidence suggests that these differences reflected the leadership of Riverside's local welfare office director. This director set a strong employment orientation, said his three top principles for running a welfare-to-work program were "selection of staff, selection of staff, selection of staff," and invested a great deal of resources in staff training (Bardach 1993).

Some other institutions that affect labor demand are also organized at the local level. National institutions such as the Federal Reserve have the strongest influence on labor demand, but local economic development agencies also influence labor demand. The tax, spending, and economic development policies of local governments can significantly affect labor demand (Bartik 1991).

How local economic development institutions are organized varies greatly from one area to another. Economic development policy is usually little influenced by neighborhood groups, which focus on housing and community development issues. A variety of city, county, and chamber-of-commerce organizations typically play a role in local economic development policies, and who does what varies greatly across the United States (Bartik 1996a). Although states also play an important role in economic development policy, states often defer to local leadership in metropolitan areas and play a more active role in rural areas, where leadership is weaker. For example, the state of Tennessee takes the lead on industrial recruitment for nonmetropolitan areas and allows the major cities to determine their own recruitment strategies and targets (Bartik 1988).

Policy Implications of Metropolitan Labor Markets and Institutions

These differences across metropolitan areas in labor market institutions and types of businesses require different antipoverty policies. The industry and firm-size mix of the MSA may affect how the average business in the area responds to wage subsidies for hiring the poor. In some MSAs, businesses have developed good working relationships with local community colleges. Such relationships may make it easier for community colleges to carry out programs to train and screen the poor for placement in private firms.

Effective labor market policies to help the poor cannot be implemented solely at the neighborhood level. The poor must be linked with firms and public and nonprofit institutions outside their home neighborhood. Neighborhood organizations may play a role in antipoverty labor market policies, but such policies must have a larger geographic scope than the neighborhood.

Although policies must differ across metropolitan areas, appropriate labor market policies should take account of the spillover effects of one area's policies on the nation. One MSA's policies may have effects on the nation as a whole through the labor market, through inter-MSA migration, through the product market, or through changes in prices. Chapter 6 returns to this topic of how labor market policies in different MSAs may affect overall national inflation.

Conclusion

This chapter has outlined five features of the low-wage labor market, focusing on those that influence the effectiveness of labor supply and demand policies in fighting poverty:

1. Despite the current U.S. economic boom, more jobs for the poor are needed and will help reduce poverty.
2. There is untapped labor supply among the poor that is potentially productive and capable of responding to increases in labor demand.
3. Labor demand increases to only a moderate extent in response to increases in the labor supply of the poor.
4. Both demand and supply policies to reduce poverty have significant spillover effects on persons not participating in these programs. In particular, both kinds of policy may reduce the employment of some nonparticipants.

5. Because the low-wage labor market is best thought of as a metropolitan area, labor supply and demand policies should be designed to reflect the particular labor market institutions and business mix of each MSA.

Other important points about the low-wage labor market that emerged include the following:

- Soft skills—such as showing up at work on time and getting along with coworkers and supervisors—are important in the low-wage labor market.
- Full-time, full-year work experience in the low-wage labor market can over time yield significant increases in wage rates. This implies that short-run increases in demand for low-wage workers can have long-run effects on earnings.
- Employers in the low-wage labor market often have poor information about the potential productivity of job seekers.
- Racial discrimination in hiring is still prevalent in the American labor market.

All these features of the low-wage labor market play a role in the discussion in subsequent chapters, which examine in more detail labor supply and demand policies. For example, chapter 4 discusses the effectiveness of job training programs and makes the point that training programs are more effective in local labor markets with lower unemployment; also, programs with closer ties to employers overcome some of the information problems facing employers and are thus more successful. Chapter 4 also discusses the spillover effects of various labor supply policies, such as welfare reform, worker wage subsidies such as the Earned Income Tax Credit, job training programs, and education programs—for example, by reducing the employment of nonparticipants.

Chapters 5 through 9 discuss various aspects of labor demand policies whose effects also depend on the features of low-wage labor markets. These chapters highlight the considerable evidence that labor demand policies can increase the employment of the poor, presumably because there is some untapped, potentially productive labor supply among the poor. A key issue discussed throughout these chapters is the potential displacement effect of labor demand policies—that is, to what extent do these policies reduce the employment opportunities of nonparticipants in labor demand programs? Another key issue is how to design labor demand policies to increase the long-run earnings of the poor more effectively. Finally, an important issue influencing the effectiveness of wage subsidies to employers for hiring the disadvantaged, discussed in chapter 8, is the information conveyed to employers by such programs. If employers avoid hiring subsidized workers in the belief that they are likely to be less productive, then this type of labor demand policy can stigmatize these workers, reducing their employment prospects. Effectively designing wage subsidies to employers, or any other labor demand or supply program, requires that policymakers take account of how low-wage labor markets work.

4

THE LABOR MARKET EFFECTS OF LABOR SUPPLY PROGRAMS

THIS CHAPTER considers programs that increase the employment or earnings of low-income Americans by increasing the quantity or quality of their labor supply or providing earnings supplements. The programs considered include welfare reform, the Earned Income Tax Credit (EITC) and other wage supplements, and education and training. What effects do these programs have on employment, earnings, and income? What spillover effects do they have on the employment and wages of those who are not program participants? How can these programs be more effective?

In this chapter, I argue that it is difficult for labor supply programs, by themselves, to increase both the employment and income of low-income Americans in both a cost-effective and fair manner. In part, these difficulties occur because most labor supply programs have displacement effects that decrease the employment and earnings of the low-income Americans who do not participate in these programs.

The labor supply of low-income Americans can be increased at little government budgetary cost by welfare reform efforts that cut welfare benefits and limit welfare eligibility, thereby pushing welfare recipients into the labor market. However, such welfare reform adversely affects some ex-welfare recipients, causing significant income declines. Programs that provide disadvantaged groups with financial incentives to work may increase income for those receiving the incentives but are estimated to have only modest effects on increasing employment. Combining financial incentives to work with some casework assistance may increase both employment and income but is costly and difficult to administer if applied to all eligible low-income Americans. If such a combination of incentives and individualized services is not offered to everyone who is eligible, significant issues of "horizontal equity" or fairness to those excluded from receiving these services are raised. Finally, all these programs that simply increase the labor force participation of low-income Americans are likely to have significant displacement effects, with from one-third to two-thirds of the new employment of program participants offset by reduced employment of low-income Americans who are not program participants.

In contrast to welfare reform or financial incentive programs, education programs seek to transform the quality of labor. Education programs can significantly increase the wages, employment, earnings, and income of low-income Americans who successfully complete them. Education programs cause some displacement, but this displacement has progressive effects on the income distribution: moving some persons from less-educated to more-educated labor markets displaces some of the original more-educated workers from jobs but increases employment for some of the less-educated persons left behind in the less-educated labor market. However, education programs are very expensive to run, at least at the scale it would take to provide the additional jobs needed for low-income Americans or to narrow significantly the distribution of wages across different education groups.

Training programs for the disadvantaged were intended to provide a "second chance" in a relatively low-cost way for those low-income Americans who did not receive adequate job skills or contacts from the "first-chance" education system. However, it has been difficult to make training programs for the disadvantaged highly effective for more than a minority of participants. In addition, training programs at best move individuals from lower-wage jobs to lower-middle-wage jobs. As a consequence, the increased employment of some training participants in lower-middle-wage jobs comes in part by displacing from employment some of the lower-middle-class Americans currently in those jobs. More successful training programs have been conducted in labor markets with strong local labor demand; these programs incorporate some demand-side components by working with specific local employers to design training curricula and help place training graduates.

Therefore, labor supply programs by themselves are insufficient, and they are more effective when complemented by labor demand programs. Efforts to increase labor demand are needed to offset some of the negative effects of labor supply programs on displacement. Strong labor demand helps to increase the effectiveness of education and training programs. Finally, some of the best labor supply programs include some demand-side components.

Welfare Reform

Federal welfare reform is pushing states to increase welfare recipients' labor supply. Several provisions of the 1996 federal welfare reform bill (the Personal Responsibility and Work Opportunity Reconciliation Act of 1996) encourage states to push welfare recipients off welfare and into the labor force by:

- imposing financial penalties on states that fail to increase the employment of welfare recipients or cut caseloads;

- imposing a five-year time limit on the receipt of federal welfare assistance by individuals;
- under the fixed federal block grants established by the 1996 bill, requiring states to pay the full cost of extra welfare spending, thus giving states an incentive to reduce caseloads.[1]

The 1996 welfare bill also continues a trend toward giving states greater flexibility in welfare administration. Prior to 1996, considerable flexibility had already been given to many states through federal waivers for welfare reforms; these waivers began under Presidents Reagan and Bush but were made broader and more radical after President Clinton took office in 1993. Given current political attitudes toward welfare reform, this greater flexibility has been used by most states to reduce caseloads and increase the labor supply of welfare recipients.

States can institute many policies and administrative procedures to increase the labor supply of welfare recipients, including:

- providing welfare-to-work services such as short-term training, counseling, and job placement;
- allowing welfare recipients to keep more of their benefits if they work;
- diverting applicants for welfare away from welfare by requiring job search before considering an application, or by providing applicants with an emergency check if they agree not to apply for welfare for some time period;
- sanctioning welfare recipients—cutting welfare benefits totally or partly—for violating rules, often for missing appointments with caseworkers.

I consider positive supports to increase labor supply—training and other services and financial support—later in this chapter. Most of welfare reform's labor supply effects so far have taken place through administrative policies that make it more difficult for individuals to get on or stay on welfare. For example, according to the U.S. Department of Health and Human Services (1998a, ch. 3), many states sanction more than 25 percent of their caseload.

Welfare reform's effects on labor supply can be seen in aggregate data. Figure 4.1 compares labor force participation for two groups: single mothers without a college degree, and other women without a college degree. As welfare rolls have declined, the labor force participation rate of single mothers has dramatically increased relative to the labor force participation of other similarly educated women. Some of this trend is due to the Earned Income Tax Credit (more on that later), but careful studies show

FIGURE 4.1 *Labor Force Participation Rates of Female Heads and Other Less-Educated Females and the Welfare Recipiency Rate, 1979 to 1998*

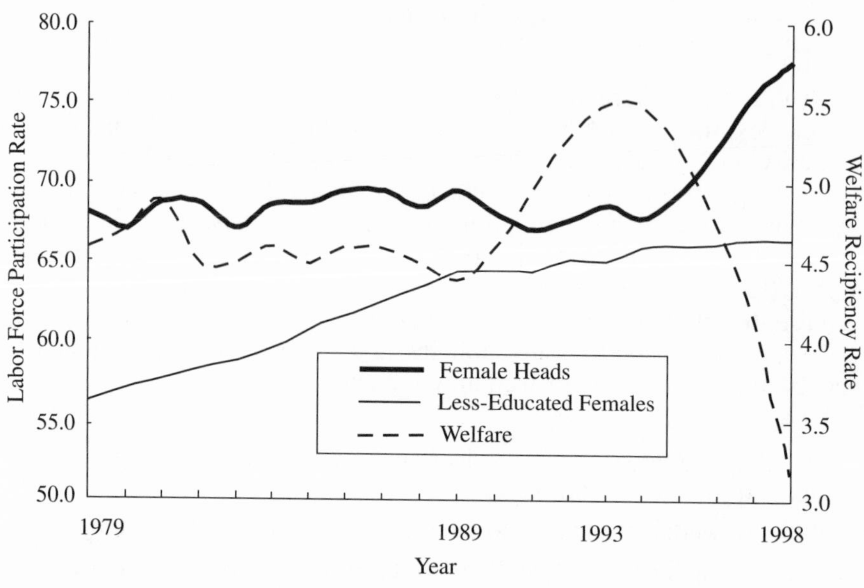

Source: U.S. Department of Health and Human Services (2000) and author's calculations.
Notes: Labor force participation data for 1979 to 1998 come from the CPS-ORG. Female heads are female heads of household, with other relatives present in the household, who are ages sixteen to forty-four and have less than sixteen years of education. This is the closest to the group "less-educated single mothers" that can be defined consistently from 1979 to 1998 for the CPS-ORG. Less-educated females are all females, ages sixteen to sixty-four, with less than sixteen years of education, except for female heads. The calculated means use CPS-ORG weights. The welfare recipiency rate is the number of welfare recipients for that fiscal year as a percentage of the U.S. population for that calendar year.

that at least one-third of this trend is due to welfare policies (Meyer and Rosenbaum 1998).

Several studies have considered how welfare reform is affecting labor supply. Table 4.1 summarizes such studies. Despite varied methodologies, the studies are consistent in their findings: from 1993 to 2008, welfare reforms will increase the labor force by between one million and two million persons. This is between .75 percent and 1.5 percent of the overall U.S. labor force, but a much larger percentage of the labor force of various groups, such as female high school dropouts (about 9 percent) and single mothers (about 10 percent).[2]

What happens to individuals forced off welfare? The available evidence suggests that some ex-welfare recipients "make it" but that others are pushed deeper into poverty. Employment rates (and therefore earnings) in-

TABLE 4.1 *Recent Estimates of the Effects of Welfare Reform on Labor Supply*

Study	Time Period	Labor Supply Effect	Brief Description of Methodology
Meyer and Rosenbaum (1998), adapted by Bartik (1998)	1993 to 1996	249,000	Estimated effects of state welfare policy variables on employment probability of single mothers versus childless single women
Bishop (1998)	1996 to 1998	571,000	Change in single-parent labor force participation rate between second quarters of 1996 and 1998 that cannot be explained by declining unemployment and trends
Daly (1997), adapted by Bartik (1998)	1996 to 1997	325,000	Labor force growth trends for women maintaining families versus U.S. population
McMurrer, Sawhill, and Lerman (1997b)	1996 to 2002	No recession: 832,000 Recession: 1,699,000	Calculated effects of 1996 welfare reform bill's escalating requirements for percentage of caseload that must be working
Chernick and Reschovsky (1996)	1996 to 2002	1,144,000	Calculated effects on state welfare spending of switching from matching grants under AFDC to block grant fixed in nominal terms under the 1996 bill.
Duncan, Harris, and Boisjoly (1998)	1996 to 2005	383,000	Calculated percentage of caseload that will reach five-year lifetime time limit on welfare receipt within eight years.
Bartik estimates (1998)	1993 to 1996 1996 to 1997 1996 to 1998 1996 to 2002 1996 to 2005 1993 to 2005	146,000 300,000 597,000 1,032,000 1,256,000 1,402,000	Estimated declines in welfare rolls that cannot be explained by unemployment, extrapolated into the future, and assumed work participation rates for participants

Source: Author's compilation.
Note: See Bartik (2000a) and Bartik (1998) for more details on the derivations of these estimates.

crease considerably, from perhaps 10 to 15 percent for women on welfare to 40 to 50 percent for women forced off of welfare (McMurrer, Sawhill, and Lerman 1997a, 1997b; Tweedie and Reichert 1998). However, unemployment rates among ex-welfare recipients are very high—for example, 30 percent in 1999 when overall national unemployment was only 4.2 percent.[3] Wage rates are low, in the $6 to $7 per hour range (Cancian et al. 1999; Bartik 2000a), and increase in real terms (after adjusting for inflation) by only 1 or 2 percent per year on average (Cancian et al. 1999; Burtless 1995). Even including individuals who voluntarily leave welfare, poverty rates remain high, at more than 40 percent five years after the recipient exits welfare (Cancian et al. 1999). In studies of reform in Iowa, the household income of 40 percent of welfare recipients forced off welfare went up, from an average of $600 a month to $1,100 per month. However, in 49 percent of the cases income went down, from an average of $884 per month to $500 per month (Fraker et al. 1997). The percentage of households with income of more than $1,000 per month went up to 22 percent (from 18 percent), but the percentage of households with income of less than $500 per month also increased, from 30 percent to 45 percent. According to surveys in South Carolina and Wisconsin, the category of deprivation that increased the most among welfare leavers was the number of families reporting that they sometimes had no way to buy food (Sherman et al. 1998; Wisconsin Department of Workforce Development 1999b). Being forced off of welfare removes a part of the social safety net; as a result, families have a longer way to fall, and some do.

What are the displacement and wage effects of the labor supply increase due to welfare reform? I considered these effects in detail in Bartik (2000a). Using a wide variety of models, I found that the displacement effects of welfare reform range from 20 to 60 percent—that is, for every ten additional ex-welfare recipients who enter the labor force because of welfare reform, two to six jobs are lost by other less-educated persons. For example, using an empirically estimated, general equilibrium model, for every ten persons entering the labor market because of welfare reform, after about ten years about two jobs are lost by single mothers with less than a college education, for a long-run displacement effect of 20 percent.[4] In contrast, under most modeling assumptions, the effects of welfare reform on wages are modest.

These significant displacement effects from labor supply shocks such as welfare reform occur because in the labor market for less-educated labor market, the short-run and medium-run responsiveness of wages and labor demand to labor supply shocks appear to be modest. As discussed in chapter 3 and in appendices 1 and 2, this moderate responsiveness of labor demand in this labor market to labor supply increases occurs under a wide variety of modeling assumptions. The resistance of relative wages for different groups to change also helps explain why welfare reform probably has only moderate effects on the wages of less-educated groups.

These adverse displacement and wage effects could be offset by expanding labor demand for the groups most affected by welfare reform, for example, through public-service employment for less-educated single mothers. An employment increase that matched the labor supply increase of welfare reform—that is, a labor demand increase of one or two million—would completely eliminate even short-run displacement effects. But most models of the labor market for the less-educated suggest that the labor market eliminates some displacement effects on its own. A more modest labor demand increase of one-fifth of the welfare reform labor supply shock, if precisely targeted at single mothers with less education, would be sufficient to offset the long-run displacement effects of welfare reform on single mothers. A welfare reform supply shock of about 1.4 million, the consensus figure used in Bartik (2000a), implies that public employment programs or wage subsidies must increase net employment by a little less than 300,000.

Government Financial Support to the Poor for Working

Several types of programs can be used to provide extra governmental assistance to the disadvantaged if they work:

1. *Tax credits targeted at the working poor:* Such tax credits are much more important to the poor if they are refundable, that is, if they are payable even if the individual has no tax liability due to ordinary exemptions and deductions. The largest such tax credit in the United States is the Earned Income Tax Credit, a refundable tax credit that provided 20 million households with an average tax credit of $1,500 in 1998 and cost the government an estimated $30 billion (Council of Economic Advisers 1998).
2. *Allowing welfare recipients to keep more of their benefits if they work:* More benefits can be paid to welfare recipients who work by various combinations of two policies: (1) increasing the initial amount of earnings that is "disregarded" when welfare benefit levels are set for a family, and (2) reducing the benefit reduction rate, that is, lowering the amount by which welfare benefits are cut for each extra dollar of earnings. For example, rather than lower benefits one dollar for each dollar increase in earnings, benefits could be cut by 50 or 67 cents for each one-dollar increase in earnings. Under the 1996 welfare reform law, earnings disregards and benefit reduction rates are now set by state governments.

3. *Special targeted wage subsidies focused on encouraging full-time work:* Full-time work can be targeted by providing a wage subsidy only if the individual's weekly work hours exceed a specific threshold. Such policies have been implemented in two experiments: Canada's Self-Sufficiency Project (SSP) and New York State's Child Assistance Program (CAP).

These supply-side wage subsidies have several goals: increasing work among the poor; increasing work hours among the poor; providing the poor with a higher net wage after the program's assistance; increasing income and reducing poverty; saving the government money by encouraging some persons to get a job and pay taxes rather than stay unemployed and collect a full welfare check; promoting fairness by providing both similar help to all the poor in similar situations and the most help to those most in need. These goals often conflict. Which goals a particular program can achieve may depend on the details of the program design.

Program Design

There are several important issues in program design:

Effects on "Budget Constraints" Most programs providing financial subsidies to the poor for working do not have the same effect as increasing their wages. To keep government spending down and to target spending on the poor, the financial subsidy is phased out above a specified earnings level—that is, it decreases as the individual's earnings increase. But phasing out the subsidy can encourage individuals to maximize the subsidy by switching from full-time to part-time work. In addition, the extra income from the subsidy allows some individuals to work only part-time or even not at all; for example, wives can drop out of the paid workforce. Therefore, although government financial subsidies for work encourage employment among those who otherwise would be outside the labor force, such subsidies usually reduce the work hours of some individuals. Whether this is a problem depends on whether one believes all adults should work full-time. For example, how upset is the average voter if, owing to government subsidies, some married women reduce their work hours or quit work? A program's effects on full-time and part-time work may depend on details of how the program affects the budget constraint.

The Perception of the Financial Subsidies Evidence suggests that financial subsidies for work that are part of welfare have less positive effects on work than subsidies for work that are perceived as "earnings" (Moffitt 1983; Meyer and Rosenbaum 1998). A plausible explanation is welfare "stigma": because of social disapproval of welfare receipt, recipients value an extra dollar of welfare benefits less than an extra dollar of earnings. Wage subsidies' effects on labor supply may also depend on whether subsidies are received with each paycheck or annually, and whether the incentives provided are understood by the recipients.

Targeting Financial subsidies for work may increase work more per dollar spent if they are targeted at those disadvantaged individuals who are most likely to respond to incentives. However, such targeting reduces the subsidies' benefits to other poor individuals. Targeting also raises the issue of "horizontal" equity: Why should one poor person receive a subsidy that is denied to another?

Generosity More generous financial subsidies are more likely to increase the work and income of the poor. But generosity costs the government money and worsens issues of fairness between program participants and similar nonparticipants.

Services Services that encourage work—for example, encouraging job search and providing job leads—may complement the effects of financial subsidy programs in encouraging work. The financial subsidies may also help caseworkers to believe that work is a good option for their clients. Of course, expanding caseworkers' services significantly adds to the costs of the program and makes delivering the program more complex and difficult. One of the appeals of financial subsidy programs by themselves is that they appear to offer an administratively simple solution, and adding casework services eliminates this appeal.

Displacement and wage effects are important issues for financial subsidy programs that increase the labor supply of the poor. As outlined in chapter 3 and in appendices 1 and 2, empirical estimates suggest that such labor supply increases have substantial displacement effects on the group whose labor supply is increased, but probably modest wage effects. Estimates from a wide variety of models suggest that a labor supply increase for a less-educated group, brought about by financial subsidies or otherwise, has displacement effects of from one-third to two-thirds. For every one hundred less-educated individuals added to the labor force by financial subsidy program, perhaps thirty-three to sixty-six low-income American workers will lose their current jobs. Labor demand will partially but not fully respond to this increase in labor supply.

The Earned Income Tax Credit

The largest U.S. financial subsidy for work is the Earned Income Tax Credit. The EITC began as Senator Russell Long's alternative to both welfare and President Nixon's proposal for a guaranteed annual income. The EITC was enacted into law on a small scale as part of a 1975 tax cut and rationalized as an offset to social security taxes on the working poor.

Strong bipartisan support for the EITC led to major expansions under Republican presidents in 1987 and 1991. President Clinton proposed, and Congress enacted, another major expansion of the EITC in 1994. With its continual expansion, however, the EITC has recently begun to attract more criticism as a "welfare" program. For example, some concerns have been raised about fraudulent EITC claims.

As of 1998, 20 million U.S. families were receiving the EITC, at a total federal cost of $30 billion (Council of Economic Advisers 1998). The EITC is now considerably larger than cash welfare expenditures; combined federal and state spending under the new welfare bill was $25 billion in fiscal year 1998 (U.S. Department of Health and Human Services 1999).[5] The EITC provides a large wage subsidy. In 1998 the maximum possible EITC was almost $4,000. Workers receive a credit of as much as forty cents for every dollar of earnings. On the other hand, as the EITC is phased out, workers pay considerably higher marginal tax rates, losing as much as twenty-one cents for every extra dollar of income.

The best estimates suggest that the EITC has modest effects on labor supply, although the precise magnitude is disputed. Positive effects on labor supply are largest for single mothers. Based on several studies, the EITC increases the labor force of single mothers by somewhere between 170,000 (Meyer and Rosenbaum 1998) and 405,000 (Liebman 1998, based on Eissa and Liebman 1996).[6] The labor supply of married men is also increased, but even more modestly (Dickert et al. 1995; Eissa and Hoynes 1999). The labor force participation rate of married women is reduced owing to the incentives of the EITC, with the largest negative estimated effect that of Eissa and Hoynes (1999), whose estimates imply that the EITC causes 161,000 married women to leave the labor force.[7] Contrary to economic theory, estimates by Eissa and Liebman (1996) suggest that the EITC does not encourage single mothers to reduce working hours from full-time to part-time. The EITC may not affect work hours because most EITC recipients receive the credit only once a year, as part of their tax refund (Eissa and Liebman 1996). Because the EITC is not received with every paycheck, single mothers may not perceive that the EITC provides incentives for working part-time rather than full-time. However, the estimates of other researchers that the EITC modestly reduces the work hours of married couples, particularly married women (Eissa and Hoynes 1999), are inconsistent with the belief that the part-time incentives of the EITC are unnoticed.

Regardless of the precise number, the point is that the EITC does not usually provide an effective work incentive or, for that matter, a work disincentive. Twenty million households receive EITC benefits. Under all these estimates, the labor force participation decisions of more than 95 percent of these people are unaffected by receiving the credit.

The EITC is somewhat more effective as a way of decreasing welfare

SIDEBAR 4.1 The Earned Income Tax Credit

The EITC provides a refundable tax credit based on the earnings of a low-income household. The credit begins at zero earnings and is then phased in at some tax credit rate up to the minimum level of earnings at which the maximum credit is received. The credit stays at the maximum over some range of earnings. The credit is then gradually phased out at some phaseout tax rate. The credit can be reduced, but not added to, by non-earnings income. Three separate credit schedules apply: for households with no children, for households with one child, and for households with two or more children.

The break points at which the credit phase-in starts, and the credit phaseout starts, are adjusted each year for inflation. This implies that the maximum credit is also adjusted each year for inflation. The schedules that applied for 1998 were:

	Type of Household		
	No Children	One Child	Two or More Children
Tax credit rate for phase-in (percentage)	7.65	34.00	40.00
Minimum earnings for maximum credit	$4,460	$6,680	$9,390
Maximum credit	341	2,271	3,756
Phaseout rate (percentage)	7.65	15.98	21.06
Income level at which phaseout begins	$5,570	$12,260	$12,260
Income level beyond which no credit is received	10,030	26,473	30,095

Source: *1998 Green Book*, updated using 1998 tax forms from IRS.

receipt and government spending on welfare. For example, some estimates suggest that as much as 20 percent of the EITC's costs are offset by savings in government spending on welfare and food stamps. The EITC is somewhat more effective as a welfare savings measure than as a work incentive for two reasons: empirical estimates indicate that perhaps three times as many families leave welfare or food stamps as join the labor force because of the EITC, and average welfare and food stamp spending per welfare recipient is two to three times the size of the average EITC benefit.[8]

The EITC is an effective wage supplement for the working poor. Estimates suggest that the EITC removed 4.4 million persons from poverty in 1998 (U.S. Census Bureau 1998). According to the President's Council of Economic Advisers (CEA), the expansion of 1993 to 1996 of the EITC probably reduced the child poverty rate by more than two percentage points

(Council of Economic Advisers 1998).[9] Because the EITC is an effective wage supplement but only modestly effective, at best, as a work incentive, most of its benefits go to the working poor and near-poor. According to Liebman's (1998) calculations, most EITC dollars go to households that are between 50 and 150 percent of the poverty line. Among households with children, the percentage receiving the EITC is 40 percent for households below 50 percent of the poverty line, increases rapidly to 80 percent for households between 100 and 150 percent of the poverty line, and then falls to almost no receipt above 300 percent of the poverty line (Liebman 1998). The EITC does not do much to increase employment among the nonworking poor, many of whom are lower on the income scale.

Because the EITC has such modest labor supply effects, any displacement and *market* wage effects are also modest. Most of the employment numbers estimated in previous studies are already corrected for any displacement effects because the studies estimate the net effect of changes in EITC provisions on some group, an effect that would include both direct and indirect effects of the EITC on labor supply. Plausible models of the wage effects of labor supply increases for single mothers suggest that the EITC probably has extremely small effects on market wages.[10] Any market wage reductions due to the EITC are quite small compared to the effective wage subsidy provided by the EITC, so there is little doubt that the EITC's effect is to truly raise net wages after taxes for many of the working poor.

Earnings Disregards and Benefit Reduction Rates

A popular welfare reform measure is to allow welfare recipients to keep more of their benefits as their earnings increase. This can be done either by increasing the earnings "disregarded" in calculating welfare benefits or by lowering the rate at which benefits are reduced as earnings increase. In 1967 a prominent federal welfare reform was enacted to increase the earnings disregard and reduce the benefit reduction rate from 100 percent (losing a dollar in benefits for every dollar in earnings) to 67 percent. In 1981 the Reagan administration partially reversed this reform by restricting it to the first four months that a welfare recipient was working, with benefits reduced dollar for dollar with earnings after that point. Subsequent federal rule changes liberalized the disregard slightly. In 1996 the federal welfare law allowed states to make their own rules about disregards and benefit reduction rates. Forty-two states now have disregard policies that are somewhat more liberal than the pre-1996 federal standard (Gallagher et al. 1998).

The research evidence suggests that increasing earnings disregards or lowering benefit reduction rates does not cause large increases in the labor supply of welfare recipients (Moffitt 1992). These work subsidies increase work hours by increasing labor force participation, but they also decrease work hours by causing some individuals to switch from full-time to part-time work. The two effects are almost equally balanced, with little net effect on work hours. The historical evidence suggests that neither the 1967 nor the 1981 changes in benefit reduction rates had large effects on the work hours of single mothers. Studies comparing states with different benefit reduction rates show little differences in the work hours of single mothers. During the late 1960s and 1970s, several negative income tax experiments tested welfare plans with different benefit reduction rates, and little net effect on work hours was shown. Finally, a recent experiment, the Minnesota Family Investment Program (MFIP), tested the use of financial incentives. The MFIP increased the percentage of single-parent welfare recipients who were ever employed during the follow-up period, by 14 percent among long-term welfare recipients and 8 percent among welfare applicants. However, most of this employment effect was in part-time employment. Because the MFIP encouraged switches from full-time to part-time employment, its earnings effects were less than its employment effects. The financial subsidies only slightly increased market earnings (by 4 percent) among single mothers who were long-term welfare recipients, and they reduced market earnings among single mothers who were new welfare applicants (Miller et al. 1997).

Allowing welfare recipients to keep more of their benefits if they work does increase income and reduce poverty for working welfare recipients. For example, the financial subsidies provided by the MFIP increased the percentage of long-term welfare recipients who escaped poverty from 15 to 24 percent and increased the percentage of welfare applicants who escaped poverty from 28 to 32 percent.

Allowing working welfare recipients to keep their benefits may be more effective in increasing work when combined with mandatory employment services. The MFIP experiment tested two "treatments": financial incentives only, and financial incentives plus some minimal but mandatory services, including developing an employment plan with a caseworker and participating in some job search classes and job clubs. The impact of financial incentives plus these services on the percentage of welfare recipients ever employed is roughly double the impact of the financial incentives alone.[11] One could argue that the services alone would be just as effective in encouraging work. However, interviews and surveys with MFIP caseworkers suggest that it would have been more difficult to convince them to make a strong "sales pitch" for employment to clients in the absence of financial incentives. With the incentives, caseworkers felt honestly that employment was in the best interest of their clients, whereas caseworkers in the regular welfare program were much less likely to feel that employment was in their clients' best interest.

SIDEBAR 4.2 The Minnesota Family Investment Program (MFIP)

MFIP was an experimental welfare reform program begun in 1994. The research compared two welfare reform "treatments" to a control group that continued under the regular welfare program. One treatment changed the financial incentives for welfare recipients to work by giving extra MFIP benefits for working and lowering the benefit reduction rate. The other treatment combined these financial incentives with mandatory participation in employment and training services.

The financial incentives under MFIP increased the rewards for working compared to not working, but reduced the rewards for working full-time versus part-time. The table shows how the regular welfare program (AFDC) compares with MFIP in monthly net income for various weekly work hours at $6 per hour. Net income in this table includes food stamps, the Earned Income Tax Credit, and federal and state taxes. The calculations are for a single parent with two children, in the fifth through twelfth month after beginning employment.

	AFDC	MFIP
Monthly income at zero work hours	$769	$769
Monthly income at twenty hours per week, $6/hour	1,024	1,261
Monthly income at forty hours per week, $6/hour	1,308	1,456
Average "wage" per hour from working forty hours rather then twenty hours	3.19	6.15
Average "wage" per hour from working forty hours rather then twenty hours	3.55	2.44

Source: Miller et al. (1997, table 1.2).

Why does MFIP offer less of a relative reward for full-time work than AFDC? Under old AFDC rules, most benefits are already phased out before a person reaches forty hours of weekly work. Hence, at some point the wage rate per hour for more work is no longer "taxed" by benefit reductions because benefits are already zero. Under a system like MFIP, which allows individuals to keep more benefits as they work, the implicit "tax" of benefit reductions continues up to higher earnings levels.

Therefore, financial incentives to work for welfare recipients combined with casework services may significantly increase both employment and income among welfare recipients. This finding from the MFIP has led to some well-deserved praise and favorable publicity for the program (Knox, Miller, and Gennetian 2000; Center for Law and Social Policy 2000). But it should be understood that this combination of financial incentives and casework services is quite expensive. For example, the MFIP is estimated to cost between $1,900 and $3,800 more per welfare family than the original Minnesota welfare system (Knox et al. 2000, 3). In addition, providing only families on welfare with such financial incentives to work and casework services raises issues of horizontal equity. Is it fair to provide such incentives and services to some low-income families while denying them to other low-income working families who are not on welfare?

New Experiments with Full-Time Work Incentives

Two recent experimental welfare reform financial incentives—the Self-Sufficiency Project (SSP) in Canada (1992 to present) and the Child Assistance Program (CAP) in New York (1988 to present)—try to avoid encouraging part-time work by targeting most of the incentives at full-time workers.[12] These two programs show that incentive programs face trade-offs. The SSP has had greater effects in increasing employment and reducing poverty but has raised issues of fairness. The CAP has saved the government money but has had only very small effects in increasing participant income.

The SSP experiment targets single parents who have been on welfare for twelve of the last thirteen months. The financial incentive for full-time work is large: half the difference between the individual's earnings and a target earnings level of $30,000 or $37,000 Canadian (about 25 percent less in U.S. dollars) *if* the individual works a minimum of thirty hours per week. The program effectively raises wages for participants by more than $3 an hour and can provide annual benefits greater than $12,000. Such benefits are so large that they raise the significant fairness issue of why other low-wage workers are not equally deserving of such wage subsidies. These large subsidies for close to full-time work have large effects on employment rates, doubling full-time employment rates in some quarters. (For example, full-time employment rates are 29.3 percent for the treatment group five quarters after program entry, compared to 14.0 percent for the control group.) Average earnings go up by more than 50 percent, family income increases more than 15 percent, and the percentage of treatment group members escaping poverty is more than double that of the control group (22.5 percent above the poverty line versus 10.2 percent in the control group) (Lin and Pan 1998).

As discussed in chapter 3, both theory and empirical models suggest that the displacement effects of such a program on other single mothers would be between one-third and two-thirds, effects that significantly reduce but do not eliminate the large employment effects of the program. If such a program were applied to all long-term welfare recipients in the United States, most labor market models suggest there would be only very small effects on the wages of single mothers. There are several reasons for these

SIDEBAR 4.3 The Self-Sufficiency Project

The Self-Sufficiency Project was a welfare reform experiment in the Canadian provinces of New Brunswick and British Columbia, starting in 1992. The traditional welfare system in Canada is quite generous compared to the U.S., but has few work incentives.

The Self-Sufficiency Project provided the treatment group with a large financial incentive to work, tied to a requirement for close to full-time work. Single-parent welfare recipients were eligible for the program if they had been on welfare at least twelve of the previous thirteen months. The experimental program agreed to provide, for a period of up to three years, half the difference between the participant's gross labor earnings and a target break-even level of $37,000 (Canadian) in British Columbia and $30,000 (Canadian) in New Brunswick. To receive the payment, however, participants had to work at least thirty hours per week and stay off the regular welfare program.

The program's payments are large. The average family supplement was more than $800 per month.

The table shows how the program changes work incentives for a single parent with two children:

	British Columbia	New Brunswick
Net annual income at zero work	$17,011	$11,782
Net annual after-tax income under regular welfare program, thirty hours per week	23,078	14,847
Net annual after-tax income under SSP, thirty-hour work week	28,267	20,184
Hourly wage rate without taxes or transfers	6.24	5.53
Hourly wage rate under regular welfare program	3.89	1.96
Hourly wage rate under SSP	7.22	5.39

Source: Lin and Pan (1998, table G.2). All dollars are Canadian; multiplying by .75 would yield approximate equivalents in U.S. dollars. The calculations allow for all taxes and tax credits. Hourly wage rates without taxes and transfers are predicted wage rates in each province for households with these characteristics.

The program has large effects on effective wage rates. At typical wage rates for program participants, the regular welfare system and other Canadian taxes impose an effective tax rate of 35 to 65 percent. The incentives provided by SSP increase wage rates by more than $3 per hour (Canadian), so that actual net wage rates are close to what they would be without any taxes or transfers.

small effects: the labor supply effects of the program, while large compared to other programs, are still only about one-sixth of those eligible for the program; only a minority of single mothers are long-term welfare recipients and hence are eligible to be targeted by the program; relative wages are resistant to change, and this labor supply shock is truly tiny compared to the overall labor force.[13]

This targeted program clearly has much larger employment effects per dollar spent than the Earned Income Tax Credit. If the SSP were applied to the entire U.S. welfare system, it would cost around $3 billion annually and would increase annual net employment by around 98,000, allowing for displacement effects.[14] The net costs would be less, perhaps cut in half, because of reduced welfare costs and increased taxes.[15] The EITC spends $30 billion annually and probably has net employment effects no greater than 405,000, and possibly as small as 36,000.[16] To put the comparison another way, the EITC causes no more than one out of twenty persons it assists to change from not participating in the labor force to participating, whereas the SSP probably causes one out of two persons it assists to start participating in the labor force.[17] The reason for these differences is that the SSP, compared to the EITC, provides a larger financial reward that is targeted at a group of individuals (long-term welfare recipients) who are unlikely to participate in the labor force, and it requires a significant change in behavior (full-time work). But if all we want is to minimize government cost for each additional person employed, current U.S. welfare reforms dominate: these welfare reforms are increasing labor supply by more than one million persons and saving money for the government, not costing money.

A variant of SSP combined the program's incentives with some services, including caseworkers and job search assistance. Financial incentives combined with services increased employment by twice as much as financial services alone.[18]

The Child Assistance Program (CAP) in New York provides much more modest incentives for full-time work for welfare recipients.[19] These modest incentives are combined with a separate casework staff whose caseloads are smaller than those of regular welfare caseworkers and who work with clients to encourage and help them find jobs. The program does not explicitly require full-time work. Rather, welfare recipients have the option of going on the conventional welfare program or going on the CAP program, which features a lower base benefit than regular welfare but a much lower benefit reduction rate. The benefit schedules of the two programs are such that it does not make sense at all to go on CAP unless one is working close to half-time, and the greatest extra incentives under the CAP go to those working twenty-five to thirty-five hours per week. The extra incentives are much smaller than those of the SSP, at most perhaps $300 per month. However, the program still increases effective wage rates (after ad-

SIDEBAR 4.4 New York's Child Assistance Program

New York's Child Assistance Program has been run as an experiment in three New York counties since 1988. The program is a voluntary alternative to regular welfare for single parents who have a valid child support order. The base grant under CAP is one-third lower than regular AFDC, but the benefit reduction rate is lower. Under AFDC, benefits were reduced dollar for dollar with earnings. Under CAP, benefits are reduced by ten cents for every dollar of earnings up to the poverty line, and by sixty-seven cents for every dollar of earnings above the poverty line.

Because the program is voluntary, and because participants can switch back and forth from AFDC to CAP, it makes no sense to go on CAP unless a participant has some minimal level of earnings. Hence, the program is effectively providing subsidies targeted at individuals working a minimum number of hours.

In addition to financial incentives, CAP provides distinct welfare-to-work services. CAP participants are assigned case managers who do not work in the same offices as regular welfare case workers and who have lower caseloads than regular welfare caseworkers.

CAP's incentives are structured so that it pays more than regular welfare only after weekly work hours exceed ten to fifteen hours (Blank, Card, and Robins 2000). The benefits of CAP tend to be maximized at weekly work hours of twenty-five to thirty-five hours. According to Blank, Card, and Robins (2000), at thirty hours per week, CAP raises hourly wage rates about $1.67 per hour.[a] MFIP raises wage rates by $2.12 per hour, and SSP by $3.59 per hour (U.S. dollars). The Canadian SSP program is far more generous than the U.S. CAP and MFIP programs.

CAP's effects on earnings were highest in Monroe County, next highest in Niagara County, and lowest in Suffolk County. The evaluators (Hamilton et al. 1996) attributed these different effects largely to differences in implementation. Monroe actively recruited harder cases and worked harder to motivate them. Suffolk made a relatively weak recruitment effort. However, it is also noteworthy that Monroe had the lowest unemployment rates during the experiment, and that the control group did worst in Suffolk County.

[a] The figures given by Blank, Card, and Robins (2000) differ slightly from those given in previous tables, no doubt because of some slight differences in the family being analyzed, the taxes considered, and so on.

justing for lost benefits, and so on) for welfare recipients who work thirty or more hours per week, by close to $2 per hour (Blank et al. 2000).

The modest subsidies and casework of the CAP lead to modest increases in employment and earnings: an increase from 26 percent to 29 percent in employment rates, and a 20 percent increase in earnings. But because clients lose welfare and food stamp benefits from work, and the

CAP subsidies are modest, income goes up relatively little, less than $200 per year for the average family assigned to the CAP. But with modest subsidies and reductions in other welfare, the CAP saves money for the government, a little more than $400 annually per family assigned to the CAP.

Displacement effects would cut the estimated effects of the CAP on single mothers' employment and earnings by one-third to two-thirds. The employment rate effects are small enough that the effects on wages of even a fully implemented CAP are negligible.

The CAP's effects varied among the three New York counties in which the experiment was implemented. The employment and earnings effects of the CAP were greatest in the county whose local welfare office was most focused on making the program work. This was also the county whose local labor market was doing best.

What role can be played by financial incentives to work? The evidence suggests that, without special design features to narrowly target the incentives at hard-to-employ groups and full-time work, financial incentives by themselves are more a way to raise the "earnings" of the poor (if incentives are considered part of earnings) than an employment incentive. Therefore, financial incentives by themselves help the working poor and do not generate additional employment for most of the nonworking poor. Financial incentives can play an important role in helping the poor, but a role that is limited because of modest effects on employment. Special design features may increase the effects of incentives on the labor supply of the poor by targeting those most likely to be out of the labor force and by targeting full-time work. But such targeting raises significant equity issues unless incentives are quite modest. Modest financial incentives may help the government budget by reducing welfare spending but are unlikely to do much to increase the economic well-being of the poor.

Financial incentives coupled with casework services may have significantly greater effects on the employment of the poor. However, such a package is significantly more costly and complex and difficult to administer. Limiting the target group of those served helps reduce the cost and complexity but raises equity concerns.

Finally, however financial incentives are designed and packaged, an analysis of their effects should take account of possible displacement effects. Plausible models of the low-wage labor market suggest that simply dumping more workers into the low-wage labor market has significant displacement effects. From one-third to two-thirds of the direct effect of these financial incentive programs on employment are likely to be offset by displacement effects on lower-income families who are currently working.

Education and Training Programs

Education and training programs already have major effects in increasing earnings and reducing poverty among many persons from disadvantaged backgrounds. Among the challenges facing these programs is how to reach more of the poor and how to improve the productivity of these complex services. Another challenge is dealing with the effect of these programs on displacement. As I discuss, stronger labor demand helps in addressing these challenges.

Several types of education and training services are available to the poor in the United States:

- *Preschool:* Head Start; other preschools that are not federally funded; and a variety of interventions designed to improve parenting or child learning (for example, visiting nurse programs).
- *K-12:* Public schools, with a variety of programs targeted at disadvantaged students; adult education programs; vocational programs; school-to-work programs.
- *Postsecondary schools:* Four-year colleges and universities; community colleges; private vocational schools.
- *Second-chance programs:* Under the Workforce Investment Act (WIA), "one-stop shops" in each local labor market are supposed to coordinate unemployment insurance, job placement services, vouchers for job training services from competing certified job training providers (including postsecondary education and adult education providers), and welfare-to-work services.

Most of the dollars go to K-12 programs. Financial support for preschool, postsecondary education, and second-chance education, training, or job placement services are insufficient to provide services to all poor individuals who might benefit from these services. For example, the federally funded Head Start preschool program is estimated to serve less than half of the children below the poverty line who are eligible.[20] Federal job training programs have generally enrolled less than 3 percent of the eligible disadvantaged population.[21]

Education

For those individuals from poor families who attain higher education, education raises wages and employment, lowers unemployment, and reduces poverty. As shown in table 4.2, finishing high school raises wages more than 40 percent, cuts unemployment in half, and cuts the poverty rate by two-thirds. Finishing college, compared to finishing high school, raises

TABLE 4.2 *Economic Outcomes Over Time for Men and Women Ages Twenty-Five to Fifty-Four, by Educational Level*

	Males			Females		
	High School Dropout	High School Graduate, Not College Graduate	College Graduate	High School Dropout	High School Graduate, Not College Graduate	College Graduate
Wages per hour						
1979	$13.91	$17.23	$21.91	$8.85	$10.99	$15.06
1998	10.26	14.94	23.26	7.67	11.51	18.60
Unemployment rates						
1979	5.9	3.3	1.7	8.9	4.7	3.5
1998	6.8	3.4	1.7	9.9	3.8	2.1
Employment rates						
1979	83.1	92.7	95.4	44.5	60.9	71.6
1998	76.4	88.8	94.4	49.0	74.4	82.4
Poverty rates						
1979	13.7	4.4	2.6	23.0	7.0	3.1
1998	21.1	6.9	2.6	34.3	10.8	2.8
Percentage of population in each education level						
1979	22.0	53.2	24.8	22.1	61.8	16.2
1998	12.9	58.2	28.9	11.4	61.2	27.4

Sources: Author's calculations of weighted means from CPS-ORG for wages, unemployment, employment; March CPS for poverty.
Note: Education definitions for 1979 based on completed years of education, for 1998 on actual degrees obtained. Evidence suggests that a small percentage of those in 1979 who completed twelve years of education did not get a diploma; from 1998 data, this number is about 1.1 percent of the female population and 1.3 percent of the male population. Hence, this table underestimates slightly the trend toward fewer high school dropouts, and if 1979 data could be adjusted for this, outcomes would look slightly better for high school dropouts and high school graduates. But adjustment would not be large; degrading the 1998 data to better match 1979 definitions only slightly changes the 1998 means.

wages more than 50 percent, cuts unemployment in half again, and cuts the poverty rate more than in half again.

Over time, education's positive effects on economic outcomes have increased. The economic outcomes of the less-educated have deteriorated, particularly for high school dropouts and males with a high school degree but not a four-year college degree. Most economists attribute these increased returns to education to increases in the economy's demand for skilled labor and to reductions in the demand for unskilled labor. As one indicator of reduced demand for unskilled labor, the table shows that even though overall unemployment declined from 5.8 percent to 4.5 percent from 1979 to 1998, unemployment among high school dropouts increased by about 1 percent for both men and women. These shifts in demand for skills are attributed by most economists to technological change, with a lesser role for increased import competition, shifts in the industrial mix away from heavy manufacturing, declining unionization, and a declining real value of the minimum wage.

An important question is whether education's correlation with economic outcomes is a cause-and-effect relationship. Most economists have traditionally believed that estimated returns to education are biased upward. Because persons with higher ability may get both more education and higher earnings, some of the measured returns to education may reflect the economic rewards of greater ability, not education. However, recent empirical work suggests that for many people, policies or events that increase educational attainment may have earnings effects that are *greater* than the usual estimated returns to education (for a review, see Card 1999). For example, some studies have examined shifts in educational attainment due to the quarter of birth, which affects years of high school completed by its interaction with state compulsory school attendance laws (Angrist and Krueger 1991). Other studies have examined shifts in educational attainment due to a person's distance from the nearest two-year or four-year college, and the tuition at that college (Card 1995a; Kane and Rouse 1993). The usual estimated return to schooling is a 5 to 8 percent increase in earnings for one extra year of schooling; the returns to schooling due to these exogenous shifts in schooling are higher, perhaps 9 to 13 percent. David Card's interpretation of these results is that *marginal* returns to education for those most affected by compulsory schooling laws and college attendance costs—that is, persons from disadvantaged families—are *greater* than *average* returns to schooling for the overall population.

The economic returns to education in part reflect labor market skills that are most likely to be learned in school. For example, Richard Murnane, John Willett, and Frank Levy (1995) find that wages are significantly affected by individuals' math test scores from their senior year in high school. The wage effects of math skills are stronger six years after high school than two years after high school, suggesting that employers only slowly learn about an employee's quantitative skills. Holding math test scores constant, educational attainment's effects on wages are cut in half. Most of the increased return to education over time is attributable to increased returns to higher skills, as evidenced by higher math test scores.

Although the current education system reduces poverty, too many still have inadequate educational attainment, and schools are not as effective in increasing skills for everyone as they need to be. These problems with the quantity and quality of education are more severe for persons from disadvantaged backgrounds. As table 4.3 shows, young people from lower-income families are significantly less likely to get a high school diploma or GED, and much less likely to get a bachelor's degree.[22] In addition, as table 4.4 shows, reading and math achievement levels are not as great as they should be for many students, even among those still in school at age seventeen or in the twelfth grade. Reading and math achievement problems are greater for students from lower-income families.

How best to make schools more effective is greatly disputed. Some policies to increase educational attainment or achievement have been supported by some empirical evidence, although the evidence in some cases is disputed. These *potentially* effective policies include:

Lower Class Size in Early Elementary Grades The Tennessee Class Size Study has shown that lower class size in kindergarten through third grade significantly raises student achievement. This experiment was rig-

TABLE 4.3 *Educational Attainment by 1992 of 1980 High School Sophomores, by Family Background and Race*

	No High School Diploma	High School Diploma or GED, No Bachelor's Degree	Bachelor's Degree or Higher
Overall percentage	5.8	70.4	23.8
1980 socioeconomic status of student's family			
Low quartile	9.0	83.8	7.2
Middle two quartiles	3.9	75.4	21.6
High quartile	1.4	47.3	51.3
By race			
White, non-Hispanic	4.9	58.6	26.5
Black, non-Hispanic	6.9	71.1	12.2
Hispanic	11.9	78.5	9.9

Source: National Center for Education Statistics (1999, table 306).

TABLE 4.4 *Some Indicators of Educational Achievement and Skills in the United States*

Percentage of Adults Ages Nineteen to Twenty-Four at Lowest Literacy Levels[a]	
Prose level 1: Cannot locate single piece of information in short text if "distractors" present (more than one alternative is possible)	14
Document level 1: Cannot match single piece of information in chart/graph/figure if "distractors" present	14
Quantitative level 1: Cannot perform single arithmetic operation using numbers stated in a text	16
Mathematics and Reading Proficiency, Seventeen-Year-Olds in School, 1996[b]	
Percentage of seventeen-year-olds *unable* to perform reasoning and problem solving involving fractions, decimals, percents, elementary geometry, and simple algebra	39.9
Percentage of students *unable* to search for specific information, interrelate ideas, and make generalizations about literature, science, and social studies material	18.6
Relative Achievement Levels of Twelfth-Grade Students from Lowest Quartile of Family Socioeconomic Status[c]	
Percentage of low quartile SES students in lowest quartile on math achievements tests	37.0
Percentage of low quartile SES students in lowest quartile on reading achievement tests	36.3

[a] Kirsch (1993).
[b] National Center for Education Statistics (1999, tables 112, 121).
[c] National Center for Education Statistics (1999, table 129). SES is socioeconomic status of student's family as measured by index that combines parent education, parent occupation, and family income.

orous, with random assignment of students and teachers to different class sizes. Lowering class size from twenty-two to twenty-five students to thirteen to seventeen students increases student achievement by third grade by about five to eight percentile points (Krueger 1999). These achievement gains persist through at least twelfth grade, even though students returned to regular-sized classes in fourth grade: students in the smaller classes in early elementary grades were more likely to graduate from high school and more likely to attend college (Pate-Bain, Fulton, and Boyd-Zaharias 1999; Krueger and Whitmore 1999). The achievement gains from lower class size are greater for students eligible for free and reduced price lunch, black students, and students in inner-city schools (Krueger 1999).

Training, Hiring, and Retaining Better Teachers The evidence suggests that good teachers are consistently able to increase student achievement during a year by one and a half grade levels, whereas bad teachers raise student achievement by only half a grade level (Hanushek 1998).

Hiring and Retaining Smarter Teachers Students learn more when taught by teachers who went to selective colleges or have higher test scores (for reviews, see Ballou and Podgursky 1997, and Ferguson 1998).

Higher Standards for Schools and Students, with Some Consequences of School or Student Performance Student achievement appears to have been increased by Dallas' elaborate system of adjusting average school tests to measure school performance, coupled with monetary rewards to schools with better performance (Ladd 1999). In Canada, students from provinces that require passing a province test for graduation tend to do better on the International Assessment of Educational Progress. In the United States, students from New York outperform students from other states on a variety of standardized tests, perhaps owing to New York's long-standing practice of awarding special diplomas to those who pass the Regents exams (Betts 1998, citing the work of Bishop 1996, 1997).

Strong Principals Case studies in the research literature on "effective schools" suggest that improving overall school performance depends greatly on the principal's leadership abilities (Lee, Bryk, and Smith 1992, and Purkey and Smith 1983, cited in Ladd 1999).

Focused Schoolwide Reform Programs A recent review cites strong evidence for the effectiveness of three schoolwide reforms: Success for All, Direct Instruction, and High Schools That Work (American Institutes for Research 1999). All three of these programs show evidence of significant academic achievement gains for students, compared to matched students, to matched schools, or to the same school before the intervention. These three schoolwide reforms are quite diverse. Success for All, developed by Robert Slavin at Johns Hopkins University, focuses on early elementary grades; this program regroups students into smaller groups for reading, requires lengthier daily instruction in reading, assesses student progress at least every eight weeks, and uses a highly structured mix of phonics and whole language instruction. Direct Instruction, developed by Siegfried Engelmann at the University of Illinois, is a highly controversial program focused on reading and math in elementary schools; it relies on teachers using scripted lessons (hence the controversy) with small homogeneous groups of students. High Schools That Work, developed by the Southern Regional Education Board, focuses on raising academic achievement among students not planning to attend college by enrolling these students in college-prep academic courses, increasing academic requirements for all students, and reorganizing the school schedules so that classes meet for longer blocks of time ("block scheduling"). Although these educational innovations are quite diverse, they do seem to have in common a strong focus on specific goals and on organizing the school day and grouping students so as to devote more time and attention to those goals.

High-Quality Preschools The Perry Preschool Project, begun in 1962, used a rigorous experiment with random assignment to test the effects of enrolling three- and four-year olds from low-income families in high-quality preschools, with low student-to-staff ratios, trained instructors, and weekly home visits. The project has followed participants through age twenty-seven. Compared to the control group, the preschool intervention increased the high school graduation rate by about one-third (from 45 percent to 66 percent) and increased earnings at age twenty-seven by more than 50 percent (Karoly et al. 1998).

High-Quality Mentorship, Tutoring, and Graduation Incentive Programs The Quantum Opportunities Program assigned one professional staff person to work intensively with twenty-five "at-risk" ninth-graders for four years. Students were provided with tutoring, motivational speakers, group cultural activities, and volunteer opportunities, as well as informal mentoring from project staff. Students were given a small stipend for participating in program activities, on the condition that the money be used for postsecondary education. Random assignment evaluation of the program indicates that the program cut the high school dropout rate in half (from 50 to 23 percent) and doubled postsecondary school attendance (from 16 to 42 percent) (Hahn 1994).

High-Quality School-to-Work Programs A few evaluations suggest that some school-to-work programs can be effective. A program jointly designed by General Motors, the United Auto Workers, the Flint, Michigan, area schools, and others to prepare high school students for skilled trades led to a 94 percent pass rate on the UAW/GM apprenticeship test, compared to 10 percent nationally. An impact study indicated that two to three years after graduation the program participants had an 80 percent employment rate at an average wage of $10.69 per hour, while a comparison group was 70 percent employed at an average wage of $5.92 per hour (National Youth Employment Coalition 1998). Evaluations of Boston's Project Protech, which tries to provide high school students with internships in industry "clusters," suggests that the program increased college attendance, employment, and wage rates (Jobs for the Future 1998).

Lower College Costs Lower college costs are estimated to have significant effects on postsecondary enrollment, particularly for students from lower-income families (Leslie and Brinkman 1988, cited in Kane and Rouse 1999; Kane 1995).[23] However, means-tested grants such as the Pell Grant Program have not been estimated to have significant effects on enrollment of lower-income students. These Pell Grant estimates may be spurious, reflecting the limited time series variation available in the program. Alternatively, lower-income families may be unaware of how much of their college costs can be covered by Pell Grants (Kane 1995).

School Choice A hotly debated topic is whether providing vouchers or some other form of greater school choice for disadvantaged students would increase or decrease student achievement. Some studies have examined the effects of vouchers on educational achievement for individual disadvantaged students who received vouchers to attend private schools, compared to a control group. These studies sometimes find achievement effects, and sometimes do not (see the review by Rouse 1998). The positive achievement effects found in some studies may be attributable in part to smaller class size in some of the private schools, as public schools with smaller class sizes in these studies show similar achievement gains, as argued by Cecilia Rouse (1998). There is also the issue of the systemwide effects of school choice and competition on all students, not just those who choose to participate in such plans. School choice and competition may put more pressure on public schools to perform, as argued by Caroline Hoxby (1998). On the other hand, under the financing systems of many states, school choice may cause significant fiscal problems for some public school systems.[24] Furthermore, if one believes there are important peer group effects in education, school choice may have negative effects on the students "left behind" in public schools.

The problem with these school reforms is that they are expensive (for example, lowering class size), complex and difficult to implement (for example, getting better teachers), both costly and complex (for example, the Quantum Opportunities Program),[25] or highly controversial as to whether they are helpful or harmful (for example, school choice).

Increases in educational attainment, due to policies or otherwise, have displacement effects. Educating some individuals moves other individuals from a low-education group to a high-education group. This has effects on four different types of individuals. First, there are the increased earnings for the newly educated. Second, among those already in the high-education group, there is some displacement and wages are reduced owing to greater competition for high-education jobs. The increased relative supply of high-education labor is offset to some extent by adjustments in relative labor demand. However, as discussed in chapter 3, empirical estimates suggest that relative labor demand is not sufficiently responsive to supply shifts to offset completely the displacement and wage effects of relative supply shifts over any short- or medium-term time period. Third, among those in the low-education group who are *not* educated, employment and wages tend to go up, because there is less supply for the available low-education jobs. This is offset partly, but not completely, by reduced relative demand for low-education workers. Finally, there are some overall effects on everyone in the labor market because educating some persons raises overall labor supply, as labor force participation rates are greater for high-education than low-education groups. Aggregate labor demand responds to this increased aggregate labor supply and to the increase in wages and earnings from educating some individuals.

The model of appendix 2 can be used to simulate these possible labor market effects of education. As described in more detail in appendix 4, the model suggests that the spillover effects on other groups of educating some individuals are large. The original more-educated group members lose earnings, and the remaining less-educated group members gain earnings.

How should we react to this significant redistribution of income away from the college-educated and toward the less-educated? Given that the income of the college-educated is significantly above the national average and is going up over time, while the income of the less-educated has been declining over time, these distributional effects should probably be viewed favorably. Increasing educational attainment for some helps offset at least some of the increased returns to education that have characterized the U.S. economy in recent years. Such a policy helps not only the less-educated who receive an education but other less-educated individuals who now find it easier to get jobs.

For all workers, educating some individuals eventually has positive effects on overall earnings. As shown in appendix 4, these positive overall effects are considerably stronger when overall unemployment is low. The aggregate demand response to the supply shock of educating some individuals is more robust when unemployment is low, because wages are more responsive when unemployment is low. Therefore, supply-side policies to increase educational attainment are more effective in helping the overall labor market if they are complemented by demand-side policies that keep overall unemployment low.

Although education can significantly increase the earnings of low-income Americans, huge and very costly and difficult increases in educational attainment would be needed to offset fully the recent regressive trends in wage or earnings differentials for different education groups or to provide the jobs needed by low-income Americans. Consider first the needed increases in educational attainment to reverse the recent declines in the relative wages of the less educated. Depending on the data set used, the relative wages or earnings of less-educated Americans probably declined by at least 15 percent from the late 1970s and early 1980s to the mid- to late 1990s.[26] As mentioned in chapter 3 and in appendices 1 and 2, most empirical models suggest that relative wages are only modestly responsive to shifts in the relative supply of different education groups. Simulations using plausible models suggest that offsetting these recent adverse wage and earnings trends would probably take an increase in the number of college graduates of at least 15 percent, or more than seven million additional college graduates (see appendix 5). This is an increase in the number of college graduates above and beyond whatever continued increase in college graduates is needed to offset future increases in the demand for skills.

One could also ask: How many additional educated individuals would be required to create the 3 to 9 million additional jobs that are needed for disadvantaged groups? (Chapter 3 calculated job needs for the poor in various ways and came up with figures in the 3 million to 9 million range.) Analysis of this question suggests that we need to educate *at least* one person to create one additional job for some less-educated group. Consider the likely employment effects of education on different groups. The employment rate of the person being educated is likely to go up, since more-educated groups have higher labor force participation rates and lower unemployment rates. However, this employment effect per person educated is considerably less than one job, since the employment rates of the less-educated are considerably more than zero and the employment rates of the more-educated are less than one. In addition, because educating someone removes that person from competing in the labor market for less-educated workers, employment opportunities for the remaining less-educated workers (those "left behind") may improve. However, this improvement for those left behind is considerably less than one job for each person educated. Not every person educated would have been employed in a less-educated job if they had not been educated, so the number of jobs potentially opened up is less than one for every one person educated. Furthermore, as the labor supply of less-educated workers is reduced, we would expect some reduction in the labor demand for less-educated workers, and that reduction in turn would further reduce the number of job openings in the less-educated labor market. Finally, education may stimulate the overall economy by adding to labor supply, hence adding to employment and overall income. Because the increase in overall labor supply is relatively modest, however, we would expect these aggregate demand effects to be modest.

Simulations using a plausible model of the labor market suggest that in the long run, for every person who gets a college degree, less-educated groups overall gain from 0.6 to 0.8 jobs (see appendix 6). This job creation figure includes the additional employment of those persons who, because of the policy, get a college degree.

Thus, to increase employment of disadvantaged groups by 3 million to 9 million jobs, we would need to provide a college education to *more* than 3 million to 9 million disadvantaged persons. For example, using the figure that providing one person with a college education increases net employment for the economy by 0.6 to 0.8 jobs, in order to increase employment of less-educated groups by 3 million to 9 million jobs, the number of college graduates would need to increase by 4 million to 15 million persons.[27] It seems reasonable to assume that the employment effects of providing lesser degrees of education (for example, increasing the number of associate's degrees from community colleges) would be less than those of increasing the number of college graduates. Hence, education policies offering lesser increments to education would need to educate even more millions to provide 3 million to 9 million jobs.

Increasing the number of college graduates above current trends by 4 million to 15 million persons (to provide the needed number of jobs) or by 7 million persons (to reverse recent wage trends for the less-educated) is a huge increase in the number of college graduates. The United States currently has about 42 million college graduates, and about 1.2 million additional persons gain a bachelor's degree each year (National Center for Education Statistics 1999, tables 9, 244). These 1.2 million college graduates per year are needed just to keep the relative wages and employment rates of less-educated workers from further deteriorating. The 4 million, 7 million, or 15 million figures represent the additional college graduates, above these current trends, who would be needed to provide the needed jobs and help bring up the wages of the less-educated. Educating more individuals through college would be very expensive, probably costing well over $100 billion.[28] In addition, attempting to increase the number of college graduates so much in the short run would run the risk of significantly decreasing the average quality of college graduates. To avoid diluting the meaning of a college degree, such a huge increase in the number of college graduates probably would require some significant improvements in the quality of K-12 education.

Training

To help low-income individuals who have not succeeded by following the normal course of the educational system, another policy option is training programs. Since the 1960s the federal government has funded a variety of training programs that provide lower-income individuals a "second chance." Some training programs are voluntary programs, open to those who meet income eligibility standards and wish to improve their chances of getting a job or getting a better job. In recent years, increasing amounts of training funds are for mandatory programs, which require participation in job training and placement activities for welfare recipients as a condition for continuing to receive full benefits. U.S. programs typically emphasize job placement or short-term training, although they occasionally also offer some basic education services. Although most funding for such programs comes from the federal government, training programs are typically administered by local boards, with state and federal regulation and accountability.

The most recent rearrangement of federal training programs was the Workforce Investment Act (WIA) of 1998. Under WIA, all training and adult education programs are to be coordinated with the job matching and placement services of state employment services (the agency that administers unemployment insurance). Individuals are supposed to learn about all these services by coming into any agency providing any one of the services ("no wrong door"), and each local area is to have one physical site where entry offices for all these services are located ("one-stop shops"). Anyone is eligible for basic job placement services, but priority for intensive placement efforts or subsidized training is supposed to be given to low-income individuals. Instead of the usual past practice of assigning individuals to already arranged training programs, under WIA individuals are given greater choice in choosing their own training program. Individuals are supposed to be given training vouchers good at all certified training providers, along with information on these training providers and programs, including information on past placement rates and wage rates.

The consensus among researchers is that training programs for low-income persons have effects on earnings that are disappointingly modest on average, with little antipoverty effect, although the programs' effects are often large enough to justify their modest costs. I argue later that this consensus is unduly pessimistic in that it overlooks the potential for some types of programs to have large effects for some individuals. But I also argue that the consensus is unduly optimistic: some training programs may cause displacement effects that decrease earnings among some of the working poor or near-poor.

As shown in table 4.5, the average effect of most voluntary training programs is to increase annual earnings by less than $1,500 per year. Mandatory programs show even smaller annual effects on earnings. On average, training increases earnings more for adult women than for adult men. Training programs seldom work for youth.

However, despite training's modest effects on annual earnings, in many cases training programs are quite cost-effective. Consider the Job Training Partnership Act (JTPA), which was the main vehicle for federal support for training programs from 1982 to 1998, before WIA. Even though JTPA increased earnings for adult men and women by only $1,000 per year, it also only cost $1,100 to $1,600 per participant (Friedlander, Greenberg, and Robins 1997). Even if the earnings gains from JTPA per-

TABLE 4.5 *Effects of Training on Earnings*

	Returns to Training for Voluntary Programs		
	Average for All Training Programs	JTPA Evaluation	Center for Employment Training
Adult men	$185 (s.e. = 467) (three programs)	$1,008	—
Adult women	1,345 (s.e. = 244) (five programs)	997	$1,803 (Minority Female Single Parent demonstration)
Youth	103 (s.e. = 207) (six programs)	−178	4,194 (JobStart demonstration)

	Returns to Training for Mandatory Programs			
	Average	National Welfare-to-Work Evaluation	Riverside-GAIN	Portland (Oregon) Welfare-to-Work Program
Adult welfare women	$558 (s.e. = $99) (three programs)	Labor force attachment approach: $930 Human capital development approach: $465	$1,416	$1,238

Source: Author's compilation.
Notes: All calculations are in 1998 dollars. All effects are for earnings in second year of program, or as close to second year as possible. Data summarizing many training programs come from Friedlander et al. (1997) and are simple averages of their estimated effects for each separate program (not study); the standard error reported is the standard error of this mean over the number of programs studied, that is, the number of observations is the number of programs. I included only programs in Friedlander et al. (1997) for which they listed (in their tables 1 and 3) classroom training or job search as first primary activity. I excluded programs that were listed as having work experience or on-the-job-training as first primary activities. However, all of the principal federal job training programs were included, even though these programs had OJT or work experience components. JTPA data also are from Friedlander et al. (1997). CET data are from Cave et al. (1993) and Zambrowski et al. (1994). National welfare-to-work data are from Hamilton et al. (1997) and are simple averages of second-year effects in Atlanta and Grand Rapids. Riverside results are from Ricco et al. (1994). Portland results are from Scrivener et al. (1998).

sisted for only a few years, the program is clearly cost-effective. For example, Daniel Friedlander and his colleagues estimated that if JTPA's earnings gains persisted for just three years, its real rate of return would be 74 percent for adult men and 41 percent for adult women, an incredibly good investment.

These high returns to some modestly priced training programs do not mean that we are guaranteed the same returns to higher-priced training programs. We do not seem to know enough about training to increase dramatically the earnings effects of training by simply spending more per trainee. For example, among the voluntary training programs for adult women reviewed by Friedlander and his colleagues (1997) (and summarized in table 4.5), several spend three to six times more per trainee than JTPA, with no significantly larger effects on average earnings. For example, the Minority Female Single Parent (MFSP) program spent an average of $6,000 per participant, around four times what was spend in JTPA per adult female participant, yet the average annual earnings effects among MFSP sites was below that of JTPA, at $824 for MFSP versus $997 for JTPA. Statistical analysis suggests only a modest relationship between spending per training participant and the earnings effects of training.[29]

Some training programs, but not all, have earnings effects that persist with little diminution for many years. For example, researchers have found evidence for several programs of real earnings effects that last at least five years after the training is completed, including JTPA programs (U.S. General Accounting Office 1996), a Baltimore welfare-to-work program (Friedlander and Burtless 1994), the Riverside, California, welfare-to-work program (Strawn 1998), and the MFSP program run by the Center for Employment Training (Zambrowski, Gordon, and Berenson 1994).[30] These programs are quite varied in the amount of training and education they provide in relation to job search and job placement assistance. It is not obvious whether there is some crucial element of a training program that helps it have long-term effects. The most that can be said is that all these programs provide services more extensive than simply urging trainees to look for a job and handing them a phone and a phone book. All these programs provide either some assistance in gaining access to job openings that the trainee might not otherwise have heard about or some assistance in obtaining job skills or credentials that qualify the trainee for a job he or she would otherwise have been unlikely to get.

Some training programs are considerably better than the average, producing much higher average earnings gains. These better training programs also appear to produce at least some small reductions in poverty rates and small gains in the percentage of individuals attaining a somewhat higher working-class status. Among voluntary programs, the training programs run by the Center for Employment Training (CET) appear to be particularly successful, in some cases increasing average annual earnings among program participants by more than $4,000. CET's Minority Female Single Parent program reduced poverty among this group, after five years, from 51 percent to 46 percent (Zambrowski, Gordon, and Berenson 1994). Although rigorous experimental evidence is unavailable, the training program run by Project Quest in San Antonio also appears to be successful. Non-experimental evaluations suggest that the program may raise annual earnings by $6,000 (Lautsch and Osterman 1998). Among mandatory programs for welfare recipients, the welfare-to-work programs run in the late 1980s by Riverside County, California, appear to be quite successful. In addition to increasing average earnings, the Riverside County programs increased the percentage earning more than $20,000 per year, during the third year after program entry, from 2.7 percent to 3.8 percent. Riverside County's program increased overall income for participants as well as earnings, with a net present value of the increase in income over three years of $1,900 per program participant (Ricco et al. 1994, 252). This improvement in income may not sound like much, but it contrasts with some welfare-to-work programs that actually lower participant income (such as the Los Angeles GAIN program), with the loss of welfare benefits outweighing relatively small gains in earnings (252). A recent evaluation also gives high marks to the Portland, Oregon, welfare-to-work program. This program increases the percentage of program participants escaping poverty to 21 percent, compared to 17 percent among the control group (Scrivener et al. 1998).

Can the success of these better training programs be explained and, perhaps, replicated? Case studies of these programs suggest that their design has three important features.

Clear Performance Goals That Pervade the Organization from the Top Down For example, Riverside County was more successful than four other counties trying the same welfare-to-work program in California and was unique among these counties in having specific job placement standards for caseworkers. According to one case study of Riverside: "'Jobs, jobs, jobs' is the motto of Riverside County DPSS Director Lawrence Townsend. . . . [H]e sold his top staff and most of his agency . . . on this mission and goal" (Bardach 1993, 24). According to a case study of the Center for Employment Training, at CET a "clear mission [is] shared among the senior staff of the organization. . . . They are in the business of getting people to work, of making the connection between disadvantaged populations and employment opportunities" (Meléndez 1996, 30, 34). The importance of clear goals is consistent with the general literature on how to make public and private management more effective. For example, Robert Behn (1991), in his book drawing lessons for public management from Massachusetts welfare-to-work programs in the 1980s, argues that effective management requires selecting a limited number of relatively simple goals, and then following through to make sure that line workers actually focus on those goals. Federal and state agencies and other central authorities can encourage local offices and local line workers to focus on goals by using well-designed performance standards, with some consequences when local offices fail to meet these standards. For example, Massachusetts' ET pro-

SIDEBAR 4.5 The Center for Employment Training

Among training organizations, the Center for Employment Training has the best record of proven success. For example, in the Minority Female Single Parent demonstration, CET was the only one of four sites to show positive results. In the JobStart demonstration, CET had the strongest performance of thirteen sites.

CET was founded in 1967 in San Jose, California, as the response of Chicano activists to the employment problems of displaced farmworkers in East San Jose. From its beginning, CET received support from Silicon Valley firms, which were growing fast and facing labor shortages. CET established affiliates throughout the Southwest in the late 1970s.

CET's training model includes the following features:

- *Strong connections with specific industries in program design and implementation:* CET talks to firms to determine which entry-level jobs have good career prospects and expanding local demand, and then targets those occupations. Each local CET sets up an industrial advisory board that provides oversight and a technical advisory committee for each targeted occupation. Instructors have experience in the industry and occupation for which they provide training. Job developers find jobs for graduates and develop long-term relationships with local firms.
- *Short-term (thirty weeks), but intense (five days a week, eight hours a day) training.*
- *An open-door policy:* CET does not screen training applicants.
- *Open-entry and -exit training:* Individuals can start training any time and stop training when they have demonstrated competency.
- *Training organized like a workplace:* Trainees use a time clock and are expected to be on time. Instructors deal with attendance problems as if the training were a real job.
- *"Integrated" and "contextual" training:* Rather than focus on basic literacy and math skills first, followed by skills training, trainees immediately train for a specific occupation and are taught basic literacy as needed.
- *Addressing the social adjustment as well as the skills needs of trainees, providing counseling as needed:* Job placement assistance is provided by instructors, working with job developers.

Source: This summary is largely based on Meléndez (1996).

gram of the 1980s succeeded in changing the culture of local welfare offices to adopt the state welfare agency's greater focus on encouraging work by using performance standards in job placement rates and wages at placement. The success of JTPA compared to many other training programs may

SIDEBAR 4.6 Project Quest

Project Quest in San Antonio is a promising training program. Although it has not been subject to a random assignment evaluation, evidence suggests that it is successful. Before-and-after comparisons of Quest trainees suggest annual earnings gains of more than $6,000. Individual case studies show that Quest has helped trainees overcome employment barriers. Interviews with community college staff and employers give high ratings to Quest.

Project Quest began operation in 1993. It was organized by two community-based organizations, both affiliated with the Industrial Area Foundations, an organization originally set up by the famed Chicago-based community organizer Saul Alinsky.

Project Quest's important features include:

- *Identifying occupations to target by talking with area employers to forecast employment needs:* Quest helped redesign training curricula for specific occupations to better meet employers' needs. More than half of Quest participants have trained for medical occupations.
- *Upgrading of some occupations through Quest intervention:* Quest discussions with banks have led to a training program for a new occupation, financial customer services. Quest discussions with hospitals led to enhanced training and higher wages for health unit clerks.
- *Training provided by community colleges:* Quest intervention led community colleges to redesign training to better fit what employers wanted.
- *Longer-term (seventeen months) training than is typical for low-income persons.*
- *Community organizations running Quest recruit participants:* Participants must have a high school diploma or GED and minimum math and reading scores.
- *Modest stipend for participants during training.*
- *Counseling provided both during and after training:* Quest provides counselors for trainees who help them with tutoring, dealing with teachers and employers, receiving financial support during training, and mandatory weekly group pep-talk/information sessions. Counselors are credited by community college staff and employers with helping trainees complete the program and stay on the job.

Source: This summary is primarily taken from Lautsch and Osterman (1998).

be due in part to JTPA's heavy reliance on performance standards for local training agencies. Clear goals were set for local training offices in increasing job placement and retention rates, while adjusting for the mix of trainees of each local training agency (for a review of the evidence on the effects of JTPA performance standards, see Bartik 1995b).

SIDEBAR 4.7 The Riverside County Welfare-to-Work (GAIN) Program

Based on a random assignment evaluation, the welfare-to-work program run by Riverside County, California, during the late 1980s and early 1990s was far more successful than supposedly similar programs in five other California counties. Riverside's three-year earnings gains for single mothers were more than twice the average effects for all the counties (Ricco et al. 1994, xxviii).

The important features of Riverside's GAIN program include:

- *A strong emphasis on jobs:* Ninety-five percent of Riverside case managers said their agency viewed quick job entry for welfare recipients as more important than education and training, whereas less than 20 percent of case managers in other California counties felt their agency emphasized quick job entry (Ricco et al. 1994, 54).
- *Performance standards for local welfare offices and individual case managers:* Unlike other counties studied, case managers, supervisory units, and district offices in Riverside County have job placement goals. Meeting goals is an important part of the evaluation of individual staff (Ricco et al. 1994, 54).
- *Job developers:* Unlike the other counties, every local welfare office in Riverside had its own job developer who worked with local employers to place welfare recipients in jobs.
- *Greater attention to staff selection and staff training:* The director of the county welfare department said that his three principles were "selection of staff, selection of staff, and selection of staff" (Bardach 1993, 26). Staff were selected based on whether they were positive people who could inspire welfare recipients to succeed. Line staff reported that the quality of staff training was extremely high (29).
- *Willingness to threaten and use sanctions (cutting benefits) for noncompliance with the program:* Riverside threatened sanctions for one-third of the caseload, more than the other counties did, although those actually sanctioned were under 7 percent (Ricco et al. 1994, 60).

Riverside's program does not appear to have been as successful in the mid-1990s as it was earlier. The program's impact on earnings was 40 to 50 percent less in the mid-1990s than it was earlier (Hamilton et al. 1997, 274). Riverside's program appears to be addressing a more disadvantaged clientele. In addition, Riverside's economy has deteriorated. In the late 1980s and early 1990s, although Riverside had the second highest average unemployment rate of the six counties studied, it also had by far the fastest employment growth rate of the six counties—an average annual rate of 4.9 percent from 1989 to 1992 (Ricco et al. 1994, 279). More recently, Riverside's employment growth has slowed down, to only 0.5 percent per year from 1992 to 1993 (Hamilton et al. 1997, 276).

A Flexible Balance Between an Employment Focus and a Focus on Obtaining Better Jobs For example, in Oregon both local welfare offices and contractors in welfare-to-work programs have standards not only for job placements but also for the average wage at placement, as well as for the proportion of those who get jobs but then return to welfare within eighteen months (Scrivener et al. 1998). CET has a strong focus on jobs but is particularly interested in jobs offering benefits and promotion possibilities (Meléndez 1996, 30). Even though Riverside greatly stressed getting a job, any job, more than 60 percent of single welfare mothers referred to Riverside were classified in need of basic education. If these individuals were unable to find a job even after help with job search, they were put through basic education classes to address some of their skill deficiencies as well as to help them deal with some of the social demands of the work world.

Better Linkage of Disadvantaged Program Participants to Employers' Hiring Networks Effective supply-side training programs require a labor demand component: working with employers to identify needed job skills, to develop a relationship of trust between the training program and the employer, and to provide individual employers with sufficient reliable information on the skills of training program graduates that employers are willing to hire them. This labor demand component is important because employers in the low-education labor market have so much trouble finding reliable, productive employees, as discussed in chapter 3. The main finding of a case study of CET was that "the CET training model is effective because it motivates students to learn job-specific skills and is part of employers' recruiting networks" (Meléndez 1996, 3). CET contacts individual employers to identify occupations with strong labor demand and good career possibilities, solicits active industry involvement on boards that help design the training curriculum, seeks to hire training instructors with extensive experience and contacts in the industry they are training for, and has an open-entry/open-exit training model under which trainees are not allowed to "graduate" until they are ready for employment in that occupation and industry. According to the case study, "interviews with CET staff and collaborating employers suggest that socialization and screening aspects of the program are tremendously important. . . . [H]iring workers from CET not only insures employers that trainees know the basic job tasks but that they have gone through the rigor of the program and are recommended by trusted instructors who 'guarantee' the reliability of their students" (15). Project Quest in San Antonio makes a similar attempt to link the program to employers' training needs and to become a trusted part of employers' customary training network: "What is unique about Project Quest . . . is the success of the project in involving employers in the design of training and the thinking through of future labor market opportunities" (Lautsch and Osterman 1998, 230). Project Quest follows a strategy very similar to CET's in that it involves employers extensively in the design of training programs for occupations that are in demand, although training services are delivered by community colleges rather than by the program itself. The welfare-to-work program in Riverside County, California, also placed a strong emphasis on changing employers' hiring patterns. Compared to less successful counties, Riverside had many more "job developers" on staff who were seeking to identify and secure job openings for its clients. According to a *Washington Post* article, Riverside's director said at a speech that "the first thing he did each year . . . was go to potential employers and lock up all the available job slots for his 'graduates'" (Rich 1993).

The modest earnings effects of training programs *on average* also conceal the strong likelihood that the effects of training are much larger for a few trainees. First, the average effects of some experimental training programs may considerably understate the average effects of the training itself, because many who are randomly assigned to the treatment group do not participate in training, and many in the control group receive training services funded from other sources (Heckman et al. 1999). For example, according to the analysis of James Heckman and his colleagues of JTPA classroom training in the National JTPA experiment, 49 percent of the adult male "treatment group" recommended for classroom training actually received the training, compared to 27 percent of the control group who received classroom training. Those in the control group who received training appeared to obtain similar hours of training as those trained in the treatment group, often from the same training providers, such as community colleges.[31] If one assumes that (a) classroom training has similar effects in the treatment and control group, and (b) that nonrecipients of JTPA training are unaffected by JTPA, then it is relatively simple to calculate the true effect of training: the estimated effects of the program are blown up by one over the difference between the treatment and control group in the proportion receiving training. Making this calculation, Heckman and his colleagues find that classroom training increases adult male earnings over five years by $17,429, and earnings over ten years by $44,454. This increase occurs even though, according to these researchers' estimates, the program itself, for adult males assigned to training, increases earnings over five years by only $3,949 and earnings over ten years by $9,755. Thus, JTPA training easily might have effects *per trainee* that exceed $4,000 per year.

Second, the effects of training and other program services surely vary greatly among program participants. For example, in the Riverside experiment, the percentage of the treatment group who were ever employed in the second year after enrollment was only 50 percent. If we assume that the treatment group members who were never employed were unaffected by the program, then all the effects of the program occur for only half of this group. If average earnings for the entire group increase by $1,416 in the second year after enrollment (table 4.5), then average earnings for the "employed" treatment group members must increase by twice as much, or by more than $2,800 on average. Or as another example, in the Minority Female Single Parent demonstration run by CET, data on the fifth year after the program show the following: of the 315 control group members responding to the survey, only one earned more than $2,400 per month on average, and that person earned less than $2,800 per month; of the 423 treatment group members, two earned between $2,400 and $2,800 per month, two earned between $2,800 and $3,200 per month, and one earned more than $3,600 per month (Zambrowski et al. 1993, 16). These data strongly suggest that at least a few CET trainees gained more than $400 per month in earnings from the program, or $5,000 per year.

More generally, one would expect program impacts to vary widely across all program participants. Even if one artificially limits the variation in program impacts by assuming that the program preserves the earnings ranking of all program participants, considerable variation in program impacts remains. Daniel Friedlander and Philip Robins (1997) make this simple assumption of perfect correlation in earnings ranks before and after treatment for various welfare-to-work programs. Under this assumption, welfare-to-work programs whose mean earnings effect is $300 to $700 per year have maximum impacts on some individuals of as much as $1,000 to $2,000 per year. Using the same assumption of perfect correlation in earnings ranks, Nancy Clements, James Heckman, and Jeffrey Smith (1994) find that although the average eighteen-month earnings impact of JTPA on adult women was $601, the standard deviation of this impact was $1,858, implying that more than 2 percent of the sample had their earnings increased by more than $4,000. Under assumptions they find more plausible about how this training program might rearrange the rank of individuals by earnings, the standard deviation of the impact increases to $4,635. Under these same assumptions, the top 1 percent of program impacts are more than $30,000.

Although program impacts almost surely are much greater for some individuals than others, this fact is useful for policy only if programs can identify who will benefit and who will not. Training could be more cost-effective if we could target training services at those unlikely to receive training without government intervention. Training could be more cost-effective if we could target training services at those who are likely to receive the largest earnings benefits. The U.S. Department of Labor currently requires state employment service offices to target special employment services at the unemployment insurance recipients who are most likely to stay unemployed long enough to exhaust their unemployment benefits. The Upjohn Institute has done some preliminary experiments in Kalamazoo in profiling welfare recipients to identify who would benefit the most from various welfare-to-work services (Eberts 1998). However, as of yet, our methods of profiling unemployment insurance recipients and welfare recipients are fairly crude, and our predictions of who will benefit the most from different services are quite imprecise. Training services could become a great deal more effective if they were to develop much better methods of determining who will benefit most from various services, possibly through more sophisticated screening and diagnostic tests.

What are the displacement effects of training programs? Training programs rarely dramatically improve skills and wages. At best, they move trainees from low-wage to lower-middle-class-wage levels, and occasionally middle-class jobs. Displacement effects from training would be similar in their pattern to the displacement effects from college education, except that the groups affected are of different relative economic status. By causing a greater availability of labor for some lower-middle or middle-class jobs, training increases unemployment and lowers wages in these labor markets. Relative labor demand responds only partially to the shifts in relative labor supply brought about by training. As discussed previously, a range of plausible models suggest displacement effects of one-third to two-thirds. But training opens up opportunities in low-wage jobs by removing some labor supply from these labor markets. As a result, labor market conditions in low-wage labor markets improve somewhat: unemployment goes down and wages go up.

Training differs from college education in that the group most negatively affected by displacement is unlikely to be above-average in income. Training probably redistributes some income away from lower-middle-class and middle-class workers and toward low-wage workers. The social benefits from such redistribution are unclear. The public is likely to perceive greater social benefits from this redistribution if the jobs targeted by training are in occupations for which employment demand is growing rapidly. Without the training services, unemployment in these occupations would have declined and wages would have increased. The training probably moderates only somewhat the magnitude of the improvements in wages and unemployment for these occupations.

Training programs that target high employment growth occupations are also more likely to elicit employer involvement in training design and to become part of employers' hiring networks more easily. As already mentioned, such links to employers are associated with the most successful training programs.

Finding high employment growth occupations is an easier task in a local labor market with faster overall employment growth. Therefore, we would expect high-productivity training programs to be more likely to arise in fast-growing labor markets. This is consistent with some case study evidence on high-productivity training programs. For example, Riverside County's welfare-to-work program in the late 1980s had by far the highest employment growth of the five California counties that participated in the evaluation, at more than twice the average rate of any of the other four countries (Ricco et al. 1994, 279). This local economic environment may have made it possible to run a welfare-to-work program that could reach out to employers and try to develop job opportunities for welfare recipients. More recent research suggests that Riverside's welfare-to-work program became less successful in the early 1990s (Hamilton et al. 1997). Annual employment growth also fell in Riverside County, from rates of around 5 percent in the late 1980s to less than 1 percent from 1992 to 1993. Riverside's strategy of "locking up" available job openings for its "graduates" may have become less viable in this low-growth environment.

Similarly, it is probably no accident that the Center for Employment Training began in Silicon Valley. According to a case study of the CET, when it began (under a different name) in 1967, CET "received immediate support from Silicon Valley and nearby companies, which were just beginning what would become an extraordinarily robust period of expansion and were facing chronic labor shortages across all occupations, including those initially requiring relatively lower skills" (Meléndez 1996, 38). As a result, as CET began it received donations of equipment, legal and accounting services, publicity materials, and personnel from numerous local companies. The CET model of close ties to industry in designing training and placing graduates was a smart response to a high-growth labor market.[32]

In sum, both training and education are complex services that are difficult to deliver effectively to enough people to reduce significantly the current poverty rate. Training programs are relatively cheap but are likely to have modest earnings effects on average. The best training programs can have much larger effects for a few individuals, but we do not know yet how to expand these effects to large numbers of trainees. Furthermore, training programs have disturbing displacement effects on lower-middle-class workers unless we target high-growth occupations. Such targeting, which may also increase the effectiveness of training, depends on a sufficiently high-growth economy to provide a good variety of appropriate high-growth occupations from which to choose. Education programs can have more dramatic effects on moving people out of poverty and into truly middle-class living standards, or higher. Education programs also can have more dramatic effects on improving the distribution of income. But education programs are likely to be not only difficult to improve and expand but also quite costly. The cost of expanding education enough to solve the employment and earnings problems of the poor by itself is likely to be prohibitive.

Conclusion

A key limitation of all these labor supply programs is that by definition they do nothing directly to create additional jobs for the poor. This limitation affects not only the scope and effectiveness of labor supply programs but may contribute to the adverse effects of these programs. In the absence of additional jobs for the poor, pushing welfare recipients into the labor force not only pushes some ex-welfare recipients deeper into poverty but may lower wages and employment rates for some of the working poor. The Earned Income Tax Credit and other wage subsidies can provide significant increases in income for the working poor, but these wage subsidies do relatively little to help the nonworking poor. Without strong job growth, training programs are more difficult to organize effectively and may lower wages and employment rates for the working poor or the middle class. Increased education has enormous potential and appeal as an antipoverty strategy. But increasing education enough to improve significantly the wages and employment of a large proportion of the poor may be impossible. It is difficult for education policy by itself to catch up with the very strong economic trends that are increasing labor demand for the more-educated and reducing demand for the less-educated.

Because of these limitations of labor supply antipoverty policies, policymakers need to examine carefully the potential of labor demand antipoverty policies. How much can labor demand policies raise the employment and earnings of the poor? What effects might labor demand policies have on displacement? Can labor demand policies be implemented without excessive inflation? What are the pros and cons of different labor demand policies, such as public-service jobs, wage subsidies to employers, and economic development programs? Subsequent chapters explore these issues.

5

THE EFFECTS OF INCREASED LABOR DEMAND

This chapter examines what increased labor demand can do for the poor. Before considering specific labor demand policies, it is appropriate to ask whether an increase in labor demand—assuming policy can bring it about—will in fact yield significant increases in the employment and earnings of the poor. Although this chapter sometimes uses evidence from specific labor demand programs, this evidence is used only to provide insights into the effects of increased labor demand. Later chapters consider the pros and cons of specific labor demand programs.

Looking at the effects of labor demand raises the following issues: What do increases in aggregate demand do for the poor? Will general increases in the economy's overall demand for labor be sufficient to help the poor, or must labor demand increases be specifically targeted at the poor? Can labor demand increases targeted at the poor increase their employment and wages enough to make meaningful reductions in poverty? Can increased labor demand increase the earnings of the poor in ways that persist in the long run, or will any benefits quickly fade? Does job creation have greater effects if the jobs created pay higher wages or are in particular industries and occupations? What are the displacement effects of increases in labor demand for the poor?

The Effects of Aggregate Demand on the Employment and Wages of the Poor

What effects do increases in aggregate labor demand have on the employment and earnings of the poor? If aggregate labor demand had extremely strong effects, perhaps lower overall unemployment by itself would solve most of the employment problems of the poor. If this were so, solving poverty through public policy would face fewer political obstacles: stronger aggregate demand helps a broad range of political interest groups. Unlike many other antipoverty policies, stronger aggregate demand does not require the poor to be singled out for special benefits. Some aggregate demand policies are simpler to administer than targeted demand policies; encouraging more jobs for everyone is easier than trying to target the poor for greater employment. (Other macroeconomic policies that increase aggregate demand, such as policies to promote long-run productivity growth and wage growth, may be more difficult to implement.)

In recent years, the aggregate economy's effects on the poor have been misunderstood. Daniel Weinberg (1993, 56), chief of the U.S. Census Bureau division that produces poverty statistics, stated in 1993 that "trickle-down is dead, that is, there has been a surprising decline in the responsiveness of earnings to the macroeconomy." In her 1997 book *It Takes a Nation,* Rebecca Blank (1997, 53), a prominent researcher on poverty issues, in a subsection of one chapter entitled "The Death of 'Trickle Down Economics,'" said: "Economic growth . . . has not been effective in reducing poverty in the United States over the past fifteen years." Weinberg's and Blank's statements contain some truth. But some policymakers might infer from these statements that macroeconomic policy no longer has important effects on poverty. Such an inference is mistaken.

The belief in the death of "trickle-down economics" is based on aggregate data that show little relationship between a stronger macroeconomy and lower poverty. For example, figure 5.1 shows that even though average U.S. family income has increased considerably since the early 1970s, the poverty rate has shown a slight upward time trend, with considerable year-to-year variation.[1]

The absence of an obvious relationship between U.S. average incomes and poverty rates is surprising. Poverty is defined as the percentage of the U.S. population (or families, depending on the type of poverty rate used) below a certain income standard. The mathematics of the income distribution are inescapable: if real mean income goes up, and the variance of income about the mean stays the same, the percentage of the population or families below any fixed real income standard *must* go down.[2] Therefore, for the trend towards increased mean family income in the U.S. to fail to reduce poverty, as shown in figure 5.1, the anti-poverty effects of increased income must have been offset by a widening in the U.S. income distribution.

Thus, because the income distribution has widened, income growth has not led to a reduction in poverty. But it does not necessarily follow from these facts that economic growth is ineffective in reducing poverty! One possibility is that even if mean income had stayed the same, the income distribution would still have widened just about as much, thus significantly increasing poverty. In this case, economic growth still reduces poverty, but this is not evident in figure 5.1 because poverty is being increased by other factors.

An alternative possibility is that the type of economic growth of the

FIGURE 5.1 *Mean Family Income and Poverty, 1967 to 1998*

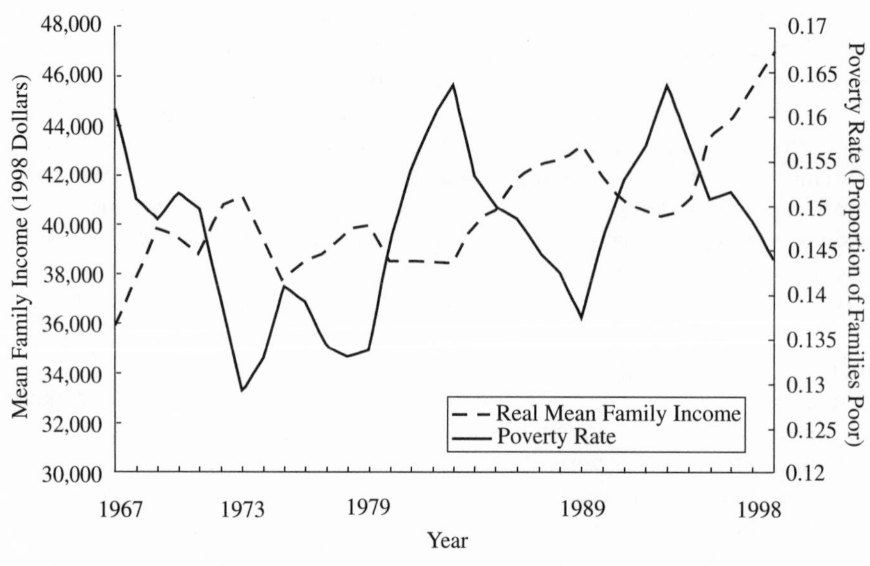

Source: Data are derived from March CPS.
Note: Poverty rate is "family" poverty rate, but with unrelated individuals included as "families." Real mean family income uses this same family definition.

modern U.S. economy inevitably causes the income distribution to widen. In this case, an increase in average incomes does not reduce poverty because this increase also increases income dispersion. From the perspective of antipoverty policy, we should be indifferent to policies that promote increases in average incomes. Some observers have explicitly argued that today's economic growth widens the income distribution. For example, the journalist Nicholas Lemann (1998, *x*), who has frequently written about poverty and racial issues, has argued: "When the economy is growing, as is the case now, the benefits go disproportionately to the well-educated people at the top of the income distribution."

To determine which of these two possibilities best describes the current U.S. economy, we would like to estimate how the economy would be different if economic growth or other changes in the macroeconomy had not occurred. But we cannot rerun U.S. history one hundred times, with randomly assigned economic growth and aggregate demand policies. The best approach to determining the effects of economic growth and aggregate demand on poverty is to compare trends in poverty rates in different U.S. regions. Have regions, states, or cities with stronger economies done better or worse in reducing poverty, or in increasing the employment and earnings of low-income groups? Has the relationship between a region's economy and its poverty rate weakened over time?

Such analyses of regional data suggest that the overall economy does have a significant effect on poverty. Furthermore, the strength of the overall economy's effects on poverty has not declined significantly over time. For example, in table 5.1, any of three indicators of the aggregate economy—unemployment, mean family income, and median family income—have statistically significant effects on poverty. The effects of these variables on poverty may have decreased a little in the 1980s, but in the 1990s the relationships between macro variables and poverty seem stronger than ever.

In fact, with some macro variables, the relationship between national trends and the national poverty rate seems as strong as ever. For example,

TABLE 5.1 *Estimated Effects of Regional Economic Conditions on Regional Poverty Rates in the United States, 1967 to 1997*

Independent Variables	Full Sample Period: 1967 to 1997	Early Sample Period: 1967 to 1979	Middle Sample Period: 1980 to 1989	Late Sample Period: 1990 to 1997
Unemployment rate	0.37 (0.06)	0.65 (0.11)	0.37 (0.08)	0.58 (0.18)
Median family income	−0.66 (0.04)	−0.65 (0.05)	−0.47 (0.05)	−0.69 (0.08)
Mean family income	−0.47 (0.04)	−0.52 (0.06)	−0.44 (0.05)	−0.59 (0.09)

Source: Author's estimates based on Bartik (2000b). Model derived from Blank and Card (1993).
Notes: Numbers in table show effects of independent variable measuring overall economic conditions in region on regional poverty rate. Standard errors of this coefficient estimate are in parentheses below estimated coefficient. Each row-column combination corresponds to a single regression. The observations in this regression are on region-year cells. The regressions differ in the independent variable used to measure region-year aggregate demand and in the years used in the estimation. The dependent variable in each regression is the mean poverty rate for a particular region-year cell. The independent variables in each regression are of three types: a complete set of year dummies; a complete set of region dummies; and a single variable measuring region-year aggregate demand and defined as some mean or median variable for each region-year cell. The means or medians for region-year cells are calculated by the author from various years of the March CPS. The twenty-one regions here are either an individual state or some grouping of states. The grouping here is arbitrarily defined based on what groupings of states one can calculate means or medians for using all the years of the March CPS from 1967 on. In calculating median or mean "family" income, I include as "families" what the Census Bureau calls "unrelated individuals." Poverty rate and unemployment rate are in percentages. Median and mean family income are in thousands of 1997 dollars. Statistical tests were done to determine whether the estimated effects in this table for particular subperiods differed from the estimated effects for the entire period. Only two subperiods are significantly different from the overall period: estimated effects of unemployment on poverty are significantly higher in the period 1967 to 1979 than for the entire period; the estimated effects of median family income on poverty are significantly smaller (in absolute value) for the period 1980 to 1989 than the estimated effect for the entire period from 1967 to 1997.

FIGURE 5.2 *Median Family Income and Poverty, 1967 to 1998*

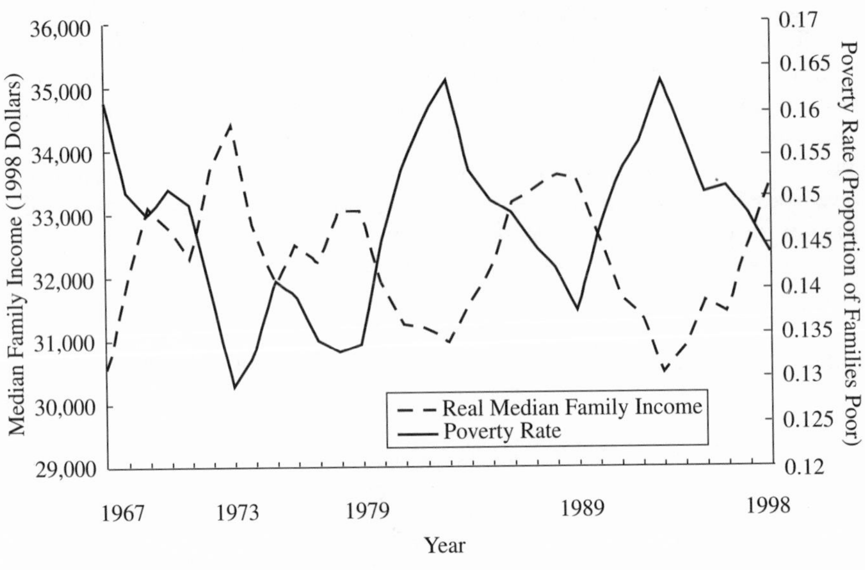

Source: Data are derived from March CPS.
Note: Poverty rate is "family" poverty rate, but with unrelated individuals included as "families." Real median family income uses this same definition.

as shown in figure 5.2, changes and trends in *median* family income appear to be quite closely correlated with changes and trends in the poverty rate. Apparently the adverse trends in income distribution that prevent increased mean income from reducing poverty at the national level are the same trends that are depressing median family income growth compared to mean family income growth.

Now that I have shown that the aggregate economy continues to affect poverty, I will focus on exactly how stronger labor demand affects the economy and the income distribution. For this chapter, we are less interested in the effects of long-term economic growth than in the effects of increased overall labor demand, as manifested by overall employment growth and a lower overall unemployment rate. Growth in median family income or mean family income, although obviously strongly affected in the short run by employment growth and lower unemployment, is also affected in the long run by many other forces distinct from aggregate labor demand, such as productivity growth. For this section, we focus on the short-term effects of increased employment growth and reduced unemployment. A later section considers the long-term effects of increased labor demand.

What would we expect the short-run effects of increases in overall labor demand, as manifested in lower overall unemployment, to be on the earnings and income of various groups? Labor market models with unemployment lead to the strong prediction that the effects will be progressive, in that the percentage effects on earnings, and perhaps on income will be much larger for lower-income groups and other groups with lower economic status (less education, racial minorities). This prediction is plausible because in a model with involuntary unemployment, we expect short-run employment growth, by lowering unemployment, to help disproportionately the groups with higher unemployment rates, which are groups with lower income and lower education, and nonwhite groups. In a model with unemployment and rationing of higher-wage jobs, we also expect increased labor demand to have some progressive effects through occupational upgrading, that is, as individuals move up into higher-paying occupations. Those on the lower end of the occupational scale have more opportunity to move up. Moderating or even possibly offsetting these progressive effects are any effects of overall unemployment on the wages of different groups. One would expect wage increases due to lower unemployment to be more broadly shared among the working population, whereas the benefits of lower unemployment on the employment rates of various groups are almost certainly concentrated on the lowest economic status groups.

Predictions based on market-clearing labor market models are less clear-cut about the progressivity of the short-run effects of aggregate labor demand growth. The effects on the wages and employment rates of different groups depend on the elasticities of labor demand and labor supply for all the various groups that define different labor submarkets. Effects may be progressive if the labor supply of low-education or other low-status groups is more elastic than that of higher economic status groups, and if relative labor demand for different groups is responsive to relative wages. This more elastic labor supply and responsive relative labor demand results in greater increases in the employment and earnings of these groups, owing to the aggregate labor demand expansion.

What is the empirical evidence on the effects of lower unemployment? Table 5.2 summarizes the empirical evidence on how lower overall unemployment influences various measures of the aggregate economy.[3] The summary includes unemployment's effects on both overall averages and aggregates and on different lower economic status groups.

As table 5.2 shows, 1 percent lower unemployment is associated with much more than 1 percent greater overall economic output; in fact, there is about a one-to-two or one-to-three relationship between unemployment and GNP. The relationship has long been dubbed "Okun's Law," after Arthur Okun, one of the first economists who rigorously explored it. Lower unemployment has more than a one-to-one relationship with overall output be-

TABLE 5.2 *Effects of Lower Unemployment*

Dependent Variable	Percentage Change in Dependent Variable for One-Percentage-Point Reduction in Unemployment Rate
Aggregate or overall average variables	
GNP	2 to 3
Labor force participation rate	0.3 to 0.6
Wage rate	0.5 to 1.5
Occupational upgrading	0.2 to 0.7
Average real earnings	1.5 to 3.5
Average real income	0.9 to 1.5
Distributional measures	
Income share of lowest income quintile	0.02 to 0.1 increase in percentage point share of national income. At mean share of 3 to 5 percent, income of lowest quintile increases by 1 to 3 percent more than average.
Poverty rate (change in rate points)	−0.3 to −0.9.
Percentage effect on earnings of bottom income quintile versus effect on overall earnings	Earnings effect on lowest income quintile is 2 to 6 percent greater than that for average family.
Various labor market variables, effects on different education groups	Percentage effects are greater on less-educated than more-educated individuals for employment rate and earnings; unclear for wages. One-point reduction in unemployment increases earnings of high school dropouts by 1 to 3 percent more than earnings of college graduates.
Various labor market variables, effects of overall lower unemployment on blacks versus whites	Most studies find greater effects on blacks than on whites in percentage terms, although the magnitude of differences varies greatly. Most of the greater effects appear to be due to effects on hours worked, not wage rates.

Source: See chapter 5, note 3, for more details.

cause lower unemployment increases labor force participation and leads to individuals moving into occupations and industries that are better paying and more productive.[4] Lower unemployment also increases wage rates for specific occupations, thus increasing wage rates more than would occur simply owing to occupational upgrading. One percent lower unemployment, because it leads to higher labor force participation and higher wage rates, results in a somewhat greater than 1 percent increase in overall average earnings. But because labor earnings are only a portion of total income, average income does not go up by as much in percentage terms as average earnings.

Lower unemployment also has a number of economic benefits for the poor and other lower economic status groups. Unemployment's *percentage* effects on the earnings of lower education groups, blacks, and the lowest income quintile are significantly greater than for the average individual. Most of these greater effects on lower economic status groups appear to be due to the greater effects of unemployment on the employment of lower economic status groups. These earnings effects on the lowest income quintile are great enough that it seems likely that lower unemployment increases the income of the lowest income quintile more than overall average income, even though earnings are a below-average share of income for the lowest income quintile. Therefore, lower unemployment probably has moderate effects on increasing the progressivity of the overall income distribution. Because the average incomes of lower economic status groups go up, lower unemployment also reduces poverty rates.

Although the short-run effects on the poor of stronger aggregate labor demand and lower overall unemployment are important, they are modest enough in magnitude that lower overall unemployment by itself clearly cannot solve the poverty problem. This can be shown in several ways. First, looking at the effects of unemployment on poverty in table 5.1 or table 5.2, a one-point reduction in unemployment reduces the poverty rate by 0.3 to 0.9 percentage points—that is, as a percentage of the total population. With an overall U.S. population of 274 million, this implies that a one-point reduction in poverty reduces the number of poor people by 0.8 million to 2.5 million. Thus, achieving 4 percent unemployment rather than 6 percent unemployment reduces the number of poor by 1.6 million to 5.0 million; keeping unemployment at 4 percent rather than going through a recession that doubles unemployment to 8 percent reduces the number of poor by 3.2 million to 10.0 million. These obviously are large numbers because they affect the quality of life of millions of people. But 34.5 million Americans were poor in 1998, when overall unemployment was 4.5 percent. Running the economy at a somewhat lower unemployment rate, while helpful, will not come close to solving the poverty problem of all these 34.5 million persons. However, preventing a recession and pursuing a goal of 4 percent employment rather than 6 percent will avoid making the problem significantly worse.

Second, consider the actual dollar effects of lower unemployment on the earnings and income of different groups. Table 5.3 shows the actual dollar effects, as well as percentage effects, of 1 percent lower unemployment on the earnings and income of different income quintiles. Even though the lowest income quintile has larger percentage gains in income and earnings from lower unemployment, the actual dollar increase in earnings and income for the lowest income quintile is quite modest. In fact, the *dollar* increase in earnings and income from lower unemployment for higher-income groups tends to be higher.

TABLE 5.3 *Effect of 1 Percent Lower Unemployment on Mean Annual Earnings, Mean Annual Income, and Share of Total Family Income, by Family Income Quintile, 1963 to 1997*

Measure	All Families	Quintile 1	Quintile 2	Quintile 3	Quintile 4	Quintile 5
Estimated effect of lower unemployment on mean earnings (standard error)	474 (55)	100 (16)	414 (49)	472 (63)	632 (72)	751 (152)
Mean earnings	32,477	2,367	11,977	25,375	42,236	80,428
Implied percentage effect	1.46	4.22	3.46	1.86	1.50	0.93
Estimated effect of lower unemployment on mean income (standard error)	473 (57)	131 (21)	351 (45)	445 (54)	571 (68)	868 (159)
Mean income	38,662	6,879	18,601	31,353	47,437	89,039
Implied percentage effect	1.22	1.90	1.89	1.42	1.20	0.97
Estimated effect of lower unemployment on quintile's percentage share of total income (standard error)	—	0.02 (0.01)	0.06 (0.02)	0.03 (0.01)	−0.01 (0.02)	−0.09 (0.04)

Source: Author's estimates using March CPS data (Bartik 2000b). Model derived from Blank and Card (1993).

Notes: Standard errors are in parentheses. Earnings data were available only for 1967 to 1997. Observations are on region-year cells, with the United States divided into twenty-one groupings of states. Quintiles are defined by family income, with an "unrelated individual" included as a "family." All dollar figures are in 1997 dollars. All regressions and calculations are weighted by 1997 population for region. All regressions include year and regional dummies.

As a result, even 4 percent lower unemployment would raise the average earnings and income of the lowest income quintile by only $400 or $500 per year. As discussed in chapter 4, it is customary to denounce job training programs for having such modest effects. This denunciation of programs for their modest "average" effects is overstated. As with training programs, increases in aggregate labor demand probably have quite significant effects for some individuals. The greater earnings and income of the lowest income quintile are probably attributable primarily to the relatively small percentage of this quintile who move from nonemployment to employment. For these individuals, the gains from lower overall unemployment are many thousands of dollars per year. However, even though some individuals in the lowest income quintile gain a great deal from a stronger economy, lower unemployment improves the *average* economic fortunes of the lowest income quintile by only a modest amount.

A third approach is to look at the extent to which lower overall unemployment helps to meet the job needs outlined in chapter 3—creating three to nine million new jobs for disadvantaged groups. Table 5.4 reports estimates of how lower unemployment in a state affects the employment rate of these less-educated groups. These effects are highly statistically significant. However, as shown in table 5.5, the estimates imply that 1 percent lower unemployment would lead to only about a 0.6 million increase in employment for these prime-age less-educated groups. Because overall unemployment in 1999 was already 4.2 percent, it seems unlikely that we can do too much more through lower overall unemployment to create the needed millions of additional jobs. However, policies to minimize or avoid recessions are needed, because a recession that increased unemployment by four percent would result in a loss of over two million jobs for less-educated persons (table 5.5).

Why do increases in aggregate labor demand have only modestly progressive effects? First, as pointed out earlier, the upgrading benefits and wage increase benefits from stronger labor demand are spread out among all income groups, education groups, and ethnic groups. Second, although unemployment is concentrated in lower-income groups, it does occur in all income groups, and thus the benefits from hiring, although progressive, are to some extent spread out. For example, table 5.6 shows that although unemployment rates are highest for the lowest income quintile, this lowest income quintile includes only 25 percent of the total unemployed. The lowest income quintile has a surprisingly low percentage of the total number of

TABLE 5.4 *Effects of 1 Percent Lower Unemployment on the Employment Rates of Different Education and Gender Groups of Prime Working-Age Individuals*

	Effects on Men	Effects on Single Women	Effects on Married Women
High school dropouts	0.676 (6.92)	0.890 (5.35)	0.728 (5.73)
High school graduates	1.030 (33.35)	1.127 (16.10)	0.803 (13.44)
College graduates	0.401 (12.83)	0.393 (4.67)	0.272 (3.52)

Source: Author's estimates.
Notes: The table is based on nine different regressions; each cell shows effect from a separate regression. *T*-statistics are in parentheses. Both employment rates and unemployment rates are measured in proportions. All regressions also include a full set of year dummies and state dummies. Regressions are weighted by estimated 1998 total state population of everyone ages twenty-five to fifty-four. Data span fifty-one states (including D.C.), and all years from 1979 to 1998. Data are weighted state means derived from CPS-ORG.

TABLE 5.5 *Effects of Lower Unemployment on Employment of Various Groups, Compared to "Needed Jobs"*

Group	Number of Needed Jobs (In Millions)	Number of Jobs Created by 1 Percent Lower Unemployment (In Millions)	Number of Jobs Created by 4 Percent Lower Unemployment (In Millions)
Male high school dropouts	0.596	0.050	0.198
Male high school graduates	1.518	0.341	1.365
Single female high school dropouts	1.082	0.027	0.108
Single female high school graduates	1.975	0.149	0.597
Total	5.171	0.567	2.268

Source: Author's estimates and calculations.
Notes: Figures for needed jobs are directly taken from table 3.2 and represent the number of jobs needed for employment rates for these four groups to change from 1998 levels to the 1979 levels of the same education group for white non-Hispanic males. Figures for job creation due to lower unemployment are taken by calculating, based on table 5.4, how much lower unemployment would increase the employment rate of each group, and then multiplying this by the change in unemployment rate and estimated size of each group in 1998.

unemployed because this income quintile of families tends to have lower labor force participation rates than overall as well as a below-average number of adults per family. To put it another way, although the unemployment problem is worse among the lowest income quintile, the demographics of the lowest income quintile, in family structure and labor force participation, reduce somewhat the numbers of lowest income quintile individuals who can immediately respond to an increase in labor demand.

What are the implications of these important but modest effects of aggregate labor demand on the employment and earnings of the poor? First, the modest magnitude of these effects implies that aggregate labor demand policies should not be considered a favored substitute for policies that more directly address the needs of the poor. For example, if a state government wants to pursue economic development policies aggressively, this will disproportionately provide earnings and income benefits to the poor. But these greater benefits for the poor are not great enough that financing state economic development programs through cuts in welfare programs is a good deal for the poor. As shown in table 5.7 (Bartik 1994a), even if cutting business taxes to spur state economic development has large effects on state employment growth, financing these tax cuts through cuts in welfare programs is a bad deal from the perspective of lower-income groups. Aggregate labor demand should be considered a *complement* rather than a substitute for programs that directly aid the poor.

TABLE 5.6 *Unemployment, Labor Force Participation, and Potential Labor Force Participants Among Different Family Income Quintiles, 1997 to 1998*

Income Quintile	Unemployment Rate	Number of Unemployed (In Millions)	Labor Force Participation Rate	Number of Labor Force Participants (In Millions)	Number of Adults Sixteen and Over (In Millions)
1 (Lowest income)	15.8	1.762	40.5	11.150	27.502
2	8.1	1.510	53.7	18.674	34.715
3	4.8	1.273	66.1	26.522	40.122
4	3.6	1.316	76.2	36.546	47.989
5 (Highest income)	2.4	1.057	80.1	44.039	54.970

Source: Author's calculations based on the March 1998 CPS.
Notes: Income quintile status is assigned based on 1997 family income, with single individuals counted as "families" (unlike Census Bureau conventions). Of course, an equal number of families are in each quintile. Unemployment and labor force status are based on employment status as of the March 1998 interview.

TABLE 5.7 *Net Distributional Effects of Local Economic Development Policies Under Alternative Cost Scenarios*

Quintile	Real Income Increase	Real Income Equivalent of Real Estate Gains	Business Tax Cuts Financed by Increases in Personal Taxes		Business Tax Cuts Financed by Reduced Welfare Spending	
			Tax Cost	Net Effect	Cost	Net Effect
1 (Lowest income)	0.787	0.071	−0.257	0.601	−2.861	−2.003
2	0.477	0.069	−0.192	0.354	−0.420	0.126
3	0.396	0.068	−0.169	0.295	−0.073	0.391
4	0.276	0.069	−0.158	0.187	−0.022	0.323
5 (Highest income)	0.166	0.086	−0.173	0.079	−0.007	0.245
Average family	0.286	0.077	−0.174	0.189	−0.174	0.189

Source: Bartik (1994a, table 3).

Notes: The elasticity of employment with regard to business tax rates is assumed to be −0.25, based on Bartik (1991). Real income increases are derived from column 2 in table 1 of Bartik (1994a). All numbers show benefits and costs, as percentages of average income in that particular quintile, of some policy that increases MSA employment by 1 percent. The policy is assumed to be a business tax cut, financed by either increasing personal taxes or cutting welfare spending. The net effect under each policy scenario sums real income gains, the annual income equivalent of real estate capital gains, and the cost of financing the policy. For example, under the tax financing scenario, the lowest income quintile's average per family income increases by 0.787 percent, its real estate value increases by an amount equivalent to a 0.071 percent increase in annual income, and its taxes increase by 0.257 percent of annual income, for a net effect of increasing the lowest income quintile's income by 0.601 percent. When the business tax cut is financed by reduced welfare spending, real income and real estate increases the same, but reduced welfare spending cuts the lowest income quintile's net income by 2.861 percent. Average family totals are calculated as weighted sums of quintile figures, using quintile shares as weights. These quintile percentage shares are: Q1, 3.91; Q2, 9.84; Q3, 16.46; Q4, 24.96; Q5, 44.83.

Second, these important but modest effects of aggregate labor demand suggest that more targeted labor demand policies may be necessary and important components of a comprehensive policy mix to increase the employment and earnings of the poor. What are the potential effects of labor demand policies targeted at the poor? We now turn to that topic.

The Effects of Increased Labor Demand on Poor Individuals

Suppose the government creates a program that targets increased labor demand at the poor, perhaps through providing public-service jobs or subsidizing private-sector jobs for the poor. Suppose the program is small-scale enough that it has no significant effect on the market wages of any group. What would we expect the effects of this program to be?

Either labor market models with involuntary unemployment or labor market models that assume that the labor market clears could explain an increase in employment resulting from this targeted labor demand program.

However, models with involuntary unemployment predict that employment rates will usually increase from such programs, whereas employment increases in market-clearing models only under special circumstances. In models with involuntary unemployment, many individuals are unemployed but willing to work at the market wage, and therefore making more jobs available to the involuntarily unemployed almost inevitably results in a net increase in employment. Employment might increase even if the new jobs pay a below-market wage.[5] In contrast, if one believes in market-clearing models, employment increases owing to the labor demand program only if both of two conditions hold: the program must pay wages above the market level; and labor supply must positively respond to wage increases. If *either* of these two conditions is unmet, the labor demand program leaves employment rates unchanged.

In either model, a targeted labor demand program has some displacement effects within the group that is given jobs, that is, some of those given jobs would have found jobs anyway. In a market-clearing model, these are individuals who would have been willing to work at the market wage but took the higher-paying program jobs; under a model with unemployment, these are individuals whose job search would have been successful anyway as vacancies opened up. The extent of displacement depends on the program's success in targeting those who would be least likely to find jobs without the program. Note that these are displacement effects within the group that participates in the program; there also may be effects on the employment of others *not* in the group, and I discuss those effects when analyzing programs that are large relative to the labor market.

Only three programs that subsidize job creation for the poor have been subjected to random assignment evaluation: the Supported Work Program; the on-the-job training (OJT) component of the Job Training Partnership Act (JTPA), the main federally funded job training program from 1982 to 1998; and the New Hope experiment in Milwaukee. Only in the Supported Work Program was the provision of subsidized jobs the primary element of treatment. In that program, the jobs provided were deliberately not normal market jobs but rather jobs that began with relatively lax work standards that were gradually tightened to market standards over the one-year duration of the work assignments. These jobs were supposed to pay below-market wages for entry-level workers with low education levels, but the lax work standards might mean that wages were high relative to the required work effort.

In the evaluations of the OJT component of JTPA, individuals were included in the evaluation if the program had recommended that they receive a placement at a private employer for six months of on-the-job training. The JTPA program reimbursed the employer for half of the client's wages during this six-month period, under the rationale that the employer

SIDEBAR 5.1 The Supported Work Program

The Supported Work Program was an experimental subsidized work program designed to increase the long-run employability of "hard-core" poor individuals. The experiment was run from 1975 to 1979 by nonprofit organizations at fifteen sites around the United States, with more than 10,000 participants. The four groups targeted by the program were long-term welfare recipients, ex-addicts, ex-offenders, and young high school dropouts.

Supported Work provided a structured work experience for up to one year, with job assignments involving gradually increasing work demands, close supervision by program staff, and peer support. Supported Work projects were usually developed and run by the local program operator, although some participants were placed at other organizations. Jobs were typically service occupations for females and construction occupations for men. One hundred percent of participant wages were subsidized, although sometimes the paid wages were financed in part by diverted welfare benefits. The wages paid were supposed to be less than the local market wage for entry-level workers. In addition to work experience, Supported Work programs provided counseling and sometimes training. After participants had acquired work experience through Supported Work projects, local program operators attempted to place them at unsubsidized jobs.

Sources: Manpower Demonstration Research Corporation (1980); Kemper et al. (1981); Couch (1992); Grossman et al. (1985).

was providing extra training. However, in many cases the training provided by employers, although perhaps valuable, was similar to what the employer would have provided any new employee; in effect, the JTPA program was providing a wage subsidy to induce employers to hire its clients. However, although individuals in the OJT portion of the JTPA evaluation were recommended for an OJT placement, only one-third received such a placement. Some of those recommended for OJT may have obtained a job without an OJT placement, others may have dropped out of the JTPA program, and for still others the program was unable to secure an OJT placement. In addition, the OJT portion of JTPA was not a pure labor demand subsidy, since individuals recommended for OJT also received many other JTPA services, such as counseling, job search assistance, basic education, and training courses.

The New Hope Program in Milwaukee is a recent innovative program that seeks to increase significantly the earnings and income of individuals in low-income Milwaukee neighborhoods. Part of the program design is the provision of short-term (up to six months initially, and perhaps six months later) jobs at community agencies, paid for by the New Hope Program. Such jobs are provided exclusively to individuals unable to obtain jobs

SIDEBAR 5.2 The New Hope Program

New Hope was an experiment that guaranteed employment at a living wage to low-income residents of two Milwaukee neighborhoods. The experiment was run from 1994 to 1998 in two Milwaukee zip codes. Those eligible were all adults in those zip codes whose family income was below 150 percent of the poverty line.

For individuals who worked at least thirty hours per week, the program provided:

- earnings supplements to increase family income to the poverty level;
- subsidized health insurance;
- subsidized child care.

For individuals unable to find full-time employment, the program provided community service jobs at nonprofit organizations for up to six months at a time, and for a maximum of twelve months during the program. In addition, project representatives provided counseling and mentoring.

Early results from the random assignment evaluation of the program indicate that New Hope's impacts depended on whether program participants were employed full-time at program entry. Among the two-thirds not employed full-time upon program entry, the program reduced the percentage never employed from 13 to 6 percent, increased market earnings by almost $700 per year, increased income by more than $1,300 per year, and reduced the percentage in poverty by an average of 7 percent. Among those already employed full-time at program entry, the program modestly reduced earnings owing to cutbacks in overtime hours. However, the cutting back on overtime hours apparently led to some improvements in parenting quality, as judged by surveys of program participants, their children, and their children's schools.

Sources: Bos et al. (1999); Brock et al. (1997).

after a job search. In addition, the New Hope Program provided other services and subsidies, including earnings supplements to participants who obtained any full-time job; a guarantee of affordable health insurance to any participant working full-time; child care subsidies for anyone working full-time; and informal counseling from New Hope representatives. Thus, the New Hope Program was not a pure labor demand subsidy but rather a mixture of a labor demand subsidy and important subsidies for increased labor supply.

Table 5.8 shows the effects of these three programs on participants' employment and earnings, and on participants' wage rates. The effects shown are the increase in employment or earnings during the program—

TABLE 5.8 *Impact of Small-Scale, Policy-Induced Demand Shocks on Employment and Wage Rates of Program Participants*

Program	Ratio of Employment and Earnings Effects on Participants to Program-Related Employment and Earnings of Participants, In-Program Period	Wage Effects
Supported Work	0.92 for AFDC mothers 0.68 for ex-addicts 0.69 for ex-offenders 0.85 for youth[b]	Changes due largely to program policy: 17 percent for AFDC mothers[a] −17 percent for ex-addicts −10 percent for ex-offenders 0 percent for youths
OJT component of JTPA	1.57 for adult women 0.77 for adult men 5.15 for female youth −1.83 for male youth non-arrestees[c]	Not available for this subgroup, but overall wage effect of JTPA appears very modest, perhaps 2 or 3 percent
New Hope[d]	0.680	Reduces wage slightly, largely owing to wage supplement policy

Source: Author's compilation.

[a] These are taken by dividing average monthly earnings for seven to nine months after enrollment by average monthly hours for experimental group, and for control group, separately (MDRC 1980).

[b] These are ratios of experimental-control differences in earnings, seven to nine months after enrollment, divided by program earnings during same time period, as reported in MDRC (1980).

[c] These figures are ratios of earnings gains for experimental versus control group for months 1 through 6 after enrollment, to twice the total OJT earning subsidies (because subsidies are half of wages) provided to that group, as reported in Orr et al. (1996). The analysis here is complicated because clearly the OJT group received more than this service, and some of the OJT subsidy occurs after the six-month period.

[d] The ratio of in-program earnings effects to program earnings is derived as the two-year effect on average earnings per participant of $646, versus two-year provisions of $945 in earnings from a community service job per participant (Bos et al. 1999).

that is, while the subsidized employment was available to participants. The effects on employment and earnings are shown in comparison to the total employment and earnings that were directly provided or subsidized by the program during the same time period. In the case of JTPA–OJT and New Hope, program components other than the subsidized employment may have affected the net employment and earnings effect reported by the program, either in a positive or negative direction. (Other program components could have a negative effect if the program led to individuals increasing their hours in training or education and thus probably reducing work hours.)

As shown in table 5.8, the evidence from these three programs suggests that targeted labor demand subsidies can increase employment and earnings, while the subsidies are in place, by a sizable amount relative to the amount of subsidized employment. The increase in employment or earnings is usually at least two-thirds of the total amount of subsidized employment or earnings. The closest to a pure labor demand subsidy is Supported Work, which consistently shows in-program effects on earnings that are sizable portions of the earnings directly provided by the program.

These increases in employment and earnings are not typically accompanied by large increases in the official wage rates paid under the programs. In some cases, employment increases even though program wages appear to be less than market alternatives. For example, employment increased in Supported Work for ex-drug addicts and ex-offenders even though the program-provided wage rates for the treatment group appear to be less than the market wages of the control group. This effect appears to be more consistent with a labor market model with involuntary unemployment than with a market-clearing model. However, as pointed out earlier, the lax work standards in Supported Work may result in higher wages relative to work effort. Furthermore, because the treatment group in Supported Work includes more workers, the reported average wage for the treatment group may be biased downward by the inclusion of more marginal workers. These marginal workers are not employed in the control group and may have obtained lower wages if they had obtained jobs.

Effects of Increasing Overall Labor Demand for an Entire Labor Market Group

Suppose the government increases labor demand for some disadvantaged group, possibly by creating public-service jobs or subsidizing private job creation, in a quantity large enough to be significant relative to the size of the labor market for that group. What employment rate and wage effects would we expect?

As discussed in chapter 3, the magnitude of the net employment rate effects and wage rate effects in the labor market for this group depend on the responsiveness of labor demand and labor supply for this group. This includes how responsive labor supply and labor demand are to the group's wage rate. In models with unemployment, the net effects of labor demand increases also depend on how responsive labor supply and labor demand are to the group's unemployment rate.

The displacement effects of large-scale publicly subsidized new jobs depend on these marketwide effects on private labor demand, in contrast to small-scale programs, in which the displacement effects for the participant

SIDEBAR 5.3 The Summer Youth Employment Program

The Summer Youth Employment Program was originally enacted as part of the War on Poverty initiatives of President Johnson in 1964. The program provides summer jobs at the minimum wage to economically disadvantaged youth at a variety of public and private contractors, with jobs typically lasting about nine weeks and averaging twenty to thirty hours per week. The program peaked in size in 1978 at 1.2 million participants. During the 1980s and 1990s, the program fluctuated between 400,000 and 800,000 participants per year, at an annual cost (in 1998 dollars) that fluctuated between $0.4 billion and $1.4 billion. The program was folded into the general block grant for employment and training provided to states and local workforce investment boards under the Workforce Investment Act enacted in 1998.

Sources: Ellwood and Crane (1984); U.S. House of Representatives (1998); U.S. Department of Labor web site.

group depend on whether they would have found jobs anyway. For programs with marketwide effects, displacement occurs because the higher wage rates for this group brought about by the publicly subsidized new jobs decrease private labor demand for this group. Displacement also occurs because the publicly subsidized jobs, by lowering the group's unemployment rate, make its labor supply less available to private labor demand, thus decreasing private labor demand for this group.

Two empirical studies have examined the labor market effects of publicly subsidized job creation for a target group: a study by David Ellwood and Jon Crane (1984) of the Summer Youth Jobs Program for disadvantaged youth, and studies by the Manpower Demonstration Research Corporation (MDRC) of the Youth Incentive Entitlement Pilot Project (YIEPP) program. The Summer Youth Jobs Program, in operation since the 1960s, provides summer jobs to disadvantaged youth. The YIEPP program was an experiment run from 1978 to 1980 that provided guaranteed jobs to all sixteen- to nineteen-year-old disadvantaged youths living in a few selected cities who stayed in school or returned to school. Neither study was run as a true experiment. A true experiment to detect marketwide effects of such programs would be difficult to run, because it would require randomly assigning different cities or states to different levels of subsidized jobs, an approach of doubtful political viability. Instead, these studies tried to determined the marketwide effects of these programs by comparing marketwide employment rates (or wage rates) for the targeted group in cities or states that received more subsidized jobs to the employment rate (or wage rate) of the targeted group in otherwise similar cities or states that received fewer

SIDEBAR 5.4 The Youth Incentive Entitlement Pilot Program

YIEPP was one of several experimental youth employment programs enacted under the 1977 Youth Employment and Demonstration Projects Act and eliminated once the Reagan administration took office in 1981. What was unique about YIEPP was that it guaranteed job availability by creating jobs, with a condition for getting the job: enrollment in a program to get a high school degree. Under YIEPP, local job training sponsors were responsible for ensuring that eligible youth were provided with *guaranteed* minimum-wage jobs, part-time during the school year and full-time during the summer, with 100 percent of the wage, of these jobs paid for by YIEPP. The program was operated as an entitlement for all disadvantaged youth in the seventeen project areas who enrolled in school or agreed to go back to school or enroll in a program to get a GED. Seventy-six thousand youth participated in these programs, on average for fifteen months. Total program cost was about $600 million in 1998 dollars. Jobs created were in both the public sector (70 percent) and the private sector (30 percent).

Evaluation of YIEPP was based on:

- interviews and surveys of youth, employer, and training sponsor views of the program;
- comparison of youth employment, earnings, and school enrollment in three project areas with three matched areas, with the matching based on similarities in local labor markets.

The evaluation suggested that it is feasible to implement a large-scale job guarantee for disadvantaged youth, in that sufficient jobs can be created and disadvantaged youth will take such jobs. Program participation was high, particularly among disadvantaged black youth, among whom more than 60 percent of those eligible participated. The program attracted more interest from in-school youths than from high school dropouts. Program sponsors were able to encourage significant private-sector participation, although job development costs were high because most private businesses were not interested in hiring disadvantaged youths. Surveys of both employers and youth participants suggest that most participants were able to do productive work rather than "make-work," and that one-fifth of participating private businesses offered regular jobs to youths they had employed through the program. Comparing project areas with matched areas, the program significantly increased the employment rates and earnings of eligible youth during the program's operation, particularly for black youth. However, the program had no effect on school enrollment. A three-month follow-up suggested that effects on earnings persisted even after the program's guaranteed jobs were gone.

Sources: Gueron (1984); Betsey, Hollister, and Papageorgiou (1985).

subsidized jobs or no subsidized jobs. The key problem here is determining what states or cities to use for comparison. Ellwood and Crane (1984) relied on the fact that the funding formula for summer youth jobs depends in a somewhat complex manner on past funding for the state and past economic conditions. As a result, they could compare states with similar overall economic conditions that happened to have different allocations for summer youth jobs owing to their past history of funding. For the YIEPP program, MDRC researchers matched each targeted city to cities that were similar, prior to the program, in a number of economic and demographic characteristics.

Both of these studies suggest that although publicly subsidized jobs lead to some marketwide displacement, such programs still lead to a considerable increase in employment rates. The estimated increase in employment rates is from half to two-thirds of the program-subsidized jobs (table 5.9). States that receive more funding for summer youth jobs have higher employment rates during the summer for nonwhite youth. In cities that were targeted for YIEPP, not only was the overall youth employment rate higher, but the employment rate gap between black and white youth virtually disappeared. For example, the program increased the average monthly employment rate of white male youth during the program from 37 to 47 percent but increased the average black male youth employment rate from 26 to 44 percent. White female youth employment rates increased from 27 to 30 percent, but black female employment rates increased from 17 to 39 percent (Gueron 1984).

These increases in employment rates were accompanied by little if any increases in wage rates in the YIEPP program. (The study of the Summer Youth Jobs Program did not examine wage rate effects.) There is no sign that wage rates for youths were much greater in YIEPP cities than in comparison cities.

The displacement and wage effects of large-scale creation of subsidized jobs can also be examined using partial equilibrium or general equilibrium simulation models. The bottom panel of table 5.9 repeats results from appendices 1 and 2 for two plausible versions of such models. The partial equilibrium model assumes various parameters for how labor demand and labor supply in the low-wage labor market react to wages and unemployment, and how wages in this labor market react to unemployment. The general equilibrium model estimates such relationships for a model that divides the labor market into five different groups, including three groups with less education. The short-run employment rate effects of policy-induced demand shocks in these models are similar to what was empirically estimated for YIEPP and the Summer Youth Jobs Program: between half and two-thirds of the program-related employment ends up

TABLE 5.9 *Short-Run Market Displacement and Wage Effects of Policy-Induced Shocks to Labor Demand*

Program	Ratio of Marketwide Effects on Employment of Target Group to Program-Related Increase in Employment: In-Program, Short-Run Effects	Wage Effects
Estimates from actual programs		
YIEPP	0.67 for school year jobs	2 percent for out-of-school youth
	0.44 for summer jobs[a]	−1 percent for in-school youth
Summer Youth Jobs	0.67 for nonwhite youth[b]	n.a.
Simulated effects		
Partial equilibrium model of appendix 1, using assumed parameters[c]	0.64	Elasticity of 0.21
General equilibrium wage curve model of appendix 2, using estimated parameters[d]		Wage elasticities of:
	0.65 for single mothers	0.14 for single mothers
	0.58 for other less-educated women	0.95 for other less-educated women
	0.64 for less-educated men	1.27 for less-educated men

[a] Author's compilation. Farkas et al. (1982, 125, table 5.8). Derived from estimated program effect in site city versus comparison city, divided by program employment in site.
[b] Ellwood and Crane (1984).
[c] Source: Table A1.1.
[d] Table A2.12. Note that results for single mothers are for a group that is a small portion of the labor market, only about 4 percent of the overall population. Results for other less-educated women and for less-educated men are for groups that are a much larger portion of the labor market, about 36 percent of the population for less-educated women, and 38 percent for less-educated men (see table A2.2).

increasing the overall marketwide employment of the target group. In the short run, the market only partially offsets the policy-induced increase in labor demand. Plausible estimates of how labor supply and labor demand behave suggest that a complete offset of the direct effects of policy on employment is unlikely. These simulation models also suggest that the market wage effects for the group targeted by the policy are likely to be modest unless the group is a large portion of the labor force. This is consistent with the modest wage effects found for the Summer Youth Jobs Program. As noted in appendix 2, empirical estimates suggest that in the short and medium run, relative wages of different groups are only modestly sensitive to shocks to labor demand for one group.

Long-Term Effects of Increased Labor Demand: The Effects of Permanent Increases in Labor Demand

What effects does increased labor demand for the poor have on their employment and earnings in the long run? In answering this question, it is important to be clear about the nature of the increase in labor demand, in particular whether it is a once-and-for-all-time increase in the level of labor demand or merely a temporary increase in labor demand. It would not be surprising that a permanent increase in labor demand would have some long-run effects. It would be surprising if temporary increases in labor demand that are later reversed have labor market effects that are permanent or at least very long-run. I argue, however, that temporary increases in labor demand can indeed cause wages and employment rates to be higher in the long run.

The long-run effects of labor demand policies obviously would be part of any good evaluation of such policies. For example, we would like to know whether, in the long run, increasing labor demand for the poor increases their employment rates, thereby helping the nonworking poor, or merely increases wages, which spreads benefits over the working poor. But if temporary increases in labor demand can have permanent effects, then labor demand policies become more attractive, not only from a benefit-cost standpoint but as a way to promote American values of autonomy and a smaller government role. If providing public jobs or subsidizing private jobs for the poor in one year can cause significant increases in employment and wages in the long run, then the government may need to provide these subsidized jobs to individuals only temporarily, not permanently. This type of temporary intervention is more attractive to many Americans: helping individuals to fish on their own rather than giving them a fish. It is the hope that government need intervene only in the short run, and that those assisted will provide for themselves in the long run, that is behind much of the traditional political support for education and job training policies. In this section, I consider the probable effects of permanent increases in labor demand for the poor; in the next section, I consider the effects of temporary increases.

Once-and-for-all increases in the level of labor demand may have long-run effects, as should be apparent from the labor market models discussed in chapter 3 and in appendices 1 and 2. Adjustments to the new, higher level of labor demand for a group may require adjustments to the equilibrium between labor supply and demand, among which may be changes in the equilibrium unemployment rate, wage rate, and labor force participation rate for the group. These adjustments in general differ going from the short run to the long run. Wage rates adjust more over time.

Private labor demand also adjusts downward more over time because of the higher wages and lesser availability of this type of worker owing to the government-supported hiring; these downward adjustments of private labor demand offset some of the initial stronger labor demand due to the government-supported hiring.

The quantitative magnitude of the long-run effects on employment and wages of permanent increases in labor demand for the poor depend on assumptions or estimates of how labor demand, labor supply, wages, and unemployment respond to one another. Appendix 7 presents one scenario that uses empirically estimated parameters to simulate some long-run effects of a shock to labor demand for one group.

As shown in the appendix, these long-run effects also depend on local labor market conditions and on how the permanent increase in labor demand affects labor supply. The displacement effects of labor demand policies are smaller if unemployment is higher. With higher unemployment, wages respond much more sluggishly to an increase in labor demand. As a result, private labor demand is not as depressed by the increase in labor demand induced by public policy, resulting in less displacement.

The displacement effects of labor demand policies are also lower if the workers hired for these jobs are still available to be hired by regular employers. Greater availability of a given group of workers, other things equal, should lead to greater hiring of this group by nonsubsidized employers. A labor demand policy can ensure that those hired are still available for regular jobs by:

- requiring a job search before making the public or subsidized job available;
- making the job temporary in duration;
- requiring periodic job searches during the job-holding period; and
- making sure that wages in the newly created job are at least slightly inferior to normal entry-level jobs.

The displacement effects of labor demand policies can also be reduced if these policies target persons who are out of the labor force. That is, the displacement effects of increased labor demand are reduced if the increased labor demand is accompanied by increased labor supply. With more labor supply as well as labor demand, the policy results in less of an initial boost to wages, and hence less of a reduction in regular employment. In addition, such a policy does not reduce the availability of the target group for regular employers.

Targeting those who are not participating in the labor force and inducing them to do so may be difficult. Presumably some nonparticipants can be induced to participate by lowering the search costs of finding a job or by making the created job more attractive in terms of wages, working conditions, or career prospects. Of these alternatives, focusing on lower search costs and assistance in finding better jobs later would have the fewest adverse impacts on the transition from the newly created jobs to regular jobs. But whatever alternative is used to induce nonparticipants to participate in the labor force, these same inducements also make the jobs that are created attractive to the unemployed, not just to nonparticipants in the labor force. If the created jobs also pay more or offer better working conditions or career prospects, then these jobs will also be attractive to those who are already employed. Thus, administrative efforts must be made to hire for those jobs the individuals who are most likely to be out of the labor force and to avoid hiring those who would otherwise be employed or unemployed. This can be done to some extent by restricting eligibility for the created jobs to groups that would be expected to have significant rates of nonparticipation in the labor force. The administrative issues in targeting labor demand policies are discussed further in chapters 7 and 8.

A final way in which the long-run displacement effects of labor demand policies can be reduced is to have these created jobs lead to long-run "human capital" accumulation. Greater human capital accumulation should increase long-run wages and employment rates. Such human capital effects of labor demand policies, however, would also occur from policies that only temporarily increase labor demand. I now consider the long-run effects from temporary shocks to labor demand.

Long-Term Effects of Increased Labor Demand: Effects of Temporary Increases in Labor Demand

How can temporary increases in labor demand have effects on the long-run equilibrium employment rates or wage rates in the labor market? Such long-run equilibrium effects of short-run forces are referred to as "hysteresis," a term originating in physics and engineering. In those fields, the term is used to describe the behavior of magnetic fields in metals. Even after removal of a magnetic force, the properties of metals are not restored to their previous state.

As discussed in chapter 3, the hysteresis effects of temporary labor demand shocks may occur because of the human capital effects, broadly defined, of short-run demand increases. That is, because someone gets a job in the short run, he or she may be better able to get a job and be productive in the long run; the short-run job thus affects the individual's long-run equilibrium wage and employment rate. There are a number of ways in which short-run labor demand shocks may increase human capital.

For most of them, there is at least some case study and anecdotal evidence supporting the possibility that these hysteresis effects can occur.

Among the possible sources of the hysteresis effects of short-run demand shocks are the following:

Learning to Show Up at Work on Time Getting a job may help some individuals develop greater discipline in conforming their schedule to the requirements of the workplace. For example, in interviews with many ex-welfare recipients who participated in the Supported Work Program, Martha Ritter and Sandra Danziger (1983, 37) heard many individuals say that the program helped them get "used to the idea of getting up every day and going to work."

Learning to Deal Productively with Coworkers, Supervisors, and Customers Workers need to learn how to deal with a complex set of relationships with those they work with or for and, in some businesses, with the customers they serve. These relationships differ from normal private relationships in that they are ongoing relationships that must be continued even if the individuals do not like one another, and they must be productive. Job experience may help individuals in learning how to better manage such relationships in the future. Ritter and Danziger (1983, 29) interviewed several ex-welfare recipients who commented on how different their work relationships were from what they were used to: "I had to get used to being among people, professional people. I was shy, more or less. . . . Before I started to work, I was more or less home all the time." In her recent study of fast-food restaurant employees in Harlem, Katherine Newman (1999, 144) found that such jobs require considerable people skills in dealing with customers:

> [T]here are many unpredictable events in the course of a workday [of a fast-food employee] that require some finesse to manage. Chief among them are abrasive encounters with customers, who . . . often have nothing better to do than rake a poor working stiff over the coals for a missing catsup packet or a batch of french fries that aren't quite hot enough. One afternoon at a [fast-food restaurant] cash register is enough to send most sane people into psychological counseling. It takes patience, forbearance, and an eye for the long-range goal (of holding on to your job, of impressing management with your fortitude) to get through some of these encounters. If ever there was an illustration of "people skills," this would be it.

Acquiring Contacts for Future Jobs and a Good Reputation with Prospective Employers Getting a job in the short run may help an individual's reputation with prospective employers. Getting a job may also help provide an individual with more contacts with people who have jobs. These contacts may know of job openings and be willing to provide leads and recommendations. For example, Newman (1999, 73) found that most of the fast-food restaurant employees she interviewed in Harlem acquired their first job experience in the Summer Youth Jobs Program: "They were able to build on this experience: they could prove to the next employer that they had some experience and drive." Most of the fast-food workers she interviewed got their job by knowing someone who already worked in the restaurant. In their interviews with Supported Work Program participants, Ritter and Danziger (1983, 68) concluded: "The provision of basic job contacts in the regular job market was . . . an obvious and crucial Supported Work contribution to these women's lives." They give several examples of participants who used such contacts: "Sarah was selling tires, but when she was robbed, she quit, and with [the Supported Work Program contractor's] assistance, was granted an interview at GM. Although Aretha left Supported Work without a job, she later used a contact she had made to get work again" (30).

Acquiring Greater Self-Confidence in One's Ability to Do a Job Well For example, Ritter and Danziger (1983, 69) found that some of the Supported Work participants "found they could make the transition to working on a daily basis; they were surprised at their own performance levels and found others encouraging and impressed with their talent and motivation. They discovered themselves to be capable and hard workers."

Acquiring Hard Skills Through Formal and Informal On-the-Job Training According to the recent comprehensive review of on-the-job-training by John Barron, Mark Berger, and Dan Black (1997, 52), nearly all newly hired workers receive at least some training. Average training hours for high school graduates without a college degree amount to almost four forty-hour weeks during the first three months of work. Most of this training is informal—that is, training is provided on an as-needed basis by supervisors and coworkers rather than through a formal program with a set curriculum, a specific time for training, and specially trained instructors (113–14). This training results in considerable productivity growth, with 10 percent more training raising productivity by 2 percent during the first three months of employment (136). According to firms, most of the skills taught during OJT are of general use outside the firm rather than applicable only to the specific firm (142).

What empirical evidence is there about the long-run effects of temporary increases in labor demand on wages and employment rates, particularly the wages and employment rates of less-educated groups? I consider three types of evidence: micro evidence from studies that look at the effects of the individual work experience of specific individuals; macro evidence from studies that look at the effects of the past labor market environment rather than the specific employment experience of individuals; and experimental evidence of the effects of programs that provide some sort of work experience.[6]

Micro Evidence of the Effects of Increased Labor Demand

One approach to examining the long-run effects of increased labor demand is to estimate empirically the effects of an individual's work experience on his or her long-run earnings, wages, or employment rate. One common approach to such estimation is implicitly embodied in the traditional approach of economists to estimating the determinants of an individual's wage rate. As mentioned in chapter 3, labor economists traditionally assume that an individual's wages at any point in time depend on the number of years of actual job experience he or she has accumulated. This specification implicitly assumes that job experience has long-run effects. In fact, this particular specification assumes that a year of job experience five or ten years ago has as much effect on current wages as a year of job experience only one year ago, because accumulated experience is included in these wage equations without any depreciation (or, for that matter, appreciation) of its assumed returns. Although most wage equations do not control for the likelihood that individuals with greater experience are more productive for unobserved reasons, studies that have tried to control for unobservable productivity characteristics of individuals continue to find that experience affects wages (Altonji and Williams 1992, 1997; Bratsberg and Terrell 1998). As mentioned in chapter 3, actual work experience seems to have similar effects for less- and more-educated persons, but less effect for females and black males compared to white males (Gladden and Taber 2000; Bratsberg and Terrell 1998).

Traditional wage equations may understate the long-run effects of a short-run increase in employment due to increased labor demand. An increase in employment in one year may also increase employment in subsequent years. Thus, the total increase in work experience from a temporary increase in labor demand may be greater than just the short-run effect on work experience. This increases the wage effects of a short-run increase in experience above that of just one more year of experience. The earnings effects are even greater if there are long-run effects on the probability of finding a job or on the annual hours worked.

Some studies have explicitly looked at how more work experience in one year affects longer-run employment and wages. Most of these studies have focused on one of two particular types of workers and employment experiences: the longer-run effects on youths of their early employment or nonemployment, and the long-run effects of being displaced from a job owing to a plant closing or large-scale layoff.

Two of the most prominent studies of the long-run effects of out-of-school youth labor market experience are Ellwood (1982) for young men and Corcoran (1982) for young women.[7] Both studies attempted to identify the effects of exogenous changes in employment for youth—that is, the effects of the employment in and of itself, holding constant observed and unobserved personal characteristics. Both studies tried to use local demand conditions as instruments to shift exogenously youths' early employment experiences, but both were unable to get precise results using this approach. As an alternative, both studies identified the effects of exogenous changes in the employment experiences of youth by imposing some assumptions about how unobservable productivity might affect wages. Ellwood found only very short-term and limited persistence in the work hours of male youths. But the early out-of-school work experience of males was found to have major long-run (four years later) effects on wages. An extra year of work was found to increase wages four years later by 10 to 20 percent. Corcoran's study of young women found more persistence in work hours in the short run than Ellwood found for young men. She found strong long-run effects of women's early work experience on wage rates, but not as strong as the effects found for men by Ellwood.

The research literature on the effects of the displacement of workers from jobs due to plant closings or mass layoffs tends to find large, persistent effects (see, for example, Jacobson, LaLonde, and Sullivan 1993; Stevens 1995). Studies of displacement due to plant closings or mass layoffs have the advantage that the change in work experience caused by such displacement is plausibly exogenous to the individual, that is, unrelated to unobserved individual characteristics that might affect future wages or employment rates. The earnings of workers are initially reduced by displacement by perhaps 20 to 40 percent, with from one-third to two-thirds of this reduction persisting after five years. (For a review that includes studies by Topel [1990] and Jacobsen, Lalonde, and Sullivan [1993], as well as her own work, see Stevens [1995].) However, the long-run effects of displacement seem considerably lower for workers with low job tenure, that is, less time on the job they lose owing to displacement. Among workers with low job tenure (less than three years), perhaps only 20 percent of the initial earnings loss persists after five years (Stevens 1995). The long-run effects of displacement are also lower for those with a high school degree or less, for whom, again, only 10 to 25 percent of the initial earnings loss persists after five years (Stevens 1995).[8] Most of the long-run effects of job displacement on earnings appear to be due to the effects on long-run wage rates.

Although studies of the youth labor market and the effects of plant closings are suggestive, it is unclear how generalizable these findings are to the effects of increased employment due to expanded labor demand under all circumstances for low-education workers. For this project, I estimated a new model, using panel data, of how much work in one year affects earnings five years later (Bartik 2000d). The estimated effects of work on future earnings are potentially biased upward by individual effects on productivity, since individuals who are more productive are likely to work more and at higher wages in many years. To control for individual productivity effects, I included a fixed effect for each individual in the sample, as well as numerous controls for time-varying individual characteristics, such as earnings prior to five years ago. Appendix 8 gives more detail on the model.

Table 5.10 reports the resulting estimates of the effects of working 2,000 hours at the average wage for each demographic group, for four demographic groups: female and males, high school dropouts and graduates. The estimated effects are reported in raw dollars and as a proportion of the original change in earnings.

These estimates imply that 10 to 25 percent of a shock to real earnings still increases earnings five years later. These results generally seem consistent with the estimates for low-tenure workers in the research literature on displaced workers.

Macro Evidence: Long-Term Effects of the Past Macro Environment

Two studies have looked at how the employment rate today depends on past levels of aggregate labor market conditions. These two studies differ from the studies reviewed earlier because they look at what is happening to the labor market's overall employment rate or unemployment rate rather than at the labor market experiences of individuals.

In Bartik (1993a), I reexamine the evidence from Blanchard and Katz (1992) on the long-run effects of a once-and-for-all shock to the level of a state's employment. Blanchard and Katz had concluded that an increase in state employment has effects on labor force participation and employment rates, but that such effects die out after five to seven years. However, their model is restrictive, because labor force participation and employment rates are affected by only two lagged years of state employment (along with two lags in the dependent variables). Reestimating these models using the same data, I found that if state employment growth is allowed to enter with as many additional lags as are statistically justified, the effects of employment growth on labor force participation become far more persistent.

Figure 5.3, derived from Bartik (1993a), contrasts the Blanchard and Katz (1992) and Bartik estimates. The effects of a onetime shock to state

TABLE 5.10 *Earnings Effects Five Years Later of Employment for 2,000 Hours per Year, at Mean Wage for Each Group, Compared to Zero Annual Work Hours*

Group	Earnings Effects Five Years Later	Earnings Effects as Proportion of Initial Earnings Shock
Female high school dropouts	$1,617	0.117
	(257)	
Female high school graduates (but not college graduates)	4,674	0.246
	(283)	
Male high school dropouts	3,191	0.125
	(1,077)	
Male high school graduates	4,559	0.133
	(1,775)	

Source: Estimates are based on model and data described more fully in Bartik (2000d) and appendix 8. Standard error of estimation is in parentheses. Estimates are based on panel data on individuals from the PSID, 1975 to 1991.
Notes: All estimates include only individuals for whom we have fifteen years of observations, and who were household head or wife during each of those fifteen years. Model regresses annual individual earnings on a number of control variables and three variables reflecting employment experiences of that individual five years before: a dummy for whether he or she worked at all during the year; the annual work hours during that year; the ln of the wage rate (annual earnings/annual hours) for those who worked five years before. Those not working are arbitrarily assigned a mean wage, but this is of no consequence because of the inclusion of the dummy for whether the individual worked five years before. Control variables include: fixed effects for year and state of residence; fixed effects for each individual; the individual's average earnings during the period from six to eight years before; discrete variables for whether the individual is married, whether the individual is black, whether the individual is Hispanic, and whether the individual has any children; the number of children; the years of education of the individual; the standard experience proxy (age − education − 6); experience squared. The model is estimated separately for the four groups included in the table. The number of individuals/observations, where an observation is an individual by year cell, are: female high school dropout: 407/6,732; female high school graduate: 665/10,940; male high school dropout: 364/5,967; male high school graduates: 217/3,530. The mean wage rates used to generate these simulations are: female high school dropout: $6.93 per hour; female high school graduate: $9.50; male high school dropout: $12.77; male high school graduate: $17.17. The simulations consider simultaneous change in two variables: the dummy for working changes from zero to one, and the annual work hours changes from zero to 2,000. The wage rate in this simulation does not change because those not working are arbitrarily assigned the mean wage anyway.

employment growth or a once-and-for-all increase in the employment level on the labor force participation rate seems to stabilize at about one-fifth of the original employment shock, with little sign of dying out after seventeen years.

It should be recalled that these are estimates of the effects of a once-and-for-all shock to labor demand, not a shock to labor demand that is later reversed. However, labor force participation rates are higher in the long run even though unemployment rates have returned to their original level. Other research suggests that overall real wages due to an employment shock at the local level are not much higher, controlling for occupation. Hence, it seems reasonable to conclude that these higher labor force participation rates are due to greater human capital accumulated by individuals in the short run owing to the shock to labor demand.

Alec Levenson (1996) uses data from the 1990 census to examine how the employment rates and annual work hours of different groups of workers ages thirty-one to forty-five are related to unemployment rates in their state of birth during the years that each worker was sixteen to twenty-five. He also controls for the individual's state of birth and age. Hence, the variation in the unemployment rate variable is coming about through variation in the state of birth's economic conditions over time. Levenson is essentially asking whether an individual who happened to enter the labor market when his or her state's economy was weak does economically worse in later life than someone who entered the labor market when his or her state's economy was strong. Levenson found some evidence that higher unemployment when entering the labor market reduced later employment of white women, black women, and black men, but not white men.

Experimental Evidence

Perhaps the ideal evidence would be experimental evidence of the effects of randomly assigned extra work experience. The closest to such an ideal study was a study of the long-run effects of the Supported Work Program by Kenneth Couch (1992). As noted earlier, Supported Work provided a very special form of work experience: work with gradually increasing stress and expectations, combined with some counseling, mentoring, and training. Furthermore, Supported Work sites deliberately tried to help participants gain long-run success by providing help in locating new jobs after the subsidized work period was over. Hence, the estimated effects of Supported Work should not be interpreted as necessarily representing the effects of any type of work experience, but rather of the type of work experience that might be provided by a generously funded government work program.

Couch's results suggest that the Supported Work Program's positive effects on the earnings of ex-welfare recipients showed little or no sign of diminishing even eight years after the subsidized jobs were over. Table 5.11 reproduces some of Couch's results for the fourth through the eighth years after the end of the subsidized jobs. As with studies of training programs, the average effects estimated here presumably represent some mix of higher and lower effects for different individuals. The constant average effects for the entire experimental group over time could reflect two conflicting trends. For some individuals, the help from Supported Work may have tended to die out in its influence over time as other more recent life

FIGURE 5.3 *Effect over Time of a 1 Percent Increase in a State's Employment on State Employment Rate and Labor Force Participation Rates: Comparing Blanchard and Katz's (1992) Estimates with Modified Estimates That Use More Flexible Specification of Possible Long-Run Effects*

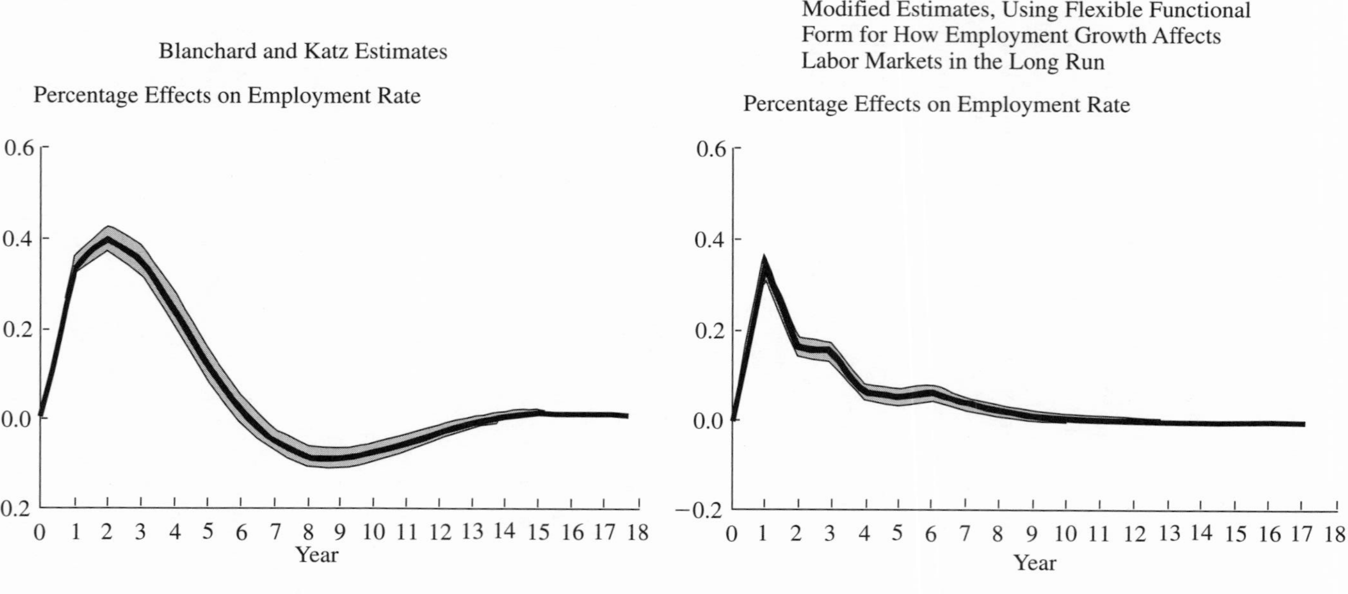

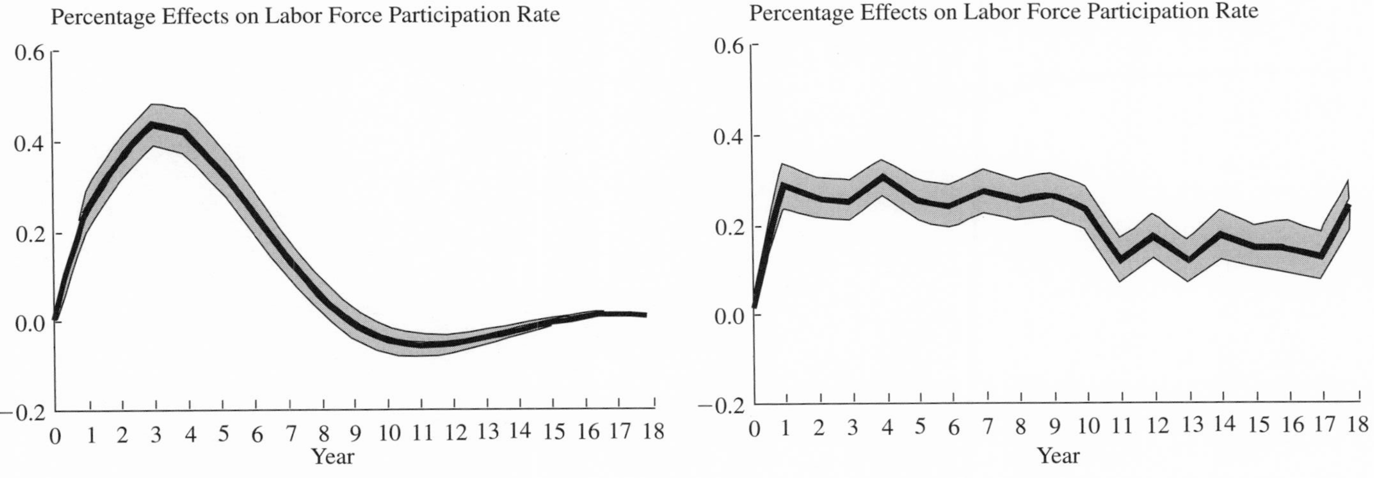

Source: Derived from Bartik (1993a).

Notes: Both sets of estimates use the same database. Blanchard and Katz (1992) allow for labor force participation and employment rates to be affected by only two lagged years of state employment; Bartik (1993a) allows for effects from up to seventeen lagged years of state employment. Figures show changes over time in employment rates and labor force participation rates in response to once-and-for-all 1 percent shock to employment. Years are years after employment increase. Employment rate is defined as employment/(labor force). One standard error to either side of point estimates is shown by the thin lines in the figure.

TABLE 5.11 *Estimates of Long-Term Average Effects of the Supported Work Program on the Annual Earnings of Female Welfare Recipients*

Year	Annual Earnings Effect (1998 Dollars)
1982 (Four years after program was over)	$1,093
	(570)
1983	1,140
	(498)
1984	1,313
	(503)
1985	1,033
	(518)
1986 (Eight years after program was over)	938
	(558)

Source: Derived from Couch (1992, table 1).
Note: Standard errors are in parentheses.

events became more important. For others, the effects of Supported Work may have tended to increase over time as they used the initial push from the program to move on to a better career ladder.

Labor Market Effects of Types of Jobs: Wages and Other Job Characteristics

As discussed in chapter 3, there is extensive evidence—albeit evidence that is not conclusive to all economists—that similar workers earn wages that differ by 10 to 20 percent in different industries and firms. Therefore, one way to increase the earnings of the poor is to increase their placement in higher-earnings industries and firms.

In addition to immediately providing higher earnings, higher-wage jobs may also promote longer-run job retention and higher earnings. Empirically, these job retention and long-run earnings benefits of higher-wage jobs may be large enough to be important. In Bartik (1997), I found that for female ex-welfare recipients, 10 percent higher wages during a given year are associated with a 1 percent greater probability of being employed the following March, and with 4 percent greater weekly earnings the next March. In Bartik (2000d; see also appendix 8), I found that among women with less than a college degree, 10 percent greater wages are associated with 1 to 4 percent greater earnings five years later, depending on the specification used and the group considered; among men with less than a college degree, 10 percent greater wages are associated with 0.2 to 3 percent greater earnings five years later (see table A8.4). Although higher-wage jobs are more desirable to retain and more likely to lead to higher future wages if retained, such jobs may also have more stringent work requirements, resulting in more firings by employers.

Although greater access by the poor to higher-wage jobs is desirable, simply increasing the proportion of higher-wage jobs in the labor market, without increasing overall labor demand, may be an ineffective strategy for improving the labor market fortunes of the poor. Several empirical studies show that, holding constant overall labor market conditions, increasing the proportion of jobs that are in manufacturing or other higher-wage jobs does increase overall earnings (Bartik 1996b, 1993b; Bound and Holzer 1993; Borjas and Ramey 1994; Juhn 1999). This increase in earnings occurs in part through higher wages and in part through higher labor force participation rates (Bartik 1993b, 1996b). However, the earnings benefits of a greater share of total employment in higher-wage jobs are concentrated among the middle class (Bartik 1996b). Holding the overall number of jobs constant, shifts in the labor market toward a greater share of jobs that are higher-wage appears to do nothing to reduce poverty (Bartik 1993b, 1996b). The smallness of the benefits for the poor from a more high-wage industrial mix may reflect the greater competition for these higher-wage jobs, because these jobs cause middle-class households to increase their labor force participation. Even with more higher-wage jobs around, the likelihood that the poor will be hired for them may be unchanged.

As discussed earlier, the access of the poor to higher-wage jobs is improved by stronger overall labor demand. Stronger labor demand significantly increases the probability that an individual with low education can be hired in a higher-wage occupation. Employers in labor markets with strong overall labor demand are forced to relax their hiring requirements.

Stronger overall labor demand in the U.S. economy or a local economy is associated with a general upgrading in job quality. When national unemployment is low, the mix of jobs actually filled shifts toward higher-wage occupations (Okun 1973; Bartik 1991). Metropolitan areas with stronger job growth shift their industrial mix toward higher-wage industries (Bartik 1993b). Presumably, in a high-growth economy, low-wage industries find it difficult to hire workers and their expansion is discouraged, while higher-wage industries and firms continue to expand. Higher-wage industries in a local economy also appear to encourage higher overall growth, perhaps by giving a greater boost to local consumer demand. Therefore, it is somewhat artificial to consider the labor market effects on the poor of either overall labor demand or industrial mix, holding the other variable constant. Growth and higher-wage jobs tend to go together.

Appropriate design of labor demand policies may also increase the access of the poor to higher-wage jobs. For example, if a local area adopts economic development policies that seek to shift the local industrial mix toward higher-wage jobs, policies that screen and place disadvantaged residents in these new jobs may be helpful. Possible mechanisms for implementing such policies are considered in chapter 9.

One could certainly imagine that other job characteristics would also be important to the labor market success of the poor. Some jobs may require skills that build on the experiences of the poor outside the labor market with child and home care, or they may provide more on-the-job-training or allow for more patience by employers as the poor develop their job skills. However, few studies have been done of how job characteristics affect job retention. In Bartik (1997), I found that among ex-welfare recipients, job retention is more likely among those who get jobs in the hospital industry and the educational services industry. Job retention is less likely for individuals who find jobs in the temporary help industry or who are employed as cashiers. Cashier jobs may involve more pressure to perform quickly and accurately. Employment as an aide in hospitals or schools may involve elder care, child care, or cleanup services, activities that are similar to the previous experiences of ex-welfare recipients at home.

Conclusion

In sum, the empirical evidence suggests that increased labor demand can significantly increase the employment and earnings of the poor. Aggregate labor demand has progressive effects, but of modest enough size that by itself aggregate demand cannot come close to solving the employment and earnings problems of the poor. More targeted labor demand policies can significantly increase the employment and earnings of the poor, with the net increase in the short run being about 60 to 90 percent of the labor demand shock. Perhaps 10 to 20 percent of the short-run increase in employment and earnings from increased labor demand persists in the long run, probably owing to increased skills, self-esteem, reputation, and job contacts of the poor who get jobs in the short run. Labor demand increases that get the poor into higher-wage jobs have greater effects on earnings, both in the short run and the long run. Finally, the displacement effects of labor demand increases can be minimized if those increases are targeted on poor persons who otherwise would be out of the labor force, and by encouraging those who gain jobs from these policies to continue searching for regular jobs. Future chapters consider how specific labor demand policies can achieve some of these goals. But before considering specific policies, the next chapter considers one perennial criticism of labor demand policies: Will labor demand policies lead to increased inflation?

6

ARE LABOR DEMAND POLICIES INFLATIONARY?

An important concern about policies that dramatically increase the employment of the poor through increased labor demand is that such policies might lead to an inflationary spiral. Lower unemployment might cause price inflation (the rate of change in prices over some time interval) to increase, resulting in an increase in inflationary expectations and, in turn, in still further increases in inflation. Inflation would continue to accelerate until unemployment increases, perhaps owing to the Federal Reserve reacting to the accelerating inflation by taking actions to increase interest rates and restrain money supply growth.

Most economists assume that although an unemployment rate that is too low may cause inflation problems, greater employment of the poor does not have inflationary effects. In contrast, I argue that labor demand policies that meet a substantial share of the job needs of low-income Americans do at least *potentially* pose inflationary problems. However, these potential inflationary problems can be minimized if labor demand policies are properly designed. This chapter outlines how labor demand policies should be designed to minimize problems with inflation.

Why Lower Unemployment Among the Poor Might Cause Inflationary Problems

Mainstream economic theory holds that there is some unemployment rate that is a NAIRU (non-accelerating inflation rate of unemployment). Policies that reduce unemployment below that unemployment rate lead to ever-accelerating inflation until unemployment is brought back to the NAIRU, through either policy actions or private market adjustments.[1] The NAIRU theory is based on the notion that unemployment below the NAIRU causes wages to increase relative to the price level that workers expect, based on either past levels of prices and inflation rates or other information workers have about inflation. These wage increases in turn cause prices to increase further relative to what workers expect, resulting in still further increases in wages. If the causal effects of wages on prices, and prices on wages, are strong enough, then any unemployment rate below the NAIRU eventually results in ever-accelerating inflation until the NAIRU is restored.[2] In fact, if we want to eliminate the "excess inflation" brought about by this unemployment below the NAIRU, the economy has to endure some period in which unemployment is above the NAIRU.

In the NAIRU model, inflation accelerates below some positive unemployment rate because there is some unemployment that is built into the workings and structure of the labor market even when effective labor demand and labor supply in the labor market are roughly in balance. A normal labor market would be expected to have some level of "frictional unemployment"—that is, unemployment that occurs as unemployed workers or new labor market entrants search for new jobs and employers with newly created jobs or vacancies in current jobs search for new workers. The level of frictional unemployment is higher as increases occur in the information problems in the labor market (discussed in chapter 3), that is, as employers have trouble finding the right workers and workers have trouble finding the right employers. Frictional unemployment is also greater in a more dynamic labor market—one with greater rates of labor force entry or new job creation. In addition, problems with the structure of the labor market may add on top of the frictional unemployment a layer of structural unemployment—unemployment that for some reason does not provide an effective source of labor supply for employers with vacancies, even if information in the labor market is perfect. For example, there may be structural mismatches between what employers demand and what unemployed workers can provide, including:

- *Skills mismatch:* Employers demand skills that the unemployed do not supply.
- *Geographic mismatch:* Employers' and workers' locations are far enough apart that the costs of mobility for either or both do not allow easy hiring.
- *Discrimination mismatch:* Some employers' arbitrary prejudices against certain groups of workers do not allow unemployed workers from these groups to be seen as adequate job candidates.

Unemployment above the level determined by frictional and structural unemployment is sometimes referred to as "demand-deficient unemployment."

If the overall unemployment rate drops below the level due to frictional or structural factors, employers are not able to find adequate supplies of labor quickly enough to match job vacancies. This puts upward pressure on wages relative to prices. In turn, increases in wages put upward pressure on prices. The upward pressure on prices puts further upward pressure on wages. If the feedback effects between wages and prices are strong enough—and there are economic theories and econometric evidence that suggest that these feedback effects are strong enough in the United States—this leads to a spiral of accelerating inflation.[3]

Despite the general acceptance of the NAIRU theory among most economists, they implicitly or explicitly assume that greater employment of the poor is not inflationary. In part, many economists implicitly assume that employment programs for the poor are unlikely under current U.S. political conditions to be large enough to affect significantly the macro economy. But another implicit assumption of economists is that even large-scale increases in employment that are targeted at the poor are not inflationary. For example, Richard Freeman and Peter Gottschalk (1998, 3), in the introduction to their edited volume on micro demand-side policies to help less-skilled workers—a volume that includes discussions of public-service jobs and wage subsidies—explicitly state that "by [micro demand-side policies] we mean policies that affect employers' demand for labor without risking the macroeconomic problems of inflation." Logically, large-scale increases in labor demand for disadvantaged groups can avoid posing inflationary problems only if at least one of the following conditions holds: (1) there is something wrong with the NAIRU theory; (2) the labor demand increases lead to increases in the labor force rather than unemployment reductions; or (3) the labor demand increases lead to reductions in structural-frictional unemployment. I agree with the opinion of most economists that labor demand increases for the poor need not be inflationary. But I think that it is important to determine precisely why and under what conditions such demand increases are not inflationary. Such an explicit understanding will help us design labor demand policies for the poor that are less likely to be inflationary.

Large-scale labor demand policies to reduce poverty could have large enough effects on overall unemployment to lead to concerns about accelerating inflation. For example, chapter 3 argued that we might need to increase the employment of disadvantaged groups by three to nine million jobs. Consider six million jobs as a midpoint estimate of the number of jobs that might be needed. If employment is expanded by six million owing to a labor demand increase, we would normally expect this to be accommodated by some combination of lower unemployment and greater labor force participation. The empirical estimates reviewed in chapter 3 suggest that normally a one-point reduction in unemployment is accompanied by a half-point increase in labor force participation. Thus, we would normally expect that for every three jobs added by an employment expansion brought about by greater labor demand, two of these jobs would be filled from the ranks of the unemployed and the other job would be filled by someone who was originally outside the labor force. Therefore, absent some special design features to the labor demand expansion, a labor demand increase targeted at the poor of six million jobs would be expected to reduce the number of unemployed by four million and to add two million participants to the U.S. labor force. An unemployment reduction of four million people, out of a U.S. labor force of 137.7 million in 1998, would be an unemployment rate reduction of 2.9 percent. With unemployment already at 4.5 percent, this would imply an unemployment rate reduction to 1.6 percent. It is certainly reasonable to be doubtful that a peacetime U.S. economy could achieve such a low unemployment rate without unsustainable inflationary pressures. Unemployment rates that low were attained in the United States only during World War II, when the country adopted stringent price controls that would be difficult to sustain in peacetime.

In this chapter I critically examine six arguments that can be made for why labor demand policies to increase the employment of the poor might *not* be inflationary, including: a stable NAIRU might not exist; the inflationary effects of job creation might be considerably reduced by targeting the new jobs at particular groups in various ways; and some demand policies, such as wage subsidies, might reduce inflation by lowering business costs. Each of these arguments has implications for the appropriate design of labor demand policies to reduce poverty.

Argument 1

A stable NAIRU might not exist.

There is no universal agreement among economists that there is some unemployment rate below which inflation endlessly accelerates. NAIRU models relate price *inflation* or wage *inflation* to the unemployment rate, with strong effects of past price inflation on future price and wage inflation.[4] Some theoretical models of wage or price setting relate wage or price *levels* to the unemployment rate, not wage or price inflation. For example, various efficiency wage models lead to a model in which the real wage *level* depends on the unemployment rate (Blanchflower and Oswald 1994).[5] In these theoretical models, lower unemployment rates in the long run lead to a higher price level, not ever-accelerating inflation.

Empirical work that tests the NAIRU model using U.S. data yields mixed results. Some empirical work on U.S. price and wage inflation supports the notion that unemployment below some NAIRU leads to an accelerating inflation spiral. But other empirical work suggests that lower unemployment, while it leads to accelerating inflation for some period of time, eventually leads either to somewhat higher but stable inflation or, in some models, to higher wages or prices but inflation no higher than it was originally (Fair 1997, 1999, 2000; Eisner 1995a, 1995b; Stock and Watson 1999).

Still, despite this uncertainty about the long-run effects of lower unemployment, both NAIRU and non-NAIRU models of the inflationary process agree that a decrease in unemployment, if accompanied by the usual changes in the economy associated with lower unemployment—such as greater capacity utilization rates for the national capital stock—is associated with prices and inflation being higher than they otherwise would be in the short run and medium run. Both NAIRU and non-NAIRU models often yield predictions for the effects of lower unemployment on prices and inflation that are similar, at least for the short and medium run. Even in NAIRU models the accelerating inflation that is predicted from unemployment being too low seems to take a while to develop.[6] Because NAIRU and non-NAIRU models make similar short-run and medium-run predictions, it is often difficult to choose between these models using the relatively short-time series available in U.S. national data.[7]

One criticism of the NAIRU model is that lower unemployment may not be the real driving force behind accelerations in inflation. Recent research by James Stock and Mark Watson (1999) suggests that there are better predictors for inflation than unemployment. In particular, capacity utilization in manufacturing, mining, and utilities—a measure of actual output in these industrial sectors relative to potential output given their capital stock—appears to do better than unemployment in predicting inflation. This is consistent with the belief that greater capacity utilization directly causes increases in price inflation, which in turn cause wage inflation to increase. Several other studies have suggested that in the United States the causation from prices to wages in the inflation process is much stronger than the causation from wages to prices (Gordon 1988, 1998; Emery and Chang 1996; Campbell and Rissman 1994; Fair 2000, 68, n. 8). It may be in the product market, not the labor market, that the crucial bottlenecks develop that give rise to inflationary pressures. This suggests that unemployment can perhaps be lowered if we can at the same time avoid increasing capacity utilization rates or other indicators of product market demand conditions.

Finally, even if there is a NAIRU, there is considerable uncertainty about exactly what it is, or how it may change. Staiger, Stock, and Watson's (1997a, 1997b) work suggests that the statistical uncertainty alone in the estimated NAIRU, assuming we know the right equation to estimate the NAIRU and that the true NAIRU is constant, may cover a range of three percentage points.[8] In addition, different procedures for estimating the NAIRU can yield point estimates of the NAIRU that may vary by 1 percent or so at a point in time. Finally, recent NAIRU models have begun estimating a "time-varying" NAIRU, which seems to better fit the data (Gordon 1997, 1998; Staiger, Stock, and Watson 1997a, 1997b). Beyond these statistical results, considerable uncertainty about the NAIRU is suggested by the recent experience in the United States of low inflation even though unemployment is well below previously hypothesized NAIRU levels.

Given this uncertainty about whether there is a NAIRU in the long run, the long time that it takes for inflationary pressures to develop, the uncertainty about what the NAIRU is, and the possibility that inflation may be driven more by product market demand conditions than by unemployment, perhaps the best advice to policymakers is to try slowly and steadily to reduce unemployment until there is some clear evidence of inflationary pressures stemming from the labor market. We may not be able to reduce unemployment dramatically from its 1999 level of 4.2 percent, but we should not seek to increase it to some hypothesized NAIRU to avoid an accelerating inflation that may never occur. Economists should be humble about pushing the NAIRU theory too far given recent experience. Our models appear to have been a misleading guide to policy. Labor market policy toward lower unemployment should be guided at least in part by actual experience, not by solely relying on uncertain models.

Argument 2

Significantly lower unemployment among disadvantaged groups might have little effect on inflation, and those effects could be offset by modest increases in the unemployment of advantaged groups, resulting in a lower overall NAIRU or structural unemployment rate.

An important reason why most economists believe that increased labor demand for the poor will have little effect on inflation is that most of them assume that this would reduce structural unemployment. If most unemployment among the poor is structural, then the characteristics of these unemployed are not well matched to employers' labor demands. The relative availability of this ill-matched labor might be expected to have little effect on wages. Labor demand policies that reduce the unemployment of the poor would not cause inflationary problems.

This argument was more formally developed some years ago by the Nobel Prize winner James Tobin, along with Martin Neil Baily (Baily and Tobin 1977, 1978). They considered a labor market divided into groups, with some groups having high unemployment rates and other groups having low unemployment rates. Unemployment is more likely to be structural among the high-unemployment groups, since their high unemployment suggests that their characteristics are not well matched to employers' labor demands. Tobin and Baily's theory relied on the intuitively plausible notion that the inflationary effects of a 1 percent reduction in unemployment are much larger at low levels of unemployment, that is, a reduction from 5 percent to 4 percent unemployment has greater inflationary consequences than a reduction from 11 percent to 10 percent.[9] There is some empirical support for this proposition in estimates of *aggregate* wage equations relating overall average wages or wage inflation to overall unemployment rates (Grubb 1986; Blanchflower and Oswald 1994).

Suppose high-unemployment and low-unemployment groups can be considered distinct groups in the labor market, with each group's wages largely determined by its own unemployment rate. In that case, one might expect the effects of lower unemployment on the high-unemployment group's wages to be lower simply because of the higher unemployment rate. The implicit assumption of this analysis is that if both groups had similar levels of unemployment, a 1 percent reduction in each group's unemployment rate would have similar effects on each group's wages. Under these assumptions, a redistribution of unemployment away from disadvantaged groups can lower overall unemployment without increasing wage inflation pressures.

Arthur Okun, who served on and then chaired President Lyndon Johnson's Council of Economic Advisers, some years ago criticized the Tobin-Baily model precisely on the grounds that different groups in the labor market might have very different reactions to changes in unemployment, starting at the same unemployment level.[10] In particular, Okun (1973) argued that the more-skilled workers might be more important for firms to retain, and hence that firms are more likely to enter into explicit and implicit long-term wage arrangements with these more-skilled workers that tend to insulate their wage rates from cyclical changes in unemployment. Because firms have less invested in the less-skilled workers, they are more willing to simply let wages for these workers be determined by current market conditions, rising and falling with the unemployment rate.

To put Okun's argument into the language of structural unemployment, it is precisely because more-advantaged groups have characteristics that are well matched to employers' demands that employers adopt wage policies that make their wages less sensitive to unemployment. The mismatch of groups with high structural unemployment means that employers may adopt wage policies that allow these groups' wages to fluctuate greatly with unemployment.

Another important point is that the wage rates of different groups may be determined more by overall unemployment in the labor market than by the relative unemployment rates of different groups. This argument was made in chapter 3, and some empirical evidence in favor of this proposition is offered in appendix 2. If this is the case, then redistributing unemployment among different groups, with overall unemployment unchanged, will not have much effect on inflationary pressures on overall wages.

In Bartik (2000c) and in appendix 9, I have estimated and simulated several models for how group wages and prices in metropolitan area labor markets are affected by local unemployment and national economic trends. These estimates also suggest that the wages of different groups in the labor force depend much less on the group's unemployment than on overall local unemployment. To the extent to which relative wages respond to relative group unemployment rates, relative wages are modestly more sensitive to relative unemployment for disadvantaged groups. Simulations using this model suggest that reducing the relative unemployment of disadvantaged groups tends to slightly increase inflationary pressures.

Therefore, it should at least be doubtful whether labor demand policies to reduce unemployment among the poor will have small inflationary effects. The unemployment of the poor may be due to structural features of the labor market, but the structure of the labor market is such that disadvantaged groups' wages increase at least as much in response to unemployment reductions as the wages of more advantaged groups.

Argument 3

Inflationary pressures from lower unemployment might be reduced by focusing the unemployment reduction on local labor markets with high unemployment, thereby allowing lower overall national unemployment without increased inflationary pressures.

As mentioned earlier, there is ample evidence that the wage increases in a local area from reducing unemployment by 1 percent tend to be somewhat lower if unemployment is initially high in the local labor market. Local wage increases also depend on national economic trends in unemployment, wages, and prices. However, the available research, reviewed in chapter 3, suggests that national economic trends are less important than local unemployment in determining local wages.

Because of this behavior of local wages, targeting an unemployment reduction at high-unemployment local labor markets, compared to lowering unemployment equally everywhere, should result in less upward pressure on average national wages. With less upward pressure on national wages, there is less upward pressure on national prices. Therefore, targeting unemployment reductions at high-unemployment areas, and offsetting this with slightly higher unemployment in low-unemployment areas, would be expected to result in no increased inflationary pressures from a lower average national unemployment rate.

In Bartik (2000c, summarized in appendix 9), I use an estimated model of group wages and prices in different metropolitan areas to simulate the inflationary effects of different geographic distributions of unemployment. These simulations suggest that targeting high-unemployment areas, instead of reducing unemployment everywhere equally, cuts inflationary pressures in half, for the same drop in overall unemployment.

Argument 4

Inflationary pressures from increased labor demand might be reduced by focusing the increase so that it increases effective labor supply, either by increasing labor force participation or reducing long-term unemployment.

If labor demand increases are targeted at nonparticipants in the labor market, it may be possible to increase employment rates with minimal effect on the unemployment rate. This should reduce inflationary effects from labor market pressures for higher wages, since research shows that wage rates are better predicted by unemployment rates than by employment rates (Bartik 2000c; Blanchflower and Oswald 1994). Of course, an increase in employment rates would still be associated with increased capacity utilization and with increased inflationary pressures from the product market. Still, the lower labor market pressures should contribute to lower overall inflationary pressures.

Layard, Nickell, and Jackman (1991) and others have argued that inflationary pressures can also be reduced by targeting unemployment reductions at the long-term unemployed. The argument is that the long-term unemployed are less effective in searching for and obtaining jobs owing to their lack of self-confidence, the deterioration in their job skills, their lack of job contacts, and their poor reputation with employers. This theory that a lower proportion of long-term unemployment results in lower inflationary pressures, for a given unemployment rate, is supported by some empirical evidence (see evidence reviewed by Layard, Nickell, and Jackman [1991, 204] and their estimates [422]).

However, in the United States a relatively small proportion of the unemployed are long-term unemployed compared to most Western European countries. For example, in 1998, 8 percent of U.S. unemployed had been unemployed more than a year, whereas the proportion of the unemployed who had been unemployed more than a year was 44 percent in France, 52 percent in Germany, and 33 percent in the United Kingdom (OECD 1999, 242, table G). These differences suggest that many people who would be long-term unemployed in European countries are out of the labor force in the United States. These differences may be attributable to greater financial support for the long-term unemployed in many European countries than in the United States; for example, unemployment benefits last much longer in many European countries than in the United States.

Even if demand increases are not particularly targeted at those not participating in the labor force or at the long-term unemployed, they may increase employment in these groups enough to allow some long-term increases in overall employment rates without inflationary pressures. As argued in chapter 5, there is considerable evidence that demand shocks lead to long-term hysteresis effects on the equilibrium labor force participation rate and the employment rate. For example, as shown in figure 5.3, demand shocks that increase the overall employment in a local labor market cause only short-run reductions in unemployment but cause both short-run and long-run increases in labor force participation rates. Therefore, even without any targeting of aggregate demand, running the economy at a generally higher level of the overall employment rate puts some upward pressure over time on the equilibrium employment rate, although it may not reduce the equilibrium unemployment rate. For example, avoiding lengthy or severe recessions in the short run may increase the labor force participation rate or employment rate that the economy can achieve in the long run.

Argument 5

The inflationary effects of public employment programs for the disadvantaged may be reduced or eliminated if these programs are designed to maximize the access of those employed to the regular job market.

Although a public employment program lowers the unemployment rate, this reduction in the unemployment rate has the usual effects on wage inflation only if it lowers the effective labor supply to employers as much as an ordinary reduction in the unemployment rate. If special requirements and services are attached to these public-service jobs, public-service employment may not lower effective labor supply to regular employers by very much. For example, public employment programs can require prior job search and periodic job search while the person has the job. Public-service jobs could be made temporary by entitling those holding them to only a limited duration of job tenure. Job search by the public job holders could be encouraged by making the wage rates of such jobs somewhat below what these individuals would be expected to make at regular jobs. The job search of those holding public-service jobs could be made more effective by the efforts of job developers to market these public-service employees to regular employers. If the public-service jobs involve progressively increasing job pressures, as in the Supported Work Program, and are designed to encourage skills development, the job holders may become employable at a wider variety of regular jobs. Because of all of these measures, those holding public-service jobs are still searching for and obtaining regular jobs and may be putting almost as much downward pressure on wages in regular jobs as they would if they were unemployed. As discussed in chapter 5, these measures would also help decrease the long-term displacement effects of public-service jobs on regular employment.

There is some evidence that some types of jobs can help reduce the inflationary effects on wages of a given level of unemployment. For example, Lawrence Katz and Alan Krueger (1999) find that in states where a larger proportion of jobs were temporary help jobs in the late 1980s, the wage inflation effects of a given level of unemployment during the 1990s were lower. Katz and Krueger argue that this may occur because temporary help agencies increase the efficiency with which workers are matched with firms, allowing a lower level of unemployment to be achieved without increasing wage inflation pressures. Programs that explicitly design public-service jobs for the disadvantaged as temporary jobs and make strong attempts to link job holders with regular employers may be similarly able to lower unemployment without increasing wage inflation pressures.

Argument 6

Wage subsidies for hiring the disadvantaged might reduce inflationary pressures by lowering employers' marginal costs.

Even though a reduction in unemployment tends to increase wage pressures, the effects of this on labor costs may be more than offset by the wage subsidy; otherwise, employment would not expand. There may be some increased short-run inflationary pressures from greater capacity utilization, but still, overall, one would expect lower unemployment achieved through wage subsidies to be less inflationary than lower unemployment achieved through normal increases in aggregate demand. In addition, because wage subsidies cause some substitution of labor for capital, any given level of unemployment is achieved at a lower capacity utilization rate, which also reduces inflationary pressures.

In theory, wage subsidies should help lower inflation only if the wage subsidy is designed so that it lowers the marginal costs of labor for many firms. As I discuss in chapter 8, wage subsidies to employers for hiring or employing disadvantaged groups can be designed in many ways. For example, a wage subsidy program might provide only a fixed number of subsidies to a relatively small number of firms. In this case, we would not expect the program to have enough effect on marginal costs for enough firms to have an effect on prices.[11] Other wage subsidies are provided as an entitlement to large numbers of firms and are more likely to put significant downward pressures on marginal costs and prices.

Little empirical research has been done on how wage subsidies to employers affect prices. John Bishop (1981) studied how the New Jobs Tax Credit of 1977 to 1978 affected retail prices in various distribution industries. The NJTC was a wage subsidy used by many firms, which were entitled to it by tax law. Hence, it is at least plausible that the NJTC would have affected pricing decisions. (Chapter 8 has more details on the NJTC.) Bishop examined the NJTC's pricing effects by estimating a time-series model that attempted to predict the retail prices in different distribution industries as a function of wholesale prices, wages, unemployment, and other variables, including a variable measuring the proportion of firms that in surveys said they were aware of the NJTC. He estimated that his NJTC variable did have some statistically significant negative effects on retail prices in some industries, in particular in the restaurant industry and in the aggregate category of "nonfood commodity (except housing) industries." He estimated that prices in industries with a lower labor share of costs, such as the grocery industry, were not significantly affected by the NJTC. Bishop estimated that the reductions in retail prices due to the NJTC were comparable in magnitude to the costs to the U.S. Treasury of this tax subsidy. However, his estimating equations account only for the direct effects of the NJTC on retail prices. The NJTC would also have had indirect positive effects on prices by reducing unemployment and raising wages. Without additional information on how the NJTC affected unemployment and wages, it is difficult to tell whether the net effect of the NJTC was to increase or reduce inflation. All that can be said is that the NJTC's effects on inflation were probably lower than those of other policies with similar downward effects on unemployment.

Conclusion

Given all these arguments, how concerned should we be about the inflationary consequences of policies to increase labor demand for the poor? My conclusion is that we should be concerned enough to take such consequences into consideration when we design labor demand policies, but that we should not assume there is some fixed NAIRU that strictly and automatically prevents us from doing much to increase overall labor demand for the poor. With appropriately designed labor demand policies for the poor, inflationary pressures may be reduced. Appropriate design of such policies includes:

- geographic targeting of aggregate demand policies at high-unemployment local labor markets, so that upward effects on wages and prices are not as great;
- demographically targeting increases in labor demand at groups that have low labor force participation rates, so that the policy adds to aggregate labor supply;

- ensuring that those employed in subsidized or public-service jobs are still available for regular jobs, so that regular employers have fewer problems finding labor and the likelihood of wage inflation is lowered;
- adding to the package of demand policies a program of wage subsidies that lowers labor costs and thus inflationary pressures.

In contrast, a poorly designed set of labor demand policies aimed at simply hiring unemployed persons among disadvantaged groups in both low- and high-unemployment labor markets for permanent public-service jobs at market wages may cause inflationary problems if carried out at the scale required to provide the jobs needed for the poor.

In addition, because of uncertainty about whether the NAIRU exists and the level of the NAIRU, and because appropriately designed labor demand policies may change the NAIRU, anti-inflation policies should not automatically assume that a particular level of unemployment is inflationary. Rather, concerns about wage inflation due to low unemployment should be based on actual experience with wage inflation and unemployment. If wage inflation due to low unemployment is occurring, we can then consider whether we need to increase unemployment in order to lower wage inflation pressures.

Chapters 5 and 6 have attempted to establish that, in principle, well-designed policies to increase labor demand for the disadvantaged can increase their employment without unacceptable displacement effects or effects on inflation. The next three chapters consider the pros and cons of specific programs to increase labor demand for the disadvantaged.

7

PUBLICLY FUNDED JOBS FOR THE POOR

THIS chapter and chapters 8 and 9 consider specific labor demand programs that seek to target the poor for increased labor demand. Here we look at publicly funded jobs.[1] Chapter 8 considers wage subsidies to private employers, and chapter 9 discusses economic development programs, labor market intermediary programs, minimum-wage regulations, and efforts to reduce employment discrimination.

Although the issues analyzed in chapters 7 through 9 vary with the program, some of the questions addressed are similar. What are the short-run and long-run effects of these programs on the employment and earnings of the poor? What effects do these programs have on the nonpoor, either by altering their employment or wages or imposing other costs? How can these programs most effectively be designed and managed? Who should be targeted by these labor demand programs?

The usual concern about labor demand programs is that they may not provide a lasting solution to poverty because they may not effectively raise the long-run ability of the poor to be economically productive. As I argue, many of these labor demand programs can be economically productive in the long run, but an equally important concern about them is whether they are politically viable. Labor demand programs inherently imply government involvement in some manner in employment decisions. In the American political tradition, such government involvement raises significant concerns from both the left wing and right wing of the political spectrum.

In this chapter, I begin with an introduction to the issues associated with public-service jobs for the disadvantaged. I then review the history, goals, and nature of these public-service jobs programs, discuss research findings about their feasibility, scale, productivity, earnings effects, and costs, and analyze the politics of public-service jobs.

An Introduction to Public-Service Jobs

By definition, a public-service employment (PSE) program for the disadvantaged provides a certain fixed amount of funding to some government or nonprofit employer to employ disadvantaged persons. The great appeal of PSE programs is that their attack on the employment problems of the poor is simple and direct. If part of the poverty problem is that insufficient numbers of the poor are employed, then hiring the poor is the commonsense solution. The limitation of PSE programs is that by their very nature they do not increase the attractiveness of employing disadvantaged persons to most employers. For example, PSE programs do not lower the wage that most employers must pay to hire disadvantaged persons. Even for government or nonprofit employers who receive PSE funds, once these funds are exhausted, the PSE program does not make it attractive to hire additional disadvantaged persons over and above those already hired under the program.[2]

Because of this design, PSE programs always face a key challenge: Will the initial increase of PSE jobs for the disadvantaged be offset because the program has not fundamentally made hiring disadvantaged persons more attractive? For example, PSE programs frequently worry about *public worker substitution:* the government and nonprofit entities have some incentive to use their PSE funds either to hire disadvantaged persons they would have hired anyway or at least to hire disadvantaged persons rather than other persons they would have hired anyway.[3] ("Public worker substitution" is sometimes called "fiscal substitution," which is imprecise terminology, or "displacement," a term that could be confused with "private-sector crowd-out," as described shortly.) The last disadvantaged worker hired still must be paid the same wage, so one might be concerned that there would be no effect of the program on overall employment or the net employment of disadvantaged workers.

PSE programs also frequently must be concerned with the *displacement* of private-sector employment of disadvantaged workers, also called *private-sector crowd-out.*[4] As mentioned, a PSE program does nothing directly to make it easier or cheaper for private-sector employers to hire the disadvantaged. But indirectly, PSE programs may make it more difficult for private-sector employers to hire the disadvantaged. The workers hired under the PSE program are no longer available for private-sector employment. This lessened availability may increase the wages of disadvantaged workers. The lessened availability of disadvantaged workers, and their higher wages, may indirectly reduce the hiring by private-sector employers of disadvantaged workers. On the other hand, if PSE programs target those who otherwise would be out of the labor force and successfully bring them permanently into the labor force, they may help expand overall employment and the economy.

Because PSE programs hire the disadvantaged for government jobs that are especially created for that purpose, these jobs may produce less output and on-the-job-training than ordinary jobs. At the extreme, if these jobs are completely unproductive make-work, then the PSE program is really a disguised income transfer program. Perhaps labeling an income transfer program a jobs program is politically advantageous, but it seems cynical, and certainly such a program is more expensive than straightforward income transfers. Make-work PSE jobs also may produce little long-run on-the-job-training and earnings benefits for the disadvantaged who are hired for them.

The long-run effects of PSE jobs on those hired is of particular concern because PSE programs are expensive. Although directly hiring the disadvantaged is the commonsense solution to the employment problems of the poor, the government must pay 100 percent of the wage costs of this hiring, plus whatever administrative and support services are required. If these jobs lead to long-run earnings benefits, then the programs can be run on a smaller scale, that is, helping smaller groups of the disadvantaged at a time and gradually increasing the overall earnings of the poor. But if these long-run earnings benefits do not occur, then PSE programs cannot achieve sufficient scale to make significant improvements in poverty without great public expense.

Hiring the disadvantaged for special government jobs also arouses political problems. Some political groups in the United States may be concerned that PSE programs will expand the size and power of government. Others may favor PSE for that very same reason. However, current government workers and their union representatives may be concerned that employing the disadvantaged in PSE jobs could threaten their own jobs.

History of Public-Service Employment of the Disadvantaged

Significant U.S. funding of public jobs for the disadvantaged and unemployed began in the Great Depression. By far the largest such program was the WPA (an acronym initially standing for the Works Progress Administration, and later for the Works Projects Administration). In its eight-year history, from 1935 to 1943, the WPA spent more than $157 billion (1998 dollars), with peak employment of 3.3 million in 1938 (Kesselman 1978, 158). The WPA was both widely popular and widely hated. It won wide support as a program that provided jobs to many who had no other alternative and that produced public works of lasting value to the nation. But it was widely opposed on the grounds that it epitomized big government, had too many "make-work" projects rather than real jobs, was subject to political corruption in who got the jobs, and unfairly competed with the private sector both in hiring workers and in producing goods.

In contrast, the smaller CCC (Civilian Conservation Corps) was much more politically popular (Kennedy 1999, 144; Kesselman 1978, 164, 166, 209–10). The CCC employed young adults, whereas the WPA employed prime-age workers who were more desirable to private employers. The CCC employed young adults in conservation projects in national parks and other natural areas, projects of little potential for private business, whereas the WPA employed older workers for highly visible public works projects in urban areas that were of much greater potential interest to private contractors.

The CCC, the WPA, and other New Deal employment programs met their demise in 1943. The full employment brought about by World War II arguably made the jobs they provided unnecessary. Furthermore, the political trends of the late 1930s and early 1940s put Congress under the control of more conservative Republicans and southern Democrats. The more conservative Congress sought to rein in the "big government" aspects of the New Deal and to restrict these jobs programs, which inherently gave greater power to the president in allocating jobs (Kennedy 1999, 783).

From 1943 until the 1970s the United States had no federal program whose goal was to create jobs for the disadvantaged or unemployed. However, beginning in the 1960s, various efforts were made to require single mothers receiving welfare to do some work in exchange for benefits. Such work requirements inherently led to some government job creation, in that the government had to find some work activity to enforce the requirement, although such work was paid in the form of continued receipt of benefits rather than in wages. For example, in 1967 Congress created the Work Incentive (WIN) program, which required all able-bodied fathers in families receiving welfare benefits to register for WIN services, including work experience programs that provided thirteen weeks of work in exchange for the welfare grant. In 1971 Congress extended the WIN registration requirement to all able-bodied welfare recipients (Brock et al. 1993). Despite such legislative requirements, in practice in most states such efforts were extremely small-scale, affecting very few welfare recipients.

In the 1970s, Congress again began funding public-service jobs programs, starting with the Emergency Employment Act of 1971 and continuing with some provisions of the Comprehensive Employment and Training Act (CETA) of 1974. Under these programs, the federal government made grants to state and local governments to hire unemployed or disadvantaged individuals. This renewed interest in public-service jobs had several

SIDEBAR 7.1 The Works Progress (Or Projects) Administration

Created in 1935, the WPA was by far the largest work relief program of the New Deal, spending more on job creation than all other New Deal programs put together (Kesselman 1978, 158). President Roosevelt thought of WPA work relief activities as a long-term activity of the federal government (Kennedy 1999, 249–50). The experience of the lengthy Great Depression suggested that the private economy would not provide an adequate numbers of jobs.

Rather than using contractors, the WPA directly administered its projects—using an average of thirty thousand employees in many local offices (Briscoe 1972, 98)—because of the perceived difficulties in getting contractors to hire the needy (Howard 1943, 151–53). A state or local government match was required on WPA projects—originally an average of a 19 percent local match, and later 25 percent (99). Seventy-eight percent of WPA projects were public works projects, including LaGuardia Airport in New York City (106).

Those hired for the WPA had to meet criteria for being considered needy, including having exhausted any unemployment benefits. It is clear that most WPA hires would not have been employed nearly as much during the Depression without the WPA. When Congress mandated an eighteen-month limit to continuous WPA employment in 1939 (with a minimum of thirty days before workers could reapply to WPA), only 13 percent of these laid-off WPA workers were employed in regular jobs when surveyed two or three months later (Kesselman 1978, 198, 203).

Workers were paid a security wage, which was supposed to exceed what could be obtained from direct cash relief yet be somewhat below prevailing private wages for that particular type of job. However, the WPA was openly willing to pay above what were thought to be unfairly low wages, particularly in the rural South. Average wages paid would be equivalent to $600 to $650 per month in 1998 dollars (Howard 1943, 158–67, 181).

The WPA was administered by local WPA offices, some of which gave substantial control over hiring to local political machines. The Memphis political boss Edward Crump required WPA workers to contribute to the local Democratic machine, and New Jersey WPA workers were required to contribute 3 percent of their wages to Frank Hague's Democratic machine (Kennedy 1999, 253).

The WPA was controversial from its beginnings. Businesses objected that the WPA was luring workers away from private-sector jobs, or producing goods or services in competition with the private sector. The WPA often had to abandon slum clearance projects because of objections from building-wrecker businesses and rat extermination projects because of opposition from exterminators (Howard 1943, 134, 166). A 1939 public opinion poll found that the WPA was cited more than any other program as both the "greatest accomplishment" of the Roosevelt administration and the "worst thing" the administration had done (Howard 1943, 105).

With conservatives beginning to take control of Congress after the 1938 elections, the WPA and many other New Deal programs were increasingly restricted in scope and size. With unemployment almost eliminated by World War II, the WPA was abolished by Congress in 1943 (Kennedy 1999, 783).

sources. First, there was some frustration with the disappointing results of some of the job training programs funded during the War on Poverty. Second, some economists argued that the problems of the poor were in part related to being relegated to a secondary labor market with high turnover and low-wage jobs with poor working conditions and little opportunity for career advancement. The creation of stable, higher-paying public-service jobs for the poor would help move the poor, they argued, into the primary labor market. Third, the recession of 1970 to 1971, followed by the recession of 1974 to 1975 induced by the policies of the Organization of Petroleum Exporting Countries (OPEC), increased congressional interest in the federal government doing something about high unemployment (Mucciaroni 1990; Sheppard, Harrison, and Spring 1972).

Although not as large as the WPA, CETA was quite sizable, creating 750,000 jobs at its peak in early 1978 (Cook et al. 1985, 10). Whatever its true economic effects (see later discussion), from a political standpoint CETA was a disaster, widely discrediting the notion of large-scale public jobs programs as a solution to unemployment and poverty. CETA was criticized by many economists on the grounds that the grants to local governments led to "fiscal substitution": local governments substituted the grants for their own funds, thus allowing lower local taxes but not increasing government employment or total employment (Johnson and Tomola 1977). CETA was also criticized because many of those hired, particularly in the early years of the program, were arguably not the most needy of the unemployed. Numerous press stories, in *Reader's Digest,* for example, chronicled various abuses of CETA, including the hiring of people for crazy jobs (one notable case was a former Black Panther activist hired "to keep an eye on the city," and another case was a "nude sculpting workshop" funded by CETA dollars [Mucciaroni 1990, 177]), embezzlement of CETA money, and the use of CETA jobs for political purposes (178). CETA was eventually replaced in 1982 by the Job Training Partnership Act, which made it official policy that federal grants to local job training groups could not be used to finance public-service jobs. (As described in previous chapters, JTPA was itself replaced in 1998 by the Workforce Investment Act, which further decentralizes decisionmaking away from the federal government—for example, by allowing job training funds to be used for job creation.)

Despite the bad reputation gained by public-service jobs from the press coverage given to CETA, in recent years there has been renewed interest in some form of public-service jobs as a part of welfare reform. The welfare reform bill of 1996 requires that certain percentages of the welfare caseload be working as of certain years. This requirement obviously raises the issue of what is to be done if the required number of welfare recipients will not or cannot find jobs. Some states and cities have begun expanding workfare-style programs, in which some welfare recip-

SIDEBAR 7.2 CETA Public-Service Employment

The Comprehensive Employment and Training Act (CETA) of 1973 was originally adopted as a compromise between President Nixon's desire to decentralize federal training programs into a block grant to state and local governments and congressional interest in expanding public-service employment. CETA set up block grants for training and PSE, distributed by formula to local agencies. Originally, CETA emphasized training over PSE, with $2.0 billion for PSE and $3.3 billion for training in fiscal year 1974 (1998 dollars) (Barnow 2000). However, as time went on, PSE took over the CETA program owing to the large recession of 1974 to 1975, the political weakness of Republicans after Watergate, and campaign commitments by President Carter. By fiscal year 1978, CETA public-service employment had expanded to $11.8 billion, versus $4.8 billion for CETA training programs (Barnow 2000).

CETA PSE funding initially was quite generous with few restrictions. Anyone who had been unemployed at least thirty days was eligible to be hired under CETA, and the federal government would pay up to $33,000 annually, with the local government permitted to supplement this amount. No duration limit was imposed on positions or on individuals funded by CETA. This led to the criticism that local governments were using this program to hire laid-off city workers, or at least workers very similar to those they would have hired anyway. The program was perceived as allowing local governments to hold down taxes rather than helping the disadvantaged get jobs (Cook et al. 1985, ch. 1; Mucciaroni 1990, ch. 7).

In response to criticisms, over time CETA PSE was made less generous and more restrictive in who could be hired and under what terms. In 1976 new CETA positions were limited to less than one year, and half of all CETA participants were required to be low-income and long-term unemployed. In 1978 federal law required that all CETA participants be low-income and long-term unemployed or welfare recipients; furthermore, individual participants couldn't be funded under CETA for more than eighteen months during a five-year period; finally, local governments could not supplement the federal CETA salary (Cook et al. 1985, 14–15).

Because of these restrictions, state and local governments became much less enthusiastic about CETA PSE. This doomed the program in the face of political opposition and bad publicity. Conservatives continued to oppose PSE on principle, and the CETA program received bad publicity for program abuses. As one congressional aide said in the late 1970s, "CETA has become a four-letter word" (Mucciaroni 1990, 162). According to Cook and his colleagues (1985, 128): "Toward the end of [the 1970s], when tighter restrictions on wages and participant eligibility limited the range of services that could be provided, we found that the program had lost much of its appeal to state and local officials. It is mainly because of this change that the Reagan administration's 1981 proposal to eliminate PSE was not more vigorously opposed." CETA was replaced by the Job Training Partnership Act (JTPA) in 1982, and JTPA forbade the use of funds for public-service employment.

ients are required to work at various government jobs in exchange for their welfare benefits. By far the most aggressive actors in the renewed workfare effort are the state of Wisconsin and the city of New York; Wisconsin's W-2 program currently has 49 percent of its caseload in workfare-type positions (Institute for Wisconsin's Future 1999), and New York City's Work Experience Program has 8 percent of its caseload in workfare positions.[5] This far exceeds what most states are doing with workfare programs; according to one survey, more than half of the workfare job slots nationwide are in Wisconsin or New York City, and most of the remainder are in other parts of New York State (Ellwood and Welty 2000).

In addition, since the 1970s liberal groups have made many attempts to resurrect some form of public-service employment that is less punitive and has greater effects on participants' earnings, both in the short term and the long term. Most of these attempts have been demonstrations and experiments with different designs of public-service job programs. In the 1970s, the Ford Foundation and several federal agencies carried out a large-scale experiment, the Supported Work Program, which explored the long-term earnings effects of providing public-service jobs to the poor that gradually increased in "stress" (responsibilities and expectations) over a one-year period and were designed to provide the training, credentials, and self-confidence for participants to get good jobs in the regular labor market (see chapter 5). In the late 1970s, the Carter administration funded two demonstration programs that provided guaranteed jobs to some groups of the poor. The Employment Opportunity Pilot Project (EOPP) was originally designed to test the effects of the guaranteed jobs portion of President Carter's welfare reform plan and hence was designed to provide guaranteed jobs to welfare recipients who were unable to find regular jobs after being trained and guided in extensive job search. Another demonstration, the Youth Incentive Entitlement Pilot Project (YIEPP), provided guaranteed full-time jobs during the summer, and part-time jobs during the school year, to disadvantaged high school–age youths in the demonstration areas who agreed to stay in school or return to school (see chapter 5). There have also been a number of small-scale revivals of the Civilian Conservation Corps of the Great Depression for youth, with disadvantaged youth being hired to do a variety of conservation and other community service projects; one of these projects, the Youth Corps, was run as an experiment. Finally, the recent New Hope Program in Milwaukee tested the employment and earnings effects on low-income adults of combining extensive earnings subsidies and guaranteed health benefits for those getting full-time jobs; this experiment provided backup community service jobs for low-income participants who were unable to find a job through job search (see chapter 5).

More recently, in light of the passage of the federal welfare reform bill in 1996, with its heavy stress on work, and the prospect of workfare efforts

SIDEBAR 7.3 The W-2 Program

Wisconsin's W-2 program is one of the most radical state welfare reforms. W-2 requires most welfare recipients to work in positions created by the program. Welfare benefits are considered a "wage" paid to a needy person for working or preparing for work. For example, W-2 payments do not vary with family size, just as wages paid by employers do not vary with family size.

W-2's enactment was in part a political accident and in part a reflection of the state's political culture. In an attempt to outdo Republican Governor Tommy Thompson in reforming welfare, Democrats in the Wisconsin legislature proposed in 1993 to abolish AFDC and replace it with a new welfare system. Governor Thompson called the Democrats' bluff by agreeing to the abolition of AFDC, and his administration then designed the W-2 with help from the conservative Hudson Institute (Kaplan 1998). W-2 was enacted in 1996 and went into effect on September 1, 1997. Its enactment reflects a state political culture in which Republicans are willing to use government aggressively and many Democrats support work requirements for the poor (Mead 1999).

Although W-2 includes several possible assignments of clients, the most common assignment (about half of all clients) is to community service jobs (CSJs). CSJ participants must work twenty to thirty hours per week, in exchange for which they receive $673 per month in W-2 benefits (plus food stamps). W-2 payments are reduced when clients have unexcused absences from their community service positions (Wiseman 1999). Local W-2 agencies develop the CSJs, generally at nonprofit employers but sometimes also at for-profit employers, public agencies, or new businesses owned by the W-2 agency (Kaplan and Rothe 1999).

W-2 has been criticized by "neoliberals" such as Mayor John Norquist of Milwaukee for not creating "real jobs," in that CSJ participants are ineligible for the Earned Income Tax Credit and do not participate in social security (Norquist 1998). More conventional liberal voices, such as the Institute for Wisconsin's Future (1998), criticize the CSJ program by arguing that these jobs provide little on-the-job-training and make it difficult for participants to have time for education and training.

in many states, some liberal groups, most notably the Center for Budget and Policy Priorities, have begun pushing for a new approach to public-service jobs for welfare recipients, labeled community service jobs (Johnson and Lopez 1997; Johnson, Schweke, and Hull 1999). Under this approach, government funds would not be used to expand government positions for welfare recipients or other disadvantaged groups but would be given to nonprofit groups in the form of grants to allow them to hire welfare recipients or other disadvantaged persons. The funded jobs would be considered temporary training positions, with limited tenure, and some effort would be made to connect these positions with permanent regular jobs. Unlike workfare positions, community service jobs, because they would

SIDEBAR 7.4 New York City's Work Experience Program

New York City is currently running the largest work experience program for welfare recipients. The program began with "home relief" recipients, the term in New York State for what in other states is called "general relief": welfare benefits for adults who do not have custody of a child and do not qualify for regular welfare programs. The program has since been extended to welfare recipients with children.

About half of New York City's work experience participants are placed in the city parks or the sanitation department (Lerman and Rosenberg 1997). Most do menial jobs. General relief recipients' work hours are determined by dividing their welfare benefits by the minimum wage, whereas welfare recipients work twenty hours per week. The types of jobs, work expectations, and implicit wage rates do not seem unusual compared to work experience programs in other states.

What is unusual about New York City's program is its size. The program has about 36,000 participants in an average month, about half of whom are welfare recipients with children and half of whom are general relief recipients. Although the welfare recipients represent only 8 percent of New York City's welfare caseload, the 36,000 work experience participants loom large compared to the total New York City workforce of 175,000. Particularly in a city that has cut back city employment in recent years, the large size of the program raises questions about whether work experience participants are replacing regular New York City workers.

Source: Most of this discussion is based on Ellwood and Welty (2000).

pay wages, would make those holding them eligible for income subsidies from the Earned Income Tax Credit; this factor would significantly increase the net income associated with community service jobs compared to workfare jobs. Some small-scale community service jobs programs have been created in a few states and cities, most notably Vermont and the state of Washington (Johnson and Headings 1998; Johnson and Kim 1999).

Finally, over the years a number of utopian programs of guaranteed jobs for all have been proposed. From the left, the Rutgers law professor Philip Harvey (1989, 5) has advocated that all persons able to work "be assured a statutory right to employment in public sector jobs paying market wages." The neoliberal journalist Mickey Kaus (1992, 125) made the following proposal in 1992: "replacing AFDC and all other cash-like welfare programs that assist the able-bodied poor . . . with a single, simple offer from the government—an offer of employment for every American citizen over eighteen who wants it, in a useful public job at a wage slightly below the minimum wage for private sector work." David Riemer (1988, 9), now chief of administration for the city of Milwaukee and a close aide to Milwaukee Mayor John Norquist, has proposed a program that would "offer

SIDEBAR 7.5 The Employment Opportunity Pilot Project

EOPP was originally designed to test the guaranteed jobs component of President Carter's 1978 welfare reform proposal, the Program for Better Jobs and Income (PBJI). PBJI envisioned requiring welfare recipients to work or enter training, with PBJI providing funding for a guaranteed public-service job or training position. PBJI planning assumed that the creation of 1.4 million jobs and training slots would be required, and EOPP was designed to test the feasibility and impacts of these guaranteed jobs.

However, Congress rejected PBJI, and EOPP was refocused on testing the impact of job search assistance, although a subsidized employment component was also included when EOPP began enrollment in mid-1979. After the Reagan administration took office in 1981, the subsidized employment component of EOPP was terminated, and EOPP was scaled back and then ended in 1981 (Brown et al. 1983, ch. 2).

EOPP was administered by local job training agencies at fourteen sites around the country. Those eligible were families that had children and were on welfare, eligible for welfare, or low-income. EOPP enrollees initially participated in five to eight weeks of self-directed job search, backed up by job club meetings and counseling. If the job search was unsuccessful, an EOPP family's "primary earner" was eligible for subsidized employment and training for up to one year. Two-thirds of those enrolled in subsidized employment got public-service jobs, one-fourth got classroom training, 14 percent were placed in a work experience position (working without pay), and 7 percent received on-the-job-training with a private employer. The average length of enrollment in public-service jobs was five months. About one-third of those participating in subsidized employment and training left it to take a regular job.

Although EOPP was supposed to provide an entitlement to a job, in practice the program did not deliver the entitlement at most sites. Most eligible non-enrollees (about 80 percent) said that they had never heard of EOPP (Brown et al. 1983, 124). Owing to administrative problems, some enrollees had to wait more than three weeks before being assigned to job search, or, after job search, being assigned to a job (Brown et al. 1983, 16). Some sites pushed subsidized employment and training more than others, with two sites enrolling more than 75 percent of those who had completed job search and two other sites enrolling less than 40 percent (Brown et al. 1983, 114).

The available non-experimental analyses of EOPP suggest that the program had positive effects on the employment rates of unmarried women. Brown and his colleagues (1983) find that EOPP raised the average employment rates of unmarried women by twelve to sixteen percentage points. Grossman and her colleagues (1985, 71) find that subsidized employment and training doubled the employment rates of female household heads during the subsidy period, and increased the employment rate of this group from 36 to 42 percent seven quarters after initial enrollment, when almost all EOPP enrollees had completed their subsidized employment.

SIDEBAR 7.6 *Community Service Jobs in the New Hope Program*

One component of the New Hope Program (see chapter 5) was community service jobs. For those eligible for the New Hope Program (low-income residents in two Milwaukee neighborhoods) who were unable to find a regular job after a search, the program provided temporary community service jobs at local nonprofit organizations. The jobs could last up to six months, paid minimum wage, and required that job holders work at least thirty hours per week, a requirement that made them eligible for the supplemental benefits of New Hope (earnings supplements, subsidized health insurance, and child care).

To create the one hundred jobs needed during the course of the program, New Hope used one job developer. The program had one coordinator for every twenty-five or thirty people working in CSJs to resolve any problems between the job holder and the employer. To make the program more attractive to employers, the local training agency, under contract with New Hope, handled the payroll for CSJ employees and paid workers' compensation for these employees, while the nonprofit agency sponsoring the CSJ job had full control over hiring, supervising, and firing the CSJ job holder.

Although some evaluation results are available for New Hope, it is impossible to separate out the effects of CSJs from the many other components of New Hope. However, about one of five CSJ participants was hired by the host agency after completing subsidized employment, suggesting that the CSJs may have had postprogram effects on employment.

Source: Poglinco et al. (1998); Kaplan and Rothe (1999).

the poor who can work community-service jobs [which he later proposes would pay minimum wages]; provide the poor who are working [both in regular jobs and community service jobs] with wage supplements sufficient to get them above the poverty line." While these proposals have never gone anywhere in the political process, they have encouraged some of the experiments and demonstrations mentioned earlier.

Goals of Publicly Funded Jobs Programs

Publicly funded jobs have had widely varied, and often contradictory, goals, and evaluations of these jobs programs reach different conclusions depending on the goals they consider. One goal of many publicly funded jobs programs has been the countercyclical goal of intervening during a recession to provide jobs to the unemployed, and perhaps to boost the economy. This clearly was the rationale for the WPA and CCC efforts of the Great Depression, and it was a key political rationale for the public-service jobs programs of the 1970s.

A second goal for some publicly funded jobs programs is simply to make a moral statement that individuals should work in return for receiving welfare benefits. For example, the W-2 welfare reform implemented in Wisconsin in 1997 requires all applicants for public assistance to do some activity for a certain number of hours per week before receiving assistance; most applicants are assigned to community service jobs. According to the official goals of W-2, the assumption of the program is that "everybody is able to work, or if not, at least capable of making a contribution to society through work activity within their abilities" (Wisconsin Department of Workforce Development 1999a).

Yet another goal of some programs has been to change the labor market for low-income Americans. Some proponents of public-service jobs programs want to change the labor market by providing jobs of last resort, which, according to Harvey (1989, 68, 74), would "probably . . . exert some upward pressure on the general level of wages, since the establishment of effective full employment would strengthen the general bargaining power of both unionized and nonunionized workers. . . . A structural change would occur in the economy involving a reallocation of productive resources from lower-wage to higher-wage industries." Others, such as Ben Harrison (1972, 67), have argued that creating permanent public-service jobs at decent wages with decent job stability would allow many more low-income Americans to move into the primary job market:

> By providing non-poverty jobs for workers now employed in the secondary labor market, a public service employment program will unquestionably compete with secondary private employers for the services of the secondary labor force. Those workers who actually move from secondary private to primary public employment will benefit directly. Moreover, there is every reason to expect that those who are left behind will benefit from the upward pressure exerted on secondary labor market wages and benefits by the competition.

Another goal has been to provide public-service jobs as temporary training opportunities so that these job holders can later move into regular private- or public-sector jobs. Clifford Johnson (Johnson et al. 1999, 7) of the Center for Budget and Policy Priorities has argued: "A diverse set of current initiatives is demonstrating that publicly-funded jobs can serve as a bridge to unsubsidized employment, providing the entry-level skills and work experience that hard-to-employ individuals often need to succeed in the regular labor market."

Types of Publicly Funded Jobs

Many types of jobs for disadvantaged workers have been funded over the years through various public-service, community service, or workfare programs.

- *WPA:* Seventy-eight percent of WPA spending went to construction and public improvements (Kesselman 1978, 207–8).
- *CETA:* CETA jobs were primarily in clerical work, public works, sanitation work, and park and recreation agencies. Thirty-four percent of jobs were with nonprofits by 1980 (Cook et al. 1985, 39–40).
- *Supported Work:* Half of Supported Work participants were employed in services, including clerical, building maintenance, food, educational, health, and human services. Twenty-nine percent were employed in construction projects. Some jobs were contracted out to for-profits (Ball 1984, esp. table 3.2).
- *Community Work Experience Program:* For women, most CWEP jobs were entry-level clerical or in day care; for men, most jobs were custodial or in grounds maintenance or garbage collection (Brock et al. 1993, 29–30).
- *New Hope:* Thirty-five percent of jobs were in office support, 13 percent in building construction or rehabilitation, 16 percent in property maintenance, 9 percent in child care, and 8 percent in food service (Poglinco et al. 1998, 5 and table 1).
- *Work Experience Program in New York City:* Over half of the jobs provided by this program were in maintenance, and about one-quarter were clerical (Lerman and Rosenberg 1997).
- *W-2:* Forty-three percent of jobs were light assembly (sorting, packing), 23 percent clerical, 15 percent cleaning, 12 percent child care, and 7 percent food service (Institute for Wisconsin's Future 1998). Some jobs were at nonprofits, some at for-profits, and some in government agencies (Kaplan and Rothe 1999, 46).
- *Maine TOPS program:* Sixty-two percent of jobs were clerical, 16 percent social services, 7 percent manual skills occupations, 5 percent food services, 4 percent health care, and 3 percent sales/cashier (Auspos et al. 1988, table 3.4).
- *Youth Corps:* Thirty-seven percent of projects were in human services, 21 were environmental/conservation, and 20 percent were educational. Two-thirds of the jobs were in nonprofit agencies (Jastrzab et al. 1997, 7).
- *YIEPP:* Of youths employed in public and nonprofit jobs, 27 percent held clerical jobs, 26 percent were in building maintenance, and 15 percent were community or recreation aides. Some were also employed at for-profits (Unicon 1982).

The programs provide the types of jobs that one might expect and are similar to the types of low-wage occupations that lower-income persons ordinarily obtain. The types of jobs obtained are often highly gender-segregated, with men tending to get more construction, building rehabilitation, and maintenance-type jobs, and women getting more clerical jobs and jobs as aides in various types of educational, health, and social service agencies. The WPA placed a greater emphasis on public works construction than seems to have been true of most subsequent efforts, which have usually been more service-oriented. This reflects shifts in the U.S. economy toward the service sector, the WPA's focus on helping the "primary earner" (in most cases, male) in each family, and the focus of subsequent efforts on welfare recipients.

Over time, public-service jobs programs have shifted from creating additional government positions in regular agencies to contracting out to nonprofit groups. Even CETA, which is often thought of as a program that mainly supported local government employment, over time was providing funding to nonprofit agencies to hire particular disadvantaged individuals for more than one-third of its jobs.

Public-service programs that create jobs by contracting out to nonprofit agencies are in many respects quite similar to wage subsidy programs that subsidize wages by making contracts with for-profit firms. In both cases, the program seeks to create jobs for particular disadvantaged persons by subsidizing some other employer to provide that job. In practice, many programs do both. For example, the Supported Work Program, which is often thought of and described as simply a public-service jobs program, sometimes placed its workers with for-profit firms. These firms would supervise the workers, typically pay a fee to cover part of the wages paid by the local Supported Work Program, and often provided some assurance that Supported Work participants who did a good job with the firm would be hired for regular jobs.

Feasibility of Large-Scale Public-Service Jobs Programs

Ellwood and Welty's (2000, 348) recent review of the research literature on public-service jobs programs concludes that creating jobs for the poor is highly feasible: "One of the striking results of reading the literature was the apparent lack of serious administrative problems for most programs in the job finding/creation parts of the PSE programs reviewed." My own reading of the research literature leads me to agree with Ellwood and Welty that creating large numbers of public-service jobs programs for the poor is highly feasible from a technical standpoint. Furthermore, on a smaller scale, it is feasible to create jobs for the poor that provide high-quality job experiences, in the sense that the job provides training that is useful to the individual's particular training needs and vocational interests. However, expanding such high-quality programs to a large scale may require some sacrifice in quality, although perhaps not so great a sacrifice as to be unacceptable. In addition, creating large-scale programs, particularly on a quick time scale, may not always be politically feasible.

Several large-scale public-service jobs programs were set up very quickly. For example, the Civil Works Administration (CWA) program, a precursor to the WPA set up during the early New Deal years, started operations in November 1933 and peaked at employment of 4.3 million workers in January 1934 before being phased out by later in 1934 (Kesselman 1978, 158). After the passage of President Carter's proposal for economic stimulus in early 1977, CETA public jobs quickly expanded from 300,000 in May 1977 to a peak of 755,000 jobs in April 1978, even though the expanded job slots had additional requirements that placed greater emphasis on targeting jobs at the disadvantaged and on contracting out jobs to short-term projects (Cook et al. 1985, 12).

However, politics may delay public-service job creation enough to make the timing of such efforts less than optimal from an antirecession or countercyclical perspective. CETA provides a good example. The recession of 1974 to 1975, which gave such an impetus to the expansion of public-service employment, reached its trough in 1975. The political response to this recession, reflected in President Carter's stimulus package, led to a peak public-service employment level in 1978, well after employment growth and economic growth had resumed. Such a political process could be short-circuited if Congress gave standby authority to the president to spend funds for public-service employment without waiting for an additional congressional appropriation of funds. But Congress has always been reluctant to grant such spending authority to any president, regardless of the political party control of either the Congress or the presidency.

In addition, it is more challenging to set up public-service jobs programs that seek to provide higher-quality job experiences for the disadvantaged, particularly if these programs seek to create such jobs by contracting out to public or nonprofit agencies, which, as discussed later, seem to be associated with higher-quality job experiences. For example, according to one of the lead researchers studying the Supported Work Program, which sought to provide very high-quality job experiences for various disadvantaged groups, designing the program involved making the judgment "that it was administratively infeasible for individual sites to reach a size in excess of a few hundred job slots" (Hollister 1984, 23). If the program had been any larger, it would have been too difficult to find a sufficient number of work projects, whether directly run by the local Supported Work agency or contracted out to various public, nonprofit, or private employers, that would provide job experiences that fit the Supported Work model of gradually increasing job stress and responsibilities. Furthermore, not all Supported Work sites were successful: one site was closed down, and another had to be completely reorganized.

In the YIEPP program, some sites were set up on a small-scale basis, providing only a few hundred jobs to disadvantaged youth, whereas other sites were set up as "saturation sites" that sought to provide jobs to all disadvantaged youth within a particular geographic area, some as large as an entire city. In both types of sites, implementing this job guarantee program provided to be administratively feasible. However, there were some greater difficulties in implementing the program at the saturation sites. For example, the waiting time for youths to get jobs at the saturation sites was thirty-four days, compared to twenty-four days at the smaller-scale sites (Diaz et al. 1982, 85). In addition, although most workplaces in both types of site were of adequate quality, audits by outside observers suggest that the smaller-scale sites had a greater proportion of very strong workplaces that provided higher-quality work experiences (112–13).

Larger-scale programs may also run into greater political problems. One of the reasons for running Supported Work programs on a small scale was to avoid the political opposition of employers or workers who might have been concerned that the programs would cause some loss of business or job loss. For example, in Supported Work, it was found that

> construction work that was small in scale, such as light housing rehabilitation, particularly if it was in disadvantaged neighborhoods, generally aroused little opposition from building trades representatives. . . . With respect to service and retail businesses, program operators sought to assure local trade associations that their work would involve relatively small production, and, therefore, relatively little pressure on the market share which local businesses enjoyed. (Ball 1984, 59)

The Need for Large-Scale Jobs Programs

As I discuss later, some advocates of creating public-service jobs to provide a job guarantee for the poor implicitly or explicitly assume that an adequate public-service jobs program must essentially provide jobs for all or almost all of the non-elderly adult poor who are not employed. But it should be recognized that even though there may be a substantial need for jobs among the poor, not everyone who is poor needs a job, and not everyone who needs a job is best served by immediately providing them with a permanent public-service job. This recognition enormously reduces the number of public-service job slots that might be needed at any point in time.

For example, consider the New Hope experiment, which provided residents of two Milwaukee neighborhoods with backup community service jobs as part of a comprehensive program to provide earnings subsidies to disadvantaged persons. Surveys indicated that of those adults in the neighborhood who would qualify on the basis of income for New Hope services, perhaps 41 percent would be likely to apply for the program.[6] The remaining 59 percent might be uninterested in New Hope for a number of reasons: they might be incapable of working; they might have alternative sources of income, either in the underground economy or in the form of various benefit programs; they might not need New Hope because their spouse or partner would be using New Hope instead; or they might be too alienated or confused to apply for any program. Of those who applied for the New Hope Program, about one-third (32 percent) at some point during the two years of the program worked in a community service job (Bos et al. 1999, 71). Some of the remaining individuals already had jobs, which they kept. Others obtained jobs during the job search that New Hope required before they would be eligible for a community service job. Some of those who were offered a community service job were uninterested. According to New Hope staff, "some participants rejected [community service jobs] out-of-hand, even if this meant that they would remain unemployed. Participants' main reason for rejecting the jobs was that they paid minimum wage" (145). Once an individual obtained a community service job, he or she could stay in the job for only six months at a stretch; participants were encouraged to search for a regular job before the community service job ran out. The upshot was that at any point in time only 8 percent of those enrolled in New Hope were employed in a community service job.[7] As a percentage of eligibles, the employment in community service jobs at any point in time would be even smaller: only 3 percent of eligibles (0.08 times 0.41). Thus, even though there is a great deal of interest among the poor in community service jobs, not everyone is interested, and a program that requires job search before making these jobs available, designs these jobs to pay only minimum wage, and sets time limits on job holding—all sensible procedures to encourage the transition to regular jobs—reduces the required number of job slots even further. This does not mean that jobs are not needed, because a much higher percentage of the eligibles will at some time take advantage of a public-service job offer.[8]

Output of Publicly Funded Jobs Projects

The stereotype is that public-service jobs are usually unproductive make-work. However, surveys from many PSE programs show that PSE employers view the work done as important and report that the disadvantaged persons hired under these programs are as productive, or almost as productive, as regular entry-level hires. For example, surveys of CETA employers found that "many employers had been pleasantly surprised at the quality of the program participants" (Cook et al. 1985, 106). In community work experience programs, "supervisors judged the work important [and] found that participants performed at comparable levels to entry-level regular employees" (Brock et al. 1993, 28). In field audits of sample work sites in the YIEPP program, the site assessor rated 87 percent of the work sites as "adequate" to "outstanding" (Diaz et al. 1982). According to one site sponsor for the New Hope Program, "The expectations are the same for all participants. The college students I have come in here on work study do the same tasks [that] the CSJ participants do. The extra hands help a lot" (Poglinco, Brash, and Granger 1998, 12).[9]

A more serious critique is that even if the public-service workers are as potentially productive as regular employees, they may not be used in as productive a manner as regular employers. In particular, to avoid displacement of regular employers, many public-service jobs projects are deliberately designed to be projects that would not have been undertaken without the public-service jobs funding. Almost by definition, such projects are less likely to be as valuable as the normal activities of the government agency or nonprofit agency.

The most serious attempt to assess the value of the output from disadvantaged workers in publicly funded jobs was the analysis done by researchers on the Supported Work Program (Kemper, Long, and Thornton 1981, 1984). These researchers attempted, for a sample of Supported Work projects, to determine the price that would be charged for the output of such projects by an alternative supplier.

Based on this analysis, the Supported Work projects produced output that was valued, in 1998 dollars, at $13.12 per hour worked by a Supported Work participant, suggesting that the projects were quite productive given the highly disadvantaged nature of the persons hired by the program. Wages plus fringe benefits for Supported Work participants averaged $14.84 per hour in 1998 dollars. Project costs (supervision, materials) averaged $8.28 per hour worked by a Supported Work participant. The overhead costs at the local site level (the management costs of raising funds, the costs of organizing projects to create appropriate jobs and of recruiting and placing participants, and supportive services for participants) averaged $6.56 per hour of work by a Supported Work participant. The central administrative costs of the Supported Work Program averaged $0.80 per hour worked by a program participant. Combining these results, the output produced by Supported Work projects offset 43 percent of the total cost of running these projects, or $13.12 per hour out of the total hourly cost of $30.48. Programs that are not run as well as Supported Work would presumably have a lower value of project output, but probably also lower overhead costs and project costs.

Another factor that in some cases may impede the economic efficiency, narrowly defined, of public-service jobs projects is the desire to maximize the job creation effects of these projects. For example, WPA projects sometimes were deliberately designed to rely more on unskilled labor than would be typical on a construction project (Kesselman 1978, 214). Although such practices may be inefficient from the narrow perspective of maximizing project productivity, they may increase social productivity by providing more jobs to the unemployed.

Employment and Earnings Effects of Public-Service Jobs Programs on Participants

As table 7.1 shows, repeating results from chapter 5, public-service jobs programs targeted at the disadvantaged can significantly raise employment and earnings during the in-program period. These programs apparently are successful in targeting for jobs those who would have little employment or earnings without the program. The increase in employment or earnings due to public-service jobs is typically 50 to 90 percent of the employment and earnings directly provided by the program to participants.[10]

What about the medium-run effects of these programs on participants, that is, the effects on employment and earnings a year or two after the public-service job experience is over? As shown in table 7.2, medium-run effects are much more varied across programs.[11] Some of the programs are able to increase postprogram annual earnings by more than $1,000. The effects on annual earnings in some of these programs is perhaps 10 to 20 percent of the earnings boost provided during the program itself. Presumably these average effects reflect considerable variation across individuals, with some individuals experiencing earnings gains after the program that are similar to or larger than the earnings gains experienced during the program, and other individuals experiencing no postprogram gains whatsoever. Other programs seem to show no significant medium-run earnings effects. In some cases, there appear to be postprogram earnings reductions, compared to what would have happened if the individual had never participated in the public-service employment program.

These postprogram earnings effects are generally similar in size to those produced by job training programs, as reviewed in chapter 4. In some cases, such as Supported Work's effects on welfare recipients and CETA PSE jobs, the postprogram earnings effects are greater than for the average training program, but no greater than for exemplary training programs,

TABLE 7.1 *In-Program Impact of Publicly Funded Jobs Programs*

Program	Comments	Ratio of Employment/Earnings Effects to Program-Induced Increase in Employment/ Earnings for In-Program Period
Supported Work	Experimental estimates. Program: employment experience with graduated stress.	0.92 for AFDC single mothers 0.68 for ex-addicts 0.69 for ex-offenders 0.85 for youth[a]
New Hope	Experimental estimates. Program: earnings and benefits supplements, community service jobs.	0.68[b]
YIEPP	Non-experimental estimates, including displacement. Program: guaranteed jobs for youth, part-time during school, full-time in summer.	0.67 for school-year jobs 0.44 for summer jobs[c]
Summer Youth Jobs	Non-experimental estimates, including displacement.	0.67 for nonwhite youth[d]
Youth Corps	Experimental estimates. Program: provided jobs in conservation or human services both summer and year-round for disadvantaged youths, ages sixteen to twenty-five.	0.57[e]

[a] These are ratios of experimental-control differences in earnings, seven to nine months after enrollment, divided by program earnings during the same time period, as reported in MDRC (1980).
[b] This is derived as the two-year effect on average earnings per participant of $646, versus two-year provisions of $945 in earnings from a community service job per participant (Bos et al. 1999).
[c] Derived from Farkas et al. (1982, 125, table 5.8), from estimated program effect in site city versus comparison city, divided by program employment in site.
[d] Ellwood and Crane (1984).
[e] Derived from Abt report (Jastrzab et al. 1996), which estimates that provided earnings of $6.76 per service hour are offset by $2.92 in reduced other earnings that treatment group would have received without program.

such as those run by the Center for Employment Training. Of course, by the very nature of these two types of programs, PSE programs produce much larger in-program employment and earnings effects than do job training programs. In addition, those who benefit the most from PSE are unlikely to be the same types of persons who benefit the most from training. As I discuss later in this chapter, PSE is likely to be of most help for individuals whose employment problems are primarily due to lack of work

TABLE 7.2 *Estimates of Postprogram Earnings Effects of Programs for the Disadvantaged with Significant Public-Service Employment/Work Experience Component*

Program	Comments	Annual Postprogram Earnings Effects (1998 Dollars)	Postprogram Earnings Effects as Proportion of Program Earnings
Supported Work Program	Experiment. Jobs with graduated stress. Four target groups: AFDC (mostly women), addicts (mostly men), offenders (mostly men), and youth.	AFDC: $2,771[a] Ex-addicts: 934 (n.s.)[b] Ex-offenders: 106 (n.s.) Youth: 531 (n.s.)	AFDC: 0.22[c] Ex-addicts: 0.10 Ex-offenders: 0.01 Youth: 0.07
CETA PSE jobs	Non-experimental results.	Adult women: 2,120[d] Adult men: −295 Young women: 1,200 Young men: −763	Adult women: 0.09[e] Adult men: −0.01 Young women: 0.05 Young men: −0.03
CETA work experience jobs	Non-experimental results.	Adult women: 568[f] Adult men: −814 Young women: −401 Young men: −2,569	—
AFDC Homemaker Home Health Aide Program	Experimental estimates. Subsidized work as welfare recipients for home health aide.	923[g]	0.25[h]
Community work experience programs	Experimental estimates. Work experience programs within welfare system. AFDC (mostly women) and AFDC-U (mostly men).	San Diego:[i] • AFDC applicants: 588 • AFDC-U applicants: (−220) (ns) Cook County: 51[i] (n.s.) West Virginia[i] (n.s.) • AFDC recipients: 1 (n.s.) • AFDC-U recipients: (−245) (n.s.)	—
WIN program: subsidized employment and training component	Non-experimental estimates. Subsidized employment or training for welfare recipients.	3,128[j]	—
Employment Opportunity Pilot Project: subsidized employment and training component	Non-experimental estimates. Subsidized employment and training for low-income persons.	878[k]	0.16[l]

(Table continues on p. 184.)

TABLE 7.2 *Continued*

Program	Comments	Annual Postprogram Earnings Effects (1998 Dollars)	Postprogram Earnings Effects as Proportion of Program Earnings
Youth Incentive Entitlement Pilot Project	Non-experimental estimates. Guaranteed jobs for disadvantaged youth.	1,306[m]	—
Maine TOPS program	Experimental estimates. Training and work experience and subsidized employment for welfare recipients.	1,243[n]	—
STETS program	Experimental estimates. Work experience plus subsidized employment for mentally retarded.	1,021[o]	—

Note: Programs considered are those in which a significant share of participants go through public employment or work experience. Where possible, I estimate the separate contribution of public employment or work experience, although this is seldom possible. In general, I estimate annual earnings effects based on earnings effects for some time period close to one year after the end of public employment or work experience. All estimates are expressed in 1998 dollars and are earnings effects per year. I also, where possible, state the earnings effects as a proportion of the earnings shock provided during the program period by the public employment or work experience. In some cases, the earnings effects can be stated only as a proportion of actual earnings paid by the program; in general that proportion is greater than the earnings shock provided by the program because participants would have had some earnings even without the program.

[a] Real earnings effects taken from various chapters of Hollister, Kemper, and Maynard (1984). Postprogram effects taken from months 25 to 27 after random assignment.

[b] n.s.: not statistically significant at 5 percent level.

[c] Earnings effects for months 25 to 27 of random assignment are taken relative to earnings effects of one to three months after random assignment.

[d] Estimates given are medians for studies summarized in Barnow (1987). For each study, I estimate effects for women and men overall by combining results for whites and minorities by assumption, based on Cook et al. (1985, 34), that 66 percent of CETA PSE participants during this period were white and 34 percent minority. For Bassi's (1993) study, I combined effects for economically disadvantaged not on welfare and those on welfare using the proportions in PSE from each group during this period from Cook et al. (1985, 34). For adult women and men, six studies are summarized. Effects for women in 1998 dollars vary from $1,160 to $3,348, effects for men from −$2,090 to $1,233. For young women and young men, only two studies are summarized, in which effects for young women in 1998 dollars are $130 and $2,530; for young men these two studies give estimates of −$518 and −$1,007.

[e] Proportions given are based on statement by Bassi (1983) that average costs of CETA PSE per participant were $23,579 (after conversion to 1998 dollars). The net earnings shock of CETA is less than this because participants would have had some earnings even without the program. Hence, figures for postprogram effects as a proportion of earnings given in the table for CETA PSE are understated relative to what effects would be as a proportion of the in-program earnings increase provided by CETA. If this displacement effect was 0.3, then the AFDC number for the proportions would be 0.13 rather than 0.09.

[f] Estimates are derived from Barnow (1987) and are medians of a number of studies. The methodology to derive these results is similar to that used for CETA PSE.

TABLE 7.2 *Continued*

[g] Estimated effects are two years after the program, for 1987, and are derived from Bell et al. (1995, 62). Effects cited are per participant.
[h] Proportion is derived as the earnings effect for 1987 (second year after program), divided by the earnings effect per participant for 1985, the main in-program year (Bell et al. 1995).
[i] Estimated effects are derived from Brock et al. (1993). AFDC-U results in West Virginia are actually nonexperimental effects based on a comparison area. Estimated effects are annual averages of effects from three months to eighteen months after random assignment. As noted in chapter 7, particularly in West Virginia, where no limit was placed on tenure in work experience assignments, this period was clearly the period during which some work in work experience jobs, which are not counted as "earnings," was taking place.
[j] These estimates come from Grossman et al. (1985) and are their figures for quarter 7 after enrollment in WIN. The Grossman estimates represent the effects of participating in the subsidized employment and training component of WIN, not WIN in general. They attempt to control for selection bias in these non-experimental estimates. It is unclear to what extent the estimates given here are effects for subsidized employment and to what extent they are effects for subsidized training.
[k] These estimates are based on Grossman et al. (1985) and are their figures for quarter 7 after enrollment in EOPP. The Grossman model shows estimated effects for participating in EOPP subsidized employment and training; they attempt to model for selection into SET and correct for selection bias. Because the most common EOPP assignment after job search was to subsidized employment, not training, we can be fairly certain that these estimates represent effects of subsidized employment.
[l] The proportion is the earnings effects for quarter 7 in Grossman et al. (1985), divided by the earnings effects for quarter 2 after random assignment.
[m] These estimates are based on the fall 1981 follow-up. I use numbers reported by Farkas et al. (1984) per YIEPP participant (xxvi); these are blown up from effects per program eligible by a factor of one over 0.73, the proportion of those eligible who participated at some point during full-scale program operations. Fall 1981 is just after the program ceased operation during the summer of 1981, but as Farkas et al. (1984) point out, the program was being phased out during 1980 to 1981 and only 13 percent of the individuals in the group followed for this estimate had a YIEPP job during this period; 43 percent had YIEPP job in 1978 to 1979, and 39 percent had YIEPP job in 1979 to 1980.
[n] This estimate is derived from the quarter 11 earnings effects of the program per experimental (Auspos et al. 1988, xxi).
[o] These estimates are derived from estimated effects on earnings twenty-two months after random assignment (Bangser 1985, 23).

experience, whereas training programs address specific skill or information deficiencies.

What about effects after four or five years, that is, in the long run? There is not much evidence on this. As shown in table 7.3, which combines information from chapter 4 with some additional studies, there generally is no dramatic falloff in program effects as we go from the medium run to the long run. Whatever falloff in earnings effects occurs appears to be concentrated in the immediate postprogram period. Thus, the key issue in determining the long-run effectiveness of these programs appears to be their medium-run effectiveness, which, as mentioned, is quite varied.

A number of factors have been explored in different research projects for their association with the postprogram effectiveness of public-service employment programs. Based on this research, the following conclusions seem warranted.

1. PSE programs are usually more effective for adult women than for adult men or youth. For evidence, see the results for Supported Work,

TABLE 7.3 *Long-Run Effects of Publicly Funded Jobs*

Program	Comments	Effects of Program Four or Five Years After Program Completion for Groups That Experienced Significant Postprogram Earnings Effects (1998 Dollars)	Long-Run Effects as Proportion of Immediate Postprogram Effects
Supported Work	Experiment. Subsidized jobs featuring graduated stress.	AFDC target group (only group with significant postprogram earnings effects): $1,140[a]	1.84[b]
AFDC Homemaker Home Health Aide Program	Experimental estimates. Subsidized work as home health aide.	585[c]	0.63[d]
WIN program: subsidized employment and training component	Non-experimental estimates. Subsidized employment and training for welfare recipients.	2,910[e]	0.93[f]

Sources: [a] Long-run effects are taken from 1983 effects in Couch (1992), the fifth postprogram year. Because Couch's estimates are taken from social security records, they probably miss considerable amounts of earnings, as noted by Grossman et al. (1985, 74). Many Supported Work participants ended up getting public-sector jobs that might during this time period have been uncovered by social security. Couch also estimates effects through 1986. Compared to 1983 annual effects of $1,140, subsequent years' effects are: 1984—$1,313; 1985—$1,033; 1986—$938 (all in 1998 dollars). There is very little sign of a falloff in the real dollar effects of Supported Work over time.

[b] This is the ratio of the earnings effects that Couch (1992) estimates for AFDC recipients in 1983 to the effects estimated by Couch for 1979. The estimates from the original Supported Work study are much higher because of uncovered earnings of Supported Work participants.

[c] Estimated effects are five years after the program, for 1990, and are derived from Bell et al. (1995, 62). Effects cited are per participant.

[d] The proportion is derived as the earnings effect for 1990 (fifth year after program), divided by the earnings effect per participant for 1987, the second postprogram year, and are derived from Bell et al. (1995).

[e] These estimates come from Grossman et al. (1985) and are their figures for quarter 15 after enrollment in WIN. The Grossman estimates represent effects for participating in the subsidized employment and training component of WIN, not WIN in general. They attempt to control for selection bias in these non-experimental estimates. It is unclear to what extent the estimates given here are effects for subsidized employment and to what extent they are effects for subsidized training.

[f] These are the estimated effects from Grossman et al. (1985) for quarter 15 after enrollment in WIN, divided by the estimated effects for quarter 7 after enrollment in WIN.

CETA PSE and work experience, and community work experience programs in San Diego, as reported in table 7.2. One hypothesis for why PSE programs are more effective for women is that the greatest employment problem of women on welfare is often, to a large extent, the simple lack of much previous work experience. The employment problems of disadvantaged youth, male ex-drug addicts, male ex-offenders, and the hard-core male unemployed may be due not so much to lack of work experience as to other problems.

2. *In some studies, participants with less prior work experience have greater postprogram benefits from PSE programs, but this finding is not universal.* For example, in the Supported Work Program, female AFDC recipients with no prior work experience gained more in postprogram earnings compared to controls with no prior work experience than did female AFDC recipients with some prior work experience (Hollister and Maynard 1984, 115). (Female AFDC recipients with no prior work experience had similar absolute levels of earnings after Supported Work to female AFDC recipients with some prior work experience who participated in Supported Work, but their earnings were higher compared to those of the relevant control group.) The effects of EOPP also appear to be greater for those with no prior work experience, although the differences across groups are not statistically significant (Grossman, Maynard, and Roberts 1985, 77). But as a counterexample, there was no sign that participants with lower levels of work experience gained more from community work experience jobs in San Diego, Cook County, Illinois, or West Virginia than those with higher levels of experience (Goldman, Friedlander, and Long 1986; Friedlander et al. 1986; Friedlander et al. 1987).[12] Also, there is no sign that subsidized employment and training in the WIN program had greater effects on those with no prior work experience (Grossman et al. 1985, 77). Perhaps the key issue is whether lack of work experience is the key problem facing an individual or merely one symptom of deeper underlying problems. If lack of work experience is the problem, it seems plausible that the work experience provided by PSE jobs provides a solution. But if lack of work experience is due to some deeper problems, then simply providing work experience may not help much.

3. *Postprogram earnings effects are generally higher in PSE programs than in workfare or work experience programs.* That is, postprogram earnings effects are often greater in programs that provide a job that is officially labeled as such, and pays a wage, as opposed to jobs in which an individual works enough hours to pay back his or her welfare benefit levels. This is true comparing CETA PSE jobs and CETA work experience jobs, and comparing results from community work experience programs in the 1980s with the results of various types of PSE experiments in the 1970s and 1980s (see table 7.2). There could be a number of explanations for this pattern. If employers take the jobs more seriously if they are labeled real jobs, then perhaps they would provide more on-the-job-training, have higher expectations, and be more likely to hire the individual permanently after the subsidized time period is over. Perhaps participants take the job

more seriously if it is labeled a real job, and perhaps succeeding at a real job has greater benefits in terms of self-esteem. Perhaps the programs themselves treat the jobs more seriously if the job slots are labeled real jobs rather than simply seen as ways of enforcing a work obligation on welfare recipients. Greater program effort may increase the quality of the work experience provided by different job slots.

4. Imposing a reasonable time limit of perhaps six months or so appears likely to increase the effects of PSE employment on employment in regular, unsubsidized jobs. For example, in the West Virginia community work experience program, no time limit was set on CWEP jobs, and as a result many West Virginia participants simply stayed in these jobs (Friedlander et al. 1986, 83–87, 179–83). This may explain in part why the program had no positive effects on earnings from regular employment. In the recent New Hope experiment,

> one concern voiced by New Hope staff was [that] some CSJ participants grew too comfortable in their jobs and did not want to leave. The project reps and CSJ staff often had to prod participants into looking for unsubsidized work, particularly as their six-month placements neared the end. Staff also suspected that some worksite sponsors tried to delay participants' transition from CSJs to unsubsidized work in order to obtain the maximum benefit from their labor. (Brock et al. 1997, 144)

Studies of Supported Work suggest that for those with "positive terminations" from the program (for example, those who went on from the program to another job or to an educational program), the positive postprogram effects of the program increased rapidly during the period from two months to six months, and also during the period from six to nine months, but did not increase thereafter. On the other hand, for those with "negative terminations" from the program (those who were fired, quit, or were incarcerated), the program had negative effects on postprogram earnings if they had participated in the program for more than six months (Hollister, Kemper, and Woolridge 1979). These findings suggest that PSE programs no longer than six to nine months in duration—provided that they are programs that make some effort to deal with participants' problems early in the program—may be of a length that maximizes postprogram effects. Budget constraints may suggest that a maximum duration closer to six months would make sense.

5. The rollover into permanent jobs provided by the work sponsors of PSE, as well as the job development efforts of program staff, appear to be important in explaining effects on postprogram earnings. A fairly sizable number of PSE participants appear to obtain postprogram jobs with their program work sponsors, that is, they "roll over" into regular positions with those sponsors. The estimated rollover percentage appeared to be about 20 percent in the CETA PSE job program of the 1970s (Cook et al. 1985, 121), as well as in the New Hope Program of the 1990s (Poglinco et al. 1998, 21). In the Supported Work Program, most of the local program sites either relied extensively on rollover into regular jobs with host agencies or used job developers extensively to help place participants with regular employers. Programs that used job developers or host agency placements tended to place half or more of program participants (Ball 1984, 72).

6. *PSE programs tend to work somewhat better if programs place participants with regular employers as host agencies rather than directly employing participants in special jobs.* This appears to be a fairly consistent result from the Supported Work Program, even though it was harder at agency-sponsored sites to consistently implement the Supported Work Program of graduated stress and work in teams (Kemper et al. 1984, 282, n. 43; Ball 1984, 66–67). Placements at host agencies may tend more often to be real jobs, with closer to real-world supervision and expectations. In addition, participants with a placement at a host agency may benefit from the greater likelihood of obtaining a permanent job through rollover.

7. *The quality of supervision matters to the long-run effects of PSE jobs, but quality can be difficult to define.* In particular, the Supported Work Program appears to have greater postprogram earnings effects for participants who were supervised by individuals who had previous experience working with the particular disadvantaged group. On the other hand, the higher education of the supervisor and the supervisor's similarity to the target group do not appear to increase the postprogram effects of the program (Hollister et al. 1979).

8. *The strength of the local labor market does not appear to have consistent effects on the postprogram effects of PSE jobs.* For example, Supported Work appeared to have greater effects on participants who entered the program when the labor market was poor (Hollister 1984, 45), whereas the San Diego work experience program had greater effects on participants who entered the program when the labor market was improving (Goldman et al. 1986, 66–80).

Public Worker Substitution and Displacement

I've already discussed in chapter 5 the displacement of other workers that may occur in the labor market as a result of an increase in the employment of the disadvantaged, such as that brought about by public-service employment programs or other labor demand policies. This discussion assumed that the net employment of the disadvantaged was initially increased by some assumed amount, and that various reactions in the labor market might in the long run cause other workers to lose their jobs and reduce the overall net employment increase from this initial amount.

But for most public-service employment programs there is also the issue of whether net public employment initially increases by as much as the jobs funded by the program. Almost all public-service employment programs involve a funding agency trying to induce another public agency or nonprofit agency to hire more disadvantaged persons. For example, the federal government provided CETA grants to local governments to encourage them to provide public jobs to the disadvantaged, and local YIEPP sponsors tried to induce local employers, mostly public-sector and nonprofit, to create additional jobs for high school–age students. In both cases, the public employers that hire the target group have some incentive, if they can get away with it, to substitute those hired from the target group for other workers they currently employ or would have employed if they had not received the funding to hire the target group. The public-service employment provides "free labor" (or almost free labor once one accounts for the employer's administrative, supervisory, or benefits costs) that allows the public or nonprofit employer to accomplish certain tasks more cheaply. This reduces the need to hire other workers and allows the public or nonprofit employer to reduce tax rates or to be less assiduous in raising funds. This reduction in net initial employment increases below the jobs funded is frequently referred to as "fiscal substitution." Ellwood and Welty (2000) use a more appropriate term for this process: "public worker substitution."

The amount of public worker substitution has been thoroughly studied for only two programs, CETA PSE jobs and YIEPP. Studies have generally relied on two methodologies: econometric estimates that attempt to determine what the public or nonprofit employer's employment level would have been without the public-service job funding; and field studies in which trained observers visit public or nonprofit employers that received public-service job funding and attempt to make a reasoned judgment about what the employer would have done without the funding. Some early econometric studies of CETA concluded that public worker substitution might be huge, in fact, essentially 100 percent within a year of the initial funding (Johnson and Tomola 1977).[13] These early estimates may reflect the design of the early CETA PSE program and its predecessor, the Public Employment Program (PEP) of 1971. These programs essentially gave local governments funds to hire any worker unemployed for more than a short length or time (as short as fifteen days in some cases) and allowed local governments to pay any wage to those workers (although the federal payment per hire was capped at some level). It is not surprising that in this case some public employers laid off some workers for a short time and then used the federal dollars to rehire them.

Later versions of CETA PSE and the YIEPP program tried to do more to minimize public worker displacement. In addition to having more regulations that explicitly prohibited public worker displacement, these later programs put more restrictions on hiring workers: those hired had to be more highly disadvantaged, funding was limited to shorter-term projects, and local governments were restricted in how much they could supplement the wages of those hired. These restrictions seem to have worked to reduce public worker substitution enormously. For example, Charles Adams, Robert Cook, and Arthur Maurice's (1983) econometric study of city payroll outlays estimates the public worker substitution effect of CETA PSE grants to be 70 percent in 1976, 23 percent in 1977, and 29 percent in 1978. After reviewing the research literature in this area, Ellwood and Welty (2000, 29) conclude that

> it appears that in at least two very different programs—the later stages of CETA, and YIEPP—we have fairly strong evidence that public substitution rates may be 25 percent or below in a reasonably tightly run program. Programs that successfully target low income, less skilled workers, provide short term employment, and pay relatively low wages appear to have far less substitution than the much more open programs of PEP and early CETA. The results also hint that displacement rates may rise over time as providers find ways to substitute the new PSE workers for unsubsidized workers.

As mentioned by Ellwood and Welty (2000), public worker substitution appears to be reduced when programs are more targeted at the disadvantaged, participant eligibility is restricted to shorter time periods, and low wages are paid. In addition, field studies suggest that whether the funder is seriously interested in enforcing regulations against public worker substitution can make a difference. For example, field studies of YIEPP (Unicon 1982) show that of the four sites studied, the Boston site had by far the largest magnitude of public worker substitution, 68 percent, whereas none of the other three sites had public worker substitution over 11 percent. Conversations with the staff of the Boston YIEPP sponsor show that the Boston site personnel were unconcerned about public worker substitution issues and probably made little attempt to force those funded not to engage in public worker substitution (Unicon 1982, 50).

Some of the field studies also suggest that the fiscal situation of the public or nonprofit agency funded may make some difference to the ease of public worker substitution (Unicon 1982). If a public or nonprofit agency has a very tight budgetary situation and is not doing much hiring, or perhaps is even laying off individuals, then it is likely that the agency could not have afforded to hire the disadvantaged persons without the public-service employment funding. If a public or nonprofit agency has a great deal of funds and is generally expanding employment, it is harder to tell whether the public-service employment funding has caused the agency to cut back on the rate at which its regular employment is expanding.

Finally, the theory of public worker substitution suggests that it is likely to be smaller if the funded number of public-service jobs is quite large relative to the size of the agency that is being funded (Gould, Ward, and Welch 1982). At an extreme, if the number of funded PSE workers is larger than the number of workers the agency would otherwise employ, it is obviously impossible for the PSE program to cause 100 percent public worker substitution. Or to put it another way, as the PSE funding gets larger relative to the size of the agency being funded, it provides more of an incentive on the margin for the agency to expand employment. PSE funding could even increase the agency's employment by more than the number of PSE jobs, by requiring the agency to hire additional supervisors because of the expanded number of workers to supervise.

The extent of public worker substitution determines only the initial labor market impact of PSE programs. The ultimate labor market impact of these programs depends on how supply, demand, and wages in the labor market respond to the initial changes brought about by the PSE program. For example, even if a PSE program involves no public worker substitution, its market effects may alter its effects on the disadvantaged. The PSE program, by initially increasing the employment of the disadvantaged, may increase wages, particularly for the disadvantaged, which discourages employers from expanding employment. In addition, the PSE program, by soaking up some disadvantaged workers, may reduce the effective supply of disadvantaged workers to other employers, which decreases the number of disadvantaged workers hired by other employers. Finally, any inflationary effects of the PSE program may lead to macroeconomic policy changes that reduce employment.

On the other hand, even if a PSE program involves complete public worker substitution, it could ultimately expand overall employment if it is targeted and designed in a way that increases labor supply. Suppose that a PSE program successfully targets a disadvantaged group that otherwise would be out of the labor force. There is 100 percent public worker substitution in that these new PSE workers are all substituted for some other group of workers. Suppose, however, that this other group of workers stays in the labor force after the PSE program, searching for other jobs. Suppose further that the new PSE workers stay in the labor force, owing to the PSE program. Then the PSE program has successfully expanded the overall labor force. As a result, we would expect wages to go down somewhat and overall employment to expand. Even though the PSE program did not expand overall employment at the employers who received the PSE grants, the program may succeed in expanding overall employment in the nation. Appendix 10 presents a simulation, using the labor market model of appendix 2, in which the *long-run* displacement effect of a PSE program depends totally on whether the program targets those who would otherwise be out of the labor force, not on the initial public worker substitution effects of the PSE program.

As summarized in chapter 5, the displacement effects of demand-side programs like PSE programs may be reduced by:

- targeting the public-service employment on persons who are out of the labor force or part of the long-term unemployed or other unemployed groups who are relatively difficult for regular employers to successfully hire;
- designing the public-service jobs to be temporary and encouraging those hired to continue searching for regular jobs, either through job search requirements or by paying below-market wages for the public-service jobs;
- designing the public-service jobs so that they increase the long-run human capital and employability of those hired;
- targeting public-service employment programs on local labor markets with high unemployment.

The Costs of Public-Service Employment Programs

What are the costs of publicly funded jobs programs? Tables 7.4 and 7.5 report the costs of variously designed public jobs programs in two different ways. Table 7.4 states costs per participant in the program. Table 7.5 states total costs of a national program, reflecting both costs per participant and the likely number of participants.

Tables 7.4 and 7.5 focus attention on the gross budgetary costs of public-service jobs programs. It is these gross budgetary costs that in most cases have to be appropriated through the legislative process.[14] As discussed, there is some considerable offset to these costs in the value of the output produced through these programs, with the value of output perhaps equal to one-half of the gross budgetary costs, depending on how well organized the program is. In addition, there may be some welfare savings associated with the program. These welfare savings are difficult to estimate and depend on many features of the design of the program. For example, does the program target those who would have gotten off welfare anyway, or those who most likely would have continued to receive regular welfare benefits without the public jobs program? If the jobs created are targeted at welfare recipients, do the jobs on net make entering welfare more or less attractive?

As tables 7.4 and 7.5 show, the costs of a public jobs program vary

TABLE 7.4 *Costs of Publicly Funded Jobs Programs*

Program	Wage Costs per Participant (1998 Dollars)	Overhead Costs per Participant (1998 Dollars)	Total Gross Costs per Participant Without Any Offsets from Reduced Welfare, Increased Taxes, Program Output, etc. (1998 Dollars)
CETA PSE	$23,579[a]	$4,257[b]	27,836
Supported Work Program	11,270[c]	12,117	23,387
AFDC Homemaker Home Health Aide Program	6,847[d]	10,376	17,223
STETS program	5,063[e]	9,901	14,964
Youth Corps	5,734[f]	8,363	14,097
New Hope Program	3,068[g]		
Youth Incentive Entitlement Pilot Project	2,815[h]	1,661	4,476
Median costs of work experience for welfare recipients participating in eight state work experience programs		1,341 for AFDC 1,271 for AFDC-U[i]	
Maine TOPS		591[j]	
New York Work Experience Program		483 to 4,800[k]	

Sources: [a] This figure is cost of CETA PSE per participant during fiscal year 1976, as reported in Bassi (1983). The cost per participant would be even greater because some participants in CETA PSE participated in more than one fiscal year.

[b] This is the midpoint figure from Ellwood and Welty (2000), derived from their statement that allowed administrative costs for CETA prime sponsors varied between 10 and 20 percent of total costs.

[c] Figures for costs are derived from nonparticipants' costs per participant from Kemper, Long, and Thornton (1984, table 8.3). Costs per service year would be higher. Costs adjusted for the value of in-program output and the value of reduced transfer payments would be lower.

[d] Cost figures per participant are derived from Bell and Orr (1994, table 3). The cost figures used are simple averages over seven state experiments considered by Bell and Orr.

[e] The costs reported here combine the costs of all phases of the program, where the program includes extensive counseling in all phases, work experience in phase 1, OJT in phase 2, and postprogram support services in phase 3. Hence, figures here overstate the costs of work experience alone in phase 1. Figures derived from Kerachsky et al. (1985, 101, table VIII.4).

TABLE 7.4 *Continued*

[f] These figures are derived from Jastrzab et al. (1996). Exhibit 3 states costs per service hour. For the four projects for which this analysis was applied, average service hours per participant appear to be 793 hours. Multiplication and then adjustment using the CPI yields the figures reported here.
[g] This is the two-year cost per New Hope participant who ever took a community service job. Thirty-two percent of New Hope participants took a community service job at some point during the experiment. Hence, the figure from Bos et al. (1999, 254, table 8.2) is divided by 0.32, and then adjusted to 1998 prices using the CPI.
[h] Costs per participant figures are derived from Gueron (1984, 10–11). Costs per participant-year would be approximately double the figures given, since the average participant participated less than half a year.
[i] These are taken from Brock et al. (1993, table 9). These are per-participant numbers; costs per experimental would be lower. Figures reported here are the median of all eight states for AFDC, four states for AFDC-U. The range is $1,133 to $2,335 for AFDC, $768 to $1,450 for AFDC-U. Brown (1997, 55) reports a range of costs for the combined categories of OJT and work experience that is toward the low range of the costs reported by Brock et al. of $384 to $1,579.
[j] This figure is derived from Auspos et al. (1988, 134, table 6.5), whose figures are for work experience costs per participant. In addition, there are costs for child care and transportation associated with work experience that are not included here. These costs are reported only in table 6.6 per experimental and are not broken out by different TOPS component. From the reported figures in table 6.6, it appears that at most, adding child care and transportation costs would approximately double the costs reported here.
[k] This is costs per FTE job of administration and supervision of WEP workers given in Lerman and Rosenberg (1997). The costs per WEP worker would be less, given that most do not work full-time. This considers only costs to agencies supervising workers and does not consider costs to the welfare department of running the program.

widely with design. These cost differences should not be interpreted as differences in the efficiency of the programs. The tables are truly comparing apples and oranges, since there are huge variations in costs owing to huge variations in the designs of public jobs programs. Among the factors affecting the costs of public jobs programs are the following:

1. The wage rate paid to participants: Some programs pay closer to market wage rates, for example, the CETA program and the Supported Work Program (75 percent of market wages was the targeted wage rate of Supported Work). Harvey's (1989) proposal (table 7.5) for guaranteed public-service jobs for the unemployed proposes paying full market wages. Other programs simply pay minimum wages, for example, YIEPP and New Hope. Kaus's (1992) proposal for guaranteed public-service jobs proposes paying slightly below the minimum wage. As mentioned earlier, paying lower wages, in addition to lowering costs, encourages participants to move to regular jobs. On the other hand, paying lower wages may encourage individuals to reject the public-service jobs in favor of other alternatives, such as crime or the underground economy.

2. The extent of job development and training offered participants before obtaining a job, and the extent of support services while on the job: Some programs, such as Supported Work, New Hope, and YIEPP, provide job developers who try to create appropriate job slots for participants in a

TABLE 7.5 *Projected National Costs of Large-Scale Publicly Funded Jobs Programs*

Program	Comments	Number of Annual Participants in National Program (Millions)	Number of Full-Time Equivalent (FTE) Jobs Created per Year by National Implementation of Program (Millions)	FTE Job Impact of Program (Millions)	Annual Cost (1998 Dollars)
Harvey's employment assurance policy[a]	Guaranteed market-wage jobs for all unemployed above 2 percent, half of discouraged workers, 90 percent of welfare parents	10.2	8.6	?	$206.5 billion gross; $37.9 billion net
Kaus's neo-WPA program[b]	Guaranteed below-minimum-wage jobs for two-thirds of welfare recipients, one-third of unemployed, one-third of "discouraged" workers	5.3	5.3	?	$104.8 billion gross; $63.6 billion net
Youth Incentive Entitlement Pilot Projects Program[c]	Guaranteed part-time jobs during school or full-time summer jobs for disadvantaged youth	1.14	0.24	0.15	$3.6 billion gross
New Hope[d]	Package of earnings supplements, guaranteed benefits, child care, and community service jobs (CSJs) for low-income persons in high-poverty neighborhoods	1.2	0.07	0.04	$0.8 billion for CSJs; $5.6 billion for entire New Hope package gross; $5.1 billion net

Antidisplacement job creation for welfare reform[e]	Jobs for welfare recipients needed to offset displacement effects in 2005 of welfare reform	1.4	0.45	0.29	$6.6 billion gross
W-2 community service jobs program on a national level[f]	Families applying for family assistance who cannot find job on own and who are considered employable by caseworkers	1.443 million at current national caseloads; 0.23 million if national caseloads reduced as much as in Wisconsin	1.082 million at current national caseloads; 0.171 million if national caseloads reduced as much as in Wisconsin	?	$16.5 billion gross, at least $4.8 billion net at current national caseloads; $2.6 billion gross, at least $0.76 billion net if caseloads reduced as much as in Wisconsin
Work experience program like New York City's on a national scale[g]	Welfare recipients who cannot find job on own and are considered employable	0.217 million if as many welfare recipients are involved as are currently involved in New York City	0.108	?	$1.6 billion $0.5 billion

[a] Derived from Harvey (1989, ch. 2). The numbers for participants and jobs used here are simply the average annual figures for the ten-year period considered by Harvey. The gross and net cost numbers are also annual averages, but updated to 1998 dollars using the CPI.

[b] Derived from Kaus (1992, 261). I updated Kaus's budget numbers based on CPI change from 1990 to 1998, rather than attempting to reestimate all the other numbers derived by Kaus.

[c] Cost projections are derived from Gueron (1984). She reports estimates that if eligibility extended to all youths below poverty standard, an estimated 976,000 youths would participate per year at a cost in 1980 dollars of $1.581 billion. But numbers she reports indicate: the average participant participates for only 0.456 of year (derived from numbers on full-year costs and per participant costs); while participating, work hours averaged about 0.467 of full-time, full-year work hours (derived from weighting average summer and school year work hours). In addition, I adjust number of participants upward by the ratio of 1998 children in poverty (less than 18) to 1980 children in poverty (U.S. Census Bureau 1999, tables B-2, B-6). Doing all these adjustments yields FTE participants as of 1997 of 0.254 million (.976 × .456 × .467 × (13.467 / 11.543)). Job impact is calculated by multiplying the FTE jobs created by the weighted average of in-program impacts reported in table 7.1 for school-year and summer jobs. I also adjusted her annual budget number by the ratio of children in poverty in 1998 and 1980, and 1998 to 1980 ratio of CPI, to get $3.6 billion ($1.581 × [14.113 / 11.543] × [163.0 / 82.4]).

[d] These projections are largely based on Bos et al. (1999) and Brock et al. (1997). According to the report by Brock et al. (1997), estimated "demand" for New Hope from these neighborhoods would be approximately 12,397 participants out of a neighborhood population of 87,968 participants. These are high-poverty neighborhoods. Assume that eligibility for a national program would be restricted to residents of neighborhoods with poverty rates of 40 percent or greater, a criterion that, according to Jargowsky (1997), included 8.5 million persons in 1990. Hence, we would expect 1.2 million participants in a na-

(Table continues on p. 198.)

tional version of New Hope. According to data in Bos et al. (1999), during the two-year follow-up, New Hope's average cost per year per participant in total was $4,704 (gross costs, not allowing for program offsets), which yields total estimated New Hope costs of $5.6 billion. Net costs per year per participant are $4,214. But average CSJ payments are only $491 per year for participants. If we assume overhead of 42 percent based on Ellwood and Welty (2000), then total CSJ costs of New Hope are approximately $.08 billion (1.2 million × $491 × 1.42). On average, only 32 percent of New Hope participants took a CSJ, for an average of 6.1 months during the two years. Jobs were generally 30 hours per week. Hence, the number of FTE jobs involved in a national program would be equal to 73,200 (1.2 million × 0.32 × [3.05 / 12] × [30 / 40]). The program was estimated to raise average annual work hours of participants by 62.7 hours per year, or 0.0314 of 2,000 annual work hours. (This average work hours effect is derived from Bos et al. [1999, 127–28, table 4.5], weighing the results by the proportion of program group in each of two initial employment statuses.) So increase in FTE employment would be 37,680 (0.0323 × 1.2 million). This is low in part because earnings supplement led some individuals to substitute part-time for full-time work.

[e] The figures here are derived from Bartik's (1998) projection that welfare reforms will add 1.4 million persons to the labor force from 1993 to 2005. Projections using the model described in appendix 2 indicate that this welfare reform will reduce employment rates among single mothers with less than a college degree by 0.21 of the shock, or 294,000. Estimates from Bartik (1999) using this same model indicate that with low unemployment, the five-year elasticity of employment of single mothers with respect to a labor demand shock to single mothers is 0.647, indicating that public-service employment of 454,000 (294,000 / 0.647) would be needed to offset the employment displacement effects of welfare reform. The calculated costs come from multiplying this number of jobs times the minimum wage of $5.15 per hour times 2,000 hours, and then adding in nonlabor costs of 42 percent (based on Ellwood and Welty 2000).

[f] Data from Wisconsin suggest that community service job placement in the spring of 1999 was 54.1 percent of W-2 placements (Institute for Wisconsin's Future 1999). The national caseload as of March 1999 was 2.668 million. Multiplying a national caseload of this amount by 54.1 percent yields national CSJ participants of 1.443 million. CSJ placements are three-quarters time, so FTE jobs involved are 1.082 million. Wisconsin pays $673 per month for CSJ placements. If we assume 42 percent overhead based on Ellwood and Welty (2000), this is gross costs of $11,468 per participant per year, at a net cost of $3,390 per participant per year. Multiplying out yields the higher gross and net costs cited in the table. But Wisconsin has had much larger reductions in welfare caseloads than the United States as whole. Using figures from Wiseman (1999), the CSJ participants in September 1998 were probably only 6.1 percent of Wisconsin's January 1988 caseload. If we multiply this by the U.S. national caseload of 3.742 million in January 1988, we would get national CSJ participants of only 0.228 million. Similar calculations yield the lower cost figures in the table. It should be noted that because most states pay much lower benefits than Wisconsin, the net agency costs of CSJs in most states would be considerably larger, because wages paid for CSJs would have to be much higher than these low benefits. On the other hand, there are other offsets to this job creation that are not considered, such as the value of services provided, any local multiplier effects, and so on.

[g] According to Ellwood and Welty (2000), New York City currently has 18,800 TANF recipients on average in its work experience program. According to Brookings Institution (1999), New York City currently has 230,942 families in its TANF caseload, so the percentage enrolled is 7.8 percent. If the same percentage of the national March 1999 caseload of 2.668 million was enrolled, this would be enrollment of 217,000. The work experience program requires work of twenty hours per week at minimum wage. One thousand hours per year at minimum wage costs about $1,118 billion. Assuming overhead of 42 percent yields net costs of $0.470 billion and gross costs of $1.588. Note that in many other states, paying for 1,000 hours at minimum wage might well exceed the cash grant, so actual budget costs of this program would be somewhere between the gross and net costs cited here.

variety of public and nonprofit agencies. For other programs, such as some of the workfare programs in which individuals work off their welfare benefits, city or state agencies are simply ordered by a mayor or governor to create job slots for workfare participants. This is easier and cheaper but probably produces more variable job quality in terms of productivity and training potential. Some programs, such as the AFDC Homemaker Home Health Aide Program and the STETS Program, provide significant training before the individual takes the job, while most other public-service jobs programs do not. Some programs provide extensive support services and supervision for participants while they are employed. At the extreme, most Supported Work projects were totally run and managed by the Supported Work agencies. In other cases, the jobs program provides less support, and participants receive whatever support and supervision is provided by their public or nonprofit employer.

3. The usual weekly hours worked by participants, and the number of weeks worked: Some programs, such as CETA and Supported Work, provided close to full-time weekly hours and often employ individuals in publicly funded jobs for as long as a year or more. Other programs provided more part-time jobs. For example, YIEPP provided disadvantaged youths with only part-time jobs during the school year, and New Hope's community service jobs were only thirty hours per week. Some programs also have lower typical lengths of participation. For example, the New Hope community service job positions could last no more than six months at a time.

4. The proportion of potentially eligible participants who are actually provided publicly funded jobs: As shown in table 7.5, some of the huge projected costs of some proposals for "guaranteed jobs," such as the proposals of Harvey (1989) and Kaus (1992), are for programs that essentially assume that most unemployed individuals will be provided with publicly funded jobs. Some publicly funded jobs programs would be considerably cheaper because they would focus on only one target group among the unemployed; for example, YIEPP focuses on disadvantaged high school–age youth. Most publicly funded jobs programs that have actually been implemented locally would have relatively low costs if implemented nationally because they provide publicly funded jobs only to a fraction of the potentially eligible population. For example, the New Hope Program provides community service jobs at any point in time to a small proportion of the eligibles in its target neighborhoods. As mentioned earlier, this occurs because some eligibles are not interested in minimum-wage jobs; eligibles who do enter the program are required to engage in some job search before being provided a community service job; and the community service jobs last only six months before the individual is required to search for a job again. As another example, the W-2 program's version of community service jobs, in the form of working off welfare benefits, while provided to more than half of all welfare recipients in Wisconsin, is being offered in a state where welfare rolls dropped by almost 90 percent from 1993 to 1998. Finally, the proposal in table 7.5 for offsetting the effects of 1.4 million welfare recipients entering the labor market from 1993 to 2005 calls for only 450,000 public-service jobs, since labor market demand is predicted to adjust to accommodate most, although not all, of the increased labor supply of welfare recipients, as described in chapter 4.

What is the cost per participant, and the total cost, that is "right" for a publicly funded jobs program? The honest answer is that we don't know. There are some difficult trade-offs among these different factors affecting costs. More expensive programs may increase the earnings and income of participants more, both while they are in the program and when they leave it. On the other hand, more expensive programs are more difficult to finance and may have to be cut back to serve fewer persons. Furthermore, if a public-service jobs program is made too attractive, it may discourage individuals from taking jobs in the private economy. We simply do not have enough operational experience to give definitive answers on the "right" cost design for a publicly funded jobs program. The right design may vary quite a bit with local economic conditions and with the wages and employment opportunities that prevail in the regular local economy.

Compared to job training programs, costs per participant for PSE programs tend to be higher. However, some lower-cost PSE programs, such as YIEPP, with more limited work hours, wages, or support services, are cheaper per participant than some of the more expensive training programs, such as the Minority Female Single Parent program, which costs more than $6,000 per participant (see chapter 4).

The Lack of a Political Consensus for Publicly Funded Jobs

Despite the potential for publicly funded jobs to increase employment and earnings, there has generally not been a strong political base capable of uniting behind a particular program and wage schedule for a large-scale, ongoing program of publicly funded jobs. The exceptions so far have been the WPA in the 1930s, CETA during the 1970s, and workfare programs in Wisconsin and New York City during the 1990s. All of these large-scale programs have been highly politically controversial. The controversy eventually killed the WPA and CETA; it may eventually undermine the programs in Wisconsin and New York City.

The WPA was frequently politically controversial because its activities were perceived as competing with private business. Given that the WPA focused on public works, its projects often did construction work that might conceivably have been done by private contractors if funds for the projects could have been found. In many cases, the WPA was forced to restrict its projects in response to political pressure from businesses that perceived a competitive threat. For example, the WPA often had to abandon slum clearance and rat extermination projects because of the opposition of private building wreckers and commercial exterminators (Howard 1943, 134, 166). In contrast, the CCC was much less controversial, in part because CCC workers usually engaged in activities, such as reforestation and park improvement, that were of little interest to private businesses.

In more recent years, publicly funded jobs projects have focused more on public services provided by government and nonprofit agencies, services that are not perceived as directly competitive with the output markets of private-sector businesses. However, a continued concern among conservatives has been that publicly funded jobs for the disadvantaged may represent a permanent expansion of government and drain labor away from the private sector, particularly if the publicly funded jobs pay wages that are "too high." During the WPA era, the WPA responded to political criticism that it was creating local labor shortages: "Entire projects would be halted in areas that were likely to experience general increases in their labor demand. Groups of workers thought to be needed by private employers were sometimes dismissed in wholesale fashion. Selective dismissals were applied to workers having experience in lines of work believed to be in demand" (Kesselman 1978, 199). During the debate over CETA, according to one history of the program, conservatives were concerned that "public employment of the unemployed, especially at competitive wages, raised the specter of draining labor and other resources from the private sector. If government acted as the employer of last resort, it could easily become the employer of first resort" (Mucciaroni 1990, 71–72). More recently, some conservative groups have strongly opposed the Clinton administration's decision that workfare positions must pay minimum wages. For example, "Robert Rector, an analyst at the Heritage Foundation, a conservative research organization in Washington, said the decision to apply minimum wage laws would cripple the work requirements [of the new welfare reform bill]. 'That's a gangland execution of welfare reform,' he said. 'You want to make welfare less attractive than low skilled jobs. You want to increase the incentive for people to get off the rolls as quickly as possible'" (DeParle 1997).

On the other side of the spectrum, labor unions and other liberal groups have been concerned that workfare programs at low wages may displace other public workers and undermine the wages of public-sector workers and other workers. For example, during the 1980s, because of opposition from local unions, work experience programs in Cook County,

Illinois, had to be carried out by nonprofits rather than by government agencies (Brock et al. 1993). The opposition of unions also led in the 1980s to a work experience program in Pennsylvania being almost completely phased out when the state faced a budget crunch. More recently, Ohio's AFSCME (American Federation of State, County, and Municipal Employees) affiliate unsuccessfully tried to include a ban on workfare in the state's plan to implement the 1996 federal welfare reform bill (Walters 1997). Activist groups such as ACORN (Association of Community Organizations for Reform Now) and the Center for Community Change have criticized workfare positions for paying below livable wages and having poor working conditions. And as mentioned earlier, the Center for Budget and Policy Priorities has extensively promoted the idea of wage-paying community service jobs rather than workfare—its key argument being that wage-paying positions would make job holders eligible for the Earned Income Tax Credit, whereas simply "working off benefits" does not.

The critical question for the political viability of publicly funded jobs is whether there is some compromise on the wages and nature of publicly funded jobs programs that would allow them to have a stable base of political support sufficient to allow them to be enacted on a large-scale basis. So far the answer is, in general, no. Many conservatives would rather have no program than one that pays wages that are "too high." Many liberals would rather have no program than one that pays wages that are "too low." There does not seem to be any wage in the middle that is just right. In fact, wages in the middle seem to often make both groups unhappy with the resulting compromise.

The political balance might be different if the unemployed and the poor had any strong voice in the matter. Both conservative and liberal groups weighing in on this issue are primarily those who already have businesses, jobs, or ideological interests that might be adversely affected by a program of publicly funded jobs. The unemployed themselves are much less likely to participate in politics or to vote than are the employed (Schlozman and Verba 1979). In the absence of direct pressure on the jobs issue from the unemployed and poor, policy debates over publicly funded jobs may tend to focus on how such programs might adversely affect the interests of other workers or of businesses.

Conclusion

Although creating public-service jobs for the disadvantaged has a bad reputation, this reputation is contradicted by most of the research. Rather than being "make-work," well-organized public-service jobs programs can produce useful output. With good administration, the substitution of subsidized PSE workers for regular public workers can be reduced to a modest percentage. PSE programs can be effectively targeted at disadvantaged persons who otherwise would not be employed. In the long run, such targeting helps expand the total number of jobs in the economy and reduces the extent to which the new workers displace other workers from jobs. The costs of public-service jobs programs can be limited to a feasible level by designing these programs appropriately, including: requiring disadvantaged persons to search for regular jobs before taking public-service jobs; making the public-service jobs short-term temporary jobs; limiting PSE jobs to less than forty hours per week; and keeping PSE wage rates close to the minimum wage. These design features also help avoid displacement by targeting the PSE jobs at those less likely to get regular jobs on their own and by encouraging PSE job holders to move on to regular jobs.

Compared to the average job training program, the average PSE program tends to be more expensive per participant. However, if measures are taken to hold costs down, PSE costs per participant can be held down to a level somewhat lower than that of more expensive training programs. PSE programs yield postprogram earnings effects that are comparable to those of job training programs. However, one of the biggest distinctions between PSE programs and job training programs is that PSE programs yield immediate increases in employment and earnings during the program period, as well as yielding useful output. In addition, the postprogram benefits of both PSE and job training are probably concentrated among a few program participants, and probably not the same types of participants. Thus, PSE and training should be viewed as complementary programs. Both types of programs may be needed to achieve the needed increases in employment and earnings among the poor.

Public-service jobs programs for the disadvantaged face strong political opposition. Labor unions fear that public-service jobs programs will undermine public-sector wage standards. Conservatives fear that public-service jobs programs will be used to expand "big government." As recommended by the Center for Budget and Policy Priorities, perhaps some of this political opposition can be avoided by revising publicly funded jobs programs to focus on subsidizing new jobs for the disadvantaged in the nonprofit sector. The nonprofit sector is less unionized and less likely to be perceived as part of "big government." In addition, because many nonprofit organizations are small, it is often easier to ensure that the subsidized jobs result in expanding the total number of jobs, rather than substituting subsidized workers for regular workers.

8

WAGE SUBSIDY PROGRAMS

An alternative to the "big government" solution of public-service jobs for the disadvantaged is the "market" solution of subsidizing private for-profit employers to hire or employ the disadvantaged. As we will see, in practice the market solution may be effective only with considerable government management.

In this chapter, I first introduce some of the issues involved in providing private employers with wage subsidies for the disadvantaged. I then consider the history of wage subsidy programs in the United States before going on to discuss research findings and analyze some proposed wage subsidy programs.

An Introduction to Wage Subsidies

Wage subsidies for the disadvantaged provide private employers with either tax credits or direct wage subsidies tied to hiring or employing individuals who meet some disadvantaged criteria. The great appeal of such an approach is that in principle it provides a simple way of encouraging the private market to solve the employment problems of the disadvantaged. If the private market on its own does not provide sufficient employment for the disadvantaged from a social perspective, the natural instinct of any economist is to subsidize the employment of the disadvantaged. Such subsidies promise to change the attractiveness of hiring the disadvantaged for all private employers.

The big disadvantage of providing wage subsidies to all private employers for hiring the disadvantaged is the potentially great cost per job created. Given the likely modest wage elasticities of labor demand for disadvantaged workers (see chapter 3), only a modest number of new jobs for the disadvantaged are likely to be created. A large percentage of the subsidies to private employers are "windfall wastage," that is, payments to private employers for hiring they would have done without the subsidies. Furthermore, at least the immediate obvious effect of these wage subsidies is to transfer public resources to private businesses. Although a full analysis would have to take account of how market wages are affected by the subsidy program, the burden of proof should be placed on those claiming that the subsidy benefit is shifted, owing to increases in market wages, from businesses to workers.

Because wage subsidies can be so costly per job created, wage subsidy policies frequently include provisions intended to reduce the costs of the subsidies or to increase the targeting of the subsidized jobs at the most needy. Rather than subsidizing all employment, wage subsidies frequently are designed as "marginal employment subsidies." Under marginal employment subsidies, the wage subsidy is provided only for the firm's additional employment, possibly of some type of worker, over some baseline level of employment. This baseline could be last year's level of employment, some multiple or fraction (say 1.02 or 0.80) of last year's employment, or the firm's previous peak level of employment. Marginal employment subsidies reduce the amount of windfall wastage, though at the cost of complicating the program and possibly providing strange incentives. For example, marginal employment subsidies may give a firm an incentive to reduce employment one year in order to increase employment the next year, although this problem is reduced if there are adjustment costs to firms that change their employment from year to year.

Wage subsidy costs can also be reduced by designing the wage subsidy as a "hiring subsidy," that is, a wage subsidy paid only for new hires of some type. Hiring subsidies are less costly per job created, but they may provide some incentive for firms to increase turnover. This incentive is limited, however, if turnover is costly for the firm because it invests heavily in training of new hires. Both marginal employment subsidies and hiring subsidies are made even less costly by limiting the subsidy to the first year or two of wages for the new hires. Although this limits costs, it makes the subsidy somewhat less valuable to the firm and does not provide as much incentive for job retention of those hired.

With wage subsidies being costly per job created, it is certainly tempting to try to target these subsidies more closely at the disadvantaged groups who are most needy or whose nonemployment causes the greatest social costs. In addition, as mentioned in chapter 5, displacement effects on the labor market of wage subsidies are reduced if these subsidies are targeted at disadvantaged groups who originally were out of the labor force or otherwise were unlikely to become employed without the subsidy. However, as wage subsidy programs increase their targeting of the most disadvantaged, the programs become less attractive to firms. Because of imperfect information in the labor market, some targeting provisions may even cause *stigma effects* that reduce the employment prospects of those targeted. Labeling an individual as extremely disadvantaged, or as someone whose nonemployment brings about large social costs, may cause some employers to believe that he or she is likely to be unproductive. The wage subsidy may be insufficient to offset the expected lower productivity, and firms may be less likely to hire the targeted individuals.

To limit the costs of wage subsidies and to try to control stigma effects, wage subsidies may also be designed as *discretionary* subsidies with a fixed budget under the control of some labor market intermediary. That is, rather than consider all employers that hire or employ those who meet some criteria to be *entitled* to a subsidy, labor market agencies would hand out subsidies only to selected employers for hiring selected disadvantaged persons. Such discretion is obviously essential for keeping a wage subsidy program to a fixed budget. In addition, such discretion may avoid stigma by:

- selecting disadvantaged persons who will have better productivity;
- allowing the intermediary to develop a reputation with employers for providing good information on the disadvantaged persons who are referred under the subsidy program;
- selecting employers who are less prone to stigmatizing disadvantaged groups.

However, such wage subsidy programs lack some of the advantages of making wage subsidies an *entitlement* program. Under a discretionary program with a fixed budget, many employers do not have lower costs for hiring additional disadvantaged workers because they cannot count on receiving wage subsidies for hiring these workers. As with public-service employment programs, discretionary wage subsidies provide the subsidized employer an incentive to use the subsidy to pay for disadvantaged workers it would have hired anyway, to substitute for similar workers it would have hired anyway, or to substitute for other workers it would have hired. Avoiding this "subsidized worker substitution" may require that the program include regulatory and monitoring provisions about which employers get subsidized and for what purpose. Even without such regulations and monitoring, discretionary wage subsidy programs may require additional government "red tape" for employers.

All of these provisions intended to reduce wage subsidy costs and target wage subsidies more precisely—marginal or hiring credits, more targeted groups, more government discretion over which employers get the subsidy for what purpose—may decrease the "employer take-up rate" for the program, that is, the number of employers who are willing to participate in the program. The provisions may still make sense by increasing the benefit-cost ratio for the wage subsidy program. However, if the take-up rate is too low, the overall net benefits of the wage subsidy program may go down even if the benefit-cost ratio is improved.

Finally, the great advantage of a wage subsidy program—that it simply has the government provide funds for the private sector to use to employ the disadvantaged—is politically problematic in the United States. Many liberal groups suspect that such government subsidies to private business will benefit the subsidized businesses and not the disadvantaged. And at least some conservative groups suspect that such government involvement will lead to undue government power over private-sector decisions.

A History of National Wage Subsidy Programs in the United States

A brief historical outline and description of national programs of wage subsidies to employers for hiring the disadvantaged is provided in table 8.1.[1] National wage subsidies to employers for hiring the disadvantaged go back to at least the early 1960s. From the beginning of federally funded job training programs under the Manpower Development and Training Act (MDTA), up through the days of the Comprehensive Employment and Training Act (CETA) and the Job Training Partnership Act (JTPA) and now the Workforce Investment Act (WIA), training agencies have funded on-the-job-training contacts with private-sector employers that hire and train specific disadvantaged clients of the training agencies. Ostensibly, these training contracts are to reimburse private-sector employers for the special training expenses involved in hiring the disadvantaged. In practice, most OJT provided to the disadvantaged has been similar to the training the employer would provide most new hires, and the OJT reimbursement has simply been some percentage of wages, most commonly 50 percent. Therefore, the OJT subsidy has essentially been a wage subsidy for hiring the disadvantaged in most cases.

Under the OJT program design, wage subsidies for hiring the disadvantaged are "discretionary" rather than "entitlements." That is, no employer is entitled to a wage subsidy just because it hires a disadvantaged person, and no disadvantaged job seeker is automatically covered by the wage subsidy program. Rather, the training agency uses available OJT funds selectively to choose disadvantaged job seekers and employers and to seek to match these job seekers and employers. Ideally, the disadvantaged job seekers chosen for OJT wage subsidies are those who are more employable than the average client of a job training agency but who are felt to have some handicaps to getting jobs on their own. The employers chosen for placements ideally are those that are thought to provide above-average job opportunities, particularly if the OJT subsidy would help alter the types of workers the company typically hires for entry-level jobs.

TABLE 8.1 *Brief Description and History of Large-Scale National Wage Subsidy Programs*

Program	Years	Brief Description	Number of Annual Participants at Peak (Millions per Year)	Annual Funding at Peak (Billions of 1998 Dollars)	Participation of Businesses
OJT component of MDTA (Manpower Development and Training Act)	1962 to 1971	Training contracts with employers to hire the unemployed or upgrade the underemployed.	0.115 (1967)	$0.2	
JOBS (Job Opportunities in the Business Sector)	1968 to 1973	Training contracts with employers for hiring young, less-educated black males from poverty backgrounds.	0.093 (1971)	0.7 (1969)	Subsidy claimed for one-third of eligible hires
WIN tax credit program	1972 to 1981	Tax credit for hiring welfare recipients participating in WIN welfare-to-work program; initially 20 percent credit, with maximum credit of $3,900 (1998 dollars) per hire.	0.028 (1976)	0.033	Credit claimed for 15 percent of eligible hires
OJT component of CETA (Comprehensive Employment and Training Act)	1974 to 1982	Training contracts with employers for hiring the disadvantaged.	0.230 (1978)	0.7	
NJTC (New Jobs Tax Credit)	1977 to 1978	Tax credit of 50 percent for the first $10,500 (1998 dollars) of wages per employee for increases in employment of more than 2 percent over previous year. No targeting.	2.15 (1978)	9.5	1.1 million firms claimed credit in 1978, over half of eligible firms

TJTC (Targeted Jobs Tax Credit)	1978 to 1994	Tax credit of various sizes over the years offered for hiring various target groups. By 1994, credit had been scaled back to 40 percent of first-year wages, up to wage of $6,600 annually (1998 dollars). Although wide variety of disadvantaged groups were targeted, disadvantaged youth were most frequently claimed.	0.622 (1985)	0.8	Of eligible youth hired, firms claimed TJTC for only 5 to 9 percent (O'Neill 1982; Katz 1998)
OJT component of JTPA (Job Training Partnership Act)	1983 to 1999	Training contracts with businesses to hire and train the disadvantaged, in exchange for 50 percent wage subsidy for six months. Continued under WIA.	0.253 (1985 to 1986)	$0.2 billion (wage subsidies); $0.7 billion including services	
WOTC (Work Opportunity Tax Credit)	1997 to present	Tax credit for hiring target groups, most recently credit of 40 percent of wages up to a $2,400 credit for individuals who retained at least 400 work hours. Eligibility simplified by tying it to receipt of food stamps or welfare rather than family income. Compared to TJTC, much more emphasis on welfare recipients: 55 percent welfare recipients in 1999 (Beverly 1999).	0.335 (1999)	0.2	
WWTC (Welfare-to-Work Tax Credit)	1998 to present	Similar to WOTC, but more generous, long-term, and targeted. Eligible group is long-term welfare recipients. Credit: 35 percent of first-year wages, 50 percent of second-year's wages, with maximum credit of $3,500 (first year) and $5,000 (second year).	0.105 (1999)	0.035	

Source: Author's compilation.

Over the years, OJT has been a consistent presence in federally funded job training programs, but one of modest size and somewhat uneasy status within the training community. OJT has never subsidized the wages of more than about 250,000 disadvantaged new hires per year, and it has never cost more than $1 billion annually. Usually less than one-quarter of job training clients have gone into OJT, and typically those who go into OJT are the more advantaged job training clients, although compared to the average job seeker OJT clients are still quite disadvantaged. During the last years of the JTPA program, OJT placements were restricted by federal rules that require more documentation by employers that substantial special training was in fact provided. Today's WIA provides substantial new freedom to state and local training agencies, and it is unclear how OJT will fare in this new policy environment.

In addition, since the early 1970s the federal government has offered one variety or another of tax credits that provide wage subsidies for hiring some group, typically a disadvantaged group. Such tax credit-based wage subsidies are entitlements in that any employer that follows the program rules for whom to hire and how long they must work is entitled to receive the subsidy. As these programs have evolved, they typically allow very little discretion to any government entity in awarding these tax-based wage subsidies. Some of these subsidies are targeted at relatively narrow categories of the disadvantaged, whereas others are more broad-based and less restrictive about eligibility.

The earliest tax-based wage subsidies were tax credits under the Work Incentive (WIN) program in the early 1970s for hiring welfare recipients. This program always operated on an extremely small scale and surprised its originators in that employers seemed to have little interest in it, even in claiming the credits when they hired an eligible person: fewer than 15 percent of the eligible welfare recipients hired were claimed as a credit by their employer. The program originally restricted eligibility to welfare recipients who were referred to employers by welfare offices, giving some control over the program to these welfare offices, but it was later modified so that subsidies were also received for welfare recipients who found jobs on their own.

Far more popular with employers was the broad-based New Jobs Tax Credit (NJTC) adopted as part of President Carter's economic stimulus package of 1977. This tax credit provided wage subsidies, up to a certain maximum per hire, and a certain maximum number of hires per firm, on new employees hired who represented an increase in the firm's employment of greater than 2 percent over the previous year. More than 50 percent of eligible firms claimed the NJTC on behalf, at its peak, of more than two million new hires, at a cost to the federal government of almost $10 billion per year (1998 dollars). The NJTC was phased out, however, within two years as the economy continued to recover from the recession of 1974 to 1975.

Hiring tax credits returned to targeting only disadvantaged job seekers under the Targeted Jobs Tax Credit (TJTC) of 1978 to 1994. As with WIN, only a minority of employers participated in this new entitlement tax credit, and they claimed it for only a small fraction of eligible hires. However, the volume of activity in this program was considerably larger than with WIN because the disadvantaged group was defined more broadly. For most of its history, the TJTC was mainly a vehicle for providing wage subsidies for employing disadvantaged youth in retail sales and clerical jobs. Even with this broadened eligibility, at its peak TJTC was claimed for only 600,000 new hires annually—less than one-third of the NJTC's level of activity.

The TJTC as initially conceived would have had local employment service and job training offices provide eligible disadvantaged job seekers with vouchers that they could present to possible employers. Upon hiring, employers would then turn in these vouchers to the local employment service office and receive a certification that would make them eligible for a tax credit. The voucher approach, however, was not particularly effective in creating a large-scale program. Many job seekers did not like using vouchers to advertise their disadvantaged status to employers. Many local employment service and job training offices did not particularly like tying up staff time in handing out vouchers to disadvantaged job seekers because this activity usually did not affect the offices' performance ratings. Hence, most TJTC certifications were instead received by employers that submitted an application for certification for a new hire after the hiring decision was made. Most employers claiming the TJTC used consultants, who would submit applications for all new hires, or for new hires who had some chance of being eligible for the TJTC, after the hiring decision was made but before the first date of employment, in order to comply with the TJTC's requirements. These procedures led to considerable criticism that many TJTC subsidies provided windfall benefits to employers for hiring the same individuals they would have hired anyway (U.S. Department of Labor 1994; Lorenz 1995).

The successors to the TJTC are the Work Opportunities Tax Credit (WOTC) and the Welfare-to-Work Tax Credit (WWTC). Partly in response to criticisms of the TJTC for providing windfalls, both these credits require that employers and job applicants fill out and sign a form on or before the date of hire that includes information suggesting that this hire is probably eligible for one of these credits. In addition, to make it easier for employers to readily determine eligibility before hiring, these credit programs in general tie eligibility to the receipt of welfare or food stamps, a status that is easier for job applicants and employers to determine than whether the applicant's income is below some standard for a "disadvantaged" level of income. In practice, this restriction to welfare or food stamp recipients has narrowed and changed the focus of these hiring tax credits, away from disadvantaged young males and toward disadvantaged single mothers. Although the level of activity in these new programs has been smaller than it was for the TJTC, the activity has been larger than under the early WIN tax credit, perhaps reflecting the stronger economy of the late 1990s and the special interest right now in welfare reform.

The bottom line of national wage subsidy programs thus far in the United States is that the targeted programs, whether discretionary or entitlement, have always operated at quite a modest scale—always affecting less than one million new hires per year, and usually at an activity level much less than that. However, this does not necessarily mean that these targeted wage subsidy programs could not pass a benefit-cost test, since these programs also do not cost very much—always costing less than $1 billion per year. It does mean that one could raise questions about whether these targeted wage subsidies have any potential for making a sizable dent in poverty without significant reform. The broader wage subsidy of the New Jobs Tax Credit was involved in far more hiring decisions, albeit at a much greater annual cost.

Local and Small-Scale Wage Subsidy Programs

In addition to these national wage subsidy programs, a number of wage subsidy programs have been operated at the state level or as small-scale demonstrations (see table 8.2). Many states over the years have set up grant diversion programs in which part or all of an individual's welfare grant can be used to subsidize a private employer to hire that individual. States also have enacted their own tax credit programs to subsidize private employers for hiring or employing the disadvantaged. With increased discretion given to state policymakers under the 1996 welfare reform bill, more states have enacted such grant diversion programs or tax credits. According to the American Public Welfare Association (APWA) (1998), thirty-two states have some sort of grant diversion program, and fifteen states have some sort of tax-based wage subsidy to private employers for hiring the disadvantaged. Most of these programs have been run on an extremely small scale.

To my knowledge, only two serious state-level attempts have been made so far to run employer wage subsidy programs on a large scale: the MEED (Minnesota Employment and Economic Development) program in Minnesota in the 1980s and the current Oregon JOBS Plus Program (see table 8.2 and appendix 12). Both programs were motivated by political ideology, in the case of MEED a liberal ideology, and in the case of Oregon JOBS Plus a conservative ideology. Social service groups and labor union groups advocated politically for the MEED program as part of an attempt to get the Minnesota state government to create many more jobs for the poor. Oregon JOBS Plus was initiated and lobbied for by conservative business interests as an attempt to demonstrate that private employment and on-the-job-training could ultimately replace government welfare benefits and job training. Because these programs are intended to be large-scale, both provide unusually generous wage subsidies to private employers for employing the disadvantaged. They differ primarily in that MEED legally includes a number of requirements for private employers to retain those hired for a certain length of time, whereas JOBS Plus includes few if any requirements for private employers. These legal differences in program requirements obviously reflect the different ideologies behind them. However, it is unclear whether in practice these different legal requirements have made any significant difference in how effectively the programs operate. Because both programs are discretionary wage subsidy programs, local program administrators can decide on their own which employers will receive subsidies, and these program administrators can determine on their own what requirements of employers are actually enforced.

Despite the generous subsidies in MEED and JOBS Plus and the intention that they be large-scale programs, both ended up being run at a moderate scale. If these programs had been run on a national scale, MEED would have had about 700,000 participants per year, and JOBS Plus about 200,000 participants. Thus, these programs were not significantly larger than the Targeted Jobs Tax Credit at its peak and were considerably smaller than the New Jobs Tax Credit.

Finally, over the years several experiments have been run that place disadvantaged clients in private jobs as well as public jobs, most notably Supported Work and YIEPP. In practice, there is not much difference between a local agency providing discretionary subsidies to a public or nonprofit employer for hiring a disadvantaged client and that same agency providing such subsidies to a private for-profit employer. In today's economy, many industries might even include some mix of public, private/nonprofit, and private/for-profit employers, so that subsidies to public and private employers might even be subsidizing quite similar types of employment. For example, it is unclear whether subsidizing the employment of a welfare recipient to work as a health aide in a hospital is a dramatically different program if the hospital is publicly owned, owned by a nonprofit, or owned by a for-profit company. What is likely to matter for the person hired is whether the job is a real job, the job's wages and working conditions, the odds of being permanently hired for the job once the subsidy runs out, and whether the training, connections, and credentials offered by the job are likely to lead to good future career opportunities.

TABLE 8.2 *Small-Scale, Local, and Experimental Wage Subsidy Programs for the Disadvantaged*

Program	Years and Places of Operation	Description	Magnitude of Subsidies	Scale of Program
Work supplementation/ grant diversion and other wage subsidies	1967 to present; various states (thirty-two at present)	Welfare department enters into contract to pay welfare grant to firm hiring welfare recipient.	Median: $2.50 per hour, typically for six to nine months.	Very small. Usually only a few thousand nationally.
State tax credits for hiring welfare recipients or other disadvantaged	Years unknown; currently fifteen states have such tax incentives	State provides credit against corporate income tax for hiring disadvantaged or welfare recipient.	Typically 20 to 30 percent of wages, with cap of less than $2,000 in credit per year per hire, but often lasts for two to three years.	No data, but probably low take-up rate.
Supported Work	Experimental program 1975 to 1978	Experiment with providing job with graduated stress. Usually public jobs, but sometimes worked in private businesses, with private businesses paying part of costs.	Probably over half of wages.	Experiment was run on a small scale.
YIEPP	Experimental program conducted from 1978 to 1981 at seventeen sites	Experiment guaranteeing jobs for disadvantaged youth; 23 percent of jobs in private sector in 1981.	100 percent wage subsidy.	Operated at saturation level in some sites. National version would have 1.1 million participants and cost $3.6 billion annually (see table 7.5)

MEED	Minnesota, 1983 to 1989	Provided wage subsidy for up to six months for employers hiring unemployed workers not receiving UI benefits for newly created jobs. Over half of placements in private sector.	Provided $6.55 per hour in wage subsidy and $1.64 per hour in subsidy for benefits (1998 dollars). Average wage subsidy exceeded 80 percent.	At peak, program spent $50 million per year and subsidized about 9,000 new job slots and had 10,700 participants. National version: $5.1 billion per year, 0.591 million new job slots, and 0.703 million participants.
Maine TOPS	Maine, 1983 to 1986	Welfare-to-work experiment, with component of OJT placements, mostly in private sector.	Wage subsidy of 50 percent	Experiment.
New Jersey Grant Diversion Program	New Jersey, 1984 to 1987	Experiment in which welfare grants used to fund OJT contracts.	50 percent wage subsidy, for up to six months.	Very small-scale program, run as experiment.
Oregon JOBS Plus Program	Oregon, 1993 to present	First a demonstration, and now a statewide program, in which welfare recipients and UI recipients are placed with participating employers who receive a wage subsidy.	Effective wage subsidy of 80 percent for up to six months.	Program is operated at modest scale: less than 4,000 per year. Similar national program would have 0.2 million participants

Source: Author's compilation.

SIDEBAR 8.1 Minnesota's MEED Program: A "Liberal" Approach to Wage Subsidies for the Disadvantaged

Minnesota's MEED[a] wage subsidy program, active from 1983 to 1989, was initiated and backed by liberal state legislators and a coalition of labor, social service, and black and Hispanic groups. Among wage subsidy programs, MEED was most distinguished by deep wage subsidies, requirements for job retention, an emphasis on economic development and job creation, and a focus on small business.

The program provided subsidies of up to $4 per hour for wages (equivalent to $6.55 per hour in 1998 dollars), and $1 per hour for fringe benefits ($1.64 per hour in 1998 dollars) for placements of the unemployed at public agencies and private businesses. At MEED's start, 60 percent of placements were at public agencies, but over time MEED's emphasis shifted to private placements, with over 75 percent of all job placements being made in the private sector. The jobs provided were required to be new jobs. Actual wages were about $1 per hour more than the MEED subsidy payment. The wage subsidies were payable for up to six months for up to forty hours per week. Private-sector employers were expected to retain subsidized workers for at least one year after the six-month subsidy was ended. If the worker quit or was fired by the employer before this period ended, the employer was supposed to either accept another MEED worker or repay most of the subsidy.

Participating workers and employers were selected and matched by local job training agencies. Eligible workers were broadly defined to include any unemployed worker who was not receiving unemployment benefits. Local training agencies were supposed to place a priority on selecting workers who were on public assistance, and in practice about half of MEED workers were public assistance recipients. Training agencies were also supposed to place a priority on nonretail small businesses, manufacturing firms, and firms that sold their product outside of Minnesota ("export-base" firms). More than 80 percent of participating private businesses had twenty or fewer full-time employees, over 20 percent were engaged in manufacturing, and 15 percent made more than half of their sales outside of Minnesota.

The Minnesota Jobs Now Coalition, a key supporter of MEED, conducted several surveys of employers who were using it. Based on these surveys and other evidence, the following observations seem warranted:

- The program's subsidies led to job creation at subsidized firms. Surveys indicate that more than 55 percent of participating employers claimed that they would not have expanded without the MEED program. Employers do not have strong incentives to lie, since the program did not require that the jobs be ones that would not have been created but for the subsidy. More than 60 percent of these businesses claimed that they had lacked sufficient cash flow or capital to expand without the MEED assistance.

SIDEBAR 8.1 Continued

- The program can be run on a large scale. At its height, during its second year, MEED placed more than 7,000 workers at private firms over a ten-month period. This is equivalent to running a national program at a level of 552,000 subsidized hires in 1998. In surveys of participating employers, more than 90 percent reported that the program had a minimum of red tape and its rules were easy to understand. More than 80 percent of participating employers were satisfied with the performance of their MEED workers.
- The long-run national political viability of approaches like the MEED program is uncertain. It was possible to run the program on a large scale in a pro-government state such as Minnesota in the aftermath of the early 1980s recession. However, even in the Minnesota political context, the program was phased out as the economy improved.
- The long-run effects of the program are uncertain. I have been unable to find any data on the long-run job retention of MEED workers. Apparently 78 percent of the MEED workers completed their six-month subsidy period plus sixty days.

Source: This summary is based on Rode (1988) and Rangan (1984).
[a] MEED originally was an acronym for Minnesota Emergency Employment Development, a name that was later changed to Minnesota Employment and Economic Development.

A Tale of Two Employers

What do wage subsidies actually look like for a specific employer? The experience of two employers illustrates both the potential and the limitations of wage subsidies for the disadvantaged.

Microboard Processing Inc. (MPI), a Connecticut-based electronics assembler with about 240 employees, makes 30 percent of its new hires from "high-risk" groups such as welfare recipients, ex-felons, and ex-drug addicts, according to a profile in the *Wall Street Journal* (Tannenbaum 1997). This hiring policy reflects the religious and social convictions of MPI's CEO, Craig T. Hoekenga.

According to the *Journal* profile, MPI has a well-developed strategy for hiring, training, and retaining employees from high-risk groups. First, the company cultivates trusted sources of workers such as churches to refer promising applicants from those groups. Second, the company puts workers through relatively intensive educational and training programs, including English lessons for some of them. Some of this training is subsidized by the state government. Third, "the company cuts employees a lot of slack on

SIDEBAR 8.2 Oregon's JOBS Plus Program: A "Conservative" Version of Wage Subsidies for the Disadvantaged

Oregon's JOBS Plus Program was initiated through political pressure from the Jeld-Wen Corporation, an important Oregon wood products manufacturer. The program reflects the belief that government income support for the poor and the unemployed can in most cases be replaced by immediate employment and on-the-job training in the private sector, although such employment may require subsidies. The designers of the program, now working for Jeld-Wen's nonprofit affiliate, the American Institute for Full Employment, include several individuals associated with welfare policy in the Reagan administration and some former affiliates of the conservative Heritage Foundation.

Among wage subsidy programs, the JOBS Plus Program is most distinguished by its extremely deep subsidies and relatively few formal requirements of participating employers. In JOBS Plus, welfare recipients and unemployment insurance recipients are placed with participating employers, which receive a subsidy of the Oregon minimum wage ($6 an hour) plus payroll taxes and workers' compensation reimbursement, for up to six months. Employers are required to pay the "trainees" the prevailing wage for similar jobs in the company (on average, this appears to be a bit less than $1 over the Oregon minimum wage); not to use the trainees to replace existing workers or fill vacancies; and to provide the trainees with a workplace mentor and appropriate OJT. After four months of wage subsidy, if the employer has not hired the trainee for a regular job, the trainee is allowed to use one paid day a week to engage in job search. Participating employers are required only to sign relatively simple forms outlining their agreement to these terms; in particular, they are not subject to any requirement to hire trainees permanently, although this happens in about one-quarter of all placements.

Based on Roberts and Padden's (1998a, 1998b) process observations of JOBS Plus, the following observations are warranted:

- Despite the deep subsidies provided under the program and the great effort to make the program employer-friendly, the program has operated on a modest scale, owing to both difficulties in recruiting employers and difficulties in finding suitable welfare recipients and other unemployed for the program. Only 7 percent of the Oregonians engaged in welfare-to-work programs are in JOBS Plus. From July 1996 to October 1997, about 3,500 participants left JOBS Plus.
- The program does appear to be more attractive to small businesses than are wage subsidies such as TJTC/WOTC and the JTPA OJT program, possibly because of the simple and limited program requirements.

SIDEBAR 8.2 Continued

- In interviews, some employers questioned aspects of the program. Specifically, some felt that the subsidies were unnecessarily large. In addition, some employers apparently felt that pre-job preparation training would sometimes have been a more effective way of developing human capital.

Source: This description is largely based on Roberts and Padden (1998a, 1998b), as well as on the American Institute for Full Employment's web site, *www.fullemployment.org*.

attendance during their first several months on the job. . . . Mr. Hoekenga says that during this period, he doesn't fire people as long as they show improvement. . . . What makes Mr. Hoekenga unique is that he has patience, says William R. Belotti, Connecticut's deputy labor commissioner. 'Most employers want people with a good work ethic, social skills and an ability to produce the first day they come to work. Craig will take people who can't produce and will wait six or nine months for them to come through.'" Finally, in a few cases, the company permanently retains some workers who will never be able to meet normal production quotas owing to significant psychological or other problems.

BMC Enterprises is Baltimore's largest black-owned business, operating fifteen Stop Shop Save grocery stores and employing approximately six hundred workers. According to a profile by Brandon Roberts and Jeffrey Padden (1998b), the company has a well-structured program for hiring and training welfare recipients and other disadvantaged groups. First, each month the company holds orientation sessions for job applicants who are referred from the Baltimore welfare department, the local job training agency, and the Baltimore Urban League. The company does rigorous screening of these referrals, including applicant interviews and drug tests. Second, those accepted into the company receive two weeks of classroom training from BMC instructors, including workplace soft skills as well as some specific skills needed at BMC, such as how to be a cashier. Third, trainees then receive four weeks of on-the-job training at a BMC store. Finally, the trainees are hired by BMC at an initial wage of six dollars an hour (as of 1997), with fifty-cents-an-hour wage increases every six months. For trainees referred by the Baltimore welfare department, BMC receives a wage subsidy for up to nine months, financed by welfare grant diversion and typically averaging about one-third of the trainee's wages. According to BMC, with the grant diversion the company can afford the costs of the training programs and it can also hire some workers whom it otherwise would not consider.

What do these two case studies suggest about wage subsidies? First, at least in these two cases, it seems clear that wage subsidies have helped support and encourage some hiring and training activities that otherwise would not have taken place at the same scale. Some disadvantaged workers are hired who otherwise might not be hired. These medium-sized companies are engaging in some special training efforts, and the subsidies do seem to help support the costs of these special services. Second, it seems likely that these wage subsidies do cause some displacement of other workers within each firm, in the sense that some of these disadvantaged new hires substitute for new hires who would otherwise have been made from other groups. It is not at all clear that these training and wage subsidies have encouraged much overall employment expansion at MPI and BMC. Finally, there is clearly some tension between encouraging the hiring of the disadvantaged and encouraging employment expansion and avoiding displacement. To the extent that policy pushes hiring more disadvantaged groups, policy is probably also reducing labor productivity, thus offsetting some of the lower labor costs brought about by wage subsidies and discouraging employment expansion.

Stigma: A Big Problem for Wage Subsidy Programs for the Disadvantaged That Are Run Stupidly

Why have there been so many problems in running targeted wage subsidy programs on a large scale? Why are wage subsidies claimed at such a low rate even for employers who do make clearly eligible hires? Most economists have a ready explanation for these problems: employers attach the stigma of low productivity to job seekers who are considered disadvantaged, and hence they are reluctant to hire these individuals.

Why might wage subsidies to employers who hire disadvantaged persons lead to stigma effects? As discussed in chapter 3, employers have poor information about the true productivity of job applicants. Because of this poor information, many employers make hiring decisions using characteristics of job applicants that are believed to signal productivity. Some employers may believe that an individual's receipt of welfare or poverty status increases the odds that the individual's productivity on the job will be low. Suppose a disadvantaged job applicant tells employers that by hiring him or her, the employer will be eligible for a special wage subsidy for hiring the disadvantaged. This information provides a monetary incentive to the employer to hire that job applicant, but it also reveals to the employer that the individual is a member of some disadvantaged class. The information that the applicant belongs to a disadvantaged group may reduce the employer's expectations about the applicant's productivity. This reduction in predicted productivity may reduce the odds that the employer will hire that job applicant. If the stigma effect of belonging to a disadvantaged group is strong enough, it might outweigh the monetary incentive, thus causing the wage subsidy to reduce the odds of that job applicant being hired.

How strong are stigma effects? A well-known article by Gary Burtless (1985) has led many economists to conclude that they are quite strong—so strong, in fact, that wage subsidies for the disadvantaged are likely to be counterproductive. Because Burtless's article has been so influential, it is worthwhile considering in some detail the evidence that underlies his conclusions.

Burtless's evidence is based on a partially completed wage subsidy experiment in Dayton, Ohio. Because of a congressional requirement, the U.S. Department of Labor in 1978 was required to conduct an experiment that tested the idea of providing disadvantaged job seekers with vouchers that they could provide to prospective employers, who could turn in the vouchers to receive a cash wage subsidy from the government. Also in 1978, Congress passed the initial version of the Targeted Jobs Tax Credit, which provided employers with tax credits for hiring the disadvantaged. One way employers could receive the TJTC was to hire workers who had received a voucher certifying their membership in the group whose hiring would result in the employer receiving the TJTC. Thus, the proposed wage voucher would seem to differ from the TJTC in only two respects: employers without tax liabilities could receive subsidies from the wage voucher program, but not the TJTC; wage vouchers would be paid off within a few months, whereas employers would have to wait until the end of their tax year to receive the TJTC. The similarities between the wage vouchers and the TJTC suggest that the differences in the effects of the two programs might be small, making it difficult for the Department of Labor to evaluate wage vouchers.

The department eventually decided to test the effects of wage vouchers and the TJTC by combining the proposed wage voucher variation with efforts to encourage disadvantaged job seekers to aggressively market the wage subsidy associated with their hiring. The Dayton experiment was targeted at welfare recipients: about half the participants were on AFDC and the other half were on general relief. All participants received two weeks of training in job search, followed by six weeks of intensive job search guided by participation in a job club that provided peer group support, advice, and social pressure. Participants were randomly divided among three treatment groups: a control group that simply received the two weeks of job search training followed by six weeks of job club; one treatment group (the "advertised TJTC group") of participants who were also given a day of extra training that suggested that they should advertise their eligibility for the TJTC to prospective employers and who were given written materials explaining the program that they were asked to give to prospective employers; another treatment group (the "advertised wage voucher group") of participants who were also given a wage voucher and told, like the other treatment group, to aggressively market their wage subsidy eligibility to employers and provided written materials on the program to give to employers. The wage and tax subsidies provided were substantial: 50 percent of wages paid during the first year of employment, up to a maximum subsidy of $5,934 (in 1998 dollars); and 25 percent of wages paid during the second year of employment, up to a maximum subsidy of $2,967.

This experiment was terminated by the Reagan administration in early 1981 before much information could be collected from employers or disadvantaged job seekers. However, before the experiment was terminated, data were collected on whether 808 welfare recipients who had gone through the program had obtained a job by the end of the initial six-week period of job club–guided job search.

To the surprise of many, the control group did much better in obtaining jobs than did either of the treatment groups. Twenty-one percent of the control group obtained jobs by the end of the six-week job club, compared to 13 percent in each of the treatment groups.[2] For those in the treatment groups who did obtain jobs, only 27 percent of their employers turned in vouchers to be redeemed for cash wage subsidies or tax credits. The other employers either did not know about the vouchers or felt that the subsidies were too small to be worth collecting. The only effect of the wage voucher was that more employers turned wage vouchers in for redemption, about 37 percent compared to 16 percent for tax credit vouchers.

Burtless's influential interpretation of these results is that they are attributable to stigma:

> An implication is that employers used the information provided by the vouchers to discriminate against target group workers. Employers may have used the vouchers to screen out job applicants known to be public assistance recipients. Alternatively, some may have reasoned that if the job applicants were so disadvantaged that they required a wage subsidy to find work, they were probably poor prospects for hiring and training. . . . Although the voucher worker was offered at a steep discount, employers appeared to interpret the voucher as implying "damaged goods." Given this interpretation, job applicants using the voucher were placed at a disadvantage in comparison to identical job applicants who refrained from identifying themselves as welfare recipients. (Burtless 1985, 112–13)

Burtless's interpretation that the Dayton treatment group members suffered from stigma effects seems reasonable. It should be noted, however, that because of limited data, we have little information on possible qualifications to his conclusion. We do not know the reactions of prospective employers when they were shown a voucher.[3] We do not know what proportion of employers in the various treatment groups were actually shown a voucher. Because of the lack of detailed data on participants or employers, we do not know whether wage subsidies helped some types of participants but hurt others, or helped with some types of employers and were counterproductive with others.

What should *not* be concluded from the Dayton experiment is that stigma effects cause all wage subsidy programs to be counterproductive. The Dayton experiment was run in such a way that it probably maximized stigma effects. The experiment provided minimal screening and training of welfare recipients and thereby provided little assurance to prospective employers that this group had any job skills. The treatment group was urged to advertise the wage subsidy to any and all employers. No attempt was made to target wage subsidies at employers that might be less prone to attaching a stigma to welfare recipients and more interested in receiving a wage subsidy.

As we will explore, discretionary wage subsidy programs can be managed so as to control what information is provided to what employers. The job seekers who participate in a wage subsidy program can be screened and trained so that employers have some assurance of some level of job skills. Job developers can market the program's participants to prospective employers. This marketing both conveys information about the job skills of program participants and screens out employers that attach a heavy stigma to an individual who is a welfare recipient or belongs to some other disadvantaged group. As Burtless mentions, the Dayton CETA program that managed the experiment was somewhat unusual in that it did not use job developers but rather used only self-directed job search via job clubs.

As discussed further later in the chapter, even entitlement wage subsidy programs for the disadvantaged in practice might have lower stigma effects than the Dayton wage subsidies. Most disadvantaged job seekers do not aggressively market their disadvantaged status to most employers. The Dayton experiment suggests that disadvantaged job seekers are wise to avoid indiscriminately advertising their disadvantaged status to all employers. Relatively few employers aggressively seek to obtain tax subsidies for hiring the disadvantaged by systematically examining whether job applicants are eligible for the various tax credits. The employers that seek out such information are those that are particularly interested in wage subsidies and less likely to stigmatize members of disadvantaged groups. Hence, in practice, entitlement wage subsidy programs such as the TJTC or WOTC are likely to be targeted at employers with lower stigma issues than was true in Dayton.

In sum, stigma is a problem, but one that can be managed. The Dayton program was run in a way that, in retrospect, was mistaken. Similar stigma problems might arise with many training and education programs. For example, one could imagine hiring problems for graduates from a training program for ex-drug addicts if these graduates are instructed to show employers a diploma listing their graduation from a training program for ex-drug addicts. Any type of program targeted at the disadvantaged, not just wage subsidy programs, must carefully consider what type of information the program conveys to prospective employers.

Implications of Studies Using Labor Market Models of Demand and Supply Behavior

I now consider what empirical estimates suggest about the likely effects of wage subsidies. I look first at studies that simulate the effects of wage subsidies based on previous estimates of demand and supply behavior, and then turn to studies that attempt to estimate the effects of actual programs.

Table 8.3 summarizes three studies that have attempted to simulate the effects of three different types of wage subsidies. These simulations are each based on specific models of the labor market and of how demand and supply behavior respond to shocks to wages.

Although the estimates differ, of course, because the wage subsidies considered are quite different, and there are also differences in the details of the models, the following points seem to be reasonable generalizations from these studies:

1. Standard labor market models of supply and demand do predict that subsidies can yield significant increases in employment. The wage subsidies considered here are modest in magnitude compared to the subsidies that have actually been proposed and used in the United States. For example, the New Jobs Tax Credit was a subsidy of 50 percent for the first $10,500 of wages, and the Targeted Jobs Tax Credit began as a subsidy of 50 percent of the first $15,000 of first-year wages, whereas the subsidies simulated in this table are all 10 percent or less. If one believes these models, the subsidies used in the United States could create millions of jobs.

2. Even when designed as subsidies to marginal employment increases, wage subsidies can be quite costly. Depending on the model considered, the cost per job created ranges from $5,000 to $44,000. Thus, if these subsidies were made large enough to create millions of jobs, their aggregate cost in wage subsidy expenditures or forgone tax revenue would be quite sizable. The costs are high because even if subsidies are provided only for marginal employment expansions, a sizable percentage of them are

TABLE 8.3 *Simulations of the Effects of Marginal Employment Tax Credits*

Study	Description of Subsidy Simulation	Annual Cost (Billions of 1998 Dollars)	Jobs Created (Millions)	Cost per Job (1998 Dollars)	Windfall Percentage
Kesselman, Williamson, and Berndt (1977)[a]	Marginal employment tax credit of 4.8 percent in manufacturing, applying to employment above 90 percent of base.	$4.5	0.101	$44,433	94.8
Hamermesh (1978)	Ten percent wage subsidy to all employment increases above base-year employment;[b] to all employment increases above 85 percent of base-year employment.	Base of 100 percent: $2.0 Base of 85 percent: $21.1	Base of 100 percent: 0.369 Base of 85 percent: 0.866	Base of 100 percent: 5,467 Base of 85 percent: 24,365	Base of 100 percent: 71.1 Base of 85 percent: 89.3
Bartik (1999)	Three different 10 percent wage subsidies, for three groups: single mothers, other women with less than a college education, and men with less than a college education. Wage subsidy assumed to apply to all employment above 80 percent of baseline.[c]	Single mothers: $1.5 Other noncollege women: $17.1 Noncollege men: $28.4	Single mothers: 0.066 Other noncollege women: 1.630 Noncollege men: 2.536	Single mothers: 22,619 Other noncollege women: 10,496 Noncollege men: 11,189	Single mothers: 92.5 Other noncollege women: 83.2 Noncollege men: 80.6

Source: Author's compilation.

[a] Kesselman et al.'s (1977) estimates are derived from estimating a translog cost function for manufacturing with three factors of production: blue-collar labor, white-collar labor, and capital. Their estimates of the own price elasticity of demand for blue-collar labor is -0.338, and -0.192 for white-collar labor. Thus, their estimates agree with most of the research literature that elasticities of demand for specific types of labor are modest.

[b] Hamermesh (1978) considers a variety of scenarios and labor demand elasticities. I consider the case where the labor demand elasticity is 0.3, which is closest to estimates later presented by Hamermesh (1993) in his book on labor demand.

[c] These estimates use the model of appendix 2 (see also Bartik 1999). In addition to these employment effects, the 10 percent wage subsidies would each cause the following effects on the market wages of the group targeted: single mothers, 0.4 percent; other noncollege women, 4.3 percent; other noncollege men, 6.1 percent. These are effects five years after the subsidy is introduced. All these estimates come from simulations reported in table A2.12, coupled with figures for total employment of three groups, except for deriving cost estimates. For cost estimates, I assume that a 10 percent wage subsidy applied to all employment above 80 percent of the base year has the same effect on employment as a 10 percent wage subsidy applied to all employment and costs the same as a wage subsidy applying to all new hires. The implicit assumptions are that a subsidy on all employment above 80 percent of base employment makes a subsidy relevant on the margin to almost all employment decisions; also, new hires each year are about 20 percent of total employment.

windfall wastage—that is, these subsidies go to firms to hire employees who would have been hired anyway. In the various models considered here, windfall wastage percentages range from 70 percent to more than 90 percent.

3. Much of the cost of these programs may be offset by increases in the market wage. The model presented in Bartik (1999) is the only one that simulates the increase in the market wage that may occur as a result of wage subsidies to employers for employing various disadvantaged groups. This model suggests that a 10 percent wage subsidy for some groups may in some cases increase the market wage of those groups by about half as much, thus transferring at least some of the costs of the program to private employers. In the specific simulation, because the wage subsidy is assumed to be applied only to new hires, whereas the wage increase occurs for all employees, more than 100 percent of the social costs of the program are in fact paid for by private employers. It should be remembered that this simulated result comes from a labor market model of how the market is thought to behave in response to a wage subsidy, not from an estimate of how the labor market actually behaves because of a wage subsidy.

4. All these calculations assume that there are no administrative problems, information problems for private employers, or stigma issues that inhibit the effective operation of these wage subsidy programs. This is a huge assumption. Actual programs probably do suffer from these problems, which would reduce the usage (and costs) of wage subsidy programs. To estimate the effects of actual programs requires data on what happens after these programs are implemented, a subject to which I now turn.

General Wage Subsidies

I first consider evaluations of the estimated impact of general wage subsidies, that is, those not strongly targeted at the disadvantaged. In the United States, the main such program was the New Jobs Tax Credit of 1977 to 1978. Table 8.4 summarizes three studies done of the NJTC.

Based on these three studies, the following conclusions seem warranted:

1. The New Jobs Tax Credit probably significantly increased the aggregate number of U.S. jobs. The NJTC may have created as many as 700,000 new jobs. If this figure is accurate, it implies a cost of roughly $13,500 per job created. Windfall wastage is about 67 percent, that is, about two dollars out of every three dollars in NJTC subsidies provided went for employment expansion that would have occurred even without the subsidy. These estimates of costs per job created and windfall wastage seem at least roughly consistent with the simulations in table 8.3 using various labor market models. On the other hand, the magnitude of the em-

TABLE 8.4 *Estimates of Effects of New Jobs Tax Credit*

Study	Methodology	Results
Perloff and Wachter (1979)	Regression analysis with some controls that compares 1976 to 1977 job growth for firms that knew about NJTC to job growth of firms that did not know; also survey of usage.	Firms that knew about credit increased employment by 3 percent more than similar firms that did not know. This implies an economywide increase in employment in 1977 of 700,000 jobs (Eisner 1989, 70). 27 percent of firms with less than 10 employees knew about NJTC, versus 89 percent of those with over 500 employees.
McKevitt (1978), as reported in Bishop (1981)	Survey of members of National Federation for Independent Businesses, asking about knowledge of NJTC and employment increases.	Of surveyed small firms, 4.1 percent said they increased employment as a result of NJTC, by an average of 2.3 employees, suggesting an aggregate employment increase of 300,000 jobs just among NFIB members.
Bishop (1981)	Time-series regression analysis of monthly data on industry employment in construction, retail industries, wholesale trade, and trucking, and its relationship to firms' awareness of NJTC.	Estimated increase in employment in these industries due to NJTC is between 225,000 and 585,000 in various models.

Source: Author's compilation.

ployment increases seems somewhat less than one would predict given that the NJTC was a 50 percent wage subsidy and that the simulations in table 8.3 consider wage subsidies of 10 percent or less. Presumably this lesser response reflects the fact that in the real world a variety of administrative and other costs to firms are involved in becoming aware of and participating in the program.

2. The New Jobs Tax Credit might have had a considerably greater impact on employment if more firms had been aware of it and willing to use it. The tax credit was claimed for only half of all eligible firms. Smaller firms were less likely to be aware of the NJTC. Of course, greater awareness of the NJTC would have been accompanied by not only a greater impact on employment but greater program costs.

3. Unfortunately, no estimates are available on whether and how the NJTC affected the employment of lower-wage and disadvantaged groups.

Because the NJTC provided a wage subsidy of new employment up to a certain maximum payroll, it provided a greater percentage wage subsidy for new employees with lower earnings. This subsidy would be expected to cause disproportionately greater percentage effects on the employment of lower-wage and disadvantaged groups, but no specific estimates are available that demonstrate and quantify the magnitude of this greater effect. If the NJTC did not disproportionately help lower-wage and disadvantaged groups, then the 700,000 jobs it created might be expected to create about 250,000 jobs for men and single women with less than a college degree, based on the estimates of chapter 5.[4]

Categorical Entitlement Wage Subsidies

I now consider studies that have looked at the effects of wage subsidies to employers that both target specific disadvantaged groups for hiring and are administered as entitlements, that is, all employers that meet the program's criteria are entitled to the wage subsidy. The results of these studies are summarized in table 8.5.[5]

Most of these studies have focused on the Targeted Jobs Tax Credit. From these studies of the TJTC and similar wage subsidies, the following summary comments seem warranted:

1. Most estimates suggest that tax credits for hiring the disadvantaged have some effect on employers' hiring decisions and employment decisions, but there are wide differences in the estimates. Some survey results suggest that only 8 percent of employers' hires under the TJTC were due to the credit (U.S. Department of Labor 1994). Some econometric results suggest that for every ten hires subsidized by the TJTC, a firm's employment increases by around two to four jobs (Bishop and Montgomery 1993; Bishop and Hollenbeck 1985, ch. 4). Other econometric results suggest that about 40 to 52 percent of the youths hired under the TJTC represent true additional hires of youth because of the credit (Katz 1998). Finally, some survey results suggest that around 50 percent of firms using the TJTC claim that their hiring and recruitment practices have been altered in some way because of it (O'Neill 1982; Christensen 1984; Copeland 1985; U.S. GAO 1991; Katz 1998). For example, many firms claim that the TJTC has changed the sources they use for recruiting new hires by increasing their use of the employment service and other sources of job seekers who are more likely to be TJTC-eligible.

These estimates can perhaps be reconciled by recognizing that the different studies answer different questions. For example, even if a firm says that a specific new subsidized hire was not hired because of his or her TJTC eligibility, the TJTC could still have increased the odds of that individual being hired by affecting the firm's recruiting sources. Thus, survey results that explicitly ask firms whether an individual was hired because of the TJTC may underestimate the influence of the credit on hiring practices; the survey-based estimate from the Department of Labor's inspector general that only 8 percent of TJTC subsidies are effective in causing a hire is likely to be an underestimate (U.S. Department of Labor 1994). On the other hand, if a firm claims in a survey that the TJTC has had some influence on hiring practices, that does not demonstrate that all hires in that firm were due to the TJTC: "some" influence might mean that one or two hires out of hundreds of TJTC hires were due to the credit. Thus, it seems likely that less than 50 percent of TJTC-subsidized hires are due to the credit. Finally, the Katz estimates, which are particularly convincing because they rely on a "natural experiment" in which a group's eligibility for a TJTC subsidy changed over time, specifically focus on whether the TJTC encouraged the hiring of disadvantaged youth. Other studies of the TJTC suggest that youth and the handicapped were perhaps the two TJTC-eligible groups that were most favorably affected by this hiring subsidy, and that the TJTC had little effect on other groups, or even negative effects (Hollenbeck, Willke, and Ershadi 1986; Hollenbeck and Willke 1991). Of course, as pointed out previously, throughout the history of the TJTC generally more than half of all certifications were of disadvantaged youth: for example, they amounted to 59 percent of all certifications in the TJTC's peak year of 1985 (Katz 1998, 32). If other targeted groups had negligible effects, then the overall effects of the TJTC would be to increase the employment of targeted groups by 24 to 30 percent of the number of subsidized jobs (0.24 to 0.30 = 0.59 times [0.40 to 0.52]). This range of effects of the TJTC is consistent with the bounds implied by other studies, such as Bishop and Montgomery (1993).

The TJTC studies suggest that windfall wastage is somewhere in the range of 50 to 92 percent; based on my earlier arguments, a reasonable point estimate is that the windfall wastage of programs such as the TJTC is about 70 percent—that is, seven out of every ten dollars goes to subsidize hires that would have occurred anyway. But the TJTC was relatively cheap per certification, with a cost per certification in its peak year of 1985 of $1,230.[6] Combining this information, the most plausible point estimate is that the cost per job created by the TJTC was $4,100 per job ($1,230/0.30), with the range of possible costs per job created extending from $2,460 up to $15,375 per job. These windfall wastage and costs per job estimates are roughly in the range of the estimates from labor market models of the costs of wage subsidy programs and estimates of the costs of the NJTC.

2. However, the TJTC and other entitlement wage subsidy programs targeting the disadvantaged have suffered from extraordinarily low take-up

(Text continues on p. 234.)

TABLE 8.5 *Empirical Studies of Entitlement Wage Subsidy Programs*

Study	Methodology	Results
Impact (1977), as reported in Hamermesh (1978)	Survey of employers using the WIN tax credit.	Less than 10 percent of employers using credit attributed their hiring of the WIN enrollee to the credit.
Wisconsin DHSS and Institute for Research on Poverty (1982)	Experimental study of effects of promotional efforts on firms' usage of WIN tax credit and TJTC.	Mail-only promotion slightly increased firms' usage of tax credits, but not statistically significant. Mail-plus-phone promotion approximately doubled firms' usage of tax credits, from 4.5 percent of firms to 9.0 percent. Twenty-three percent of firms with more than one hundred employees used credit, versus less than 4 percent for firms with fifty or fewer employees.
O'Neill (1982)	January 1980 survey of 720 firms.	Sixty-three percent of firms had heard of TJTC, 38 percent had used or planned to use TJTC, of whom 26 percent said use of TJTC would increase employment level, and 46 percent said they substituted target hires for similar nontarget hires. Both knowledge and usage or planned usages of TJTC were lower for small firms.
Christensen (1984)	Random survey of firms in 1980 and 1982.	Thirty-four percent of employers who used credit claimed it affected their hiring decisions significantly, 22 percent claimed it had some effect. TJTC usage was much greater among large establishments than small establishments. Probability of TJTC usage was 32 percent higher among firms contacted and asked to accept a specific referral. Firms that had received TJTC in 1980 or 1981 increased share of youth in total employment by 6 to 20 percent more than other firms. But employment growth was not statistically significantly greater in firms that used TJTC compared to firms that did not. Finally, for every increase of one in state vouchering activity in 1982, there was a 0.4 increase in employment for eligible youth as of March 1983.
Bishop, in Bishop and Hollenbeck (1985, ch. 4)	Regression analysis of employment of around 3,000 firms, December 1980 to June 1982.	Based on typical number of certifications associated with TJTC participation, for every ten TJTC-subsidized jobs at firm, there were three to four extra jobs, and six or seven displaced, with probably most of those displaced being nonsubsidized youth (four or five).

Bishop, in Bishop and Hollenbeck (1985, ch. 5)	1982 survey of stratified random sample of firms.	Eighty percent of TJTC certificates are at firms that claim they tried to select TJTC eligibles. But only 18 percent of firms reported that job applicant's eligibility influenced hiring decisions "a great amount," and only 15 percent reported that it influenced their decision "a moderate amount."
Bishop, in Bishop and Hollenbeck (1985, ch. 7)	1983 interviews in which 850 employers were asked to rate eleven imaginary job applications, with TJTC status of application randomly assigned.	On average, TJTC status only slightly increased employer's rating, by 1.9 points on average.
Copeland (1985); Hollenbeck, in Bishop and Hollenbeck (1985, ch. 8)	Case studies of thirty-five firms heavily using TJTC.	Twenty-six percent of firms reported giving hiring preference to TJTC applicants. Nine percent reported creating openings to hire TJTC applicants. Seventy-five percent of firms used consultants to screen applicants for eligibility and arrange for certification. Only 11 percent felt TJTC workers were less productive than other workers. Fifty-five percent of firms had monetary incentives to encourage local managers to hire and certify TJTC workers.
Bishop and Montgomery (1986)	Analysis of 1980 survey of 5,279 establishments.	Proportion using a program went up if firm learned of WIN tax credit from government rep: this increased WIN participation rate by 70 percent and TJTC participation rate by 53 percent.
Lorenz (1988)	Comparison of earnings of three groups: those vouchered and then hired under TJTC; those submitted for TJTC certification upon hire; and those vouchered but not hired under TJTC during first six months of 1982, in Maryland and Missouri.	Higher earnings during TJTC period for groups hired under TJTC, but earnings differentials eroded over time.

(Table continues on p. 232.)

TABLE 8.5 *Continued*

Study	Methodology	Results
Hollenbeck and Willke (1991); Hollenbeck, Willke and Ershadi (1986)	Comparison of change in average annual earnings and employment of vouchered TJTC eligibles in states with average voucher penetration rate of eligible population to performance of nonvouchered eligibles in states with zero penetration rate.	Vouchered youth and handicapped generally gained, with average annual real earnings gain of $462 (1998 dollars) for youth and $1,940 for handicapped. Most of earnings gain appeared to be due to employment increases. Among youth, white females gained most. But there was lots of displacement: losers included nonvouchered black male youth, both vouchered and nonvouchered black males, black females, and white females on welfare, and both vouchered and nonvouchered black veterans.
Bishop and Kang (1991)	Survey data on 3,412 establishments collected in 1982, with oversampling of large firms in low-wage industries.	Government offer to refer eligible workers increased expected number of TJTC hires five to twelve times, depending on year. Government contact without referral offer increased number of TJTC hires by 43 percent to 87 percent, depending on year. Prior involvement with other government wage subsidies significantly increased TJTC usage.
U.S. General Accounting Office (1991)	Interviewed sixty employers among top TJTC users in four states.	Forty-five percent of employers made special efforts to recruit, hire, or retain TJTC-eligible workers, including developing relationships with agencies supplying TJTC eligibles, giving incentives to local managers for hiring and retaining TJTC eligibles, and being more lenient in job standards with TJTC hires.
Bishop and Montgomery (1993)	Regression analysis of the percentage change in individual firms' employment from end of 1980 to 1981 as a function of change in TJTC hires as a proportion of previous level of employment.	TJTC estimated to increase total firm employment by 13 to 30 percent of certifications.
U.S. Department of Labor (1994)	Selected sample of 983 TJTC workers. Asked employers whether TJTC worker would have been hired without tax credit.	Only 8 percent of TJTC certificates were hired by their employers because of their TJTC status.

Tannery (1998)	Compared treatment group of youth and welfare recipients in Pennsylvania from 1988 to 1994 who were hired and successfully certified with controls whose certification was not processed owing to technical errors.	In general, certification was estimated to increase earnings of disadvantaged youth from $2,000 to $4,000 per year and to increase earnings of welfare recipients by about $1,600 per year.
Katz (1998)	Differences-in-differences-in-differences estimator based on restriction in 1989 that made disadvantaged twenty-three- to twenty-four-year-olds no longer eligible for TJTC.	TJTC estimated to increase employment rates of disadvantaged twenty-three- to twenty-four-year-olds by 3.4 to 4.3 rate points. Suggests that 40 to 52 percent of TJTC certifications created jobs for group targeted. If this were applied to all TJTC, TJTC would have created 249,000 to 322,000 jobs for disadvantaged groups that it targeted at its peak in 1985.
Woodbury and Spiegelman (1987); Spiegelman and Woodbury (1987); Dubin and Rivers (1993)	Experimental data, seeing how weeks of unemployment vary for UI recipients for whom bonus was paid to employers hiring them within eleven-week period.	Bonus reduced initial spell of unemployment by statistically significant two-thirds of a week on average. But take-up rate was also very small: only 5 percent of sample submitted “notice of hire” to state of Illinois—less than one-fourth of 21 percent of experimental group that was eligible for bonus

Source: Author’s compilation.

rates. Less than 10 percent of eligible hires are typically claimed on employers' tax returns. Take-up rates are lower for smaller establishments and firms. Because of low take-up rates, the government resources devoted to these wage subsidy programs are quite modest, but the participation and job creation potential of these programs is also modest. For example, if we take the point estimate that the TJTC has affected perhaps 30 percent of the hiring decisions that it has subsidized, then the program at its peak created only 187,000 jobs per year for disadvantaged groups. This may not be even as many jobs as the number of jobs created for disadvantaged groups by the much broader wage subsidy of the NJTC.

3. Aggressive government outreach can significantly increase firm take-up rates for employment tax credits for the disadvantaged. Personal government contact about these tax credits significantly increased take-up rates (Bishop and Montgomery 1986; Wisconsin DHSS and Institute for Research on Poverty 1982). Subsidized hires are increased even more if the government contact is accompanied by specific referral of a disadvantaged client (Bishop and Kang 1991; Christensen 1984). It is quite feasible that more aggressive government outreach could double activity in these tax credit programs.[7]

4. Some studies suggest that the TJTC has led to displacement. The TJTC as it evolved ended up being mainly used by employers interested in hiring disadvantaged youth, particularly employers in retail industries such as fast-food restaurants. Several estimates suggest that disadvantaged youth were helped. But one study suggests that in states that more aggressively promoted the TJTC by aggressively issuing vouchers of TJTC eligibility, although the employment of disadvantaged youth was increased, such policies hurt the employment prospects of some disadvantaged blacks and welfare recipients. This finding is consistent with Burtless's argument that being identified as a welfare recipient to all employers may reduce a welfare recipient's probability of being hired because of stigma effects.

5. Although the new WOTC and WWTC credits are superficially quite similar to the TJTC, there are enough differences in perhaps crucial administrative details that the effects of these new programs might be quite different. For example, the new law focuses eligibility on individuals who are currently receiving welfare benefits or food stamps, partly in order to make it easier for employers to determine eligibility before hire. In practice, this has led to much more emphasis on welfare recipients as an eligible group than was true under the TJTC, and less emphasis on youth, particularly young males. In addition, the new credits require that the employer and job seeker fill out a form establishing the likely eligibility of the individual for the tax credit on or before the date of hire. This provision is intended to increase the likelihood that tax credit eligibility will be considered in making the hiring decision. Whether this provision is having its intended effect is unknown.

6. The reliability of the results of most of the studies of entitlement wage subsidies are questionable because these studies use nonexperimental data. The one experimental study of an entitlement wage subsidy program is the study by Spiegelman and Woodbury (1987; a portion was also published as Woodbury and Spiegelman 1987) of employer tax credits for hiring individuals receiving unemployment insurance benefits within eleven weeks of starting benefits. It is reasonable to assume that the general group of unemployment benefit recipients is more advantaged and less stigmatized in the eyes of employers than are welfare recipients. However, even in this case, the take-up rate is very small: less than one-quarter of those hired within the eleven weeks had an employer that submitted a "notice of hire" in order to claim the employer subsidy. This finding suggests that more than stigma is involved in the low take-up rates of employer wage subsidies. Perhaps some employers and job seekers are simply reluctant to get involved with government programs. However, the low take-up rate does not mean that the program is not effective per dollar spent. The employer bonus under unemployment insurance (UI) appears to have a windfall wastage percentage of only 26 percent, and an annual cost per full-time equivalent job created of $3,000.[8] In the case of the employer bonus, enough is saved on UI benefits paid that these gross costs are probably more than offset by reduced receipt of unemployment insurance benefits. The employer bonus results are perhaps somewhat more favorable than those for most entitlement wage subsidies for the disadvantaged, but not by much. However, as with the wage subsidies for disadvantaged groups, the low take-up rate limits the potential national benefits of the program. For example, I project that a universal employer bonus program would probably increase full-time equivalent employment by only about 5,000 annually (see appendix 13).

Categorical Discretionary Wage Subsidies

I now consider studies of wage subsidy programs that subsidize private employers to hire disadvantaged groups but award these subsidies in a discretionary manner, with some labor market agency choosing which disadvantaged job seekers and employers will receive subsidies. These studies are summarized in table 8.6.[9]

Based on these studies, the following conclusions seem justified:

1. Because of the individual-focused nature of discretionary programs, these studies generally focus on the effects of wage subsidies on subsidized versus unsubsidized individuals rather than on their effects on subsidized versus unsubsidized employers. A few studies do report results that indicate effects on employers. These studies imply that discretionary wage subsidies have displacement effects of 40 to 60 percent on the disadvantaged—that

TABLE 8.6 *Estimates of Effects of Discretionary Wage Subsidy Programs*

Study	Methodology	Results
Various studies of MDTA OJT, summarized by Perry et al. (1975)	Four different studies comparing earnings gains of MDTA trainees who participated in OJT to some comparison group.	Average earnings effects in first post-OJT year across all studies and groups was $1,834 (1998 dollars). Effects were generally greater for women than men, blacks than whites. OJT effects were generally greater than institutional training.
Farber (1971), as reported in Perry et al. (1975)	Comparison of 1969 earnings of 1968 JOBS contract participants to matched comparison group.	Overall average effect on earnings was an increase in annual earnings of $1,188 (1998 dollars). Effects on females were five times greater than for males, effects on blacks two or three times greater than for whites.
Ball et al. (1981)	Variation in YIEPP wage subsidy offer from 50 to 100 percent	100 percent wage subsidy: 18.2 percent agreed to participate and hire disadvantaged youth. 75 percent wage subsidy: 10.0 percent agreed to participate. 50 percent wage subsidy: 4.7 percent agreed to participate.
Ball et al. (1981)	Participating firms asked to allocate work hours of youths among those who displaced persons who would otherwise be employed and those whose hiring allowed firm to expand employment	Median reported displacement rate was 50 percent. Displacement was significantly higher at worksites whose quality was rated higher by outside observers.
Unicon (1982)	Case studies by outside observers of twenty-nine firms.	Sixty percent displacement.
Gould et al. (1982)	Regression analysis of effects on firm's employment growth of YIEPP hires.	For every ten YIEPP workers hired by for-profit firms, net employment of firms went up by about eight jobs, but about three of these were extra supervisors. Net employment of nonsupervisory personnel went up only by around five.

Farkas et al. (1984)	Non-experimental data comparing youth at sites participating in YIEPP to youth at previously similar sites not participating in YIEPP.	Annual earnings effect a few months after YIEPP program terminated (although it had been mostly phased out a year earlier): \$1,306 (1998 dollars) for young black cohort. This effect is overall YIEPP effect; subsidized private for-profit jobs were only 23 percent of YIEPP jobs.
Bishop, in Bishop and Hollenbeck (1985, ch. 4)	Regression analysis of employment of around 3,000 firms, December 1980 to June 1982 as a function of dummy variable for whether firm participated in CETA-OJT.	For every ten OJT slots at a firm, there will be three extra jobs at the firm.
Barnow (1987), summary of various studies	Regression analyses of postprogram annual earnings of CETA-OJT participants, compared to matched individuals.	Adult women: \$1,572 Adult men: \$1,851 Female youth: \$1,636 Male youth: −\$172
Bishop and Montgomery (1986)	Analysis of 1980 survey of 5,279 establishments.	Among establishments familiar with OJT, the proportion using OJT was increased by 85 percent if firm first learned of WIN tax credit from government representative.
Rangan (1984), Rode (1988)	Survey data on participating MEED employers.	In 1988, 56 percent claimed they would not have expanded to current size without MEED subsidy; in 1984, 59 percent claimed they would not have expanded to current size without MEED subsidy.
Auspos et al. (1988)	Experiment in which welfare recipients randomly assigned to treatment sequence of prevocational training, then work experience, then OJT wage subsidy.	Net annual earnings impact of entire program sequence per experimental was \$1,243 (in 1998 dollars). Program statistics indicate that about seven out of ten OJT placements roll over into regular positions with same employer.

(Table continues on p. 238.)

TABLE 8.6 *Continued*

Study	Methodology	Results
Freedman et al. (1988)	Experiment in which single-mother welfare recipients were randomly assigned to group eligible for OJT wage subsidies.	Annual earnings impact (1998 dollars) during immediate postprogram period was $929 per experimental. Since only 43 percent of all experimentals participated in OJT, and other differences in services received between experimentals and groups were small, the average earnings impact per OJT participant was $2,160. During the main period in which experimentals received OJT subsidies, employment effects on experimentals were from 38 to 46 percent of the OJT-subsidized employment, suggesting that OJT led to increased employment for a little less than half of OJT sample. Fifty-six percent of OJT participants completed their trial employment period, and all but one of those who completed the trial employment period rolled over into a regular job with same employer.
Orr et al. (1996)	Random assignment experiment in which individuals were randomly assigned to treatment and control after having been divided into one of three service strategies: OJT, classroom training, or other services.	Effects (in 1998 dollars) in months 19 through 30 after enrollment in JTPA were $1,342 for adult females, $1,479 for adult males, −$1,182 for female youth, and −$1,575 for male youth. Youth effects were not statistically significant. Effects for adult females on welfare at enrollment appeared to be about twice as great as for average adult female. OJT effects were generally more positive than classroom training results for adults.

Source: Author's compilation.

is, of every ten jobs subsidized, four to six would already have been available to the disadvantaged, with the remainder representing true net increases in job opportunities for the disadvantaged (Ball et al. 1981; Unicon 1982; Rangan 1984; Rode 1988).

2. There is less agreement on the overall displacement effects of discretionary wage subsidies. The study of the YIEPP program by William Gould and his colleagues (1982) suggests that wage subsidies under YIEPP may encourage some expansion of job opportunities as supervisors for the nondisadvantaged. Hence, the effects on net employment of ten subsidized jobs may be as high as eight new jobs, with two to four of those new jobs going to supervisors. In contrast, John Bishop (Bishop and Hollenbeck 1985, ch. 4) suggests that for every ten jobs subsidized by CETA-OJT, net employment at a firm goes up by only three new jobs. Finally, the YIEPP experiment with different wage subsidy offers implies net employment effects somewhere in the middle of these results from Gould and his colleagues and from Bishop. For example, these estimates suggest that at a 75 percent wage subsidy, 10 percent of employers agreed to participate, and at a 50 percent wage subsidy, 4.7 percent agreed to participate. (Of course, these responses represented employers' initial response to a proposed wage subsidy, and it is unclear how results would vary if we had data on what employers actually ended up deciding to do.) If we extrapolate these responses to a zero percent wage subsidy, these results imply that 2.2 percent of employers would have hired disadvantaged youth without any subsidy. This suggests that a 50 percent wage subsidy has a private worker substitution of about 2.2/4.7 = 47 percent, or every ten subsidized jobs yield about five new jobs.

3. Many of the studies examine the effects on subsidized versus unsubsidized individuals. Only a few report data during the wage subsidy period to see how much of the subsidized employment represents a real increase in employment for those subsidized, and how much of the subsidized employment merely replaces, or "displaces," employment that the individual would have obtained anyway. It should be emphasized that this sort of displacement is quite different from the displacement estimates of how employers behave. A wage subsidy program that involves only a portion of the disadvantaged population could have sizable effects on the employment experiences of those subsidized, but every new job for the subsidized group could come totally at the expense of the unsubsidized disadvantaged group, with employers not expanding at all the total number of job slots for the disadvantaged. In any event, the best evidence on effects during the subsidy period comes from the New Jersey Grant Diversion/OJT study; this program was a true random assignment experiment in which the treatment was almost purely OJT. (In other studies, either the study did not use random assignment or the program studies involved a number of services in addition to OJT or the wage subsidy.) Based on the New Jersey study, about 40 percent of the OJT-subsidized jobs represent job opportunities that the welfare recipients would not have obtained without the program, whereas about 60 percent of the subsidized jobs replace or substitute for jobs that these individuals would have obtained anyway. Other studies suggest similar substitution effects for individuals.[10] The percentage of "new" job opportunities for individuals seems somewhat lower for discretionary wage subsidies than for the public-service jobs numbers in table 7.1, where, for example, Supported Work showed in-program effects as high as 92 percent of the subsidized jobs. Wage subsidies to private for-profit employers may tend to target a somewhat less disadvantaged group, with greater alternative job opportunities.

4. *Most of the studies of discretionary categorical wage subsidies to employers focus on the earnings effects of the programs during periods after the wage subsidy has run out.* Again, the most useful study is that of New Jersey's OJT program for welfare recipients because it is a random assignment experiment with pure OJT provided. The New Jersey experiment suggests that OJT participation increases average postprogram annual earnings by around $2,000. Both the Maine TOPS (Training Opportunities in the Private Sector) program and the JTPA-OJT strategy component study are random assignment experiments that involve OJT but provide more services than just OJT. If one assumes that all of the effects of these programs are due to their OJT components, then these studies imply annual postprogram earnings effects of OJT participation of $4,000 (Maine) and $3,000 (JTPA), but these figures are overestimates of the effects of OJT if other program components also affect postprogram earnings. Average postprogram earnings effects are generally between $1,000 and $2,000 for some of the older OJT and wage subsidy programs (MDTA, JOBS [Job Opportunities in the Business Sector], CETA-OJT), just slightly below those estimated in the New Jersey random assignment experiment. Postprogram earnings effects of OJT and similar discretionary wage subsidies are generally greater in percentage terms for women than for men, and sometimes greater in absolute dollars for women than for men. Effects are greater for adults than for youth, and in fact, in some studies OJT has zero or even negative effects on youth (JTPA for both male and female youth, CETA-OJT for male youth). In contrast, the YIEPP program showed postprogram earnings effects on youth of around $1,300 per year, from a program that was about 23 percent subsidized private for-profit employment and 77 percent subsidized employment in public and nonprofit agencies. The postprogram earnings effects of discretionary wage subsidies to for-profit private employers are on average of similar size to those of public-service jobs and the average job training program. Some wage subsidy

programs have had larger postprogram effects. For example, the JTPA experiment indicates that for adults the OJT strategy produces greater postprogram earnings effects than the classroom training strategy, at no greater costs per participant (Orr et al. 1996, 194). Of course, wage subsidies (and public-service jobs) by design have greater in-program effects on employment and earnings than job training programs. In addition, it seems reasonable to assume that these average postprogram effects of discretionary wage subsidy programs are concentrated on a small proportion of all the disadvantaged persons participating in these programs. The participants who benefit the most from wage subsidy programs may be those whose greatest needs are for job experience and a chance to prove themselves with a specific employer; those who benefit the most from job training programs may have specific skill needs.

5. Most of the postprogram earnings effects of all these programs are probably due to rollover: after the wage subsidies run out, employers continue to employ many of those who were subsidized. In New Jersey, rollover was 56 percent, in Maine 70 percent, and in the YIEPP program, rollover was somewhere between 19 and 57 percent.[11] Rollover appears to be somewhat greater for discretionary wage subsidies to for-profit private employers than for public-service jobs programs, possibly because for-profit private employers may have more flexibility in hiring a proven worker than do public-sector employers.

6. Discretionary wage subsidies are conceptually similar to PSE jobs programs, except that subsidies are provided to private for-profit employers and usually cover only some percentage less than 100 percent of wage costs. Hence, the long-run displacement effects of discretionary wage subsidies on overall employment, and employment for the disadvantaged, depend to a great degree on whether they succeed in increasing the labor supply of some group that otherwise would be out of the labor force, as discussed in chapter 5 and chapter 7.

Longer-Run Effects

Little research has been done on the long-run effects of wage subsidy programs—say, after five years. Generally studies do not find much change in the effects of OJT in the first two years after OJT is over (Prescott and Cooley 1972; Auspos et al. 1988). One study of the MDTA found some deterioration in the effects of OJT. The average effects of OJT on earnings during a five-year period after OJT was completed were about 28 percent lower than effects during the first year after OJT was completed (Perry et al. 1975, 166, table VII-5). The long-term studies of the JTPA do not find much deterioration in its effects over time, but these studies have not separately examined the different service strategies under the JTPA, such as OJT (U.S. GAO 1996).

Recent Proposals for Large-Scale Wage Subsidy Programs

Over the past few years, several prominent economists have advocated large-scale wage subsidy programs to address the problems of the unemployed and the disadvantaged. I briefly consider here the proposals made by Edmund Phelps (1997), Robert Haveman (1988, 1997), and Dennis Snower (1994). Phelps's proposal is for a universal wage subsidy program for all employment that would offer a greater percentage of wages for lower-wage workers. Haveman's proposal is for a revival of the New Jobs Tax Credit. Snower's proposal is for a "benefit transfer" scheme that would encourage employment growth yet be self-financing.

Under Phelps's proposal, a wage subsidy would be paid to employers for every hour of employment of full-time workers, with the wage subsidy set quite high for low-wage workers and then phased out. Phelps's proposal starts out at a subsidy of $3 when the employer pays $7 and is totally phased out for employer wages above about $12 per hour. Updating to 1998 wage rates suggests that this subsidy might start at $4.61 per hour when the employer pays $8.61 and be phased out by a wage of about $15 per hour.

Phelps estimates that this wage subsidy program would cost $125 billion in 1997. Updating this to 1998, based on the changes in wage and salaries from 1997 to 1998, suggests an annual cost in the 1998 economy of $132 billion. Phelps argues that this cost is totally offset by reduced costs of crime, Medicaid, welfare, unemployment benefits, the EITC, and increased tax collections. However, as pointed out in a number of reviews of his book, he gives no detailed simulations of how his proposal would affect these government programs to prove his case. For example, John Kennan's (1999, 1202) review in the *Journal of Economic Literature* argues that "the claim that the subsidy would pay for itself is based more on wishful thinking than on hard analysis." Daniel Hamermesh's (1999, 153) review in *Economica* points out that "there is no doubt that Phelps's identification of the possible cost savings is in the right direction. But without an estimate of the employment effects [of Phelps's proposal], any estimate of the savings even from reduced transfers is not credible. That is truer still for any possible savings from reductions in crime, etc. These difficulties vitiate the argument for the programme being self-financing."

As pointed out by Hamermesh, Phelps presents no explicit estimates of his proposal's impacts on wages and employment. His implicit model appears to be one in which the long-run demand for all types of labor is perfectly elastic. In that case, subsidies are totally passed on to workers in the form of higher wages. The resulting change in employment depends on the different unemployment rates of different groups that are needed to bring about these changes in wages, and also on the changes in labor force participation that occur in response to higher wages and lower unemployment. Phelps appears to believe that these resulting changes in employment would have to be fairly large to be compatible with such large changes in market wages.

In appendix 15, I use the model of appendix 2 to simulate the employment and wage effects of Phelps's proposal. Based on these simulations, Phelps's proposal would be predicted to have quite sizable employment and wage effects. In fact, the wage effects are clearly sufficient to more than offset the costs of the employer subsidies.[12]

Why, then, should we not immediately adopt Phelps's proposal? First, there is always reason to be hesitant about assuming that the real world would so neatly follow these models. As pointed out in the analysis of actual wage subsidy programs, the actual take-up rates and responses to wage subsidy programs have frequently deviated from what have been predicted. Any predictions using such models implicitly assume that all firms will use the wage subsidy and will respond to it. If these assumptions are untrue, the actual employment and wage effects of the model could be much less.

Furthermore, unlike some other wage subsidy models, even if the employment and wage effects are much less than predicted, most of the costs of Phelps's wage subsidies stay the same. The proposal subsidizes all employment, not just marginal changes in employment. Hence, implementing the Phelps proposal would be far riskier than implementing some other wage subsidy proposals.

Third, Phelps's proposal appears to encourage low-wage employers in ways that may raise both substantive and political concerns. As his proposal is designed, employers receive a larger subsidy for their employment if they pay lower wages. The implicit, standard economics model that Phelps is using essentially assumes that wage rates paid by employers are largely dictated by the job skills of the workers they hire. But in some other models, as discussed in chapter 3, firms have considerable choice over which wage strategy to follow. Firms may choose to pay low wages and accept higher worker turnover and lower worker productivity, or they may pay higher wages and hope to make up for the extra costs with lower worker turnover and higher worker morale and effort. As discussed in chapter 3, there is indirect evidence for some control of individual firms over wages, in that a significant proportion of wage variation across firms cannot be explained by standard human capital variables or compensating differentials for firm amenities. In any event, the point is that if firms have some choice over their wage strategy, Phelps's proposal would reward firms for following a low-wage strategy. Presumably some firms would adjust to this by paying lower wages to their workers. It is unknown how large such firm responses might be. Even if one believes that such firm responses would be small, the political perception that Phelps's proposal encourages "low-road" employers would be deadly to the proposal. I suspect that this element of the proposal alone would destroy any hope of widespread public support for it.

Haveman proposes reviving the New Jobs Tax Credit of the late 1970s. Such a revived NJTC might cost $9 billion to $17 billion per year.[13] Appendix 15 also uses the model of appendix 2 to simulate the employment and wage effects of the Haveman proposal. The model using these assumptions projects that a revived NJTC would create 4.5 million jobs after five years. Average annual job creation per year is 900,000 jobs, a figure that seems roughly consistent with estimates of the effects of the original NJTC. In addition, the Haveman proposal would increase overall wages about 5 percent. This wage increase far exceeds in dollar value the budgetary cost of the program.[14]

As with Phelps's proposals, it is reasonable to question how much one should rely on a few estimates from a model in deciding on an ambitious wage subsidy program. However, the downside risk with the Haveman proposal is much less. The overall cost of the program is much less because it subsidizes only marginal increases in employment. Furthermore, the less successful the proposal is in creating jobs, the less it will cost.

Dennis Snower, an economist at the University of London, has argued for the position that wage subsidies to employers for hiring the disadvantaged can in some cases be undertaken for "free"—that is, the savings in welfare costs and extra taxes collected might be enough to offset any subsidy costs. Snower has proposed offering wage subsidies through benefit transfer programs as a way to lower unemployment in the United Kingdom and other European countries, as well as in the United States. In other words, instead of paying unemployment or welfare benefits, we could "transfer" or convert some of these benefits to subsidies to employers for hiring the unemployed. Snower argues that such wage subsidies could be some significant percentage of wages and still offer a cost savings over welfare and unemployment benefits, and could have significant effects on overall unemployment.

Whatever the merits of Snower's position for European economies, with much higher welfare and unemployment benefits that last a long time, it is much more difficult in the U.S. context to run a self-financing wage subsidy program for welfare recipients and other disadvantaged persons, for several reasons. First, the fact that welfare benefits tend to be lower in the United States compared to wages makes the feasible level of subsidies lower. Second, eligibility for welfare benefits and unemployment benefits is more restricted, and even individuals who do not obtain jobs may find themselves thrown off welfare. Third, the United States has a number of welfare benefits that continue (like food stamps and Medicaid) or even kick in (the Earned Income Tax Credit) for a disadvantaged person who gets a job.

Appendix 16 presents a discussion of Snower's mathematical model using plausible U.S. figures. There I conclude that it is unlikely, in the U.S. context, that a wage subsidy system would be self-financing, particularly for any wage subsidy rate greater than 10 percent. The wage subsidies might justify themselves in labor market benefits but probably would not lower social welfare costs or raise tax collections enough to pay for themselves.

The Politics of Wage Subsidies

At the national level in the United States, wage subsidies to employers for hiring the disadvantaged have never had a strong coalition of political supporters who are primarily interested in making sure that such subsidies significantly add to the labor market opportunities of disadvantaged persons. The primary national advocates for wage subsidy programs have been business groups, which, although they may have altruistic motives, are primarily interested in how the program can help make their businesses more profitable. Groups on the political left that see themselves as advocates for the disadvantaged have generally been suspicious of wage subsidy programs and have called for either ending the programs or putting such restrictions on them that they would probably be unworkable.

As an example of this political pattern, Edward Lorenz (1995) shows that over the years most of those testifying on the various reauthorizations of the Targeted Jobs Tax Credit have been representatives of businesses that heavily use the credit and the management assistance companies that contract with firms to help them use the credit. This pattern has continued with the more recent reauthorizations of the Work Opportunity Tax Credit. For example, in the July 1999 hearings on the WOTC held before the House Committee on Ways and Means, six out of seven of the nongovernmental witnesses represented employer groups. Testimony was heard from representatives of the National Employment Opportunities Network (NEON) (the lobbying group for the management assistance companies), the National Council of Chain Restaurants, and the Job Opportunities Business Symposium (described as "a coalition of major employers who use the Work Opportunity and Welfare to Work tax credits"). In addition to lobbying for extension of the WOTC, these groups called for various changes to make the program easier to use. For example, NEON argued for changes so that the program could be used to hire more young males, for example, by allowing WOTC eligibility for anyone living in a household where a child is on welfare, not just for those officially listed as part of the welfare case.

It is unclear whether this change is a good idea or not, but it certainly suggests the possibility of more windfalls to companies for hiring they would have done anyway; windfall wastage, however, is not a big concern for these business groups.

The one non-employer group to testify at these July 1999 hearings was a representative of the Center for Community Change, which describes itself as "a national non-profit organization that provides technical assistance to community based organizations in low-income and predominantly minority community around the country." The CCC's testimony brings up concerns about windfalls for businesses from the WOTC program (Espinosa 1999). The CCC's suggested revisions included a requirement that employers that receive the WOTC report retention rates of participants, and also a requirement that the federal government list companies receiving more than $100,000 per year in WOTC credits. Although these proposals may have merit, if adopted by themselves they would seem likely to discourage business participation in the program enormously. These disclosure rules would seem likely to generate potential organizing opportunities for local low-income advocacy organizations, as was the case with the Community Reinvestment Act (CRA) for the banking industry. However, unlike the case with the CRA, businesses can avoid these disclosure PR problems by simply not participating in the WOTC.

As mentioned earlier, only in two states, Oregon and Minnesota, has any political coalition succeeded in pushing through a sizable wage subsidy program to employers for hiring the disadvantaged. Both of these programs were adopted under somewhat peculiar circumstances. In Oregon, a large company had an ideological commitment in showing that employment in the private sector could solve social problems without government, yet that company was willing to do so through a partnership with the state government in providing generous government subsidies. In Minnesota, a coalition of liberal groups interested in aggressively promoting full employment was able to come up with a program that was extremely generous to business and at the same time had enough regulations about targeting small businesses and requiring retention of those subsidized that it was congruent with liberal political beliefs. These mixtures of strong ideological beliefs with a great deal of pragmatism seem absent from national political debates over wage subsidies to employers.

Conclusion

Many labor economists believe that wage subsidies to private employers to employ the disadvantaged cannot be effective because of stigma effects. But the research evidence suggests that if properly designed, employer wage subsidies for hiring the disadvantaged can be effective in increasing the employment and earnings of the disadvantaged. These positive effects occur with several designs of wage subsidies: general wage subsidies for net employment increases, entitlement wage subsidies for hiring the disadvantaged, and discretionary wage subsidies handed out by local agencies for hiring selected disadvantaged persons. What does not work is encouraging all disadvantaged persons to randomly market their disadvantaged status to random employers by handing out wage subsidy vouchers.

The positive employment and earnings effects of wage subsidies are equal to or somewhat greater than those of most training programs. The costs of wage subsidies can be held down by designing them to be marginal subsidies, tied to hiring decisions or net employment increases. Even though most of the subsidies reward employers for employment decisions they would have made anyway, resulting in windfall wastage, marginal wage subsidies can be made cheap enough to result in reasonable costs of wage subsidies per job created.

The biggest limitation of wage subsidies that target the disadvantaged is their generally low take-up rate by employers. No targeted wage subsidy to employers has ever subsidized as many as 700,000 hires in a year. Take-up rates can be increased by moving to more general wage subsidies, but then fewer of the benefits of the wage subsidy program are targeted at the disadvantaged. Take-up rates may also be increased by aggressive marketing of wage subsidies. Some combinations of general wage subsidies with aggressive marketing of targeted wage subsidies may be needed to make a significant dent in the task of creating the millions of jobs needed by the poor.

Compared to public-service jobs, wage subsidies to private employers offer both advantages and disadvantages. The research suggests that subsidizing private employers may have higher worker substitution effects than subsidizing public employers, that is, the subsidized workers are more likely to be substituted for other workers the employer would have employed. In addition, compared to public-service jobs, wage subsidies to private employers for hiring the disadvantaged appear more likely to employ persons who would have been employed anyway. Thus, private employers appear a little more adept than public employers at using employment subsidies to meet their goals rather than the goals of the employment subsidy program. On the other hand, compared to public-service jobs, subsidies to private employers appear to be more likely to lead to the subsidized employee being "rolled over" to a regular job.

Perhaps wage subsidies to private employers and public employers should be seen as complementary policies. Public-service jobs programs may be better able to hire the most disadvantaged of the poor. Subsidies to private employers may be able to provide access to somewhat broader employment opportunities for the more modestly disadvantaged of the poor.

Both wage subsidies to for-profit employers and public-service jobs should be seen as complementary to training programs. Subsidized jobs can help those whose main employment needs are work experience, job contacts, and credentials. Training programs can help those whose main employment need is to deal with skills problems that are best addressed through more formal training and education.

Whatever the merits of wage subsidies, an important issue is whether wage subsidies to employers can be made politically viable on a large scale. Perhaps wage subsidies to employers can be made more politically popular by targeting more of these subsidies at small businesses. Historically, targeting small businesses has been more successful under discretionary wage subsidies than under tax credit programs. Local training agencies have been able to target small businesses for OJT or wage subsidy slots. Obviously, it is conceptually possible to design employment tax credit programs so that more of the subsidies go to smaller businesses. However, tax-writing committees have wanted to allow all businesses to use employment tax credits. In practice, this has resulted in heavier usage of these credits by more sophisticated, larger businesses. Increasing the participation of small businesses in these tax credit programs would require either restricting these credits more to smaller businesses or much more aggressively promoting these credits to small businesses.

9

OTHER LABOR DEMAND POLICIES THAT MAY AFFECT THE POOR

This chapter considers several labor demand policies that have a primary purpose other than aiding the poor but that may nonetheless have potential for helping the poor. In contrast, the demand-side policies discussed in previous chapters—public-service jobs and employer wage subsidies—are primarily rationalized as ways of increasing the earnings of the poor and disadvantaged.

The policies considered in this chapter include: state and local economic development policies, with special attention to enterprise zones; labor market intermediary policies; antidiscrimination policies; and minimum-wage and living wage policies. All of these policies would have plausible rationales even if they had no effect on the poor. However, all of them could be reformed in ways that would make them more effective in helping the disadvantaged and poor.

State and Local Economic Development Policies

Over the past thirty years, state and local governments have devoted increasing resources to a wider variety of policies designed to encourage economic development. Economic development policies, which were aggressively pursued in the 1930s by Mississippi and other southern states seeking to attract new manufacturing branch plants, have now spread to all states. From an initial focus on recruiting manufacturing branch plants, economic development efforts have spread to a wide variety of policies designed to encourage employment growth in new branch plants, new business start-ups, existing businesses, and small businesses.

Current economic development policies provide a wide variety of financial incentives and nonfinancial services to many different types of businesses (see table 9.1). Most public attention goes to financial incentives, many of them in the form of tax breaks: property tax abatements for new or expanding businesses, corporate income tax credits for the payroll

TABLE 9.1 *A Typology of State and Local Economic Development Policies*

Traditional Economic Development Policies
(Targeted at Recruitment and Expansion of Larger Businesses)

1. Marketing area as branch plant location
   - Industrial development advertising
   - Marketing trips to corporate headquarters
   - Provision of site information to prospects
2. Financial incentives
   - Industrial revenue bonds
   - Property tax abatements
   - Other tax relief
   - Provision of land at below-market prices
3. Nonfinancial incentives
   - Customized training
   - Expedited provision of site-specific roads and utilities
   - Help with regulatory problems

"New Wave" Economic Development Policies
(Targeted at Small or Start-Up Businesses)

1. Capital market programs
   - Predominantly government-financed loan or equity programs
   - Government support for predominantly privately financed loan or equity programs
2. Information/education for small businesses
   - Small business ombudsman and information office
   - Community college classes in starting a business
   - Small business development centers
   - Entrepreneurial training programs
   - Small business incubators
3. Research and high technology
   - Centers of excellence in business-related research at public universities
   - Research-oriented industrial parks
   - Applied research grants
   - Technology transfer programs and industrial extension services
4. Export assistance
   - Information and training in how to export
   - Trade missions
   - Export financing
5. Networking programs
   - Networks of small businesses working with local community colleges to define training needs and create specialized courses for particular industries (a different variety of "customized training")
   - Cooperative arrangements among small firms with similar but not directly competing products to share services such as consultants, shipping, and marketing

Source: Author's compilation.

associated with new or expanding plants, and so on. Financial incentives also include subsidized loans or financing. Not all economic development policies provide financial incentives; many offer special low-cost or free services to businesses instead, including: public infrastructure such as utility lines or access roads; a wide variety of information and advice, particularly for small and medium-sized businesses, on modernization, exporting, and general productivity and marketing improvement issues; and various types of customized job training.

Although precise statistics are hard to come by, state and local governments appear to be devoting substantial resources to economic development, particularly in the form of tax breaks. Some recent estimates suggest that federal resources devoted to economic development amount to $6 billion annually (National Academy of Public Administration 1996, 65–66). State resources devoted to economic development are estimated to be $16 billion per year, with local resources thought to be at least another $16 billion annually (Corporation for Enterprise Development and Harrison Institute for Public Law 1999, 83). This $32 billion estimate for state and local resources for economic development is very rough, because most state and local resources for economic development take the form of tax expenditures. Estimates are that tax expenditures exceed direct spending by a ratio of at least three to one. Thus, despite the recent attempt to reorient economic development policy toward services to small and medium-sized businesses, the bulk of economic development resources probably still go to tax breaks for the new or expanding plants of large corporations.

Why do state and local governments pursue economic development? What are the goals of economic development? The most important immediate economic development goal of most cities and states is simply to create more jobs. For example, a 1994 survey by the National League of Cities (NLC) of city elected officials showed that "increasing jobs located in city" was by far the most common number-one priority of economic development policies, with almost half of elected officials listing this as a number-one goal and almost two-thirds listing it as one of the top three goals of economic development policy (Furdell 1994). In a 1993 survey of local economic development organizations, 50 percent stated that the "number of jobs created" was the key criterion in determining when economic development incentives would be used (National Council for Urban Economic Development 1993).

But simply increasing jobs is not obviously and inherently good in and of itself. Increasing jobs is a proximate goal, not an ultimate goal. Why do state and local governments want to increase the number of jobs in their jurisdiction? At least three possible benefits of more jobs seem important to most state and local officials. First, increasing local jobs is thought to improve the local tax base and local fiscal conditions. In various surveys over the years of local elected officials, "increasing the tax base" has been generally listed as one of the top three goals of economic development by around half of the respondents.[1]

Second, an important, though usually unstated, benefit of increasing the number of jobs is to increase the revenues and property values of local businesses and landowners. Among the key political backers of local economic development are various business and landowner interests that benefit from greater local economic activity. These key political backers of economic development include many local businesses that sell mainly to the local market, including newspapers, banks, chambers of commerce and their many retailer members, and land developers (Bartik 1991, ch. 3).

Third, increasing the number of jobs is thought to create job opportunities for the local unemployed and poor. In a 1994 NLC survey, 13 percent of local elected officials said that "reducing poverty in the city" was one of the top three goals of local economic development policies (Furdell 1994).

The belief that local job growth helps the unemployed and the poor is consistent with research evidence on mobility across local labor markets. As reviewed in chapter 3, mobility across metropolitan areas is limited in the short run. This limited mobility is probably due in part to the attachments that people have to the familiar people and places of their home area. As a result, it is at least plausible that increases in job availability in a metropolitan area would improve labor market outcomes for local residents.

What does research suggest about the effectiveness of state and local economic development policies? It is convenient to divide the research evidence into two parts: the extent to which state and local economic development policies affect local business activity, and the extent to which increases in local business activity help to achieve the goals of economic development policies.

On the first point, the research evidence suggests that economic development policies can increase local business activity, but that the costs of doing so may be large. I have extensively reviewed the research evidence on this elsewhere (Bartik 1991, 1992, 1994b, 1994c, 1995a, 1996a), so I merely hit some of the highlights here. First, the extensive research evidence on taxes and tax breaks suggests that changes in state and local taxes, holding public services constant, do have statistically significant but modest effects on state and local business activity. These modest effects imply that creating one more job in a state or metropolitan area may require forgoing $5,000 per year in tax revenue for the life of the job.[2]

Research evidence is much more sparse on the effects of various economic development services. The evidence is sparse in part because economic development programs have generally not encouraged evaluation. In addition, rigorous evaluation of such programs is difficult because economic development officials are understandably reluctant to randomly assign businesses to different economic development regimes. Among the findings of the studies that have been done are the following:

1. Several surveys suggest that programs that give information and consulting advice to small and medium-sized businesses on modernization and other issues can be useful. For example, surveys of clients of Ohio's Edison Technology Center program show that about one-third of client businesses report positive effects on sales, profits, market share, and employment (Mount Auburn Associates 1992); in surveys of business clients of Pennsylvania's Industrial Resource Center program, almost half of the businesses reported cost reductions due to the program (KPMG Peat Marwick 1993); surveys of clients of small business development centers in Oregon indicate that about one-fourth of the businesses thought the program had greatly increased their profits (Public Policy Associates and Brandon Roberts & Associates 1992). Although economists are usually suspicious of survey responses, it is not clear in this case that the surveyed businesses have strong incentives to lie and claim that an ineffective program is effective. Moreover, these survey results generally jibe with the findings from focus groups.
2. Econometric studies of manufacturing extension centers, for which federal support was enormously expanded under President Clinton, suggest that firms that received advice from a local center increased their productivity growth faster (by 7 to 16 percent over a five-year period) than similar firms that did not receive advice because they happened to be located in an area without a center (Jarmin 1999).[3]
3. A research study with a randomly chosen treatment and control group suggests that individuals who went through entrepreneurial training were much more likely to start a successful small business than individuals who were also interested in starting a small business but were randomly assigned to a control group that was not eligible for free training in entrepreneurship (Benus, Wood, and Grover 1994).
4. Research on a customized job training program for firms modernizing in Michigan suggests that firms that received modernization grants, compared to similar firms that applied too late to receive a grant, were more likely to achieve a significant reduction in the product scrappage rate (Holzer et al. 1993).

So there is some evidence that economic development policies can increase state and local business activity. What effects does this increased activity have on the fiscal, political, and antipoverty goals of economic development policy? The main issue for this book is the potential effect of economic development policies on the poor and disadvantaged. However, for completeness, I should mention that the findings on the fiscal and political goals of economic development policy are mixed. It is not at all clear that increases in local business activity generally pay off fiscally once one takes into account the population migration that occurs because of increased business activity and the resulting need for increased infrastructure spending by all the affected state and local governments, not just the local jurisdiction where the new business activity is located (Bartik 1996a; Altshuler and Gomez-Ibanez 1993). On the other hand, there is substantial evidence that increased local business activity does have substantial effects on local landowners by causing very large capital gains (Bartik 1991). For example, GM's location of the Saturn plant in Tennessee may have increased local land values by $200 million to $400 million.

To return to the key issue for this book, the research literature shows that increases in local employment do have statistically significant and important effects on local labor markets. Empirical research shows that an increase of 10 percent in a metropolitan area's employment increases average real earnings per person by around 4 percent. Half of this increase in real earnings occurs because local residents who otherwise would be out of the labor force get jobs. The other half of the increase in real earnings occurs because growth allows some individuals to be promoted to better-paying occupations (Bartik 1991).

The effects of local growth on real earnings appear to be long-term (Bartik 1991, 1993a). These long-term effects of local growth are consistent with hysteresis effects (see chapters 3 and 5). Because of limited short-run mobility across MSAs, a shock to local employment provides the opportunity for additional employment experiences to the original local residents. This additional local experience allows local residents to enhance their skills, self-confidence, and reputation with employers. As a result, local residents attain greater employability and wages in the long run.

These benefits of local growth are greater, in percentage terms, for lower-income persons, less-educated persons, and blacks. For example, an increase in MSA employment has about twice as great a percentage effect on income for families in the bottom income quintile as it does for the average family (Bartik 1994a). All of these findings on the effects of a stronger local economy are perfectly compatible with the evidence discussed in chapter 5 on how shifts in aggregate labor demand and overall unemployment affect different groups. In fact, the effects of local employment growth and other local economic variables on different groups provide some of the best evidence for the effects of general economic conditions on different groups.

The limitation of local employment growth as an approach to helping the poor is that even though the effects of growth are progressive, the actual dollar effects on the poor are modest. For example, a policy that increases local employment by 1 percent would be estimated to reduce the local poverty rate by only 0.1 to 0.3 percent of the population (Bartik 1993b; Bartik 1996b). A policy that increases local employment by 1 percent would increase the real earnings of the lowest income quintile by four times as much as it would average overall earnings (1.6 percent versus 0.4 percent), but actual annual real earnings for the lowest income quintile would go up by only $40 annually (Bartik 2000b). Local employment growth thus has some of the same limitations as an antipoverty tool as changes in aggregate demand and unemployment.

There are several reasons for this limited effect of local employment growth on the poor and disadvantaged. The first is unique to local employment growth: to a considerable degree, local employment increases result in increases in net migration that reduce considerably the labor market effects of the increased demand. The best estimates suggest that in the short run between 30 and 50 percent of new local jobs are absorbed by increased net migration, whereas in the long run between 60 and 90 percent of new local jobs are absorbed by increased net migration (Bartik 1993a).[4] Thus, in the long run perhaps as few as 10 percent of the new jobs result in increased employment for the local unemployed. The other reasons are identical to those given in chapter 5 for why aggregate demand has limited effects on the poor and the disadvantaged. One reason is that many of the new jobs, rather than going to the unemployed, go to those already employed who are seeking better jobs. Job openings eventually trickle down to the unemployed, but this trickling-down process reduces somewhat the net wage of the jobs taken by the unemployed. A second reason is that, although unemployment is concentrated among the lowest income quintile, it is not as concentrated as much as one would think among this quintile. Many lower-income-quintile families include only one adult, and they often have low labor force participation rates. Thus, more of the unemployed than one would think come from upper-income quintiles, even though unemployment rates are very high for the lowest income quintile.

What can be done to make state and local economic development more effective in increasing the earnings of the poor and disadvantaged? Somehow economic development assistance must be tied explicitly or implicitly to some attempt by assisted firms to hire disadvantaged persons who are screened or trained so that they are suitable job-ready hires for firms. A variety of state and local economic development policies attempt to do just this. Some of these policies offer "carrots" in the form of extra economic development incentives or services to encourage new and expanding firms to hire the disadvantaged, while others are more "stick" policies that attempt to require companies that receive economic development assistance to hire the disadvantaged.

One commonly used type of policy usually goes under the label of a "first-source" program, and it is usually perceived as a "stick" policy. Under first-source policies, firms that receive economic development assistance from a city or state are required to make some type of effort to at least consider, and in some cases hire, local unemployed or disadvantaged residents. Many cities formally have first-source policies, but these policies are seldom enforced because cities are fearful that strict enforcement would be a deterrent to economic development.

To make first-source programs viable as part of an economic development strategy, the first-source "stick" needs to be linked to a "carrot": a screening and training program run well enough that businesses can use it to hire workers for entry-level jobs who are at least as good as, and perhaps better than, the workers the business could hire on its own. One such program was the JobNet program in Portland, Oregon. By investing a considerable amount in job networking and screening, the JobNet program was able to operate at a fairly high level of activity. If a similar program had been run at a national level in 1998, the program would have had annual placements of around 541,000. However, although the program model of JobNet was viable, it is unknown exactly how much JobNet affected hiring behavior by firms and to what extent JobNet affected the economic development of Portland. We simply do not know whether overall the JobNet program was perceived by business as making Portland more or less attractive as a business location. In addition, JobNet also lacked strong political support in the end.

A second policy that can be used to increase the hiring of the disadvantaged as part of an economic development strategy is some version of a customized training program. Customized training programs, sometimes called "employer-focused training programs," are becoming an increasingly prominent economic development tool used by states. According to a recent survey sponsored by the National Governors Association (NGA), states in 1998 spent more than $575 million on employer-focused training programs (Regional Technology Strategies 1999).

Under these programs, the state heavily subsidizes training or provides free training that is designed in close cooperation with an employer or a group of employers. The training may be targeted to new or expanding firms as part of an economic development incentive package, or it may be provided to existing firms to help increase their competitiveness and long-run viability as an employer in the state. Such training programs become tools for increasing hiring of the disadvantaged to the extent to which state governments are able to include more disadvantaged persons in the training process than the business would have hired on its own. Among the states that are large providers of customized training are Iowa, California, Texas, and North Carolina.

Among the issues in making development-related customized training

SIDEBAR 9.1 Portland's JobNet

Until recently, JobNet in Portland, Oregon, was still active and providing one of the most sophisticated programs linking economic development with jobs for disadvantaged persons. Companies receiving economic development aid from the Portland Development Commission (PDC), the leading regional economic development agency, were required to sign a "first-source" agreement with PDC under which the company had to use PDC as a first source of applicants for entry-level jobs. The first-source agreements were administered by JobNet, a division of PDC.

From 1978 to 1998, JobNet worked with local training agencies, the employment service, local community colleges, and neighborhood agencies to identify disadvantaged persons who were suitable for entry-level jobs. JobNet would ensure that disadvantaged persons were screened and/or trained for entry-level jobs in firms receiving economic development aid. Firms were required to consider these candidates but were not required to hire any particular candidate or any fixed number of candidates from JobNet. However, if a firm was not making a good-faith effort to hire JobNet referrals, incentives for that firm could be revoked.

JobNet's design combines a stick with a carrot. In addition to penalizing uncooperative firms, JobNet was rewarding cooperative firms with easier access to high-quality job applicants. JobNet saw itself as having two sets of clients: disadvantaged job seekers and firms locating or expanding in Portland. JobNet's services met the needs of both sets of clients.

JobNet's design combined labor supply with labor demand programs. To offer disadvantaged people meaningful access to higher-skill jobs, the program provided customized training. For example, JobNet worked with Portland semiconductor firms to set up specialized training institutes.

JobNet operated at a high activity level. From 1989 to 1996, it placed 5,123 job seekers, or around 700 persons a year. In 1994 to 1995, one of JobNet's peak years, 1,235 job seekers were placed. On a national scale, this would have been equivalent to 541,000 placements per year.[a]

JobNet's placements helped many disadvantaged persons to get jobs that paid above-average wages. Forty-two percent of JobNet's placements in the fiscal year 1995 were minorities, and 52 percent had low income. The median hourly wage of those placed was $9.35 per hour (in 1998 dollars).

These results were achieved at a modest cost to JobNet itself of about $353 per placement (in fiscal year 1995). However, JobNet's partners (community colleges, neighborhood groups, training agencies, the employment service) also had costs, which are unknown. On a national scale, the costs of a JobNet program would be around $191 million annually.

A case study suggests that firms were favorably impressed with JobNet. One manufacturer had "initial doubts about working with JobNet staff and . . . concerns about the flexibility he would lose in advertising for covered positions. . . . [But] the company's human resource manager found JobNet to be very responsive and communicative throughout the firm's hiring process" (Molina 1998, 41). In addition, some

SIDEBAR 9.1 Continued

firms used JobNet's services voluntarily; indeed, 42 percent of JobNet's 1995 placements were at such firms.

However, JobNet in the end proved politically vulnerable because it lacked grassroots support. As Oregon moved to a "one-stop" consolidated approach to workforce development in 1997 and 1998, JobNet as a training program was removed from the PDC and has not yet been re-created at the new workforce development board. Although some neighborhood groups and education and training agencies protested JobNet's demise, no one was willing to make JobNet a key issue. This lack of support may reflect JobNet's weak ties to most neighborhood groups. Early in JobNet's history, it was thought that neighborhood groups would be a key source of job candidates. However, most neighborhood groups did not have the resources needed to identify or train qualified job candidates and therefore had little organizational investment in JobNet.

Sources: Molina (1998); Lisa Nisenfeld, former head of JobNet division of PDC, interview with the author, December 1999.

[a] This is based on extrapolating JobNet's 1994 to 1995 placements per capita in Multnomah County (the PDC was responsible for business recruitment throughout the Portland area, and thus JobNet to some extent was active throughout the local labor market, not just the city of Portland) to the U.S. population in 1998.

more effective in increasing the earnings of the disadvantaged are the following:

1. To what extent is the training subsidized by customized training programs new training that firms would not otherwise do? The only research so far that has addressed this issue is the study by Harry Holzer and his colleagues (1993), who report that under a now-defunct Michigan program, firms that received training grants from the state appeared to do much more training than firms that had applied for such grants but not received a grant because funds had been exhausted for the fiscal year. There is some reason to be concerned that in many cases the subsidized training may simply subsidize training the firm would have done anyway. Based on the NGA data, state training grants appear to be less likely to go to smaller firms: 24 percent of state customized training dollars go to business establishments with fifty or fewer employees, whereas 38 percent of nonretail U.S. employment is in business establishments with fifty or fewer employees (Regional Technology Strategies 1999, 10). Data on OJT show consistently that smaller firms are much less likely to engage in training on their own than larger firms (Barron et al. 1997). Hence, there is certainly a greater risk that customized training grants to larger firms substitute for training they already do.

SIDEBAR 9.2 North Carolina's Community College Programs for Business and Industry

North Carolina's industrial training programs help achieve two goals: orienting the state's community colleges toward the needs of employers, and encouraging firms to hire a more diverse workforce. Overall, North Carolina spent $44 million on industrial training programs in 1998, and 319,000 workers received such training in 1997. On a national scale, this would have been equivalent to spending $654 million annually and training 4.8 million workers.[a]

The business and industry program in North Carolina's fifty-eight community colleges offers three training programs: New and Expanding Industry Training (NEIT), Occupational Continuing Education (OCE), and Focused Industry Training (FIT).

NEIT goes back to the late 1950s, when North Carolina became the first state to use customized training to attract new branch plants. The state set up industrial education centers to deliver this training. These centers became the nucleus for many community colleges when North Carolina in 1963 consolidated its twenty industrial education centers and six community colleges.

Firms are eligible for NEIT if they are creating at least twelve jobs in some industry that exports goods or services outside the state. Eighty percent of NEIT clients are in manufacturing. Half are firms new to the state, and half are expanding firms. NEIT is offered to new firms by development agencies and marketed to existing firms by community colleges. Under NEIT, the college places ads for employers and screens trainees, often subcontracting to the local employment service office the tasks of reviewing applications and administering tests. The firm chooses trainees from among those screened. The firm typically provides the equipment, while the community college provides the facilities and the trainers. NEIT typically provides eighty to five hundred hours of training. The firm decides which trainees will be hired.

The NEIT program is totally funded by state dollars. Its 1998 budget was $10.1 million. Twenty-five thousand workers, almost all new hires, were trained in 1997, at an average cost (in 1998 dollars) of $391 per trainee.

OCE provides more short-term and limited training, but with fewer eligibility requirements. For a fee of $35 per course, the community colleges offer courses that provide occupationally relevant training. Sixty percent of the courses are arranged by employers, and 40 percent by individual workers. Courses are customized to the needs of an individual firm if there are at least ten to twelve trainees from the firm. Forty percent of those trained under OCE programs are new hires.

OCE's budget in 1998 was $31 million. In 1997, 285,000 workers were trained under OCE, at an average cost per trainee of only $86 (in 1998 dollars). Community colleges are reimbursed the next fiscal year, including overhead, for the number of OCE trainees they enroll.

FIT was set up to provide customized training to smaller manufacturers that do not have sufficient numbers of potential trainees to justify customized training under

SIDEBAR 9.2 Continued

either of the other two programs. Only manufacturers are eligible, and the training must be arranged by the employer. The state funds FIT up front. Spending on FIT in 1998 was $3.1 million. Nine thousand workers were trained by FIT in 1997, at an average cost of $384 each (in 1998 dollars).

North Carolina's industrial training programs are not explicitly targeted at the disadvantaged. However, by using community colleges so extensively in the screening and training process, many firms end up hiring a somewhat more diverse workforce. Enrollment in North Carolina's community college system is 20 percent black. Community colleges often administer local job training agencies, and half of North Carolina's "one-stop shop" training centers under the Workforce Investment Act are located at community colleges. Batt and Osterman's (1993, 34) case study argues that community colleges can sometimes use their multiple roles to give some disadvantaged persons access to better jobs. For example, "because [Durham Technical Institute] administers JTPA and state welfare-to-work programs, it has the opportunity to mainstream more disadvantaged students in these [industrial] training programs and has done so. Mothers on welfare, for example, have received training and placement in electronic assembly jobs through [NEIT] without being stigmatized or isolated for special treatment."

Sources: Regional Technology Strategies (1999); Batt and Osterman (1993); Osterman and Batt (1993).

[a] This is calculated by simply extrapolating North Carolina's per capita numbers based on total U.S. population in 1998.

2. *To what extent does the customized training result in firms employing more disadvantaged persons than they would hire on their own?* Overall, most of the customized training dollars (58 percent) now go to train workers who were already employed by the firm at the start of training (Regional Technology Strategies 1999, 5). It seems unlikely that such training investments would have much effect on the firm's decisions about whom to employ. It is more likely that customized training affects the firm's employment of the disadvantaged if the training is targeted at new hires, particularly unemployed new hires: 34 percent of customized training dollars go for new hires who were elsewhere employed, and 8 percent of customized training dollars go for trainees who were unemployed prior to training. For training targeted at new hires, the state training program can affect the pattern of hiring either explicitly, by making the funding conditional on who is trained, or implicitly, by using the opportunity presented by training to include some disadvantaged job seekers in the hiring and training pool. As an example of an explicit link, California in 1998 devoted $20 million of its $112 million for customized training to projects that helped firms train workers who were receiving or had recently received

welfare benefits (Regional Technology Strategies 1999, 21). As an example of an implicit link, in the North Carolina program the community colleges are the key training providers to employers; they also provide training services to many low- and moderate-income households, including training services under federally funded job training for the disadvantaged and welfare-to-work programs. According to Rosemary Batt and Paul Osterman's (1993) case study, some community colleges in North Carolina are able to mainstream welfare recipients into the state's economic development job training programs. For example, some welfare mothers have received training and placement in electronic assembly programs under the state's New and Expanding Industries Program.

3. Customized training and placement programs are also sometimes run locally as part of local or community-run economic development efforts. For example, the WIRE-Net organization is an economic development program focused on several West Side neighborhoods in Cleveland and run by a coalition of community development corporations and various small manufacturing firms located in these neighborhoods. This organization provides various services to encourage the retention of manufacturing businesses in this neighborhood, such as providing firms with advice on modernization, personnel management, and marketing, referring local firms to reliable consultants, and helping link up firms into small peer groups that can provide informal advice. In addition, WIRE-Net sponsors a "Hire Locally" program. Under this program, WIRE-Net helps screen, train, and refer local residents to job openings at local manufacturers.[5]

4. Finally, some economic development training programs, rather than train disadvantaged workers for specific firms, train disadvantaged workers for occupations that are thought to be in high demand by a number of firms. For example, Florida's economic development program is running the Performance Bonus Incentive Fund, which gives bonuses to local community colleges for training and placements in occupations that are thought by the state to be in high demand by new and expanding businesses, with extra bonuses if the training is provided to welfare recipients and other disadvantaged individuals.

Enterprise Zones

Enterprise zones have frequently been proposed and tried as one way of targeting economic development policies at the disadvantaged.[6] "Enterprise zone" (EZ) is a generic term for any policy that seeks to encourage business activity in a small spatial area, such as a neighborhood.

The enterprise zone concept originated among conservative thinkers in

SIDEBAR 9.3 Florida's Performance-Based Incentive Funding Program

Florida's Performance-Based Incentive Funding (PBIF) program is an interesting experiment in incentives to motivate educational institutions to pursue economic development and workforce development goals, with special attention to the needs of the disadvantaged. So far the program would have to be given a grade of "incomplete, but promising."

PBIF was established by the Florida legislature in 1994. The program is administered by Enterprise Florida, the public-private entity that administers Florida's economic development efforts. Under PBIF, extra funds are allocated to local community colleges and school districts that enroll students in occupationally specific training programs and place them in these occupations, if these occupations are designated as high-demand and high-wage. High-demand occupations are designated annually by Enterprise Florida. High-wage is defined as $9 per hour in general, but $7.50 per hour for welfare recipients. Extra incentives are provided for those in various disadvantaged groups (economically disadvantaged, disabled, displaced workers, limited English proficiency). Incentives are allocated based on *increases* since a base year in program enrollment, program completion, and occupational placement.

In the 1995 to 1996 program year, the PBIF program handed out $10 million in incentive grants. Overall placements in PBIF-designated occupations of those who completed the program increased from 10,213 in the 1992 to 1993 baseline year to 16,851 in the 1995 to 1996 program year. Placements for disadvantaged groups increased from 2,118 in the baseline year to 5,077 in the 1995 to 1996 program year. However, only 240 of these PBIF placements were welfare recipients.

Has this program been successful? The program has increased educational activity in the designated occupations. However, it is unclear whether the program has led to changes in educational institutions to better meet the needs of disadvantaged students. For example, it is unclear whether placements of disadvantaged students have really increased or schools are just keeping better track of whether a student is in a target group. The small number of welfare recipients placed is distressing. Some community colleges have set up special courses for welfare recipients. However, there have been no major changes in outreach, support services, entrance requirements, or course design.

Sources: Roberts and Padden (1998b); Florida Office of Program Policy Analysis and Government Accountability (1998); Switzer (1999).

England in the early 1980s, and then was pushed in the United States by the conservative Republican congressman Jack Kemp. In their original conservative incarnation, enterprise zones were supposed to revitalize inner-city neighborhoods by eliminating most or all of the taxes and regulations of liberal welfare states in those neighborhoods. Eliminating regulations was soon dropped from most enterprise zone proposals, since there is not much support among any groups, including inner-city residents, for dramatically reducing environmental or worker health and safety regulations among inner-city businesses.

No federal EZ bill was enacted in the 1980s, but many states began their own EZ programs. Some state EZ programs focused on cutting business taxes, but other more "liberal" EZ programs also increased public services and infrastructure: job training, child care services, police protection, streets and sidewalks.

Finally, in 1993 the Clinton administration succeeded in getting Congress to adopt a bill setting up a very small number of "empowerment zones," and a much larger number of "enterprise communities." Clinton definitely tilted toward the more liberal version of enterprise zones, proposing tax breaks coupled with grants to each zone for enhancing various services ($100 million in grants for each empowerment zone, $3 million each for the enterprise communities).

Two issues can be raised about enterprise zones that are quite similar to the issues raised about economic development programs in general. First, do enterprise zones encourage a greater level of business activity in the zones than would otherwise occur? The theoretical literature on economic development suggests that the answer is uncertain. In general, one would expect that for an *average* neighborhood in a metropolitan area, with property zoned for businesses, the volume of business activity would be quite sensitive to business tax costs and other costs in that neighborhood. In particular, business activity should be more sensitive to a neighborhood's taxes than to the average tax rate of the MSA or state (Bartik 1991, 1992). Within an MSA, the average neighborhood has many close substitutes from a business perspective, and so business activity in the neighborhood should change a great deal in response to minor cost changes. But enterprise zones by definition are not "average neighborhoods." Enterprise zones are chosen precisely because they are thought to be much harder than the average neighborhood to redevelop. Even large changes in taxes or other business costs in an enterprise zone might not be enough to allow business activity to profitably increase there.

Before discussing evaluation findings, it should be said at the outset that enterprise zones are difficult to evaluate because they are far from randomly chosen (Bartik and Bingham 1997). It is difficult to find suitable comparison areas for zones, and it is unclear how this may bias evaluations. Enterprise zones might do worse than comparison areas because policymakers select the worst neighborhoods for EZ designation. Alternatively, enterprise zones might do better than comparison areas because there is nowhere for the zone area to go but up.

Having admitted the limitations of evaluation research on enterprise zones, the empirical literature on them generally has negative findings, although some studies find some effects. Recent studies by Robert Greenbaum (1998), Alan Peters and Peter Fisher (in press), Marlon Boarnet and William Bogart (1996), and Daniele Bondonio and John Engberg (1999) all fail to find significant effects of enterprise zones on business activity. On the other hand, Leslie Papke (1994) finds some evidence that enterprise zones in Indiana have reduced unemployment claims, and Barry Rubin and Margaret Wilder (1989) find some evidence that the Evansville, Indiana, enterprise zone has helped increase employment in the zone. One study suggests that enterprise zone success seems greater in states that designate fewer zones (Erickson and Friedman 1991). Another study suggests that enterprise zone success is associated with greater staffing efforts to administer the zones (Elling and Sheldon 1991). Perhaps zones have worked, not in general, but in a few states or cities. For example, Indiana's EZ program may be more successful than programs in other states because Indiana's zones receive a percentage of the zone tax breaks to help support EZ staff.

Even if enterprise zones succeed in increasing business activity in the zone neighborhood, they may not help the disadvantaged residents of the neighborhood to get jobs. As discussed in chapter 3, neighborhoods are not labor markets. Most individuals, even disadvantaged individuals, do not work in the same neighborhood in which they live. Thus, we would not expect most of the jobs that locate in a zone to go to the residents of the zone. Recent research by Peters and Fisher (in press) illustrates this problem. These researchers show that for most zones most of the jobs in the zone are held by persons living in other neighborhoods, including many affluent neighborhoods. Helen Ladd's (1994, 207) review of the research on enterprise zones concludes that the cost of these programs, per job created for a zone resident, is probably at least $40,000 to $60,000.

What, if anything, can be done to solve these problems with enterprise zones? Rather than focusing on simply increasing business activity in a neighborhood, we might instead focus on trying to increase the employment of everyone in a low-income neighborhood, even at firms outside the neighborhood. This is the strategy taken by programs such as YIEPP and New Hope, which try to target the residents of low-income neighborhoods and improve their employment. Employment programs may have administrative reasons to target neighborhood residents: such targeting is less stigmatizing than targeting individuals because they are on welfare. Moreover, there may be some neighborhood "spillovers" in that greater employment success for one neighborhood resident may provide a role model or a job contact for other neighborhood residents. For example, one could imagine an enterprise zone proposal in which wage subsidies to employers would be paid for employing residents of the zone, but these wage subsidies could go to employers regardless of the employer's location, rather than only to employers located in the zone. Such a wage subsidy was part of President

Clinton's original empowerment zone proposal before it was modified by Congress. At the same time, various community development activities could be pursued in zone neighborhoods: fixing up housing and the infrastructure, improving public services, and encouraging the growth of local businesses and local business leadership. Such community development activities are the focus of much of the Clinton administration's empowerment zone program. However, we should expect these community development activities to improve only the quality of life and morale of distressed neighborhoods. These activities would be less important in improving the employment rates of local residents than broader efforts to connect neighborhood residents with the metropolitan labor market.

Labor Market Intermediaries

As described earlier, one way to make economic development policies more beneficial for disadvantaged persons is to link such policies with labor market intermediaries (LMIs) that seek to place them in jobs in firms that receive economic development assistance. But LMI programs can also operate on their own, without being tied to economic development programs.

A labor market intermediary can be defined as an organization, program, or group of organizations or programs that seeks to link up individuals who need jobs with employers who need workers. Such programs can help job seekers at all income levels. For this book, I am primarily interested in how intermediaries can help the disadvantaged and the poor, although not necessarily through an LMI program that is restricted to the disadvantaged and the poor.

By their very definition, labor market intermediaries are both labor supply and labor demand policies, in that the intermediaries interact with both job seekers and employers to at least marginally affect their behavior. Labor market intermediaries are more demand-oriented the more they interact with employers and the more they seek to alter employer behavior that is relevant to the labor market success of job seekers. Labor market intermediaries may seek to alter employer behavior along a number of dimensions:

- *Who employers hire, what sources employers use for hiring, and the process used for hiring:* For example, an LMI may seek to increase employer use of the LMI for screening and providing the employers with job candidates from disadvantaged groups.
- *How jobs are defined, the career path associated with those jobs, and how the job skills needed for those jobs are credentialed:* For example, LMIs may work with employers to set up new job classifications, with

defined advancement opportunities that require a particular credential from a newly designed training program.

- *Supervisory practices of frontline managers:* For example, LMIs may work with employers to help frontline managers more effectively deal with the problems faced by new employees who come from disadvantaged backgrounds and have spotty previous employment experience.

The longest-standing U.S. labor market intermediary is the U.S. Employment Service (ES), run by state governments under federal rules (Balducchi, Johnson, and Gritz 1997). The ES was permanently established in 1933. During the Great Depression the service was primarily active in helping to place unemployed workers in the WPA and other New Deal employment programs. With the establishment of the federal-state unemployment insurance program in 1935, the ES began to play one of its primary roles: providing a way to operationalize the "work test" under UI. Under the UI work test, unemployed individuals who receive UI benefits are required to register with the ES and accept suitable job referrals that it provides. During World War II the ES helped recruit and place workers in defense industries.

The main service consistently provided by the U.S. Employment Service is labor exchange—that is, job seekers register with the ES, employers voluntarily list job openings with the ES, and the ES refers job seekers to suitable job openings. In addition to job referrals, the ES sometimes provides counseling and testing services to job seekers as well as job development services—that is, it contacts employers to see whether they have any suitable job openings for the job seeker. In addition, during the 1960s and early 1970s, the ES was the key agency providing a large part of federally funded job training services for the disadvantaged and for dislocated workers. Typically the ES was asked, as part of various training programs, to do screening and referral of job applicants and some job development; sometimes the ES also provided job readiness training. However, with the passage of CETA in 1974, job training services for the disadvantaged were moved to separate local agencies from the local ES office, and the role of the ES in helping the disadvantaged diminished. In addition, real funding for the ES's basic labor exchange service, after staying constant in real terms in the 1970s, has declined by 20 percent in real terms since 1984 (Balducchi et al. 1997, 469).

The Employment Service's reputation among both job seekers and employers is generally poor. The ES is regarded as providing minimal services and as dealing mostly with low-quality workers and jobs. Despite this reputation, research suggests that core ES services are cost-effective. ES job referrals seem to particularly help women. For example, studies have estimated that women receiving ES job referrals, compared to similar women who do not receive ES referrals, return to work about three weeks sooner and obtain 25 percent higher earnings in the short run (Balducchi et al. 1997, 484). Although these benefits are quite modest, the benefits of these services clearly outweigh the costs, because ES costs per referral are low.

However, owing to its poor reputation and sparse services, the ES does not have a large share of labor market placements. This modest share of labor market placements, together with the ES's modest effects on employment, limits its overall effects. For example, in 1994, although 18.8 million people were ES registrants, only 8.1 million received an ES referral, and only 2.7 million ES registrants were placed in jobs by the ES, about 15 percent of all ES registrants (U.S. Department of Labor 1998b, 320–22). Even if employment effects were the same for all ES registrants who received a referral as studies show they were for women, ES effects would be equivalent to an increase in full-year employment of only about half a million jobs.[7] Only 2.9 million of the 18.8 million ES registrants were economically disadvantaged, even though certainly more than 2.9 million economically disadvantaged individuals were in need of a job at some time during 1994.

In part because of the market opportunity left open by the ES's poor reputation and low market share, and in part because of firms' increased demand for labor flexibility and determination to reduce labor costs, the role of temporary help agencies has greatly increased in recent years. For example, from 1982 to 1998, employment in the help supply industry, as a percentage of all employment, increased from 0.5 to 2.3 percent (Houseman 1999). Many firms increasingly use temporary help services as a screening device: more and more workers are hired through "temp-to-perm" placements. Firms may use temp agencies in this way because they feel that contracting out to a specialist improves the quality of screening. Firms may also believe that it is easier to not convert a temp hire to a permanent hire than it is to fire a new regular employee during a probationary period. Not retaining a temporary employee may be easier psychologically for supervisors, pose less risk of lawsuits, and have less of an effect on the morale of other workers.

Is the increased role of temporary help services a good or bad trend for disadvantaged workers? On the one hand, the growth of temp services may make it harder for disadvantaged workers to get good permanent jobs. On the other hand, temp-to-perm screening may be more rational and less prejudiced as a screening device than has typically been the case when individuals are directly hired for permanent jobs. However, it should always be kept in mind that temporary help agencies receive their fees from employers and hence must reflect the views and interests of employers. There is anecdotal evidence that temporary help agencies are frequently asked to not refer blacks. For example, one community-based nonprofit temporary agency in Chicago, Suburban Job Link, claims that racially biased job orders from employers were more common in the late 1990s than they were in the mid-1980s (Seavey 1998, 59). Furthermore, because of who pays their fees, there are limits to the costs of services that temporary help agencies are willing to offer job seekers to help make them more employable.

Some states have recently begun to pay temporary help agencies to place welfare recipients and other disadvantaged groups in jobs, a strategy that would change the incentives facing temporary help agencies, at least for that program (Houseman 1999). No research evidence is available on the success of these demonstrations.

Community-based nonprofit organizations are increasingly attempting to play a role as labor market intermediaries promoting the employment of the disadvantaged. Why might community-based organizations have some advantage as LMIs? First, because of their political base in the community, these organizations have some built-in incentive to make sure their programs are meeting the needs of their constituents. Second, they may be better than other LMIs at screening disadvantaged job seekers and providing them with mentorship services. There is some precedent for community-based organizations being better able to screen disadvantaged persons than other organizations in the housing area, where they seem to be better at managing low-income housing projects than the government and other organizations, in part because they are better at screening tenants and dealing with problem tenants.

The community-based nonprofit organizations trying to be labor market intermediaries are following a wide variety of models. Some community-based approaches, like Minneapolis NET, focus simply on providing job market information. Other organizations, such as the Milwaukee Careers Cooperative, set up nonprofit temporary help agencies for placing the disadvantaged. Finally, other community-based nonprofit organizations are seeking to provide LMI services as part of a wide variety of other services seeking to affect the labor market for the disadvantaged.

One comprehensive community-based approach to improving labor markets for the disadvantaged, with LMI services as a core component, is what is called a "sectoral employment development program." This approach to increasing the employment and earnings of the disadvantaged has been significantly supported by a number of foundations, in particular the Mott Foundation. Under the sectoral employment development approach, the community-based organization seeks to affect the labor market for the disadvantaged by targeting a particular "sector," by which is meant a somewhat narrowly defined group of occupations within a particular industry. The organization then seeks to provide valued LMI, training, and other

SIDEBAR 9.4 The Minneapolis Neighborhood Employment Network

The Minneapolis Neighborhood Employment Network (NET) was started in 1981 as a first-source program: firms that received assistance from the Minneapolis city government were required to use this program as a source for entry-level job hiring. However, over time NET has come to rely little on requirements placed on employers. Rather, NET appeals to employers by offering an easier source of high-quality labor supply for new hires, in the context of a high-aggregate-demand local labor market. NET appeals to its affiliates by offering access to jobs throughout the local labor markets and providing cost savings by having many neighborhood groups share services, ideas, and peer support.

The NET director or job broker is located in the Minneapolis mayor's offices. NET has eleven neighborhood affiliates. It employs two job developers who aggressively search out new job listings. Information on these job listings is distributed through a computer network with links to each neighborhood. After receiving a job listing, neighborhood affiliates recruit and screen appropriate job candidates and directly contact the employer. NET affiliates regularly meet with the director to discuss common problems. According to a case study of NET (Molina 1998, 28), "there is considerable peer pressure among the partners to refer only good matches in order to retain employers' credibility in the whole network." Funding for the NET affiliates comes from the Job Training Partnership Act (JTPA) and the federal Community Development Block Grant program. The NET director's position is funded by private funds.

No formal evaluation has been done of NET, but the program has succeeded in achieving a significant number of job placements for relatively disadvantaged persons, at modest costs. In the fiscal year 1996, the program placed 1,706 persons. This is equivalent to making 1.3 million job placements nationally in 1998.[a] All those placed have household income less than 80 percent of median household income in the Twin Cities metropolitan area. Thirty-five percent of those placed received some type of welfare assistance before being placed. The cost of the NET director and the NET affiliates per placement is $790 (in 1998 dollars). The total cost of an equivalent national program would be $1.0 billion (in 1998 dollars).

Source: Molina 1998.

[a] This is calculated by extrapolating Minneapolis's per capita job placement rate to the U.S. population in 1998.

services within that sector and to use the value of these services to change how employers hire in that sector and to upgrade wages and job quality within that sector.

For example, Project Quest, profiled in chapter 4, is sometimes called a sectoral employment development program because it has sometimes be-

SIDEBAR 9.5 The Milwaukee Careers Cooperative

The Milwaukee Careers Cooperative (MCC) is a nonprofit, temporary-to-permanent placement agency that specializes in placing workers in light industrial work and primarily serves young African American male workers in five neighborhoods in central Milwaukee. MCC was founded in 1987 by a group of church congregations and community organizations.

MCC's staff of six includes one developer-account executive who solicits job orders from area employers for MCC, just as is done by ordinary temp agencies. Job seekers go through job retention training and some screening. MCC places these workers with employers under thirty- to ninety-day contracts, but only if a permanent job is available at the end for those who perform satisfactorily. As with a regular temp agency, the employer pays MCC a fee, and MCC pays the worker during the contract period. No extra fee is charged for a permanent placement. One week after workers are placed, MCC runs a Saturday morning workshop for workers providing advice on job retention and an opportunity to discuss problems that might have developed on the job. MCC workers are provided with transportation to work via a van service for up to six months after being permanently placed. The van service allows MCC workers to be available at odd shift times, giving them an important comparative advantage with suburban industrial employers.

MCC has achieved fairly high placement levels and has provided services valuable enough that employers have been willing to pay substantial fees. In the 1996 fiscal year, MCC placed 1,132 persons, or 61 percent of those who came to MCC seeking jobs. This is equivalent to making 516,000 placements nationally in 1998.[a] Most MCC clients are twenty to twenty-four years old, two-thirds are males, and 86 percent are African American. The costs of MCC, including paying wages to its temp workers, are about $1,468 per placement (in 1998 dollars). Seventy-five percent of MCC's costs are covered by employer fees, and the remaining costs are covered by government and foundation grants, area congregations, and individual contributions.

Source: Seavey (1998).

[a] This is calculated by extrapolating MCC's placement rate as a percentage of Milwaukee's population in 1996 to the national population in 1998.

come intimately involved with the details of how a particular occupation or industry is structured. Project Quest finances and organizes employment services for the disadvantaged in San Antonio. These employment services feature customized training (carried out at community colleges), screening, and referral services for particular occupations and industries. In some cases, Project Quest's consultations with industries in attempts to customize its training, screening, and referral process have led to some restructuring and upgrading of jobs in particular sectors. For example, Project Quest's discussions with banks led to the creation of a new job title and training program—financial customer services—and its discussions with hospitals led to the beefing up of the expected training and credentials for the position of unit clerk, as well as wage increases for this position.

Other examples of sectoral employment programs include:

- The Chicago Manufacturing Institute (CMI) is a for-profit spinoff from Chicago Commons, a community-based human services agency. CMI works with a group of local metalworking businesses to set up training, screening, and referral for various occupations associated with metalworking. CMI also provides industrial extension advice to these firms on how to use the latest technology and has helped upgrade training standards in its client businesses (Clark and Dawson 1995).
- Cooperative Health Care Associates (CHCA) in the South Bronx is a for-profit, worker-owned cooperative that provides home health care aides, usually on contract to major hospitals or other larger visiting nurse agencies. CHCA typically hires minority women who were previously on welfare and provides intensive training. CHCA provides health insurance benefits and tries to pay its worker-owners 10 to 20 percent more than other agencies pay home health aides. The idea is to make up for these extra costs with better quality and lower worker turnover (Clark and Dawson 1995; Dawson 1998; Elliott and King 1999).

Another example of a comprehensive community-based approach to the employment problems of the disadvantaged, with a strong emphasis on labor market intermediary services, is the Jobs Initiative of the Annie E. Casey Foundation (AECF). Under the Jobs Initiative, the AECF is providing $30 million over eight years to partly fund efforts by coalitions of community groups, government, and other organizations in six large cities to address the employment problems of low-income residents of designated low-income neighborhoods. The coalition groups at various Job Initiative sites are often intervening as a labor market intermediary to attempt to affect how employers hire employees and how they structure jobs. For example, the Denver group is providing training for businesses in how to supervise disadvantaged entry-level workers (Jobs for the Future and Burness Communications 1999).

The development of the Internet and other computer technology is beginning to affect LMI services. For example, the U.S. Department of Labor has sponsored the development of America's Labor Market Information System (ALMIS), which includes Internet access to job listings across the United States and the résumés of job seekers.[8] However, because employers want to know whether disadvantaged workers have particular soft skills, which are hard to evaluate by looking at a résumé, it is unclear whether the developments of such computerized job exchanges will significantly help the employment opportunities of the disadvantaged.

A recent major reform that may dramatically affect LMI services for disadvantaged workers is the Workforce Investment Act, enacted in 1998.[9] Under WIA, the labor exchange services of the ES are supposed to once more be reintegrated with the wide variety of training services for different disadvantaged groups. This reintegration is supposed to be supervised at the local level by business-led workforce investment boards (WIBs), which will oversee the operation of "one-stop" centers at which job seekers are supposed to be able to learn about all the labor exchange and job training services available in that area.

At these one-stop centers, job seekers will be able to obtain three levels of services. "Core services," for which all job seekers are automatically eligible, include basic assessment of the job seeker's skills and interest and information on job openings, the local labor market, and available training and education services and the ordinary financial aid available for those services. "Intensive services" and "training services" may be offered to any job seeker, but local WIBs are supposed to target these services at low-income individuals. "Intensive services" include more extensive assessments and testing, counseling, case management, short-term job readiness and job search classes, and paid or unpaid work experience. "Training services" are provided through vouchers at local certified training providers.

This new system is supposed to achieve overall accountability by state and local performance standards, which are subject to some negotiations between the state and federal government. In addition, eventually training providers, in order to be certified, will have to provide information on various performance measures, and that performance will have to be judged to be satisfactory.

As of this writing, it is not clear exactly how WIA will be implemented, or what difference it will make in how labor exchange services and training services are provided. At least two key issues face WIA and these various community-based initiatives seeking to provide labor market intermediary services. First, will these efforts be funded well enough to provide adequate LMI and related services to the disadvantaged? Providing LMI services to the disadvantaged is expensive and requires screening efforts, which can also be expensive, and extensive time spent with job seekers by caseworkers. Without sufficient funds, not much training can be provided and these programs find that they have to screen out many of the hard-to-serve and reduce the number of people they can help. LMI programs are likely to reach more employers and to have a greater effect on employment opportunities if they involve extensive job development, which, again, requires significant monetary investment in hiring job developers. In addition, such programs are more likely to be successful with employers if they can provide postplacement casework services.

Second, there is the issue of performance. LMI services are complex services to deliver. Programs must consider both employers and disadvantaged job seekers as clients and seek to balance and fulfill the interests of both groups. It is difficult for one agency to see itself as serving both employers and job seekers, and yet services to both must be coordinated, however difficult that is to do with multiple agencies.

We do not yet have ideal solutions to these problems. The issue of money depends on the politics of job training and on whether a political coalition can be constructed that will advocate for funding WIA and other efforts at a serious level. Much will depend on the details of how the performance standards for state and local agencies are written, and what pressures this process puts on these agencies to perform. But top-down performance standards are probably usefully supplemented by pressure at the local level by the poor and disadvantaged to make sure these programs are effective in improving their employment opportunities.

Antidiscrimination Policies

As discussed in chapter 3, there is strong evidence that blacks and other minorities continue to be subject to widespread employment discrimination. Evidence of employment discrimination comes from employment "audits," or "tests," in which an antidiscrimination group or government agency sends matched pairs of white and nonwhite "testers" to apply for the same job. Evidence of employment discrimination also comes from studies in which interviewers have found that many employers admit that they are less likely to hire blacks, particularly black males from inner-city neighborhoods. Employment discrimination in part is motivated by simply racial prejudice. Discrimination often can be sustained because of extremely imperfect information about job seekers' true productivity. Finding it extremely difficult to hire productive workers, and often having poor information about job seekers, many employers are prone to "grasp at straws," using race, welfare receipt, or other characteristics of job seekers as possible signals of productivity. Research on hiring patterns by different employers is consistent with the hypothesis that racial discrimination is more prevalent in small businesses (Holzer 1996, 102), which may face more serious information problems in hiring job seekers or be more prone to adopt the prejudices of the business owner.

Policies to combat employment discrimination in the United States largely rest on two foundations: Title VII of the Civil Rights Act of 1964, and Executive Order 11246 from 1965 (Jaynes and Williams 1989). Title VII of the Civil Rights Act made racial discrimination illegal in hiring, pay, and promotion. Title VII also set up the Equal Employment Opportunity Commission (EEOC), which has the power to investigate discrimination complaints, help mediate such complaints, and bring suit against employers who discriminate. If the EEOC decides not to sue a particular employer, it may authorize individuals to bring their own suits. Executive Order 11246, from the Johnson administration, restated and beefed up an earlier Kennedy administration executive order requiring federal contractors to undertake "affirmative action" to increase the employment of racial minorities and other "protected groups." These requirements are monitored and enforced by the U.S. Department of Labor's Office of Federal Contract Compliance Programs (OFCCP). Affirmative action plans, which outline steps in recruitment and hiring practices to increase the employment of minorities and sometimes have numerical targets for these revised practices to achieve, also can result from court cases brought by individuals or the EEOC.

From a philosophical perspective, we can distinguish between antidiscrimination policies that simply seek to eliminate any racial preference in hiring, firing, and promotions and affirmative action programs, which in some cases have been interpreted as setting quotas for how many minorities must be hired or employed in particular jobs. However, in practice it has often been difficult to enforce policies against discrimination without at some point asking for some sort of numerical proof that the employer is not engaged in discrimination. The search for such accountability naturally leads to the adoption of some sort of affirmative action plan with at least loose numerical targets.

On the whole, the evidence suggests that antidiscrimination policies have made a significant difference to the employment prospects of blacks. Some time-series studies present evidence that the employment prospects of blacks, particularly in the South, were significantly improved by the Civil Rights Act of 1964 and the change in legal rights and social attitudes it represented (Freeman 1973; Donohue and Heckman 1991). Other studies have argued that improvements in the education of blacks were more important in explaining black economic gains in the 1960s (Smith and Welch 1989). Some studies have found evidence that during the 1960s and 1970s the employment of blacks improved more at government contractors than at noncontractors (Leonard 1990). The progress of blacks at government contractors seemed to slow down or even halt during the 1980s and 1990s, owing possibly to reduced enforcement activities or to increased court and public resistance to affirmative action plans (Leonard 1990; Holzer and Neumark 1999b). Other studies that compared firms that use affirmative action in recruiting or hiring to those that do not have found that affirmative action usage is significantly associated with increased employment of blacks (Holzer and Neumark 1998).

In several recent studies, Harry Holzer and David Neumark (1998, 1999a) have looked in greater depth at the effects of affirmative action on employment practices, comparing firms that use affirmative action in recruitment or hiring with similar firms that do not. Their findings suggest that employers using affirmative action policies adopt a variety of employment practices that may reduce or eliminate any possible deleterious effects of those policies on productivity or efficiency. Firms using affirmative action use a wider variety of personnel recruitment tools, engage in more on-the-job training, and use more formal personnel evaluation tools. Affirmative action is associated with some drop in the educational credentials of the blacks who are hired. However, affirmative action does not seem to result in any drop in employers' assessment of the actual productivity of the blacks who are hired.

What is the potential of antidiscrimination policies in increasing the employment of the poor? As of now, we simply do not have enough information on how the labor market works to make a reliable estimate. As some have pointed out (for example, Heckman 1998), even if we know from cross-section studies of firms that are subject to antidiscrimination policies to varying degrees how these cross-sectional variations are related to the firms' employment patterns, we do not know the aggregate effects of antidiscrimination policies applied to just some firms on black employment over all firms. We would presume that the increase in black employment at firms that are federal contractors or use affirmative action for some other reason would result in some reduction in available black labor supply to other firms, thus reducing black employment at these firms to some degree. Net black employment would increase somewhat less than the estimated increase in black employment at the subset of firms subject to antidiscrimination policies. To put it another way, if all firms used antidiscrimination policies such as affirmative action, we would expect the overall percentage effect on black employment to be less than what we observe today at the subset of firms that currently use such policies. Firms today that use such policies are to some extent reducing black employment at other firms, an effect that would not be possible if all firms used such policies.

On the other hand, most of the estimates of how antidiscrimination policies are associated with differences in black employment across firms may be only partial measures of the effects of those policies. For example, in comparing contractor with noncontractor firms, even noncontractor firms are subject to the Civil Rights Act of 1964. Furthermore, many noncontractors may at some point become contractors and have to change their employment policies. It is very difficult to determine what employment practices firms would follow if none of the U.S. antidiscrimination policies were in place.

In addition, it is unclear from current research what proportion of the effects of antidiscrimination policies accrue to lower-income blacks compared with other groups. Finally, some of the benefits for lower-income blacks from antidiscrimination policies may come at the expense of lower-income whites.

If we ignore all these qualifications, the employment effects of antidiscrimination policies are potentially large. Jonathan Leonard (1990), for example, estimates that contractor status seems to increase black female employment about 10 percent and black male employment about 5 percent (see also Holzer and Neumark 1999b). If we could assume that effects of this magnitude would occur if all firms followed antidiscrimination policies, and if we compared a world with universal antidiscrimination policies to a world with no such policies, then black employment in aggregate would be about one million higher. If all of these jobs went to blacks with lower incomes, and no jobs were lost by whites with lower incomes, then universal antidiscrimination policies would indeed have a sizable net effect on the employment problems of the poor in the United States. But, for the reasons given earlier, there are problems with all these simplifying assumptions. It is not clear whether antidiscrimination policies have a net employment effect on blacks that is greater or less than one million. Furthermore, these net employment effects would certainly not all be on lower-income blacks, and they would in fact probably have some adverse effects on lower-income whites.

The current U.S. political climate limits the role of antidiscrimination policies, particularly the antidiscrimination policies that would most help lower-income blacks. Polls show that only a minority of U.S. whites believe that there continues to be a problem with employment discrimination against blacks: for example, one survey found that only 37 percent of whites thought that a black job applicant who was equally qualified as a white applicant would be less likely to get a job offer (Bendick 1999, 54). Affirmative action is clearly politically vulnerable. Although public opinion polls on affirmative action get very different results depending on how the questions are phrased (in particular, whether the questions describe affirmative action as "preferences" or "quotas," or as more aggressive recruitment practices), there has often been sufficient opposition to affirmative action to repeal these programs (Holzer and Neumark 1999b). The 1996 referendum passage in California of Proposition 209, which prohibited governmental institutions in California from giving "preferential treatment" to any individual or group on the basis of race, is a recent example. The courts have also increasingly ruled that some affirmative action programs are unconstitutional.

With the retreat of affirmative action, antidiscrimination policy is forced to rely more on the litigation of individual employment discrimination cases, but this legal strategy is not the best way to help unemployed or lower-income blacks. The problem is that individual litigation of employment discrimination tends to focus on issues such as promotion denial or wrongful discharge; job applicants are not in a good position to tell whether their failure to be hired was due to racial discrimination. For example, hiring discrimination claims amount to only 6 percent of the claims filed annually with the EEOC (Bendick 1999, 61). The problem is that addressing hiring discrimination is obviously more helpful to unemployed blacks than addressing problems once on the job.

As suggested by Marc Bendick (1999), one solution to some of these problems with antidiscrimination policies is to implement widespread employment testing. Such testing would both help shape public opinion and provide evidence for broadened antidiscrimination litigation. Under this proposal, both government agencies and community organizations would frequently send matched pairs of employment testers to various firms in different industries to see whether employers treat job applicants differently in making hiring decisions. Widely publicizing any strong evidence of employment discrimination based on race might change opinion among the white public about whether employment discrimination against blacks and other minorities is an ongoing problem. Changes in public attitudes might give more support for governmental and private efforts to combat discrimination. In addition, recent legal rulings from the EEOC indicate that findings from employment testing can be used as the basis for litigation. Such litigation could affect recruitment and hiring practices and would help the unemployed and poor more than litigation over promotion and discharge decisions.

Policies against employment discrimination are also likely to be more effective if they can be tied to overall efforts to improve employers' personnel management or other aspects of employer productivity. For example, a company is likely to be better able to implement an antidiscrimination program in hiring if it has access to a labor market intermediary that reliably supplies productive minority and nonminority job candidates. As another example, research suggests that diversity training efforts to make employers' practices more supportive of the success of minority employees are more likely to be successful if employers see how these efforts might improve their organization's productivity and profitability (Bendick, Egan, and Lofhjelm 1998).

Minimum Wages and Living Wages

Increasing the minimum wage is often proposed as a way to solve poverty. However, as the review here will show, research suggests that at best minimum-wage increases have only modest antipoverty effects. Minimum-wage regulations should be seen not as an antipoverty policy but as a way to protect the wage standards of working-class and lower-middle-class workers.

Minimum-wage regulation in the United States began with state efforts, starting with Massachusetts in 1912, to establish minimum wages for women and minors (Card and Krueger 1995). These state minimum-wage regulations, which had spread to sixteen states by the early 1920s, were declared unconstitutional by the Supreme Court in 1923. But the Supreme Court reversed itself in 1937, opening the way to the Federal Fair Labor Standards Act of 1938, which established federal minimum-wage regulations for men and women regardless of age in most industries, occupations, and firms. Since 1938, these minimum-wage standards have sporadically been increased by Congress, usually after a period of years during which the real value of the federal minimum wage has eroded. Congress has typically increased the minimum wage in response to lobbying by labor unions and allied liberal social activist groups. In addition to federal minimum-wage regulations, some states at some points in time have had minimum wages higher than the federal standard, typically as a response to state political pressure during a period in which the nominal federal minimum wage standard had been eroded by inflation.[10]

In the 1990s, community activists and public-sector unions successfully pushed many local communities to adopt a narrower version of minimum wages: local living wages. Under local government living-wage ordinances, minimum wages are typically set higher than federal or state minimums, but only for firms that have some dealings with the local government, such as firms that receive city contracts above some dollar value, or firms that receive economic development subsidies above a certain dollar value. The first strong living-wage ordinance was adopted by the city of Baltimore in 1994. As of mid-1999, at least thirty-five local governments had adopted living-wage ordinances, including such prominent ones as the cities of Los Angeles, Boston, Detroit, Oakland, Minneapolis, Saint Paul, and San Antonio, and Los Angeles County and Miami-Dade County. Of the thirty-five current ordinances, eighteen cover only firms that have service contracts with the city, seven cover only firms that receive economic development subsidies from the city, and ten cover both contractors and subsidized firms (ACORN 1999a, 1999b).

How minimum wages affect employment is a perennially popular topic among economists. Economists are interested in minimum wages because the employment effects of minimum wages seem to pose a near-ideal test of a central proposition of economic theory: that demand responds to prices. Despite great efforts by many economists, it has often been surprisingly hard to find large effects of minimum wages on employment. David Card and Alan Krueger (1995) have recently argued, using evidence from U.S. states on responses to changes in state and federal minimum wages, that the employment effects of increased minimum wages are zero or even positive. Their work has been vigorously challenged by many economists, however, particularly in a number of studies by David Neumark and William Wascher (for example, Neumark and Wascher 1997). But even studies finding statistically significant negative effects of minimum wages tend to find modest effects. For example, most studies that find negative effects of minimum wages on teenage employment or young adult employment tend to get elasticities in a range from −0.1 to −0.3, that is, a 10 percent increase in the minimum wage would reduce the employment of teenagers or young adults by 1 to 3 percent (Neumark 1999).[11]

What might explain why the employment effects of minimum wages are modest? As discussed in chapter 3, an increase in wages may have effects on productivity that offset some of the increased employment costs due to higher wages. Workers may be motivated to work harder if paid higher wages. Higher wages may reduce worker turnover, reducing firms' hiring and training costs. As a result of the productivity benefits of higher wages, higher minimum wages may not reduce the incentive to hire workers as much as might be expected simply from how much monetary payments to workers are increased.

Card and Krueger (1995) offer a more sophisticated theoretical argument that may even explain why increased minimum wages could cause some firms to increase employment. Suppose that owing to imperfect information in the labor market, some low-wage firms effectively face an upward-sloping supply curve of labor. That is, in order to hire and maintain a higher employment level, an individual firm might need to pay higher wages. With the high employee turnover that is common in the low-wage labor market, and the quite imperfect networks linking employers and job seekers, an individual low-wage employer is always hiring. The firm would be able to increase employment levels only by holding down quit rates or increasing hire rates, and this might be most easily done in some cases by increasing wage rates.

If this is true, some firms may avoid having to pay higher wages to all their workers by deliberately holding back on employment levels and hiring. Employment is not expanded even if the marginal or additional worker hired would produce more than he or she would cost in wages, because hiring this additional worker would require increasing wages for all existing workers.[12] For firms in this situation, a modest increase in the minimum wage might cause employment levels and hiring to expand. If the firm is going to have to pay all its workers more anyway, it might as well hire workers as long as their productivity exceeds the wage that will have to be paid.

Even though minimum wages do not have large effects in reducing the employment of low-wage workers, the net antipoverty effects of modest increases in the minimum wage are likely to be modest as well. The antipoverty effects of minimum wages are limited because only some of the poor can benefit from increases in the minimum wage. As discussed in chapter 3 (see table 3.3), 43 percent of poor families in 1998 did not include anyone who had worked during that year. Obviously one would expect increased minimum wages to have little effect if any on this group, unless minimum wages somehow spurred an increase in employment. In two-thirds of the remaining 57 percent of poor families, the individuals who are working are working only part-time or for part of the year. These low annual work hours also limit the earnings increases for the poor from an increased minimum wage. Finally, of the poor who do work, many earn more than politically feasible minimum-wage levels. For example, in March 1994, when the debate was over whether to increase the minimum wage from $4.25 per hour to $5.15 per hour, only 37 percent of the "working poor" had wages in the range of $4.25 to $5.15 per hour, the group that was most likely to be significantly affected by a minimum-wage increase (Houseman 1998, 177). Fifty-four percent of the working poor had wages above $5.15 per hour and would experience only modest "spillover" effects of higher minimum wages on wage structures. (The other 9 percent had wages below the old prevailing minimum wage of $4.25, and it is quite unclear whether they would be affected by a higher minimum wage.)

These limited antipoverty effects do not imply that minimum-wage increases necessarily fail to have progressive effects on the income distribution. Minimum-wage increases probably do have disproportionate benefits for the poor compared to their share in the population. It is just that the benefits of minimum-wage increases are not so concentrated on the poor that modest minimum wage-increases can do that much. For example, as shown in table 9.2, workers in "working poor families" are estimated to have received 19 percent of the benefits from the 1990 to 1991 increase in the minimum wage from $3.35 to $4.25 per hour. This is a modest share of the benefits of the minimum-wage increase, but it is disproportionately concentrated on the working poor, since working poor workers are only 6 percent of the workforce. Upper-income families gain disproportionately less from a minimum-wage increase. For example, more than 60 percent of all workers are in families that earn more than three times the poverty line, but they receive only one-third of the benefits from a minimum-wage increase. Hence, minimum-wage increases clearly distribute their benefits progressively, but the benefits are spread out to some extent across all workers. A fair number of workers earning close to the minimum wage are in families above the poor or near-poor class. For example, of those workers affected by the 1996 to 1997 increase in the minimum wage from $4.25 to $5.15 per hour, 68 percent were in families at 150 percent or more of the poverty line (Houseman 1998).

TABLE 9.2 *Share of Benefits from Minimum-Wage Increases Going to Workers at Different Levels of Family Income*

Income-to-Needs Ratio of Worker's Family	Percentage of All Workers	Percentage Share of Benefits from Minimum-Wage Increase
Less than 1.00	6.1	19.3
1.00 to 1.25	2.8	8.4
1.25 to 1.50	3.3	6.4
1.50 to 2.00	8.2	12.2
2.00 to 2.99	17.9	21.2
3.00 and above	61.7	32.5

Source: Burkauser et al. (1996, 550, table 2).
Notes: The minimum-wage hike considered is the 1990 to 1991 hike from $3.35 per hour to $4.25 per hour. The income-to-needs ratio is ratio of family income to poverty line for that family size. The benefits from a minimum-wage increase are calculated assuming that there are no employment or hours effects, and that wages for everyone in the range from $3.35 to $4.25 per hour go up to $4.25 per hour owing to the minimum-wage hike, but that no other wages change. The underlying data are calculated by Burkauser et al. (1996) from the March 1990 CPS-ORG.

Empirical studies that have estimated the effects of increased minimum wages on poverty also usually find modest effects. Some studies simply simulate the effects of increases in the minimum wage on poverty, typically under the assumption that employment and work hours are unaffected. For example, Susan Houseman (1998) simulates that the 1996 to 1997 minimum-wage increase reduced poverty rates among workers by about 0.1 or 0.2 percentage rate points, from 4.94 percent of all workers to either 4.86 or 4.79 percent, depending on whether workers below the old minimum wage were assumed to be affected or not.[13] Other studies have simply directly estimated the effects of minimum-wage increases on poverty, typically by examining the effects on poverty of cross-state variations in minimum-wage increases. For example, Card and Krueger (1995) estimate a statistically insignificant effect of the 1990 to 1991 minimum-wage increase in reducing poverty among adults. The statistically insignificant point estimate suggests that the 1990 to 1991 minimum-wage increase reduced poverty rates among all adults by about two-tenths of 1 percent. Effects of one-tenth or two-tenths of 1 percent of all workers, or of all adults, are "large" in that in a country with as large a population as that of the United States, the minimum-wage increase would be bringing hundreds of thousands of people out of poverty. However, the effects are modest in that feasible minimum-wage increases are unlikely to make a major dent in poverty rates.

What about the effects of living-wage ordinances? Because these ordinances apply only to a few narrow categories of firms, they affect far fewer workers than minimum-wage regulations. Hence, living wages, compared to minimum wages, must have effects on poverty that are much smaller. For example, in a study of the living-wage ordinance in Los Angeles by proponents of the living wage, the estimate is that the ordinance, even if fully implemented and enforced, will affect fewer than eight thousand workers in a metropolitan area with more than four million workers (Pollin and Luce 1998). The workers in Los Angeles affected by a living-wage ordinance are less than 1 percent of the workers potentially affected by a minimum-wage increase.

What about the costs of a living-wage ordinance compared to a minimum-wage increase? We need to consider separately the two categories of firms targeted by living-wage ordinances—firms receiving economic development subsidies and firms receiving city contracts—because the likely responses by these two categories of firms are quite different. For the predominantly manufacturing firms receiving economic development subsidies, living-wage ordinances could easily lead to changes in their business location decisions. If only one city in a metropolitan area imposes a living-wage requirement, firms can usually find similar locations elsewhere in the metropolitan area that offer similar access to labor and markets and probably similar levels of economic development subsidies. We would expect business location decisions within a metropolitan area to be quite sensitive to even minor variations in the costs of alternative locations, and in fact the empirical literature suggests that intrametropolitan business location decisions are extremely sensitive to even small property tax differentials (Bartik 1991).

As a result, a living-wage requirement imposed by one city on firms receiving economic development subsidies may lead many of these firms to choose other locations within the metropolitan area. This may not be much of a problem if the city has high demand for its existing industrial sites and can easily fill its available industrial sites with higher-wage firms. But for cities with more troubled economies, it may be much harder to find other firms to locate in the city, and the living-wage requirement may lead to a net reduction in industrial employment in the city, with possible adverse effects on the city's tax base. Whether it has adverse labor market consequences for city residents depends on whether city residents have ready access, via car or mass transit, to the jobs in firms that have been driven outside the city by the living-wage requirement. As discussed in chapter 3, problems with job access are likely to be more acute in metropolitan areas above 800,000 in population, particularly those with weaker mass transit systems.

For firms bidding on city contracts, living-wage requirements are likely to have quite different effects. Unlike development subsidies, living-wage requirements for city contractors cannot be easily evaded. Although some industrial sites may be unused for industry because of living-wage requirements, city contracts still in general have bidders. Part of the cost of the living-wage requirement may, however, be passed on to city taxpayers in the form of higher bids. If higher wages result in increased productivity or lower worker turnover for city contractors, however, we would not expect 100 percent of the costs of living wages to be passed on to city taxpayers.

There is little good empirical evidence on how much living-wage requirements raise city contract costs. Only three studies have focused on this issue; all three consider the city of Baltimore, and all are sponsored by strong proponents or opponents of living wages. Two studies conclude that the ordinance did not raise city contract costs (Weisbrot and Sforza-Roderick 1996; Niedt et al. 1999), while the third study disputes this finding (Employment Policies Institute 1998). In general, it is difficult to do a good comparison over time of a city's contract costs because the types of contracts tend to change significantly. It is unclear whether any of these three studies have been able to control adequately for changes in the terms and conditions of city contracts.

Even if city contract costs do go up, it would not necessarily be irrational for city voters to believe that the benefits of living-wage requirements for city contractors might exceed the costs. Living-wage requirements on city contractors at least help improve the wages of some workers, a fair number of whom are low-income. Living-wage requirements for city contractors may also help protect the wage standards of city workers. However, given the small number of workers affected, any effect in reducing city poverty rates must be tiny.

In sum, minimum wages and living-wage standards have only modest antipoverty effects. What role, then, can these policies have? At least two possible roles come to mind, both of which are relevant to antipoverty policy.

First, the political campaigns to increase the minimum wage or pass living-wage ordinances can help mobilize a broad political coalition that may then be able to address poverty issues in a more effective manner. According to a recent article in *Governing* magazine on the living-wage movement, "the living-wage battle has been a tremendous success for the groups behind it. . . . The simple message—that working people should not live in poverty—has an appeal that is a magnet for all kinds of groups looking to energize their members. In city after city, labor unions, community organizations, religious groups and others are forming coalitions and rallying under the living-wage banner" (Swope 1998, 25). According to one organizer for the group ACORN, which seeks to create and mobilize community organizations around the United States, the living-wage campaign is "about raising issues, building alliances, and having strength in numbers. In Boston, the mayor's office wouldn't return our calls last year, and now we're in regular meetings" (25). Once a broad coalition is mobilized and has gained political strength, it can consider a broader program to address the issues of poverty and low earnings.

Second, the minimum wage and living wage can be seen as ways of protecting the wage standards of the working class and lower-middle class. Card and Krueger (1995, 288–97) present empirical findings suggesting that minimum-wage increases in a state have significant effects in increasing at least the bottom 10 percent of wage rates in the state. As table 9.2 shows, simulations of the minimum wage's impact do show significant benefits for workers whose families are between the poverty line and three times the poverty line, concentrated on those workers between the poverty line and twice the poverty line. Living-wage ordinances, even if they only directly help a few workers for city contractors, can help protect the wage standards of city workers as cities move increasingly toward privatizing some city services. According to Gerald McEntee, president of the American Federation of State, County, and Municipal Employees (AFSCME), the motivations for living-wage ordinances are clear: "We fight for these people, to bring up their wages, benefits and health care, first because it's good for them, but also so they're not in direct competition with folks in the public sector" (Swope 1998, 25).

This protection of wage standards may be important as part of a comprehensive strategy to increase the earnings of the poor that could have broad public support. As we adopt policies to increase the employment of the poor, through training programs, community service jobs, wage subsidies, and job placement programs, we face a natural concern about the effects of these added workers from low-income families on wage standards. Minimum-wage and living-wage standards set at reasonable levels may be part of an overall antipoverty strategy, a way of reassuring lower-middle class workers that these new workers will not undermine their wages.

Conclusion

The demand-side policies considered in this chapter are quite diverse. Among the limitations of these policies in dealing with poverty are the following:

- Economic development's benefits are spread widely among the population, with only a modest proportion of benefits going to the poor.
- Labor market intermediary programs tend to be underfunded and are complex services that are difficult to deliver in a high-quality fashion.
- Antidiscrimination policies in their current form have severe political limitations on how much they can address hiring discrimination.

- Minimum wages and living wages have at best modest antipoverty effects and may have some adverse employment consequences.

Possible solutions to these limitations are equally diverse:

- Economic development programs should be linked with customized training programs and other LMI programs to make sure a greater proportion of economic development's benefits go to the poor.
- LMI programs must attract the political attention they need to be funded at a higher level and to be closely scrutinized to improve performance. This may require linking LMI programs with policies that have broader political appeal, such as economic development programs.
- Antidiscrimination policies need to address hiring discrimination through employment testing programs and through being linked to broader improvements in personnel practices.
- Minimum-wage and living-wage political campaigns should keep requests for increases reasonable, but these campaigns should be used to mobilize support for a broader antipoverty agenda.

10

A SUGGESTED PACKAGE OF LABOR DEMAND POLICIES

GIVEN this book's findings, what labor demand policies would most effectively increase the employment and earnings of low-income Americans? This concluding chapter focuses on answering this question. The demand policy proposed here emphasizes a program of short-term labor demand subsidies, to both public and private employers, that are targeted at low-income Americans who otherwise would be out of the labor force.

As argued in this book, a labor demand policy to increase the employment and earnings of the poor is needed because current employment rates for the poor are much too low and labor supply policies by themselves cannot sufficiently increase these employment rates. Labor demand for many low-income groups in many local labor markets is too low. As discussed in chapter 5, research shows that stronger labor demand can significantly increase the employment and earnings of low-income Americans.

Policies to increase aggregate labor demand can help deal with the employment problems of the poor but by themselves are inadequate. This chapter proposes a revised version of the New Jobs Tax Credit, a program used from 1977 to 1978 and reviewed in chapter 8. This revised NJTC would provide subsidies to both public and private employers for expanding total employment—not just employment of the poor—when unemployment in the local labor market is high. During a recession, the revised NJTC would apply throughout the nation and would play a significant countercyclical role in helping to minimize the depth and length of the unemployment impact of the recession. During national economic peak periods, the revised NJTC would help to promote overall employment expansion in depressed local labor markets. However, expansions in aggregate employment, while they help the poor, cannot by themselves solve the employment problems of the poor, since too few of the new jobs go to the poor.

To supplement aggregate demand policies, more targeted labor demand policies are needed. Based on research reviewed in this book, the greatest long-run employment impacts will come from a program that targets labor demand subsidies at low-income Americans who otherwise would be out of the labor force or not employed. The program should subsidize short-run employment of about six months, in jobs and for employers that seem most likely to lead to "rollover" of the subsidized hires into regular jobs. Both public and private employers should be included, since both are part of the labor market, and one or the other type of job may be more appropriate for a particular placement. To improve the political support for these targeted demand subsidies, subsidies should be targeted at small businesses and small nonprofit organizations. To avoid displacement of other workers and promote local economic development, the subsidies should be aimed at newly created jobs. Given all these criteria for targeting, the targeted demand program needs to be administered in a discretionary fashion, by agencies that can choose which employers and low-income persons to involve in job matches. The administering agencies should be free to organize the program to best suit the needs of each local labor market, given that local area's mix of employers and labor market institutions. Given the many requirements for employers participating in the program, including that employers hire particular target groups for subsidized jobs and "roll over" some of these hires into regular jobs after the subsidy period, the subsidies for the program should be generous enough to induce large-scale employer participation. This targeted demand program could be considered a revised version of the MEED program used in Minnesota in the 1980s (see chapter 8).

To deal with the employment needs of the poor, a revised NJTC and a targeted labor demand program will have to be run on a large scale, with the targeted labor demand program perhaps employing one and a half million workers on average. Such a large-scale program will cost tens of billions of dollars annually but is clearly affordable if U.S. governmental institutions have the political will to pursue the objective of full employment for all. Political support for labor demand policies requires a political consensus, from both conservatives and liberals, that increasing the employment of the poor is a sufficiently important goal to justify a significant use of scarce public resources, and that these policies can help us achieve this goal.

The remainder of this chapter considers the rationale and design of this proposed labor demand program in more detail.

Why Labor Demand Policies Are Needed

Even when the U.S. economy is booming, as it was in the late 1990s and 2000, millions of additional jobs are still needed for low-income Americans. As reviewed in chapter 3, the employment rates of lower-income groups in the United States, compared either to the past or to the earnings needs of these groups, are low enough to suggest a need for three million to nine million additional jobs. For the purposes of this chapter, I pick a middle figure of six million as the number of jobs needed by low-income Americans.

As reviewed in chapter 4, labor supply policies by themselves are insufficient to create six million more jobs for low-income Americans. Wage subsidy programs for workers can significantly boost earnings for the poor but have only modest effects in increasing employment for the nonemployed. For example, the largest wage subsidy program for workers, the Earned Income Tax Credit, probably increases the labor supply of disadvantaged household heads by no more than half a million persons, at a cost of $30 billion annually. Most job training programs are cheap enough to pass a benefit-cost test but have effects on employment and earnings that are modest for the average trainee, whose annual earnings are increased, mostly through increased work, by less than $1,500 per year. Job training programs that do better require strong ties to employers that are motivated by strong labor demand conditions. Education programs can significantly increase the earnings of those participating, but they have more modest effects on overall labor supply unless they are vastly expanded at huge cost. Welfare reform policies force at least one million people off welfare rolls and into the labor force, but at a huge social cost to the half of all ex-welfare recipients who do not make it in the labor market. Finally, all these labor supply programs, by encouraging additions to the labor supply of the disadvantaged, have displacement effects: because of the jobs gained by these new entries to the labor force, there is some loss of job opportunities for the current employed. As reviewed in chapter 3, plausible economic models suggest that displacement is in the range of one-third to two-thirds; that is, for every three jobs gained by disadvantaged persons entering the labor market, one or two jobs are lost by disadvantaged persons who are already employed.

Even with a booming American economy, labor demand for many of the poor is too low. The booming economy includes pockets of high unemployment for less-educated groups and minorities and in some city labor markets. As reviewed in chapter 5, studies show that increases in labor demand for the disadvantaged can have major effects on their employment. Demand policies that subsidize increased employment for lower-income groups frequently cause immediate increases in employment and earnings for these groups of at least two-thirds of the program-related employment and earnings.

Perhaps the most important effects of increased demand are long-run: short-run increases in labor demand for disadvantaged groups can have long-run hysteresis effects, increasing the permanent employment and earnings of these groups. As reviewed in chapter 3, employers in low-wage labor markets place great emphasis on the soft skills of being able to deal with customers, coworkers, and supervisors. Low-wage labor markets also are characterized by poor employer information about whether job seekers have these needed soft skills. As a result of the importance of soft skills and information problems in low-wage labor markets, short-run increases in work experience for lower-income groups can significantly increase their long-run earnings. These long-run effects occur because an individual's short-run work experience improves his or her soft skills, self-esteem, and reputation with employers. Empirical estimates suggest that 20 percent of short-run increases in employment and earnings for disadvantaged groups may be reflected in long-run increases in their employment and earnings.

Policy to Increase Aggregate Labor Demand

Contrary to what is sometimes claimed, stronger aggregate labor demand conditions continue to have important effects on increasing the progressivity of the income distribution and reducing poverty. For example, as reviewed in chapter 5, a one-point reduction in the overall unemployment rate will reduce the poverty rate by between 0.3 and 0.9 points (that is, by 0.3 to 0.9 percent of the population).

To increase aggregate labor demand, the United States should adopt a policy of providing subsidies to all employers for increased overall employment of all types of labor, not just disadvantaged groups. Cost-effective, non-inflationary subsidies to employers for aggregate labor demand should include the following design features:

- *Subsidize only employment at the margin.* To save scarce funds, subsidies to employers should go only for expansions to aggregate employment, not for all current employment. As reviewed in chapter 8, aggregate labor demand subsidies for all employment can cost hundreds of billions of dollars.
- *Target subsidies on high-unemployment local labor markets.* Aggregate labor demand policy should help encourage employment expansion in the high-unemployment local labor markets that need jobs the most. As shown in chapter 6, such geographic targeting helps to minimize the inflationary effects of aggregate labor demand policies during periods in which the overall national labor market is tight.
- *Design subsidy legislation so that employment subsidies can be quickly implemented in response to an economic downturn.* To be effective in

helping to increase aggregate labor demand during a recession, employer subsidies must be quickly implemented once a recession starts.

- *Subsidize all employers.* Subsidies for employment expansion should go to all employers, not just large corporations. Subsidies should encourage employment expansion not just at profitable large corporations but also at public employers, nonprofit employers, unincorporated businesses, and temporarily unprofitable businesses.

Such a subsidy policy could be described as a revised version of the 1977 to 1978 New Jobs Tax Credit. The NJTC as originally designed provided income tax credits to for-profit firms that expanded employment by some percentage over their base year's employment level. In addition, the credit applied only to an individual's wages up to some cap, which tended to provide an above-average subsidy of jobs for lower-skill and lower-wage workers. The program had a very high take-up rate, with over half of eligible firms claiming the credit. As reviewed in chapter 8, there is good research evidence that the NJTC was successful in significantly increasing employment growth.

One objection to reviving the NJTC is that such a credit is hardly needed for the nation as a whole, as least as of the 1998 to 2000 period, when U.S. unemployment has been consistently very low at close to 4 percent. However, as reviewed in chapter 3, unemployment rates are still high in some metropolitan areas and large central cities. Therefore, a revised NJTC should modify the program so that the credit is tied to the unemployment rate of the local labor market. That is, employers would get a credit only for expanding employment in high-unemployment local labor markets. Under this design, such a tax credit would apply to few local labor markets when the U.S. economy is strong, but to most of the nation when the U.S. economy is weak.

An important issue is how to define "local labor markets"—that is, the relevant geographic area to use in defining the unemployment rate to be used to determine eligibility for the tax credit. As reviewed in chapter 3, for smaller metropolitan areas, it is clear that the local labor market should be defined as the metropolitan area as a whole. Metropolitan areas above 800,000 in population, however, often seem to present significant spatial mismatch problems, suggesting that unemployment conditions in an area smaller than the MSA might also be considered. One possibility is to allow cities above some minimum size cutoff, perhaps 500,000 or so, to use the city unemployment rate in determining the generosity of the credit to employers for expanding local employment. Such a design would allow the credit to help alleviate spatial mismatch problems by encouraging employment expansion in relatively distressed central cities.

The old NJTC was enacted into law as a political response to the recession of 1974 to 1975 and therefore did not go into force until the 1977 to 1978 period, well after the U.S. economy had begun its recovery. A revised NJTC should be permanently enacted into law, with a formula that ties its implementation in each local labor market to current or quite recent unemployment rates. Because of necessary lags in obtaining unemployment rate data, the credit would not be of much use in brief recessions, but it would help to boost employment if the United States experienced a lengthy recession.

Finally, a revised NJTC should be designed to apply to employment expansions by all employers, not just profitable businesses. One way to do this is to allow all employers to take the credit against the payroll tax, as previously suggested by Carcagno and Corson (1982). The social security and Medicare trust funds would be reimbursed from general funds to make up for the loss in revenue. Such a modification obviously would be controversial because it might be perceived as a threat to the health of these trust funds. However, this option would allow the jobs credit to encourage the expansion of public-service employment and nonprofit employment in economically distressed local labor markets. Rather than being restricted to for-profit employers, the jobs credit would encourage employment expansions of all types. Such an expansion might also gain the credit a wider base of political supporters.

What are the potential effects and costs of this revised NJTC? First, let us consider the possible effects and costs of the revised NJTC during a significant national economic recession, when the credit would apply to almost all the nation. As reviewed in chapter 8, estimates suggest that a revised NJTC might increase aggregate employment by 900,000 per year, or 1.8 million over a two-year period. Of these new jobs, only a portion would go to disadvantaged groups. For example, estimates in chapters 5 and 8 suggest that a nationwide NJTC might create about 260,000 jobs in one year, and 520,000 jobs in two years, for adult heads of household, ages twenty-five to fifty-four, with less than a college education.[1]

Such an employment boost clearly would not solve all the employment problems resulting from a recession, but it would help. A recession that increased overall unemployment rates by 4 percent would result in a loss in the U.S. labor market of about 7.8 million jobs overall.[2] Of this 7.8 million in lost jobs, 2.3 million would be lost by adult heads of household, ages twenty-five to fifty-four, with less than a college education (see table 5.5). Therefore, over a two-year period during which a serious recession might significantly depress the labor market, a revised NJTC might deal with one-fourth of the employment loss caused for less-educated groups, and for the nation as a whole.

Therefore, other expansionary fiscal and monetary policies should also continue to be used to deal with serious, long-lasting, national recessions in the United States. One possible criticism of a revised NJTC is that if these other expansionary fiscal and monetary policies are used, why is there any special need for a revised NJTC? Perhaps our traditional fiscal and monetary policies (Federal Reserve policies, automatic stabilizers such as the tax and unemployment insurance system) can take care of the problems of recession just as well as the more complicated NJTC program. One argument for the revised NJTC is that this employment subsidy focuses the expansion of aggregate demand on the labor market. Compared to other fiscal and monetary policies, an NJTC policy focuses more of the demand expansion on increased employment rather than on increases in capital utilization. This may be important for a recession that takes place during an inflationary period (and in some cases, a recession may actually have occurred because of Federal Reserve actions to slow down economic activity to reduce inflation). As reviewed in chapter 6, some inflation models suggest that overall inflation is related more to capacity utilization (use of the capital stock relative to maximum feasible use) than to unemployment rates. During "stagflation" periods, with both high unemployment and high inflation, it might be prudent to try to target demand increases more on the labor market to minimize further pressures on capacity utilization and inflation.

In addition, an NJTC policy on the margin should focus more of the employment expansion on more disadvantaged groups. Following the precedent of the original NJTC, a revised NJTC should calculate the subsidy as a percentage of an individual's wages up to some cap. With such a cap, an NJTC policy provides a greater percentage subsidy for employment expansions for lower-wage jobs. This should encourage a greater portion of the employment expansion to result in new jobs for less-educated workers and other disadvantaged groups.

The estimated costs of this revised NJTC, when implemented on a national basis during a serious recession, are $19 billion per year.[3] Such an expenditure is quite reasonable and affordable as part of a package of federal policies to alleviate a serious economic recession.

What about the effects and costs of a revised NJTC when the overall U.S. labor market is doing well? The revised NJTC would then apply only to high-unemployment local labor markets. This revised NJTC would be a policy to reduce structural unemployment by helping to focus more U.S. employment growth on high-unemployment local labor markets, thereby better matching labor demand with labor supply. As discussed in chapter 6, focusing employment growth and lower unemployment on high-unemployment local labor markets allows lower overall U.S. unemployment, with no greater inflationary pressures.

The exact effects and costs of the structural role of a revised NJTC depends on how much of the United States is assumed to suffer from high local unemployment and on the time period considered in the analysis. Suppose we assume that even at time periods of low overall national unemployment perhaps 20 percent of the U.S. labor market is part of local labor markets with high unemployment, for which the revised NJTC would be implemented. Suppose we further consider the likely long-run effects of the structural part of a revised NJTC—say, after ten years. Then a rough estimate is that the structural component of a revised NJTC would provide about half a million of the needed six million jobs for disadvantaged groups.[4] This is a significant effect, but it does not come close to solving the employment problems of low-income Americans.

With the assumption that the structural part of the revised NJTC would apply to 20 percent of the United States, the total national costs of the NJTC, during periods of low national unemployment, would be about $4 billion per year.[5] This is easily affordable in our current national economy, given current federal budget surpluses. It could be financed without expanding overall federal spending by cutting current federal economic development programs, which cost about $6 billion annually (National Academy of Public Administration 1996, 65–66).

A Proposed Targeted Labor Demand Policy

Therefore, an aggregate labor demand policy, while it can help deal with recessions, can deal only with a small portion of the employment problems of low-income Americans that persist even during business cycle periods. As discussed at the beginning of this chapter, even when the U.S. economy is doing well, low-income Americans need about six million additional jobs. As discussed earlier, a revised NJTC might provide, when the labor market is strong, about half a million of these jobs. An NJTC policy is limited in what it can do because only a modest portion of the labor demand increase caused by the policy goes to disadvantaged groups. Even with a permanent NJTC, at least five and a half million additional jobs are needed for low-income Americans. To develop these five and a half million additional jobs will require a significant role for a more targeted labor demand policy—in that the policy seeks to tightly target its labor demand increase on disadvantaged groups.

Based on the findings of this book, a good targeted labor demand policy should reflect the following principles of design:

1. Target the labor demand groups at disadvantaged persons who otherwise would probably be out of the labor force or not employed. Whether a person meets this criterion for targeting should be based in part on their previous work experience, but it should also be based on a demonstrated difficulty in finding a job in the current labor market. *Employing some of this target group may require complementary supply-side programs to provide counseling or training.*

As discussed in chapters 5, 7, and 8, targeted increases in labor demand for a disadvantaged group are likely to have maximum employment effects when these policies target groups of people who otherwise would not be employed. This minimizes providing employment to disadvantaged persons who could have readily found a job on their own. In the long run, labor market models suggest that the displacement effects of targeted labor demand depend a great deal on whether the policy adds to labor supply. If the policy adds to labor supply, then it has fewer adverse effects on the labor demand of regular employers, avoiding the problems that occur if subsidized jobs reduce the availability of disadvantaged workers to regular employers. As discussed in chapter 6, targeted labor demand policies that add to labor supply are likely to have fewer inflationary effects, because they do not reduce overall unemployment as much. A targeted labor demand policy adds more to labor supply if it targets persons who would be outside of the labor force. Requiring a prior job search is a useful way of testing whether a person is unlikely to be employed in a regular job. Finally, although many disadvantaged persons without a job may be able to benefit immediately from job experience, others may need some counseling or training before they can make the best use of a job opportunity.

2. *Design the subsidized job slots to encourage workers to transition to the regular job market by making the subsidized job slots short-term and paying subsidized workers below-market wages.* As shown in chapters 5 and 7, the displacement effects of a labor demand policy are reduced if subsidized workers are more readily available for regular jobs; labor demand from regular employers is thus encouraged because the policy provides a greater effective labor supply. As discussed in chapter 6, the inflationary effects of a labor demand policy are also reduced if subsidized workers are more readily available for regular jobs, because the labor supply shortages for regular employers that might lead to wage inflation pressures are reduced. Greater availability of subsidized workers for regular jobs is increased by making the subsidized jobs short-term, although short-term jobs also provide less work experience. The evidence from the Supported Work Program (chapter 7) suggests that subsidized job slots of about six months in length might best balance the trade-off between the value of lengthier subsidized work experience and the need to transition quickly to regular jobs. Paying below-market wages not only encourages subsidized workers to transition to regular jobs but is a market test for whether the subsidized worker is unable to find a job at market wages; taking a subsidized job at below-market wages would not make sense for someone who could readily obtain a regular job paying market wages. Finally, keeping subsidized jobs relatively short-term and paying below-market wages helps to hold down the costs of a subsidized jobs program.

3. Target subsidized jobs at employers that encourage rollover of subsidized employees to regular jobs or otherwise provide work experiences that increase long-run employability and wages. As reviewed in chapters 3, 5, and 7, the short-run work experiences provided by subsidized employment can have long-run effects on employment and earnings by increasing a worker's job skills, self-esteem, and reputation with employers. As I discuss later in this chapter, significant long-run effects of a subsidized employment program are crucial if the program is to address the employment needs of the poor at a reasonable cost and scale. As outlined in chapters 7 and 8, much of the long-run effect of subsidized employment occurs because subsidized workers roll over into regular jobs with the same employer.

4. Agencies administering subsidized employment programs should aggressively seek to limit "subsidized worker substitution": the substitution by employers of subsidized workers for incumbent workers. Such administrative policies are most easily implemented if subsidized employment is limited to newly created jobs. Targeting new jobs also may attract political support for a subsidized employment program, since the program may be perceived by state and local governments as a potential economic development tool. As discussed in chapter 7, such substitution is a key part of the political resistance to subsidized employment by unions and others interested in the employment of incumbent workers. Research suggests that aggressive administration can enormously limit such substitution. If the subsidized jobs are new jobs, then by definition the subsidized employment cannot eliminate the employment of incumbent workers. (Although, of course, the subsidized jobs might have been created even without the subsidy and might then have gone to other workers.) If the subsidized employment program targets not only new jobs but jobs in "export-base" businesses—businesses that "export" their goods and services outside of the local labor market—then state and local governments may see subsidized employment as encouraging their jurisdiction's economic development.

5. To maximize political support and the employment effects of subsidized employment, target small businesses and small nonprofit agencies. As discussed in chapters 7 and 8, political opposition to subsidized employment comes from both conservatives opposed to subsidizing big government and liberals opposed to subsidizing big business. Targeting small businesses and nonprofits helps to alleviate political fears about the expanded power of large organizations. In addition, an employment subsidy of a fixed modest size is more likely to affect labor costs on the margin for smaller organizations than for larger organizations and thus is more likely to encourage overall employment expansion. Finally, smaller organizations are more likely than large organizations to have some difficulties in financing an employment expansion, and thus employment subsidies may have greater effects on employment expansion for them.

6. *Administer subsidized employment as a discretionary program in which targeted workers and employers are selected and matched by the administering agency.* It would be extremely difficult for any entitlement wage subsidy program, in which employers are automatically entitled to a wage subsidy for employing a target group, to achieve the best degree of targeting at workers who otherwise would not be employed. Under an entitlement system, employers tend to hire, from whatever target groups are identified, those who are most readily employable in regular jobs—precisely the individuals who should not be targeted by the subsidized demand policy if its employment effects are to be maximized. In addition, administering the subsidized employment program in a discretionary manner helps to reduce stigma effects by ensuring that the worker and employer are a reasonable match and that the employer has good information about the worker's characteristics. A discretionary program also allows the administering agency to target employers that are more likely to encourage rollover or otherwise provide job opportunities that lead to long-run effects on earnings. On the other hand, research suggests that direct employment of subsidized workers by the administering agency is less effective in increasing long-run earnings, possibly in part because such subsidized jobs are less likely to resemble regular jobs, and certainly because such subsidized jobs are less likely to roll over into regular jobs.

7. *Make the employment subsidy large enough to attract employers to a program with many targeting requirements and expectations for long-run earnings effects.* The design principles outlined earlier suggest that an employment subsidy program should target individuals who are unlikely to be employed in regular jobs, put them in a subsidized job for six months, and encourage them to roll over or transition into regular jobs. This design expects much of employers during a six-month subsidized employment period. Employers certainly have to exercise a great deal of patience working with these new subsidized employees to overcome any deficiencies in soft skills. Given the expectations, the subsidy needs to be large enough to encourage employer participation and to make them feel that the subsidy program is worthwhile. Cheaper subsidies may appear to offer a lower cost per subsidized job but are less cost-effective in providing additional employment experience that otherwise would not occur. Thus, cheaper subsidies are less effective in providing employment experience that increases long-run earnings.

8. *Aggressively market the subsidized employment program to employers using job developers.* As discussed in chapter 8, a common problem with wage subsidy programs is low take-up rates by employers. However, research shows that aggressively marketing the subsidy program through direct personal contacts with employers, offering specific workers as job candidates, can greatly increase take-up rates. In addition, by learn-

ing a great deal about the needs and characteristics of employers, job developers can help identify job candidates who are better job matches and suggest possible changes in employer personnel practices that will better assist the new worker in becoming more productive.

9. Run the subsidized employment program so that it can flexibly respond to the characteristics of the local labor market. Choosing employers and disadvantaged persons to target, marketing the program to employers, and matching employers and possible workers are program goals that require intimate knowledge of the local labor market. This knowledge is probably best achieved through a program that is administered, with substantial discretion, at the local labor market level.

10. Include a performance measurement system or evaluation system to improve accountability. The fact that a complex, customized employment subsidy program must be administered with a great deal of discretion raises the obvious possibility that some local programs will be poorly run. To address this possibility, targeted employment demand programs should include provisions for measuring performance in terms of what the subsidized employment actually added to net employment and what long-run effects resulted from the short-run employment experience.

Based on these ten principles, the targeted demand program I propose would most resemble a significantly revised version of the MEED program. As discussed in chapter 8, the MEED program, funded by the state of Minnesota in the 1980s, provided large wage subsidies for a short term (up to six months) to selected employers who hired targeted long-term unemployed individuals in newly created jobs. The program was run in a discretionary fashion by local job training agencies, which selected the employers and unemployed to be matched in the program. The target group was relatively broad: it included all long-term unemployed, but local agencies were supposed to give a preference to public assistance recipients. The program included subsidies to both public and private employers. In awarding subsidies, local agencies gave a preference to small businesses and businesses that exported their product outside Minnesota. Subsidies were relatively generous: 100 percent of wages and fringes up to a cap of $6.55 per hour for wages (1998 dollars) and $1.64 per hour for fringes (1998 dollars). Employers were required to pay subsidized workers the prevailing wage. Private employers receiving subsidies were required to retain subsidized workers for at least one year after the six-month subsidy period was over; if they did not, either the employer would be required to hire another MEED-subsidized worker or part of the subsidy had to be repaid.

As discussed in chapter 8, there is some evidence from employer surveys that the MEED program had a substantial effect on job creation: more than half of the subsidized jobs probably would not have been created without the program. In addition, the program was run at a sizable scale, equivalent to running a national program with 600,000 subsidized workers participating in the program in a year.

The revisions I would suggest to the MEED program are significant enough that perhaps the program should be given a new name: the NEED (National Employment and Economic Development) program. One of the most important revisions would be to target the program more rigorously at disadvantaged persons who are unlikely to be immediately employed in regular jobs throughout the program. As mentioned earlier, perhaps all persons considered for the program would be required to first search for a regular job. In addition, if a more disadvantaged group is targeted, the NEED wage subsidies should be accompanied by significant expenditures of supply-side subsidies to increase the employability of the target group, including funds for counseling and job training. In addition, targeting a less readily employable group might require relaxing the MEED program's job retention "clawback" provision. Perhaps rollover and job retention should be encouraged through a "carrot" rather than required through a "stick": employers that successfully retained a subsidized employee for some post-subsidy period might receive a modest bonus payment.

If the NEED program includes significant spending on supply-side subsidies, should it still be described as a labor demand policy? I would argue that the NEED program is still primarily a labor demand policy in that it first seeks to modify employer behavior to create enough jobs, and then seeks to see what can be done to fit disadvantaged persons into those jobs. The program first makes sure that the jobs are created before providing supply-side services. Current supply-side programs train or otherwise prepare disadvantaged persons for jobs and just hope that the jobs will be available once the training and preparation are completed.

Another important issue centers on the wage rate paid by employers and the wage rate received by workers under NEED. In general, the subsidy to employers should be less than 100 percent—no more than 80 or 90 percent—to give employers some economic incentive not to simply claim that the "prevailing wage" is the maximum subsidy amount. In addition, the wage received by subsidized workers should be less than the market wage. However, it would certainly be politically desirable for employers to pay the prevailing or market wage. To achieve this, the program should impose a special "tax" or mandatory savings to create a gap between the wage paid by employers and the wage received by subsidized workers. Some of the wage paid by employers would not go immediately to the worker but instead would be placed in a special fund. Some of the proceeds from this fund could be paid out as a bonus to the worker if he or she stays employed for a certain period of time, thereby providing the subsidized worker with a greater incentive for job retention. Alternatively, some of the proceeds from this fund could be paid out later as a voucher to the worker to be used for further job training. Finally, perhaps some of the fund could be used to finance insurance for the workers against common problems that could impede work, such as a car in need of modest repairs.[6]

It should be recognized that many of the specific design features of the NEED program would benefit from considerable experimentation. There should be some experimentation with the formulas for providing wage subsidies, the amounts of supply-side services that are likely to be needed, how best to target disadvantaged workers who are unlikely to be employed, and so on. This experimentation would ideally involve random assignment evaluation to assess the impact of different NEED designs on the immediate employment effects of the program during the subsidy period and the long-run effects on employment. As part of this experimentation, performance indicators for the program should be developed to allow ongoing accountability without continuously doing random assignment experiments. For example, it may be possible to design statistical models, using individual characteristics and local labor market characteristics, to adjust statistically the measured short-run and long-run employment experiences of program participants and to give a rough indicator of the true "value added" of the NEED program. A similar performance indicator system has long been used for the JTPA program, with some success (see Bartik 1995b).

What scale is the NEED program likely to require? What are the costs likely to be? Will the required scale and costs be feasible? The required scale depends a great deal on what is assumed about how many of the five and a half million required jobs for disadvantaged persons (the six million jobs estimated in chapter 3 minus the half a million provided by the revised NJTC) the NEED program is asked to create, over what time period. The required scale also depends on how successful the NEED program is in increasing employment for participants during the program and on the long-run effects of this employment experience. Suppose, as seems reasonable based on research, that in a well-run NEED program about two-thirds of the subsidized employment represents employment that otherwise would not occur for these participants. Suppose that 20 percent of this extra employment is reflected in long-run increases in employment for participants. Under these assumptions, and some other reasonable assumptions, for a NEED program to increase employment of the disadvantaged by 5.5 million at the end of ten years, it would need to subsidize, at any given point in time, about 1.3 million job slots and to have 3.1 million workers participating in the program during an average year.[7]

Is such a scale of operation for NEED either feasible or desirable? This level of activity is about five times the level of activity of the MEED program, and that vast difference in scale suggests that it might be difficult to get the NEED program to the required scale. It might be possible, however, to at least reach some appreciable percentage of the needed jobs with a NEED program. For example, if it proved feasible to double the scale of MEED, then a NEED program could over ten years meet one-third of the calculated job needs of the disadvantaged. On the other hand, the scale of the program is not necessarily out of line compared to some past jobs programs or to other countries. CETA public services at their peak employed 800,000 persons at one time, and the CWA program (a precursor to the WPA during the New Deal) peaked at employment of 4.3 million workers (see chapter 7). To have 3.1 million annual participants in NEED would involve a little more than 2 percent of the U.S. labor force, and as noted in chapter 2, several Western European countries have regularly involved at least that great a percentage of their labor force in labor demand programs.

One could also raise the question of whether this scale of operations is needed. Must labor demand policies provide all of the six million jobs needed by disadvantaged groups? Perhaps it will be found that some of these job needs can be met by regular training and other labor supply approaches, with no need for subsidized employment.

An important point is that the required scale of operations is quite sensitive to the assumptions about the in-program employment effects of the program, and the long-run employment effects. For example, keeping all the same baseline assumptions, but assuming that only 50 percent (rather than 67 percent) of the job slots create additional employment for participants, the required scale to create 5.5 million additional jobs after ten years increases to 4.1 million annual participants and 1.7 million job slots at any point in time. Returning to the baseline assumptions for how many in-program jobs are additional jobs, but instead assuming that long-run effects are only 10 percent (rather than 20 percent) of the added in-program employment, the required number of annual participants is 4.9 million, and 2.1 million job slots are required at any point in time.[8] These calculations emphasize the point that it is important to run the program to maximize its net employment impact, both in-program and long-term.

What about the costs of the NEED program? This is sensitive to all the assumptions made about the required scale, plus two additional assumptions: how large are average wage subsidies, and how much will be spent on supply-side training and support services? Suppose it is assumed that the average wage subsidy is $8 per hour. Suppose it is assumed that each dollar spent on the wage subsidies is matched by a dollar spent on supply-side services, a practice that is roughly consistent with other demand-side programs that have tried to include supply-side services (see table 7.4). Then the NEED program, in order to increase employment of the disadvantaged by 5.5 million after ten years, would cost about $21 billion annually in wage subsidies and another $21 billion in supply-side services, for a total of $42 billion per year.[9]

Spending $42 billion per year on NEED is certainly economically feasible when, as in 1999, the federal government is running huge budget surpluses and the U.S. GDP is $9.0 trillion (U.S. Department of Commerce 2000, 1). The program could also be financed in part by reallocating related spending to the NEED program. Some funds could come from extra welfare block grant funds. As of the end of fiscal year 1998, the unobligated portion of states' welfare block grants from the federal government was running at $2.7 billion per year (U.S. Department of Health and Human Services 1999, 26, table 2.5). As mentioned in chapter 9, state and local resources—both explicit spending and tax breaks—devoted to encouraging economic development probably amount to $32 billion per year. Some portion of this amount could plausibly be diverted to the NEED program, since creating job opportunities for the unemployed and disadvantaged is supposed to be one of the primary goals of economic development programs. But ultimately the decision to devote $42 billion annually to a program such as NEED is a matter less of feasibility than of political will.

Why Labor Demand Policies to Help the Poor Make Sense

What would provide the political will to enact a significant program of labor demand policies to help low-income Americans? What might convince conservatives to consider such significant government activism? What would make liberals willing to focus government activism on employment for the poor rather than other goals? I believe that the political case can be made in part by citing the empirical evidence on three points:

1. Full employment for all, including the poor, is a crucial social goal.
2. Full employment for all is achievable.
3. Full employment for the poor requires a greater use of labor demand policies.

This book has addressed all three of these points, paying particular attention to the third point.

The importance of the goal of full employment for all rests in part on values. I agree with the many social critics, on both the left and right, who have argued that in American culture employment for disadvantaged groups is crucial if these groups are to garner social respect and political power (Wilson 1996; Mead 1992; Kaus 1992; Ellwood 1988). But there is also empirical evidence on the importance of employment. Because we have taken steps to "make work pay" by expanding the Earned Income Tax Credit, full-time, full-year work for all the heads of poor families can enormously reduce poverty (see Sawhill 1999, discussed in chapter 3). Furthermore, if a disadvantaged person can keep working full-time and full-year, the empirical evidence suggests that this work experience will lead to steady wage gains (see, for example, Gladden and Taber 2000, discussed in chapter 3). Full employment for the poor does not come close to immediately providing most of the poor with middle-class status. But it moves many of the poor immediately out of poverty and, over time, allows the poor to gradually improve their standard of living.

Full employment for all is achievable. Recent U.S. experience has refuted conventional wisdom among economists and shown that overall unemployment rates can be reduced far more than was thought possible without causing economic disaster. Numerous experiments and demonstrations of labor demand programs have shown that if we expand labor demand, the employment rates of welfare recipients, black teenagers, and many other disadvantaged groups can be greatly increased to match the employment rates of the American mainstream.

Finally, labor demand policies can help significantly increase the employment rates of the poor. This is what the bulk of this book has sought to show with empirical evidence. Other economists have also sought recently to make a case for labor demand policies, such as Katz (1998) on wage subsidies and Ellwood and Welty (2000) on public-service jobs. I make a detailed case for a specific program of labor demand policies throughout this book, but the case for *some* sort of labor demand policy to help the poor should simply be common sense. Expanded employment for the poor requires changes in both sides of the labor market: more of the poor must be willing and able to work, and more employers must be willing to hire them. Surely it is common sense that public policy should work on both sides of the labor market. Public policy must be involved in both labor supply and labor demand to be most effective in increasing the employment and earnings of the poor.

Appendix 1

A THEORETICAL MODEL OF THE DISPLACEMENT AND WAGE EFFECTS OF LABOR SUPPLY AND DEMAND POLICIES IN LABOR MARKETS FOR LESS-EDUCATED WORKERS

IN THIS appendix, a theoretical partial equilibrium model of labor markets is used to simulate the effects on the employment and wages of less-educated workers of various types of labor supply and demand policies. The most important implication of these simulations is that policies that increase the quantity of labor supplied or demanded in labor markets for less-educated workers have significant displacement effects. Such "quantity" policies significantly increase the net employment of less-educated workers, but by significantly less than the quantity added to labor supply or demand, implying that the extra labor supply or demand displaces some less-educated workers from jobs. These significant displacement effects are robust to a range of plausible assumptions about demand and supply behavior. The other robust result is that the short-run and medium-run effects of supply and demand policies on market wages are likely to be modest in size.

The theoretical model used is a partial equilibrium model in that it describes only the behavior of the low-wage labor market by itself. The model includes four equations:

$$\text{(Labor supply) } L^s = L^s(W,U) \tag{A1.1}$$

$$\text{(Labor demand) } L^d = L^d(W,U) \tag{A1.2}$$

$$\text{(Definition of unemployment rate) } L^s\,(1 - U) = L^d \tag{A1.3}$$

$$\text{(Wage curve) } W = W(U) \tag{A1.4}$$

where L^s is the labor supply of less-educated workers, L^d is the labor demand for less-educated workers, W is the wage rate of less-educated workers, and U is the unemployment rate of less-educated workers.

The model used assumes unemployment. This assumption seems realistic for several reasons. First, we observe unemployment in the labor market, and in particular we observe high unemployment rates in labor markets for less-educated and other disadvantaged groups. Second, exhaustive research suggests that in the short term and the medium term, wages are better predicted by unemployment than by other variables, suggesting that unemployment is an economically meaningful category that helps determine the equilibrium in a labor market (Blanchflower and Oswald 1994; Card 1995b).

Unemployment can be theoretically rationalized in many ways. One of the most popular theoretical rationales is provided by so-called efficiency wage or wage curve models (Blanchflower and Oswald 1994; Akerlof and Yellen 1986; Solow 1990; Davidson 1990; Weiss 1990; Layard, Nickell, and Jackman 1991; Card 1995b). In these models, employers find it profitable to set wages above the level that would clear the market. Above-market-clearing wages result in unemployment because the higher wage increases labor supply and reduces labor demand. Above-market-clearing wages are profitable because they allow employers to get their workforce to be more productive. If the market wage resulted in zero unemployment, workers could easily find another similar job. Worker turnover would be extremely high, increasing firms' hiring and training costs and lowering productivity.[1] Therefore, in order to lower this turnover, firms increase wages above the market-clearing level. This results in unemployment, which enables firms to hire better workers, lower worker turnover, and motivate workers to be more productive to avoid being fired. In addition, workers may have standards of wage fairness. If wages are considered unfair, workers may be unwilling to work hard. Employers may wish to pay a fair wage, thereby encouraging better worker morale and productivity, even if this wage is above the market-clearing wage.

Unlike standard market-clearing models of the labor market, in wage curve models the equilibrium wage is *not* set where supply equals demand. Therefore, wage curve models require another equation to close the model. To provide this equation, wage curve models assume a stable empirical relationship between unemployment and wages, dubbed the "wage curve." Lower unemployment increases wages for several reasons. With lower unemployment, fewer workers are available in the market and it is easier to find jobs. Therefore, with lower unemployment, wages must be set higher to keep hiring and turnover costs down and to motivate greater worker productivity. Lower unemployment also is associated with higher business profits, which may cause workers to believe that a wage increase is fair.

In a wage curve model, equilibrium wages, employment, and labor supply are determined by an interaction of three relationships: the labor demand curve, the labor supply curve, and the wage curve. (The fourth equation simply defines the relationship between labor supply, labor demand, and the unemployment rate). Labor supply and demand are more complicated to describe because they may depend not just on wages but also on unemployment, as can be seen in equations A1.1 and A1.2. Because workers cannot all immediately obtain a job at the market wage, labor force participation decisions depend on the unemployment rate, not just the wage rate. Employers now face an additional choice: whom to hire from among those looking for jobs. Who is hired may depend on who is looking, for example, if a greater proportion of the available labor supply is from a less-educated group, then a greater proportion of less-educated candidates may be in the interview pool, and a less-educated candidate is more likely to be the first candidate to be judged acceptable for a particular job opening, other things equal. Higher unemployment of some type of labor may reduce the quantity supplied of that labor type and increase the quantity demanded. Therefore, a key empirical parameter determining the effects of demand and supply policies is the effect of unemployment on labor supply and demand.

The conventional market-clearing labor market model can be described as a limiting case of the above model. If we specify the wage curve equation so that wages are infinitely sensitive to unemployment rates, then wages completely adjust to prevent any fluctuations in the unemployment rate in response to any shock to labor supply or demand. The unemployment rate essentially becomes fixed at some "frictional" level of unemployment, and the effects of unemployment on labor supply or demand become irrelevant.

To use the model for simulation, we first add policy-induced proportionate shocks to the quantity demanded, the quantity supplied, the wage paid by demanders, and the wage received by suppliers. Totally differentiating this model, one obtains the following equations for the equilibrium change in wages and employment in the low-wage labor market in response to the various supply and demand policies:

$$(dW/W) = (-hD_p + D_q - eS_p - S_q)/(\text{Denominator}) \tag{A1.5}$$

$$dE/E = [(-hD_p + D_q)F + (eS_p + S_q)G]/(\text{Denominator}) \tag{A1.6}$$

where:

$$\text{Denominator} = F + G$$

$$F = [(1/(1 - U))(1/g) + e + a(1/g)]$$

$$G = [-h - b(1/g)]$$

and e is the elasticity of labor supply with respect to wages, h is the elasticity of labor demand with respect to wages, a is the percentage change in labor supply due to a one-point increase in the unemployment rate, b is the percentage change in labor demand due to a one-point increase in the unemployment rate, and g is the percentage change in wages for a one-point increase in the unemployment rate. D_p is the wage subsidy to employers as a proportion of the market wage, D_q is the proportionate shock to employment from a quantity demand shock as a proportion of the preshock employment level, S_p is the wage subsidy to workers as a proportion of the market wage, and S_q is the shock to employment from a quantity supply shock as a proportion of the preshock employment level.

Therefore, the employment and wage effects of labor supply and demand policies depend on a wide variety of behavioral parameters. What do we know about these behavioral parameters? As mentioned in chapter 3, recent research suggests that the elasticity of the labor supply of low-wage men with respect to the wage, allowing for changes in labor force participation, is probably higher than previously thought, at perhaps 0.4 (Juhn, Murphy, and Topel 1991). This is consistent with research evidence on the wage elasticities of the labor supply of single mothers (Moffitt 1983). Other research suggests that a one-point reduction in the unemployment rate increases labor force participation for most groups by about one-half of 1 percent (Bowen and Finegan 1969; Bartik 1999).

As mentioned in chapter 3, the most convincing evidence on the elasticity of labor demand for less-educated workers with respect to wages comes from the minimum-wage literature. This research literature suggests that the elasticity of demand for less-educated workers may be in the modest range of -0.1 to -0.6. However, other researchers disagree with this low elasticity and believe that the elasticity of demand for less-educated workers may be much greater (in absolute value). For example, George Johnson (1998), in his work on the labor market effects of immigration, assumes empirical parameters that imply an elasticity of demand for less-educated workers of around -1.5 (see also Bartik 2000a). Much less is known about the elasticity of demand for less-educated workers with respect to the unemployment rate. The estimates from Bartik (1999), which are also presented in appendix 2, suggest that a one-point reduction in the unemployment rate of a less-educated group may increase labor demand for that group by 1.5 percent in the medium run (that is, three to five years after the change in unemployment rate), and by about -0.75 percent in the short run (the immediate effect of the shock).

The wage curve literature, exhaustively researched and summarized by Blanchflower and Oswald (1994), concludes that the elasticity of overall wages for all workers in a labor market with respect to the overall unemployment rate is around -0.1. At about 5 percent unemployment, this corresponds to a one-point reduction in the unemployment rate, causing about a 2 percent increase in wages. However, evidence presented in Bartik (1999) and Bartik (2000c) and summarized in appendix 2 and appendix 9, suggests that for a particular group's labor market, changes in unemployment for that group alone have much lower effects on relative wages. A reasonable estimate of the medium-run effects of unemployment of a group on wages, for a group that is about 10 percent of the overall labor market, is that a one-point reduction in that group's unemployment rate, by itself, increases the wages of that group by about 0.6 percent.[2] Finally, as already mentioned, if one wanted to assume a market-clearing model, or at least assume that in some long run the unemployment rate will return to some fixed equilibrium level, this can be done by assuming that the elasticity of wages with respect to unemployment is minus infinity.

Using equations A1.5 and A1.6, table A1.1 presents the effects of the various labor supply and demand policies on wages and employment. The effects shown are on the wages and employment of less-educated workers. These workers are assumed to make up a distinct labor submarket, with elasticities in that submarket as assumed in the table, based on the discussion earlier in this appendix. The policies are assumed to be aimed at this labor submarket and are assumed to be policies that either increase the quantity of labor supplied or demanded in the submarket or subsidize the wages of employers or workers in the submarket. The elasticities shown are the percentage changes in market wages or employment in this labor submarket for less-educated workers, for a 1 percent increase in the quantity of labor supplied or demanded or a 1 percent wage subsidy, with all percentages expressed in relation to the original employment and market wage in the labor submarket.

The scenario row labeled "baseline" gives results that use what I regard as the most plausible behavioral parameters for the medium-run effects of these policies, that is, the effects of these policies on wages and employment three to five years after the policy is enacted. (The research behind these assumed parameters is summarized earlier in this appendix.) The other rows give alternative elasticity calculations for the effects of these policies and typically alter just one behavioral assumption from the baseline results.

The baseline results show displacement effects of both labor supply and demand policies. A quantity shock to either labor supply or demand results in a net employment increase that is about half of the size of the original shock. That is, for every two additional persons whose labor is supplied to the market because of the policy, or whose labor is demanded in the market because of the policy, net employment goes up by only about one person. This implies that some other person's employment is displaced by the policy. In addition, the wage effects of all the policies are modest.

TABLE A1.1 *Implications of Demand and Supply Elasticities for the Effects of Demand and Supply Policies on the Wages and Employment of Less-Educated Workers*

		Employment and Wage Elasticities of Various Policies[b]							
		Quantity Increase in Labor Demand		Quantity Increase in Labor Supply		Demand-Side Wage Subsidy to Employer		Supply-Side Wage Subsidy to Worker	
Scenario	Assumptions About Demand and Supply Behavior[a]	Employment	Wage	Employment	Wage	Employment	Wage	Employment	Wage
Baseline	Elasticity of demand with respect to wage of −0.5, elasticity of demand with respect to unemployment rate of 1.5, elasticity of wages with respect to one-point increase in unemployment rate of (−0.6).	0.50	0.16	0.50	−0.16	0.25	0.08	0.20	−0.07
Short run	Same as baseline, but elasticity of demand with respect to one-point increase in unemployment rate of 0.75.	0.64	0.21	0.36	−0.21	0.32	0.10	0.15	−0.08
Greater response of demand to unemployment	Same as baseline, but elasticity of demand with respect to one-point increase in unemployment rate of 3.0.	0.36	0.12	0.64	−0.12	0.18	0.06	0.26	−0.05

Greater response of wages to unemployment	Same as baseline, but elasticity of wages with respect to one-point increase in unemployment rate of (−2.0).	0.49	0.41	0.51	−0.41	0.24	0.20	0.20	−0.16
Greater response of labor demand to wages	Same as baseline, but elasticity of labor demand with respect to wages of (−1.5).	0.43	0.14	0.57	−0.14	0.65	0.21	0.23	−0.06
Long-run effects with unemployment returning to long-run frictional level	Same as baseline, but elasticity of wages with respect to one-point increase in unemployment rate of (−1,000).	0.44	1.11	0.56	−1.11	0.22	0.55	0.22	−0.44
Long-run market-clearing model with high elasticity of demand	Same as long-run model, but with elasticity of labor demand with respect to wages of (−1.5).	0.21	0.53	0.79	−0.53	0.32	0.79	0.32	−0.21

Source: Author's calculations.
Note: See appendix for model and equations used to produce these numbers.
[a] All simulations assume unemployment of eight percent, elasticity of labor supply with respect to wages of 0.4, and elasticity of labor supply with respect to a one-point change in unemployment of −0.5.
[b] Percentage change in employment or wages of less-educated workers for a 1 percent increase in labor quantity or a 1 percent wage subsidy.

These modest effects on wages reflect the relatively modest effects of unemployment on wages in this model. The model ends up being heavily influenced by how sensitive both supply and demand are to changes in unemployment, since wages do not adjust that much. Because these unemployment effects on labor supply and demand are both of moderate size, we can conclude that supply or demand shocks both have some significant effects on employment, though nothing close to a one-for-one effect.

As mentioned earlier, the empirical estimates presented in appendix 2 suggest somewhat lower responses of labor demand to unemployment in the very short run, that is, the immediate effect. The second row of table A1.1 presents these short-run results, which are somewhat more favorable to labor demand policies. A government policy to hire one hundred persons results in a short-term net employment increase of sixty-four persons, implying displacement from employment of thirty-six persons. In contrast, a government policy to add one hundred persons to the labor market implies a net employment increase of thirty-six persons, implying that around fifty-six persons are displaced from employment.[3] These more favorable results for labor demand compared to labor supply policies occur because the short-term parameters involve labor demand being less responsive to labor supply; by implication, labor demand and hence employment can be more responsive to policy-induced shocks to labor demand. However, the difference between these short-run and medium-run results is not overwhelming. In either case, both supply and demand quantity policies involve considerable displacement and wage effects of policies are modest.

The next three scenario rows examine how robust these results are to possible changes in assumptions about behavior. I consider greater responsiveness of demand to unemployment, wages to unemployment, and labor demand to wages. Under all three scenarios, both labor supply and demand policies that increase the quantity supplied or demanded have significant effects in increasing employment, but also considerable displacement effects, of roughly similar magnitude to the employment and displacement effects of the baseline scenario. Wage effects are still in all cases fairly modest, although somewhat higher, as one would expect, in the scenario that allows wages to respond more to unemployment.

Finally, I considerable possible long-run effects of labor supply and demand policies, under the assumption that in the long run one could assume that market forces bring unemployment back to some equilibrium level. Under what I consider the most plausible behavioral parameters, the employment and displacement effects of policies that increase the quantity of labor supplied or demanded are quite similar to the previous scenarios. However, the wage effects of the various policies are far greater under this long-run scenario, under which unemployment changes cannot bear any of the burden of adjustment to the policies. Thus, more of the adjustment is forced into changes in market wages. However, because both labor supply and demand are assumed to have modest elasticities in response to wages, both labor demand and supply policies that increase quantities can increase net employment significantly, and by similar amounts, but with significant displacement effects.

Finally, I consider a long-run scenario that also increases the elasticity of labor demand with respect to wages to a level more consistent with the views of some economists (for example, Johnson 1998). Under this scenario, quantity increases in labor supply become more effective in increasing employment relative to quantity increases in labor demand. Private demand is more responsive in adjusting upward in response to the lower wages brought about by quantity increases in labor supply, as well as more responsive in adjusting downward in response to the higher wages brought about by quantity increases in labor demand.

Considering all these scenarios, it seems quite likely that policies that induce increases in the quantity of labor supplied or demanded in low-wage labor markets have both significant employment effects and significant displacement effects. Employment increases in response to these policies, but by perhaps only one-third to two-thirds of the original shock to labor supply or demand. The wage effects of all these labor supply and demand policies are likely to be modest. Under plausible assumptions, short-run and medium-run reactions to supply and demand policies are dominated by changes in unemployment and the effects of these changes on labor supply and demand, rather than by large changes in wages. Because both labor supply and demand are moderately affected by unemployment under a wide variety of plausible scenarios, the employment effects of either policy are moderate, implying some displacement. The long-run effects of labor supply and demand policies are somewhat more uncertain, but under the most plausible assumptions, they still involve both significant employment and significant displacement effects. However, the short-run and medium-run effects on employment are likely to be quite important in determining the long-run effects of policy on the wages and employability of these less-educated groups, by affecting the accumulation of human capital. These human capital effects are not incorporated into these simple partial equilibrium models. However, considerable evidence, discussed in both chapters 3 and 5, suggests that the human capital effects of short-run changes in work experience are likely to be important in the long run.

Appendix 2

DESCRIPTION OF AN EMPIRICALLY ESTIMATED, DYNAMIC GENERAL EQUILIBRIUM MODEL WITH UNEMPLOYMENT OF A LABOR MARKET WITH DIFFERENT GROUPS OF LABOR, WITH SIMULATION RESULTS FOR VARIOUS LABOR SUPPLY AND DEMAND POLICIES

THIS appendix describes and presents estimates for a dynamic general equilibrium model of a labor market model with five groups of labor. It also presents some simulations of how employment and wages in this model respond to various types of labor supply and demand policies. More details on this model and the simulations are in Bartik (1999).

Throughout this book, the endnotes present simulation results from this appendix or other simulation results from this model for the effects of various policies. These simulation results are meant to be illustrative, not definitive. As discussed in this appendix, where this model is estimating parameters for which we have some previous empirical evidence, the parameter estimates seem reasonable. However, the model is also estimating parameter estimates for which we have little previous empirical evidence, so we should be cautious about assuming that these parameter estimates are robust. In addition, constructing and estimating this model involved many choices about how to structure and identify the model. It is unclear how robust the simulation results would be to other ways of structuring and identifying the model. Despite these limitations, the simulations do illustrate the plausible effects of labor supply and demand policies in a model that is plausible and consistent with the empirical literature. The model provides specific simulation estimates that back up more general qualitative statements in the text that a particular policy could plausibly have displacement or wage effects that are large or small. The model estimates are usually presented in the notes to avoid having the text place too much reliance on the results from this one particular model.

The most important implication of this model is that the spillover or displacement effects of labor supply and demand policies are likely to be significant. In general, five years after a policy has increased the labor supply or demand of a particular less-educated group, these policies are estimated to cause significant increases in employment for that group, but by considerably less than 1 percent for a 1 percent increase in quantity supplied or demanded, a finding that implies significant displacement effects.

Description of Structural Model and Data

The model is estimated using pooled time-series cross-section data. The model's observations are means or aggregates of labor market variables for a state/year cell. The data encompass all fifty states and the District of Columbia and all years from 1979 to 1997. The data come from the Outgoing Rotation Group of the Current Population Survey (CPS-ORG). The model's twenty-three equations are estimated using weighted least squares, with 1979 state population for weights. Fixed effects for state and year are included in all equations to reflect the omitted characteristics of states or time periods. The model includes equations for five groups: female heads of household who are not college graduates, have other relatives present in the household, and are between the ages of sixteen and forty-four ("female heads");[1] other women ages sixteen and sixty-four who are not college graduates ("other less-educated females"); female college graduates ages sixteen to sixty-four ("more-educated females"); males between the ages of sixteen and sixty-four who are not college graduates ("less-educated males"); and male college graduates ("more-educated males"). The model can be divided into five different sectors: six labor demand equations, one for each group and one overall; six wage equations; five labor force participation rate equations, one for each group; five population equations; and one equation explaining state personal income. The model's estimates are used to simulate the effects of labor supply shocks and demand shocks.

The model includes unemployment, which makes it more realistic: we observe unemployment, and unemployment varies greatly over time, across different groups, and across different local markets. Empirical evidence shows that unemployment predicts wages.[2]

The model is estimated using local data, not national data. Using local data provides more observations, allowing more precise estimates. In addition, empirical evidence suggests that labor market outcomes are more influenced by local variables than by national variables (Blanchflower and Oswald 1994; Bartik 1994a). State data are used rather than metropolitan data, even though metropolitan areas are closer to true local labor markets.

States are chosen for data reasons. MSA boundaries change greatly over time, making it difficult to define consistent variables. In addition, sampling for the CPS is designed to produce reliable estimates at the state level (for example, by oversampling smaller states) but not for smaller metropolitan areas.

The model identifies cause-and-effect relationships by lagging right-hand-side variables and including lagged dependent variables as controls. We would like to allow right-hand-side variables to have immediate effects. However, almost all the right-hand-side variables are endogenous, and it is difficult to find good instruments for so many endogenous variables. The identifying assumption that labor market behavior responds to other variables with a lag seems plausible. Including lagged dependent variables as well as lagged independent variables allows the dynamic behavior of the model to be more complex. Lagged dependent variables also control for recent state trends. Controlling for such unobserved trends, the estimated effects of other variables on the dependent variable are more likely to represent a true causal influence.

Table A2.1 summarizes the model. The demand equations impose the restrictions that overall labor demand depends on average wages and that relative demand for each type of labor depends on each type's relative wage. This specification can be derived from a production function in which labor enters in aggregate form, with that labor aggregate produced by a subproduction function that is constant-elasticity-of-substitution in the five labor types. Less restrictive specifications, in which demand for each labor type depends on all five wages, resulted in estimates that were too imprecise.

Employers with a job opening may base hiring in part on who is in the labor pool, not just on wages. To allow for this, the equations for the relative labor demand for each group also include the labor force share of each group. The current values of labor force share are included, because hiring should depend on the current labor pool. Because measurement error in labor force share is correlated with measurement error in employment share (both variables are measured using the CPS-ORG data), lagged labor force share is used as an instrument for current labor force share.

A shock to labor force share, holding past trends in labor demand share constant, implies a shock to the relative unemployment rates of different groups. Therefore, the specification used here is just a variant of the specification used in appendix 1, which allowed labor demand for a particular group to be affected by the group's unemployment rate. The elasticity of labor demand for a particular group with respect to its labor force share implies an elasticity with respect to unemployment of that group.[3]

The overall wage curve in the model is standard, but it implicitly assumes that overall wages depend on overall unemployment, not on the

TABLE A2.1 *A Wage Curve Model of State Labor Markets*

Type of Equation	Dependent Variable	Independent Variables[a]
Overall labor demand (one equation)	ln(state employment)	ln(wage) ln(personal income)
Employment share demand (five equations)	ln(share of employment in group)	ln(wage of group/overall wage) *Current* value only of ln(labor force share of group) [endogenous, lagged labor force share used as instrument]
Overall wage curve (one equation)	ln(wage)	ln(unemployment rate)
Relative wage curves (five equations)	ln(wage of group/ overall wage)	Some function of relative unemployment of group, with functional form chosen for each group after preliminary testing
Labor force participation rate (five equations)	ln(labor force participation rate of group)	ln(wage of group) Unemployment rate of group ln(AFDC benefits for female-head group)
Migration (five equations)	ln(population of group)	Same as for labor force participation rate
Income (one equation)	ln(state personal income)	ln(wage) ln(employment) ln(population) Includes current as well as lagged values of these variables

Source: Author's compilation.
Notes: All estimates are based on pooled annual time-series cross-section data for all states, 1979 to 1997. All estimates are weighted by 1979 state population and use weighted least squares except employment share demand, which is weighted 2SLS.
[a] These are independent variables in addition to year and state dummies, and two lags of dependent variable. All independent variables are included with two lags and no current values unless otherwise noted.

relative unemployment of different groups. The relative wage equations assume that the relative wage is affected by relative unemployment. Less restrictive specifications, in which each group's wage rate depends on all the groups' unemployment rates, were too imprecise.

Some experimentation was done with the functional form by which unemployment affects wages. For each wage curve, four different specifications were estimated, each with a different functional form for unemployment: linear; unemployment and unemployment squared; the natural logarithm of the unemployment rate; and one over the unemployment rate. The specification that minimizes the Akaike Information Criterion (AIC) was chosen for use in simulations.

The labor force participation equations and "migration" (or population) equations are standard. An income equation is included, and income is included in the labor demand equation, to allow for multiplier effects. As state employment increases, income increases, increasing local output demand and thus further increasing local labor demand. The income equation includes current right-hand-side variables because income increases immediately if wages, employment, and population in the state increase. The system is still identified because income enters with a lag in the overall labor demand equation.

The equation system seems sparse because only a few continuous variables are included in each equation. Because state and year dummies are included, the model does control for many variables. The state dummies control for variables that vary among states but not much over time. The year dummies control for variables that change over time in a similar manner for different states.

The model is estimated using weighted least squares, with 1979 state populations as weights. Using state population as weights increases the precision of estimates, because CPS-ORG samples are larger for the larger states. By using state population as weights, the estimates also describe the behavior of the "average" state, where "average" reflects the relative population in each state. State populations from 1979 are used as weights, rather than populations for each state/year cell, to ensure that the weighting variable is not endogenous.[4]

These estimated equations are used to simulate the impact of various shocks to the labor supply or demand of different groups. Because the wage curve equations are nonlinear, the model requires assumptions about the baseline unemployment rate. With lower unemployment, wages respond more to shocks, thus affecting other variables. The simulations in this appendix consider only a low-unemployment baseline, but later simulations presented in the endnotes consider both low-unemployment and high-unemployment baselines. For the low-unemployment baseline, unemployment rates for each group are taken from national averages for the lowest unemployment year (1997) in the sample; for the high-unemployment baseline, unemployment rates are from the highest unemployment sample year (1982).

This appendix focuses on the national effects of labor supply or demand shocks, that is, the average effects in all states of labor supply or demand shocks that take place in all states. Such an analysis should incorporate spillover effects across states. I explored modeling spillover by adding national variables to the equations; to do so I had to change from fixed to random year effects, but in most cases the national variables had counterintuitive signs. This may reflect the limited number of available national observations (eighteen years).

To estimate national effects, simulations suppress the migration effects of supply or demand shocks. This approach approximates the national effects of a shock if migration is the main spillover effect across states. The assumption is that if a shock takes place in all states, the resulting adjustments should not involve significant migration. Simulations have also been done allowing for migration effects. These simulation results differ only modestly, as the empirical estimates suggest that migration has only modest responses to changes in a state's wages or unemployment.

Table A2.2 summarizes the means of some variables for the five groups. The means show the pattern one would expect, with less-educated groups having lower wages, lower labor force participation, and higher

TABLE A2.2 *National Means of Labor Market Outcomes for Five Demographic Groups and Overall Population Ages Sixteen to Sixty-Four, 1997*

	Female			Male		
	Household Heads Ages Sixteen to Forty-Four, Other Relatives Present, Less Than College Education	Ages Sixteen to Sixty-Four, Less Than College Education, Excluding First Group	College Graduates, Ages Sixteen to Sixty-Four	Less Than College Education, Ages Sixteen to Sixty-Four	College Graduates, Ages Sixteen to Sixty-Four	Overall Population, Ages Sixteen to Sixty-Four
Proportion of population	0.0399	0.3569	0.1091	0.3782	0.1159	1.0000
Wage rate	$ 8.49	$ 8.80	$15.19	$10.85	$18.85	$11.29
Unemployment rate (1982 rate in parentheses)	11.0 (15.4)	5.4 (10.2)	2.2 (4.2)	6.0 (12.0)	1.9 (3.1)	5.0 (9.9)
Labor force participation rate	75.7	66.5	82.8	81.5	93.1	77.4

Source: All data are taken from 1997 Merged Outgoing Rotation Group data tape of the CPS, with the exception of the unemployment rate data for 1982.

Notes: All means are weighted national means using appropriate weights from tape. Mean wage rate is actually exp(mean ln[hourly wage]). Over sample period of 1979 to 1997, 1997 is the year with the lowest national unemployment rate for sixteen- to sixty-four-year-olds, and 1982 is the year with the highest national unemployment rate. The patterns of unemployment in these two years are used as alternative baselines in simulating the effects of supply and demand shocks.

unemployment rates than more-educated groups, and women having lower wages and labor force participation rates than men.

Parameter Estimates

Tables A2.3 through A2.9 present the parameter estimates from estimating the twenty-three equations in this model. Because of the complex dynamic nature of the estimated equations, these raw parameter estimates are difficult to interpret completely. The next section helps in this interpretation by presenting the implications of these parameter estimates for various important behavioral elasticities. However, the raw parameter estimates do suggest that the model has an overall good fit, with parameter estimates often highly significant and of reasonable sign.

There are several important conclusions to be drawn from these raw parameter estimates:

The model's equations have good explanatory power. R-squared statistics are generally high, always over 0.5 and often over 0.9, indicating that the model's variables do a good job of tracking a state's differential trends in employment, wages, labor force, population, and income during this period from 1981 to 1997.

TABLE A2.3 *Overall Labor Demand Equation (Dependent Variable: ln(Employment))*

Independent Variable	Coefficient (*t*-statistic)
Lag ln(employment)	0.6900 (19.49)
Second lag	−0.0567 (−1.72)
Lag ln(wage)	−0.0779 (−1.74)
Second lag	−0.2210 (−4.85)
Lag ln(personal income)	0.4377 (9.50)
Second lag	−0.1524 (−3.12)

Source: Author's estimates.
Note: The estimation is based on 867 observations, for fifty states plus D.C., times seventeen years (1981 to 1997). Independent variables also include complete vectors of year dummies (sixteen variables) and state dummies (fifty variables) to control for fixed time period and state effects; coefficients on these variables are not reported to save space. The estimation uses 1979 state population as weight for each state-year cell observation. R-squared is 0.9996.

TABLE A2.4 *Relative Labor Demand Equations (Dependent Variables: ln(Employment of Group/Total Employment))*

Independent Variable	Female Heads	Other Less-Educated Females	More-Educated Females	Less-Educated Males	More-Educated Males
Lag ln(employment share of group)	0.2713 (2.66)	0.0719 (2.34)	0.3549 (4.40)	0.3999 (5.15)	0.3864 (5.62)
Second lag	−0.0434 (−1.64)	0.0032 (0.25)	−0.0227 (−0.92)	−0.0291 (−1.27)	−0.0685 (−2.83)
Lag ln(relative wage of group)	−0.0915 (−1.41)	−0.0502 (−2.50)	0.0923 (1.93)	−0.0333 (−0.99)	0.0340 (1.03)
Second lag	0.0015 (0.02)	−0.0124 (−0.65)	−0.0647 (−1.26)	−0.1170 (−3.29)	−0.0810 (−2.52)
Current ln(labor force share of group)	0.3752 (1.56)	0.8503 (14.00)	0.3008 (1.96)	0.4277 (3.44)	0.4009 (3.98)

Source: Author's estimates.

Notes: A *t*-statistic is in parentheses below each coefficient estimate. Each column shows estimates for one equation; this equation's dependent variable is the ln(employment share) for the group given in the column headings. The estimations in each of five equations presented here are based on 867 observations, for fifty states plus D.C., × seventeen years (1981 to 1997). Independent variables also include complete vectors of year dummies (sixteen variables) and state dummies (fifty variables) to control for fixed time period and state effects; coefficients on these variables are not reported to save space. The estimation uses 1979 state population as weight for each state-year cell observation. Estimation is by 2SLS, with current labor force share treated as endogenous and lagged labor force share used as instrument. R-squared not reported because this statistic is not meaningful for 2SLS. In the first stage of 2SLS, the *t*-statistic on the lagged labor force share instrument for each of the five equations is as follows: female head, 2.98; other less-educated females, 5.62; more-educated females, 4.65; less-educated males, 5.36; more-educated males, 6.05.

As shown by the t-statistics, many coefficient estimates are statistically significant. Both lagged dependent variables and other independent variables are often highly statistically significant. Often the second lag as well as the first lag is statistically significant. This suggests that the model's independent variables are good variables for predicting the dependent variables, and that the dynamic structure of the model is quite complex.

Two-stage least squares results appear to rely on instruments that predict well. As mentioned in the notes to table A2.4, the instrument used to predict current labor force share (lagged labor force share) has a high t-statistic in the first-stage prediction equation. This suggests that these 2SLS estimates are unlikely to suffer the bias toward OLS estimates that may occur when first-stage instruments are poor predictors (Bound, Jaeger, and Baker 1995).

TABLE A2.5 *Overall Wage Equation (Dependent Variable: ln(Wage))*

Independent Variable	Coefficient (*t*-statistic)
Lag ln(wage)	0.7318 (20.29)
Second lag	0.1030 (2.96)
Lag ln(unemployment rate plus 0.005)	−0.0314 (−6.71)
Second lag	−0.0217 (−4.52)

Source: Author's compilation.
Notes: The estimation is based on 867 observations, for fifty states plus D.C., × seventeen years (1981 to 1997). Independent variables also include complete vectors of year dummies (sixteen variables) and state dummies (fifty variables) to control for fixed time period and state effects; coefficients on these variables are not reported to save space. The estimation uses 1979 state population as weight for each state-year cell observation. R-squared is 0.9816. The unemployment rate is defined as ln(labor force − ln(employment). The specification then takes the logarithm of this unemployment rate definition. 0.005 is added to avoid problems with occasional zeros for some smaller groups. The logarithmic specification was chosen by Akaike Information Criterion over linear specification, specification with 1 / unemployment rate, and specification with unemployment rate and unemployment rate squared.

The signs of the raw estimates generally appear reasonable.[5] In all the estimating equations, lagged dependent variables have positive effects, but effects of less than one, suggesting that there is some lagged adjustment of these variables in response to shocks. In the overall demand equation, wages have negative effects on labor demand, and state personal income (a proxy for output or product demand) has a positive impact, as would be expected. In the relative labor demand equations, relative wages generally have significant negative effects on employment share, with the exception of the equation for female heads and more-educated females. Current labor force share affects the employment share significantly, with the exception of the female head employment share equation. In the overall wage equation, unemployment has significant negative effects on overall wages. The log specification chosen suggests that these effects are nonlinear, with a one-point reduction in unemployment having greater positive effects on wages when unemployment is low. In the group relative wage equations, higher relative unemployment rates have negative effects on relative wages. (Note that in the female heads and less-educated females equations, the unemployment rate variable is specified as 1/UR, so the positive coefficients imply negative effects of relative unemployment on relative wages.) In the labor force participation rate equations, unemployment rates have

TABLE A2.6 *Relative Wage Curves (Dependent Variables: ln(Wage of Group/Average Wages Overall))*

Independent Variable	Female Heads	Other Less-Educated Females	More-Educated Females	Less-Educated Males	More-Educated Males
Lag ln(relative wage)	0.2332 (6.47)	0.3227 (9.05)	0.3090 (8.81)	0.3592 (10.31)	0.4426 (12.67)
Second lag	−0.0463 (−1.28)	0.0862 (2.44)	−0.0139 (−0.39)	0.1555 (4.48)	0.0146 (0.42)
Lag ln(relative unemployment variable)	0.001035 (4.35)	0.000567 (1.75)	−0.1150 (−1.54)	−0.0419 (−0.61)	0.0539 (0.49)
Second lag	−0.000045 (−0.22)	0.000496 (1.51)	−0.1021 (−1.37)	−0.1422 (−2.06)	−0.2779 (−2.51)

Source: Author's estimates.

Notes: A *t*-statistic is in parentheses below each coefficient estimate. Each column shows results from estimating a different equation; the dependent variable for each equation is the ln(relative wage) for the group named in the column heading. The estimation of each of the five equations presented in this table is based on 867 observations, for fifty states plus D.C., × seventeen years (1981 to 1997). Independent variables also include complete vectors of year dummies (sixteen variables) and state dummies (fifty variables) to control for fixed time period and state effects; coefficients on these variables are not reported to save space. Estimation uses 1979 state population as weight for each state-year cell observation. R-squared for each estimated equation is as follows: female heads, 0.5334; other less-educated females, 0.8279; more-educated females, 0.8906; less-educated males, 0.9261; more-educated males, 0.7549. The relative unemployment variable specification in each equation was chosen separately, based on Akaike Information Criterion, among the following possible unemployment rate transformations: linear (UR_g − UR); log-linear ($\ln[UR_g]$ − ln[UR]); one over UR specification ($1 / UR_g$ − 1/ UR); and quadratic. Optimal specification was 1/UR for female heads and other less-educated females, linear for all others.

negative effects on labor force participation for all groups. Wage rates generally do not have significant effects on labor force participation, with the exception of a negative effect on labor force participation for more-educated females. AFDC benefits have negative effects on labor force participation for female heads of household. In the migration or population equations, relatively few variables except lagged population have significant effects. The exceptions are that wages appear to have significant effects on population for more-educated females and more-educated males, unemployment rates appear to have significant negative effects on population for more-educated males, and AFDC benefits have some positive effects on population for female heads. In the personal income equation, employment has significant positive effects, while the sum of the coefficients on either the wage rate or population is close to zero. This is consistent with interpreting the personal income equation as a proxy for output. Changes in

TABLE A2.7 *Labor Force Participation Rate Equations (Dependent Variables: ln(Labor Force Participation Rate for That Group))*

Independent Variable	Female Heads	Other Less-Educated Females	More-Educated Females	Less-Educated Males	More-Educated Males
Lag ln(lfpr for group)	0.4140 (11.62)	0.4923 (13.88)	0.3246 (9.53)	0.4324 (12.14)	0.2730 (7.58)
Second lag	−0.0227 (−0.63)	0.1131 (3.80)	−0.0808 (−2.39)	−0.0044 (−0.12)	−0.0802 (−2.24)
Lag ln(wage rate for group)	0.0169 (0.39)	0.0188 (0.48)	0.0160 (0.64)	−0.0149 (−0.77)	0.0177 (1.45)
Second lag	0.0448 (1.05)	−0.0323 (−0.83)	−0.0595 (−2.40)	0.0332 (1.76)	0.0013 (0.11)
Lag ln(unemployment rate for group)	−0.1482 (−3.04)	−0.2527 (−3.85)	−0.1990 (−2.47)	−0.1124 (−3.46)	−0.1136 (−2.20)
Second lag	−0.0351 (−0.72)	−0.0387 (−0.58)	0.0876 (1.10)	−0.1068 (−3.18)	−0.0270 (−0.52)
Lag ln(AFDC benefit level)	−0.1201 (−2.17)	—	—	—	—
Second lag	0.0153 (0.30)	—	—	—	—

Source: Author's estimates.

Notes: A *t*-statistic is in parentheses below each coefficient estimate. Each column shows empirical estimates for a different equation; the dependent variable for this equation is the ln(labor force participation rate) for the group named in the column heading. The estimate of each of the five equations presented in this table is based on 867 observations, for fifty states plus D.C., × seventeen years (1981 to 1997). Independent variables also include complete vectors of year dummies (sixteen variables) and state dummies (fifty variables) to control for fixed time period and state effects; coefficients on these variables are not reported to save space. Estimation uses 1979 state population as weight for each state-year cell observation. R-squared for each equation is as follows: female heads, 0.8370; other less-educated females, 0.9533; more-educated females, 0.7449; less-educated males, 0.9063; more-educated males, 0.5608. AFDC benefits allowed to affect only labor force participation of female-head group, on argument that this is the only group of the five that is very likely to be eligible for welfare benefits. Estimated welfare receipt rate for female-head group is 28.6 percent; the estimated receipt rate for other groups is: other less-educated women, 2.5 percent; more-educated women, 0.3 percent; less-educated men, 0.5 percent; more-educated men, 0.1 percent. These are based on welfare receipt rates from March 1997 CPS, blown up by 1.33 based on Blank's (1997) estimates of how much of welfare receipt is underreported.

TABLE A2.8 *Migration Equations (Dependent Variables: ln(Population for That Group))*

Independent Variable	Female Heads	Other Less-Educated Females	More-Educated Females	Less-Educated Males	More-Educated Males
Lag ln(population for group)	0.5839 (16.40)	0.7782 (22.13)	0.6112 (17.54)	0.8547 (23.95)	0.7084 (20.06)
Second lag	−0.0935 (−2.61)	0.0872 (2.56)	−0.0348 (−1.03)	0.0400 (1.14)	−0.0604 (−1.77)
Lag ln(wage rate for group)	−0.1098 (−1.63)	0.0427 (1.02)	0.1628 (3.01)	0.06451 (1.72)	0.1664 (3.39)
Second lag	0.0379 (0.56)	−0.0629 (−1.53)	−0.0595 (−1.10)	−0.0739 (−2.00)	−0.0147 (−0.29)
Lag ln(unemployment rate for group)	−0.0509 (−0.66)	−0.0153 (−0.22)	−0.1422 (−0.81)	−0.0583 (−0.89)	−0.7644 (−3.64)
Second lag	−0.0104 (−0.14)	−0.0664 (−0.94)	−0.0624 (−0.36)	−0.0842 (−1.30)	−0.3288 (−1.56)
Lag ln(AFDC benefit level)	0.0255 (0.30)	—	—	—	—
Second lag	0.0989 (1.24)	—	—	—	—

Source: Author's estimates.
Notes: A *t*-statistic is in parentheses below each coefficient estimate. Each column shows coefficient estimates for a different equation; the dependent variable for the equation is the ln(state population) for the group named in the column heading. The estimate of each of the five equations presented in this table is based on 867 observations, for fifty states plus D.C., × seventeen years (1981 to 1997). Independent variables also include complete vectors of year dummies (sixteen variables) and state dummies (fifty variables) to control for fixed time period and state effects; coefficients on these variables are not reported to save space. Estimation uses 1979 state population as weight for each state-year cell observation. R-squared for each equation is as follows: female heads, 0.9925; other less-educated females, 0.9995; more-educated females, 0.9975; less-educated males, 0.9994; more-educated males, 0.9978.

wages should not have any permanent effects on output, rather, changes in wages would redistribute income among different claimants to the income resulting from production.

Estimation Results: Behavioral Elasticities Implied by the Model

In this section, I present the implications of the model's estimates for the elasticities of labor demand, supply, and other labor market behavior. The most important conclusion is that where the model is estimating behavioral

TABLE A2.9 *Personal Income Equation: (Dependent Variables: ln(State Personal Income))*

Independent Variable	Coefficient (t-statistic)
ln(Wage rate)	0.1862 (5.30)
Lag	−0.0903 (−2.12)
Second lag	−0.1126 (−3.37)
ln(Employment)	0.2670 (7.31)
Lag	−0.0053 (−0.12)
Second lag	−0.1350 (−3.62)
ln(Population)	−0.1539 (−3.18)
Lag	−0.0600 (−1.01)
Second lag	0.1492 (3.28)
Lag ln(Personal income)	1.0651 (28.72)
Second lag	−0.1688 (−4.20)

Source: Author's estimates.
Notes: The estimation is based on 867 observations, for fifty states plus D.C., × seventeen years (1981 to 1997). Independent variables also include complete vectors of year dummies (sixteen variables) and state dummies (fifty variables) to control for fixed time period and state effects; coefficients on these variables are not reported to save space. Estimation uses 1979 state population as weight for each state-year cell observation. R-squared is 0.9999.

elasticities for which there is much previous research, the model estimates are roughly consistent with the previous research literature.

The model's elasticity of overall labor demand with respect to wages is summarized in figure A2.1.[6] The figure shows the elasticity both with income held fixed and with income allowed to vary. The estimates here of income-constant elasticities (of −0.2 or −0.4 in the short run, and −0.8 after eight years or so) are consistent with estimates of output-constant labor demand elasticities in the literature (Hamermesh 1993). When per-

FIGURE A2.1 (− 1) Times Elasticity of Overall Employment Demand with Respect to Overall Wages, with and Without Income Varying

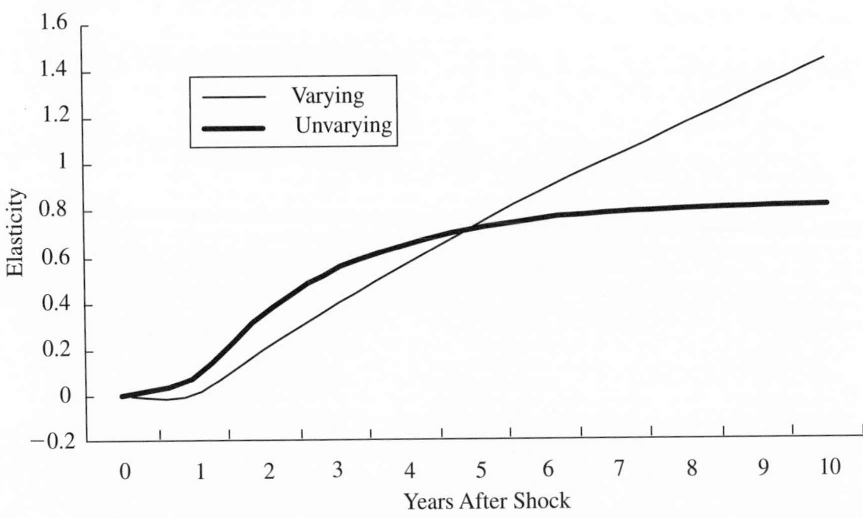

	Income Not Allowed to Vary	Income Allowed to Vary
Five years	0.717	0.722
	(11.22)	(5.84)
Ten years	0.808	1.431
	(12.43)	(4.48)

Source: Author's estimates.

Notes: Pseudo *t*-statistics, derived from 1,000 Monte Carlo repetitions of simulations, are in parentheses. Elasticities are derived from decreasing overall wages by 10 percent. The "income not allowed to vary" elasticities are based on simulations using only the overall labor demand evaluation of the model. Simulations with "income allowed to vary" also allow the income equation in the model to become operational, with feedback between labor demand and income equations.

sonal income is allowed to vary, the model implies that labor demand elasticities with respect to wages head off toward infinity in the very long run. This is consistent with economic theory: if production is constant returns to scale in capital and labor, and if in the long run capital is assumed to be perfectly elastically supplied at some fixed rate of return, and output is allowed to vary, then the long-run elasticity of labor demand with respect to the wage has to be infinite. Or to put it another way, only one wage rate, for a given technology, is consistent under these assumptions with a long-run general equilibrium, so any labor supply shock must be accommodated

FIGURE A2.2 *(– 1) Times Elasticity of Relative Labor Demand for Each Group with Respect to That Group's Relative Wage*

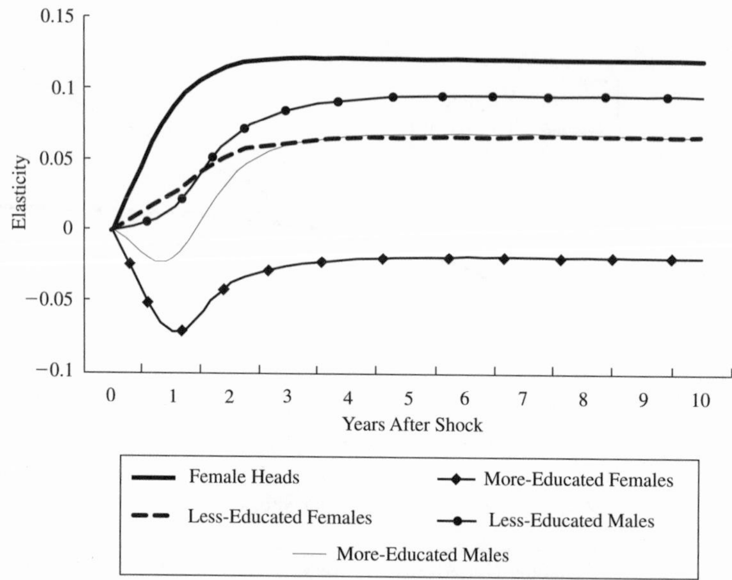

	Female Heads	Other Less-Educated Females	More-Educated Females	Less-Educated Males	More-Educated Males
Five-year elasticity	0.122 (1.29)	0.067 (4.24)	−0.019 (−0.26)	0.096 (3.58)	0.068 (1.79)

Source: Author's estimates.
Note: Pseudo *t*-statistics are in parentheses, derived from 1,000 Monte Carlo repetitions of effects of shock. Effects are (−1) times elasticity of ln(employment in group/employment overall) with respect to ln(wage of group/overall wage). Elasticities are derived from decreasing the wage of the group by .10, with resulting effects multiplied by ten to generate table and figure. Each simulation allows only the group's relative demand equation to become operational.

by adjustments in the capital stock and labor demand at the same wage rate. A wage decrease increases employment, greater employment increases income, greater income further increases employment, and so on.

Estimates of relative labor demand elasticities for labor types with respect to relative wages are shown in figure A2.2. Estimates of relative demand elasticities are modest, about 0.1 in absolute value after five years for most groups. These estimates are consistent with the minimum-wage literature (Katz 1998), although toward the low end of the demand elasticities implied by this literature.

Estimates of how relative labor demand responds to relative labor supply, holding relative wages constant, are presented in table A2.10. These effects of relative labor supply are large, consistent with the argument made in both appendices 1 and 2. There is no previous research that suggests a plausible size for such estimates.

Estimates of the elasticities of labor supply of different groups with respect to wages or unemployment are presented in table A2.11. Wages are estimated to have little effect on labor supply, with the exception of modest effects on the migration of male and female college graduates. This is consistent with the traditional conventional wisdom in economics, but inconsistent with more recent research by Juhn and his colleagues (1991). Unemployment rates have large effects on both labor force participation and migration. The effects on labor force participation and population migration are consistent with previous research (Bowen and Finegan 1969; Herzog, Schlottmann, and Boehm 1993).

As figure A2.3 shows, reductions in unemployment have large effects on wages. These effects on wages unfold gradually, so that the wage inflation rate is higher for a while after an unemployment reduction, resulting in a short-run Phillips curve. The nonlinearity of the wage curve implies that

TABLE A2.10 *Sensitivity of Relative Labor Demand to Relative Labor Supply, Holding Relative Wages Constant*

Group	Short-Run (Immediate) Elasticity	Implied Long-Run Elasticity
Female heads	0.375 (1.56)	0.486
Other less-educated females	0.850 (14.00)	0.919
More-educated females	0.301 (1.96)	0.451
Less-educated males	0.428 (3.44)	0.680
More-educated males	0.401 (3.98)	0.588

Source: Author's estimates.
Notes: Effects are derived directly from parameter estimates in relative labor demand elasticities. Short-run effect is from equation explaining ln(employment share of group) and is coefficient on ln(labor force share of group). A *t*-statistic is in parentheses below each coefficient estimate. Long-run effect is this short-run effect ÷ 1 − (sum of coefficients on two lagged dependent variables in equation).

TABLE A2.11 *Medium-Run Elasticities of Labor Supply with Respect to Wages and Unemployment*

	Female Heads	Other Less-Educated Females	More-Educated Females	Less-Educated Males	More-Educated Males	All Five Groups
Wage elasticities after five years						
Labor force participation rate	0.098	−0.025	−0.057	0.030	0.024	0.021
	(1.38)	(0.51)	(1.89)	(1.64)	(1.58)	(1.05)
Population	−0.140	−0.039	0.236	0.012	0.397	0.048
	(1.06)	(0.45)	(2.24)	(0.15)	(3.29)	(0.98)
Total labor force	−0.042	−0.064	0.178	0.042	0.421	0.069
	(0.28)	(0.66)	(1.63)	(0.49)	(3.44)	(1.33)
(−1) times unemployment elasticities after five years						
Labor force participation rate	0.298	0.661	0.149	0.374	0.173	0.492
	(3.18)	(5.15)	(1.07)	(8.02)	(2.04)	(8.92)
Population	0.121	0.262	0.447	0.508	2.769	0.632
	(0.66)	(1.17)	(0.89)	(2.60)	(3.83)	(4.25)
Total labor force	0.420	0.923	0.596	0.882	2.943	1.124
	(1.98)	(3.60)	(1.14)	(4.33)	(4.05)	(6.93)

Source: Author's compilation.
Notes: Estimates are derived from 1,000 Monte Carlo repetitions of two different simulations: one where all ln(wages) are increased by 0.10, the other where all unemployment rates are reduced by 0.01. Each simulation allows the labor force participation and population equation for that group only to become operational. Elasticities are change in natural logarithm of the three labor force variables divided by change in the wage or unemployment rate variable, and, for unemployment, multiplied by (−1). Absolute values of pseudo t-statistics are in parentheses below elasticity estimates and are equal to the absolute value of the mean elasticity from 1,000 repetitions divided by the standard deviation of elasticity in 1,000 repetitions. Estimates are elasticities after five years; elasticities slowly change only after five years. For example, the elasticity of the total overall labor force after ten years with respect to wages is 0.039 ($0.52 = t$), from 0.069 ($t = 1.33$) after five years. The elasticity of the overall total labor force after ten years with respect to unemployment is 1.408 ($t = 6.15$), compared to 1.124 ($t = 6.93$) after five years.

if unemployment is initially lower, a reduction in unemployment has effects on wages that are greater. The estimated size of the effects of unemployment on wages is consistent with the extensive research evidence presented in Blanchflower and Oswald (1994). They find a similar nonlinearity in estimated wage curves. However, unlike Blanchflower and Oswald, I estimate that unemployment's effects on wages unfold only gradually, since lagged wages are significant in the overall wage curve that I

FIGURE A2.3 *Elasticity of Overall Wages with Respect to Unemployment Under Conditions of High and Low Initial Unemployment*

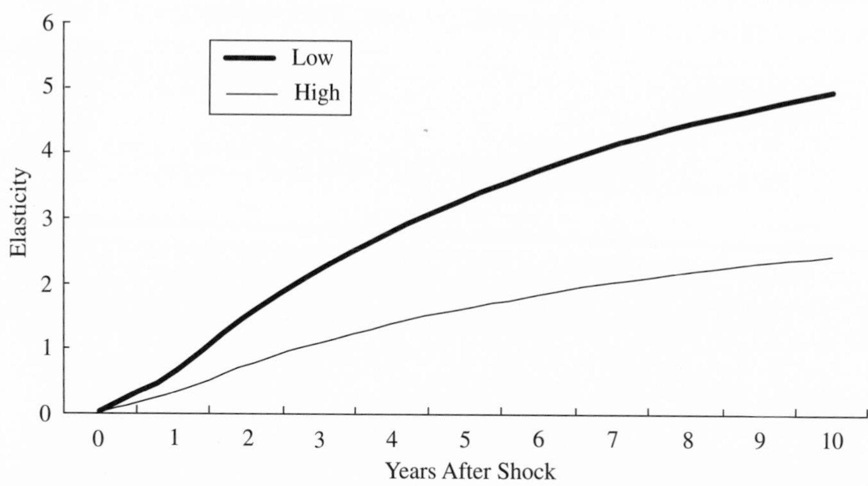

Elasticity of Wages with Respect to 1 Percentage Point Reduction in Unemployment Rate	Low Unemployment at Baseline	High Unemployment at Baseline
After five years	3.317	1.629
	(15.13)	(15.13)
After ten years	4.959	2.435
	(12.40)	(12.40)

Source: Author's estimates.
Notes: Results are change in ln(wage) × 100, for 1 percent reduction in unemployment rate of all five groups. A change from a 6 percent to a 5 percent unemployment rate is a 1 percent change in the unemployment rate. Base unemployment rates in low unemployment baseline are actual national unemployment rates for the five groups in 1997. For high unemployment baseline, actual national unemployment rates for the five groups as of 1982 were used. 1982 and 1997 were highest and lowest unemployment years in nation from 1979 to 1997. See table A2.2 for the actual values of unemployment rates for each group in 1982 and 1997.

estimate. This is consistent with more recent research by Blanchard and Katz (1997) on the wage curve.

Figure A2.4 shows that a change in unemployment of one group has effects on relative wages that are small, regardless of the initial unemployment rate. A 1 percent unemployment reduction for a group increases the group's relative wage by less than one-third of 1 percent after five years. Effects of overall unemployment on overall wages are five to ten times as great. The estimates are consistent with labor market institutions and cus-

FIGURE A2.4 *Group-Specific Elasticity with Respect to Unemployment for Group-Specific Wages Relative to Overall Wages Under Conditions of Low Initial Unemployment*

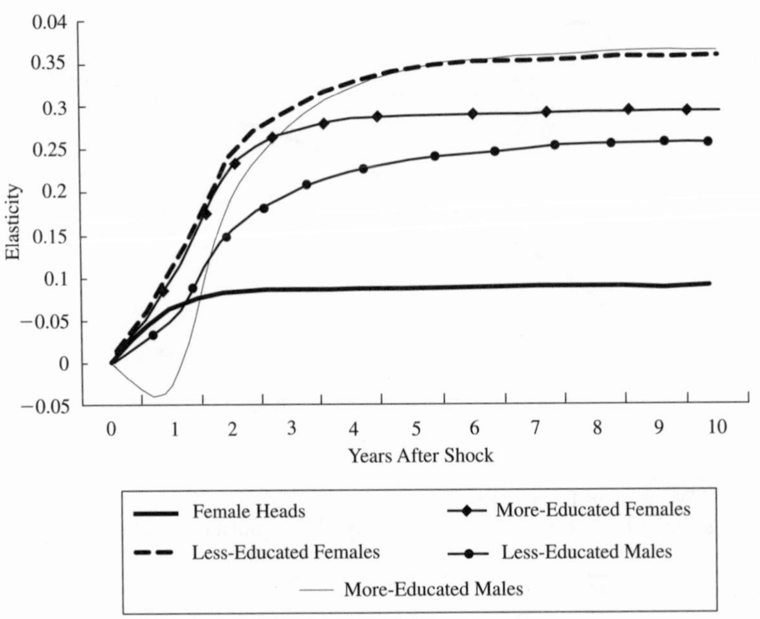

	Female Heads	Other Less-Educated Females	More-Educated Females	Less-Educated Males	More-Educated Males
Low unemployment baseline	0.085	0.341	0.287	0.236	0.342
	(3.70)	(3.02)	(2.97)	(3.70)	(2.27)
High unemployment baseline	0.047	0.142	0.273	0.173	0.322
	(3.84)	(3.86)	(2.83)	(3.18)	(2.15)

Source: Author's estimates.
Notes: Pseudo t-statistics are in parentheses, derived from 1,000 Monte Carlo repetitions of simulation. Simulation shows effect on 100 times ln(wage of group / average overall wage) of reduction of 1 percent in unemployment of that group, with unemployment rates for other groups staying unchanged.

toms that resist changes in relative wages. However, no previous empirical research has examined relative wage curves, so it is unclear whether this result would be robust to a variety of data and modeling assumptions.

The estimated wage curves, and the effects of unemployment on labor

FIGURE A2.5 *Complete Labor Supply Elasticities with and Without Population Adjustment Under Conditions of High (Bold Lines) and Low (Regular Lines) Initial Unemployment*

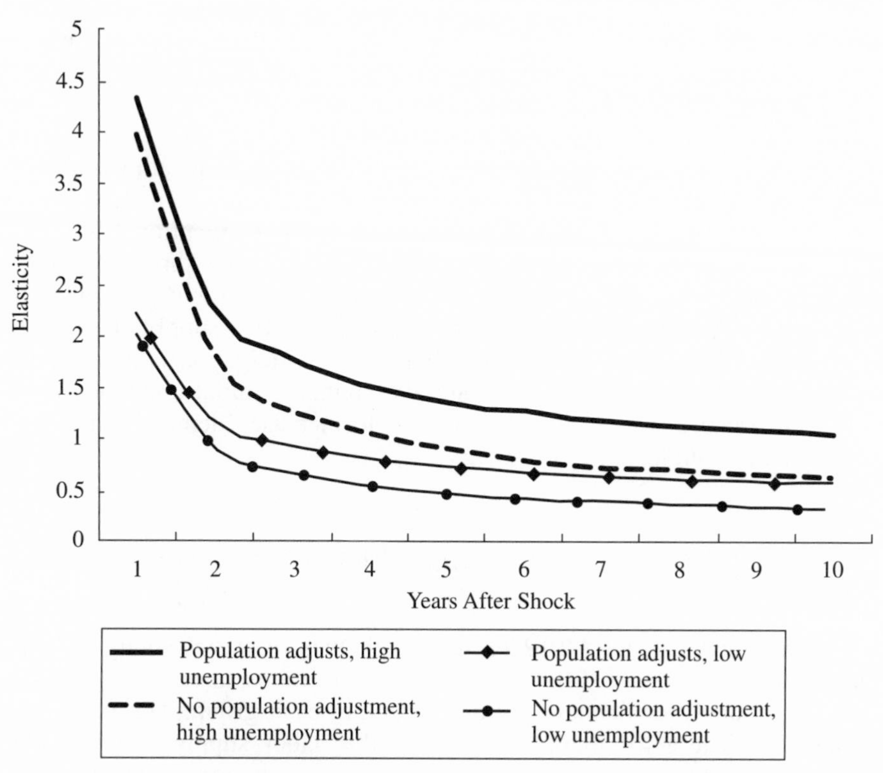

	Low Initial Unemployment Rate, No Population Adjustment Allowed	Low Initial Unemployment Rate, with Population Adjustment	High Initial Unemployment Rate, No Population Adjustment Allowed	High Initial Unemployment Rate, with Population Adjustment
Effective labor supply elasticity after five years	0.473 (12.71)	0.725 (10.14)	0.912 (12.94)	1.351 (10.12)

Source: Author's estimates.

Notes: These numbers are derived from a simulation that specified an exogenous 1 percent reduction in the unemployment rate for all groups and used wage curve equations, labor force participation rate equations, and population migration equations to simulate the effects of this change on wages and the labor force. The labor demand side of the model is suppressed for this exercise and is not allowed to adjust. The effective labor supply elasticity is the ratio of the change in the natural logarithm of the overall labor force to the change in the average log wage. Pseudo *t*-statistics from 1,000 Monte Carlo repetitions of simulation are in parentheses. Low initial unemployment rates are national unemployment rates of 1997(overall average: 5.0 percent), and high initial unemployment rates are national unemployment rates of 1982 (overall average: 9.9 percent).

force participation and migration, imply that the model's effective labor supply elasticity with respect to wages is much greater than the tiny wage elasticities of labor supply in table A2.11. An effective labor supply elasticity can be calculated by estimating the effect of a demand-induced change in unemployment on employment and wages. The ratio of the percentage change in employment to the percentage change in wages from this exercise is an effective labor supply elasticity.

Effective labor supply elasticities are shown in figure A2.5. These supply elasticities are large, particularly in the short run. In a wage curve model, short-run elasticities are large because employment adjusts faster than wages. Elasticities decline over time as wages adjust, although long-run elasticities are still higher than suggested by the conventional wisdom in economics, since labor supply increases can take place through adjustments in unemployment rates and adjustments in labor force participation in response to changes in unemployment rates. Effective supply elasticities are higher if population as well as labor force participation is allowed to adjust. Effective supply elasticities are also higher if initial unemployment is higher, because wages are less sensitive to increased demand when unemployment is high.

Empirical Results: Simulated Elasticities in Response to Labor Supply and Demand Policies

Using this model, table A2.12 presents estimates of the elasticity of employment and wages of different less-educated groups in response to various labor supply or demand policies targeting each group. The most important implication of these estimates is that labor supply and demand policies have significant employment effects, but also significant displacement effects.

The estimated elasticities show how a group's employment or market wages change five years after the policy is implemented. Five years is chosen as a reasonable medium-term effect that should be well measured by the model, allowing the model dynamics to work out for a bit without being too heroic about assuming that we understand the long-run dynamics perfectly. The model is identified by the assumption that the current values of most independent variables do not matter, so short-run estimates (zero to two years, for example) may tend to yield understated effects, since the model imposes the assumption that very short-term effects are zero. On the other hand, a model that has only two lags in all variables may not capture the truly long-run effects of policies, after ten years or so.

The impact estimates captured in table A2.12 essentially compare market wages and employment for a group in two worlds, one in which a

TABLE A2.12 *Simulations, Based on an Empirically Estimated Dynamic Model, of Elasticities After Five Years of Wages and Employment of Various Less-Educated Groups in Response to a Supply or Demand Policy Targeting That Group*

	Employment and Wage Elasticities for Group from Policy Targeting That Group[a]							
	Quantity Increase in Labor Demand		Quantity Increase in Labor Supply		Demand-Side Wage Subsidy to Employer		Supply-Side Wage Subsidy to Worker	
Group	Employment	Wage	Employment	Wage	Employment	Wage	Employment	Wage
Less-educated female heads of household	0.65 (3.21)	0.14 (4.89)	0.42 (1.75)	−0.11 (−5.61)	0.16 (1.57)	0.04 (3.60)	0.04 (0.99)	−0.01 (−1.32)
Other less-educated females	0.58 (7.84)	0.94 (11.97)	0.69 (10.56)	−0.67 (−11.72)	0.40 (11.12)	0.43 (6.15)	−0.01 (−0.46)	0.01 (0.27)
Less-educated males	0.64 (7.28)	1.27 (12.44)	0.66 (8.04)	−0.91 (−5.67)	0.47 (10.93)	0.61 (5.88)	0.01 (1.14)	−0.02 (−1.07)

Source: Author's estimates.

Notes: See appendix 2 for the model and equations used to produce these numbers. Elasticities are calculated as change in ln(employment) or ln(market wage) of group, divided by the effect that the policy initially has on the natural log of the appropriate variable for the policy for that group. The divisor for elasticities is the initial shock due to policy to ln(employment of group) for quantity increase in labor demand, initial shock due to policy to ln(wage paid by employers for group) for wage subsidy to employers, initial shock due to policy to ln(labor force of group) for quantity increase in labor supply, and initial shock due to policy to ln(wage received by workers in group) for wage subsidy to workers. Estimated elasticities are effects after five years of running models for each of these twelve shocks (four different types of policies, each of three groups). Population-migration equations in the model are suppressed to approximate the "national" effects of implementing the policy in all states; the implicit assumption is that if all states pursue the same policy, there would be no incentives for in- or out-migration. Pseudo t-statistics in parentheses are derived from 1,000 Monte Carlo repetitions of simulation, with each repetition randomly choosing a set of parameter estimates from the estimated distribution of the model's parameter estimates. Pseudo t-statistics are ratio of mean results from 1,000 Monte Carlo repetitions to standard deviation of results in these 1,000 repetitions. Estimates are based on initially low-unemployment rate scenario, where overall unemployment situation for 1997 is used, with overall unemployment of 5 percent, and unemployment rate for various groups as given in table A2.2.

[a] Percentage change in employment or wages of each group for a 1 percent increase in labor demand or supply for that group, or a 1 percent wage subsidy to workers in that group or to employers of that group.

policy targeting that group is implemented, and the other in which that policy is not implemented. The impact estimates are derived by simulating the model one thousand times, with each simulation randomly drawing a set of parameter estimates from the estimated statistical distribution of parameter estimates. These one thousand repetitions of the models can be used to generate pseudo standard errors and t-statistics for these estimated impacts.

As mentioned earlier, the elasticity estimates are derived from a model that omits the migration equations and essentially treats population as exogenous. The argument is that suppressing migration captures the elasticities that would occur if every state simultaneously pursued the same policy, or the "national" effects of a "national" policy. If just one state pursued a labor market policy, the impact on that state of the policy would be in part determined by population in- or out-migration, and that migration in turn would have spillover effects on labor markets in other states. But if every state simultaneously pursued the same policy, the incentives for any migration would be much less, and perhaps even zero, as assumed. If migration is the main way in which labor market policies have spillover effects across states, then this suppression of migration is the right way to capture the effects of a policy that is pursued throughout the nation.

The model elasticities depend on the initial unemployment rate, since this affects the sensitivity of wages to unemployment. The results presented in table A2.12 assume that unemployment rates are at the lowest levels observed nationally during the estimation period, which occurred in 1997, when overall unemployment was 5 percent and the different groups' unemployment rates were as given in table A2.2. The simulations were also run when unemployment was at its highest national level during the estimation period, which occurred in 1982, when overall national unemployment was 9.9 percent. The high-unemployment simulation results are somewhat more favorable to labor demand policies, and somewhat less favorable to labor supply policies, since overall wages are less sensitive to unemployment changes when unemployment is high. However, the difference in the relative effectiveness of labor demand and supply policies between the low- and high-unemployment baselines is modest.

The estimated elasticities reported in table A2.12 generally are consistent with the theoretical elasticities calculated in appendix 1. However, there are some interesting differences between the estimated elasticities and the theoretical calculations, differences that in part reflect differences in behavioral elasticities and in part reflect the differences between the general equilibrium model estimated in this appendix and the partial equilibrium model used in appendix 1.

Notable results in table A2.12 include the following:

The model estimates significant employment and displacement elasticities. The model estimates that a quantity shock to the labor demand or supply of a group generally causes an employment impact of about two-thirds the size of the shock. The implied displacement effect is about one-third the size of the shock. The employment effects of both demand and supply policies are larger in the empirical model than in the theoretical calculations of appendix 1 because of the multiplier effects incorporated in this general equilibrium model. Particularly for the groups that make up a larger share of the labor market, labor supply and labor demand policies, by expanding overall employment, cause an expansion in overall income via the income equation of the model, which in turn feeds back into further employment expansion. This multiplier effect also explains why the employment elasticities of the demand and supply quantity shocks no longer sum to one, whereas in the theoretical model of appendix 1 the sum of the employment elasticities of demand and supply quantity shocks must be exactly one.

A supply-side wage subsidy has few effects. In table A2.12, supply-side wage subsidies to workers have few effects on either employment or market wages. This reflects this model's empirical estimates that the wage elasticity of labor supply is small. Even though labor supply does not respond much to wages, demand-side policies can still have considerable effects on employment by lowering unemployment and by increasing labor force participation through lower unemployment.

Demand-side wage subsidies can have significant effects on employment for groups that make up large shares of the labor force. In contrast to the theoretical results in appendix 1, in table A2.12 demand-side wage subsidies have substantial effects on the employment of other less-educated females and less-educated males. These groups are each a sizable share of the labor market (36 percent of the population for other less-educated females, and 8 percent for less-educated males). The substantial effects of wage subsidies on employment for these groups occur despite the very small elasticities of relative employment shares in response to relative wages that are estimated in this model. But because these two groups are relatively large shares of the overall labor force, wage subsidies to these groups have substantial effects on overall labor demand, thus boosting employment for all groups, including the group subsidized.

Wage rate effects of policies tend to be larger for groups that are a larger share of the labor force. In contrast to the theoretical model of appendix 1, the wage rate effects of policies tend to be considerably larger for the groups that are a large share of the labor force. Even though relative wages are little affected by changes in relative unemployment rates, these groups are a large enough share of the labor force that supply or demand policies applied to them have substantial effects on overall unemployment and overall wages.

Thus, in general the results are consistent with the theoretical model of appendix 1 except in two respects. First, labor supply or demand policies applied to a group that is a substantial share of the labor force may have important general equilibrium or macro effects that are not taken account of in appendix 1 but are in table A2.12. Second, the estimated model in table A2.12 has tiny wage elasticities of labor supply, whereas the theoretical model of appendix 1 has modest wage elasticities of labor supply; as a result, this appendix's appraisal of supply-side wage elasticities is more pessimistic than the appraisal in appendix 1.

Conclusion

The empirical model presented, estimated, and simulated in this appendix suggests, consistent with appendix 1, that labor demand or supply policies that directly increase the quantity of labor demand or supply have substantial employment effects, but also substantial displacement effects. The model constructed and estimated here suggests that considerable variation in group unemployment rates, and a consequent variation in labor force participation and employment, is likely to occur in the short run and the medium run in response to policies affecting labor supply or demand. These variations in unemployment rates are substantially but not completely offset by the variations in labor demand that occur in response to changing unemployment rates. As a result, both employment and displacement effects are substantial. In contrast, the effects of wage subsidies on labor supply or demand are more uncertain and depend crucially on what one estimates or assumes about the wage elasticities of labor demand and supply for different groups or for overall labor.

The results should be interpreted as suggestive rather than definitive. Many of the empirical parameters estimated here have not been extensively researched in previous studies. In addition, more research needs to be done to see how robust these results are to alternative model structures, data sets, or estimation techniques. However, it is certainly quite plausible that group unemployment rates may vary in response to policies that successfully provide some initial boost to labor supply or demand, and that such unemployment effects are not close to being completely offset by demand responses in the short run or the medium run. Hence, the qualitative result—that quantity policies in general have substantial employment and displacement effects—should be taken seriously, even if there is considerable uncertainty about the exact magnitude of such effects or the dynamics of how such effects evolve over time. Finally, it should be noted that the model constructed here is not really appropriate for addressing the very long-run effects of policies. The model does not include crucial features that might help determine such long-run effects. For example, the model does not in any serious way incorporate the possibility that short-run and medium-run employment experiences have long-run human capital effects on the employability or wages of less-educated persons. As discussed in the text, these hysteresis effects are probably important in determining long-run effects of supply and demand policies.

Appendix 3

SIMULATED DISPLACEMENT AND WAGE EFFECTS OF WELFARE REFORM, BASED ON AN EMPIRICALLY ESTIMATED GENERAL EQUILIBRIUM MODEL OF A LABOR MARKET WITH MULTIPLE GROUPS

I HAVE recently (Bartik 2000a) used the model presented in Bartik (1999) and appendix 2 of this book to estimate the displacement and wage effects of welfare reform. This model divides the labor market into five groups and estimates labor supply, labor demand, and wage curves for each of these five groups. The effects of welfare reform in this model are estimated based on assumptions about how welfare reform will affect the labor supply of different groups over the period 1994 to 2008. The largest percentage effects of welfare reform are on the labor supply of the "less-educated female heads of household," or "single mother," group in this labor market model. Welfare reform will have a peak effect on this group of increasing its labor supply by 12 percent in 2004.

What does this model suggest will be welfare reform's labor market effects? For average wages and unemployment for the overall population, welfare reform's effects are modest and quickly dissipated (Bartik 2000a). Overall effects are modest because welfare reform's effect on labor supply is a modest percentage of overall labor supply; furthermore, overall labor demand responds strongly to a labor supply shock, because a supply shock increases overall output. Effects are larger for the group whose labor supply is most affected by welfare reform—single mothers with modest education. As shown in figure A3.1, although this group's wages never decline more than 2 percent owing to welfare reform, unemployment of this group goes up and stays up owing to welfare reform, increasing in some years by more than four points. This four-point increase is for a group that in 1993 already was experiencing 12 percent unemployment. Wage rate effects for single mothers are modest because the model suggests, consistent with the discussion in chapter 3, that relative wages are resistant to change; because overall wages are not much affected by welfare reform, the wage rates of

FIGURE A3.1 *Percentage Impacts of Welfare Reform on Wage Rate and Unemployment Rate of Female Heads*

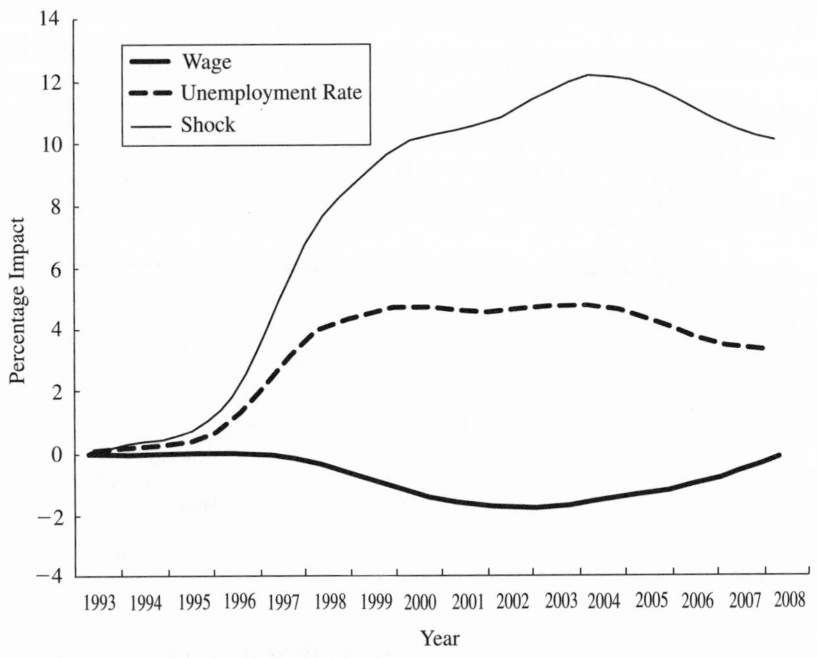

Source: Estimates derived by simulating model of appendix 2 and Bartik (1999) for welfare reform shock, as described in Bartik (2000a).
Notes: Effects on logarithmic variables are multiplied by 100 to get effects in percentage terms. For comparison, figure also reports labor supply shock on females heads as percentage of baseline labor force of female heads. "Female heads" are female heads of household, with other relatives present, with less than a college degree.

single mothers cannot decline much. However, the model also suggests, consistent with chapter 3, that employers' relative demand for different groups is not very sensitive to relative wages or relative labor supply. As a result, labor demand for single mothers does not increase enough to match the increased labor supply of this group caused by welfare reform.

Because welfare reform increases the unemployment of single mothers, welfare reform has displacement effects on this group. Table A3.1 shows displacement rates for different groups and overall. These displacement rates are the ratio of the jobs lost by those individuals who were working prior to welfare reform to the jobs gained by the individuals forced into the labor market by welfare reform. As the table shows, in the short run welfare reform has considerable *overall* displacement effects,

TABLE A3.1 *Displacement Effects of Welfare Reform*

Group	2000	2004	2008
Female heads	0.29	0.26	0.21
	(2.69)	(2.41)	(2.03)
Other women with less than a college degree	0.31	0.01	−0.34
	(6.89)	(0.10)	(2.96)
Women with college education	0.03	−0.10	−0.26
	(1.49)	(2.96)	(4.73)
Men with less than college education	0.21	−0.14	−0.50
	(3.95)	(1.64)	(3.96)
Men with college education	0.05	−0.08	−0.23
	(2.46)	(2.35)	(4.32)
Overall average	0.89	−0.06	−1.10
	(18.14)	(0.32)	(3.43)

Source: Estimates derived by using the model presented in Bartik (1999) and appendix 2 to simulate the effects of welfare reform, as described by Bartik (2000a).
Notes: Displacement is defined in this table as: [(−1) × change in employment of original members of group] / (total change in employment of those entering labor force due to welfare reform). That is, the denominator is the same for all five groups, and the sum of the displacement numbers for each group is equal to overall average displacement. Numbers in parentheses are absolute values of pseudo *t*-statistics for testing whether estimated displacement is zero, and are derived by dividing the estimates by the standard deviations from 1,000 Monte Carlo simulations of model.

with eighty-nine employed individuals losing their jobs for every one hundred ex-welfare recipients who obtain jobs.[1] But in the long run this displacement disappears. In the long run welfare reform has multiplier effects on the overall economy, with expanded national income due to extra labor supply expanding overall national employment *more* than the number of ex-welfare recipients who get jobs. However, displacement among single mothers stays high. For every one hundred ex-welfare recipients who get jobs owing to welfare reform, more than twenty single mothers who otherwise would be employed are without jobs.

For more details on this model, see Bartik (1999) or appendix 2. For more details on the application of this model to welfare reform, see Bartik (2000a).

Appendix 4

THE LABOR MARKET EFFECTS OF EDUCATION

THE DISPLACEMENT effects of education can be simulated with the empirically estimated general equilibrium model of a five-group labor market developed in Bartik (1999) and described in appendix 2. Six simulations were done, three for a low-unemployment baseline and three for a high-unemployment baseline. For each unemployment baseline, simulations were done for three different scenarios: moving 0.1 percent of the population from the less-educated female head group to the more-educated female group; moving 0.1 percent of the population from the other less-educated female group to the more-educated female group; and moving 0.1 percent of the population from the less-educated male group to the more-educated male group.

Table A4.1 summarizes the main features of these simulation results. The table shows earnings effects on different groups, and for the entire population ages sixteen to sixty-four, in comparison to earnings effects on the 0.1 percent of the population that is educated in each simulation. Earnings effects are measured as the change in the product of wages times the employment rate for each group. (Changes in weekly work hours are ignored because weekly work hours are not used in or calculated in this model.) The 0.1 percent of the population that receives a college education in each scenario approximately doubles its earnings.

As the table shows, educating some groups has spillover effects on other groups that are quite large. For example, the ratio of the earnings effects on the more-educated group that the newly educated join to the earnings effects on the group educated is always a negative number somewhat greater than one in absolute value. For example, consider the effects after five years of providing less-educated female heads of household with a college education, assuming a low-unemployment baseline. For this case, the ratio of the earnings effects on the group joined to the earnings gain for the group educated is given in the table as −1.555. In other words, for every dollar in earnings gained by the female heads of household who receive a college education, women who already were college-educated

TABLE A4.1 *Effects of Education on Earnings of Different Groups*

	Low Unemployment Rate, Effects After Five Years	Low Unemployment Rate, Effects After Ten Years	High Unemployment Rate, Effects After Five Years	High Unemployment Rate, Effects After Ten Years
Female heads				
Ratio: (earnings effects on group left)/(earnings gains for group educated)	0.596 (2.28)	0.615 (2.35)	0.550 (2.30)	0.557 (2.33)
Ratio: (earnings effects on group joined)/(earnings gains for group educated)	−1.555 (3.30)	−1.445 (3.09)	−1.486 (3.31)	−1.445 (3.21)
Ratio: (total earnings effects for population)/(earnings gains for group educated)	−0.280 (0.91)	0.635 (1.90)	−0.051 (0.27)	0.259 (1.38)
Other less-educated females				
Ratio: (earnings effects on group left)/(earnings gains for group educated)	0.113 (0.98)	0.481 (3.19)	0.133 (1.42)	0.265 (2.62)
Ratio: (earnings effects on group joined)/(earnings gains for group educated)	−1.443 (3.31)	−1.275 (2.95)	−1.355 (3.27)	−1.295 (3.13)
Ratio: (total earnings effects for population)/(earnings gains for group educated)	−0.438 (1.53)	1.001 (2.37)	−0.072 (0.43)	0.413 (1.96)
Less-educated males				
Ratio: (earnings effects on group left)/(earnings gains for group educated)	0.420 (3.02)	0.673 (4.57)	0.424 (3.46)	0.496 (4.16)
Ratio: (earnings effects on group joined)/(earnings gains for group educated)	−1.320 (4.55)	−1.165 (4.17)	−1.224 (4.54)	−1.163 (4.44)
Ratio: (total earnings effects for population)/(earnings gains for group educated)	−0.007 (0.04)	0.668 (3.07)	0.139 (0.99)	0.365 (2.58)

Source: Author's estimates.

Notes: These results are estimated from the five-group model described in appendix 2 and Bartik (1999). The table presents ratios of the effects on "earnings" (dollar effects on earnings, defined as the change in the product of wage times employment rate) of different groups to effects on earnings of individuals who are "educated" by leaving a low-education group and joining a higher-education group. Absolute values of pseudo *t*-statistics are in parentheses and are derived from 1,000 Monte Carlo repetitions of simulations. The earnings effects analyzed are for the low-education group that loses some population, the high-education group that gains some population, and for everyone. The earnings effects calculated for the group receiving education assume that this group before and after being switched from one population to another has wages and an employment rate similar to whatever group it is in at the moment. Three different education switches are considered: switching some female heads to the college-educated female group; switching some less-educated females to the more-educated female group; switching some less-educated men to the more-educated male group. Simulations are all for switch of one-tenth of 1 percent of overall population. Generally, the group that is educated approximately doubles its average earnings, mostly owing to gaining wages from switching to college-educated group. Initial unemployment rates that are low and high correspond to 5.0 percent and 9.9 percent overall unemployment, the lowest and highest unemployment rates in the 1979 to 1997 sample period for which this model is estimated. See Bartik (1999) and appendix 2 for more details.

lose about $1.56 in earnings, owing to reductions in both their employment rate and their wage rate. The employment rate and wage rate of this already-educated group go down because of the added competition from the additional labor supply of college-educated women.

Providing a college education to some groups also has spillover effects on persons who do not receive a college education. Consider again the case of the effects after five years of providing some female heads of household with a college education, under a low-unemployment rate scenario. The table reports the ratio of the earnings effects on the non-college-educated group left behind to the earnings effects on the female heads who receive a college education is 0.596. For every dollar of earnings gained by female heads who receive a college education, the less-educated female heads who do *not* receive a college education also reap an earnings gain of $0.60, owing to increases in both their employment rate and their wage rate. The employment rate and wage rate of this group go up because of the reduced labor supply of non-college-educated women.

The table also reports the sum of these earnings effects across all five groups in the labor market. This total earnings effect is also reported as a ratio to the earnings gains for the group that is educated. As the table shows, these total earnings effects vary a great deal over time and with the initial unemployment rate. In general, after five years the model estimates that there are few aggregate earnings effects of education. Education mostly redistributes earnings across different groups. But after ten years, education does have considerable net earnings effects over the entire population. These net earnings effects are higher when unemployment is initially low. When unemployment is initially low, overall wages are more responsive to the labor supply increases brought about by providing some persons with a college education, since under low unemployment wages are more responsive to unemployment changes (see appendix 2). This greater responsiveness of wages causes aggregate labor demand to be more responsive to the increased labor supply caused by education.

More details on this simulation are provided in Bartik (1999).

Appendix 5

PROCEDURES FOR DETERMINING THE CHANGES IN EDUCATION LEVELS NEEDED TO REVERSE RECENT U.S. TRENDS IN EARNINGS AND WAGE DIFFERENTIALS

I FIRST use the empirically estimated general equilibrium wage curve model with five labor force groups of appendix 2 to calculate the change in education needed to move college versus noncollege earnings differentials from 1998 values back to 1979 values. This elaborate calculation is done in the following way.

1. First, we calculate earnings differentials for non-college-educated and college-educated males, based on table 4.8. Using appropriate weights, we calculate the average wage of male nongraduates and the average employment rate of male nongraduates. We take the product of this figure and multiply by 2,000 hours to get annual earnings of $29,235. Similar calculations yield a male graduate annual earnings figure of $41,804. The ratio is 1.430. The differential in logarithmic terms is ln(1.43) = 0.3577.
2. Similar calculations for 1998 yield annual earnings numbers of $24,390 for male nongraduates and $43,915 for male graduates. The ratio is 1.801, and the logarithmic differential is 0.5883. The logarithmic differential between male graduates and nongraduates grew by (0.5883 − 0.3577 = 0.2306) between 1979 and 1998.
3. The empirical estimates in the simulation for the effects of education are for a switch of 0.001 of the overall population between the ages of sixteen and sixty-four from male nongraduates to male graduates. The estimated elasticities (the ratio of change in ln[earnings], where ln earnings is sum of ln[wage] and ln[employment rate]) are 1.649 for nongraduates and −5.393 for graduates. If we assume that the effects are approximately log linear, as suggested by experiments, then the needed switch in male nongraduates to graduates is the solution to the following equation: (1.649 + 5.393)Pm = 0.2306. Solving for Pm

yields 0.0327—that is, a switch of about 3.3 percent of the population age sixteen to sixty-four would be needed to bring ratios between male graduate and nongraduate earnings back to their 1979 levels.

4. For women, I first calculate earnings figures for each year and each group (nongraduates and graduates). These figures for 1979 are $11,803 (nongraduate) and $21,566 (graduate), and for 1998, $15,363 (nongraduate) and $30,653 (graduate). The log differential grew from 0.6028 to 0.6908, an increase of 0.088.
5. Applying the empirical estimates from the simulations is more difficult because the model has two female groups with less than a college education: female heads (FH) and other less-educated females (LEF). I assume that the education shock from nongraduate to graduate comes from each group in proportion to its share of the female nongraduate group. These shares are 0.101 (FH) and 0.899 (LEF). Elasticities for the switch from FH to female graduate are 17.12 for FH and −8.35 for graduate. Elasticities for the switch from LEF to graduate are 1.45 for LEF and −7.85 for graduate. The relevant equation using the weights is: Pf [0.101(17.12 + 8.35) + 0.899(1.45 + 7.85)] = 0.088. Solving this yields Pf = 0.00805. Restoring the 1979 ratio of graduate to nongraduate earnings among females would require a switch of eight-tenths of 1 percent of the sixteen-to-sixty-four population between female nongraduates and graduates.
6. As of July 1, 1998, there were 173.7 million Americans between the ages of sixteen and sixty-four (www.census.gov). Hence, the required number of new male college graduates is 5.68 million, and the required number of female college graduates is 1.40 million, for a total of 7.08 million. As of 1997, there were 42.5 million college graduates in the U.S. population (National Center for Education Statistics 1999, table 9). So this increase of 7.08 million is an increase of 16.7 percent in the number of college graduates. If we imagine such an increase happening over the nineteen years from 1980 to 1998, the annual number of additional graduates is 373,000 (7.08/19). Over that time period, 20.01 million bachelor's degrees were awarded in the United States (National Center for Education Statistics 1999, table 244), so this would be an average annual increase of 35.4 percent in the number of bachelor's degrees awarded.
7. Average annual educational and general expenditure per student in higher education was $11,319 (in 1998 dollars) from 1995 to 1996 (National Center for Education Statistics 1999, table 336). If we assume that the 7.08 million graduates would each on average need four additional years of education, the total spending required would be four times 7.08 million times $11,319, or $320.6 billion. If this were spent over nineteen years, the average annual expenditure would be $16.9 billion. This compares with total educational general expenditures from 1995 to 1996 (in 1998 dollars) of $161.4 billion (National

Center for Education Statistics 1999, table 336). Thus, the required expenditure increase in annual educational spending is around 10.5 percent. This percentage increase is considerably less than the percentage increase in bachelor's degrees because many students in U.S. universities are not in the process of successfully earning a bachelor's degree—either they are getting some other degree or they will drop out before receiving a bachelor's degree.

Using the model of Borjas, Freeman, and Katz (1997), I do a similar calculation of the needed increase in college graduates to move graduate-nongraduate wage ratios from their 1995 level back to their 1980 level. Borjas, Freeman, and Katz (1997) report an increase in this log wage ratio of 0.191 from 1980 to 1995. They also report an estimate that the elasticity of response of this log wage ratio to the log of the relative labor supply of college-equivalent versus high school–equivalent labor is −0.709. (Their college-equivalent category is all college graduates plus half of those with some college; high school equivalents are all those with a high school degree or less plus half of those with some college). Hence, to reduce this wage ratio by 0.191 would require an increase in the log labor supply ratio of college-equivalent to high school–equivalent labor of 0.269 ([−0.191]/[−0.709]). They report that 42.6 percent of American workers are college equivalents. Using these figures, a little algebra shows that increasing the log labor supply ratio of college equivalents to non-equivalents by 0.269 would require increasing the number of college equivalents by 15.7 percent. The estimated number of college equivalents as of 1995 was 53.2 million. So the increase in the number of college equivalents required is 8.3 million. This could be accomplished if 8.3 million persons with a high school degree or less acquired a college degree, or if 16.6 million persons with some college got a college degree. Either way, the required increase in college graduates and the associated expense are enormous.

Appendix 6

SIMULATIONS OF THE EFFECTS OF EDUCATION ON EMPLOYMENT

THESE simulations use the model of appendix 2 and Bartik (1999). The education simulations are the same as those in appendix 4: three different education scenarios, each moving 0.1 percent of the population from a less-educated category to a college-educated category. For this appendix, I consider only results from a low-unemployment baseline and focus on effects ten years after the education shock.

Table A6.1 summarizes the results, which are reported as ratios of the number of jobs gained by different groups to the numbers of persons educated. In other words, these ratios show how many jobs are gained per person educated. As the table shows, the number of jobs gained by the group that is educated is between 14 and 19 percent of the number of persons educated. This effect is modest because employment rates for these persons before they had a college degree were considerably more than zero, and their employment rates after attaining a college degree are still less than one. In addition, the decline in labor supply of less-educated workers because of the education program opens up some job opportunities for the remaining less-educated workers. The number of additional jobs for the remaining less-educated workers is estimated in this model to be between 32 and 41 percent of the number of persons receiving a college degree. The effects are considerably less than one for one, but considerably more than zero: when labor supply leaves the less-educated market, demand in this market does decline significantly but not by as much as the drop in labor supply, thus offering some additional job openings for those remaining, but less than the numbers of those educated. The net effect is that for each person educated, the number of jobs for less-educated workers, including those educated, goes up by between 0.6 and 0.8 jobs.

TABLE A6.1 *Effects of Education on Employment of Low-Education Groups*

Group	Employment Effects per Person Educated of Educating Single Mothers	Employment Effects per Person Educated of Educating Other Women	Employment Effects per Person Educated of Educating Men
Employment effects on group being educated	0.165 (109.4)	0.192 (129.6)	0.139 (187.2)
Employment effects on group "left behind"	0.362 (2.40)	0.320 (3.61)	0.405 (5.02)
Sum of employment effects on all less-educated groups (including those who gain education)	0.709 (3.88)	0.817 (4.47)	0.643 (6.08)
Sum of employment effects on entire labor force (including those who are more educated)	0.305 (2.10)	0.507 (3.47)	0.300 (3.74)

Source: Author's estimates.

Notes: Employment effects stated are *ratio* of net increase in jobs for indicated group or groups to number of people who gain education. The columns consider the effects of providing a college education to some number of individuals from three groups: single mothers ages sixteen to forty-four with less than a college education (column 1); other women ages sixteen to sixty-four with less than a college education (column 2); men with less than a college education (column 3). Rows consider effect on: employment of group that is educated (row 1); employment of those who do *not* receive a college education in the group that is educated (row 2); total employment of all those who originally, before the education program, had less than a college education (row 3); total employment of everyone (row 4). Estimates are derived from three simulations, in each of which 0.1 percent of the population in some less-educated group is switched to a more-educated group. Simulation assumes that initially unemployment is low, at 5.0 percent (1997 actual level). The estimated employment effects are effects ten years after the education "shock" occurs. Numbers in parentheses are pseudo t-statistics on estimates, derived from 1,000 Monte Carlo repetitions of simulation.

Appendix 7

AN ILLUSTRATIVE SIMULATION OF HOW LONG-RUN DISPLACEMENT EFFECTS OF LABOR DEMAND POLICIES VARY WITH LABOR MARKET CONDITIONS AND HOW THE POLICY AFFECTS LABOR SUPPLY

THIS appendix uses the model of appendix 2 to look at how the long-run displacement effects of labor demand policies vary under different assumptions about local labor market conditions and about how the policy is conducted. As discussed in appendix 2, this model is an empirically estimated general equilibrium model of the labor market that divides the labor force into five groups and incorporates involuntary unemployment. Because the model includes only two lags in the various independent variables and two lagged dependent variables in most equations, it is somewhat heroic to assume that the model accurately represents long-run effects. In particular, with only two lags, the model has a tendency to impose the assumption that employment rates return to their original equilibrium after some time. For example, the model's assumptions that only two lags in labor force participation matter to future labor force participation makes it difficult for the model to show any long-run hysteresis effects of work experience on the labor force's employability. However, the model is useful for showing how long-run effects of demand shocks in a simulation model can vary greatly with the local unemployment rate and with how the demand shock affects labor supply.

For this illustration, I use the model to simulate the displacement effects after ten years of a permanent labor demand increase for the model group called "less-educated males," which is all males ages sixteen to sixty-four with less than a college education. In the baseline scenario, I assume that the unemployment rate is low. I assume that the jobs created are permanent jobs paying market wages, and that the jobs are filled simply by hiring from the ranks of unemployed less-educated males. Under these assumptions, after ten years, for every job created for less-educated males, hiring by regular employers of less-educated males is reduced by one, resulting in 100 percent displacement and zero net increase in employment for less-educated males (table A7.1). In addition, other persons also lose their jobs, so on net the program after ten years slightly reduces overall employment. These effects occur owing to a combination of the low unemployment rate and the implications of the government reducing the pool of unemployed less-educated men. With low unemployment, wage rates are more sensitive to labor demand increases, resulting in a larger initial increase in wages and hence a greater reduction in overall labor demand. Because the program hires unemployed less-educated male workers for permanent jobs paying market wages, it reduces the supply of unemployed less-educated male workers to other employers. As vacancies are created over time, a lower proportion of these vacancies are filled by less-educated male workers. As mentioned earlier, because the model allows only two lags in labor force participation to affect future labor force participation, the model allows only a limited scope for long-run effects of work experience, so the model may miss some long-run effects of short-run work experience in positively affecting the employment rate of less-educated males.

As mentioned in chapter 5, the long-run displacement effects of labor demand policies are smaller if unemployment is higher. With higher unemployment, wages respond much more sluggishly to an increase in labor demand. As a result, private labor demand is not as depressed by the increase in labor demand induced by public policy, resulting in less displacement. For example, the second row of table A7.1 considers the displacement effects of a labor demand policy that increases demand for less-educated males, if unemployment is initially high. With initially high unemployment, after ten years, for every two jobs for less-educated men created by the policy, other employers create one less job opportunity for less-educated men, and overall employment of less-educated males increases by one. The displacement effects are about half of what they are under low-unemployment conditions. The range of unemployment conditions considered in the table corresponds to the lowest and highest unemployment years observed in the United States from 1979 to 1997. The highest unemployment year was 1982, at 9.9 percent, and 1997 was the lowest unemployment year, at 5.0 percent. Under more typical unemployment conditions, displacement rates would be somewhere between these extremes.

The displacement effects of labor demand policies are also lower if the workers hired for these jobs are still available to be hired by regular employers. The third row of table A7.1 considers the case where the unemployment rate is low, as was assumed initially, but the less-educated males hired by the policy are still available to be hired by regular employers. (As noted in chapter 5, a public-service jobs policy could encourage such availability of workers to regular employers by making PSE jobs temporary, requiring periodic job searches for regular jobs, or paying below-market

TABLE A7.1 *Long-Run Displacement Effects of Increase in Labor Demand for Less-Educated Males Under Various Assumptions*

Scenario	Displacement of Other Less-Educated Males (Pseudo *t*-Statistic for Displacement Estimate)	Overall Displacement Rate (Pseudo *t*-Statistic for Displacement Estimate)
Baseline scenario: Low unemployment rate, jobs created are permanent and pay market wages, hiring is done from unemployed less-educated males	0.974 (7.07)	1.545 (4.74)
High unemployment scenario: Baseline except high unemployment	0.484 (4.15)	0.386 (1.40)
Public-service job scenario with continued availability of PSE workers for regular jobs: Baseline except jobs created are assumed to not reduce supply of labor to regular jobs	0.526 (3.70)	1.616 (4.77)
Targeting nonparticipants scenario: Baseline, except jobs created go to less-educated males who otherwise would not be in the labor force	−0.128 (−1.44)	−0.295 (−1.36)

Source: Author's estimates.

Notes: All estimates are taken from simulations of the model described in appendix 2 and in Bartik (1999). Pseudo *t*-statistics are derived as ratios of average effects to standard deviations of effects from 1,000 Monte Carlo simulations of model. These long-run effects are the effects occurring ten years after the shock to labor demand. Less-educated males are males with less than a college degree. Estimates are all derived from a shock to labor demand of less-educated males of 0.001 of overall population. Displacement rate of less-educated males is loss of employment to less-educated males not directly hired by the shock, divided by the number of jobs created; if this number is negative, it indicates a gain in employment. Overall displacement is loss of employment to all in population other than those directly hired by the policy, divided by the number of jobs created. Low unemployment is the unemployment rate that prevailed in 1997 (5.0 percent overall). High unemployment is unemployment rate that prevailed in 1982 (9.9 percent overall). Baseline scenario assumes that those directly hired by the policy effectively decrease available labor supply to regular employers. The third scenario (row 3) assumes that created jobs do not reduce available labor supply to regular employers, perhaps by design features of the policy that encourage transition to regular jobs. The scenario in row 4 assumes that for each job created, labor supply of less-educated males increases by one person.

wages.) Under these assumptions, the displacement rate drops from 100 percent to 50 percent for less-educated males: for every two less-educated males hired under the labor demand policies, regular employers reduce their employment of less-educated males by one, and net employment of less-educated males goes up by one.[1] Overall displacement is still high because of the assumptions made in the model: that the relative availability of different groups of unemployed workers affects the mix of workers who are hired by employers, but that the overall number of workers hired is based on wage rates and output demand, not the number of unemployed workers available.[2]

As noted in chapter 5, the displacement effects of a labor demand policy can also be reduced if this policy targets for hiring persons who are out of the labor force. As a result, the increased labor demand is accompanied by increased labor supply. The increased labor supply reduces the labor demand policy's effects on increasing wages, and as a result the labor demand policy causes less of a reduction in overall regular employment. In addition, because of the increased labor supply, the increased labor demand does not reduce the availability of the target group for regular employers. For example, consider row 4 of table A7.1. The simulation underlying this row assumes that the unemployment rate is initially low, but that the hiring of less-educated male workers is accompanied by an equal increase in the labor supply of less-educated male workers, presumably because the policy targets for hiring workers who are currently out of the labor force. Under these assumptions, the demand policy (or labor demand policy accompanied by labor supply policies) results in little or no displacement, either for the less-educated male target group or overall.

The fourth-row scenario can also be seen as an ad-hoc way to bring hysteresis effects into the model. The hysteresis hypothesis is that short-run labor demand shocks increase the long-run employability and effective labor supply of some workers by increasing their short-run work experience. The fourth-row scenario makes the extreme assumption that such effects are 100 percent: for every worker hired owing to the policy, long-run labor supply goes up by one person. Under this extreme assumption, the displacement effects of labor demand policies are not a problem. Under less extreme assumptions, where short-run work experience has long-run effects only for some workers, displacement effects would be somewhere in between the estimates of row 1 and row 4. Labor demand policies would have long-run employment effects for the targeted group of workers to the extent to which the policies were able to raise their effective labor supply.

Appendix 8

EMPIRICAL ESTIMATES USING INDIVIDUAL PANEL DATA ON THE LONG-RUN EFFECTS OF SHOCKS TO EMPLOYMENT AND EARNINGS

WHAT are the long-run effects of having a job? How do they vary across different education and gender groups? To what extent are these effects related to the wage rate of the job? As discussed elsewhere in this book, these questions are extremely relevant to determining the long-run effects of labor demand policies. We know less about the long-run effects of exogenous shocks to employment than we would like. The empirical work described in this appendix adds to our knowledge using data from the Michigan Panel Survey of Income Dynamics (PSID) database.

The empirical model estimated is a regression model using PSID data. Observations are annual data on a panel of individuals, with a number of observations on each individual. The dependent variable is the individual's real annual earnings. The explanatory variables that I focus on are whether the individual worked five years before, his or her annual work hours, and his or her wage rate. Controls include state and year dummies, demographic characteristics of the individual, average earnings prior to five years before, and, in some regressions, individual fixed effects. Regressions are estimated separately for six groups defined by gender and education level.

Specifically, the estimation equation can be written as:

$$Y_{ist} = B_0 + B_s + B_t + B_x X_{ist} + F_i + B_e E_{ist-5} + B_h H_{ist-5} + B_w \ln(W_{ist-5}) + U_{ist}$$

Y_{ist} is annual real earnings of individual i living in state s during year t. B_s and B_t are fixed effects for each state and year. X_{ist} represents a set of controls for the individual's characteristics, including controls for marital status, the presence of any children, the number of children, whether the individual is black or Hispanic, the individual's years of education, the standard experience proxy (age − education − 6), experience squared, and the individual's average real earnings during the period from six to eight years before. F_i is a fixed effect for the individual that is included in some regressions reported here. To avoid bias due to estimating fixed effects with too short a panel, observations are included only for individuals with at least fifteen estimable years of data; to ensure comparability, the same restriction is imposed on models that omit fixed effects. There are three key variables of interest: a dummy E_{ist-5} for whether the individual's work hours were positive five years before; H_{ist-5}, the annual work hours of the individual five years before; and $\ln(W_{ist-5})$, the natural logarithm of the individual's "wage" five years before, defined as annual earnings divided by annual work hours five years before. Individuals who were not working are arbitrarily assigned an ln(wage) of zero; such an assignment does not affect the estimates because of the inclusion of a dummy variable for whether the person was working. U_{ist} is the disturbance term. The model is estimated separately for men and women, divided into three education groups: high school dropouts, high school graduates who are not college graduates, and college graduates. To be in the sample, individuals must be between the ages of twenty-two and sixty-four (as of the date of the dependent variable) and must be either a household head or the spouse of a household head (since the PSID reports data more consistently for people in those categories).

The estimated model uses data from the PSID because the PSID is the longest panel with data on the general U.S. population. The specific data actually used in estimation span 1975 to 1991, with the relatively late early year required because of the number of lagged variables used in the estimation.

Without any controls, clearly the estimated effects for employment and wages five years before are biased by individual effects. One would expect individuals who had higher employment and wages five years before to tend to be more productive, a tendency that would positively affect annual earnings today. Thus, individual effects tend to positively bias the estimated effect of employment and wages five years before on real earnings today. The many demographic controls and the control for lagged real average annual earnings for the years from six to eight years before are intended to control for many unobservable variables affecting annual earnings. By controlling for these many individual variables, the goal is to minimize bias from individual effects and to come closer to estimating the true causal effects of shocks to the person's employment and wage rate five years before. The fixed effect controls for any additional unobservable individual effects that are fixed over time. These fixed effects could result in downward bias in the estimated effects of employment and wages five years before, since measurement error biases tend to be more extreme with fixed effects. Fixed effects are equivalent to differencing all variables from individual averages. This differencing eliminates much true variation in the lagged employment and wage variables. This increases the ratio of measurement error to true variation in the lagged employment and wage variables, tending to bias these estimates toward zero.

I also attempted to avoid the problems with individual effects by using instrumental variables. As has been done by others (for example, Ellwood 1982), I used state economic conditions in different years as an instrument to exogenously shift employment and wages five years before. Although these variables did a reasonable job of predicting lagged employment and wages, the resulting 2SLS estimates were too imprecise to be informative.

Obviously, given that we do not have experimental data or perfect instruments that cause clearly exogenous shocks in lagged employment and wages, the results from estimating this model must be interpreted cautiously. However, the estimates from models that control for so many individual characteristics—in particular, earnings from six to nine years before—must be taken as suggestive at the very least of the true causal effects of employment and wages. The estimates that control for fixed effects may even result in estimates that underestimate the true causal effects of lagged employment and wages.

Table A8.1 provides some descriptive statistics for some of the key variables. The patterns of work, real earnings, and wages are as one would expect, increasing with education, and being higher for men than for women. The real wage statistic used is a rough measure of real wages, since it is based on dividing reported annual earnings by reported annual work hours.

Table A8.2 presents coefficient estimates for some of the key variables. Each panel reports estimates for six different groups, with results for each group reflecting a separate regression. In general, most of the coefficient estimates are sensible.[1] F-tests on the three variables for employment and wages five years before are always statistically significant. The effects of the person's wages five years before is always statistically significant, except for the fixed effects estimates for male high school dropouts.

To make the estimates easier to interpret, table A8.3 reports the effects of switching from zero to two thousand hours of work five years before, and working at various values of ln(wage): the average ln(wage) for that group from five years before, and the twenty-fifth and seventy-fifth percentiles of wages for that group from five years before. (Table A8.1 gives values for these wage variables.) In addition to the dollar effect on earnings today and the standard error of that dollar effect, the table reports the earnings effects as a proportion of the initial shock to earnings.

In general, the model suggests that from one-tenth to one-half of a

TABLE A8.1 *Descriptive Statistics for Key Variables for Different Groups Used in Estimation*

Group	Number of Individuals in Sample (Number of Panel Observations on Person-Year Cells)	Mean Annual Real Earnings	Mean Annual Work Hours Five Years Before	Mean Wage Five Years Before, Real Dollars per Hour [Twenty-Fifth Percentile, Seventy-Fifth Percentile]
Female high school dropouts	407 (6,732)	$6,752	834	6.93 [5.24, 9.51]
Female high school graduates	665 (10,940)	13,523	1,215	9.50 [6.82, 12.83]
Female college graduates	177 (2,895)	23,986	1,310	16.14 [10.81, 21.26]
Male high school dropouts	264 (4,332)	25,574	1,789	12.77 [8.73, 18.15]
Male high school graduates	364 (5,967)	38,548	2,071	17.17 [12.64, 22.10]
Male college graduates	217 (3,530)	63,994	2,228	21.69 [16.11, 29.85]

Source: Author's estimates.
Notes: Real wages are calculated as annual real earnings / annual real hours. All real earnings and real wage figures are in 1995 dollars.

shock five years before is reflected in higher earnings today. Most of the fixed effects estimates are lower than the non–fixed effects estimates. As previously explained, it is unknown which estimates are better, since the fixed effects estimates, while controlling better for individual effects, may accentuate measurement error. The fixed effects estimates (at the mean wage rate) are the ones reported in table 5.10 to be conservative.

As shown in the table, the wage rate paid on a job does make a difference to its effects on current earnings. Higher wages do make a difference to long-run effects, and this difference is generally statistically significant, as already shown in the results reported in table A8.2. However, the effects of higher wages are modest, particularly in the fixed effects estimates.

The modest effects of wages can also be seen by calculating the elasticity of current real earnings with respect to wages. This is done in table A8.4. These results are the basis for the statements in chapter 5 about the effects of 10 percent higher wages five years later.

In sum, the estimates presented in this appendix suggest that work experience does have both substantively and statistically significant posi-

TABLE A8.2 *Parameter Estimates from Two Models of Earnings, for Six Demographic Groups (Dependent Variable: ln(Real Annual Earnings))*

(a) Models Without Individual Fixed Effects

	Female			Male		
Independent Variable	High School Dropouts	High School Graduates	College Graduates	High School Dropouts	High School Graduates	College Graduates
Five years before: dummy for whether worked during year	−4,218 (511)	−8,079 (609)	−14,857 (1887)	−14,825 (1905)	−33,171 (2979)	−67,673 (12840)
Five years before: annual work hours	2.491 (0.179)	3.641 (0.186)	4.593 (0.533)	2.848 (0.389)	5.010 (0.456)	6.004 (1.678)
Five years before: ln(average real wage = annual real earnings/annual work hours)	2,621 (246)	4,598 (261)	6,686 (663)	5,881 (629)	10,607 (775)	20,468 (2487)
F-test (probability) for three five-years-before variables	140.7783 (0.0001)	307.8882 (0.0001)	58.5700 (0.0001)	35.5826 (0.0001)	72.4473 (0.0001)	22.7189 (0.0001)

(b) Models with Individual Fixed Effects

	Female			Male		
Independent Variable	High School Dropouts	High School Graduates	College Graduates	High School Dropouts	High School Graduates	College Graduates
Five years before: dummy for whether worked during year	−865 (415)	−2,460 (496)	−3,354 (1601)	1,038 (1842)	−4,898 (2571)	−18,402 (12210)
Five years before: annual work hours	0.627 (0.148)	1.954 (0.153)	0.905 (0.453)	0.263 (0.351)	2.129 (0.406)	1.524 (1.760)
Five years before: ln(average real wage = annual real earnings/annual work hours)	634 (197)	1,433 (209)	1,725 (567)	639 (569)	1,828 (694)	8,559 (2568)
F-test (probability) for three five-years-before variables	14.7935 (0.0001)	101.3081 (0.0001)	5.3637 (0.0011)	3.197 (0.0225)	10.6008 (0.0001)	3.8943 (0.0086)

Source: Author's estimates.

Notes: Standard errors are in parentheses below coefficient estimates. All models also include year dummies and state dummies; dummy variables for whether married, whether have kids, whether black, whether Hispanic; continuous variables for "experience" and "experience squared," years of education, and average real earnings from years 6 through 8. Coefficients and standard errors for these variables are not reported to save space and focus on variables of interest. Panel b models also include fixed effects for each individual. Each panel is reporting results from six regressions, one for each of six groups. Dependent variable in each regression is annual real earnings (1995 dollars).

TABLE A8.3 *Estimated Real Earnings Effects Five Years Later of Working Full-Time at Various Wage Rates*

(a) Models Without Individual Fixed Effects

Group	Twenty-Fifth Percentile	Mean Wage for That Group	Seventy-Fifth Percentile
Female high school dropouts	$5,107 (269) [0.487]	$5,839 (288) [0.421]	$6,669 (326) [0.351]
Female high school graduates	8,031 (293) [0.589]	9,555 (320) [0.503]	10,937 (361) [0.426]
Female college graduates	10,246 (952) [0.474]	12,926 (1,050) [0.401]	14,768 (1,149) [0.347]
Male high school dropouts	3,614 (951) [0.207]	5,851 (1,014) [0.229]	7,919 (1,115) [0.218]
Male high school graduates	3,758 (1,902) [0.149]	7,007 (1942) [0.204]	9,684 (1,997) [0.219]
Male college graduates	1,224 (9,700) [0.038]	7,312 (9,752) [0.169]	13,848 (9,869) [0.232]

(b) Models with Individual Fixed Effects

Group	Twenty-Fifth Percentile	Mean Wage for That Group	Seventy-Fifth Percentile
Female high school dropouts	$1,440 (247) [0.137]	$1,617 (257) [0.117]	$1,818 (282) [0.096]
Female high school graduates	4,199 (268) [0.308]	4,674 (283) [0.246]	5,104 (311) [0.199]
Female college graduates	2,561 (871) [0.118]	3,253 (936) [0.101]	3,728 (1,010) [0.088]
Male high school dropouts	2,948 (1,053) [0.169]	3,191 (1,077) [0.125]	3,416 (1,139) [0.094]

TABLE A8.3 *Continued*

(b) Models with Individual Fixed Effects

Group	Twenty-Fifth Percentile	Mean Wage for That Group	Seventy-Fifth Percentile
Male high school graduates	3,999	4,559	5,020
	(1,735)	(1,775)	(1,828)
	[0.158]	[0.133]	[0.114]
Male college graduates	8,435	10,981	13,714
	(9,315)	(9,406)	(9,576)
	[0.262]	[0.253]	[0.230]

Source: Author's estimates.
Notes: Table reports effects on real earnings (in 1995 dollars) in a given year of working full-time five years before at various wage rates, compared to not working at all. The estimates are based on the models reported in table A8.2. The estimates are based on switching the values of three variables: the employment dummy (from zero to one), the annual hours worked variable (from zero to 2,000), and the ln(wage) variable (from one to whatever value is assumed). Standard errors are in parentheses and are based on estimated variance-covariance matrix for the estimates in table A8.2. Brackets show the estimated dollar effects on real earnings as a proportion of the initial shock to earnings. The various percentiles of wages used in the simulations are calculated separately for each of the six groups and are based on the wage distribution of each group; the actual wage numbers used are reported in table A8.1.

tive effects on real earnings five years later, although the precise magnitude of these effects varies with the specification. The wages of the job also make a difference, although this is less important than whether a person works full-time compared to not at all.

TABLE A8.4 *Elasticities of Current Real Earnings with Respect to Wage of Job Taken Five Years Before*

Group	Nonfixed Effect Estimates	Fixed Effect Estimates
Female high school dropouts	0.39	0.09
Female high school graduates	0.34	0.11
Female college graduates	0.28	0.07
Male high school dropouts	0.23	0.02
Male high school graduates	0.28	0.05
Male college graduates	0.32	0.13

Source: Author's estimates.
Notes: These elasticities are derived by dividing the coefficient estimates on five-year lagged wages, from table A8.2, by the mean value of current real earnings for that group, reported in table A8.1.

Appendix 9

SIMULATIONS OF THE INFLATIONARY EFFECTS OF DIFFERENT PATTERNS OF LOWERING UNEMPLOYMENT, USING AN ESTIMATED MODEL OF LOCAL GROUP WAGE CURVES AND PRICES

THIS appendix outlines and reports estimates of a model that relates the local wages of two education groups and of local prices to local unemployment rates for the groups and national economic trends. More details on the model and more estimates are in Bartik (2000c). The model is used to perform two sets of simulations of the inflationary effects of lowering unemployment in different patterns. In the first set of simulations, I consider the inflationary effects of lowering overall national unemployment by more or less targeting this reduction on the less-educated group. In the second set of simulations, I consider the inflationary effects of lowering overall national unemployment by more or less targeting this reduction on high-unemployment local areas.

The theoretical basis for the wage curve and price curve models estimated here are models in which firms maximize profits by choosing wage or price levels, with that choice based in part on some demand indicator such as the level of the local unemployment rate. Wage curve models, which relate the level of wages of some group to the level of local unemployment, local prices, and other variables, can be based on a variety of labor market models in which workers and firms have some ties to each other, such as efficiency wage models or bargaining models (Blanchflower and Oswald 1994; Blanchard and Katz 1999; Mortensen and Pissarides 1994). In all these models, firms have some reasons to set wages higher to retain their current workforce and increase its productivity, with the unemployment level influencing the wage level they choose. Price curve models, which relate the level of prices to some demand indicator such as unemployment, and also to wages, can be based on imperfect competition models in which the firm must maximize profits by following some price-setting strategy (Fair 2000; Tirole 1988). In general, any model in which firms have some market power in the product and labor markets, whether owing to imperfect information or ties between firms and workers or customers, naturally leads to a model in which firms choose some optimal wage and price levels, with that choice based in part on demand indicators such as unemployment.

The model has three equations: one to explain metropolitan area prices, and the other two to explain MSA nominal wages for the two education groups making up the labor market: college graduates and nongraduates.[1] Local prices and wages are explained by lagged prices and wages, and local overall unemployment and local unemployment of each group are explained by lagged national prices and wages. The model is estimated using pooled time-series cross-section data, where each observation is an MSA average for a particular year. Twenty-five MSAs are included, for all years from 1979 to 1998. The model treats national effects as random effects and includes a lagged national wage or price variable in each equation if it is statistically significant.[2] All equations include MSA fixed effects. Simulations examine the effects of changes in group unemployment rates. Models with national wage or price variables can be simulated under some assumptions about how unemployment changes throughout the nation.

A typical set of estimating equations in the model can be written as:

$$\ln P_{mt} = A_0 + A_1(L)\ln P_{mt-1} + A_2\ln W_{mt} + A_3 f_p(U_{mt}) + A_m + A_t + A_4\ln P_{t-1} + e_{pmt} \quad \text{(A9.1)}$$

$$\ln W_{gmt} = B_{0g} + B_{1g}(L)\ln P_{mt-1} + B_{2g}(L)\ln W_{gmt-1} + B_{3g}(L)\ln W_{mt-1} + B_{4g} f_g(U_{gmt}) + B_{5g} f_g(U_{mt}) + B_{gm} + B_{gt} [+ B_{6g}\ln W_{gt-1}] + e_{gmt} \quad \text{(A9.2)}$$

Coefficients followed by an (L) indicate a polynomial in the lag operator, with lags of the variable to the right included. The first equation explains prices in MSA m and year t. The second equation stands for the two groups' wage equations, with the dependent variable being nominal wages in MSA m and year t for group g, with each group having its own coefficients. Several lags in local prices are included in all three equations. Current wages are included in the price equation, and lags in both group and overall wages are included in the group wage equations. For the price equation, some functional form for overall MSA unemployment is included, and in the group wage equations, some functional form in both group and overall unemployment is included. All equations include MSA fixed effects (A_m or B_{gm}). All equations include random national year effects (A_t or B_{gt}). The price model also includes lagged national prices, and the group wage equation for college graduates also includes lagged national wages for that group. National variables were insignificant in the group wage equation for nongraduates and were dropped from the equation. The disturbance terms, represented by e, are assumed to be independent and identically distributed.

Functional forms and lag lengths are chosen through experimentation. Economic theory says that price setting and wage setting should be related to the levels of unemployment, but it says little about the functional form for this relationship or about how this relationship changes over time. In Bartik (2000c), all models were first estimated treating national effects as fixed. Using this fixed effects specification, functional forms and lag lengths were chosen. These optimal functional forms and lag lengths were then carried over into the random effects specification.

For unemployment in the price equation, I considered the following functional forms: the unemployment rate (UR); ln(UR); 1/(UR); 1/(UR squared); and UR squared. For each functional form of unemployment, I considered entering only the current value, entering only the value lagged one year, or entering the current and lagged values together. The chosen specification was the lag of (1/UR), which minimized the Akaike Information Criterion.[3]

For each of the two group wage equations, I considered the same alternative specifications as in the price equation for unemployment, except that each wage equation included both overall unemployment and that group's unemployment. Although the specification varied across the two groups, in each equation I assumed that overall and group unemployment followed the same functional form and lag. The chosen specifications minimized the AIC. The chosen specification for nongraduates includes both the current and lagged values of the log of the unemployment rate. The chosen specification for college graduates is the lag of the unemployment rate squared. For nongraduates, the chosen specification implies that unemployment has greater effects on wages at low unemployment than high unemployment, whereas for college graduates, unemployment has smaller effects at low unemployment than high unemployment.

Other aspects of the specification also were subject to experimentation. I considered entering from one to eight lags in the local price variable in each of the three equations. I ended up choosing to enter five annual lags in the local price variable in all equations. This minimized the AIC for the price equation and exceeded the AIC-minimizing lag length for the two wage equations.[4] Including five years of past prices is consistent with the theoretical notion that price expectations may depend in a complicated way on recent price trends. It is also consistent with empirical work that uses national data to find that relatively long lags in price data help explain inflation (for example, Gordon 1998).

For wage equations, I considered fewer lags, for two reasons: I have more years of price data than wage data, and including one more lag in wages requires sacrificing twenty-five observations, one for each MSA; evidence from national data suggests that fewer lags in wages are needed to predict prices and wages (Gordon 1988, 1998). For the price equation, I considered adding an additional lag in overall local wages, but it was clearly insignificant. For the wage equations, I considered having one to three lags in both group and overall wages. The second lag in wages was statistically significant in both wage equations, but the third lag was not statistically significant and was dropped.

After I settled on the specifications with year fixed effects, I considered random effects specifications with various national variables. Entering more than one national variable at a time led to extremely imprecise results. This probably occurs because there are only eighteen years of national data (once a few years are dropped because of lags) with which to estimate the effects of national variables. Therefore, I decided to include only a maximum of one national variable in each equation. Entering lagged national prices in the price equation, and each group's lagged national wage in the group wage equation, is appealing because inter-MSA trade and migration would force local prices or wages to respond to changes in the same variable at a national level. Some tests showed that no other national variables had significantly better explanatory power than choosing one lag in the analogous national variable.[5]

National group wages were statistically significant only in the college graduate wage equation. For nongraduate wages, national group wages were statistically insignificant, as were other national variables.[6]

These findings suggest that labor markets for nongraduates, who make up the majority of the labor force, are in some sense fundamentally local, in that local wages respond mainly to local trends in wages, unemployment, and prices. National trends do have important indirect effects on these groups' local wages by influencing local prices and local unemployment. In contrast, local wages of college graduates are significantly affected by national wage trends. This may reflect the greater migration across MSAs of the college-educated compared to other labor market groups (see chapter 3). In addition, the significant influence on local prices of national price trends may reflect interregional trade.

Wage and unemployment data come from the Outgoing Rotation Group of the Current Population Survey (CPS-ORG). Price data come from the U.S. Bureau of Labor Statistics. Wage and unemployment data exclude some observations that are imputed or that yield implausible wages. The wage means used are regression-adjusted means, using standard explanatory variables in a wage equation with MSA means. The unemployment means are not regression-adjusted. Price data were adjusted so that price levels were comparable across MSAs as well as over time. Some adjustments were done to make MSA boundaries more consistent over time and more consistent between the wage, unemployment, and price data sets. For more details on all these adjustments, see Bartik (2000c).

Table A9.1 lists means and standard deviations of unemployment and wages, as well as overall unemployment for each MSA as of 1998, the lowest unemployment year in the sample. These data show the expected pattern of higher unemployment and lower wages for nongraduates. The data also emphasize that the variation in unemployment across MSAs and years is large. Furthermore, recent unemployment in some MSAs has been quite low. This suggests that these data may reveal how much inflation is caused by unemployment that is lower than the current (as of 1999) national unemployment rate of 4.2 percent. One problem in studies using national data is the difficulty of determining the inflation effects of unemployment as low as current levels because we have rarely experienced such low unemployment in recent years at the national level. This is not true at the local level.

The actual equation estimates are presented in table A9.2. The estimates generally seem plausible. All the unemployment rate variables, considered together, have a statistically significant combined effect in each of the three equations. Group unemployment is always statistically significant in explaining the wages of either group. Overall local unemployment is statistically significant in explaining college graduate wages, but not nongraduate wages. For nongraduates, the estimates cannot say whether the group unemployment or the overall unemployment rate variables are significant in explaining wages. Each group's wages are strongly influenced by overall local wages and, to a lesser extent, by local prices. Local prices are only modestly influenced in the short run by local wages, national prices, and local unemployment rates, but these effects increase greatly in the long run owing to the large coefficients on lagged prices in the local price equation.[7]

These estimates are consistent with a view that local labor markets for different groups are strongly integrated with each other. Because group wages are only weakly affected by group unemployment rates and are strongly affected by overall wages, the relative wages of different groups tend not to change drastically in response to various shocks.

The next step is simulating the effects on national inflation of various ways of lowering unemployment. One set of simulations considers the effects of allocating a given national reduction in unemployment differently among the two education groups. The second set of simulations considers the effects of allocating a given national reduction in unemployment in different ways among MSAs with different unemployment rates.

Specifically, all simulations consider various ways of lowering na-

TABLE A9.1 *Descriptive Statistics on Local Unemployment and Wage Data for Twenty-Five Metropolitan Areas, 1979 to 1998*

(a) Means and Standard Deviations

	Proportion of Labor Force, Average Across All Years and MSAs	Mean of MSA Unemployment Rates, All Years and MSAs	Mean of MSA ln(Adjusted Real Wage) (1979 Dollars)
Overall	1.000	6.4	1.639
		(2.2)	(.064)
Noncollege graduate	0.723	7.6	1.555
		(2.5)	(.067)
College graduate	0.277	2.8	1.943
		(1.2)	(.080)

Notes: The means here are "means" of means; that is, they are unweighted means and standard deviations across observations on MSA-year means for twenty-five MSAs and all years from 1979 to 1998. The underlying data are calculated from the CPS-ORG, as described in the text. The unadjusted means for unemployment for each MSA-year are calculated using CPS sampling weights. The regression-adjusted means for ln(wage rate) are based on preliminary regression of ln(real wage) on a variety of wage predictors. Standard deviations are in parentheses.

(b) 1998 MSA Means for Overall Unemployment Rate

MSA	1998 Unemployment Rate
Atlanta	2.9
Baltimore	5.3
Boston	2.6
Buffalo	2.9
Chicago	5.0
Cincinnati	3.8
Cleveland	3.1
Dallas	3.8
Denver	3.1
Detroit	4.2
Houston	4.2
Kansas City	3.4
Los Angeles	6.8
Miami	7.0
Milwaukee	3.4
Minneapolis-St. Paul	1.8
New York	6.2
Philadelphia	5.2
Pittsburgh	4.2
Portland (Oregon)	4.8
St. Louis	5.0
San Diego	5.5
San Francisco	3.9

(Appendix continues on p. 366.)

TABLE A9.1 *Continued*

(b) 1998 MSA Means for Overall Unemployment Rate	
MSA	1998 Unemployment Rate
Seattle	2.8
Washington, D.C.	3.2

Source: Author's estimates.
Note: The official national unemployment rate in 1998 was 4.5 percent. The simple mean across these twenty-five MSAs in 1998 was 4.2 percent.

tional unemployment from 4.5 percent to 3 percent. In the first set of simulations, I arbitrarily assume that all MSAs are identical and that the United States consists only of MSAs. The wage and price effects for a representative MSA then show national wage and price effects and can be entered back into the wage and price equations in the simulations. I consider two ways of lowering national unemployment to 3 percent, differing in the way the education groups' unemployment is lowered. In the first, unemployment rates of college graduates and nongraduates are reduced as they normally are when unemployment drops from 4.5 percent to 3 percent.[8] In the second, both groups' unemployment rates are equalized at 3 percent.

Figure A9.1 shows the results of these simulations over time, and table A9.3 presents simulation results for one year. As can be seen in the figure and table, compared to the customary pattern of lowering unemployment across groups, equalizing group unemployment rates tends instead to increase prices more over time, although the difference is modest. As the table shows, wages go up somewhat more in the equalizing scenario, particularly for the nongraduate group. These results occur because of the strong link between wages for the two groups in the model estimated here; that link tends to limit changes in relative wages. In addition, wages for nongraduates are quite sensitive to unemployment rates, so lowering unemployment for this group, if anything, helps increase wage pressures.

In the second set of simulations, I arbitrarily assume that the nation is divided into two equal parts: MSAs with an unemployment rate of 6 percent, and MSAs with an unemployment rate of 3 percent. The averages of two representative MSAs then show national wage and price effects and can be entered back into the wage and price equations of each type of MSA in the simulations. I consider two different ways of lowering national unemployment to 3 percent, differing in the geographic pattern. In the first, overall unemployment in both types of MSAs is lowered by 1.5 percent. In the second, overall unemployment in the high MSAs only is lowered to 3 percent.

TABLE A9.2 *Selected Coefficient Estimates from Wage and Price Equation Models*

	Mean ln(Wage) of Persons with Less Than College Education in That MSA and Year	Mean ln(Wage) of College Graduates in That MSA and Year	ln(Average Consumer Prices) in That MSA and Year
Functional form of unemployment on right-hand side	ln(UR)	UR squared	1/UR
Coefficient on:			
Lagged national variable	—	0.382 (2.82)	0.121 (3.11)
Current unemployment rate, group	−0.0278 (−1.44)	—	—
Lag unemployment rate, group	−0.0058 (−0.29)	2.464 (0.96)	—
Current local unemployment rate	0.0107 (0.53)	—	—
Lag local unemployment rate	−0.0235 (−1.11)	−3.492 (−4.30)	0.000472 (3.91)
Lag ln(wage group)	0.229 (2.38)	0.188 (3.14)	—
Second lag ln(wage group)	0.237 (2.46)	−0.202 (−3.41)	—
Current overall wage	—	—	0.0644 (4.31)
Lag ln(overall wage)	0.449 (4.30)	0.305 (2.76)	—
Second lag ln(overall wage)	−0.129 (−1.20)	0.233 (2.13)	—
Lag 1 ln(price)	0.371 (3.51)	0.037 (0.20)	0.978 (22.11)
Lag 2 ln(price)	−0.092 (−0.61)	0.322 (1.30)	−0.246 (−3.99)
Lag 3 ln(price)	−0.061 (−0.41)	−0.089 (−0.37)	0.074 (1.19)
Lag 4 ln(price)	−0.028 (−0.19)	0.133 (0.57)	0.082 (1.37)
Lag 5 ln(price)	−0.064 (−0.75)	−0.262 (−1.73)	−0.125 (−3.22)
F-test probability:			
All unemployment rate variables	0.0001	0.0001	0.0001
Unemployment rate for group	0.3468	0.3381	—
Unemployment rate overall	0.4793	0.0001	0.0001

(Appendix continues on p. 368.)

TABLE A9.2 *Continued*

	Mean ln(Wage) of Persons with Less Than College Education in That MSA and Year	Mean ln(Wage) of College Graduates in That MSA and Year	ln(Average Consumer Prices) in That MSA and Year
Wage for group	0.0002	0.0002	—
Wage overall	0.0001	0.0001	0.0001
Prices	0.0002	0.0712	0.0001

Source: Author's estimates.
Notes: Observations are on MSA-year cell means for labor market variables. Each column corresponds to one of the three equations estimated. The dependent variable for the equation is listed at the top. The second row lists the functional form for unemployment used on the right-hand side of that equation. Unemployment rate variables are defined as proportions, not percentages. Subsequent rows list various right-hand-side variables and give the estimated coefficients on these variables in each equation, with *t*-statistics in parentheses. National variable included is lagged group wage for college graduate wage equation, lagged national price for price equation. All equations also include dummies for each MSA and random effects for each year. Last six rows list relevant F-test probabilities in each equation for variables of a particular type.

Figure A9.2 shows the results from this set of simulations over time, and table A9.4 shows results for one selected year. As the figure shows, targeting high-unemployment regions for unemployment reductions results in about half the inflationary pressure of lowering unemployment equally in all regions. As shown in the table, lowering unemployment equally in all regions results in huge upward price pressures in low-unemployment regions. Targeting high-unemployment regions reduces these upward price pressures in low-unemployment regions, at a modest cost in more price pressures in high-unemployment regions.

Before concluding, I briefly consider possible challenges to the validity of these simulations. The first challenge is to ask whether it is reasonable to think that these kinds of wage equations and price equations are likely to be stable in response to the types of policy-induced shocks to unemployment considered here. Returning to the underlying theory, the price equation theory is using unemployment only as a demand indicator. It is certainly arguable that there might be better measures of the demand facing firms in the product market. The simulated effects on prices are valid to the extent to which other demand measures in the various simulations continue to change in their customary way with variations in overall unemployment. Although this seems a reasonable assumption, it is untestable. For the wage equations, the underlying theory is that wages are set based on a particular set of labor market institutions and firm-worker relationships. The model estimates how wages vary with unemployment with various rates of group unemployment; those rates alter the levels of wages that are optimal for firms to set. The simulated effects on wages are valid

FIGURE A9.1 *Price Effects of Lowering Overall Unemployment from 4.5 to 3.0 Percent, with Two Different Ways of Distributing Unemployment Reduction: Lowering Unemployment Among Both College Graduates and Nongraduates According to Customary Patterns, and Equalizing Both Groups at 3.0 Percent*

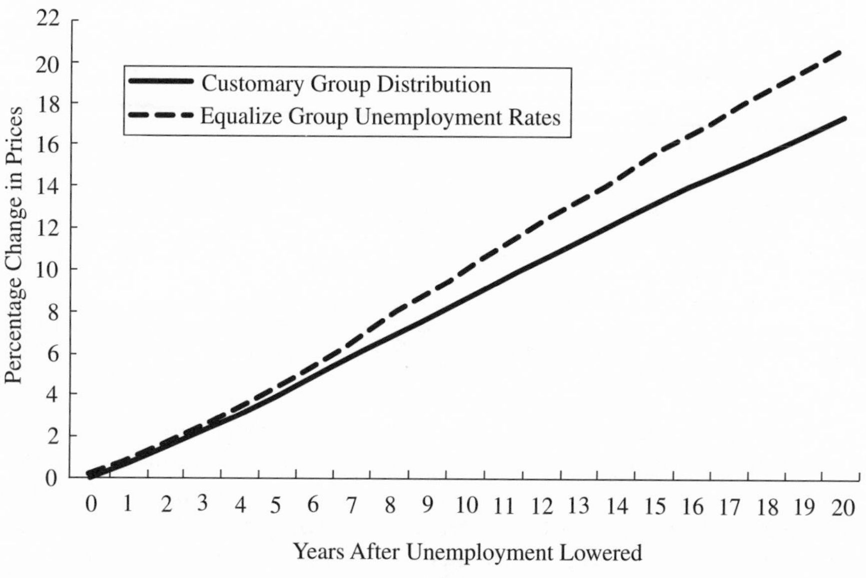

Source: Author's estimates.
Note: Both simulations start out with a college graduate unemployment rate of 2.1 percent, and a nongraduate unemployment rate of 5.4 percent. Simulation using customary distribution lowers graduate unemployment rate to 1.5 percent, and the nongraduate unemployment rate to 3.6 percent. Other simulation equalizes both groups' unemployment rates at 3 percent.

to the extent to which wage-setting institutions continue to react to unemployment reductions as they have been observed to do during this sample period. This seems reasonable for the simulations involving different geographic patterns of lowering unemployment. This assumption seems more questionable for the simulations in which unemployment for college graduates and nongraduates is equalized, since this unemployment equalization is not observed in the real world. Hence, such simulations require the assumption that the patterns of wage variation with unemployment observed during the sample period can be *extrapolated* to a dramatically different pattern of group unemployment rates.

TABLE A9.3 *Estimated Effects on Prices and Real Wages After Ten Years of Two Different Patterns of Lowering Unemployment Among Different Groups*

Variable	Customary Pattern of Lowering Group Unemployment Rates (College Grads to 1.5 percent, Non-Grads to 3.6 percent)	Equalizing Group Unemployment Rates at 3 percent
ln(price)	0.0868	0.0999
	(4.62)	(4.04)
ln(overall real wage)	0.0606	0.0867
	(2.36)	(2.15)
ln(real wage non-graduates)	0.0641	0.0915
	(2.39)	(2.12)
ln(real wage college graduates)	0.0517	0.0746
	(1.52)	(1.57)

Source: Author's estimates.
Notes: Initial unemployment rates: college graduates, 2.1 percent, nongraduates, 5.4 percent, overall unemployment, 4.5 percent. Both simulations lower overall unemployment from 4.5 to 3 percent. Pseudo *t*-statisitics are in parentheses, from 1,000 Monte Carlo repetitions of simulation.

The second challenge is to ask whether we can infer national price and wage trends from the local price and wage equations estimated in this model. National wage and price trends are *defined* as the average of local wage and price trends, so the inferences are valid if we have the model right. The key issue here is whether the model accurately estimates the feedback effects from national variables to local variables. The economet-ric problem is that such estimation is based in this model on only eighteen years of national data (albeit for twenty-five MSAs), hence it is hard to be confident of the robustness and stability of the national feedback effects. To some extent, this is reflected in the standard errors on the national variables in the wage and price equation. However, it should be noted that in general the model does not show strong, overpowering immediate effects of na-tional variables on local wage and price trends. Hence, it seems unlikely that national feedback effects could be so overwhelmingly strong as to seriously change the simulation results reported here. The model strongly suggests that local wages of different groups tend to vary closely together. The model also strongly suggests that local wages and prices are more sensitive to unemployment reductions when local unemployment is low. These strong findings of the model would yield results similar to those in the simulations, under a wide variety of assumptions about national feed-back effects, as long as these national feedback effects are of only moder-ate size or smaller.

FIGURE A9.2 *Price Effects of Lowering Unemployment from 4.5 to 3.0 Percent, Under Two Different Methods of Distributing Unemployment Reduction Among Regions: Lowering Unemployment Equally Everywhere, and Focusing Unemployment Reduction in High-Unemployment Regions*

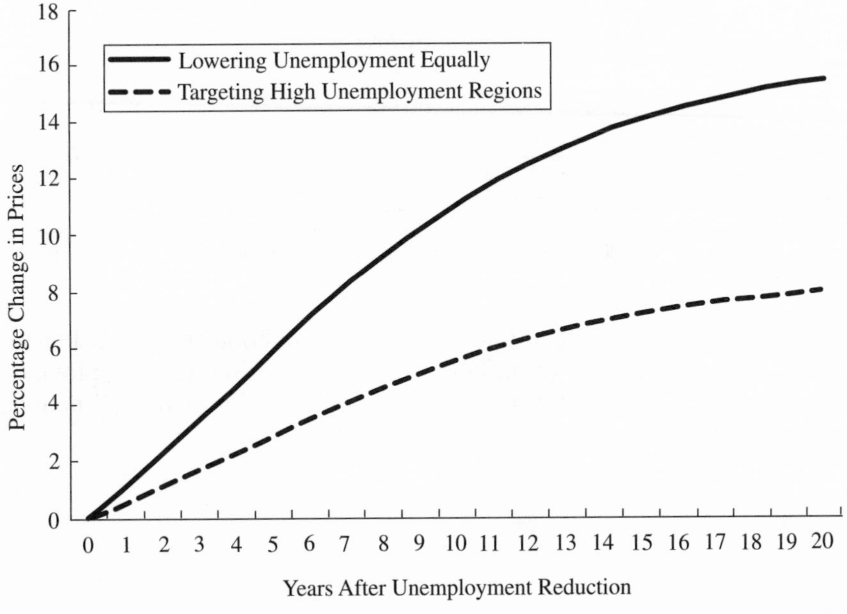

Source: Author's estimates.
Notes: In both simulations, the economy is initially divided into two equal-sized regions, one with unemployment of 6 percent, the other with unemployment of 3 percent. In one simulation, overall unemployment is lowered to 3.0 percent by lowering unemployment in both regions by 1.5 percent. In other simulation, overall unemployment is lowered to 3 percent by lowering unemployment in high-unemployment regions only.

In conclusion, the model presented in this appendix suggests that wages for different groups, as well as local prices, are strongly influenced by overall local unemployment, and not so strongly by the unemployment of different groups. As a result, there is limited scope for redistribution of unemployment among different groups to reduce wage and price pressures. The model also suggests that reductions in overall local unemployment have significantly stronger wage and price effects at lower unemployment rates. As a result, there is some reason to think that targeting unemployment reductions at high-unemployment areas could significantly reduce up-

TABLE A9.4 *Estimated Effects on Prices After Ten Years of Two Different Patterns of Lowering Unemployment Across Geographic Areas*

Variable	Lowering Unemployment in Both Regions by 1.5 Percent	Lowering Unemployment in High-Unemployment Region to 3 Percent
ln(National prices)	0.1114 (4.40)	0.0563 (4.83)
ln(Prices in high-unemployment region)	0.0709 (3.38)	0.0897 (5.70)
ln(Prices in low-unemployment region)	0.1519 (4.77)	0.0230 (2.33)

Source: Author's estimates.
Notes: Initial unemployment rates: high-unemployment region, 6 percent; low-unemployment region, 3 percent; overall national unemployment 4.5 percent. Both simulations lower overall unemployment from 4.5 to 3 percent. Pseudo *t*-statistics are in parentheses, from 1,000 Monte Carlo repetitions of simulations.

ward pressures on wages and prices, for given reductions in national unemployment rates. For a given inflation target, redistributing unemployment away from high-unemployment areas could allow a lower overall national unemployment rate.

Appendix 10

SIMULATIONS OF THE DISPLACEMENT EFFECTS OF PSE PROGRAMS UNDER VARIOUS SCENARIOS

THIS appendix presents simulations of how displacement effects of a PSE program might vary with unemployment, public worker substitution, and increased labor force participation induced by the program. Figure A10.1 illustrates some of these possibilities using an empirically estimated general equilibrium model of the labor market with five labor market groups and unemployment (see also appendix 2; Bartik [1999]). In these particular simulations, I consider a PSE program that targets less-educated single mothers. I consider four possible scenarios, varying along two dimensions: either the PSE jobs are assumed to initially all be net new jobs, or the PSE jobs for less-educated single mothers are all assumed to be offset 100 percent by reduced numbers of jobs for other less-educated women; either the single mothers hired for the PSE jobs are assumed to all be in the labor force initially, or the single mothers are all assumed to enter and stay in the labor force because of the PSE program. The figure and table A10.1 show overall displacement rates, that is the loss in other jobs due to the PSE jobs, where a displacement rate of one means that no net jobs are created by the PSE program, a displacement rate of zero means that all the PSE jobs represent a net addition to employment, and negative displacement rates mean that the PSE jobs have some multiplier effects on other jobs.

As the figure shows, initially the displacement rate depends on public worker substitution, that is, on whether the jobs created are new jobs or merely reshuffle who gets the available jobs. If there is a lot of public worker substitution, initially displacement rates are near one, whereas if the jobs are all new jobs, there are some multiplier effects of the PSE program. However, as time goes on, the displacement effects depend more on whether the PSE program has succeeded in adding to effective labor supply. If the program has added new workers to the labor force, displacement rates in the long run tend to be zero or negative. If new workers have not been added to the labor force, in the long run displacement rates tend to be close to one, particularly if unemployment rates are low.

TABLE A10.1 *Displacement Effects After Five Years of Publicly-Funded Jobs for Single Mothers Under Four Scenarios*

Demand Shock Scenario	Displacement Rate for Overall Employment, Low Baseline Unemployment Rate	Displacement Rate for Overall Employment, High Baseline Unemployment Rate
Scenario 1: increase in labor demand for female heads	−0.012 (−0.06)	−0.349 (−2.61)
Scenario 2: increase in labor demand for female heads, targeted at female heads who otherwise would be out of the labor force	−0.652 (−5.32)	−0.675 (−5.32)
Scenario 3: increase in labor demand for female heads, offset by equal-sized reduction in labor demand for other less-educated females	1.008 (64.01)	1.007 (114.07)
Scenario 4: increase in labor demand for female heads, offset by equal-sized reduction in labor demand for other less-educated females, but increased demand for female heads is targeted at persons who otherwise would be out of the labor force	0.383 (2.58)	0.686 (8.97)

Source: Author's estimates.

Notes: Pseudo *t*-statistics on estimated overall displacement rates are in parentheses, derived from 1,000 Monte Carlo repetitions of simulations. Reported displacement rates are equal to 1 − (actual change in overall employment in five years due to scenario / initial change in employment of female heads brought about by demand shock). A displacement rate of one implies that overall employment did not go up at all owing to the demand shock, and hence that each job gained by a female head owing to the demand shock is offset completely by a job lost to someone else. A displacement rate of zero implies that the actual change in overall employment is equal to the initial demand shock to female heads, so that there is no net gain or loss to others from the initial demand shock to female heads. A negative displacement rate implies that there is actually a net gain to others from the initial demand shock to female heads. To generate the scenarios, the following assumptions are made: in scenario 1, added demand for female heads reduces effective supply to private demanders; in scenario 2, the added demand also generates an added supply of female heads to the overall labor market; in scenario 3, two demand shocks occur, a positive demand shock to female heads and a negative demand shock of equal size to other less-educated females, with corresponding changes in the effective supply of each type of labor to private demanders of labor; in scenario 4, in addition to the two demand shocks, there is a positive supply shock for female heads.

FIGURE A10.1 *Displacement Effects of Publicly Funded Jobs for Single Mothers Under Four Scenarios*

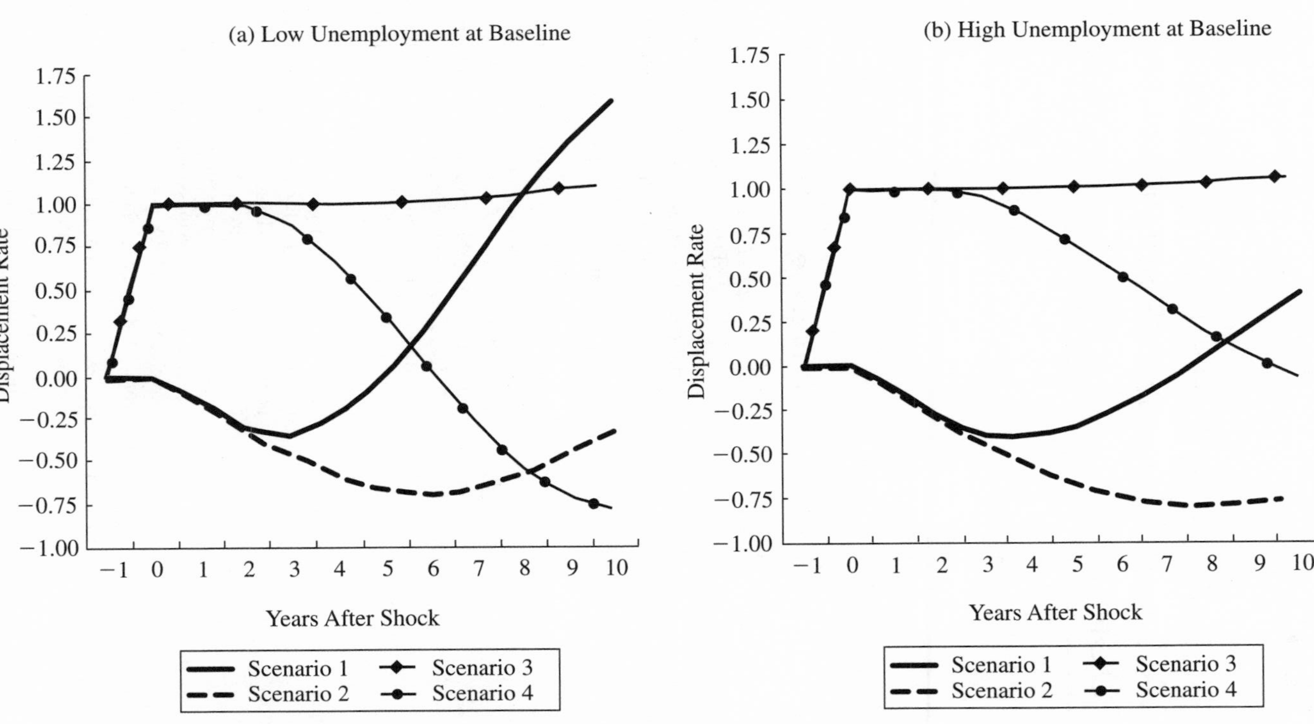

Source: Author's estimates.

Notes: The figure is derived from simulating the model of appendix 2 under four scenarios times two different baselines for overall unemployment, a low-unemployment baseline and a high-unemployment baseline. Each scenario estimates the effects of policy (publicly funded jobs) that increases labor demand for female heads of household with less than a college degree. In each scenario, what is estimated is the displacement rate: how much employment of all others (except those employed directly in these jobs) is affected by policy. Four scenarios are described in table A10.1, which also gives actual numbers for displacement effects five years after the policy is implemented.

Appendix 11

DESCRIPTION AND HISTORY OF LARGE-SCALE NATIONAL WAGE SUBSIDY PROGRAMS

TABLE A11.1 *Description and History of Large-Scale National Wage Subsidy Programs*

Program	Years	Description
OJT component of MDTA (Manpower Development and Training Act)[a]	1962 to 1971	Training contracts entered into with employers to hire the unemployed or upgrade the underemployed, with wages paid by employers and training costs paid by the government. Generally administered by the Department of Labor's Bureau of Apprenticeship, which was not enthusiastic about the program given its ties to established union apprenticeship programs. Grew rapidly to 1967. Eventually most OJT was ceded to the JOBS program in 1968, and OJT components of both programs were formally merged in 1971.
JOBS (Job Opportunities in the Business Sector)[b]	1968 to 1973	Sponsored by federal government in cooperation with National Alliance of Business; targeted at young and less-educated workers from poverty backgrounds; most were black males; federal government provided contracts to private business with up to $12,600 per placement (1998 dollars). Grew rapidly from 1968 to 1971, then declined.
WIN tax credit program[c]	1972 to 1981	Tax credit for hiring welfare recipients participating in WIN welfare-to-work program; initially provided 20 percent wage credit, with maximum credit of $3,900 (1998 dollars) per hire, and credit cut in half for firm whose annual credit exceeded

TABLE A11.1 *Continued*

Program	Years	Description
		$98,000. Initially only for hires placed by WIN offices, the program was expanded in 1973 to include WIN hires who found jobs by themselves. Initially required two-year retention, which was reduced to ninety days in 1975. The credit amounts were liberalized in 1978 to be the same as those adopted for TJTC in that year. Folded into TJTC in 1981.
OJT component of CETA (Comprehensive Employment and Training Act)[d]	1974 to 1982	Training contracts with employers, ostensibly to reimburse for extra training and supervision costs associated with high-risk hires. Typically about 12 percent of CETA training participants received OJT (Levitan and Gallo 1988). Decline in OJT in latter years of MDTA, early years of CETA, before increasing until 1978 and then declining with rest of program.
NJTC (New Jobs Tax Credit)[e]	1977 to 1978	Tax credit of 50 percent for the first $10,500 (1998 dollars) of wages per employee for increases in employment of more than 2 percent over previous year. Total credit could not be claimed for more than about forty-seven employees per firms, so there were no marginal incentives for large growing firms. Replaced by TJTC.
TJTC (Targeted Jobs Tax Credit)[f]	1978 to 1994	Tax credit of various sizes over the years offered for hiring various target groups. Originally offered tax credit of 50 percent of first-year wages and 25 percent of second-year wages, up to wage of $15,000 annually (1998 dollars). By 1994, credit had been scaled back to 40 percent of first-year wages, up to wage of $6,600 annually (1998 dollars). Among target groups usually included under the program were economically disadvantaged youth, veterans, and ex-offenders; disabled individuals undergoing vocational rehabilitation; and recipients of various forms of welfare assistance. Youth in cooperative education programs were originally included but then cut out in 1981. Generally more than half of those certified have been disadvantaged youth.

(Appendix continues on p. 378.)

TABLE A11.1 *Continued*

Program	Years	Description
		Originally employers could request retroactive certification of hires, but over the years the credit was amended so that certification had to be requested prior to first date of employment and employer was supposed to make good-faith effort to determine eligibility prior to hiring. Also, over the years, requirements were added that credit was paid only for employees who lasted for at least 120 hours of work. About 70 percent of employers participating in TJTC have job hires screened by consultants who handle paperwork, usually screening after hiring decision is made. Characteristics of TJTC jobs (U.S. Department of Labor 1994): occupations: 39 percent clerical/sales, 38 percent service; industries: 66 percent wholesale/retail. Thirty-seven percent of jobs pay minimum wage, 65 percent no fringes, 61 percent part-time. Seventy-six percent no longer with same firm five quarters after hire. From U.S. GAO (1991): 59 percent retail store and restaurants; 75 percent service or clerical/sales occupations; 75 percent of jobs pay within $1 of minimum wage. Expired, replaced after lapse by WOTC.
OJT component of JTPA (Job Training Partnership Act)[g]	1983 to 1999	Under the Job Training Partnership Act, one service option, in addition to various job search and training options, was to provide on-the-job-training. This typically involved job developers from JTPA locating employers for JTPA clients and entering into contracts with them to provide OJT for six months, in exchange for a wage subsidy for 50 percent of wages. Employers entering into OJT contracts were generally expected to retain trainees at the end of the six months if their performance was satisfactory. Employers who were felt to be abusing the system to get wage subsidies could be excluded from future OJT placements. An important point is that these wage subsidies under OJT, unlike most of the tax-based wage subsidies, were discretionary in that there

TABLE A11.1 *Continued*

Program	Years	Description
		was no entitlement by any employer to receiving an OJT subsidy unless the local JTPA service provider voluntarily decided to enter into a contract with that provider. Over time, regulations were tightened to require more substantive training and more documentation by employers, causing OJT to decrease in importance. Initially OJT was larger under JTPA than under CETA. Over time, JTPA shrank in size, and OJT declined as a proportion of the program. For example, the percentage of OJT participants was 22 to 23 percent for most of the 1980s but went down to 15 percent by 1991 to 1992. Will probably be continued under WIA.
WOTC (Work Opportunity Tax Credit)[h]	1997 to present	Generally similar to TJTC, but with differences in potentially crucial design details. Slight changes from 1996 to 1998, but in most recent design, provides credit of 40 percent of wages up to a $2,400 credit for individuals retained at least 400 work hours, 25 percent up to $1,500 for individuals employed 125 to 400 hours. Good-faith effort is more specifically defined as employer completing a prescreening eligibility form on or before date job offer is made, basically stating that employer believes hire is eligible. Eligibility is also simplified by tying it to receipt of food stamps or welfare rather than family income. Eligible groups include welfare and SSI recipients; eighteen- to twenty-four-year-olds in families receiving food stamps or living in empowerment zones or enterprise communities; vocational rehabilitation referrals; veterans receiving food stamps; and ex-felons who are members of low-income families. Compared to TJTC, WOTC puts much more emphasis on welfare recipients: 55 percent welfare recipients in 1999 (Beverly 1999).
WWTC (Welfare-to-Work Tax Credit)[i]	1998 to present	Similar to WOTC, but much more generous, long-term, and targeted. Eligible group is

(Appendix continues on p. 380.)

TABLE A11.1 *Continued*

Program	Years	Description
		welfare recipients who received welfare at least eighteen months. Credit is 35 percent of first-year wages, 50 percent of second-year wages, with maximum credit of $3,500 of first year wages and $5,000 of second year wages. Benefits can be counted in wage base. Has same requirements as WOTC for employer to do written eligibility screen on or before hiring date

Source: Author's estimates.

Note: This appendix presents more detailed program descriptions corresponding to table 8.1. It also gives the sources and methods used to derive the costs and size figures used in table 8.1.

[a] Perry et al. (1975, 152–53, table VII–I). Total cost figures are derived from costs per enrollee figures in Mangum (1968, 121) for fiscal year 1967.

[b] Hamermesh (1978) and Perry et al. (1975).

[c] Hamermesh (1978) and O'Neill (1982).

[d] OJT enrollment figures are derived from U.S. Department of Labor (1979, 32). Total cost per OJT participant is derived using Taggart (1981, 25, 46), a calculation that implies fiscal year 1978 costs per participant of $3,180 (1998 dollars). This cost figure takes service year costs and adjusts them to per participant costs by average length of training and ratio of participants to slots.

[e] Katz (1998), Perloff and Wachter (1979), and Bishop (1981). In addition to what is noted in the table, the credit could be no larger than 50 percent of excess total wages over 105 percent of the previous year's wages, to limit the ability of firms to maximize the credit by getting rid of full-timers and replacing them with part-timers.

[f] Katz (1998), U.S. House of Representatives (1998), and Bishop and Montgomery (1993).

[g] Various issues of the *Training and Employment Report* of the U.S. Department of Labor, in particular the report for program year 1986 (U.S. Department of Labor 1990). Figures on costs are extra wage subsidy costs of OJT. This is derived from Orr et al. (1996). I take costs per OJT participant from the different groups and weight each group by the proportion of OJT participants. In addition, I looked at the costs of the OJT strategy versus other strategies. It is difficult to determine true relative OJT costs with associated services, since the OJT strategy in Orr et al. (1996) has only 30 percent of that group actually using OJT. However, in looking at the OJT strategy, the average cost of incremental training services across all four groups for this strategy appears to be $1,235, whereas the average cost across all four groups of classroom training is $1,195. OJT is expensive, but so is classroom training. So I assume that on average OJT is only slightly more expensive than average service, and hence might cost 30 percent of total JTPA spending on Title II-A.

[h] Participation figures come from U.S. Department of Labor, (2000). Budget figures for tax expenditures come from U.S. Office of Management and Budget (1998, 333). Note that some WOTC costs are delayed, and because program is being phased in, the ongoing costs of running a program at 1999 size would be higher than $0.2 billion, perhaps between $0.3 billion and $0.4 billion based on OMB projections.

[i] as for WOTC; see note *h*.

Appendix 12

SMALL-SCALE, LOCAL, AND EXPERIMENTAL WAGE SUBSIDY PROGRAMS FOR THE DISADVANTAGED

TABLE A12.1 *Small-Scale, Local, and Experimental Wage Subsidy Programs for the Disadvantaged*

Program	Years and Places of Operation	Description	Magnitude of Subsidies	Scale of Program
Work supplementation/ grant diversion and other wage subsidies[a]	1967 to the present, various states. At present, thirty-two states have some sort of wage subsidy program. Some recent interesting programs are listed below separately.	Welfare department pays welfare grant, or sometimes welfare grant plus food stamps, as wage subsidy to private employer that hires welfare recipient for some period of time. This is a discretionary program in that the employer receives subsidy only if it enters into a contractual arrangement with the state welfare department.	Quite variable across programs, typically in range of $1 per hour to $5 per hour. Across thirteen states for which explicit wage subsidy can currently be calculated, median is $2.50 per hour. Length of subsidy is typically a maximum of six or nine months. Of the twenty-two states that report this feature of their program, eleven have a maximum of six months, and seven have a maximum of nine months.	Although these programs have commonly been created in various waves of welfare reform, they usually are run at a very small scale. For example, under the JOBS program in 1994, sixteen states ran the Work Supplementation Program, but total participation across all states was only 1,011.[b]
State tax credits for hiring welfare recipients or other disadvantaged	Years unknown; currently fifteen states have such tax incentives. (Five offer only in enterprise zone areas.)	State provides credit against corporate income tax for hiring disadvantaged or welfare recipient. Such tax credits are an entitlement in that any firm that meets the requirements of the tax credit is entitled to it.	Quite variable, but typically the subsidy is less per hour of work but longer-lasting than for grant diversion. Across five states that calculate incentives as percentages, percentage is 20 to 30 percent of wages in first year. Credit is typically capped during the first year, with a median cap of $1,500. Of ten states	There is little data on the take-up rate of these programs, but experience with TJTC and WOTC would suggest that the take-up rate is modest.

			with incentives, three have them for the first three years of employment, two for the first two years, and five for just the first year.	
Supported Work[c]	Experimental program, 1975 to 1978.	Although in most cases SW workers were directly employed by SW agency in public-service or nonprofit-type jobs, some SW workers were employed either as subcontractors to private business or directly under the supervision of private business, with private business reimbursing for part of the costs.	On average Supported Work covered 16 percent of its costs by income from selling goods or services, implying extremely large wage subsidy when contracting with private businesses.	Experiment was run on a small scale.
YIEPP	Experimental program conducted from 1978 to 1981 at seventeen sites.	Guaranteed part-time job during school year, and full-time job during summer, for disadvantaged youth ages sixteen to nineteen, living in eligible areas, who stayed in school or returned to school. The proportion of jobs in the private sector grew over time, reaching 23 percent by the last year of the experiment.	An essentially 100 percent wage subsidy was provided for the duration of a youth's eligibility, although some experiments during the program tested using 50 percent and 75 percent wage subsidies.	Operated at saturation level in some sites. Response to program suggests that a national program would have about 1.1 million participants and cost about $3.6 billion annually (see table 7.5).

(Appendix continues on p. 384.)

TABLE A12.1 *Continued*

Program	Years and Places of Operation	Description	Magnitude of Subsidies	Scale of Program
MEED[d]	Minnesota program conducted from 1983 to 1989.	Provided wage subsidy for up to six months for employers hiring unemployed workers not receiving UI benefits for newly created jobs. Initially 60 percent of placements were in the public sector, but over time 75 percent were in the private sector. Private-sector employers were required to retain subsidized workers for at least one year after the subsidy expired; if not, they had to hire another subsidized worker or repay a portion of the subsidy. Workers and employers were recruited and selected by local JTPA agencies. Priority was placed on employers that were nonretail small businesses and businesses that exported outside Minnesota. Priority was placed on unemployed persons receiving public assistance.	Provided $4 per hour in subsidy for wages and $1 per hour in subsidy for benefits (equivalent to $6.55 per hour for wages and $1.64 per hour for benefits in 1998 dollars). Actual wage paid averaged slightly less than $1 more than the subsidized wage, so the average wage subsidy exceeded 80 percent.	At peak, program spent $50 million per year and subsidized about 9,000 new job slots and had 10,700 participants. A national program of the same scale relative to population would spend $5.1 billion per year (1998 dollars), be associated with 0.591 million new job slots, and have 0.703 million participants.[e]

Maine TOPS[f]	Maine program conducted from 1983 to 1986.	Random assignment experiment in which individuals who had received welfare for at least six months, had volunteered for the program, were thought by program staff to be suitable for employment, and were randomly selected into the treatment group were offered sequenced "treatment" of (1) two to five weeks of prevocational training in job search and job-holding skills; (2) half-time work experience positions in the public and nonprofit sectors for up to twelve weeks; (3) OJT positions in private for-profit (73 percent) or public or nonprofit sector (27 percent) for up to six months.	OJT period provided wage subsidy of 50 percent to employers, partly financed by welfare grant diversion and partly by JTPA funds. MDRC evaluation comments that those hired seem to receive no more training than most workers receive, and seem as productive as the average new worker, so OJT subsidy is really a hiring subsidy, not compensation for extra costs. Average OJT subsidy per OJT participant was $1,900 (1998 dollars).The total cost of the program per participant in any program component was $4,481, $626 of which was OJT wage subsidy costs (reduced from $1,900 because less than half of those participating in the program used OJT).	The program was run as an experiment but ended up being smaller-scale than anticipated when it was set up, in part because the program was thought to be suitable for only a portion of the caseload, in part because of the complexity of delivering all the services in the prescribed sequence and recruiting employers. Only 30 percent of the treatment group members actually received the OJT wage subsidy.

(Appendix continues on p. 386.)

TABLE A12.1 *Continued*

Program	Years and Places of Operation	Description	Magnitude of Subsidies	Scale of Program
New Jersey Grant Diversion Program[g]	New Jersey program conducted from 1984 to 1987.	Random assignment experiment in which welfare recipients who were single parents, volunteered for OJT, and were believed to be suitable for OJT were randomly assigned either to a control group, which received normal welfare-to-work services, or to a treatment group, which also was eligible for OJT.	50 percent wage subsidy, for up to six months. Average subsidy lasted ten weeks. Forty-three percent of experimental sample actually received OJT subsidy. Costs per OJT participant (per experimental) of OJT wage subsidy itself was $1,269 ($518) in 1998 dollars. Administrative costs of OJT program per OJT participant (per experimental) were $1,823 ($744) in 1998 dollars. Administrative costs included the costs of hiring job developers to find jobs for OJT participants.	Very small-scale program run as an experiment. In the first year, there was an average eight-week waiting period for locating OJT positions; it declined in the second year to four weeks.
Oregon JOBS Plus Program[h]	Oregon program conducted from 1993 to the present.	First a demonstration and now a statewide program in which welfare recipients and UI recipients are placed with participating employers, which receive a wage subsidy for hiring them for up to six months.	Wage subsidy is $6 per hour plus payroll taxes and workers' compensation costs. Firm is supposed to pay prevailing wage for the job; on average, firms pay a bit less than $1 more, making the effective average	Program is operated on a modest scale. Seven percent of Oregonians engaged in welfare-to-work programs are in JOBS Plus. From July 1996 to October 1997, 3,500 persons left JOBS Plus. A similar program in per

		wage subsidy over 80 percent. Wage subsidy is up to six months. After four months on the job, if employer has not hired the participant, employer must allow that person to search for a job one day a week, thus reducing effective subsidy.	capita size, run on a national scale, would have had about 0.220 million graduates in 1998.

Source: Author's estimates.
Note: This table expands on table 8.2 and lists the sources for its figures.
[a] American Public Welfare Association (1998), on both state wage subsidies and state tax credits for hiring the disadvantaged.
[b] Savner and Greenberg(undated).
[c] Ball (1984); the 16 percent figure is from page 75.
[d] Rangan (1984) and Rode (1988).
[e] These calculations are based on projecting Minnesota's per capita spending levels and participation levels in 1984 to the nation for 1998.
[f] Auspos, Cave, and Long (1988).
[g] Freedman, Bryant, and Cave (1988).
[h] Roberts and Padden (1998a, 1998b).

Appendix 13

DETAILED DESCRIPTION OF EMPIRICAL STUDIES OF ENTITLEMENT WAGE SUBSIDY PROGRAMS

TABLE A13.1 *Detailed Description of Empirical Studies of Entitlement Wage Subsidy Programs*

Study	Methodology	Results
Impact (1977), as reported in Hamermesh (1978)	Survey of employers using the WIN tax credit.	Less than 10 percent of employers using credit attributed their hiring of the WIN enrollee to the credit.
Wisconsin DHSS and Institute for Research on Poverty (1982)	Experimental study of the effects of promotional efforts on firms' usage of WIN tax credit and TJTC. 1,405 firms were involved with test of mail-only promotion (sending brochure), and about 284 firms were involved with test of mail-plus-phone promotion (mailing brochure, plus follow-up phone call). About half of the firms were randomly assigned to treatment in each case, half to controls. The brochure emphasized money savings to the firm, a lack of red tape, and who to contact. Phone contact emphasized these features plus survey findings that most employers had been pleased with the quality of the subsidized workers. The dependent variable was whether the firm made a certified hire for tax credit during the five months after promotional efforts were	Mail-only promotion slightly increased firms' usage of tax credits, but not to a statistically significant extent. Mail-plus phone promotion approximately doubled firms' usage of tax credits, from 4.5 percent of firms to 9.0 percent. This increase is statistically significant at the 5 percent level in an analysis that adds in other firm characteristics. Because of the study design, it is unclear whether the extra effect of the mail-plus-phone promotion was due to the personal nature of the phone contact or the extra message of the phone contact (that most firms found that workers hired under these tax credit programs were of good quality). Firm size was highly correlated with the use of tax credits: 23 percent of firms with more than one hundred employees used the credit, versus less than 4

TABLE A13.1 *Continued*

Study	Methodology	Results
	undertaken (March 1 to July 31, 1981).	percent for firms with fifty or fewer employees.
O'Neill (1982)	January 1980 survey of 720 firms.	Sixty-three percent of firms had heard of TJTC, 38 percent had used or planned to use TJTC, of whom 26 percent said that using TJTC would increase employment level, and 46 percent said they substituted target hires for similar nontarget hires. Both knowledge and usage or planned usages of TJTC are highly correlated with firm size, with usage particularly low among firms with twenty or fewer employees; usage or planned usage was 22 percent in this group, versus 37 percent for firms with twenty-one to sixty employees, 42 percent for firms with sixty-one to one hundred, and 48 percent for firms with more than one hundred employees.
Christensen (1984)	Random survey of 5,301 firms in 1980 and 3,710 firms in 1982. Underlying data come from various studies led by Bishop and his colleagues (cited later in this table), although statistical analysis is different. The survey both directly asked firms how TJTC affected their employment decisions and ran regression models to estimate determinants of TJTC usage and how credit affected employment growth and change in share of youth employment. Survey also analyzed CPS data on employment in March 1983 of youth eligible for TJTC in 1982 and looked at how these youth were affected by state vouchering activity in 1982. Because there were no controls for endogeneity of state vouchering activity in this approach, doubts are raised about the results.	Thirty-four percent of employers who use credit claim it affects their hiring decisions significantly, and 22 percent claim it has some effect on hiring decisions. TJTC usage is much greater among large establishments than small establishments, with 45 percent of those above two hundred in employment size using TJTC, versus 16 percent for those with five to nineteen employees. Probability of TJTC usage was 21 percent greater among firms contacted by the government about TJTC, and 32 percent higher among firms contacted and asked to accept a specific referral. Firms that had received TJTC in 1980 or 1981 increased their share of youth in total employment by 6 percent to 20 percent more than other firms, even when we instrument for TJTC usage using a variable for whether firm had been contacted by government employment agencies about TJTC. But employment

(Appendix continues on p. 390.)

TABLE A13.1 *Continued*

Study	Methodology	Results
		growth is not statistically significantly greater in firms that use TJTC compared to firms that do not. Finally, for every increase of one in state vouchering activity in 1982, there was a 0.4 increase in employment for eligible youth as of March 1983. Because there were about 45 percent as many certificates as vouchers, one could argue that each certificate for a youth was associated with about one job for each youth. No sign that TJTC had a significantly negative effect on employment for nondisadvantaged youth.
Bishop, in Bishop and Hollenbeck (1985, ch. 4)	Regression analysis of employment of around 3,000 firms, December 1980 to June 1982, and the proportion of employment of youth as a function of a dummy variable for whether the firm participated in TJTC. Attempts to instrument for TJTC participation were unsuccessful.	Based on typical number of certifications associated with TJTC participation, for every ten TJTC-subsidized jobs at a firm, there will be three to four extra jobs, and six or seven displaced, with probably most of those displaced being nonsubsidized youth (four or five).
Bishop and Hollenbeck (1985, ch. 5)	1982 survey of stratified random sample of firms.	Eighty percent of TJTC certificates are at firms that claim they tried to select TJTC eligibles. Eighty percent of TJTC certificates are at firms that claimed they had contacted ES or other government agencies to request referrals of TJTC eligibles. But only 18 percent of firms reported that job applicant's eligibility influenced hiring decisions "a great amount," and only 15 percent reported that it influenced their decision "a moderate amount."
Bishop, in Bishop and Hollenbeck (1985, ch. 7)	1983 interviews in which 850 employers were asked to rate 11 imaginary job applications on a scale from 0 to 200, in which 50 was the worst applicant ever hired, 100 was average, and 150 was the best applicant. TJTC status of application was randomly assigned.	On average, TJTC status only slightly increased employer's rating, by 1.9 points on average. TJTC eligibility helped much more for firms that provided more general training and paid low wages. TJTC was more helpful for applicants with low schooling.

TABLE A13.1 *Continued*

Study	Methodology	Results
Copeland (1985); Hollenbeck, in Bishop and Hollenbeck (1985, ch. 8)	Case studies of nonrandom sample of thirty-five firms in industries that heavily use TJTC, with oversupply of firms that heavily use TJTC.	Twenty-six percent of firms reported giving hiring preference to TJTC applicants. Nine percent reported creating openings to hire TJTC applicants. Twenty-nine percent screen for TJTC eligibility before making hiring decision. Forty percent claim TJTC increased use of ES. Seventy-five percent of firms use consultants to screen applicants for eligibility and arrange for ES certification. Only 11 percent felt TJTC workers were less productive than other workers. Eight percent felt TJTC workers had higher turnover. Fifty-five percent of firms had monetary incentives to encourage local managers to hire and certify TJTC workers.
Bishop and Montgomery (1986)	Analysis of 1980 survey of 5,279 establishments. Particularly focused on the 20 percent familiar with TJTC and the 31 percent familiar with WIN tax credits (see table 8.6 for analysis of CETA-OJT). Focused also on models for explaining determinants of establishment's familiarity with each program and explaining determinants of usage of each program, conditional on establishment being familiar with that program.	Among establishments familiar with the particular subsidy program, the proportion using it in each case goes up significantly if the firm first learned of the WIN tax credit from a government representative. This increases the WIN participation rate by 70 percent (mean participation rate is 0.15) and increases the TJTC participation rate by 53 percent (mean participation rate is 0.07). Among all establishments, a 10 percent increase in other establishments at site that learned of WIN via government increases proportion familiar with these three programs by 8 percent for WIN and 9 percent for TJTC. Both familiarity with programs and usage conditional on familiarity were significantly greater for larger establishments.
Lorenz (1988)	Comparison of earnings of three groups: those vouchered and then hired under TJTC, those submitted for TJTC certification upon hire, and those vouchered but not hired under TJTC during first six months	The earnings of the groups were quite similar in the 1981 period. As one might expect, the groups that were hired for TJTC jobs in early 1982 had considerably higher earnings in the period from July 1, 1982 to

(Appendix continues on p. 392.)

TABLE A13.1 *Continued*

Study	Methodology	Results
	of 1982, in Maryland and Missouri. Three groups were compared for three types of TJTC eligibles: disadvantaged youth, welfare recipients, and Vietnam veterans. Sample was followed for one year prior to hire, and five years after hire. No attempt was made to control for unobserved differences across groups that might explain why the first two groups were hired in TJTC jobs in early 1982.	June 30, 1983. These earnings differences tended to erode over time, although differentials tended to stay higher for the youth group. Differentials in favor of TJTC hires were concentrated on those whose employers ended up receiving full TJTC credit. This result also could be due to selection bias.
Hollenbeck and Willke (1991); Hollenbeck, Willke, and Ershadi (1986)	Comparison of change in average annual earnings and employment from two years before potential vouchering to two years after potential vouchering, for vouchered TJTC eligibles in states with average voucher penetration rate of eligible population versus nonvouchered eligibles in states with zero penetration rate. Comparisons were the same for the displacement analysis, except that it looked at nonvouchered TJTC eligibles in states with average voucher penetration rates.	Vouchered youth and the handicapped generally gain, with average annual real earnings gain of $462 (1998 dollars) for youth and $1,940 for the handicapped. Most of the earnings gain appears to be due to employment increases. Among youth, white females gain the most. But there are many indications of displacement: losers include nonvouchered black male youth, both vouchered and nonvouchered black males, black females, white females on welfare, and both vouchered and nonvouchered black veterans. These are results without correction for nonrandom nature of vouchering, but with controls for standard demographics, controls for area economic conditions, and implicit controls due to changes specification for prior economic status. Corrections for selection bias yield implausible results.
Bishop and Kang (1991)	Analysis of cross-sectional data on 3,412 establishments collected in 1982, with oversampling of large firms in low-wage industries. Asked questions about number of employees hired under TJTC in 1980, 1981, and 1982. Estimated Poisson model of determinants of number of TJTC hires by establishment, as	Government offer to refer eligible workers increased expected number of TJTC hires five to twelve times, depending on year. Government contact without referral offer increased number of TJTC hires by 43 percent to 87 percent depending on year. Prior involvement with other government wage subsidies significantly

TABLE A13.1 *Continued*

Study	Methodology	Results
	function of characteristics of establishment and firm and interactions with government.	increased TJTC usage. An establishment that used NJTC, WIN tax credit, and CETA-OJT in the past, compared to an establishment that used none of these programs, had a three to ten times greater number of TJTC hires. In 1980 and 1981, larger establishments were much more likely to make more TJTC hires; in 1981 and 1982, larger firms were much more likely to make more TJTC hires.
U.S. General Accounting Office (1991)	Interviewed sixty employers among top TJTC users in four states.	Forty-five percent of employers made special efforts to recruit, hire, or retain TJTC-eligible workers, including developing relationships with agencies that supplied TJTC eligibles, giving incentives to local managers for hiring and retaining TJTC, and being more lenient in job standards with TJTC hires.
Bishop and Montgomery (1993)	Regression analysis of the percentage change in individual firm's employment from end of 1980 to 1981, as a function of change in TJTC hires as a proportion of previous level of employment. The marginal effect of TJTC is allowed to vary with proportion, with spline at proportion of .50. This regression overestimates the effects of TJTC because growth increases new hires, increasing TJTC in turn. Hence, the study also estimated growth as a function of the ratio of TJTC hires to all new hires, an estimate that should be biased downward. It also examined the effect of TJTC hires on youth's share of total employment.	In specification that is biased upward, TJTC was estimated to increase total firm employment by 30 percent of certifications for certifications up to 50 percent of total employment, with zero marginal effect for certifications above 50 percent. In specification that is biased downward, TJTC was estimated to increase total firm employment by 13 percent of TJTC certifications (up to 50 percent proportion, with marginal effect beyond assumed to be zero), but estimate is not significantly different from zero. TJTC was also estimated to increase the number of young workers hired, by just slightly less than TJTC effect on overall employment. This implies that TJTC has at most slight displacement effects on adults, although it may have displacement effects within youth group.

(Appendix continues on p. 394.)

TABLE A13.1 *Continued*

Study	Methodology	Results
U.S. Department of Labor (1994)	Selected sample of 983 TJTC workers. Asked employers whether TJTC worker would have been hired without tax credit. If employer did not answer, assumed that if applicant said eligibility was checked before hire, then TJTC caused hire.	Only 8 percent of TJTC certificates were hired by their employers because of their TJTC status. Average starting wage was $4.96 (1992 dollars). Thirty-seven percent were paid minimum wage or below. Sixty-five percent of jobs had no fringe benefits.
Tannery (1998)	Compared treatment group of youth and welfare recipients in Pennsylvania who were hired from 1988 to 1994 and then management assistance companies applied for certification on their behalf and received that certification, with control group of individuals for whom certification was not processed owing to technical paperwork errors (for example, missing signatures or data). The comparison uses a sparse set of demographic controls but does not control for prior earnings or employment. Also, it is apparent from data that the control group is significantly different from the treatment group in a number of respects; the source of these differences is unknown. Finally, it is not clear what "treatment" amounts to in this analysis: both groups were employed by an employer who submitted them to be certified; the only difference was that at some later date the certification was not received. Are the differences detected due to certification yielding more job retention or to the possibility that firms that made errors were different sorts of employers?	In general, certification is estimated to increase earnings of disadvantaged youth between $2,000 and $4,000 per year, and it increases earnings of welfare recipients by about $1,600 per year. Certification is also associated with more quarters of employment during the 1988 to 1994 period, increasing the quarters worked by 2 percent to 6 percent for various groups. However, as noted under "Methodology," it is not clear what "treatment" means in this study, and it is not clear that the controls do not differ from the treatment group in the types of firms in which they were employed.
Katz (1998)	Uses difference-in-difference-in-differences estimator that is based on restriction in 1989 that made disadvantaged twenty-three- to twenty-four-year-olds no longer eligible for TJTC. Looks at trends in	TJTC was estimated to increase employment rates of disadvantaged twenty-three- to twenty-four-year-olds by 3.4 to 4.3 rate points. Suggests that 40 to 52 percent of TJTC certifications create jobs for the

TABLE A13.1 *Continued*

Study	Methodology	Results
	relative employment rates of disadvantaged and nondisadvantaged twenty-three- to twenty-four-year-olds versus trends in relative employment rates of disadvantaged and nondisadvantaged eighteen- to twenty-two-year-olds (disadvantaged in this group stayed eligible for TJTC) and trends in relative employment rates of disadvantaged and nondisadvantaged twenty-five- to twenty-nine-year-olds (never eligible for TJTC). Also does some regression adjustment for demographic changes in one estimate.	group targeted. If this were applied to all TJTC, TJTC would have created 249,000 to 322,000 jobs for the disadvantaged groups it targets at its peak in 1985. *Caveat:* there is some sign that the relative employment of disadvantaged twenty-three- to twenty-four-year-olds started declining in 1988, before TJTC eligibility was eliminated.
Woodbury and Spiegelman (1987); Spiegelman and Woodbury (1987); Dubin and Rivers (1993)	Experimental data, comparing UI benefits collected and weeks of unemployment of two groups of UI recipients: treatment group whose employers would get $757 bonus (1998 dollars) if UI recipient was reemployed within eleven weeks and stayed employed for four months; control group who were subject only to regular UI benefits and rules.	Bonus reduced initial spell of unemployment by statistically significant two-thirds of a week on average, but reduction in unemployment over entire benefit year is only marginally significant (probability of 0.19) reduction of 0.36 weeks. Take-up rate is also very small: only 5 percent of sample submitted "notice of hire" to the state of Illinois, which is less than one-fourth of the 21 percent of the experimental group that was reemployed within eleven weeks. If experimental effects were concentrated within this group, this implies that experiment reduced weeks of unemployment of this group by about thirteen weeks, compared to control group mean of twenty weeks. Effects on overall benefit year unemployment are statistically significant for white women. Effects of employer bonus appear to be stronger for high school dropouts, those previously employed in clerical or sales jobs, persons with below-average prior earnings, and those who get jobs in wholesale and retail trade. Participation in program in sense of agreeing to participate is greater for those with lower prior earnings. Although

(Appendix continues on p. 396.)

TABLE A13.1 *Continued*

Study	Methodology	Results
		employment bonus has effects, they are so small (or rather, the take-up rate is so small) that a universal national program would have very small effects on total employment. A national program today might increase average employment levels by 5,000 persons and cost perhaps $17 million per year.[a]

Source: Author's estimates.
Note: This appendix presents a more detailed description of the results from empirical studies reviewed in table 8.5.
[a] National figures are derived in the following way. Based on Spiegelman and Woodbury (1987), over the sixteen-week period in which the Illinois experiment was conducted, approximately 12,000 new claimants came in who met the experimental criteria, in an area in which weekly unemployment averaged 300,000. Hence, over a fifty-two-week period, the number of persons eligible for an employer bonus-style treatment averages about 13 percent of average total unemployment. Average unemployment in the United States nationally now is about 6 million, so the number of persons to whom this treatment might be applied is 780,000. We would expect treatment to increase employment for this group by an average of .36 of a week over a year. Multiplying 780,000 times .36 over 52 results in an increase in employment of about 5,400. Also, of 780,000, only 2.8 percent would claim bonuses, which average $757 in 1998 dollars. Multiplying this out, we have 21,840 claiming bonuses and a total bonus cost of $16.5 million.

Appendix 14

DETAILED SUMMARIES OF ESTIMATES OF EFFECTS OF DISCRETIONARY WAGE SUBSIDY PROGRAMS

TABLE A14.1 *Detailed Summaries of Estimates of Effects of Discretionary Wage Subsidy Programs*

Study	Methodology	Results
Various studies of MDTA OJT, summarized by Perry et al. (1975)	Four different studies, comparing earnings gains of MDTA trainees who participated in OJT to some comparison group of nontrainees.	Average earnings effects in first post-OJT year across all studies and groups is $1,834 (1998 dollars). Effects were generally greater for women than men, and greater for blacks than whites. OJT effects generally were greater than institutional training in studies looking at both.
Farber (1971), as reported in Perry et al. (1975)[a]	Comparison of 1969 earnings of 1968 JOBS contract participants to matched comparison group based on preprogram earnings from social security.	Overall average effect on earnings is increase in annual earnings of $1,188 (1998 dollars). Effects on females are five times those on males, effects on blacks two or three times those on whites. Annual earnings effects on black females estimated to be $3,319 (1998 dollars).
Ball et al. (1981)	During latter part of YIEPP, job developers for YIEPP in Detroit and Baltimore varied the wage subsidy offered among different private businesses. In Detroit, the wage subsidy varied between 100 percent and 75 percent based on random assignment; in Baltimore, it varied between 100 percent and 50 percent based on lo-	Regression adjusted participation rates (verbal agreement to hire youth under program; firms might have changed mind later, in either direction): under the 100 percent wage subsidy, 18.2 percent agreed to participate and hire disadvantaged youth; under the 75 percent wage subsidy, 10.0 percent agreed to par-

(Appendix continues on p. 398.)

TABLE A14.1 *Continued*

Study	Methodology	Results
	cation of firm. Regression model estimated pooling both cities, and estimating firm's decision to participate as function of subsidy offered, and a variety of firm characteristics. Tests indicate two cities can be pooled in regression.	ticipate; and under the 50 percent wage subsidy, 4.7 percent agreed to participate. These differences are statistically significant. Participation is also significantly higher for younger businesses, growing businesses, and businesses with prior experience with youth. Participation did not vary significantly, controlling for other factors, with size of business, prior experience with government employment and training programs, and financial condition or profitability of firm.
Ball et al. (1981)	Participating firms were asked to estimate the percentage of youths' work hours that resulted in displacement of other workers, versus the percentage that represented a net increase in total work hours for the firm. These survey responses were then adjusted by researchers to be internally consistent and to add up to 100 percent. Note that YIEPP program rules are supposed to prohibit "displacement" or "substitution" in the sense of directly laying off one worker to hire a YIEPP worker, although program rules could not prevent a firm from hiring a YIEPP worker instead of another worker.	Mean reported displacement rate is 49.9 percent among 111 surveyed firms, and median displacement rate is 50 percent. That is, for every two youths subsidized by YIEPP at private firms, overall employment is estimated to increase by one. It is not clear whether displacement is of other youths, other disadvantaged, or adults or nondisadvantaged. Displacement is significantly higher at worksites whose quality was rated higher by outside observers. (Compared to "inadequate" worksites, displacement is higher by 14 percent at adequate sites, 18 percent at good sites, and 22 percent at "outstanding" sites.) Displacement is lower for full-time summer work than for part-time school-year work, by 17 percent.
Unicon (1982)	Trained observers visited twenty-nine participating firms at four different sites, interviewed managers of firms, and attempted to judge whether hiring a YIEPP worker had resulted in a net increase in employment or displaced some nonsubsidized worker.	Weighted mean estimate from four cities is 60 percent displacement in the private sector, implying that for every ten YIEPP jobs in the private sector, net business employment increases by four. It is unclear for whom the 60 percent displacement substitutes.
Gould, Ward, and Welch (1982)	Nonlinear regression analysis of employment data for 410 to 514 for-profit firms (depending on period examined), and of how their em-	Net displacement is estimated to average around 19 percent, but this low figure is in part due to the estimate that each YIEPP worker leads to an

TABLE A14.1 *Continued*

Study	Methodology	Results
	ployment during YIEPP is related to pre-YIEPP employment, revenue growth, and ratio of YIEPP workers to predicted total workers, with YIEPP to total workers allowed to have nonlinear effect on net employment. The effect of YIEPP on employment as YIEPP-to-non-YIEPP ratio approaches infinity is assumed to reflect effects of YIEPP on requiring extra supervisors. There were some problems with the quality of the employment data owing to some firms being confused about whether total employment includes YIEPP workers.	extra .28 of a supervisor. Hence, displacement of nonsupervisory workers is estimated to be 47 percent. So, for every ten YIEPP workers hired by for-profit firms, the firm's net employment goes up by about eight, but about three of these are extra supervisors. Net employment of nonsupervisory personnel goes up only by around five.
Farkas et al. (1984)	Non-experimental data comparing youth at sites participating in YIEPP to youth at previously similar sites not participating in YIEPP.	Annual earnings effect a few months after YIEPP program was terminated (although it had been mostly phased out a year earlier): $1,306 (1998 dollars) for young black cohort. This effect is overall YIEPP effect; subsidized private for-profit jobs were only 23 percent of YIEPP jobs.
Bishop, in Bishop and Hollenbeck (1985, ch. 4)	Regression analysis of employment of around 3,000 firms from December 1980 to June 1982, and the proportion of employment of youth, as a function of dummy variable for whether firm participated in CETA-OJT. Attempts to instrument for OJT participation were unsuccessful.	Based on typical number of OJT slots associated with CETA-OJT participation, for every ten OJT slots at a firm there are three extra jobs at the firm. OJT participation has insignificant effects on youth share of employment.
Barnow (1987)	Summary of various studies. Generally, regression analysis of postprogram annual earnings of CETA-OJT participants compared to individuals matched on pre-OJT earnings and other characteristics.	Adult women:[b] $1,572 Adult men: $1,851 Female youth: $1,636 Male youth: −$172
Bishop and Montgomery (1986)	Analysis of 1980 survey of 5,279 establishments. Particularly focused on the 57 percent familiar with CETA-OJT (see table 8.5 for analysis of TJTC and WIN tax credits). Focus is on models for explaining	Among establishments familiar with OJT, the proportion using OJT was increased by 85 percent if the firm first learned of the WIN tax credit from a government representative (mean participation rate is .075).

(Appendix continues on p. 400.)

TABLE A14.1 *Continued*

Study	Methodology	Results
	determinants of establishment's familiarity with OJT and explaining determinants of usage of OJT, conditional on establishment being familiar with OJT.	Among all establishments, a 10 percent increase in other establishments in area that learned of WIN via the government increases the proportion familiar with OJT by 11 percent. Familiarity with the program increases significantly for larger establishments, but usage conditional on familiarity increases significantly for smaller establishments. Authors speculate that this may occur because local training offices tend to spread referrals among employers.
Rode (1988) and Rangan(1984)	Survey data on participating MEED employers, asking whether they would have expanded to their present size without the MEED subsidy.	In 1988, 56 percent claimed they would not have expanded to their current size without the MEED subsidy; in 1984, 59 percent made this claim. It should be noted that the average number of MEED placements per business was 2.8 in 1984 and 1.8 in the latter period, so in most cases the issue is whether the firm would have added one worker without MEED. As noted in chapter 8, MEED was focused on small businesses: more than 80 percent of the private businesses participating had twenty or fewer full-time employees.
Auspos, Cave, and Long (1988)	Random assignment experiment in which welfare recipients who volunteered and who were felt to be suitable were randomly assigned to a treatment sequence of prevocational training, then work experience, then OJT wage subsidy.	The net annual earnings impact of the entire program sequence, per experimental, was $1,243 in 1998 (after OJT). Only 30 percent of the treatment group participated in OJT, so if OJT causes the entire impact, then the impact of OJT would be much greater. During quarters four and five after random assignment, when prevocational training and work experience are mostly over and OJT is near its peak, the employment impact of program is between two-fifths and two-thirds of OJT employment. This is consistent with the belief that OJT in fact leads to employment for

TABLE A14.1 *Continued*

Study	Methodology	Results
		some who otherwise would not find employment. Program statistics indicate that about seven out of ten OJT placements "roll over" into regular positions with the same employer.[c]
Freedman, Bryant, and Cave (1988)	Random assignment experiment in which single-mother welfare recipients who volunteered and were felt to be suitable were randomly assigned to a group eligible for OJT wage subsidies.	The annual earnings impact (1998 dollars) during the immediate postprogram period is $929 per experimental. Since only 43 percent of all experimentals participated in OJT, and other differences in services received between experimentals and groups were small, the average earnings impact per OJT participant was $2,160. During the main period in which experimentals received OJT subsidies, employment effects on experimentals were from 38 percent to 46 percent of the OJT-subsidized employment, suggesting that OJT leads to increased employment for a little less than half of OJT sample. Fifty-six percent of OJT participants completed their trial employment period, and all but one of those who completed the trial employment period rolled over into a regular job with the same employer.[d]
Orr et al. (1996)[e]	Random assignment experiment in which individuals were randomly assigned to treatment and control after they had been divided into one of three service strategies: OJT, classroom training, or other services. Each strategy received multiple services; for example, only 30 percent of the OJT strategy group received OJT, and 5 percent of the other two groups received OJT. Estimates reported here are for OJT strategy and are effects per enrollee.	Effects (in 1998 dollars) in months 19 to 30 after enrollment in JTPA are $1,342 for adult females, $1,479 for adult males, −$1,182 for female youth, and −$1,575 for male youth. Youth effects are not statistically significant. Effects for adult females on welfare at enrollment appear to be about twice as great as for average adult female. OJT effects are generally more positive than classroom training results for adults. However, for women, the "other services" category had higher earnings effects than the OJT service

(Appendix continues on p. 402.)

TABLE A14.1 *Continued*

Study	Methodology	Results
		strategy. Key services in "other services" appear to be job search and work experience.

Source: Author's compilation.
Note: This appendix presents more detailed summaries of the studies listed in table 8.6.
[a] Perry et al. (1975, 198, table VIII-2), data on net changes, contract trainees versus controls.
[b] These figures are based on studies summarized in various studies. To combine results from different studies, I aggregated each study up to overall effects on adult women, adult men, female youth, and male youth. To aggregate, I assume, based on Taggart (1981), that CETA-OJT was 21 percent welfare recipients, 79 percent nonrecipients, 60 percent white, and 40 percent minority. The numbers reported in this table are means of the various studies in 1998 dollars of annual earnings effects. The means are based on six studies for men and women and two studies for youth. The range of effects reported in 1998 dollars are: adult women, $88 to $2,205; adult men, –$908 to $5,527; female youth, $782 to $2,490; and male youth, –$870 to $527.
[c] The long-run effects, in percentage terms, of the program on earnings are greater than the effects on the proportion "ever employed" in a quarter. This finding is difficult to interpret. These greater percentage earnings effects could be due to higher wages, more full-time employment, or steadier employment during the quarter for those employed.
[d] The impact of the program on those "ever employed" in a given quarter tends to fade over time, even though the earnings impact does not. It is difficult to know what to make of this. The earnings impact could be due to effects on wages, effects on weekly work hours, or effects on weeks employed during the quarter for those who are employed.
[e] For impact figures, I use months 19 to 30, because this is clearly a period after OJT would be expected to have ended, whereas months 7 to 18 may also include OJT enrollment for some participants. Impact figures are per enrollee in JTPA, not assignee. On the other hand, figures are not per enrollee in OJT. If all these effects were assumed to be due to OJT participation of 30 percent of OJT enrollees who received OJT, the numbers in the table would have to be multiplied by around three.

Appendix 15

ESTIMATES OF THE EMPLOYMENT AND WAGE IMPACTS OF SOME RECENT WAGE SUBSIDY PROPOSALS

THIS appendix uses the labor market model of appendix 2 (see also Bartik 1999) to simulate the employment and wage effects of recent proposals for wage subsidies by Edmund Phelps and Robert Haveman. Models are estimated for Phelps's proposal by applying his formula for wage subsidy to the mean ln(wage) of each of five groups to calculate the subsidy, with the subsidy set equal to zero for two high-education groups because the calculated subsidy would be extremely small. Final subsidies ended up as 16.7 percent for female heads, 14.4 percent for other less-educated women, and 5.3 percent for less-educated men.

The wage subsidies to be entered into the model under Haveman's proposal require a more elaborate calculation. I first calculated subsidies based on an updated NJTC formula as a percentage of the mean ln(wage) of the group. These initial subsidies were then multiplied by 0.16 to reflect the fact that subsidies would be received only on employment in excess of 102 percent of the previous year's employment. The very conservative assumption here is that faced with a floor on the wage subsidy that requires 2 percent growth, firms act is if they have made a once-and-for-all-time choice of a certain higher employment level in response to the subsidy, and that the up-front subsidy is equivalent to an ongoing subsidy of 0.16 as high if the firm uses a real discount rate of about 0.12 and an assumed inflation rate of 0.04 (Bartik 1996a; Summers and Poterba 1994). This is a quite conservative assumption. Simulations by Daniel Hamermesh suggest that the actual employment impact of a subsidy with a floor of 102 percent might be 40 percent of the subsidy with no floor. (For example, see in Hamermesh [1978] how the employment effect varies as one goes from a subsidy on employment in excess of 85 percent of the previous year's employment to a subsidy on employment in excess of 100 percent of the previous year's employment.) In any event, the final subsidies used for the Haveman simulation were: female heads, 4.95 percent; other less-educated

TABLE A15.1 *Estimated Five-Year Effects of Phelps and Haveman Proposals*

	Phelps's Proposal	Haveman's Proposal
Impact on overall employment after five years	9.002 million jobs (10.89)	4.518 million jobs (11.01)
Impact on overall wages after five years	14.9 percent (4.44)	5.0 percent (5.96)

Source: Author's estimates derived from simulations using model of appendix 2.
Notes: Numbers in parentheses are pseudo *t*-statistics, calculated as ratio of mean effects to standard deviation of these effects from Monte Carlo repetitions of simulation. Percentage impact on overall wages is actually 100 times impact on ln(average overall wage). Wage effects for each of the five groups is quite similar in this model, within a few tenths of a percent except for the female head group, whose market wage goes up somewhat less. Most of the new jobs go to three non-college-educated groups in this model (7.1 million in Phelps model, 3.6 million in Haveman model).

females, 4.77 percent; more-educated females, 2.76 percent; less-educated males, 3.87 percent; and more-educated males, 2.23 percent.

Table A15.1 presents the estimated effects on employment and wages, after five years, for the Phelps and Haveman proposals.

Appendix 16

AN ANALYSIS OF SNOWER'S PROPOSAL FOR A "SELF-FINANCING" WAGE SUBSIDY SYSTEM FOR EMPLOYING THE DISADVANTAGED

This appendix presents an analysis for the United States of Dennis Snower's proposal for a wage subsidy system that, he argues, may be able to pay for itself in some European countries.

Snower's mathematical analysis is useful for illustrating some of the difficulties in having self-financing wage subsidies for the disadvantaged in the United States. Let us consider, as he does, a single period for which we are trying to determine the maximum feasible wage subsidy we can pay that can be financed by the resulting reduction in welfare benefits. A modified version of Snower's equation for the maximum feasible self-financing wage subsidy can be written as follows:

$$s = S/W = (1 - D)(1 - d)(p_n B_n - p_e B_e)/W$$

where s is the wage subsidy as a proportion of wages, S is the dollar amount of the wage subsidy, W is the dollar amount of the wage over that time period, D is the proportion of the individuals subsidized who would have gotten jobs anyway, d is the displacement rate due to subsidized individuals getting a job, B_n is the benefits the person collects from welfare or unemployment insurance if they do not work, p_n is the probability that they will collect those benefits if they do not work, B_e is net welfare benefits (net of payroll and other taxes paid) collected if the individual works, and p_e is the probability that the person will collect those welfare benefits. Perhaps reflecting a European perspective, Snower's equation is simpler: p_n is implicitly set equal to one, p_e and B_e are set equal to zero, and the maximum feasible subsidy is some fraction of the benefit replacement rate (B_n/W), where that fraction is assumed to depend on windfall wastage D and displacement d.

In the U.S. context, there are a number of differences from the European context. First, in general the replacement rate B_n/W is smaller. Welfare benefits are frequently quite small in the United States. For example, average TANF benefits in the median state, for a family of three, come to only $379 per month, or $4,548 per year (U.S. House of Representatives 1998, 525). This is only 38 percent of an individual's annual wage at a $6 per hour job worked for 2,000 hours. Many, perhaps most, poor people who are unemployed must rely on welfare rather than social insurance such as unemployment benefits, which tend to have higher benefit levels. Of course, individuals on welfare in the United States also get food stamps and Medicaid. But those who work at low-wage jobs also tend to get food stamps and, with various allowances allowed, often get almost as much as they would have received on welfare.[1] Furthermore, to encourage work, families on welfare who go to work are supposed to continue receiving Medicaid for some period of time.

Second, in addition to continuing to receive Medicaid and food stamps, a U.S. working family also would become eligible for the EITC. At $12,000 in earnings, this would be a payment of $3,641 for a family of three, as of 1997 (U.S. House of Representatives 1998, 408), almost as much as the welfare benefit they got when they were not working.

Third, even if the family did not work, in the U.S. context there is a good chance that for one reason or another they would no longer be on welfare. Particularly with many states aggressively attempting to reduce welfare rolls, P_n might be considerably less than one. The probability of receiving various welfare benefits if employed may also be considerably less than one for some of these benefits, although receipt rates of eligibles are actually quite high for the United States.

The net result from such a simple single-period analysis is that the maximum feasible self-financing wage subsidy may be quite low for the United States. Snower assumes that $(1 - D)(1 - d) = 0.5$. Judging from the research reported in chapter 8, this assumption may be a bit high, though not necessarily implausibly high. But if one plugs in plausible numbers for some of the other figures, it is easy to get a maximum feasible self-financing wage subsidy rate of less than 10 percent of wages.[2]

Of course, we can justify much larger wage subsidies as self-financing if we are willing to assume that a onetime hiring subsidy has quite persistent effects on the individual's benefit receipt. On the whole, there is no strong evidence that wage subsidies for increased private employment produce extremely persistent effects in reducing welfare receipt. The effects of subsidized jobs on earnings, and in some cases on employment, seem to be quite persistent. But in many cases, the effects on welfare dependence seem to fade over time.

NOTES

Chapter 2

1. A well-known result in economics is that if the labor market is perfect, subsidies to either side of the market will have identical effects on employment and on net wages received by workers and net wages paid by employers.
2. If the original supply of workers was not sufficient to accommodate the extra labor demand, then market wages may go up. The resulting increase in labor supply and (partial) reduction in labor demand brings labor demand and labor supply back into equality at a higher wage.
3. The figures in table 2.4 are derived in the following way. All data on GDP come from Council of Economic Advisers (1999). Federal job training programs include the Job Training Partnership Act (JTPA) Title II-A for adults, II-C for youth, 23 percent of JTPA Title III for dislocated workers (23 percent of JTPA Title III participants had wages less than $7.50 per hour), Job Corps, and summer youth jobs. JTPA data come from Social Policy Research Associates (1999), Job Corps and summer youth job data from U.S. House of Representatives (1998). JTPA funds are allocated to labor demand based on the proportion of participants in OJT and work experience; Job Corps is considered labor supply, and summer youth jobs are considered labor demand. Welfare-to-work programs include both TANF (Temporary Assistance for Needy Families) and welfare-to-work grant program. For TANF, labor demand is assumed to be total TANF spending times the proportion of the caseload participating in subsidized work, public-service employment, community jobs, or OJT, based on U.S. Department of Health and Human Services (1999, 41, table 3.5). Supply-side spending is assumed to be equal to the proportion of the caseload not participating in demand-side efforts times TANF funds allocated to encouraging work activities. For welfare-to-work grant program, grants are allocated to the demand side based on the estimated proportion of the grant funds allocated to "supported work activities" (OJT, work experience, subsidized jobs, community service), plus the funds allocated to employer mediation and workplace mentors (Perez-Johnson and Hershey 1999, 31, table D.1). Employment service data from the president's 2000 budget for the U.S. Department of Labor (available as one of the appendices to the budget at http://www.access.gpo.gov/usbudget/fy2000/app_down.html). Head Start, Title I, Pell Grants, and state need-based aid for college come from National Center for Education Statistics (1999, tables

361, 322, 323). To calculate the amount of general K-12 spending that goes to the disadvantaged, I take total spending on public K-12 schools (National Center for Education Statistics 1999, table 164), subtract Title I to avoid double-counting, and then multiply by the estimated proportion of all elementary and secondary students who receive Title I services (National Center for Education Statistics 1999, table 374). Subsidies to higher education are calculated as the difference between student tuition and fees paid (table 329) and instructional spending (table 337) for public institutions, with four-year institutions considered to include Research I, Research II, Doctoral, Master's, and Baccalaureate, and two-year institutions considered to be Associate's. The subsidy amount is $7.8 billion for four-year colleges and $5.0 billion for two-year colleges. The proportion going to the disadvantaged is equal to the proportion of eighteen- to twenty-four-year-olds who are dependent family members and who come from a family with annual income less than $15,000 (derived from series P20-500 of Census Bureau, now published only electronically at the Census Bureau web site: http://www.census.gov/population/www/socdemo/school.html). Data on federal economic development programs come from National Academy of Public Administration (1996). Estimated state and local economic development spending comes from Corporation for Enterprise Development and Harrison Institute for Public Law (1999, 83). Data on the amount of wages transferred by the 1990–91 increase in the minimum wage are from Card and Krueger (1995); estimates for the proportion that goes to workers with family income less than 150 percent of the poverty line come from Burkhauser, Couch, and Wittenburg (1996). Estimated total administrative and compliance costs for equal employment opportunity laws are from Conrad (1995); as a rough guess, I assume that the proportion that benefits blacks with family income less than 150 percent of the poverty line is equal to the proportion of blacks ages eighteen to sixty-four with family income less than 150 percent of the poverty line (U.S. Census Bureau 1999, P60-207, table 2).

Chapter 3

1. Married women might also need jobs, of course, but I excluded them from this calculation to be conservative. The target white male employment rate in 1979 was calculated separately for high school dropouts and high school graduates (non-college-graduates). One could argue against using a lower target employment rate for high school dropouts than for high school graduates, but I wanted to restrict the calculation to employment rates that had actually been achieved for a particular education level.
2. Source is 1999 figures from the U.S. Census Bureau, accessed July 8, 2000, from the Census Bureau web site: http://www.census.gov/hhes/poverty/threshld/99prelim.html.
3. In a recent survey of leading labor economists, their median estimate of the uncompensated labor supply elasticity, which is what I am discussing in the text, was 0 for men and 0.3 for women (Fuchs, Krueger, and Poterba 1998).

4. This line of critique of the labor supply literature has been emphasized in a review article by the well-known labor economist James Heckman (1993).

5. These results from the late 1980s are from Juhn, Murphy, and Topel (1991), using data from the March Current Population Survey (CPS).

6. These wage elasticities are responses to market wages and therefore are appropriate for evaluating how the labor supply of the poor responds to increased demand. However, as discussed further in chapter 4, these wage elasticities might not apply to government supply-side wage subsidies to workers. Some research suggests that changes in welfare that provide implicit wage increases—that is, more income for extra work—may not affect labor supply as much as market wage increases (Moffitt 1983; Meyer and Rosenbaum 1998). This may explain why the wage elasticities estimated using data from the Negative Income Tax Experiments (Robins 1985) are much smaller than those estimated by Juhn, Murphy, and Topel (1991) or by Moffitt (1983).

7. These figures come from the March 1999 CPS and are discussed more in table 3.3. Similar figures come from other studies. According to Rebecca Blank's recent book on U.S. poverty, *It Takes a Nation,* 63 percent of all families who are poor during a given year include at least one individual who worked sometime during that year, although in two-thirds of these families the individual did not work full-time year-round (Blank 1997, 31–32). Similar figures are cited in Citro and Michael (1995), Lazere (1997), and U.S. Census Bureau (1999). According to Citro and Michael (1995, NRC 260), 51 percent of poor families under the current poverty measure included one or more workers in 1992. According to Lazere (1997), from 1994 to 1996, 65 percent of nondisabled, nonretired poor families with children included at least one worker (19); the average number of weeks worked in families with a worker (including all workers) was forty-one weeks (21); 25 percent of these nondisabled poor families had a full-time, year-round worker (23); 52 percent of these nondisabled, nonretired poor families had earnings as a majority of their cash income (26). According to the Census Bureau (1999), of all individuals between the ages of eighteen and sixty-four who were poor during 1998, 49 percent worked and 16 percent worked full-time, full-year (thirty-five or more hours for fifty or more weeks) (calculated from page 17, table 3). These figures seem compatible, varying according to the families and individuals included in the calculations, and according to whether the focus is on individuals working or everyone working.

8. Many welfare mothers work, but again, not usually full-time. Edin and Lein's figures imply that those welfare mothers who do unreported work on average do so for only a few hours per week. The point is that these welfare mothers can do productive work and potentially could work more.

9. This self-assessment asked welfare recipients to assess their own anxiety, depression, loss of emotional control, and psychological well-being.

10. The skills test was the Armed Forces Qualification Test, which has been shown to be correlated with wage rates and earnings.

11. These are regression-adjusted estimates that hold constant various demographic characteristics of the person. The particular estimates are for an AFDC (Aid to Families with Dependent Children) recipient (as of seven to ten months before) who is single, black, female, living in an urban census tract, twenty-five to thirty-four years old, the mother of one child under two, and the recipient of welfare for seven years.
12. This figure is derived by adding up their percentages using appropriate weights for the different groups in their survey. For women with higher test scores, around two-thirds worked year-round.
13. The gap between actual work experience and potential work experience may explain why wages for ex-welfare recipients on average grow quite slowly with time (Cancian et al. 1999; Burtless 1995). In the five years after leaving welfare, less than 5 percent work full-time year-round for all five years, and only 25 percent are working full-time year-round by the fifth year (Cancian et al. 1999).
14. Black unemployment rate data from U.S. Department of Labor (1999, 52); high school dropout rate calculated by author from the Outgoing Rotation Group of the CPS (CPS-ORG), 1998; the welfare recipient unemployment rate, calculated by author from March 1998 CPS, is the unemployment rate in March 1998 of single mothers who received welfare sometime during 1997.
15. This is Katherine Abraham's (1983) conclusion based on regressions of vacancy rates on unemployment rates. I did similar regressions of vacancy rates on unemployment rates using Harry Holzer's twenty-eight local sites (Holzer 1989, table 3.2, 32). This regression had an R-squared of 0.22, a constant term of 3.00 (standard error = 0.71), and a coefficient on the unemployment rate of −0.212 (standard error = 0.077). The implied unemployment rate at which the vacancy rate and the unemployment rate are equal is 2.48 percent. In Holzer's database, the lowest unemployment rates are 4.7 percent, so this prediction requires some extrapolation beyond the range of the data. For Abraham's data, some significant numbers of local area observations in some of the databases are below 3 percent unemployment, and these actual observations indicate that unemployment rates and vacancy rates tend to be equal at slightly below 3 percent unemployment.
16. The "typical" wage differentials across industries and firms referred to in these studies correspond to the standard deviation of unexplained wage differentials across industries and firms after controlling for observed worker and job characteristics.
17. This agrees with Hamermesh (1993, 136): "Knowledge of the extent of substitution among various groups of workers is not well developed."
18. There is much dispute in the minimum-wage literature, but it is over whether minimum-wage increases have zero or even positive employment effects (Card and Krueger 1995), or whether minimum wages have modest negative employment effects (Neumark 1999).
19. This estimate is taken from Katz (1998), who in turn bases his estimate on dividing the effects of minimum wages on teenage employment that are stan-

dard in the literature outside Card and Krueger (1995) by the effects of minimum wages on teenage wages that are estimated by Card and Krueger. Therefore, the elasticity cited is for employment with respect to wages, not employment with respect to changes in the minimum wage. Katz assumes that a reasonable range of elasticities of teenage employment with respect to the minimum wage is -0.05 to -0.2, whereas Card and Krueger's results suggest that average teenage wages increase by one-third to one-half of typical increases in the minimum wage. A recent paper (Baker, Benjamin, and Stanger 1999) finds slightly higher long-run elasticities of teenage labor demand with respect to the minimum wage in Canada, of about -0.25. However, it also appears that minimum wages may be somewhat more binding in Canada on teenage wages. This suggests that teenage wages may increase more with the minimum wage in Canada than in the United States. Baker and his colleagues do not report elasticities of teenage wages with respect to the minimum wage. However, if the effect were one-half, toward the upper end of Card and Krueger's estimates, the implied labor demand elasticity from their estimates would be -0.5.

Reductions in the wage of less-educated workers will also have output expansion effects, but these are less important, since less-educated workers' contribution to output is only a small portion of the contribution of all labor.

20. Berg, Olson, and Conrad (1991) cite similarly high job loss rates in other welfare-to-work programs. For example, the Enterprise Jobs program had a 31 percent job loss rate one month after the job was started, and 73 percent by six months. The Massachusetts ET program, which is widely considered a highly successful welfare-to-work program, found that twelve to sixteen months after a job was started, 62 percent of the program participants were no longer at their original job.
21. More evidence of the importance of referrals is in Granovetter (1994).
22. All migration data come from the U.S. Bureau of the Census, series P20, figures for the 1996 to 1997 period from the March 1997 Current Population Survey (U.S. Census 1997, tables 25 and 28).

Chapter 4

1. Previously, federal welfare assistance to states was provided on a matching basis, so that the federal government paid part of the costs of extra welfare spending.
2. The percentage increase in the labor force for each group is calculated based on the estimated labor force entries for that group alone from welfare reform (see Bartik 2000a).
3. Unemployment figures for ex-welfare recipients—that is, single mothers who received welfare sometime during 1998—are calculated by the author from the March 1999 CPS.
4. See appendix 3 for more information on this modeling result, and Bartik (2000a) for more details on this simulation.

5. Of this total, $13.9 billion was federal dollars and $11 billion was state dollars. This total does not include unobligated federal dollars but does include federal dollars obligated but not actually spent in fiscal year 1998, as well as TANF funds (TANF is the new acronym for welfare, standing for "Temporary Assistance to Needy Families") transferred to child care and social service programs (U.S. Department of Health and Human Services 1999, table 2.5). The state total includes both state maintenance of effort funds in the TANF program and in separate state programs (table 2.12).

6. The estimates of Dickert, Houser, and Scholz (1995) imply that 182,000 single parents will enter the labor force because of the EITC expansion between 1993 and 1996. The Meyer and Rosenbaum (1998, table 11) estimates cited here use the estimated effect on the employment rate of changes in "income taxes if work" from the period 1984 to 1996 of 0.0232. This is multiplied by the estimated number of single mothers without a college degree from Bartik (1999) of 6.86 million, and in turn multiplied by 1/0.913, where 0.913 is Meyer and Rosenbaum's figure for single mothers who do not have a college degree.

   As noted by a reviewer of a draft of this book, one can argue about whether these effects of the EITC on the labor force participation of single mothers are "large" or "modest." For example, Liebman's (1998) estimate that the EITC increased the number of single mothers working by 405,000 appears to be an increase in the number of single mothers working by between 5 and 10 percent. (It is difficult to be sure because Liebman does not detail his intermediate calculations and assumptions.) This can be viewed as a large effect. On the other hand, the implication of this estimate is that the labor force participation of an overwhelming majority of single mothers who receive the EITC is unaffected by the EITC.

7. According to Eissa and Hoynes (1999), the EITC causes the labor force participation rate of low-education husbands to go up by 0.2 points and that of wives to go down by 1.2 points. Twenty million taxpayers receive the EITC; Eissa and Hoynes say that one-third are married couples. If, as they assert, 60 percent of low-education married couples are eligible for the EITC, probably about half of such couples actually receive it. That means that the actual labor force effect of the EITC on the group of low-education couples receiving it is twice what Eissa and Hoynes estimate, or 0.4 points for husbands and -2.4 points for wives. (I assume that only those who receive the EITC have their labor supply affected). Of the 6.7 million married couples receiving the EITC, some are low-education, and some are not. Let's assume that the labor supply effect of the EITC on married couples receiving it is the same whether or not they are a high-education couple. Then the labor supply effect of the EITC on wives is a reduction of 2.4 percent of 6.7 million, or 160,800. The labor supply effect of the EITC on husbands is an increase of 0.4 times 6.7 million, or 26,800.

8. This 20 percent cost saving figure is a rough extrapolation of the results of Dickert and her colleagues (1995). Their figures show welfare and food

stamp cost savings due to the EITC expansion of 1993 to 1996 of $3.3 billion. The 1993 expansion roughly doubled the size of the EITC, so these results imply that the overall program might save $6 billion of the $30 billion overall costs. The suggestion that the 1993 expansion roughly doubled the labor market behavior effects of the EITC is also consistent with estimates by Meyer and Rosenbaum (1998). The estimates of Dickert and her colleagues do not seem to calculate changes in welfare spending for individuals who stay on welfare. Their $3.3 billion cost savings reflects their estimates that the number of families leaving welfare and food stamps owing to the EITC expansion exceeded 500,000, even though the estimated EITC effect on the labor force was an increase of only 186,000. Also, average welfare and food stamp benefits for the typical single-parent family leaving welfare owing to the EITC are more than three times their EITC benefits; for the typical two-parent family, welfare and food stamp benefits are a little less than half their EITC benefits.

9. The Council of Economic Advisors (1998, 6) claims that the child poverty rate, including the EITC, declined by five points from 1993 to 1997, and that "over half of the decline in child poverty between 1993 and 1997 can be explained by changes in taxes, most importantly the EITC."

10. Simulations using the general equilibrium model of appendix 2 suggest that the EITC would at most reduce the market wage of single mothers by only nine-tenths of 1 percent. In this model, the estimated labor supply of less-educated female heads of household is 5.19 million. A labor supply shock of 405,000, the maximum estimated by Liebman (1998), would be a labor supply increase of 7.8 percent. According to table A2.12, the elasticity of market wages after five years for labor supply shocks to female heads of household is -0.11. This implies a decline in market wages for this group of -0.9 percent.

11. Consider the effects on long-term single-parent welfare recipients. In quarters 2 through 7 after program intake, the percentage of the control (AFDC) group ever employed was 59.0 percent, the percentage of the MFIP-incentives-only group ever employed was 66.8 percent, and the percentage of the MFIP-incentives-plus-services group ever employed was 76.0 percent (Miller et al. 1997, table 4.3).

12. Another recent experiment, the New Hope Program, also targets earnings supplements at full-time workers. However, these supply-side work incentives are coupled with guaranteed community service jobs, a labor demand policy. The New Hope Program is discussed in chapter 7, which reviews public-service jobs programs.

13. Assuming welfare recipients are 30 percent of single mothers (Bartik 2000a) and that long-term (more than one year) welfare recipients are 84 percent of welfare recipients (U.S. House of Representatives 1998, 531), a labor supply shock of 15 percent implies a labor supply shock of about 3.8 percent to female heads. (These long-term figures are a bit high in terms of the Canadian criterion, because they refer to receipt over several spells rather than the

current spell.) Because single mothers with less than sixteen years of education are about 4 percent of the overall population, this is a labor supply shock of about one-sixth of 1 percent to overall labor supply. Applying the elasticities in table A2.12, this labor supply shock of 3.8 percent should reduce female head wages about four-tenths of 1 percent. Table A2.12 also suggests displacement of 58 percent. As noted in appendices 1 and 2, other models suggest displacement rates between one-third and two-thirds.

14. The average number of TANF families with one adult recipient was 2.14 million as of the July-September 1997 quarter (U.S. Department of Health and Human Services 1998b). Assuming that 84 percent of these families have cumulative welfare receipt of greater than one year, about 1.8 million families would be eligible for a U.S. SSP program. According to Lin and Pan (1998), monthly Canadian spending per SSP participant was $196 (table 3.7); annualizing this and multiplying by 0.75 to convert to U.S. dollars gives annual spending per SSP participant of $1,764. Multiplying by 1.8 million families gives total spending of $3.2 billion. During the same months, the SSP reached its peak employment impact of a change in the employment rate of 0.13 per participant (Lin and Pan 1998, table 3.1). Multiplying this by 1.8 million gives an impact of 234,000 extra workers. The five-year displacement rate in table A2.12 is 58 percent; multiplying 234,000 by 0.42 gives 98,000 as the net boost to employment.

15. In Canada net spending per SSP participant is cut from $196 per month to $55 per month after allowing for reductions in welfare spending and increases in income tax revenue. However, one would expect U.S. savings in welfare spending to be less because of our less generous welfare benefits.

16. The largest employment increase estimated for the EITC is an increase of 405,000 in the employment of single mothers (Liebman 1998). But there are probably negative effects on the employment of wives that exceed any positive effects on husbands, and Liebman's estimate is on the high side. If we use Meyer and Rosenbaum's (1998) estimate of a positive employment effect of 170,000 for single mothers, and Eissa and Hoynes' (1999) estimates to get effects of a reduction of 161,000 for wives and an increase of 27,000 for husbands (see note 7), the net employment effect of the EITC is only 36,000.

17. In the fifth quarter, the monthly average of the treatment group receiving supplement payments was 23 percent (Lin and Pan 1998, 45). The net increase in the employment rate in the fifth quarter was 13 percent (table 3.1).

18. Financial incentives alone increased employment rates by 8.6 percent in the fifth quarter after random assignment, from 32.3 percent among controls to 40.9 percent among the financial services treatment group. Annual earnings increased by $518, from $2,227 among controls to $2,745 among the financial-incentives-only group. Financial incentives plus services increased employment rates by 15.5 percent, and annual earnings by $1,113. According to Blank, Card, and Robins (2000), the somewhat different effects of financial incentives in this comparison have to do with the different sample that was used.

19. Information on the CAP, unless otherwise noted, comes from Hamilton et al. (1996).

20. Different sources give different proportions of eligibles served in Head Start. According to the Children's Defense Fund web site, one-third of eligible children are served. According to the President's Council of Economic Advisers, Head Start gives slots to 40 percent of those eligible (CEA 1997). The numbers look somewhat better for specific ages. For example, for Head Start's peak year of age four, it appears to enroll about 60 percent of those eligible (see *1998 Green Book;* Karoly et al. 1998, 112, statistics on children born into poverty annually).

21. For example, in 1990 the estimated number of adults who were economically disadvantaged enough to be eligible for JTPA services was 23.9 million (Loprest and Barnow 1993). Of those 23.9 million, 2.2 million were unemployed and 12.5 million were out of the labor force. In contrast, JTPA in 1990 had only 307,000 adult terminees (U.S. House of Representatives 1998). Even if we ignore eligibles who were employed, JTPA is graduating only 2.1 percent of the eligible.

22. Table 4.3 understates the percentage of high school dropouts. The table is based on a sample of high school sophomores, and some have already dropped out of school by tenth grade. The table counts GED recipients as high school graduates, even though some research argues that the GED is not worth very much as an educational credential (Cameron and Heckman 1993).

23. According to Kane and Rouse's (1999) summary of Leslie and Brinkman (1988), a $1,000 reduction in tuition increases postsecondary enrollment among eighteen- to twenty-four-year-olds by 4.4 percentage points.

24. For example, under the state-controlled school finance system in Michigan, all school operating funding is provided on a per-student basis by the state, with the per-student amount in each district based on historical spending patterns in each district and some state attempt to bring up the lowest-spending districts. When urban districts lose a student to a charter school or a private school, they lose their "average cost" funding for that student. Yet their true costs probably decline by much less given the fixed costs of running schools and the fact that the marginal teacher who is laid off or not hired is paid a beginning teacher's salary. For example, in Kalamazoo public schools, the director of finance estimates that the cost savings from losing a student are only about one-third of the loss in the state operating subsidy.

25. The Quantum Opportunities Program costs $10,000 to $15,000 over the four years and requires high-quality dedicated staff to run effectively. As evidence, in one of the five sites in which the program was implemented, the program essentially collapsed in its second year because of poor management.

26. My own calculations in appendix 5, based on table 4.2, show that the log earnings differential between male college graduates and nongraduates increased by 0.2306 between 1979 and 1998, and the log earnings differential

between female college graduates and nongraduates increased by 0.0880 from 1979 to 1998. Borjas, Freeman, and Katz (1997) calculate that the log wage differential between college graduates and nongraduates grew by 0.191 from 1980 to 1995.

27. The 4 million is derived by dividing 3 million by 0.8, and 15 million by dividing 9 million by 0.6.

28. Average annual educational and general expenditures per student in higher education was $11,319 from 1995 to 1996 (National Center for Education Statistics 1999, table 336), in 1998 dollars. Take the low 4 million figure for the needed additional graduates. If producing these college graduates requires only two years of additional education on average, then the needed additional expenditure would be $90 billion (4 million × 2 years × $11,319 per year). Most plausible variations in assumptions would enormously increase this figure.

29. Friedlander et al. (1997) look at five voluntary training programs for adult females for which they have both second-year earnings effects and cost per participant. Regressing second-year earnings effects on cost yields a coefficient of 0.110, with a standard error of 0.074. Spending another dollar on training thus seems on average to yield a return of eleven cents in extra earnings in the second year after training is completed. If this earnings effect were persistent over time, it would be large enough that spending extra money on training would be a reasonable policy option. However, this return to spending extra on training is quite modest compared to the 70 percent or greater annual returns of some low-cost training programs. Furthermore, this extra return is modest enough that even the most expensive training programs rarely have average annual earnings effects greater than $2,000.

30. There is some confusion about how to interpret these results. Even in the most rigorous experimental studies, the standard errors of the experimental-control differences in earnings tend to grow as we move further away from the training period. This occurs because both experimentals and controls are subject to random shocks to their earnings, and these shocks accumulate over time. As the variability of earnings increases over time, our uncertainty about the true average earnings of each group increases. For example, in the GAO's study of the long-term effects of JTPA, the earnings effects (and standard errors) for adult women in the five years after assignment were: year 1—$379 (145); year 2—$658 (178); year 3—$583 (196); year 4—$556 (218); year 5—$402 (225). (Note that these effects are in current dollars, not constant dollars.) Because the earnings effects for year five are only 1.79 times the standard error of the estimated earnings effect, the GAO's report emphasized that JTPA's five-year earnings effects were not statistically significant (which is true at the 5 percent level, but not the 10 percent level). This is clearly a biased way to interpret the results. Given how standard errors go up over time, even if earnings effects are unchanged, eventually it is inevitable that the *t*-statistic will fall below whatever cutoff we might use. It seems more appropriate to note that earnings effects appear to diminish only slightly over time as we go from year two to year five.

31. One could argue that one mystery of the JTPA experiment is why JTPA has any effect on the receipt of classroom training. According to Thomas Kane (1995), after allowing for Pell Grants, the average cost to a control group member of classroom training similar to what JTPA offered would be only $60. Kane argues that information and paperwork problems in learning about financial aid and filling out forms might explain why JTPA increases the receipt of classroom training. This seems consistent with the important role of counselors in Project Quest in helping participants deal with the complexities of financial aid.

32. It is not clear that all types of training and placement programs are more successful in high-demand local labor markets. For example, San Diego's job search program for welfare recipients appeared to be more successful when labor market conditions in San Diego were depressed. Also, the Supported Work Program, operated at fifteen sites around the United States, appeared to be more successful in times when the overall job market was depressed (Gueron and Pauly 1991, 186). In both of these cases, although program graduates did better when labor market conditions were stronger, the control group did even better, reducing the program's net impact. I am making a more limited point: if one is setting up a program that will interact with industry to design a curriculum and place program graduates, it is easier to set up and implement such a program if there are more fast-growing occupations from which to choose.

Chapter 5

1. Similar diagrams have been published elsewhere, for example, in Blank (1997, 55).

2. This has been pointed out most prominently by Gottschalk and Danziger (1985), and Danziger and Gottschalk (1995), who provide formulas for predicting exactly how much an increase in mean income, holding the variance of income constant, will reduce poverty, for various assumed parameters of the income distribution and positions of the poverty line relative to mean income.

3. The sources for each row in table 5.2 are as follows: *GNP:* Okun's Law (see, for example, Okun 1973) as updated most recently by Bluestone and Harrison (2000, 281–82, 73). *Labor force participation rate:* Arthur Okun (1973) estimates that a one-percentage-point reduction in unemployment increases labor force participation by 0.6 percent, based on Perry (1971). William Bowen and Aldrich Finegan (1969) estimate that a 1 percent decrease in unemployment increases labor force participation by perhaps half a percent. My own estimates (Bartik 1991) are from underlying models of how unemployment and labor force participation rates both respond in the short run to shocks to a metropolitan area's employment growth. Dividing the labor force participation rate effect by the unemployment rate effect gives a short-run effect of 0.3 to 0.4, which grows over time. My results (Bartik 1999) suggest

that the labor force participation rate increases by half a percent after five years in response to a one-point reduction in the unemployment rate.

Wage rate: Blanchflower and Oswald (1994) conclude that the elasticity of ln(wage) with respect to ln(unemployment rate) is −0.1. At an unemployment rate of 6 percent, this implies that a one-point reduction in unemployment increases wages about 1.8 percent. However, because Blanchflower and Oswald generally use annual earnings as a dependent variable, as pointed out in Card (1995b), this is an overestimate of the likely effect of unemployment on *hourly* wages. Card reviews the macro literature on the cyclicality of real wages, restricting his attention to studies that control for changes in labor force composition by using panel data, and he concludes that the elasticity is −0.08 to −0.09; at an unemployment rate of 6 percent, this implies that a one-point reduction in unemployment increases wages by 1.4 to 1.6 percent. Card's own estimates of state wage curves suggest an elasticity of −0.08, implying that a one-point reduction in unemployment increases wages by 1.4 percent. Olivier Blanchard and Lawrence Katz's (1997) inclusion of lagged wages suggests that the short-run elasticity of wages is considerably less than the long-run elasticity. Their estimated short-run elasticity is −0.04, implying that the short-run effect of a one-point reduction in unemployment is to raise wages by 0.7 percent. The coefficient on lagged wages is 0.91 to 0.92, however, so this initial effect rapidly grows over time. In making my own estimates (Bartik 1991, 166, table 7.3; 92) of the effect of MSA employment growth on unemployment, occupational real wages, changes in wages due to occupation switches, and overall wages, dividing the total wage effect by the change in the unemployment rate yielded an effect of 0.6 percent for a one-point reduction in the unemployment rate brought about by MSA employment growth. I have also estimated (Bartik 1999) wage curves with two lags in wages and unemployment. The coefficient on the first lag in unemployment implies a short-run elasticity of −0.03, which implies that a one-point reduction in unemployment increases wages by 0.5 percent. However, the effect of unemployment rapidly grows over time in this specification, to a value of 1.6 to 3.3 after five years. Taken altogether, it seems likely that the short-run percentage effect on wages of a one-point reduction in the unemployment rate is somewhere in the range of 0.5 to 1.5, with lower values more plausible for the immediate effect and higher values after two or three years.

Occupational upgrading—increases in real wages due to moving up to better-paying occupations: Okun (1973) estimates upgrading effects of 0.7 percent; his estimates, admittedly speculative, are based on comparing estimated changes in real output with estimated changes in real labor input (235). In making my own estimates (Bartik 1991), I looked at changes in occupations held by workers, controlling for worker demographic characteristics, and at how those changes would be expected to change real wages based on national norms for those occupations. These estimates were derived by dividing change in this "occupational rank" variable (166) due to MSA growth by change in the unemployment rate due to MSA growth (166). My tables suggest an upgrading effect of 0.2 percent based on ordinary least squares (OLS) estimates of the effects of employment growth, and 0.4 based on two-stage least squares (2SLS) estimates of the effects of employment growth due to demand shocks to an MSA's export base.

Average real earnings: My estimates (Bartik 1991) are derived by dividing the short-run effect of MSA employment growth on real earnings (OLS estimates) by the short-run effects of MSA employment growth on unemployment; depending on which of two unemployment rate effect estimates are used, one gets effects in the range of 2.6 to 3.6 percent. Card (1995) estimates the elasticity of annual earnings with respect to unemployment of -0.20, a result that translates into a percentage effect of 3.6 percent for a one-point reduction in unemployment at 6 percent unemployment. Using pooled time-series cross-section data on nine census regions, Blank and Card (1993) estimate that a one-point reduction in the unemployment rate increases overall average real earnings by 1.7 percent. I update these estimates (Bartik 2000b) with more recent data, using twenty-one somewhat smaller states or state groupings, and obtain an estimated effect of 1.5 percent. I have also estimated (Bartik 1994a) the effects of MSA employment growth on earnings: using various measures of the effects of employment growth on unemployment from earlier work (Bartik 1991), I found that the implied percentage effect of a one-point reduction in unemployment on earnings is 1.8 to 2.3 percent. (These are effects on nominal earnings, but results in Bartik [1991] indicate that the immediate effect of employment growth on prices is slight.) Recently (Bartik 2000b), I updated these estimates using more recent data, and using states rather than MSAs; I got somewhat lower estimates of the effects of employment growth on overall earnings. These somewhat smaller estimates imply that a one-point unemployment reduction has an effect on average earnings of 1.3 to 1.8 percent.

Average real income: Using pooled time-series cross-section data on the nine census regions, Blank and Card (1993) estimate that a one-point reduction in unemployment increases average real income by 1.4 percent. I have updated these estimates (Bartik 2000b), using twenty-one groupings of states, and estimate that a one-point reduction in unemployment increases average real income by 1.2 percent. Previously (Bartik 1994a), I used MSA data to estimate the effect of employment growth on real income. Using various estimates of the effects of MSA employment growth on unemployment (−0.32 and −0.442, from Bartik [1991]), I estimated an effect of a one-point reduction in unemployment on real income of 1.1 to 1.4 percent. Recently (Bartik 2000b), I updated these estimates, using state data, and these estimates imply that a one-point reduction in unemployment increases average real income by 0.9 to 1.2 percent. Finally, I have estimated (Bartik 1996) how MSA employment growth affects the real income-needs ratio, with a data set following the same individual from year to year. The estimates correspond to an effect of a one-point reduction in unemployment increasing average income by 1.2 to 1.5 percent.

Income share of lowest income quintile: Studies using regional data are less likely to be biased by unobserved national trends than are studies using national data. Estimates from specific studies using regional data include: 0.06, from Bartik (1994a), using MSA data; 0.10, from Bartik (1996b), using

MSA data and individual panel data to control for unobserved individual effects and compositional effects; 0, from Blank and Card (1993), using nine census regions; 0.02, from Bartik (2000b), updating Blank and Card (1993) and using twenty-one regions; 0.04 to 0.05 (depending on which coefficient from Bartik [1991] is used to convert employment growth effects into unemployment effects), from Bartik (2000b), updating Bartik (1994a), using state data, and with employment growth as demand shock. Estimates from studies using national data include: −0.02 to 0.05, from Romer and Romer (1999); 0.02 to 0.04 (not statistically significant), from Mocan (1999), using national data and separating unemployment into cyclical and structural components (cyclical effects used here); 0.06, from Blank (1989); 0.10, from Blank and Blinder (1986); 0.15, from Cutler and Katz (1991); and 0.09, from Jäntti (1994).

Poverty rate (change in rate points): Estimates from studies using regional data include: −0.7 to −0.9, depending on which coefficient is used to convert employment growth effects to unemployment effects, from Bartik (1996b), using MSA growth as a demand indicator and panel data on individuals to control for unobservable individual effects; −0.3, from Bartik (1994a), using MSA growth as a demand indicator; −0.3, from Blank and Card (1993), using nine census regions; −0.7, from Tobin (1994), using states; −0.5 to −0.6 (depending on how state employment growth is converted to unemployment effects; effects were a little lower in the 1990s at −0.3 to −0.4), from Bartik (2000b), redoing Bartik (1994a) by using states. Updating Blank and Card (1993) and using twenty-one regions, I recently (Bartik 2000b) got −0.4 for the overall sample, −0.7 for 1967 to 1979, −0.4 for 1980 to 1989, and −0.6 for 1990 to 1997. In results using national data, Tobin (1994) gets −0.4; Blank (1993), using GNP growth, and converting these numbers to unemployment rate effects using Okun's Law yields −0.8 for 1963 to 1969, and −0.3 for 1983 to 1989; Powers (1995), in results using GNP growth and the conventional poverty rate as a dependent variable, gets results, converted to unemployment rate effects using Okun's Law, of −1.1 for 1960 to 1969, −0.8 for 1970 to 1979, and −0.8 for 1980 to 1989; Romer and Romer (1999) get results of −0.4 to −0.5; using per capita GNP growth, Cain (1998) gets results that translate, using Okun's Law, into unemployment rate effects of −0.8 from 1959 on, and −0.7 from the 1970s on; using simple regressions involving GDP growth, Haveman and Schwabish (1999) get results that translate, using Okun's Law, into unemployment rate effects of −0.7 from 1960 to 1975, −0.3 from 1976 to 1982, −0.5 from 1983 to 1992, and −0.7 from 1993 to 1997. Other studies, such as Blank and Blinder (1986), Blank (1993), Cutler and Katz (1991), and some of the results in Haveman and Schwabish (1999) and Cain (1999), also report effects of unemployment on poverty, but usually controlling for variables such as the ratio of mean or median income to the poverty line. This makes it difficult to determine the full effect of a shock to aggregate demand, which would in general affect incomes and unemployment simultaneously.

Percentage effect on earnings of bottom income quintile versus effect on overall earnings: The estimates of Blank and Card (1993), using nine census regions, imply that a one-point reduction in unemployment increases earnings by about 2 percent more for the lowest income quintile than for the average family. I redid these estimates (Bartik 2000b) using updated data and twenty-one groupings of states and estimated that the effect of a one-point reduction in unemployment is to increase earnings by about 3 percent more for the lowest income quintile than for the average family. I estimated the effects of MSA growth on earnings by quintile (Bartik 1994a), and these estimates imply, depending on how growth effects are translated into unemployment effects, that 1 percent lower unemployment increases the earnings of the bottom income quintile about 4 to 6 percent more than for the average family. I redid these estimates (Bartik 2000b) using updated data and state data, and the new estimates imply that 1 percent lower unemployment increases the earnings of the bottom income quintile about 3 to 4 percent more than for the average family.

Various labor market variables and effects on different education groups: In recent work (Bartik 1996b), I calculated a significantly greater effect of MSA growth on less-educated men than on more-educated men (although not for women), which translates into 1 percent lower unemployment increasing annual earnings by 2 to 3 percent more for men with ten years of schooling compared to sixteen years of schooling. These greater effects appear to be mainly due to effects on annual hours, not on hourly wages. In Bartik (1994a), I estimated significantly greater effects of MSA growth on high school dropouts than on those with at least a high school degree, effects that translate into a 1 percent reduction in unemployment having a 1 percent greater effect on the annual earnings of dropouts. In Bartik (1991), I estimated significantly greater effects of MSA growth on less-educated men, effect that translated into unemployment having a 0.4 percent greater effect on the annual earnings of men with ten years of education compared to those with sixteen years. Freeman (1991) estimated effects of unemployment on younger workers implying that a 1 percent reduction in unemployment causes about a 2 percent greater effect on the employment of those with less than twelve years of school than on those with sixteen years or more of school (dividing Freeman's effects on absolute employment-population ratios by the means of these ratios), and 1 percent lower unemployment appears to have about a 3 percent greater effect on the weekly earnings of high school dropouts compared to college graduates. Topel (1986, table 8, column 4) estimates that a six-year change in education causes a change in the effects of MSA growth that implies that a one-point reduction in unemployment would increase weekly earnings by about 3 percent more for men with ten years of education compared to men with sixteen years of education. Blanchflower and Oswald (1994) calculate an effect of unemployment on the annual earnings of different education groups that implies that there is about a 2 percent greater effect on the annual earnings of individuals with eleven years or less of schooling than those with thirteen years or more of schooling. Card's (1995b, table 3, column 6) elasticity estimates imply that a reduction from 6 percent to 5 percent unemployment would increase annual earnings by about 2 percent more for individuals with less than twelve years of education than for those with sixteen or more years of education; these different effects appear to be due completely to different effects on annual hours, not on hourly wages.

Various labor market variables and effects of overall lower unemployment on blacks versus whites: Bound and Holzer (1993) find effects of growth in overall MSA employment-population ratios that, if translated into effects of unemployment, imply that a one-point drop in unemployment has 3 to 4 percent greater effects on the employment of blacks than that of whites, but that unemployment rate effects on wages do not differ much. In Bartik (1994a), I find effects of MSA growth on blacks compared to whites that imply that a one-point lower unemployment rate increases annual earnings about 1 percent more for blacks than for whites. In Bartik (1996b), I do not find any significant differences between the responses of black and white labor market variables to greater MSA growth. In Bartik (1991), I find that the annual earnings of blacks increase by more than they do for whites in response to MSA growth, corresponding to about a 0.2 percent greater increase in annual earnings in response to a one-point unemployment reduction; this effect is primarily due to greater effects on hourly wages. Blank and Blinder (1986) found that a one-point reduction in unemployment reduced unemployment about 2.5 times as much for nonwhite males, and 1.2 times as much for nonwhite females, a finding that suggests that unemployment has a 1.5 percent greater effect on the employment of nonwhite males, and a 0.2 percent greater effect on the employment of nonwhite females. On the other hand, unemployment rate effects on the annual earnings of those employed do not differ much by race. Blanchflower and Oswald (1994) find unemployment increases the annual earnings of blacks by only perhaps 0.1 percent more than for whites.

4. Also, average weekly work hours tend to go up.

5. Readers with a background in the history of economic thought will recall that this is John Maynard Keynes's criterion for whether unemployment is involuntary: Would a drop in the market wage result in an increase in employment or not?

6. One could also estimate the long-run effects of temporary increases in labor demand using the model of appendix 2. But it should be noted that this model, with only two lags in all variables, is not necessarily well suited to detecting small long-run hysteresis effects of increased human capital development on long-run employment rates and wage rates. These effects of human capital are better measured by models that are less restrictive in how employment in one time period affects long-run labor market outcomes.

7. There is also a research literature on the long-run effects of the in-school work experience of youth, but I do not discuss it here because it seems to raise issues that are somewhat different, including the issue of how such work experience might interfere with schooling.

8. Stevens's (1995) analysis of workers with low job tenure (less than three years) or low education (high school or less) finds negative but statistically insignificant long-run effects on earnings, but statistically significant effects on wages. My own interpretation is that these findings suggest long-run effects on earnings owing to the effects on wages.

Chapter 6

1. For example, in most standard macro models, the inflationary spiral reduces the real money supply unless Federal Reserve policy is completely accommodative. This reduction in the real money supply reduces aggregate economic activity and increases unemployment.
2. Technically, the condition for wage and price interactions to be strong enough to justify a NAIRU model is that in a model of price inflation (or wage inflation), the sum of the coefficients on lagged price inflation (or wage inflation) must equal one rather than being less than one. As shown by Blanchard and Katz (1999), this condition is equivalent to the sum of the coefficients on lagged real wages, in a model of the expected real wage, being one.
3. In Blanchard and Katz's (1999) review, the evidence suggests that these feedback effects are strong enough to result in accelerating inflation below a NAIRU in the United States, but not in most Western European countries.
4. The condition for a NAIRU is that the sum of the coefficients on lagged inflation equals one (Gordon 1997).
5. As Blanchard and Katz (1999) point out, models relating real wage levels to unemployment also result from many other models of wage setting, such as bargaining models (for example, Mortensen and Pissarides 1994). Ray Fair's (2000) well-known macroeconomic model is based on the theory that each firm is an imperfect competitor that sets price levels based on expectations of demand, possibly indicated by the unemployment level, and other firms' price policies. As Fair notes, a model with the price level as a dependent variable and the unemployment level as an explanatory variable can also be derived from a duopoly model with imperfect information (Tirole 1988).
6. For example, in Robert J. Gordon's (1998) recent paper on why inflation is so low, his model using a constant NAIRU of 6.0 percent predicts a consumer price index (CPI) annual inflation rate for the second quarter of 1998 of 3.2 percent, whereas the actual figure was 1.6 percent. Even though unemployment in the second quarter of 1998 was 4.4 percent, and it had been below the 6 percent NAIRU since September 1994, even Gordon's predicted inflation rate of 3.2 percent is not much above the actual 1994 inflation rate of 2.6 percent. It takes a while for below-NAIRU unemployment rates to drive up the inflation rate dramatically in most estimated NAIRU models.
7. That is, it is often difficult to tell whether the sum of the coefficients on lagged inflation is one or merely close to one, and this difficulty makes an enormous difference for the resulting long-run equilibrium.
8. That is, the 95 percent confidence interval for the NAIRU for a given estimation model often spans a 3 percent range in unemployment for the NAIRU estimated as of a given time.
9. Richard Layard, Stephen Nickell, and Richard Jackman (1991, 201), citing Hall's (1977) formal statistical analysis, develop the following argument for

why a one-point reduction in unemployment affects inflation more at lower unemployment rates. Intuitively, if the number of unemployed workers competing for every vacancy goes from two to one, this is much more important, from the perspective of both employers and workers, than if the number of unemployed workers competing for every vacancy goes from six to five. A reduction from two to one in the unemployment-vacancy ratio causes a huge increase in the probability of an unemployed worker quickly finding a suitable job, and a huge decrease in the probability of a firm with a vacancy finding a suitable hire. A reduction from six to five in the unemployment-vacancy ratio does not dramatically change the odds of firms and workers finding suitable job matches; at either ratio, it is easy for firms to find suitable workers, and very hard for workers to find suitable jobs. Hence, we would expect a given reduction in the number of unemployed to have much larger effects on wages at low levels of unemployment.

Tobin and Bailey also used the argument that the average worker in a low-unemployment group would be a higher-productivity worker who would use more capital stock than the less-productive average worker in a high-unemployment group. Because of this greater use of capital by workers from low-unemployment groups, greater relative employment for these groups puts more pressure on usage of the capital stock for a given level of overall unemployment. More shortages of capital put upward pressure on prices.

10. See Okun comments in Bailey and Tobin (1977, 577), as well as Okun (1973, 245–46).

11. The wage subsidy in this case may still have effects on the employment of the disadvantaged, for example, by targeting firms that otherwise would be unlikely to hire the disadvantaged and by targeting disadvantaged persons who otherwise would be unlikely to be employed. Chapter 8 provides a fuller discussion of different types of wage subsidies.

Chapter 7

1. An excellent recent study that looks at publicly funded jobs is Ellwood and Welty (2000), which provides an alternative view of some of the same issues considered in this chapter. Their study has influenced my own thinking about publicly funded jobs, as I indicate through various citations, although I go beyond their analysis in various ways. Another good recent review of the PSE literature is Gottschalk (1998).

2. That is, in economics terminology, a PSE program is a closed-end grant program for select employers that does not change wage rates at the margin for most and perhaps all employers.

3. I have adopted the term "public worker substitution" from Ellwood and Welty (2000).

4. The term "private-sector crowd-out" is adopted from Ellwood and Welty (2000).

5. Ellwood and Welty (2000) report that New York City has 18,800 welfare recipients on average in work experience programs. According to Katz and Allen (1999), New York City has 231,000 families in its welfare caseload.
6. This figure comes from Wiseman (1997, 36). I assume that those likely to use New Hope were the estimated 12,397 who were projected from the sample survey to respond that New Hope would interest either themselves or their spouse/partner "a great deal," out of the 30,077 adults in these neighborhoods estimated to be eligible for New Hope.
7. This figure is derived by multiplying the 32 percent of those who ever held a community service job during the twenty-four-month follow-up period by the average 6.1 months they held such a job, divided by 24 months (Bos et al. 1999, 117).
8. Thus, I disagree with Burtless and Haveman's (1984) interpretation of the results of the Employment Opportunity Pilot Project (EOPP) that there is not much interest among the poor in public-service job guarantees. They emphasize that in EOPP, among those eligible, only 18 percent enrolled; of those, only 62 percent received job search assistance; of those 62 percent, one-third obtained unsubsidized jobs; and of the two-thirds of those who did not obtain unsubsidized jobs, only about half ended up accepting an offer of subsidized employment or training, two-thirds of which took the form of public-service jobs. The net result is that less than 3 percent of those eligible for EOPP ended up getting a public-service job. But there are two factors at work here. First, the emphasis that EOPP, like most programs of public-service jobs for the poor, puts on first encouraging individuals to find jobs on their own reduces enormously the demand for public-service jobs. Second, EOPP suffered from a number of administrative problems that enormously reduced demand for the public-service job slots. Among other things, the percentage of eligible EOPP non-enrollees who had never heard of the program was apparently around 80 percent (Brown et al. 1983, 123). In addition, as the EOPP program evolved, less stress was placed on the guaranteed jobs portion of the program and more on the job search aspects; this shift of focus, combined with funding shortfalls, may have encourage some sites not to market the public-service jobs aggressively.
9. More evidence for the productivity of PSE jobs and PSE workers comes from the following studies and programs:

   - *PSE programs generally:* "We suspect a more reasonable estimate [of the value of output in PSE programs] is perhaps 75 percent of the pay of workers plus program-provided supervision and benefits in well-run programs. But that estimate is highly speculative" (Ellwood and Welty 2000, 46).
   - *WPA:* "One study of FERA [Federal Emergency Relief Administration] work relief construction projects in New York state for the winter of 1934 to 1935 found them to average 75 percent of the efficiency achieved under private contract. A sample study of WPA construction projects in late 1939 found their total costs about 13 percent greater than the estimated

costs under contract. WPA authorities reported instances where the use of machinery could have reduced the costs of performing tasks by as much as two-thirds" (Kesselman 1978, 214).

- *Supported Work:* "The value of output produced was equal to more than 50 percent of the per-participant costs" (Hollister 1984, 31).
- *Community Work Experience Program (CWEP):* "The majority of participants were positive about their assignments and believed they were making a useful contribution" (Brock et al. 1993, 28). "On average, 83 percent of supervisors thought that the work was necessary and should not be delayed. Similarly, approximately 80 percent of the participants also thought that their work was necessary" (32).
- *New Hope:* "It appears that New Hope achieved the goal of developing CSJs [community service jobs] that were 'real' jobs." Quotes from site sponsors: "The participants here served us well, and there are a multitude of tasks for the kinds of office support positions that we need here most" (Poglinco et al. 1998, 12).
- *New York City (Work Experience Program):* The quality of employees was reported to be slightly below that of city workers on average in these relatively menial jobs (Lerman and Rosenberg 1997).
- *The work experience component of the Maine Training Opportunities in the Private Sector (TOPS) program:* "The majority of supervisors found the participants to be at least as productive as regular new employees, if not more so" (Auspos, Cave, and Long 1988, 52).
- *Youth Corps:* "Almost 80 percent of the sponsoring agencies rated the quality of corpsmembers' work as 'good' or 'excellent.' . . . Sixty-nine percent of [service] beneficiaries rated the quality of the work performed to be good, very good, or excellent" (Jastrzab et al. 1996, 11).
- *YIEPP:* Ninety-two percent of the work sponsors found the youths' work to be of value (Diaz et al. 1982).

10. As noted in chapter 5, the non-experimental estimates and the experimental estimates include different effects in the assessment of the net impacts of these programs during the in-program period. The experimental estimates studies compare participants with nonparticipants and essentially ask whether participants could have obtained a job even without the program. The non-experimental estimates studies compare areas with large usage of the program to areas with small or no usage. Therefore, the non-experimental estimates reflect both the net impact on participants plus the market displacement effects of the program in the short run.

11. Most of the programs shown in table 7.2 have already been described in the text or in sidebars. More descriptions of programs are provided in the notes to the table. The AFDC Homemaker Home Health Aide Program provided short-term training as a home health aide for welfare recipients, followed by a year of subsidized employment as a home health aide. The Maine TOPS program was a welfare-to-work program for welfare recipients that combined a sequence of services: a few weeks of prevocational training, followed by up to twelve weeks of part-time work experience, and then followed in some cases by up to six months of subsidized OJT/employment in the private sector. Sixty-eight percent of TOPS enrollees participated in the work experi-

ence, and 31 percent in OJT. The Structured Training and Employment Transitional Services (STETS) program was an employment program for the mentally retarded with three phases. Phase 1 was assessment and half-time work experience in a sheltered workshop or public or nonprofit agency. Phase 2 was OJT/subsidized employment with a regular employer. Phase 3 was postplacement support services for up to six months. Phases 1 and 2 together were supposed to last less than one year.

12. Goldman et al. (1986) report larger effects for female AFDC applicants with no prior work experience, but this is for the job search/work experience treatment compared to controls receiving no services. If one looks at their table 3.8 (92), there is no sign that the differential between the job-search-only treatment and the job-search-plus-work-experience treatment is greater for those with no prior work experience.
13. As Ellwood and Welty (2000) point out, citing Borus and Hamermesh (1978), this conclusion is sensitive to the details of the econometric estimation.
14. One possible exception is workfare programs in which individuals are assigned to a job in order to "work off" their welfare check. Legislative approval of such programs may merely be a matter of approving the incremental administrative costs of locating and creating job slots, referring welfare recipients to these slots, and monitoring their participation in the workfare slots. The extra supervisory costs may be passed on to the agencies in which workfare participants are employed. The costs of the welfare benefits paid for this work may not be counted as an extra cost of the program, even though in some cases it may be just that if the program leads to additional participation in the welfare program.

Chapter 8

1. A more detailed version of table 8.1 is in appendix 11.
2. The exact percentages are 20.6 percent for the control group, 13.0 percent for the TJTC group, and 12.7 percent for the wage voucher group.
3. However, another experimental study does suggest that it was showing the employers the voucher that caused labor market problems. A small study in Racine and Eau Claire examined a program that encouraged welfare recipients and other disadvantaged groups to advertise to employers that their hiring would make the employer eligible for a tax credit. This treatment group was compared to a randomly chosen control group. Of the control group, 21.1 percent obtained a certified job (one for which the employer applies for the tax credit) within sixty days of entering the study, versus 12.0 percent of the treatment group; this difference was statistically significant at the 10 percent level after controlling for other client characteristics. A follow-up with a small subsample asked whether the client had told employers about the credit. The treatment group was more likely than controls to have

told employers about the credit, but some of the treatment group did not tell employers, and some of the control group did tell employers about the credit. Of those clients who told employers about the credit, 6.3 percent obtained a certified job, compared to 21.7 percent of those clients who did not tell employers about the credit; this difference was statistically significant at the 10 percent level after controlling for other client characteristics. Furthermore, after statistically controlling for whether the client told employers about the credit, the client's treatment group status had no significant effects on his or her success in obtaining a job. Thus, the training seems to harm clients because it increases the odds that they will tell employers about their eligibility for the credit (Wisconsin Department of Health and Social Services and Institute for Research on Poverty 1982).

4. The calculation behind this figure is as follows: 700,000 jobs is about 0.7 percent of the U.S. labor force in 1977. Table 5.2 indicates that labor force participation might go up by 0.3 to 0.6 percent when the unemployment rate declines by 1 percent. Use 0.45 percent as a midpoint figure for the response of the labor force. From differentiation, one can derive a formula that shows that the change in the unemployment rate from a shock to employment will be given by $dU = -(dE/L)/(1 + 0.45(1 - U))$, where U is the unemployment rate, E is employment, and L is the labor force. Based on this formula, the 700,000 jobs in 1977 would have lowered the unemployment rate by 0.50 percent. Applying this to table 5.5 suggests that such a lower unemployment rate would increase employment for men and single women, ages twenty-five to fifty-four, with less than a college degree, by 283,000 jobs. This 283,000 figure is how many jobs would be created today from such an unemployment reduction. It needs to be scaled back a bit to account for somewhat lower population in the past. Using statistics from the *Digest of Education Statistics* (National Center for Education Statistics 1999, 17, table 8) and the *U.S. Statistical Abstract* (U.S. Census Bureau 1998, 15, table 14), I estimate that the total population without a college degree, ages twenty-five and over, increased from 108.4 million in 1980 to 120 million in 1997. This suggests scaling back the 283,000 estimate to about 250,000 jobs in 1977.

5. A more detailed description of the results of these studies is in appendix 13.

6. This is based on dividing the tax expenditure in 1985 ($0.765 billion, in 1998 dollars), derived from Bishop and Montgomery (1993), by the number of 1985 certifications (622,000).

7. Unfortunately, given the nonlinear nature of the estimation in the various studies that have been done, it is difficult to make precise simulations of exactly how much employment tax credit usage would change owing to various policy initiatives to increase government outreach. A precise simulation would require the use of the original data, with all the information on the characteristics of each firm. But, for example, the Bishop and Kang (1991) study estimates that offering a referral to a firm increases the number of TJTC hires by that firm five- to twelvefold. Use a midpoint estimate of eightfold. Twenty-one percent of all firms reported receiving a government

offer of a referral. Suppose firms are identical except for receiving a government referral. Then the 21 percent of firms that received a government offer of a referral would have 76 percent of the TJTC hires (0.76 = (8 × 0.21)/[(8 × 0.21) + 0.79] = 1.68/2.13). To double the number of TJTC hires would require increasing the proportion of firms receiving an offer of a referral by 0.30 (2.13/7).

8. Of those assigned to the employer bonus, 2.8 percent had an employer who successfully claimed a bonus. (Some employers who submitted a notice of hire did not retain the employee long enough to receive the bonus.) The bonus experiment increased the proportion of those hired within eleven weeks (the eligibility period) by 2.1 percent, so the deadweight loss is 0.7/2.8 = 25 percent. Also, the program cost $21.50 per participant (1998 dollars); the average participant reduced his or her number of weeks in the program during the benefit year by 0.36 weeks, or about 0.7 percent of a full-year employee. So the cost for increasing employment by fifty-two weeks is $21.50/0.007, or $3,000.

9. Appendix 14 presents a more detailed description of the studies summarized in table 8.6.

10. For example, the results from Maine TOPS suggest that when OJT is near its peak, the employment impact of the TOPS program is between two-fifths and two-thirds of OJT employment. The JTPA study, in which about one-half of enrollees participate in OJT at some point, has earnings effects during its first six months (the peak months for OJT) of 18 percent for women and 9.4 percent for men. If 50 percent of enrollees actually participated in OJT for all of these first six months (surely an overestimate), and if all the earnings effects of the JTPA-OJT strategy are due to employment increases associated with OJT (probably also an overestimate), then about 36 percent (women) or 19 percent (men) of OJT jobs represent a net expansion in job opportunities for JTPA clients. Finally, in the YIEPP program, as shown in table 7.1, the employment impact of school-year jobs is 67 percent of the jobs created, whereas the employment impact of summer jobs is 44 percent of the jobs created.

11. According to Joseph Ball and his colleagues (1981, 59–60, and table 18), 19 percent of surveyed work sponsors had hired one or more YIEPP youth after the subsidy ended, and 38 percent intended to hire one or more YIEPP youth. The 38 percent who "intended" to hire YIEPP youth includes both those who wanted to hire a youth but the youth quit and those who were currently receiving a YIEPP subsidy but intended to hire that youth for a regular permanent position. Hence, some of this 38 percent represents rollover and some does not, but it is impossible to be more precise than that.

12. The model used in appendix 15 predicts an annual cost of $170 billion for Phelps's proposal. This exceeds his prediction of $132 billion, probably because the model does not distinguish between full-time and part-time employment, and Phelps wants to restrict subsidies to full-time employees. At the model's prevailing wages for overall labor, the subsidy would add $457

billion in overall wages. The model simulation indicates that wages tend to overshoot their equilibrium level at five years and to gradually come back down over time.

13. Haveman (1988) estimates \$5 billion to \$10 billion per year. Updating to 1998 by the change in wage and salaries from 1988 to 1998 gives the \$9 billion to \$17 billion figure.
14. The increase in wages would have an estimated value of \$146 billion. The estimated annual budgetary costs of the non-windfall part of the program, based on a 50 percent wage subsidy of the first \$10,500 in wages, or an annual subsidy of \$5,250, times annual job creation of 900,000, yields annual budgetary costs of \$4.7 billion. If the program cost \$9 billion to \$17 billion, this implies deadweight loss of 48 to 61 percent, which seems roughly compatible with previous research results.

Chapter 9

1. In a 1987 NLC survey, 56 percent of mayors listed "improving the city's tax base" as one of their city's top three economic development goals (Bowman 1987). In a 1994 NLC survey, 43 percent of local elected officials listed "increase tax base/revenues" as one of the most important goals of local economic development activity (Furdell 1994).
2. As discussed in Bartik (1996a, 310, n. 55), the revenue lost per job gained from a change in the state and local business tax rate is given by the following formula: $dR/dJ = (R/J)[1 + (1/E)]$, where R is state and local business tax revenue, J is number of jobs, and E is the elasticity of the number of jobs with respect to the business tax rate. (To prove this, use the following equations: $dR/R = dT/T + dJ/J$, where T is the business tax rate defined as a tax rate per job, for small changes in T and J, as $R = T \times J$; $E = (dJ/J)/dT/T)$, from definition of elasticity.) I have previously derived annual state and local business tax revenue estimates that when updated to 1998 dollars are \$2,148 per job. Furthermore, the research suggests an elasticity of business activity with respect to the overall state and local business tax rate of around (-0.3) (Bartik 1991, 1992). Substituting in gives a figure for revenue lost per job created from state and local business tax rate cuts of \$5,012.
3. In other words, Ronald Jarmin (1999) uses the presence of a center in the MSA where the firm is located as a key identifying variable to correct for the endogeneity of firms choosing to be center clients.
4. The impact of local employment growth on net migration versus local employment rates cannot easily be ascertained by simply looking at who gets the new jobs at firms that locate or expand in the area. For example, suppose a new plant locates in an area and employs all local residents. In general, some of those local residents are opening up job vacancies by quitting other local jobs to take jobs at the new plant. These vacancies may be filled by in-migrants even though none of the original jobs were. In addition, some unemployed local residents who take jobs at the new plant might have other-

wise left the area. Finally, one would generally expect the new plant to have multiplier effects on other employment, and one should look at the impact of these jobs on net migration and local employment rates.

5. For more on WireNet, see Ma and Proscio (1998), Mayer (1998), and Elliott and King (1999).
6. For more on enterprise zones and their history, see Ladd (1994).
7. This is derived by multiplying 8.1 million by three weeks divided by fifty-two weeks, to translate the effects of ES services into person-years of employment.
8. For more information, see the ALMIS information web site at http://www.doleta.gov/almis/index.htm.
9. This description of the WIA is based on information from the U.S. Department of Labor (1998a), Savner (1999), Schade et al. (1999), and National League of Cities (1999).
10. State minimum wages, even at the same level as the federal minimum wage, also cover industries and types of employers that are not covered by federal minimum-wage regulations.
11. As mentioned in chapter 3, such elasticities of labor demand with respect to minimum wages imply somewhat larger (in absolute value) elasticities of labor demand with respect to wages for teenagers and other disadvantaged groups (Katz 1998). Because research indicates an elasticity of average teenage wages with respect to the minimum wage of perhaps one-third to one-half, the implied elasticity of teenage labor demand with respect to average teenage wages is perhaps two to three times the elasticity of teenage labor demand with respect to the minimum wage. If one believes Neumark's range of minimum-wage elasticities of −0.1 to −0.3, the implied labor demand elasticity with respect to average teenage wages would be in the range of −0.2 to −0.9. If one believes Katz's range of minimum-wage elasticities of −0.05 to −0.2, then the implied labor demand elasticity with respect to average teenage wages would be in the range of −0.1 to −0.6.
12. Essentially the argument is that various imperfections in the labor market cause individual employers to have some market power over the wages they pay, and that they face an upward-sloping labor supply curve. This leads to the standard analysis of how a buyer with monopsony power responds to a floor on the price of the product he or she buys.
13. This is consistent with the results of Isabel Sawhill (1999), who finds that even if all family heads worked full-time, full-year, an increase in the minimum wage from the current $5.15 per hour to $6 per hour would reduce the poverty rate only from 3.6 percent to 3.4 percent.

Chapter 10

1. See chapter 8, note 4, for a similar calculation. Nine hundred thousand jobs today, using the same procedures as in chapter 8, note 4, would lower overall

unemployment by 0.46 percent. Applying this to table 5.5, the number of jobs for men and single women without a college education, ages twenty-five to fifty-four, would go up by 261,000 jobs.

2. This relies on the assumption that a one-point increase in unemployment reduces labor force participation by 0.45 points. As noted in note 1, this results in a 900,000 loss in jobs being associated with a 0.46 point increase in the unemployment rate. Multiplying 900,000/0.46 times 4 gives 7.8 million jobs.

3. This number is derived in two steps. First, actual NJTC annual costs in 1978 are updated to 1998 using figures on the growth in nongovernmental wage and salaries from 1978 to 1998 (Council of Economic Advisers 1999, 358, table B-28). Second, it has been estimated that nonprofit revenues are about 8 percent of GDP (Hines 1998). Assume then that nonprofit employment is about 8 percent of total employment. I then used this to calculate how much additional employment would be covered by an NJTC that included nonprofit employers and state and local governments, as opposed to an NJTC that covered only the private business sector (Council of Economic Advisers 1999, 380–81, table B-46).

4. The calculation goes as follows. As discussed in chapter 8, a revised NJTC on a national basis might create a total of 4.5 million jobs after five years. If the revised NJTC was implemented in a low-unemployment environment and applied to only 20 percent of the nation, it might create only 20 percent as many jobs, or 900,000 jobs, after five years. (Perhaps some additional jobs would be reallocated from low- to high-unemployment areas, but one could argue that these reallocated jobs should be ignored, since disadvantaged workers in both locations would suffer offsetting effects.) Based on estimates in Bartik (1991, 236), employment adjustment in local labor markets is such that the ten-year effect of some local cost factor is about 1.625 times the five-year effect ($1.625 = [1 - .9104^{10}]/[1 - .9104^{5}]$, based on estimated employment adjustment factors from Helms's [1985] business location study). Hence, the ten-year effects on aggregate jobs would be estimated to be 1.462 million jobs (1.462 = 1.625 times 0.9 million). Previous calculations have suggested that jobs for less-educated prime-age workers, as a proportion of total jobs created, would be 0.29 (261,000/900,000). Hence, the total number of estimated jobs created for less-educated prime-age workers would be 0.424 million (0.29 times 1.462 million), which I round to half a million. Obviously this is a rough calculation, but it seems unlikely that revising some of the assumptions could greatly increase the estimated job creation.

5. Twenty percent of the $19 billion cost for a full nationwide NJTC is $3.8 billion.

6. Because the worker would ultimately benefit from all these uses of the wage fund, one could argue that the worker is still receiving the market wage. However, given that low-income workers are likely to have significant discount rates, and that these training vouchers and car repair insurance spend-

ing are mandatory and unlikely to be engaged in voluntarily by most workers, it is likely that workers place an immediate value on the wage fund amounts that are less than the dollars they are forced to put into the fund. As a result, the effective net wage, including the subjective value that workers place on the fund dollars, is likely to be less than the market wage.

7. The calculation goes as follows. Call x the required number of participants per year to attain the goal of 5.5 million additional jobs after ten years. Assume that two-thirds of the participants actually increase their employment because of the program, and that they participate for an average of five months. Then the in-program employment effect of the program, in terms of full-time, full-year employment, is $x(.67)(5/12)$. Suppose that in the remaining six months of the year about half the original participants are still employed because of the program. Then the remaining incremental program, in full-time, full-year job units, during the same year, is $x(.67)(0.5)(0.5)$. Suppose that the long-term employment effect of the program is 20 percent of the original shock to employment for the original participants, for each of the next ten years. Then the program, running in steady state, will be producing after ten years additional full-time, full-year employment of $x(.67)(.20)(10)$. We then sum these three terms, set equal to the target goal of 5.5 million jobs, and solve for x, which gives 3.1 million participants per year. Because each of these participants is in the program for an average of only five months out of the year, the average number of participants at a point in time is 1.3 million (3.1 million times (5/12)).
8. These figures are derived by just substituting the assumed numbers in the equation used in note 7.
9. A subsidy of $8 per hour, covering 1.3 million full-time job slots on average during the year, would cost (8)(2,000 hours)(1.3 million) = $20.8 billion.

Appendix 1

1. Hiring and training costs are substantial. For example, according to Barron, Berger, and Black (1997), firms on average screen more than nine applicants before making a job offer, conduct five to seven interviews, and spend an average of 19 hours evaluating applicants. Newly hired workers on average receive 140 hours of training, most of it informal training.
2. This relies on the finding, presented in figures A2.1 and A2.2, that at low unemployment rates, the five-year elasticity of relative wages with respect to a one-point change in unemployment for less-educated groups is about -0.3, and that the five-year elasticity of overall wages with respect to a one-point change in overall unemployment is about -3. For a group that is about 10 percent of the overall labor market, the elasticity of the group's wages for a one-point change in the group's unemployment rate would be $-0.6 = -0.3 + (0.1)(-3)$.

3. The assumed unemployment rate is 8 percent, so of the one hundred persons added to the labor market, ninety-two will get jobs. But net employment goes up by only thirty-six persons. So fifty-six other persons must no longer be employed because of the policy.

Appendix 2

1. This is the closest one can come to consistently defining single mothers using CPS-ORG data.
2. Unemployment predicts wages better than employment-population ratios, which would fit a market-clearing model (Blanchflower and Oswald 1994).
3. The relevant formula showing the relationship between the elasticity of labor demand with respect to a one-point change in the unemployment rate (E_u), versus the elasticity of labor demand with respect to labor supply (E_s), at a given unemployment rate U, is $E_u = [E_s/(1 - E_s)][1/(1 + U)]$.
4. Because all equations include a state fixed effect, state population from any year can be used as a weight without bias as long as the weight does not vary across years for a state.
5. Except where noted, all statements in this section about the statistical significance of some group of variables in a particular equation are backed up by F-tests for that group of variables that indicate statistical significance at the 5 percent level.
6. Estimates in the figures and tables are based on one thousand Monte Carlo repeated simulations of the model, with each simulation based on one random draw from the distribution of parameter estimates for the twenty-three estimated equations. These one thousand Monte Carlo repetitions are used to generate average elasticities and effects, standard errors of such effects (the standard deviation of the effect in the one thousand repetitions), and pseudo *t*-statistics for the effects (the ratio of the average effects to the standard deviation of the effects). This approach is used because of the difficulty in generating analytical standard errors in this complicated nonlinear model.

Appendix 3

1. Someone who “loses” his or her job owing to welfare reform is someone who would have been employed in some alternate universe in which welfare reform did not occur, not necessarily someone who was employed prior to welfare reform.

Appendix 7

1. The assumptions made in the first and third rows of table A7.1 are implemented as follows. In the first row, for every worker of a given group hired by

the policy, it is assumed that the effective supply of that worker is reduced by one in the equations explaining relative labor demand. As shown in appendix 2, the relative labor supply of the different groups enters the relative labor demand equations. In contrast, in the third-row simulations, the hiring of additional workers from one group has no effect on the relative employment of different groups by regular employers, that is, the relative labor supply of different groups in the relative employment equations is unaffected.

2. That is, in appendix 2, although the labor force share of different groups affects relative hiring of the different groups, the overall labor force (or the overall unemployment rate) does not affect overall labor demand.

Appendix 8

1. In interpreting the coefficient on employment, it should be remembered that the ln(wage rate) is defined as zero when the individual was not employed at all five years before, and that the model also includes annual work hours five years before. Thus, the employment dummy implicitly measures the effect of working less than one hour five years before at a wage of $1 per hour.

Appendix 9

1. In the full paper from which these results are taken (Bartik 2000c), two other groupings of the labor force are used: white non-Hispanics versus other races, and central-city residents versus suburban residents.
2. In Bartik (2000c), half of the estimates use a model in which national effects are treated as fixed; doing so requires dropping the national price or wage variable from the equation. Fixed effects and random effects estimates are not significantly different. The fixed effects estimates are more precise but do not allow any simulation of the national effects of lowering unemployment in many MSAs, since these estimates do not allow feedback from national trends to local prices and wages.
3. I also tested whether group unemployment rates help explain prices. This test examines Baily and Tobin's (1977, 1978) hypothesis that a group's unemployment has fewer effects on prices if the group's wage rate is low. The group unemployment rate was added in the same functional form and lag as overall unemployment. The unemployment of nongraduates is statistically insignificant in the price equation.
4. The AIC-minimizing lag lengths for nongraduates was four, and one for college graduates.
5. For example, the national price lagged one period had a *t*-statistic of 3.11 in the price equation. For this equation, I also looked at lagged national wages and the lagged national unemployment rate. The best national variable was the national wage lagged one year, which had a *t*-statistic of 3.12. In the wage equation for college graduates, the *t*-statistic on the national wage is 2.82. In

this equation, I also tried several specifications that each entered a different national variable, including lagged national overall wages, lagged national prices, and lagged national overall unemployment rate. The best *t*-statistic was for overall national wages, the coefficient on which had a *t*-statistic of 2.83.

6. The *t*-statistic on lagged national wages of nongraduates in that group's local wage equation was 1.36. I also tried other national variables: national overall wages lagged one year; national prices lagged one year; and the overall national unemployment rate lagged one year. These variables were always clearly statistically insignificant.

7. For example, because the sum of the coefficients on lagged prices in the price equation is 0.763, the long-run effect of local wages on local prices is 0.272 (.0644 coefficient on local wages/[1 − 0.763]). This is reasonable given that some estimates suggest that local value added for most of the retail goods that are part of the local CPI is about 35 to 50 percent (Bartik 1991, 129) and probably somewhat greater for local goods such as housing.

8. This normal reduction is derived from estimates of the correlation between the unemployment rates of college graduates and nongraduates in an MSA, controlling for MSA and year fixed effects. With estimated covariances and variances of group unemployment rates, one can derive an equation to predict each group's unemployment given overall unemployment. The actual unemployment reductions are from 5.4 percent for nongraduates and 2.1 percent for graduates when overall unemployment is 4.5 percent, to 3.6 percent and 1.5 percent, respectively, when overall unemployment is 3 percent.

Appendix 16

1. For example, according to a Congressional Research Service (CRS) study reported in the *1998 Green Book* (U.S. House of Representatives 1998, 408), in Pennsylvania a family of three with no earnings would receive $2,746 per year in food stamps as of January 1997, whereas a family of three with earnings of $12,000 per year would receive food stamps of $2,102 per year.

2. For example, on the basis of the CRS study already mentioned, let's assume 100 percent receipt of all benefits both while employed and unemployed. AFDC benefits are $5,052 per year with no earnings, and food stamp benefits are $2,746 with no earnings. The EITC is $3,640 at $12,000 in earnings, and food stamps would be $2,102. Medicaid is still received for some period of time, whether or not the family is employed. Then filling in numbers in this equation yields $s = (0.5)(\$2{,}055/\$12{,}000) = 0.086$.

REFERENCES

Abraham, Katherine G. 1983. "Structural-Frictional Versus Deficient Demand Unemployment: Some New Evidence." *American Economic Review* 73(4): 708–24.

Adams, Charles F., Jr., Robert F. Cook, and Arthur J. Maurice. 1983. "A Pooled Time-Series Analysis of the Job-Creation Impact of Public Service Employment Grants to Large Cities." *Journal of Human Resources* 17(2): 283–94.

Addison, John T., and McKinley L. Blackburn. 1999. "Minimum Wages and Poverty." *Industrial and Labor Relations Review* 52(3): 393–409.

Akerlof, George A. 1982. "Labor Contracts as Partial Gift Exchange." *Quarterly Journal of Economics* 97: 543–69.

Akerlof, George A., and Janet L. Yellen, eds. 1986. *Efficiency Wage Models of the Labor Market*. New York: Cambridge University Press.

Altonji, Joseph G., and Nicolas Williams. 1992. "The Effects of Labor Market Experience, Job Seniority, and Job Mobility on Wage Growth." Working Paper 4133. Cambridge, Mass.: National Bureau of Economic Research.

———. 1997. "Do Wages Rise with Job Seniority?: A Reassessment." Working Paper 6010. Cambridge, Mass.: National Bureau of Economic Research.

Altshuler, Alan A., and José A. Gomez-Ibanez, with Arnold M. Howitt. 1993. *Regulation for Revenue: The Political Economy of Land Use Exactions*. Washington, D.C.: Brookings Institution.

American Institutes for Research. 1999. *An Educator's Guide to Schoolwide Reform*. Arlington, Va.: Educational Research Service.

American Public Welfare Association. 1998. *Welfare Check to Paycheck: State Incentives for Businesses to Hire Welfare Clients*. Washington, D.C.: American Public Welfare Association.

Anderson, Barbara. 1999. "First-Source Hiring Agreements." Available at: *http://www.senate.state.oh.us/horn/march99.htm*.

Angrist, Joshua D., and Alan B. Krueger. 1991. "Does Compulsory School Attendance Affect Schooling and Earnings?" *Quarterly Journal of Economics* 106: 979–1014.

Association of Community Organizations for Reform Now. 1999a. "Living Wage Successes: A Compilation of Living Wage Policies on the Books." Washington, D.C.: ACORN.

———. 1999b. "Living Wage Ordinance Stats at a Glance." Available at: *http://www.livingwagecampaign.org/lw-stats.html.*

Auspos, Patricia, George Cave, and David Long. 1988. *Maine: Final Report on the Training Opportunities in the Private Sector Program.* New York: Manpower Demonstration Research Corporation.

Bailey, Martin Neil, and James Tobin. 1977. "Macroeconomic Effects of Selective Public Employment and Wage Subsidies." *Brookings Papers on Economic Activity* 2: 511–44.

———. 1978. "Inflation-Unemployment Consequences of Job Creation Policies." In *Creating Jobs: Public Employment Programs and Wage Subsidies,* edited by John L. Palmer. Washington, D.C.: Brookings Institution.

Baker, Michael, Dwayne Benjamin, and Shuchita Stanger. 1999. "The Highs and Lows of the Minimum Wage Effect: A Time-Series Cross-Section Study of the Canadian Law." *Journal of Labor Economics* 17(2): 318–50.

Balducchi, David E., Terry R. Johnson, and R. Mark Gritz. 1997. "The Role of the Employment Service." In *Unemployment Insurance in the United States: Analysis of Policy Issues,* edited by Christopher J. O'Leary and Stephen A. Wandner. Kalamazoo, Mich.: W. E. Upjohn Institute for Employment Research.

Ball, Joseph. 1984. "Implementation of the Supported Work Program Model." In *The National Supported Work Demonstration,* edited by Robinson G. Hollister Jr., Peter Kemper, and Rebecca A. Maynard. Madison: University of Wisconsin Press.

Ball, Joseph, Carl Wolfhagen, David Gerould, and Loren Solnick. 1981. *The Participation of Private Businesses as Work Sponsors in the Youth Entitlement Demonstration.* New York: Manpower Demonstration Research Corporation.

Ballou, Dale, and Michael Podgursky. 1997. *Teacher Pay and Teacher Quality.* Kalamazoo, Mich.: W. E. Upjohn Institute for Employment Research.

Bangser, Michael R. 1985. *Lessons on Transitional Employment: The STETS Demonstration for Mentally Retarded Workers.* New York: Manpower Demonstration Research Corporation.

Bardach, Eugene. 1993. *Improving the Productivity of JOBS Programs.* New York: Manpower Demonstration Research Corporation.

Barnow, Burt S. 1987. "The Impact of CETA Programs on Earnings: A Review of the Literature." *Journal of Human Resources* 22(2): 157–93.

———. 2000. "Job Creation for Low-Wage Workers: An Assessment of Public Service Jobs, Tax Credits, and Empowerment Zones." In *The Low-Wage Labor Market: Challenges and Opportunities for Economic Self-sufficiency*, edited by Kelleen Kaye and Demetra Smith Nightingale. Washington: U.S. Department of Health and Human Services.

Barron, John M., Mark C. Berger, and Dan A. Black. 1997. *On-the-Job Training.* Kalamazoo, Mich.: W. E. Upjohn Institute for Employment Research.

Bartik, Timothy J. 1988. "Tennessee." Three chapters in *The New Economic Role of American States: Strategies in a Competitive World Economy,* edited by R. Scott Fosler. New York: Oxford University Press.

———. 1991. *Who Benefits from State and Local Economic Development Policies?* Kalamazoo, Mich.: W. E. Upjohn Institute for Employment Research.

———. 1992. "The Effects of State and Local Taxes on Economic Development: A Review of Recent Research." *Economic Development Quarterly* (February): 102–10.

———. 1993a. "Who Benefits from Local Job Growth—Migrants or the Original Residents?" *Regional Studies* 27(4): 297–311.

———. 1993b. *Economic Development and Black Economic Success*. Upjohn Institute Technical Report 93–001. Kalamazoo, Mich.: W. E. Upjohn Institute for Employment Research.

———. 1994a. "The Effects of Metropolitan Job Growth on the Size Distribution of Family Income." *Journal of Regional Science* 34(4): 483–501.

———. 1994b. "What Should the Federal Government Be Doing About Urban Economic Development?" *Cityscapes* 1(1): 267–91.

———. 1994c. "Jobs, Productivity, and Local Economic Development: What Implications Does Economic Research Have for the Role of Government?" *National Tax Journal* 47(4): 847–61.

———. 1995a. "Economic Development Strategies." Upjohn Institute Staff Working Paper 95–033. Available at: *http://www.upjohninst.org*.

———. 1995b. "Using Performance Indicators to Improve the Effectiveness of Welfare-to-Work Programs." Upjohn Institute Staff Working Paper 95–36. Available at: *http://www.upjohninst.org*.

———. 1996a. "Strategies for Economic Development." In *Management Policies in Local Government Finance,* 4th ed., edited by J. Richard Aronson. Washington, D.C.: International City/County Management Association.

———. 1996b. "The Distributional Effects of Local Labor Demand and Industrial Mix: Estimates Using Individual Panel Data." *Journal of Urban Economics* 40: 150–78.

———. 1997. "Short-term Employment Persistence for Welfare Recipients: The Effects of Wages, Industry, Occupation, and Firm Size." Upjohn Institute Staff Working Paper 97–046. Available at: *http://www.upjohninst.org*.

———. 1998. "The Labor Supply Effects of Welfare Reform." W. E. Upjohn Institute for Employment Research Staff Working Paper 98–053. Available at: *http://www.upjohninst.org*.

———. 1999. "Aggregate Effects in Local Labor Markets of Supply and Demand Shocks." Working Paper 99–57. Kalamazoo, Mich.: W. E. Upjohn Institute for Employment Research.

———. 2000a. "The Displacement and Wage Effects of Welfare Reform." In *Finding Jobs: Work and Welfare Reform,* edited by Rebecca M. Blank and David Card. New York: Russell Sage Foundation.

———. 2000b. "The Changing Effects of the Economy on Poverty and the Income Distribution." Working Paper. Kalamazoo, Mich.: W. E. Upjohn Institute for Employment Research.

———. 2000c. "Group Wage Curves." Working Paper. Kalamazoo, Mich.: W. E. Upjohn Institute for Employment Research.

———. 2000d. "Long-run Effects of Short-run Shocks to Employment." Working Paper. Kalamazoo, Mich.: W. E. Upjohn Institute for Employment Research.

Bartik, Timothy J., and Richard D. Bingham. 1997. "Can Economic Development Programs Be Evaluated?" In *Dilemmas of Urban Economic Development: Is-*

sues in Theory and Practice, edited by Richard D. Bingham and Robert Mier. Thousand Oaks, Calif.: Sage Publications.

Bassi, Laurie J. 1983. "The Effect of CETA on the Postprogram Earnings of Participants." *Journal of Human Resources* 18(4): 539–56.

Batt, Rosemary, and Paul Osterman. 1993. "Workplace Training Policy: Case Studies of State and Local Experiments." Working Paper 106. Washington, D.C.: Economic Policy Institute.

Behn, Robert D. 1991. *Leadership Counts: Lessons for Public Managers from the Massachusetts Welfare, Training, and Employment Program*. Cambridge, Mass.: Harvard University Press.

Bell, Stephen H., and Larry L. Orr. 1994. "Is Subsidized Employment Cost Effective for Welfare Recipients?: Experimental Evidence from Seven State Demonstrations." *Journal of Human Resources* 29(1): 42–61.

Bell, Stephen H., Larry L. Orr, John D. Blomquist, and Glen G. Cain. 1995. *Program Applicants as a Comparison Group in Evaluating Training Programs*. Kalamazoo, Mich.: W. E. Upjohn Institute for Employment Research.

Bendick, Marc, Jr. 1999. "Adding Testing to the Nation's Portfolio of Information on Employment Discrimination." In *A National Report Card on Discrimination in America: The Role of Testing,* edited by Michael Fix and Margery Austin Turner. Washington, D.C.: Urban Institute.

Bendick, Marc, Jr., Mary Lou Egan, and Suzanne Lofhjelm. 1998. *The Documentation and Evaluation of Antidiscrimination Training in the United States*. Geneva: International Labor Office.

Benus, Jacob M., Michelle Wood, and Neelima Grover. 1994. *A Comparative Analysis of the Washington and Massachusetts UI Self-Employment Demonstrations*. Report prepared for U.S. Department of Labor, ETA/UIS, by Abt Associates, Bethesda, Md.

Berg, Linnea, Lynn Olson, and Aimee Conrad. 1991. *Causes and Implications of Rapid Job Loss Among Participants in a Welfare-to-Work Program*. Evanston, Ill.: Center for Urban Affairs and Policy Research.

Berger, Mark. 1983. "Changes in Labor Force Composition and Male Earnings: A Production Approach." *Journal of Human Resources* 18: 177–96.

Betsey, Charles L., Robinson G. Hollister Jr., and Mary R. Papageorgiou, eds. 1985. *Youth Employment and Training Programs: The YEDPA Years*. Washington, D.C.: National Academy Press.

Betts, Julian R. 1998. "The Two-Legged Stool: The Neglected Role of Standards in Improving America's Public Schools." *Economic Policy Review* 4(1): 97–116.

Beverly, John R. 1999. "Hearing on the Work Opportunity Tax Credit." Testimony before the Subcommittee on Oversight of the House Committee on Ways and Means, July 1, 1999.

Bishop, John H. 1981. "Employment in Construction and Distribution Industries: The Impact of the New Jobs Tax Credit." In *Studies in Labor Markets,* edited by Sherwin Rosen. Chicago: University of Chicago Press.

———. 1993. "Improving Job Matches in the U.S. Labor Market." *Brookings Papers: Microeconomics,* 335–400.

———. 1996. "The Impact of Curriculum-Based External Examinations on School Priorities and Student Learning." *International Journal of Education Research* 23: 653–752.

———. 1997. "The Effect of National Standards and Curriculum-Based Exams on Achievement." *American Economic Review* 87: 260–64.

———. 1998. "Is Welfare Reform Succeeding?" Cornell University ILR School Working Paper (August).

Bishop, John, and Kevin Hollenbeck. 1985. *The Effects of TJTC on Employers.* Task 4 Final Report. Columbus: National Center for Research in Vocational Education, Ohio State University.

Bishop, John H., and Suk Kang. 1991. "Applying for Entitlements: Employers and the Targeted Jobs Tax Credit." *Journal of Policy Analysis and Management* 10(1): 24–45.

Bishop, John H., and Mark Montgomery. 1986. "Evidence on Firm Participation in Employment Subsidy Programs." *Industrial Relations* 25(1): 56–64.

———. 1993. "Does the Targeted Jobs Tax Credit Create Jobs at Subsidized Firms?" *Industrial Relations* 32(3): 289–306.

Blanchard, Olivier, and Lawrence F. Katz. 1992. "Regional Evolutions." *Brookings Papers on Economic Activity* 1: 1–75.

———. 1997. "What We Know and Do Not Know About the Natural Rate of Unemployment." *Journal of Economic Perspectives* 11(1): 51–72.

———. 1999. "Wage Dynamics: Reconciling Theory and Evidence." *American Economic Review* 89(2): 69–74.

Blanchflower, David G., and Andrew J. Oswald. 1994. *The Wage Curve*. Cambridge, Mass.: MIT Press.

Blank, Rebecca M. 1989. "Disaggregating the Effect of the Business Cycle on the Distribution of Income." *Economica* 56(22): 141–63.

———. 1993. "Why Were Poverty Rates So High in the 1980s?" In *Poverty and Prosperity in the USA in the Late Twentieth Century,* edited by D. B. Papadimitriou and E. N. Wolff. New York: Macmillan.

———. 1997. *It Takes a Nation: A New Agenda for Fighting Poverty*. New York: Russell Sage Foundation.

Blank, Rebecca M., and Alan. S. Blinder. 1986. "Macroeconomics, Income Distribution, and Poverty." In *Fighting Poverty: What Works and What Doesn't?,* edited by Sheldon H. Danziger and Daniel H. Weinberg. Cambridge, Mass.: Harvard University Press.

Blank, Rebecca M., and David Card. 1993. "Poverty, Income Distribution, and Growth: Are They Still Connected?" *Brookings Papers on Economic Activity* 2: 285–339.

Blank, Rebecca M., David Card, and Philip K. Robins. 2000. "Financial Incentives for Increasing Work and Income Among Low-Income Families." In *Finding Jobs: Work and Welfare Reform,* edited by Rebecca M. Blank and David Card. New York: Russell Sage Foundation.

Bluestone, Barry, and Bennett Harrison. 2000. *Growing Prosperity: The Battle for Growth with Equity in the Twenty-First Century*. Boston: Houghton Mifflin.

Boarnet, Marlon G., and William T. Bogart. 1996. "Enterprise Zones and Employment: Evidence from New Jersey." *Journal of Urban Economics* 40(2): 198–215.

Bondonio, Daniele, and John Engberg. 1999. "Enterprise Zones and Local Employment: Evidence from the States' Programs." Heinz School of Public Policy Management Working Paper. Available at: *http://www.heinz.cmu.edu/heinz/wpapers*.

Borjas, George J., Richard B. Freeman, and Lawrence F. Katz. 1997. "How Much Do Immigration and Trade Affect Labor Market Outcomes?" *Brookings Papers on Economic Activity* 1: 1–90.

Borjas, George J., and Valerie A. Ramey. 1994. "The Relationship Between Wage Inequality and International Trade." In *The Changing Distribution of Income in an Open U.S. Economy,* edited by J. H. Bergstrand. New York: North-Holland.

Borus, Michael E., and Daniel S. Hamermesh. 1978. "Estimating Fiscal Substitution by Public Service Employment Programs." *Journal of Human Resources* 13(4): 561–65.

Bos, Johannes M., Aletha C. Huston, Robert C. Granger, Greg J. Duncan, Thomas W. Brock, and Vonnie C. McLoyd. 1999. *New Hope for People with Low Incomes: Two-Year Results of a Program to Reduce Poverty and Reform Welfare.* New York: Manpower Demonstration Research Corporation.

Bound, John, and Harry J. Holzer. 1993. "Industrial Shifts, Skills Levels, and the Labor Market for White and Black Males." *Review of Economics and Statistics* 75: 387–96.

Bound, John, David A. Jaeger, and Regina M. Baker. 1995. "Problems with Instrumental Variables When the Correlation Between the Instruments and the Endogenous Explanatory Variable Is Weak." *Journal of the American Statistical Association* 90(430): 443–50.

Bowen, William G., and T. Aldrich Finegan. 1969. *The Economics of Labor Force Participation*. Princeton, N.J.: Princeton University Press.

Bowman, Ann O. 1987. *The Visible Hand: Major Issues in City Economic Policy*. Washington, D.C.: National League of Cities.

Bratsberg, Bernt, and Dek Terrell. 1998. "Experience, Tenure, and Wage Growth of Young Black and White Men." *Journal of Human Resources* 33(3): 658–82.

Briscoe, Alden T. 1972. "Public Service Employment in the 1930s: The WPA." In *The Political Economy of Public Service Employment,* edited by Harold L. Sheppard, Bennett Harrison, and William J. Spring. Lexington, Mass.: D. C. Heath and Co.

Brock, Thomas, David Butler, and David Long. 1993. *Unpaid Work Experience for Welfare Recipients: Findings and Lessons from MDRC Research*. MDRC Working Papers. New York: Manpower Demonstration Research Corporation.

Brock, Thomas, Fred Doolittle, Veronica Fellerath, and Michael Wiseman. 1997. *Creating New Hope: Implementation of a Program to Reduce Poverty and Reform Welfare.* New York: Manpower Demonstration Research Corporation.

Brookings Institution. 1999. "The State of Welfare Caseloads in America's Cities: 1999." Center on Urban and Metropolitan Policy Survey Series (February).

Brown, Amy. 1997. *Work First: How to Implement an Employment-Focused Approach to Welfare Reform.* New York: Manpower Demonstration Research Corporation.

Brown, Charles, James Hamilton, and James L. Medoff. 1990. *Employers Large and Small*. Cambridge, Mass.: Harvard University Press.

Brown, Randall, John Burghardt, Edward Cavin, David Long, Charles Mallar, Rebecca Maynard, Charles Metcalf, Craig Thornton, and Christine Whitebread. 1983. "Employment Opportunity Pilot Project: Analysis of Program Impacts." Project Report 83–03. Princeton, N.J.: Mathematica Policy Research.

Burkhauser, Richard V., Kenneth A. Couch, and David C. Wittenburg. 1996. "'Who Gets What' from Minimum Wage Hikes: A Re-estimation of Card and Krueger's Distributional Analysis in *Myth and Measurement: The New Economics of the Minimum Wage*." *Industrial and Labor Relations Review* 49(3): 547–52.

Burtless, Gary. 1985. "Are Targeted Wage Subsidies Harmful?: Evidence from a Wage Voucher Experiment." *Industrial and Labor Relations Review* 39(1): 105–14.

———. 1995. "Employment Prospects of Welfare Recipients." In *The Work Alternative: Welfare Reform and the Realities of the Job Market,* edited by Demetra Smith Nightingale and Robert H. Haveman. Washington, D.C.: Urban Institute Press.

Burtless, Gary, and Robert H. Haveman. 1984. "Policy Lessons from Three Labor Market Experiments." In *Employment and Training R&D: Lessons Learned and Future Directions*. Kalamazoo, Mich.: W. E. Upjohn Institute for Employment Research.

Cain, Glen G. 1998. "The State of the Economy and the Problem of Poverty: Implications for the Success or Failure of Welfare Reform." Discussion Paper 1183–98. Madison: University of Wisconsin, Institute for Research on Poverty.

Cameron, Stephen V., and James J. Heckman. 1993. "The Nonequivalence of High School Equivalents." *Journal of Labor Economics* 11(1): 1–47.

Campbell, Jeffrey R., and Ellen R. Rissman. 1994. "Long-run Labor Market Dynamics and Short-run Inflation." *Federal Reserve Bank of Chicago Economic Perspectives* 18(2): 15–27.

Cancian, Maria, Robert Haveman, Thomas Kaplan, Daniel Meyer, and Barbara Wolfe. 1999. "Work, Earnings, and Well-being After Welfare: What Do We Know?" In *Welfare Reform and the Macro-Economy,* edited by Sheldon Danziger. Kalamazoo, Mich.: W. E. Upjohn Institute for Employment Research.

Carcagno, George J., and Walter S. Corson. 1982. "Administrative Issues." In *Jobs for Disadvantaged Workers: The Economics of Employment Subsidies,* edited by Robert H. Haveman and John L. Palmer. Washington, D.C.: Brookings Institution.

Card, David. 1995a. "Using Geographic Variation in College Proximity to Estimate the Return to Schooling." In *Aspects of Labour Market Behaviour: Essays in Honour of John Vanderkamp,* edited by Louis N. Christofides, E. Kenneth Grand, and Robert Swidinsky. Toronto: University of Toronto Press.

———. 1995b. "The Wage Curve: A Review." *Journal of Economic Literature* 33: 785–99.

———. 1999. "The Causal Effect of Education on Earnings." In *Handbook of Labor Economics,* vol. 3A, edited by Orley Ashenfelter and David Card. Amsterdam, New York, and Oxford: Elsevier Science, North-Holland.

Card, David, and Alan B. Krueger. 1995. *Myth and Measurement: The New Economics of the Minimum Wage*. Princeton, N.J.: Princeton University Press.

Cave, George, Hans Bros, Fred Doolittle, and Cyril Toussaint. 1993. *JOBSTART: Final Report on a Program for School Dropouts.* New York: Manpower Demonstration Research Corporation.

Center for Community Change. 1999. "Jobs and Welfare Reform." Available at: *http://www.communitychange.org/jobswelfare.htm.*

Center for Law and Social Policy (CLASP). 2000. "Minnesota and Canadian Demonstrations: Decrease Poverty and Increase Well-being." *CLASP UPDATE* (June): 2–4.

Chernick, Howard, and Andrew Reschovsky. 1996. "State Responses to Block Grants: Will the Social Safety Net Survive?" Technical Paper. Washington, D.C.: Economic Policy Institute (July 31).

Christensen, Sandra. 1984. "The Targeted Jobs Tax Credit." Congressional Budget Office staff memorandum (May).

Citro, Constance F., and Robert T. Michael. 1995. *Measuring Poverty: A New Approach.* Washington, D.C.: National Academy Press.

Clark, Peggy, and Steven L. Dawson. 1995. *Jobs and the Urban Poor: Privately Initiated Sectoral Strategies.* Washington, D.C.: Aspen Institute.

Clements, Nancy, James Heckman, and Jeffrey Smith. 1994. "Making the Most out of Social Experiments: Reducing the Intrinsic Uncertainty in Evidence from Randomized Trials with an Application to the National JTPA Experiment." Technical Working Paper 149. Cambridge, Mass.: National Bureau of Economic Research.

Conrad, Cecilia A. 1995. "The Economic Cost of Affirmative Action." In *Economic Perspectives on Affirmative Action,* edited by Margaret C. Simms. Washington, D.C.: Joint Center for Political and Economic Studies.

Cook, Robert F., Charles F. Adams Jr., V. Lane Rawlins, and Associates. 1985. *Public Service Employment: The Experience of a Decade.* Kalamazoo, Mich.: W. E. Upjohn Institute for Employment Research.

Copeland, Joseph. 1985. "Case Studies: Employer Usage of TJTC." Working Paper. Columbus: Ohio State University, National Center for Research in Vocational Education (November).

Corcoran, Mary. 1982. "The Employment and Wage Consequences of Teenage Women's Nonemployment." In *The Youth Labor Market Problem: Its Nature, Causes, and Consequences,* edited by Richard B. Freeman and David A. Wise. Chicago: University of Chicago Press.

Corporation for Enterprise Development and Harrison Institute for Public Law at Georgetown University. 1999. *International Investor Rights and Local Economic Development.* Washington, D.C.: Corporation for Enterprise Development.

Couch, Kenneth A. 1992. "New Evidence on the Long-term Effects of Employment Training Programs." *Journal of Labor Economics* 10(4): 380–88.

Council of Economic Advisers. 1997. "The First Three Years: Investments That Pay." Available at: *http://clinton3.nara.gov/WH/EOP/CEA/First_Years/.*

———. 1998. "Good News for Low Income Families: Expansions in the Earned Income Tax Credit and the Minimum Wage." Available at: *http://clinton4.nara.gov/media/pdf/eitc.pdf.*

———. 1999. *Economic Report of the President.* Washington: U.S. Government Printing Office.

Cutler, David M., and Lawrence F. Katz. 1991. "Macroeconomic Performance and the Disadvantaged." *Brookings Papers on Economic Activity* 2: 1–74.

Daly, Mary. 1997. "Labor Market Effects of Welfare Reform." Federal Reserve Bank of San Francisco Letter 97–24 (August 29). Available at: *http://www.frbsf.org/econrsrch/wklyltr/e197–24.html.*

Danziger, Sandra, Mary Corcoran, Sheldon Danziger, Colleen Heflin, Ariel Kalil, Judith Levine, Daniel Rosen, Kristin Seefeldt, Kristine Siefert, and Richard Tolman. 1999. *Barriers to the Employment of Welfare Recipients.* Ann Arbor, Mich.: Poverty Research and Training Center.

Danziger, Sheldon, and Peter Gottschalk. 1995. *America Unequal.* New York and Cambridge, Mass.: Russell Sage Foundation and Harvard University Press.

Davidson, Carl. 1990. *Recent Developments in the Theory of Involuntary Unemployment.* Kalamazoo, Mich.: W. E. Upjohn Institute for Employment Research.

Dawson, Steven L. 1998. "Start-ups and Replication." In *Jobs and Economic Development: Strategies and Practice,* edited by Robert P. Giloth. Thousand Oaks, Calif.: Sage Publications.

DeParle, Jason. 1997. "White House Calls for Minimum Wage in Workfare Plan." *New York Times,* May 16.

Diaz, William A., Joseph Ball, and Carl Wolfhagen, with Judith Gueron, Stephanie Sheber, and Albert Widman. 1982. *Linking School and Work for Disadvantaged Youths: The YIEPP Demonstration: Final Implementation Report.* New York: Manpower Demonstration Research Corporation.

Dickens, William T., and Lawrence F. Katz. 1987. "Inter-Industry Wage Differences and Industry Characteristics." In *Unemployment and the Structure of Labor Markets,* edited by Kevin Lang and Jonathan S. Leonard. London: Basil Blackwell.

Dickert, Stacy, Scott Houser, and John Karl Scholz. 1995. "The Earned Income Tax Credit and Transfer Programs: A Study of Labor Market and Program Participation." In *Tax Policy and the Economy 9,* edited by James M. Poterba. Cambridge, Mass.: National Bureau of Economic Research and MIT Press.

Donohue, John, and James Heckman. 1991. "Continuous Versus Episodic Change: The Impact of Civil Rights Policy on the Economic Status of Blacks." *Journal of Economic Literature* 29(4): 1603–43.

Dubin, Jeffrey A., and Douglas Rivers. 1993. "Experimental Estimates of the Impact of Wage Subsidies." *Journal of Econometrics* 56: 219–42.

Duncan, Greg J., Kathleen Mullan Harris, and Johanne Boisjoly. 1998. "Time Limits and Welfare Reform: How Many Families Will Be Affected?" Working Paper. Chicago: Northwestern University and University of Chicago, Joint Center for Poverty Research (March 9). Available at: *http://www.nwu.edu/IPR/publications/nupr.*

Dunn, L. F. 1979. "Measuring the Value of Community." *Journal of Urban Economics* 6: 371–82.

Eberts, Randall W. 1998. "The Use of Profiling to Target Services in State Welfare-to-Work Programs: An Example of Process and Implementation." Working Paper 98–052. Kalamazoo, Mich.: W. E. Upjohn Institute for Employment Research. Available at: *http://www.upjohninst.org.*

Edin, Kathryn, and Laura Lein. 1997. *Making Ends Meet: How Single Mothers Survive Welfare and Low-Wage Work*. New York: Russell Sage Foundation.

Eisner, Robert. 1989. "Employer Approaches to Reducing Unemployment." In *Rethinking Employment Policy,* edited by D. Lee Bawden and Felicity Skidmore. Washington: Urban Institute Press.

———. 1995a. "A New View of the NAIRU." Working Paper. Chicago: Northwestern University.

———. 1995b. "Our NAIRU Limit: The Governing Myth of Economic Policy." *American Prospect* 21: 58–63.

Eissa, Nada, and Hilary Williamson Hoynes. 1999. "The Earned Income Tax Credit and the Labor Supply of Married Couples." Discussion paper, 1194–99. Madison, Wisconsin: Institute for Research on Poverty. Available at *http://www.ssc.wisc.edu/irp*.

Eissa, Nada, and Jeffrey B. Liebman. 1996. "Labor Supply Response to the Earned Income Tax Credit." *Quarterly Journal of Economics* 111: 606–37.

Elling, Richard C., and Ann Workman Sheldon. 1991. "Determinants of Enterprise Zone Success." In *Enterprise Zones: New Directions in Economic Development,* edited by Roy E. Green. Newbury Park, Calif.: Sage Publications.

Elliott, Mark, and Elisabeth King. 1999. *Labor Market Leverage.* New York: Public/Private Ventures.

Ellwood, David T. 1982. "Teenage Unemployment: Permanent Scars or Temporary Blemishes?" In *The Youth Labor Market Problem: Its Nature, Causes, and Consequences,* edited by Richard B. Freeman and David A. Wise. Chicago: University of Chicago Press.

———. 1988. *Poor Support: Poverty in the American Family.* New York: Basic Books.

Ellwood, David T., and Jon Crane. 1984. "Summer Youth Employment Program: Private Job Supplement or Substitute." Report prepared for the U.S. Department of Health and Human Services.

Ellwood, David, and Elisabeth Welty. 2000. "Public Sector Employment and Mandatory Work: A Policy Whose Time Has Come and Gone and Come Again?" In *Finding Jobs: Work and Welfare Reform,* edited by Rebecca M. Blank and David Card. New York: Russell Sage Foundation.

Emery, Kenneth M., and Chih-Ping Chang. 1996. "Do Wages Help Predict Inflation?" *Federal Reserve Bank of Dallas Economic Review* (First Quarter 1996): 2–9.

Employment Policies Institute. 1998. *The Baltimore Living Wage Study: Omissions, Fabrications, and Flaws.* Washington, D.C.: Employment Policies Institute.

Erickson, Rodney A., and Susan W. Friedman. 1991. "Comparative Dimensions of State Enterprise Zone Policies." In *Enterprise Zones: New Directions in Economic Development,* edited by Roy E. Green. Newbury Park, Calif.: Sage Publications.

Espinosa, Carlos. 1999. "Hearing on the Work Opportunity Tax Credit." Testimony before the Subcommittee on Oversight of the House Committee on Ways and Means, July 1.

Fair, Ray C. 1997. "Testing the NAIRU Model for the United States." Working Paper. New Haven, Conn.: Yale University.

———. 1999. "Does the NAIRU Have the Right Dynamics?" *American Economic Review* 89(2): 58–62.

———. 2000. "Testing the NAIRU Model for the United States." *Review of Economics and Statistics* 82(1, February): 64–71.

Farber, David J. 1971. *Highlights—First Annual Follow-up: 1968 JOBS Contract and Noncontract Programs.* Unpublished report. Washington: U.S. Department of Labor.

Farkas, George, Randall Olsen, Ernst W. Stromsdorfer, Linda C. Sharpe, Felicity Skidmore, D. Alton Smith, and Sally Merrill. 1984. *Post-Program Impacts of the Youth Incentive Entitlement Pilot Projects.* New York: Manpower Demonstration Research Corporation.

Farkas, George, D. Alton Smith, Ernst W. Stromsdorfer, Gail Trask, and Robert Jerrett III. 1982. *Impacts from the Youth Incentive Entitlement Pilot Projects: Participation, Work, and Schooling over the Full Program Period.* New York: Manpower Demonstration Research Corporation.

Ferguson, Ronald F. 1998. "Can Schools Narrow the Black-White Test Score Gap?" In *The Black-White Test Score Gap,* edited by Christopher Jencks and Meredith Phillips. Washington, D.C.: Brookings Institution Press.

Fix, Michael, and Raymond J. Struyk, eds. 1992. *Clear and Convincing Evidence: Measurement of Discrimination in America.* Washington, D.C.: Urban Institute Press.

Florida Office of Program Policy Analysis and Government Accountability. 1998. "Follow-up Report on the Enterprise Florida Jobs and Education Partnership." Report 98–03. Tallahassee: OPPAGA. Available at: *http://www.oppaga.state.fl.us.*

Fraker, Thomas M., Lucia A. Nixon, Jan L. Losby, Carol S. Prindle, and John F. Else. 1997. *Iowa's Limited Benefit Plan.* Washington, D.C.: Mathematica Policy Research.

Freedman, Stephen, Jan Bryant, and George Cave. 1988. *New Jersey: The Demonstration of State Work/Welfare Initiatives.* New York: Manpower Demonstration Research Corporation.

Freeman, Richard B. 1973. "Changes in the Labor Market for Black Americans 1948–1972." *Brookings Papers on Economic Activity* 1: 67–120.

———. 1991. "Employment and Earnings of Disadvantaged Young Men in a Labor Shortage Economy." In *The Urban Underclass,* edited by Christopher Jencks and Paul E. Peterson. Washington, D.C.: Brookings Institution.

Freeman, Richard B., and Peter Gottschalk, (eds). 1998. *Generating Jobs: How to Increase Demand for Less-Skilled Workers.* New York: Russell Sage Foundation.

Friedlander, Daniel, and Gary Burtless. 1994. *Five Years After: The Long-term Effects of Welfare-to-Work Programs.* New York: Russell Sage Foundation.

Friedlander, Daniel, Marjorie Erickson, Gayle Hamilton, and Virginia Knox. 1986. *West Virginia: Final Report on the Community Work Experience Demonstrations.* New York: Manpower Demonstration Research Corporation.

Friedlander, Daniel, Stephen Freedman, Gayle Hamilton, and Janet Quint. 1987. *Illinois: Final Report on Job Search and Work Experience in Cook County.* New York: Manpower Demonstration Research Corporation.

Friedlander, Daniel, David H. Greenberg, and Philip K. Robins. 1997. "Evaluating

Government Training Programs for the Economically Disadvantaged." *Journal of Economic Literature* 35: 1809–55.
Friedlander, Daniel, and Philip K. Robins. 1997. "The Distributional Impacts of Social Programs." *Evaluation Review* 21(5): 531–53.
Fuchs, Victor R., Alan B. Krueger, and James M. Poterba. 1998. "Economists' Views About Parameters, Values, and Policies: Survey Results in Labor and Public Economics." *Journal of Economic Literature* 36(3): 1387–1425.
Furdell, Phyllis A. 1994. *Poverty and Economic Development: Views from City Hall.* Research Report on America's Cities. Washington, D.C.: National League of Cities.
Gallagher, L. Jerome, Megan Gallagher, Kevin Perese, Susan Schreiber, and Keith Watson. 1998. "One Year After Federal Welfare Reform: A Description of State Temporary Assistance for Needy Families (TANF) Decisions as of October 1997." Occasional Paper 6. Washington: Urban Institute.
Gladden, Tricia, and Christopher Taber. 2000. "Wage Progression Among Less Skilled Workers." In *Finding Jobs: Work and Welfare Reform,* edited by Rebecca M. Blank and David Card. New York: Russell Sage Foundation.
Goldman, Barbara, Daniel Friedlander, and David L. Long. 1986. *Final Report on the San Diego Job Search and Work Experience Demonstration.* New York: Manpower Demonstration Research Corporation.
Gordon, Robert J. 1988. "The Role of Wages in the Inflation Process." *AEA Papers and Proceedings* 78(2): 276–83.
———. 1997. "The Time-Varying NAIRU and Its Implications for Economic Policy." *Journal of Economic Perspectives* 11(1): 11–32.
———. 1998. "Foundations of the Goldilocks Economy: Supply Shocks and the Time Varying NAIRU." *Brookings Papers on Economic Activity* 2: 297–333.
Gottschalk, Peter. 1998. "The Impact of Changes in Public Employment on Low-Wage Labor Markets." In *Generating Jobs: How to Increase Demand for Less-Skilled Workers,* edited by Richard B. Freeman and Peter Gottschalk. New York: Russell Sage Foundation.
Gottschalk, Peter, and Sheldon H. Danziger. 1985. "A Framework for Evaluating the Effects of Economic Growth and Transfers on Poverty." *American Economic Review* 75: 153–61.
Gould, William, Michael Ward, and Finis Welch. 1982. *Measuring Displacement: An Econometric Approach.* Final Report on the Major Research Outputs for the Study of the Labor Market Effects of the Youth Incentive Entitlement Pilot Projects. Santa Monica, Calif.: Unicon Research Corporation (December 21).
Granovetter, Mark S. 1994. *Getting a Job: A Study of Contacts and Careers.* Chicago: University of Chicago Press.
Grant, James. 1979. "Labor Substitution in U.S. Manufacturing." Ph.D. diss., Michigan State University.
Greenbaum, Robert T. 1998. "An Evaluation of State Enterprise Zone Policies: Measuring the Impact on Business Decisions and Housing Market Outcomes." Ph.D. diss., Carnegie Mellon University.
Groshen, Erica L. 1991. "Five Reasons Why Wages Vary Among Employers." *Industrial Relations* 30(3): 350–81.

Grossman, Jean Baldwin, Rebecca Maynard, and Judith Roberts. 1985. "Reanalysis of the Effects of Selected Employment and Training Programs for Welfare Recipients." Project Report. Princeton, N.J.: Mathematica Policy Research.

Grubb, David B. 1986. "Topics in the OECD Phillips Curve." *Economic Journal* 96(381): 55–79.

Gueron, Judith M. 1984. *Lessons from a Job Guarantee: The Youth Incentive Entitlement Pilot Projects.* Research Report. New York: Manpower Demonstration Research Corporation.

Gueron, Judith M., and Edward Pauly. 1991. *From Welfare to Work.* New York: Russell Sage Foundation.

Hahn, Andrew. 1994. "Evaluation of the Quantum Opportunities Program (QOP): Did the Program Work?" Report. Waltham, Mass.: Brandeis University (June).

Haimson, Joshua, Alan Hershey, and Anu Rangarajan. 1995. *Providing Services to Promote Job Retention.* Off Welfare and Into Work Report Series of the Postemployment Services Demonstration. Princeton, N.J.: Mathematica Policy Research.

Hall, Robert E. 1977. "An Aspect of the Economic Role of Unemployment." In *The Microeconomic Foundations of Macroeconomics,* edited by G. C. Harcourt. London: Macmillan.

Hamermesh, Daniel S. 1978. "Subsidies for Jobs in the Private Sector." In *Creating Jobs: Public Employment Programs and Wage Subsidies,* edited by John L. Palmer. Washington, D.C.: Brookings Institution.

———. 1993. *Labor Demand.* Princeton, N.J.: Princeton University Press.

———. 1999. Review of E. S. Phelps, *Rewarding Work: How to Restore Participation and Self-Support to Free Enterprise. Economica* (February): 152–53.

Hamilton, Gayle, Thomas Brock, Mary Farrell, Daniel Friedlander, Kristen Harknett, and others. 1997. *Evaluating Two Welfare-to-Work Program Approaches: Two-Year Findings on the Labor Force Attachment and Human Capital Development Programs in Three Sites.* New York and Washington: Manpower Demonstration Research Corporation, U.S. Department of Health and Human Services, and U.S. Department of Education.

Hamilton, William L., Nancy R. Burstein, August J. Baker, Alison Earle, Stefanie Gluckman, Laura Peck, and Alan White. 1996. "The New York State Child Assistance Program: Five-Year Impacts, Costs, and Benefits." Project Report. Cambridge, Mass.: Abt Associates (November).

Hanushek, Eric A. 1998. "Conclusions and Controversies About the Effectiveness of School Resources." *Economic Policy Review* 4(1): 11–27.

Harrison, Bennett. 1972. "Public Employment and the Theory of the Dual Economy." In *The Political Economy of Public Service Employment,* edited by Harold L. Sheppard, Bennett Harrison, and William J. Spring. Lexington, Mass.: D. C. Heath and Co.

Harvey, Philip. 1989. *Securing the Right to Employment: Social Welfare Policy and the Unemployed in the United States.* Princeton, N.J.: Princeton University Press.

Haveman, Robert. 1988. *Starting Even: An Equal Opportunity Program to Combat the Nation's New Poverty.* New York: Simon & Schuster.

———. 1997. "The Welfare State and Full Employment." Paper presented at the

Fourth Annual Research Seminar on Issues in Social Security, Sigtuna, Sweden (June 14), and University of Essex, England (June 20).

Haveman, Robert, and Jonathan Schwabish. 1999. *Macroeconomic Performance and the Poverty Rate: A Return to Normalcy?* Discussion Paper DP 1187–99. Madison: University of Wisconsin, Institute for Research on Poverty.

Heckman, James J. 1993. "What Has Been Learned About Labor Supply in the Past Twenty Years?" *American Economic Review* 83(2): 116–21.

———. 1998. "Detecting Discrimination." *Journal of Economic Perspectives* 12(2): 101–16.

Heckman, James, Neil Hohnmann, Jeffrey Smith, and Michael Khoo. 1999. "Substitution and Dropout Bias in Social Experiments: A Study of an Influential Social Experiment." Working Paper 9819. London: University of Western Ontario.

Helms, L. Jay. 1985. "The Effect of State and Local Taxes on Economic Growth: A Time Series Cross Section Approach." *The Review of Economics and Statistics* 67: 574–82.

Herzog, Henry W., Jr., Alan M. Schlottmann, and Thomas P. Boehm. 1993. "Migration as Spatial Job-Search: A Survey of Empirical Findings." *Regional Studies* 27(4): 327–40.

Hines, James R., Jr. 1998. "Nonprofit Business Activity and the Unrelated Business Income Tax." Working Paper 6820. Cambridge, Mass.: National Bureau of Economic Research.

Hollenbeck, Kevin, and Richard J. Willke. 1991. "The Employment and Earnings Impacts of the Targeted Jobs Tax Credit." Working Paper 91–07. Kalamazoo, Mich.: W. E. Upjohn Institute for Employment Research. Available at: *http://www.upjohninst.org*.

Hollenbeck, Kevin, Richard Willke, and Jamal Ershadi. 1986. "The Effects of TJTC on Disadvantaged Populations." Task 2 Final Report. Columbus: Ohio State University, National Center for Research in Vocational Education.

Hollister, Robinson G., Jr. 1984. "Introduction." In *The National Supported Work Demonstration,* edited by Robinson G. Hollister Jr., Peter Kemper, and Rebecca A. Maynard. Madison: University of Wisconsin Press.

Hollister, Robinson G., Jr., Peter Kemper, and Rebecca A. Maynard, eds. 1984. *The National Supported Work Demonstration.* Madison: University of Wisconsin Press.

Hollister, Robinson G., Jr., Peter Kemper, and Judith Woolridge. 1979. "Linking Process and Impact Analysis: The Case of Supported Work." In *Qualitative and Quantitative Methods in Evaluation Research,* edited by Thomas D. Cook and Charles S. Reichardt. Beverly Hills, Calif.: Sage Publications.

Hollister, Robinson G., Jr., and Rebecca A. Maynard. 1984. "The Impacts of Supported Work on AFDC Recipients." In *The National Supported Work Demonstration,* edited by Robinson G. Hollister Jr., Peter Kemper, and Rebecca A. Maynard. Madison: University of Wisconsin Press.

Holzer, Harry J. 1989. *Unemployment, Vacancies, and Local Labor Markets.* Kalamazoo, Mich.: W. E. Upjohn Institute for Employment Research.

———. 1996. *What Employers Want: Job Prospects for Less-Educated Workers.* New York: Russell Sage Foundation.

Holzer, Harry J., Richard N. Block, Marcus Cheatham, and Jack H. Knott. 1993. "Are Training Subsidies for Firms Effective?: The Michigan Experience." *Industrial and Labor Relations Review* 46(4): 625–36.

Holzer, Harry J., and Sheldon Danziger. 1998. "Are Jobs Available for Disadvantaged Workers in Urban Areas?" Working Paper. East Lansing and Ann Arbor: Michigan State University and University of Michigan.

Holzer, Harry J., and Keith R. Ihlanfeldt. 1996. "Spatial Factors and the Employment of Blacks at the Firm Level." *New England Economic Review*(May/June): 65–82.

Holzer, Harry, and David Neumark. 1998. "What Does Affirmative Action Do?" Discussion Paper 1169–98. Madison: University of Wisconsin, Institute for Research on Poverty.

———. 1999a. "Are Affirmative Action Hires Less Qualified?: Evidence from Employer-Employee Data on New Hires." *Journal of Labor Economics* 17(3): 534–69.

———. 1999b. "Assessing Affirmative Action." Working Paper W7323. Cambridge, Mass.: National Bureau of Economic Research.

Houseman, Susan N. 1998. "The Effects of Employer Mandates." In *Generating Jobs: How to Increase Demand for Less-Skilled Workers,* edited by Richard B. Freeman and Peter Gottschalk. New York: Russell Sage Foundation.

———. 1999. "Flexible Staffing Arrangements." Report Executive Summary. Available at: *http://www2.dol.gov/dol/asp/public/futurework/conference/staffing/exec_s.htm.*

Howard, Donald S. 1943. *The WPA and Federal Relief Policy.* New York: Russell Sage Foundation.

Hoxby, Caroline M. 1998. "What Do America's 'Traditional' Forms of School Choice Teach Us About School Choice Reforms?" *FRBNY Economic Policy Review* (March): 47–59.

Ihlanfeldt, Keith R. 1992. *Job Accessibility and the Employment and School Enrollment of Teenagers*. Kalamazoo, Mich.: W. E. Upjohn Institute for Employment Research.

Ihlanfeldt, Keith R., and David L. Sjoquist. 1998. "The Spatial Mismatch Hypothesis: A Review of Recent Studies and Their Implications for Welfare Reform." *Housing Policy Debate* 9(4): 849–92.

Impact (Institute for Manpower Policy Analysis). 1977. *An Assessment of WIN and Welfare Tax Credits.* Minneapolis: Impact.

Institute for Wisconsin's Future. 1998. "The W-2 Job Path: An Assessment of the Employment Trajectory of W-2 Participants in Milwaukee." Working Paper. Milwaukee: Institute for Wisconsin's Future.

———. 1999. *W-2 Connection.* Vol. 2, no. 2. Milwaukee: Institute for Wisconsin's Future.

Jacobson, Louis, Robert LaLonde, and Daniel Sullivan. 1993. *The Costs of Worker Dislocation.* Kalamazoo, Mich.: W. E. Upjohn Institute for Employment Research.

Jaeger, David A., and Ann Huff Stevens. 1999. "Is Job Stability in the United States Falling?: Reconciling Trends in the Current Population Survey and Panel Study of Income Dynamics." *Journal of Labor Economics* 17(4): S1–28.

Jäntti, Markus. 1994. "A More Efficient Estimate of the Effects of Macroeconomic Activity on the Distribution of Income." *Review of Economics and Statistics* 76: 372–78.

Jargonsky, Paul A. 1997. *Poverty and Place: Ghettos, Barrios, and the American City*. New York: Russell Sage Foundation.

Jarmin, Ronald S. 1999. "Evaluating the Impact of Manufacturing Extension on Productivity Growth." *Journal of Policy Analysis and Management* 18(1): 99–119.

Jastrzab, JoAnn, John Blomquist, Julie Masker, and Larry Orr. 1997. "Youth Corps: Promising Strategies for Young People and Their Communities." Studies in Workforce Development and Income Security 1–97. Cambridge, Mass.: Abt Associates (February).

Jastrzab, JoAnn, Julie Masker, John Blomquist, and Larry Orr. 1996. "Impacts of Service: Final Report on the Evaluation of American Conservation and Youth Service Corps." Evaluation of National and Community Service Programs. Cambridge, Mass.: Abt Associates.

Jaynes, Gerald David, and Robin M. Williams Jr., eds. 1989. *A Common Destiny: Blacks and American Society.* Washington, D.C.: National Academy Press.

Jobs for the Future. 1998. "School-to-Career Initiative Demonstrates Significant Impact on Young People." Available at: *http://www.jff.org*.

Jobs for the Future and Burness Communications. 1999. "Innovations and Products at the Casey Jobs Initiative Sites." Baltimore: Annie E. Casey Foundation. Available at: *http://www.aecf.org/jobsinitiative*.

Johnson, Clifford, and Mark Headings. 1998. "Vermont's Community Service Employment Program." Washington: Center on Budget and Policy Priorities.

Johnson, Clifford, and Lana Kim. 1999. "Washington State's Community Jobs Initiative." Washington: Center on Budget and Policy Priorities. Available at: *http://www.cbpp.org/520wtw.htm*.

Johnson, Clifford, and Ana Carricchi Lopez. 1997. "Shattering the Myth of Failure: Promising Findings from Ten Public Job Creation Initiatives." Washington: Center on Budget and Policy Priorities. Available at: *http://www.cbpp.org/1222jober.htm*.

Johnson, Cliff, William Schweke, and Matt Hull. 1999. *Creating Jobs: Public and Private Strategies for the Hard-to-Employ.* Washington, D.C.: Corporation for Enterprise Development.

Johnson, George E. 1998. "The Impact of Immigration on Income Distribution Among Minorities." In *Help or Hindrance: The Economic Implications of Immigration for African Americans*, edited by Daniel Hamermesh and Frank D. Bean. New York: Russell Sage Foundation.

Johnson, George E., and James D. Tomola. 1977. "The Fiscal Substitution Effects of Alternative Approaches to Public Service Employment Policy." *Journal of Human Resources* 12(Winter): 3–26.

Juhn, Chinhui. 1999. "Wage Inequality and Demand for Skill: Evidence from Five Decades." *Industrial and Labor Relations Review* 52(3): 424–43.

Juhn, Chinhui, and Dae Il Kim. 1999. "The Effects of Rising Female Labor Supply on Male Wages." *Journal of Labor Economics* 17(1): 23–48.

Juhn, Chinhui, Kevin Murphy, and Robert Topel. 1991. "Why Has the Natural

Rate of Unemployment Increased over Time?" *Brookings Papers on Economic Activity* 2: 75–142.

Kane, Thomas J. 1995. "Rising Public College Tuition and College Entry: How Well Do Public Subsidies Promote Access to College?" Working Paper 5164. Cambridge, Mass.: National Bureau of Economic Research.

Kane, Thomas J., and Cecilia Elena Rouse. 1993. "Labor Market Returns to Two- and Four-Year Colleges: Is a Credit a Credit and Do Degrees Matter?" Working Paper 4268. Cambridge, Mass.: National Bureau of Economic Research.

———. 1999. "The Community College: Educating Students at the Margin Between College and Work." *Journal of Economic Perspectives* 13(1): 63–84.

Kaplan, Thomas. 1998. "Wisconsin's W-2 Program: Welfare as We Might Come to Know It." Discussion Paper 1173–98. Madison: University of Wisconsin, Institute for Research on Poverty.

Kaplan, Thomas, and Ingrid Rothe. 1999. "New Hope and W-2: Common Challenges, Different Responses." *Focus* 20(2): 44–48.

Karoly, Lynn A., Peter W. Greenwood, Susan S. Everingham, Jill Houbé, M. Rebecca Kilburn, C. Peter Rydell, Matthew Sanders, and James Chiesa. 1998. *Investing in Our Children: What We Know and Don't Know About the Costs and Benefits of Early Childhood Interventions.* Washington, D.C.: Rand Corporation.

Katz, Bruce, and Katherine Allen. 1999. *Survey: The State of Welfare Caseloads in America's Cities: 1999.* Washington, D.C.: Brookings Institution.

Katz, Lawrence F. 1998. "Wage Subsidies for the Disadvantaged." In *Generating Jobs: How to Increase Demand for Less-Skilled Workers,* edited by Richard B. Freeman and Peter Gottschalk. New York: Russell Sage Foundation.

Katz, Lawrence F., and Alan B. Krueger. 1999. "The High-Pressure U.S. Labor Market of the 1990s." *Brookings Papers on Economic Activity* 1: 1–65.

Katz, Lawrence F., and Lawrence H. Summers. 1989. "Industry Rents: Evidence and Implications." *Brookings Papers on Economic Activity: Microeconomics*: 209–90.

Kaus, Mickey. 1992. *The End of Equality.* New York: Basic Books.

Kazis, Richard, and Hilary Kopp. 1997. *Both Sides Now: New Directions in Promoting Work and Learning for Disadvantaged Youth.* Boston: Jobs for the Future.

Kemper, Peter, David A. Long, and Craig Thornton. 1981. *The Supported Work Evaluation: Final Benefit-Cost Analysis.* New York: Manpower Demonstration Research Corporation.

———. 1984. "A Benefit-Cost Analysis of the Supported Work Experiment." In *The National Supported Work Demonstration,* edited by Robinson G. Hollister Jr., Peter Kemper, and Rebecca A. Maynard. Madison: University of Wisconsin Press.

Kennan, John. 1999. Review of Edmund S. Phelps, *Rewarding Work: How to Restore Participation and Self-Support to Free Enterprise. Journal of Economic Literature* 37: 1202–3.

Kennedy, David M. 1999. *Freedom from Fear: The American People in Depression and War, 1929–1945.* New York: Oxford University Press.

Kerachsky, Stuart, Craig Thornton, Anne Bloomenthal, Rebecca Maynard, and Susan Stephens. 1985. *The Impacts of Transitional Employment for Mentally*

Retarded Young Adults: Results from the STETS Demonstration. New York: Manpower Demonstration Research Corporation.

Kesselman, Jonathan R. 1978. "Work Relief Programs in the Great Depression." In *Creating Jobs: Public Employment Programs and Wage Subsidies,* edited by John L. Palmer. Washington, D.C.: Brookings Institution.

Kesselman, Jonathan R., Samuel H. Williamson, and Ernst R. Berndt. 1977. "Tax Credits for Employment Rather Than Investment." *American Economic Review* 67(3): 339–49.

Kirsch, Irwin S. 1993. *Adult Literacy in America: A First Look at the Results of the National Adult Literacy Survey.* Washington: U.S. Department of Education, Office of Educational Research and Improvement.

Kirschenman, Joleen, and Kathryn M. Neckerman. 1991. "'We'd Love to Hire Them, but . . .': The Meaning of Race for Employers." In *The Urban Underclass,* edited by Christopher Jencks and Paul E. Peterson. Washington, D.C.: Brookings Institution.

Kleppner, Harry J., and Nikolas Theodore. 1997. *Work After Welfare: Is the Midwest's Booming Economy Creating Enough Jobs?* DeKalb, Ill.: Northern Illinois University, Office for Social Policy Research.

Knox, Virginia, Cynthia Miller, and Lisa A. Gennetian. 2000. *Reforming Welfare and Rewarding Work: A Summary of the Final Report in the Minnesota Family Investment Program.* New York: Manpower Demonstration Research Corporation.

KPMG Peat Marwick. 1993. *Customer Satisfaction Survey of the Pennsylvania Industrial Resource Centers.* Harrisburg: Pennsylvania Department of Commerce.

Krueger, Alan B. 1999. "Experimental Estimates of Education Production Functions." *Quarterly Journal of Economics* 114(2): 497–532.

Krueger, Alan B., and Diane M. Whitmore. 1999. "The Effect of Attending a Small Class in the Early Grades on College Attendance Plans (Executive Summary)." Working Paper. Available at: *http://www.telalink.net/~heros.*

Ladd, Helen F. 1994. "Spatially Targeted Economic Development Strategies: Do They Work?" *Cityscape* 1(1): 193–218.

———. 1999. "The Dallas School Accountability and Incentive Program: An Evaluation of Its Impacts on Student Outcomes." *Economics of Education* 18: 1–16.

Lane, Julia I., Alan G. Isaac, and David W. Stevens. 1997. "Firm Heterogeneity and Worker Turnover." Working Paper. Washington, D.C.: American University.

Lautsch, Brenda A., and Paul Osterman. 1998. "Changing the Constraints: A Successful Employment and Training Strategy." In *Jobs and Economic Development: Strategies and Practice,* edited by Robert P. Giloth. Thousand Oaks, Calif.: Sage Publications.

Layard, Richard, Stephen Nickell, and Richard Jackman. 1991. *Unemployment: Macroeconomic Performance and the Labor Market.* New York: Oxford University Press.

Lazere, Edward B. 1997. *The Poverty Despite Work Handbook: Data and Guidelines for Preparing a Report on the Working Poor in Each State.* Washington: Center on Budget and Policy Priorities.

Ledebur, Larry C., and William R. Barnes. 1993. "All in It Together: Cities, Suburbs and Local Economic Regions." Research Report. Washington, D.C.: National League of Cities.

Lee, Valerie E., Anthony S. Bryk, and Julia B. Smith. 1992. "The Organization of Effective Secondary Schools." *Review of Research in Education* 19: 171–267.

Lemann, Nicholas. 1998. "Foreword." In *The New Dollars and Dreams: American Incomes and Economic Change,* by Frank Levy. New York: Russell Sage Foundation.

Leonard, Jonathan S. 1990. "The Impact of Affirmative Action Regulation and Equal Employment Law on Black Employment." *Journal of Economic Perspectives* 4(4): 47–63.

Lerman, Robert, and Eric Rosenberg. 1997. "The Benefits and Costs of New York City Workfare." Washington, D.C.: Urban Institute. Unpublished paper.

Leslie, Larry, and Paul Brinkman. 1988. *Economic Value of Higher Education.* New York: Macmillan.

Levenson, Alec R. 1996. "Persistence in the Labor Market: The Effect of Early Career Labor Market Conditions on Future Job Prospects." Working Paper 96–1. Santa Monica, Calif.: Milkin Institute for Job and Capital Formation.

Levitan, Sar A., and Frank Gallo. 1988. *A Second Chance: Training for Jobs.* Kalamazoo, Mich.: W. E. Upjohn Institute for Employment Research.

Liebman, Jeffrey B. 1998. "The Impact of the Earned Income Tax Credit on Incentives and Income Distribution." In *Tax Policy and the Economy 12,* edited by James M. Poterba. Cambridge, Mass.: National Bureau of Economic Research and MIT Press.

Lin, Winston, and Elsie C. Pan. 1998. *When Financial Incentives Encourage Work: Complete Eighteen-Month Findings from the Self-Sufficiency Project.* Ottawa: Social Research and Demonstration Corporation.

Loprest, Pamela J., and Burt S. Barnow. 1993. "Estimating the Universe of Eligibles for Selected ETA Programs." Project Report. Washington, D.C.: Urban Institute Project (October).

Lorenz, Edward C. 1988. "The Targeted Jobs Tax Credit in Maryland and Missouri: 1982–1987." Report 88–18. Washington, D.C.: National Commission for Employment Policy.

———. 1995. "TJTC and the Promise and Reality of Redistributive Vouchering and Tax Credit Policy." *Journal of Policy Analysis and Management* 14(2): 270–90.

Ma, Patricia, and Tony Proscio. 1998. *Working Close to Home.* Philadelphia: Public/Private Ventures.

Mangum, Garth L. 1968. *MDTA: Foundation of Federal Manpower Policy.* Baltimore: Johns Hopkins University Press.

Manpower Demonstration Research Corporation. 1980. *Summary and Findings of the National Supported Work Demonstration.* Cambridge, Mass.: Ballinger.

Mayer, Neil S. 1998. *Saving and Creating Good Jobs: A Study of Industrial Retention and Expansion Programs.* Washington, D.C.: Center for Community Change.

McKevitt, J. 1978. Testimony before the Senate Finance Subcommittee on Administration of the Internal Revenue Code and Select Committee on Small Business (July 26).

McMurrer, Daniel P., Isabel V. Sawhill, and Robert I. Lerman. 1997a. "Welfare Reform and Opportunity in the Low-Wage Labor Market." Working Paper 5, Opportunity in America Series. Washington, D.C.: Urban Institute.

———. 1997b. "Spreadsheets Used to Estimate Effects of Welfare Work Participation Requirements." Washington, D.C.: Urban Institute (July 1).

Mead, Lawrence M. 1992. *The New Politics of Poverty: The Nonworking Poor in America.* New York: Basic Books.

———. 1999. "Statecraft: The Politics of Welfare Reform in Wisconsin." Discussion Paper 1184–99. Madison: University of Wisconsin, Institute for Research on Poverty.

Meléndez, Edwin. 1996. *Working on Jobs: The Center for Employment Training.* Boston: Mauricio Gastón Institute for Latino Community Development and Public Policy.

Meyer, Bruce D., and Dan T. Rosenbaum. 1998. "Welfare, the Earned Income Tax Credit, and the Employment of Single Mothers." Working Paper. Chicago and Cambridge, Mass.: Northwestern University and National Bureau of Economic Research (October).

Milbank, Dana. 1997. "Under the Underclass." *New Republic,* August 4, 1997. Available at: *http://www.tnr.com/magazines/tnr/archive/08/080497/milbank080497.html.*

Miller, Cynthia, Virginia Knox, Patricia Auspos, Jo Anna Hunter-Manns, Alan Orenstein. 1997. *MFIP, Making Welfare Work and Work Pay: Implementation and Eighteen-Month Impacts of the Minnesota Family Investment Program.* New York: Manpower Demonstration Research Corporation.

Miller, Shazia Raffiullah, and James E. Rosenbaum. 1996. "The Missing Link: Social Infrastructure and Employers' Use of Information." Working Paper WP-96-15. Chicago: Northwestern University, School of Education and Social Policy.

Mocan, H. Naci. 1999. "Structural Unemployment, Cyclical Unemployment, and Income Inequality." *Review of Economics and Statistics* 81(1): 122–34.

Moffitt, Robert. 1983. "An Economic Model of Welfare Stigma." *American Economic Review* 75(3): 1023–35.

———. 1992. "Incentive Effects of the U.S. Welfare System: A Review." *Journal of Economic Literature* 30(1): 1–61.

Molina, Frieda. 1998. *Making Connections: A Study of Employment Linkage Programs.* Washington, D.C.: Center for Community Change.

Mortensen, Dale, and Christopher Pissarides. 1994. "Job Creation and Job Destruction in the Theory of Unemployment." *Review of Economic Studies* 61(3): 397–416.

Mount Auburn Associates. 1992. "An Evaluation of Ohio's Thomas Edison Technology Centers." Final report submitted to the Ohio Department of Development. Somerville, Mass.: Mount Auburn Associates.

Mucciaroni, Gary. 1990. *The Political Failure of Employment Policy, 1945–1982.* Pittsburgh: University of Pittsburgh Press.

Murnane, Richard J., John B. Willett, and Frank Levy. 1995. "The Growing Importance of Cognitive Skills in Wage Determination." *Review of Economics and Statistics* 77(2): 251–66.

Murphy, Kevin M., and Finis Welch. 1990. "Empirical Age-Earnings Profiles." *Journal of Labor Economics* 8(2): 202–29.

National Academy of Public Administration. 1996. *A Path to Smarter Economic Development: Reassessing the Federal Role.* Washington, D.C.: National Academy of Public Administration.

National Center for Education Statistics. 1999. *Digest of Education Statistics 1998.* NCES 1999–036. Washington: U.S. Department of Education.

National Council for Urban Economic Development. 1993. *Survey of Public Economic Development Agencies.* Washington, D.C.: National Council for Urban Economic Development.

National League of Cities. 1999. *Workforce Investment Act of 1998: Local Officials' Guide.* Washington, D.C.: National League of Cities.

National Youth Employment Coalition. 1998. *PEPNet '98: Lessons Learned from Forty-three Effective Youth Employment Initiatives.* Washington, D.C.: National Youth Employment Coalition.

Neumark, David. 1999. "The Employment Effects of Recent Minimum Wage Increases: Evidence from a Pre-Specified Research Design." Working Paper 7171. Cambridge, Mass.: National Bureau of Economic Research.

Neumark, David, and William Wascher. 1997. "Do Minimum Wages Fight Poverty?" Working Paper 6127. Cambridge, Mass.: National Bureau of Economic Research.

Newman, Katherine S. 1999. *No Shame in My Game: The Working Poor in the Inner City.* New York: Alfred A. Knopf and Russell Sage Foundation.

Newman, Katherine, and Chauncy Lennon. 1995. "The Job Ghetto." *American Prospect Online.* Available at: *http://www.prospect.org/archives/22/22newm.html.*

Niedt, Christopher, Greg Ruiters, Dana Wise, and Erica Schoenberger. 1999. "The Effects of the Living Wage in Baltimore." Working Paper 119. Washington, D.C.: Economic Policy Institute.

Norquist, John O. 1998. *The Wealth of Cities: Revitalizing the Centers of American Life.* Reading, Mass.: Addison-Wesley.

Okun, Arthur M. 1973. "Upward Mobility in a High-Pressure Economy." *Brookings Papers on Economic Activity* 1: 207–61.

Olson, Krista, and LaDonna Pavetti. 1996. "Personal and Family Challenges to the Successful Transition from Welfare to Work." Project Report. Washington, D.C.: Urban Institute.

O'Neill, Dave M. 1982. "Employment Tax Credit Programs: The Effects of Socioeconomic Targeting Provisions." *Journal of Human Resources* 17(3): 449–59.

Orr, Larry L., Howard S. Bloom, Stephen H. Bell, Fred Doolittle, Winston Lin, and George Cave. 1996. *Does Training for the Disadvantaged Work?: Evidence from the National JTPA Study.* Washington, D.C.: Urban Institute Press.

Organization for Economic Cooperation and Development. 1999. *OECD Employment Outlook.* Paris: Organization for Economic Cooperation and Development.

Osterman, Paul. 1999. *Securing Prosperity: The American Labor Market: How It Has Changed and What to Do About It.* Princeton, N.J.: Princeton University Press.

Osterman, Paul, and Rosemary Batt. 1993. "Employer-Centered Training for International Competitiveness: Lessons from State Programs." *Journal of Policy Analysis and Management* 12(3): 456–77.

Papke, Leslie E. 1994. "Tax Policy and Urban Development: Evidence from the Indiana Enterprise Zone Program." *Journal of Urban Economics* 54: 37–49.

Pate-Bain, Helen, B. DeWayne Fulton, and Jayne Boyd-Zaharias. 1999. "Effects of Class-Size Reduction in the Early Grades (K-3) on High School Performance." Working Paper. Available at: *http://www.telalink.net/~heros*.

Perez-Johnson, Irma, and Alan M. Hershey. 1999. "Early Implementation of the Welfare-to-Work Grants Program." Report to Congress. Princeton, N.J.: Mathematica Policy Research.

Perloff, Jeffrey M., and Michael L. Wachter. 1979. "The New Jobs Tax Credit: An Evaluation of the 1977–78 Wage Subsidy Program." *American Economic Review* 69(2): 173–79.

Perry, Charles R., Bernard E. Anderson, Richard L. Rowan, Herbert R. Northrup, Peter P. Amons, Stephen A. Schneider, Michael E. Sparrough, Harriet Goldbert, Larry R. Matlack, and Cornelius A. McGuinness. 1975. *The Impact of Government Manpower Programs: In General, and on Minorities and Women.* Philadelphia: University of Pennsylvania Press.

Perry, George L. 1971. "Labor Force Structure, Potential Output, and Productivity." *Brookings Papers on Economic Activity* 3: 533–65.

Peters, Alan H., and Peter S. Fisher. In press. *State Enterprise Zone Programs: Have They Worked?* Kalamazoo, Mich.: W. E. Upjohn Institute for Employment Research.

Peterson, Paul E., and David Myers. 1998. "An Evaluation of the New York City School Choice Scholarship Programs: The First Year." Working Paper (October). Available at: *http://data.fas.harvard.edu/pepg/NewYork-First.htm*.

Phelps, Edmund S. 1994a. "A Program of Low-Wage-Employment Tax Credits to Pull up the Employment and Wage Rates of the Disadvantaged." Working Paper 55. Washington, D.C.: Russell Sage Foundation.

———. 1994b. "Raising the Employment and Pay of the Working Poor: Low-Wage Employment Subsidies Versus the Welfare State." *AEA Papers and Proceedings* 84(2): 54–58.

———. 1997. *Rewarding Work: How to Restore Participation and Self-Support to Free Enterprise.* Cambridge, Mass.: Harvard University Press.

Poglinco, Susan M., Julian Brash, and Robert C. Granger. 1998. "An Early Look at Community Service Jobs in the New Hope Demonstration." Evaluation Paper. New York: Manpower Demonstration Research Corporation.

Pollin, Robert, and Stephanie Luce. 1998. *The Living Wage: Building a Fair Economy.* New York: New Press.

Powers, Elizabeth T. 1995. "Growth and Poverty Revisited." *Economic Commentary* (April 15): 1–4.

Prescott, Edward C., and Thomas F. Cooley. 1972. "Evaluating the Impact of MDTA Training Programs on Earnings Under Varying Labor Market Conditions." Report prepared for Office of Policy, Evaluation, and Research, Manpower Administration, U.S. Department of Labor.

Public Policy Associates and Brandon Roberts & Associates. 1992. *Oregon Small*

Business Services Evaluation. Final Report. Lansing, Mich.: Public Policy Associates.

Purkey, Stewart C., and Marshall S. Smith. 1983. "Effective Schools: A Review." *Elementary School Journal* 83(4): 427–52.

Quint, Janet C., Judith S. Musick, and Joyce A. Ladner. 1994. *Lives of Promise, Lives of Pain: Young Mothers After New Chance.* New York: Manpower Demonstration Research Corporation.

Rangan, Asha. 1984. *MEED Means Business: Private Employers Assess the State Jobs Program.* Minneapolis: Jobs Now Coalition.

Raphael, Steven. 1998. "The Spatial Mismatch Hypothesis and Black Youth Joblessness: Evidence from the San Francisco Bay Area." *Journal of Urban Economics* 43(1): 71–111.

Regional Technology Strategies. 1999. *A Comprehensive Look at State-Funded, Employer-Focused Job Training Programs.* Washington, D.C.: National Governors Association.

Reingold, David A. 1999. "Inner-City Firms and the Employment Problem of the Urban Poor: Are Poor People Really Excluded from Jobs Located in Their Own Neighborhoods?" *Economic Development Quarterly* 13(4): 291–306.

Ricco, James, Daniel Friedlander, and Stephen Freedman. 1994. *GAIN: Benefits, Costs, and Three-Year Impacts of a Welfare-to-Work Program.* New York: Manpower Demonstration Research Corporation.

Rich, Spencer. 1993. "Runaway Training: Why Educating Poor, Unskilled Workers Won't Land Them Jobs." *Washington Post,* February 7.

Riemer, David R. 1988. *The Prisoners of Welfare: Liberating America's Poor from Unemployment and Low Wages.* New York: Praeger.

Ritter, Martha, and Sandra K. Danziger. 1983. "After Supported Work: Post-Program Interviews with a Sample of AFDC Participants." Research Report. New York: Manpower Demonstration Research Corporation.

Roberts, Brandon, and Jeffrey D. Padden. 1998a. *Welfare to Wages: Strategies to Assist the Private Sector to Employ Welfare Recipients.* Vol. 1. Flint, Mich.: Mott Foundation.

———. 1998b. *Welfare to Wages: Strategies to Assist the Private Sector to Employ Welfare Recipients.* Vol. 2. Flint, Mich.: Mott Foundation.

Robins, Philip K. 1985. "A Comparison of the Labor Supply Findings from the Four Negative Income Tax Experiments." *Journal of Human Resources* 20(4): 567–82.

Rode, Peter. 1988. *MEED Means More Business: Job Growth Through Minnesota's Wage Subsidy Program.* Minneapolis: Jobs Now Coalition.

Rogers, Cynthia L. 1997. "Job Search and Unemployment Duration: Implications for the Spatial Mismatch Hypothesis." *Journal of Urban Economics* 42(1): 109–32.

Romer, Christina D., and David H. Romer. 1999. "Monetary Policy and the Wellbeing of the Poor." *Federal Reserve Bank of Kansas City Economic Review* (First Quarter).

Rouse, Cecilia Elena. 1998. "Schools and Student Achievement: More Evidence from the Milwaukee Parental Choice Program." *Economic Policy Review* 4(1): 61–76.

Rubin, Barry M., and Margaret G. Wilder. 1989. "Urban Enterprise Zones: Employment Impacts and Fiscal Incentives." *Journal of the American Planning Association* 55(4): 418–31.

Savner, Steve. 1999. "Key Implementation Decisions Affecting Low-Income Adults Under the Workforce Investment Act." Working Paper. Washington: Center for Law and Social Policy (August).

Savner, Steve, and Mark Greenberg. Undated. *State Usage of Work Supplementation Under JOBS and Section 1115 Waivers.* Washington, D.C.: Center for Law and Social Policy.

Sawhill, Isabel. 1999. "From Welfare to Work: Toward a New Antipoverty Agenda." *Brookings Review* 17(4): 27–30.

Schade, Linda, Carlos Espinosa, Mary Ochs, and Lisa Ranghelli. 1999. *Getting Good Jobs: An Organizer's Guide to Job Training.* Washington, D.C.: Center for Community Change.

Schlozman, Kay Lehman, and Sidney Verba. 1979. *Injury to Insult: Unemployment, Class, and Political Response.* Cambridge, Mass.: Harvard University Press.

Scrivener, Susan, Gayle Hamilton, Mary Farrell, Stephen Freedman, Daniel Friedlander, Marisa Mitchell, Jodi Nudelman, and Christine Schwartz. 1998. *National Evaluation of Welfare-to-Work Strategies: Implementation, Participation Patterns, Costs, and Two-Year Impacts of the Portland (Oregon) Welfare-to-Work Program.* New York: Manpower Demonstration Research Corporation.

Seavey, Dorie. 1998. *New Avenues into Jobs: Early Lessons from Nonprofit Temp Agencies and Employment Brokers.* Washington, D.C.: Center for Community Change.

Sheppard, Harold L., Bennett Harrison, and William J. Spring, eds. 1972. *The Political Economy of Public Service Employment.* Lexington, Mass.: D. C. Heath and Co.

Sherman, Arloc, Cheryl Amey, Barbara Duffield, Nancy Ebb, and Deborah Weinstein. 1998. "Welfare to What: Early Findings on Family Hardship and Wellbeing." Washington, D.C.: Children's Defense Fund and National Coalition for the Homeless (November).

Smith, James P., and Finis R. Welch. 1989. "Black Economic Progress After Myrdal." *Journal of Economic Literature* 27(2): 519–64.

Snower, Dennis J. 1994. "Converting Unemployment Benefits into Employment Subsidies." *AEA Papers and Proceedings* 84(2): 65–70.

Social Policy Research Associates. 1999. *PY 97 Standardized Program Information Report (SPIR) Data Book.* Report prepared for U.S. Department of Labor, Employment and Training Administration, Office of Policy and Research. Menlo Park, Calif.: Social Policy Research Associates.

Solow, Robert M. 1990. *The Labor Market as a Social Institution.* Cambridge, Mass.: Basil Blackwell.

Spiegelman, Robert G., and Stephen A. Woodbury. 1987. *The Illinois Unemployment Insurance Incentive Experiments.* Kalamazoo, Mich.: W. E. Upjohn Institute for Employment Research.

Staiger, Douglas, James H. Stock, and Mark W. Watson. 1997a. "The NAIRU,

Unemployment, and Monetary Policy." *Journal of Economic Perspectives* 11(1): 33–49.

———. 1997b. "How Precise Are Estimates of the Natural Rate of Unemployment?" In *Reducing Inflation: Motivation and Strategy,* edited by Christina D. Romer and David H. Romer. Chicago: University of Chicago Press.

Stevens, Ann Huff. 1995. "Long-term Effects of Job Displacement: Evidence from the Panel Study of Income Dynamics." Working Paper 5343. Cambridge, Mass.: National Bureau of Economic Research.

Stock, James H., and Mark W. Watson. 1999. "Forecasting Inflation." Working Paper 7023. Cambridge, Mass.: National Bureau of Economic Research.

Strawn, Julie. 1998. "Beyond Job Search or Basic Education: Rethinking the Role of Skills in Welfare Reform." Working Paper. Washington, D.C.: Center for Law and Social Policy.

Summers, Lawrence, and James Poterba. 1994. "Time Horizons of American Firms: New Evidence from a Survey of CEOs." In *Capital Choices: Changing the Way America Invests in Industry,* edited by Michael Porter. Boston: Harvard Business School Press.

Switzer, Michael. 1999. "Weekly Workforce Updates." Available at: *http://workforce.floridajobs.org*.

Swope, Christopher. 1998. "The Living-Wage Wars." *Governing* (December): 23–25.

Taggart, Robert. 1981. *A Fisherman's Guide: An Assessment of Training and Remediation Strategies.* Kalamazoo, Mich.: W. E. Upjohn Institute for Employment Research.

Tannenbaum, Jeffrey A. 1997. "Making Risky Hires into Valued Workers." *Wall Street Journal* (June 29): Section B, 1.

Tannery, Frederick J. 1998. *Targeted Jobs Tax Credits and Labor Market Experience.* Washington: Employment Policies Institute.

Tirole, Jean. 1988. *The Theory of Industrial Organization.* Cambridge, Mass.: MIT Press.

Tobin, James. 1994. "Poverty in Relation to Macroeconomic Trends." In *Confronting Poverty: Prescriptions for Change,* edited by Sheldon H. Danziger, Gary D. Sandefur, and Daniel H. Weinberg. Cambridge, Mass.: Harvard University Press.

Topel, Robert H. 1986. "Local Labor Markets." *Journal of Political Economy* 94: S111–43.

———. 1990. "Specific Capital and Unemployment: Measuring the Costs and Consequences of Job Loss." *Carnegie-Rochester Conference Series on Public Policy* 33: 181–214.

Triest, Robert K. 1990. "The Effect of Income Taxation on Labor Supply in the United States." *Journal of Human Resources* 25(3): 491–516.

Tweedie, Jack, and Dana Reichert. 1998. "Tracking Recipients After They Leave Welfare: Summaries of State Follow-up Studies." National Conference of State Legislatures Report. Available at: *http://www.ncsl.org/statefed/welfare/followup.htm*.

Unicon Research Corporation. 1982. *Measuring Displacement: A Field Monitoring Approach.* Final Report on the Major Research Outputs for the Labor Market Effects of the Youth Incentive Entitlement Pilot Projects. Santa Monica, Calif.: Unicon Research Corporation (December 21).

U.S. Bureau of the Census. 1997. *The Current Population Survey, March 1997: Geographic Mobility, March 1996 to March 1997 (Update).* Available at: *http://www.census.gov/population/www/socdemo/migrate.html.*

———. 1998. "Poverty 1998." Table F, March 1999 Current Population Survey. Available at: *http://www.census.gov/hhes/poverty/poverty98/tablef.html.*

———. 1999. *Poverty in the United States: 1998.* Current Population Reports, Series P60–207. Washington: U.S. Government Printing Office.

U.S. Department of Commerce. 1993. *1990 Census of Population: Social and Economic Characteristics, United States.* Washington: U.S. Government Printing Office.

———. 1998. *Statistical Abstract of the United States 1998.* Washington: U.S. Government Printing Office.

———. 2000. "Business Situation." *Survey of Current Business* 80(4): 1–8.

U.S. Department of Health and Human Services. 1998a. "Temporary Assistance for Needy Families (TANF) Program." First Annual Report to Congress. Available at: *http://www.acf.dhhs.gov/news/welfare/congress/index.htm.*

———. 1998b. "Characteristics and Financial Circumstances of TANF Recipients, July-September 1997." Washington: DHHS/ACF/OPRE (December 14).

———. 1999. "Temporary Assistance for Needy Families (TANF) Program." Second Annual Report to Congress. Available at: *http://www.acf.dhhs.gov/news/welfare/congress/index.htm.*

———. 2000. The Administration for Children and Families. "Temporary Assistance for Needy Families (TANF): Percent of Total U.S. Population, 1960–1999." Available at: *http://www.acf.dhhs.gov/news/stats/6097rf.htm.*

U.S. Department of Labor. 1979. *Training and Employment Report of the Secretary of Labor.* Washington: U.S. Government Printing Office.

———. 1990. *Training and Employment Report of the Secretary of Labor.* Washington: U.S. Government Printing Office.

———. 1994. *Targeted Jobs Tax Credit Program: Employment Inducement or Employer Windfall?* Washington: U.S. Department of Labor, Office of Audit, Office of the Inspector General.

———. 1998a. *Workforce Investment Act of 1998.* Employment and Training Administration. Available at: *http://usworkforce.org/runningtext2.htm.*

———. 1998b. *Training and Employment Report of the Secretary of Labor.* Washington: U.S. Government Printing Office.

———. 1999. *Monthly Labor Review* (August).

———. 2000. "Work Opportunity and Welfare-to-Work Tax Credits." Education and Training Administration. Available at: *http://workforcesecurity.doleta.gov/employ/updates.asp.*

———. Undated. "Testers Pilot Program Executive Initiative." Employment Standards Administration, Office of Federal Contract Compliance Programs Special Report. Available at: *http://www.dol.gov/dol/esa/public/media/reports/ofccp/testers.htm.*

U.S. General Accounting Office. 1991. *Targeted Jobs Tax Credit: Employer Actions to Recruit, Hire, and Retain Eligible Workers Vary.* Report HRD-91-33. Washington: U.S. General Accounting Office.

———. 1996. "Job Training Partnership Act: Long-term Earnings and Employment Outcomes" (March).

U.S. House of Representatives, Committee on Ways and Means. 1998. *1998 Green Book: Background Material and Data on Programs Within the Jurisdiction of the Committee on Ways and Means.* Washington: U.S. Government Printing Office.

U.S. House of Representatives, Congressional Budget Office. 1984. "The Targeted Jobs Tax Credit: Staff Memorandum." Washington: U.S. House of Representatives.

U.S. Office of Management and Budget. 1971. "Budget of the United States." Washington: Executive Office of the President.

———. 1998. "Budget of the United States Government." Washington: Executive Office of the President.

Walters, Jonathan. 1997. "Why Unions Hate Workfare." *Governing* (November): 35–39.

Weinberg, Daniel H. 1993. "Comment on Rebecca Blank, 'Why Were Poverty Rates So High in the 1980s?'" In *Poverty and Prosperity in the USA in the Late Twentieth Century,* edited by Dimitri B. Papadimitriou and Edward N. Wolff. New York: St. Martin's Press.

Weisbrot, Mark, and Michelle Sforza-Roderick. 1996. *Baltimore's Living Wage Law: An Analysis of the Fiscal and Economic Costs of Baltimore City Ordinance 442.* Washington, D.C.: Preamble Center for Public Policy.

Weiss, Andrew. 1990. *Efficiency Wages: Models of Unemployment, Layoffs, and Wage Dispersion.* New York: Harwood Academic Publishers.

Wilson, William Julius. 1996. *When Work Disappears: The World of the New Urban Poor.* New York: Alfred A. Knopf.

Wisconsin Department of Health and Social Services and the Institute for Research on Poverty. 1982. "Jobs Tax Credits: The Report of the Wage Bill Subsidy Research Project, Phase II." Madison: Department of Health and Social Services.

Wisconsin Department of Workforce Development. 1999a. "Wisconsin Works (W-2) Philosophy and Goals." Available at: *http://www.dwd.state.wi.us//desw2/philosop.htm.*

———. 1999b. "Survey of Those Leaving AFDC or W-2, January to March 1998." Preliminary Report. Available at: *http://www.ncsl.org/statefed/welfare/leavers.htm.*

Wiseman, Michael. 1997. "Who Got New Hope?" Working Paper. New York: Manpower Demonstration Research Corporation.

———. 1999. "In Midst of Reform: Wisconsin in 1997." Assessing the New Federalism Discussion Paper 99-03. Washington, D.C.: Urban Institute.

Woodbury, Stephen A., and Robert G. Spiegelman. 1987. "Bonuses to Workers and Employers to Reduce Unemployment: Randomized Trials in Illinois." *American Economic Review* 77(4): 513–30.

Zambrowski, Amy, Anne Gordon, and Laura Berenson. 1993. *Evaluation of the Minority Female Single Parent Demonstration: Fifth-Year Impacts at CET.* New York: Rockefeller Foundation.

Zedlewski, Sheila R. 1999. "Work-Related Activities and Limitations of Current Welfare Recipients." Assessing the New Federalism Discussion Paper 99-06. Washington, D.C.: Urban Institute.

Index

Boldface numbers refer to figures and tables.